Howard Hawks

HOWARD HAWKS

The Grey Fox of Hollywood

TODD McCARTHY

GROVE PRESS
New York

Published simultaneously in Canada
Printed in the United States of America

FIRST EDITION

Library of Congress Cataloging-in-Publication Data

McCarthy, Todd.
    Howard Hawks : the grey fox of Hollywood / Todd McCarthy. — 1st ed.
      p.   cm.
    Filmography: p.
    Includes bibliographical references and index.
    ISBN 0–8021–1598–5
    1. Hawks, Howard, 1896–1977   2. Motion picture producers and directors—United States—Biography. I. Title.
PN1998.3.H38M33   1997
791.43'0233'092—dc21
[B]

                    96–49075

Design by Laura Hammond Hough

Grove Press
841 Broadway
New York, NY 10003

10 9 8 7 6 5 4 3 2 1

TO SASHA AND MADELEINE

Contents

Howard Hawks

Introduction:

The Engineer as Poet

Howard Hawks is the most important of the classical Hollywood directors of whom there has been no biography. Certainly, he has long since emerged from his status as the exclusive property of film cultists and buffs to become recognized as one of the half dozen great American filmmakers whose careers began in the pre–World War II era. At the very least, a dozen of his pictures are as universally admired as any produced by the major studios. He pursued the requisite colorful life filled with sport, drink, and women; befriended the rich, famous, and talented; possessed ego to burn; and lived long enough to, however casually, build and bend the facts of his life into legend.

But the fact remains that Howard Hawks, despite having had his name above the title virtually from the beginning of his career, was never as well known as such contemporaries as Alfred Hitchcock, Frank Capra, John Ford, Cecil B. De Mille, William Wyler, or Billy Wilder. He was only once nominated for an Oscar, which he did not win. Although between 1939 and 1949 Hawks enjoyed a remarkable unbroken string of hits that placed him in the commercial front rank, this success helped brand him as a reliable supplier of entertainment, discoverer of new talent, and director of big stars, not as an American artist of the first caliber. To become a brand-name Hollywood filmmaker in that era, one either had to appear in one's own films (Chaplin, Stroheim, Keaton, Welles), win awards (Ford, Capra, Wyler, McCarey, Wilder, Kazan, Stevens), exclusively specialize in a certain kind of production (Hitchcock, De Mille, Lubitsch, Sternberg for a while), or cultivate a reputation as a social commentator of rare and bold seriousness (Stanley Kramer). Superficially, at least, Hawks specialized in diversity; and since every bone in his body opposed pretension, politics, and pompousness in pictures, the public has always had trouble automatically associating his name with specific films.

Going one step further, the Hawks style is, at a glance, invisible. His films' visuals are the least distinctive of any of the major directors, his work

3

less immediately identifiable than that of most masters. Ironically, Hawks was one of the most stylized of all filmmakers, but the stylization had more to do with rituals, behavior, dialogue delivery, performance, and abstracting the action from the real world than with distinctive camera angles, editing patterns, a regular stock company, repeated settings, or anything else that would breed familiarity in the viewer. In other words, the stylization was disguised by a deceptive directness, by humor, by the openness of the characters and the liveliness of the players. This remarkable achievement meant that Hawks would not even be recognized as an artist for much of his career, but in this he was only the most prominent among many.

In the late 1960s a small film magazine published a cover article called "Who the Hell Is Howard Hawks?" The very title of Robin Wood's piece, which appeared in advance of his seminal critical book on the director, mocked the lack of serious appreciation of Hawks's work, a situation that was to be rectified over the following few years. Ironically, "Who the Hell Was Howard Hawks?" could easily serve as the title for any investigation of Hawks the man. It is far easier to read Hawks, to get a strong sense of what he was all about, through his work than it was in life even for those closest to him. Many people are conveniently called enigmas, but even Hawks's friends referred to him that way. He was Sphinxlike, remote, cold, private, intimidating, self-absorbed, a man with eyes like blue ice cubes. He was, like any director worthy of the profession, crafty and controlling, and he never lost self-control. At the same time, the frigid blue eyes could quickly turn warm and impudent. He was invariably a gentleman of impeccable elegance, taste, judgment, and style, a director of infinite generosity to his performers and crew, a friend of great loyalty, a man of intelligent discrimination. But that there was always a sense of distance, of not really knowing this man, was freely admitted even by those who spent months and years with him.

This distance alone could be enough to discourage any biographer, as could the fact that Howard Hawks was not a man of letters. The few literary exchanges that do exist are remarkably unrevealing and unconfidential, generally dotted by Hawks's apologies for not being a better correspondent. Nor did the director keep diaries, memos, or even helpful datebooks. Simply put, Hawks left no contemporaneous record of what he was thinking, feeling, or doing throughout his life, and the material he did leave behind was spotty and virtually accidental.

For the most part, Hawks's legacy exists in the form of the interviews he so readily granted late in life, in which he expounded to acolytes about his career and accomplishments. To anyone with an interest in his work, or in American films in general, these testimonies are fascinating not only for their anecdotal richness but also as a revelation of Hawks's innate intelligence, of how much thought and theory he put into what were long regarded variously as examples of Hollywood escapism, star vehicles, and assembly-line products. In their own way, however, the interviews create yet another barrier to an accurate view of Hawks's life and career, for they go beyond ego in their self-aggrandizement into an advanced realm of imagination and fantasy. Many people have taken Hawks's beguiling stories at face value, and many of Hawks's tall tales involved people who were already dead for twenty-five years when Hawks related the incidents in which he was, coincidentally, the only surviving witness. When cursory research proved Hawks's versions of events to be exaggerations at best and blatant lies at worst, it served notice that just about everything he ever said would need to be doubted, investigated, corroborated—when possible.

But this detour provides its own reward, in the sense that it leads one to the substance of Hawks's nature. That Hawks was a natural storyteller may be a handicap to objectifying his life but a linchpin to defining his character. His disinclination to keep a record of his life anywhere other than in his own head did not represent a deliberate attempt to frustrate later chroniclers, as it has been with certain self-conscious, self-tailoring artists; nothing could have been further from his mind. Hawks's account of his own life—in which everything revolved around him, in which he was always right, in which he told Hemingway, Faulkner, Cooper, Grant, Bogart, Wayne, Hepburn, Bacall, and Monroe what was best for them and told Mayer, Warner, Cohn, Goldwyn, Hughes, Wallis, and Zanuck where to get off—was merely the fantastic flip side of the imagination that went into his film stories.

The other happy truth is that while he may not have done everything he said he did, Hawks also accomplished a great deal. As the photographer Robert Capa said, "There are two kinds of mythomaniacs: The ones who are that way because they have never done anything, and the ones who have done so much they can never be satisfied with anything. Howard Hawks is the prototype of the second category." It remains impossible to know why Hawks felt compelled to insist that he was the one who told Josef von Sternberg how to dress Marlene Dietrich or that he instructed his friend Victor Fleming how to direct *Gone with the Wind* or that he was once asked by TWA to take the controls of a commercial airliner when the pilot took ill midflight. Such preposterous claims were laughed off by his friends during his lifetime but tend to be taken more seriously when put down in black-and-white by interviewers and film scholars who didn't choose to challenge Hawks on most of his improbable assertions.

Howard Hawks was born to wealth and privilege. The oldest of five children, he was told he could do anything he wanted to do and was pampered and endlessly spoiled by his maternal grandfather. As a very young man he was among the first Americans to race cars and fly planes. It was his grandparents, and not his genteel parents, who had boldly sought opportunity in the Midwest and built the family fortune on both sides, and it was with them that he identified most strongly. Outside of his spectacle of antiquity, *Land of the Pharaohs,* and the second half of *Come and Get It,* and except for some individuals in his comedies, the characters in his films are essentially classless, working men and women who establish their personal worth by how well they do their jobs and how they relate to one another. Many writers and several of the greatest filmmakers have made of their work a sweeping autobiography, disguised to greater or lesser degrees. Hawks's oeuvre does not represent an autobiography; rather, it constitutes a massive self-projection, a portrait of his fantasy of himself as a great flier, racer, soldier, explorer, pioneer of industry, detective, criminal, lover, hunter, and sheriff. All these purposeful men of action served as good characters for the movies, but they were also ideal vehicles for Hawks to explore his own notions of excellence.

To achieve this within the structure of the commercial film industry, which became increasingly rigid, stratified, and dominant during the period he was building his position in it, Hawks clearly needed to establish a reputation and the power to steer his own course. In this line, he pursued a singular strategy with, arguably, greater success than any other director of his era. Hawks officially directed forty feature films, eight of them silents, far fewer than such contemporaries as John Ford, Raoul Walsh, Michael Curtiz, Frank Borzage, King Vidor, and W. S. Van Dyke, all of whom got a head start in silents by roughly ten years, but more than Capra, McCarey, Milestone, and Mamoulian, who began their careers at roughly the same time. But Hawks maintained a more resolute control over his projects than any of them, making a remarkably small number of pictures that were not of his own choosing and only occasionally finding himself on the losing end of a battle with a studio boss (usually Sam Goldwyn). Of the nonwriters among major Hollywood directors, only Cecil B. De Mille, Alfred Hitchcock, and William Wyler had as much or more say over their productions as Hawks did for as long a period, which in his case was nearly forty years.

With rare exceptions, Hawks created or chose his stories, selected his writers and worked very closely with them, enjoyed decisive influence over casting, shot to his heart's content while constantly reworking his scripts, and kept compromises with the studios to a remarkable minimum.

What drove him to achieve this was an insistent, overpowering will to independence. What enabled him to do it was a potent mixture of arrogance, intelligence, wealth, antiauthoritarianism, skill at intimidation, impudence, and willingness to walk away. Few were able to play the studio heads better than Hawks; he could be as cagey as they were, and even though they were the absolute bosses in Hollywood, Hawks represented the refined, accomplished, well-mannered, Ivy League, blue-blooded WASP whose acceptance they craved. They must have felt Hawks's condescension; they were dealing with a man who, from the beginning of his career, conveyed the impression of independent wealth even when he was virtually broke. In the tycoons' minds, this guy could take it or leave it; he didn't *need* them, which made his bargaining position with them all the greater. Little did they know that he felt so insecure as a director on his first few pictures that he regularly had to pull his car over on his way to work in order to vomit. Only later would the imperious confidence become entirely genuine, after years of practice and expert bluffing.

But what gave Hawks his real ace in the hole with his bosses is that his aims were at one with their own. He wanted to make good films with big stars and bring in a lot of money. His idea of a great film story was one in which a handsome, tough, masculine man, in a risky predicament and normally at the center of a small professional group, performed valiantly and stoically under great pressure and won a beautiful young woman while doing it. What could be more appealing to a wide audience than such a story? For Hawks, there was something wrong with a picture if it didn't go over with the public. Unlike John Ford, his drawer was not full of difficult, uncommercial, socially conscious scripts that he thought perhaps he would be allowed to make if he would play ball with the studios. No, the issue with Hawks was that he wanted to make his films *his* way and on his own terms. Very early on, he discovered that his own tastes and those of the public were remarkably in sync; if he liked an actor, audiences tended to like him; if he thought something was funny, other people tended to laugh as well. This conviction bolstered his position with the studio heads and fostered his belief that he should just be left alone to make his movies, that he would deliver something the studio bosses and the public would like. And he nearly always did.

Hawks spent his entire career first forging, then trying to expand his ability to make pictures within the system yet independently of studio surveillance and interference. His methods and variable success at doing so form one of the main themes of this book, and it was not for nothing that he always retained a special fondness for *Scarface*. The reason was not so much artistic as circumstantial; Hawks and Howard Hughes felt like partners in crime on that maverick production, which they made not only separate from but in defiance of the established industry. Making a film independently of the mainstream was an exceedingly difficult matter during the decades Hawks was active, and whenever Hawks managed to do so, he proved to be his own worst enemy in terms of fiscal responsibility. Objectively, the armchair observer can postulate that Hawks was better off working under conditions of creative tension with Jack Warner and Hal Wallis, or with Harry Cohn, than by his own devices. No matter: the point is that Hawks constantly strove to be as free from the bridle as possible; when he felt it at all, he bit and kicked. In practice, this led him to break contracts and jump studios with fearless regularity—in the sound era, only once did he direct more than two films in a row at a given studio, a rare occurrence in those years of long-term contracts.

Hawks fought hard for the right to tell stories his way, to not be bossed or pushed or compromised. But to what end? Did he really possess the soul of an artist who simply had to create, an artistic urge that can be compared seriously to those of his friends Hemingway and Faulkner or to compulsive, self-consciously artistic filmmakers like Welles, Bergman, and Godard? Would Hawks even have entered the arts at all in another era, without the combined allure of fun, luxury, big money, elite status, beautiful women, social power, and, incidentally, self-expression offered by the movies? When assessing the early lives and biographies of most of the cinema's pioneering artists, one develops the collective impression of a bunch of clever but somewhat aimless types who were lucky enough to stumble onto a good thing at the right time. Certainly, for people born in the last decade of the nineteenth century, the cinema, such as it was, did not yet exist as something anyone would aspire to as a profession. In any event, one rarely, if ever, hears of an American who set out in the late 1910s or 1920s with serious artistic ambitions that could be achieved only in films.

For his part, Hawks intended to be an engineer. He did read widely, but he was never drawn toward music, drama, creative writing, or newspaper work. The impulse toward artistic self-expression seemed not to be there. But when, in his own way, he stumbled into movies, when he began to see how vividly moving images could convey fantasies of action and accomplishment and distilled, idealized renditions of human behavior, he began to understand what he might be able to do. Hawks had always found that he could do most things better than most other people, so he rightly reasoned that it would be that way with movies as well. Only later would he see that everything he believed and everything that excited him could be conveyed through the stories he told in pictures.

Hawks, then, was an intuitive, rather than an intentional, artist, in the sense that he did not set out to make statements about life, the condition of mankind, politics, war, history, or social conditions. Although he thought very highly of himself, Hawks—like Ford, Walsh, and a few other rugged pioneers who started in the silent cinema—always positioned himself as a craftsman. "All I'm doing is telling a story," he invariably said. If you wanted to call him an artist, that was your privilege, but he was never going to be the one to do it. He steered clear of anything that smacked of the highbrow, the literary, or the intellectual. Although they are both often referred to as prototypical macho and cynical men of action, Hawks was, as a director, almost the diametrical opposite of John Huston. For all his personality, skill, and distinction, Huston spent much of his career adapting important works of literature for the screen and trying to be "faithful" to them. Nothing could have been further from Hawks's intent in making a movie; he couldn't be bothered to read Melville, Joyce, McCullers, O'Connor, Lowry, or, for that matter, Freud, much less make a film inspired by them. On the rare occasions—arguably, only three or four times—when Hawks tackled the work of a distinguished author, he made it a point to be as unfaithful and irreverent as possible, never more so than with *To Have and Have Not*. When Huston tackled an estimable preexisting work, there was usually, although not always, the impression of the original being pared, hammered, twisted, chopped, and remolded so it would fit into a cinematic box. When Hawks took on a property that had succeeded in a previous incarnation (notably *Twentieth Century*; *The Front Page*; *To Have and Have Not*, despite its minor reputation; *The Big Sleep*; *The Big Sky*; and *Gentlemen Prefer Blondes*), the feeling was more that the original had been entirely dismantled, cleverly rethought, and meticulously reassembled in accordance with the logic of the cinema and the imperatives of Hawks's own personality. And in all cases, despite the presence of diverse writers, it was Hawks who directed the rethinking and the enormous changes that were made to each one, and he, not the original authors or subsequent scenarists, determined the films' personalities.

In the received literary sense, Hawks's life of the mind was not that of an intellectual; he did not follow intellectual pursuits, and he displayed or feigned astonishment at many of the exalted qualities some critics found in his work. What, then, is one to make of François Truffaut's observation that Hawks "is one of the most intellectual filmmakers in America"? Only that Hawks had an extremely well worked out set of theories, convictions, and principles about how to make movies and was articulate enough to express them in a simple, direct manner. Hawks thought long and hard about his profession, about what worked and what did not, just as he might have about engineering, architecture, design or construction of any kind. Hawks knew how to take apart and reassemble cars, motorcycles, and planes. He could expertly copy any piece of furniture. His innate taste told him how to dress himself, and his advice helped his second wife become the best-dressed woman in the United States. Perhaps it was not such a great a leap for him to be able to expertly construct, or reconstruct, a story for films, to design an inexperienced woman's look, voice, and behavior to powerful effect on the screen, to know how a man should act in extremis. A great mystique has always surrounded film directing. Partly for that reason, Hawks aspired to the position early on, and he was incredibly fortunate to be able to achieve it and build the rest of his life around it. But he approached it as a job, even as it allowed him to express his poetic flair for dramatizing Hemingway's "grace under pressure."

Hawks was concerned with men in action but he was not, per se, an action director. The scenes in his films of battles, flying, deep-sea fishing, logging, cattle driving, river boating, singing and dancing, pyramid build-ing, animal chasing, auto racing, and train crashing were usually done by second-unit directors and were often noticeably divorced from the fabric of the picture. Rather, Hawks was a master of events played out within tight quarters among a handful of people in a limited period of time; despite his reputation as an outdoorsman, as a director he was most comfortable in a drawing room, an office, a home, or a hotel. These enclosed settings mag-nified the importance of every gesture and look, every remark, every deci-sion, to the point where meaning, if you were looking for it, was densely packed into every moment.

Although often conceived of as a naturalistic director because of his relatively plain, straightforward, eye-level visual approach and his affinity for Hemingway's stripped-down narrative storytelling technique, Hawks was actually the most stylized Hollywood director this side of Josef von Sternberg, with whom he had more in common than anyone imagined at the time. At their best, Hawks's films, like Sternberg's, conveyed a beautifully wrought philosophy of life entirely through action, embodied in characters who enact certain behavioristic rituals in a remote setting artfully detached from the real world. Many critics have attempted to define this philosophy, which takes the form of a highly entertaining but nonetheless fatalistic variety of adolescent existentialism, one devoid of sentimentality, false hope, or religious reassurance. Man is the measure of all things in Hawks's tough and sometimes bitter universe, but there is compensation to be had in friendship, unity of the group, the assertion of intelligence over dumb brute force, and the rewards of a job well done. Perhaps the critic Molly Haskell put it best when she ventured, "In Hawks, the pioneer hubris, and rashness and naïveté, of the American converges with the austere, man-centered morality of ancient Greece." In his work, she wrote, one sees "the picture of man poised, comically or heroically, against an antagonistic nature, a nothingness as devoid of meaning as Samuel Beckett's, but determined nonetheless to act out his destiny, to assert mind against mindlessness."

That Hawks shunned deep analysis yet employed extensively developed theories in his work, that he was an outdoorsman of action and at the same time a filmmaker most at home in highly stylized interiors, that he was an autocratic elitist who nonetheless reveled in the classlessness of his characters' group pursuits—these are just three of the paradoxes in Hawks's character. Among the others: he was not an intellectual yet he was very intelligent (not so unusual); he possessed the wisdom of his years but remained an adolescent in his enthusiasms even in old age; he was innately conservative in his worldview yet daring and inclined to risk; he was the very definition of a modern twentieth-century man but stuck to tried-and-true formulas; he was embraced by many feminists in the 1970s for liberating his women characters from the home and placing them on the same field with men, yet he held an utterly conventional view of women's role in his own life; he was stoic but reckless, reserved but excessive; he was celebrated but little known; he was a pragmatist but a poet; and he had the mind of an engineer but the subconscious of an artist.

He was, above all, a modern artist. Of all the classical Hollywood directors, he is the one whose work has dated the least, for whom no excuses or explanations need be made. His visual style was straightforward, unmannered, unrooted in a specific era except for that of the classical Hollywood cinema in the most general sense. His lack of interest in topical matters, politics, social issues, and the like also serves to liberate him from the concerns of the times in which he worked, except, again, in the broadest sense of dealing with existing conditions such as Prohibition and World War II. What decisively set Hawks apart from 98 percent of his contemporaneous filmmakers was his complete lack of sentimentality. At every opportunity, he cut against conventional expectations in emotional moments and had acute antennae for anything that could be considered soft, schmaltzy, cloying, or indulgent.

Much of this difference stemmed from his female characters, who, in so many cases, talked back; were at least as smart as the men; refused to be condescended to; wore uniforms, smartly tailored outfits, or pants more often than dresses; were not used as ornaments or mere objects of men's desires; and didn't simply want to get married and have kids. Putting aside for the moment the ongoing debate over how truly liberated Hawks's women were, it remains indisputable that they represent a uniquely vibrant, free-spirited, and intelligent group, not only in Hollywood terms but by any standard. The frankness with which male-female attraction was presented, the feeling of mutual respect and equality-as-ideal that is generated between the best of Hawks's couples, represents the most moving thing in his work and would play as a model of contemporary sexual relations in any era. Although several of his best films conclude with a couple getting together after having hurdled many obstacles, Hawks always avoided the climactic romantic clinch, the typical happy ending. The last moments of *Only Angels Have Wings* and *To Have and Have Not*, for example, show the central couples embarking on a "happy" future, giving the films upbeat endings that provide great audience satisfaction. When one deeply considers the circumstances, however, it is hard to imagine a prolonged, satisfying future even for these beautiful couples, much less for many of the others in Hawks's films; the other factors working upon their lives would seem to stack the cards against them for anything but the short term. And surely in the work of no other significant Hollywood director of the Production Code era have family and children played so marginal a role. In only one of his sound films, *Monkey Business*, are the central characters married throughout the picture. Edward G. Robinson and Zita Johann marry, unhappily, partway through *Tiger Shark*; Edward Arnold is encumbered in a passionless match in the second half of *Come and Get It*; Cary Grant and Rosalind Russell were formerly wed in *His Girl Friday*; Cary Grant and Ann Sheridan's wedding precipitates all the ensuing frustrations and complications of *I Was a Male War Bride*; Dewey Martin unwittingly finds himself wed to Indian girl Elizabeth Threatt toward the end of *The Big Sky*, and Jack Hawkins's Pharaoh seals his own fate when he takes Joan Collins for a second wife in *Land of the Pharaohs*. In stark opposition to Hollywood convention, mothers appear with the utmost infrequency in Hawks's work — briefly in *Scarface*, *Sergeant York*, and *Land of the Pharaohs*, marginally in *Come and Get It*. The only remotely normal and appealing kids in Hawks's films — and their screen time is momentary — are the young Matthew Garth in *Red River* and Pharaoh's son; the others, the little boys in *The Ransom of Red Chief*, *Monkey Business*, and *Gentlemen Prefer Blondes*, are grotesques. Otherwise, all of Hawks's main characters are basically unattached, single men and women free to pursue their interests and goals in life, as well as each other. For his wily way with women, Hawks was tagged with the nickname "the godamned grey fox of Brentwood," by his friend John Ford.

Throughout his career, Hawks was well known as a star maker, a shrewd spotter of new talent, male and female. He can fairly be said to have discovered, or used effectively for the first time on the screen, Paul Muni, George Raft, Carole Lombard, Frances Farmer, Rita Hayworth, Jane Russell, Lauren Bacall, Dorothy Malone, Montgomery Clift, Joanne Dru, Angie Dickinson, James Caan, and Jennifer O'Neill. He worked repeatedly with five of the greatest male stars in the business — James Cagney, Gary Cooper, Cary Grant, Humphrey Bogart, and John Wayne; used Edward G. Robinson, Richard Barthelmess, and Joel McCrea twice; and relied upon such regular supporting players as Walter Brennan, Vince Barnett, Charles Coburn, and Arthur Hunnicutt. On only two occasions, however, did he use a leading lady a second time, with Ann Dvorak and Lauren Bacall; unlike Sternberg, his Svengali instinct was generally used up after one go-round with a given actress.

Hawks left a legacy not only directly through his own work and the people he brought into the business but through his influence on a surprising number of contemporary filmmakers. Hawks's modernity can be read in large measure through the extent to which his work remains a keystone and an inspiration for directors around the world; aside from Orson Welles and Alfred Hitchcock, both of whom had styles that were much bolder and immediately impressive and imitable, it is arguable that no director has been more widely cited as a positive and instructive influence than Hawks. Jean-Luc Godard and Bernardo Bertolucci each referred explicitly to Hawks in early features. Martin Scorsese had the leading characters in his first film go see *Rio Bravo*, which they then discussed at length, and he may have based Sharon Stone's character in *Casino* on Joan Collins's in *Land of the Pharaohs*. Peter Bogdanovich excerpted *The Criminal Code* in his first film and *Red River* in his second, and lifted bodily from *Bringing Up Baby* for his third. John Carpenter twice remade Hawks's films, the first time unofficially, the second time with credit. Brian De Palma, in between Hitchcock homages, remade *Scarface*. Walter Hill, John Milius, and, less obviously, Robert Benton owe a great deal to Hawks. François Truffaut considered *Hatari!* to be a disguised film about the filmmaking process and a model for his own *Day for Night*. Quentin Tarantino attended an entire Hawks retrospective while writing *Pulp Fiction*. There are, and no doubt will be, more, for the reason that Hawks's films live in the present more vitally than those of most filmmakers from any country or any era.

In a related way, Hawks has also inspired some of the most lucid and impressive writing from the relatively large number of critics who have written about him; just as Hawks collaborated with the best writers, he has brought out the best in those who respond to his work. Hawks's films have been assessed, analyzed, defended, and canonized in unusually eloquent and expressive fashion, first by the *Cahiers du Cinéma* critics and Manny Farber, then by Peter Bogdanovich and Andrew Sarris, and more recently by Robin Wood, Gerald Mast, Joseph McBride, Molly Haskell, Peter Wollen, John Belton, Gerald Peary, Richard Thompson, Jean-Pierre Coursodon, William Paul, Bruce Kawin, Gilbert Adair, and David Thomson, who went so far as to state that if he had the usual ten films to take to a deserted island, they would all be by Hawks. Wood's book stands as a model of insightful, persuasively argued critical analysis, while only a handful of directors ever produced a body of work that could inspire and actually support the sort of exhaustive explication Mast conducted in his scrupulously scholarly study of Hawks. Very few negative assessments of the director have appeared in the past twenty years, the only notable one having been Raymond Durgnat's conspicuously unconvincing article *Hawks Isn't Good Enough*. Hawks's career even inspired one of the most astonishingly esoteric critical books ever published, Clark Branson's *Howard Hawks: A Jungian Study*. What remains impressive is how Hawks's body of work provokes and sustains such a considerable volume and diversity of study and analysis, generally at a very high level of appreciation and intelligence, and how the work easily accommodates this multitude of interpretations. This, one can only insist, further attests to the great life and relevance Hawks's films still possess.

The overriding reason for writing a biography of Howard Hawks, of course, lies in the extraordinary films he made. In all the books, interviews, and articles about him, what has never been explained is how he succeeded in controlling his career to the remarkable extent he did, why the films turned out the way they did, and how he was able to use the Hollywood system to his own end for four decades. Any lingering notions that just because he didn't impose his name on the screenplays to his films he was not the "author" of them will be eliminated in short order. But it is also very much to the point that he could never have done it alone. Without his collaborators, Howard Hawks probably would have designed planes or automobiles for a living. The way he selected, and then used, those he worked with was an intrinsic part of Hawks's artistic process. For this reason, a considerable emphasis has been placed on the characters and talents of his important writers and actors, as well as on his process of working with them. In terms of his working method, Hawks stood with such contemporaries as Leo McCarey and Gregory La Cava, two directors he greatly admired, and in the opposite camp from Hitchcock, whom he also liked. When he was working in the manner he preferred, any Hawks picture was the result of a continual process of experimentation, adjustment, and discovery based on the personalities and talents of those involved, all channeled through the rigorous prism of Hawks's taste and selectivity. A film director is best compared not to a solitary artist such as a novelist, poet, painter, or sculptor but to an orchestra conductor or a chef, someone who puts an indelible personal stamp on a work by organizing, choosing, interpreting, and synthesizing a certain set of materials.

Unfortunately, the vast majority of Hawks's most important collaborators, especially the writers, died years ago, making direct questioning impossible. Jules Furthman, Ben Hecht, Charles MacArthur, William Faulkner, Leigh Brackett, Seton Miller, Dudley Nichols, Charles Lederer, Nunnally Johnson, Harry Kurnitz—it would be difficult to offer a more impressive list of literary collaborators, but they are all long gone, having left behind little or, in most cases, nothing in the way of detailed notations on their work with Hawks. Also departed without ever having been questioned extensively or at all about Hawks, or having written about him in memoirs, were such important actors as Gary Cooper, Humphrey Bogart, Paul Muni, Joan Crawford, John Barrymore, Fredric March, Walter Brennan, Montgomery Clift, Danny Kaye, Ann Sheridan, Marilyn Monroe, and Rock Hudson; all the studio heads, from Warner, Mayer, and Zanuck to Cohn, Goldwyn, and Hughes; most of his producers and cameramen; his closest friends through much of his life, Victor Fleming and Charles K. Feldman; and all of his brothers and sisters. For reasons of their own, his three wives all declined to share their memories: the first, Athole, due to mental fragility that would have been unduly disturbed, her daughter said, by resurrecting troubling events from decades before; the second, Slim, because she was working on her own memoirs, which were published posthumously; and the third, Dee, who said that she is saving everything for a book she plans to write, revealing things only she knows about Hawks and her late brother-in-law, Groucho Marx. We shall see.

Even if Hawks had lived a hundred years, he would never have sat down to write his memoirs. For him, the interview format represented the ideal means to relate his anecdotes and embellish his own stature. He was a great storyteller, both in films and in person, and regaling admiring interrogators was easy. The impediments he placed in the way of a biographer stemmed more from negligence than intention: by casually leaving his collection of papers, scripts, and photographs in his garage, he put them at the mercy of the elements, which got to them, initially and massively in the early 1950s, then again in the 1970s, destroying much of whatever he had put aside. The remainder, which has been lovingly inventoried and stored at Brigham Young University, simply because the archivist there, James D'Arc, was the first person to ask for it, represents a tantalizing but highly fragmentary glimpse into the entirety of Hawks's life and career.

Fortunately, there have been other ways to go—often on very long roads but ending up, one trusts, at basically the same destination. Many circumstances work against this biography being a view of Hawks from the inside, a full reading of his mind and emotions: he was not a man of letters or diaries; he was temperamentally opposed to revealing his inner thoughts and feelings, even to his wives and others closest to him; and he was never questioned extensively by his interviewers about his early and personal life and was not challenged on the incongruities, distortions, and outright fabrications of his oft-told tales—who knew better at that time, or cared to confront the great man? An interior study of Hawks could only be wildly speculative, given his personality and assiduous disinclination from shared introspection. By necessity, much of the early life remains much sketchier than one would like; by terrible coincidence, his early Wisconsin academic records burned along with the school that housed them, some of his high school documents got lost in various transfers, Cornell University disposed of student transcripts dating back that far, and his army records were destroyed, along with so many others, in St. Louis. There is no way to corroborate Hawks's accounts of his amateur auto-racing career, his alleged athletic exploits, his early flying days, or even some of his initial filmmaking ventures. Inevitably, the life comes into sharper focus a bit later on, when the adult Hawks embarks upon his serious career, but some areas, such as his private dealings with bookies and the full extent of his gambling, remain beyond research, just as they were unknowable even to his family and inner circle.

Endlessly forthcoming on one level but unreachable on another, Hawks was the sort of man for whom the term *enigma* was invented, and no end of critical analysis or biographical excavation may change that. Upon being told that one of my aims with this book was to sort out the truth from Hawks's own versions and set things straight, Hawks's longtime associate Paul Helmick said, "Then you'd be the only one." Toward the end, Hawks acknowledged, "I've had a helluva good life." For once, he was not exaggerating.

1

Origins

Settle your father and your brother in the best of the land; let them dwell in the land of Goshen. —Genesis 47:6

The big news in Goshen, Indiana, on Decoration Day, May 30, 1896, was the melee at August Fausch's saloon. Things got so out of hand that at 8:30 that Saturday night Marshal Rigney shot and killed the chief perpetrator, Richard Van Tassel, commonly known as Dick Simmons, a hulking man who was considered "prone to drink." The tempers that night at Fausch's merely matched the weather, however, as a heavy storm was ripping through central and northern Indiana, the wake of a major cyclone that had hit St. Louis, killing more than four hundred people.

In a quieter part of town, in a stately, handsome house on the corner of Fifth and Jefferson, there was big news of a happier, more intimate nature: a first child was born to Frank W. Hawks, the thirty-one-year-old scion of Goshen's most prominent and successful family, and his wife, the former Helen Howard, the twenty-four-year-old daughter of one of Wisconsin's leading industrialists. Given his mother's surname and his father's middle name, Howard Winchester Hawks represented the joining of two affluent, business-minded, British-blooded Midwestern families of similar traditions, each of which had made its fortune in local industry in the second half of the nineteenth century.

If you did business in Goshen in 1896, you had to do business with the Hawkses; they had basically made the town, and they virtually owned it. The mainstay of the local economy, the exceedingly profitable Goshen Milling Company, had been incorporated, and was controlled, by four Hawks men, including Frank's father, Eleazer, who had owned an earlier incarnation of the firm, C. & E. Hawks, with his brother Cephas. If you wanted to buy or rent a house, you had to go to the real estate office of Hawks Bros. & Co., downtown at Lincoln and Main. If you then wished to furnish your home, you headed up to Jefferson to see Edwin Hawks at the Hawks Furniture Company. If you needed some financing, you could make an appointment with City National Bank Vice President Frank E. C. Hawks, who might also be able to help you out with your heating problems, as he doubled as president of the Hawks Coal Company. If you developed indigestion or a headache from worrying about how you were going to afford your new home, Dwight Hawks, the town's leading pharmacist over at Hawks & Egbert, might be able to assist you. Anything you might need to fix the place up could be found at the magnificent Hawks, Messick & Company hardware store, and you could supply it with all the latest items from Chicago and New York at Joel P. and William H. Hawks's well-stocked dry goods and notions store on Lincoln. And if you didn't know how much postage it would take to send that box of Hawks buckwheat to Mom back in Michigan, you could have a word with Ida Hawks, the assistant postmaster at the main post office over on Pike.

Having been in the area for precisely sixty years before Howard was born, the Hawkses were among the founding families of the Elkhart County area, and they played the critical imaginative and economic role in putting Goshen on the map. But the family had been in North America for more than 260 years before the birth of its most famous member.

Early in 1630, ten years after the original Pilgrims landed in Plymouth, the brothers John and Adam Hawks were among a Massachusetts Bay Company expedition of six hundred settlers to the New World. After landing on June 12 at Salem, they eventually settled on the Shawmut Peninsula, where Boston soon grew. Like many of the new colonists, the Hawks brothers had arranged to pay for their voyage through an indentured work agreement. After four years of labor in the Boston settlement of Dorchester, the Hawks brothers were declared free men at the General Court of the Massachusetts Bay Colony on September 3, 1634.

Adam disappeared from history at this point, but John moved on to the Colony of Connecticut, to the settlement of Windsor. He married Elizabeth Brown, a niece of Nathaniel Ward, with whom he had several children, including the sons Eliezer and Gershom. As adults the two brothers were caught in the thick of the first war between the English colonists and the native Indians. Eliezer Hawks was one of the few whites to escape unscathed from one major battle, at the Falls, in 1676.

Shortly thereafter, Eliezer moved about twelve miles north of Hadley to the new settlement of Deerfield, where he married Judith Smead. The couple's son, named after his father, was born on December 26, 1693, and grew up to marry, in 1714, Abigail Wells. Eliezer Jr. moved down the road to Wapping and began a family that grew to at least four sons. In 1743, he bought five hundred acres of land at Charlemont, about sixteen miles northwest of Wapping on both sides of the Deerfield River. In the early 1750s, his first three sons, Gershom, Joshua, and Seth, built separate homes in this densely forested section of the Berkshire Mountains, which lay directly on the Mohawk Trail and was the scene of considerable skirmishing with Indians as well as with the French. To protect their new homes, the brothers built a stockade, which was dubbed "Hawks Fort." Looming above Charlemont, immediately west of the modern Berkshire East Ski Area, is Hawks Mountain.

Taking over his father's farm at Wapping was a younger son, Paul, who had served in the French wars and was married to Lois Wait. Their large family included the sons Eleazer, Joseph, and Cephas. After the Phelps and Gorham purchase opened up land in western New York, these three sons were among the many New Englanders who decided to move west in the 1790s, settling in Ontario County, midway between Syracuse and Rochester.

Moving away from the farming that the family had traditionally practiced, Cephas partnered with two other settlers in building a gristmill in about 1799. Ten years later, he constructed a large woolen factory at White Springs, near Geneva, and made a great deal of money very quickly. However, prices plunged and the economy bottomed out after the War of 1812, wiping out his profits.

In the meantime, Cephas Hawks had married Chloe Chase and started what was to become a family of eleven children. Remarkably, the first six kids—Frank, Albert, Dwight, Cephas Jr., Eleazer, and Joel—were all boys, while the next five—Eliza, Calista, Sarah, Mary, and Harriet, who died as a child—were all girls. With prospects in the area unlikely to improve, Cephas moved the family in the early 1820s to the growing village of Ypsilanti, Michigan, fifteen miles east of Ann Arbor. Trying a new field, Cephas opened a distillery there in 1826 with four other men. Over time, he also became quite successful in the cattle business, accumulating enough capital to consider other enterprises. In 1835, he and his son Cephas Jr. undertook a prospecting tour of neighboring areas and bought two hundred acres of land near Middlebury, Indiana, just south of the Michigan line, about 125 miles southwest of Ypsilanti.

The state of Indiana had been created just nineteen years before, in 1816. As of 1822, the southern half of the state had been settled and carved up into counties, but the northern third was still owned by Indians; the peaceful mound-building Pottawattomi tribe occupied what became Elkhart County. By coercive treaty, the Indians were forced to give up their land in 1828, at which time it was opened up to homesteaders. The first settlers in what became Goshen put down stakes that year, Elkhart and St. Joseph counties were established in 1830, and the first industry at what became Waterford, on the Elkhart River about fifteen miles south of the Michigan line, as well as on the Goshen-Logansport Road, came into being three years later.

Cephas and Cephas Jr. had been so impressed by the potential they saw in Indiana that they promptly moved the entire family to burgeoning Waterford in early 1836. Cephas found 99.4 acres of land, including a grist-mill and ample water power created by a dam the previous owner had put up across the Elkhart River. After a series of transactions, in March 1836 the land ended up in the hands of Cephas, Cephas Jr., and a friend from Ypsilanti named David Ballentine, and in 1838 they officially founded the town of Waterford.

The gristmill Cephas bought was the first frame mill in the county and quickly became known for making the finest flour in the region. So successful was C. Hawks & Sons that in 1847 Cephas, Cephas Jr., and the latter's younger brother Eleazer built a much larger mill on the same site along the river. This mill had a vastly increased capacity over the old one, able to process fifty barrels of flour per day.

Well before he had spent a decade in the area, Cephas Hawks, with the help of his sons, had turned Waterford into quite a thriving little manu-facturing center. The family owned a sawmill, a woolen mill, a brewery, and the town's main store, which had such a varied and plentiful stock of merchandise that citizens of much larger towns, such as South Bend and Elkhart, came to Waterford to trade. Cephas Hawks also ran a tannery and an ashery in the bargain, and, in the judgment of an official record of Elkhart County, "the family whose interests most completely identified them with the early history of Waterford was that founded here in the thirties by Cephas Hawks Sr."

No matter how industrious the Hawks men were, however, or how superior was their mill, Waterford was fighting a losing battle with Goshen for economic and political dominance in the area. Established as the seat of Elkhart County, the four-by-five-block town of Goshen had just been poking along until 1852, when the first railroad line, the Lake Shore & Michigan, came through. This spelled Waterford's doom just as it signaled Goshen's future. Three years later Cephas Jr. and Eleazer opened a hard-ware store, and the Hawks family began shifting its base to the bigger town.

Well before this, it had become clear that of all of Cephas's ten sur-viving offspring, these two boys were the ones best suited to carry on their father's smart business ways and ambitious thinking. The fourth-born son, Cephas Jr. always worked closely with his father and in all ways was the natural heir apparent to the family businesses. He married a Vermont native, Dalinda B. Bliss, in 1841, and over the next twelve years they had six children: Calista C., Frank E. C., Eveline, who died as a child, Mary E., Edwin W., and Harriet, who also died very young.

Cephas Sr.'s next son, Eleazer, also followed easily into the family business ventures. Eleazer, however, experienced repeated tragedy in his domestic life. His first wife, Margaret Thomas, after at least eight years of marriage, died suddenly at the age of thirty on March 16, 1857. Three years later, Eleazer wed a woman known only as Eliza Ann, but within a year she too was dead, at thirty-five. The circumstances of both women's deaths are nowhere recorded. Then, on October 1, 1863, Eleazer tried a third time, marrying thirty-one-year-old Jennie L. Goff. Little more than one year later, on October 16, 1864, at the advanced age of forty-five (for then, at least), Eleazer became a father for the first time when Jennie gave birth to Franklin Winchester Hawks, who was to become Howard Hawks's father. In 1868, a daughter, Grace L., was born, while a subsequent daughter died in infancy.

In 1844 Cephas Sr.'s sixth and final son, Joel P., at age twenty-two, married Sarah J. Brown of New York State; her father, Ebenezer Brown, became sheriff of Elkhart County. They had a son, Dwight, in 1851, but the following year, in hopes of striking it rich in the Gold Rush, Joel left for California and was gone for three years. Like most other prospecting hopefuls, Joel failed to make his fortune, but the agreeable climate did improve his health. In short order, Joel and Sarah had five more children—Joel P. Jr., Alice and Minnie, both of whom died in childhood, and Emma and Mabel.

While Joel was away, his mother, Cephas Sr.'s prim, charitable, God-fearing wife, died, on Christmas Day 1853, three days short of her seventy-third birthday. By the time Joel returned home in 1855, his father was eighty-one, still energetic and involved in business, but comfortable and proud to see his sons so capably following in his footsteps; ten years before, he had signed official ownership and control of the mill over to Cephas Jr. and Eleazer. Cephas Sr. essentially represented the prototypical success story of his generation, having been born before the birth of the nation, pushing westward several times before settling upon his chosen place, building that into a thriving mercantile community, then leaving behind many descendants to further what he had made into a respected name. He died on May 18, 1859, at eighty-five, having decidedly made his mark in the world.

The year their father died, Cephas Jr. and Eleazer constructed the biggest building yet seen in Goshen, a three-story commercial structure into which they moved the hardware store and gradually installed many of the major Hawks concerns, including the dry goods operation in 1865, the grocery store soon thereafter, the real estate office, the Hawks Coal Company, and the Hawks Electric Company.

Looking ahead in the mid-1860s to how he could further enhance the economic outlook for the little Midwestern empire his father had founded, Cephas Jr. realized that improved transportation in and out of Goshen could considerably expand his pool of potential customers. Opening Goshen up to year-round boat transport seemed the best bet, and to do this meant building a hydraulic canal. He encountered a surprising amount of opposition from other local businessmen, but he promoted the idea tirelessly until he not only won approval but secured a contract from the city to build it himself.

So it came as little surprise when, after the canal was completed, Cephas and Eleazer announced that they would move their milling operations from Waterford to Goshen. More than ever, due to the increased capacity and improved transportation, the Hawks mill thrived: the facility was greatly enlarged, the latest equipment was continually replacing the old, and the company cranked its capacity up to five hundred barrels of flour every twenty-four hours, making it one of the biggest operations of its type in the country. As one local historian put it, "No other concern in Goshen contributes more to the prosperity of Goshen than does the Goshen Milling Co."

By this time, the other dominant family industry was the Hawks Furniture Company. Established in 1873 by Cephas, Eleazer, Joel, and partner Daniel Fravel, the operation started small, with eight employees, making inexpensive, unfinished bedstands and tables. But it grew quickly into the second most important business in Goshen, turning out ornate chamber suites of mahogany, bird's-eye maple, and quartered oak that went out to customers worldwide.

As the century was drawing to a close, the Hawkses so completely dominated Goshen life and business that writers of the city's history could barely contain themselves paying them homage. The *Manual of Goshen* proclaimed that the Hawks brothers' talent for business was so great that "one almost believes they have a perpetual royalty on doing things at precisely the right time, which largely accounts for their bags of golden sheckels. . . . The historian, like sensible people generally, will join in the refrain, 'Pass up more Hawkses if you would supplant poverty by plenty.'"

* * *

The year 1891 was a year of wrenching personal loss for the Hawks family. On May 19, Grace, the only surviving daughter of Eleazer and Jennie, who had lost a later daughter in infancy, died suddenly at the age of twenty-three. Exactly a week later, on May 26, Eleazer passed away, at seventy-two. This double loss left Jennie devastated and, with time, increasingly irrational and difficult; it also left Frank Winchester Hawks a very wealthy twenty-six-year-old. Although involved in the family businesses since graduating from the University of Michigan at Ann Arbor, Frank had not yet shown either the zeal or the traditional Hawks industriousness to integrate himself into the inner circle of management. With Cephas now seventy-eight, and as involved with his voracious reading as he was with business, control of the Hawks industries was falling into the hands of Cephas's eldest son, Frank E. C. Hawks, who was now forty-three.

With his father dead and living with his grieving, inconsolable, unreasonable mother at the large frame house on Fifth and Jefferson, young Frank Winchester Hawks was at sixes and sevens throughout 1891, faithfully tending to his mother as best he could but increasingly looking for a place for himself in the Hawks's well-built, well-to-do, insular universe. Destined to become the first Hawks to leave Goshen, he would meet the woman who would give him a way out the following year.

The leading lights of young society in Neenah, Wisconsin, in the early 1890s were unquestionably Theda Clark and Helen Howard. Theda, born in 1871, was the daughter of Charles B. Clark, cofounder, in 1872, of Kimberly, Clark & Co., which was on its way to becoming one of the most successful paper companies in the United States and, as the inventor of Kleenex, certainly the most famous. Helen, born the following year, was the daughter of Charles W. Howard, also from impoverished origins, who had similarly worked his way up to an exalted position in the paper business. In east-central Wisconsin at the southern, upriver end of the Fox River and the northwest tip of Lake Winnebago, Neenah was one of the economic miracles of the 1890s, a town with a local industry so strong that it barely felt the terrible depression of 1893–97. During this period, there were twenty large paper mills along thirty-seven miles of the Fox River—all successful. Like the city-building pioneers of New England, the founders of the factory towns of the Fox River Valley used as their models the industrial giants of Great Britain, Birmingham and Manchester. When their communities didn't reach those proportions, they scaled back their ambitions, settling for contented, Republican, enormously profitable, immensely comfortable stability at a time when—before the sweeping democratic reforms of Governor Robert La Follette in the 1900s—power in Wisconsin was completely in the corrupt hands of the few men at the top of the state's leading industries.

Charles W. Howard arrived at this growing community in 1862, when he was seventeen. The son of Charles Howard, a native of the Isle of Man, and Hannah Hopkins, of Maine, he was born in Gardiner, Maine, on May 7, 1845. No other information has come down about his parents or early life, perhaps by his own design, as he set the style his famous grandson was to emulate in the fabrication of tall tales and outrageous lies that everyone knew were phony but no one dared challenge to his face. In 1866, he married Euphemia Brown, who was born March 10, 1844, to Scottish natives. During his twenties, Charles ran a harness shop, one of several catering to the extensive horse-and-buggy trade and located on the working-class western end of Wisconsin Avenue, a world away from the affluent eastern section of the avenue, to which he would eventually rise. As of 1870, the Howards still lived at 19 Boarding Street, and the value of their personal estate totaled a mere three hundred dollars.

But Charles kept saving and looking for angles, and by 1874 he was able to become a partner in the A. W. Patten Mill, where he learned the business and reaped the benefits of the mill's unique system of using old paper stock for its raw material; for a while, its capacity of three tons of paper every twenty-four hours bested by fifty percent even what Kimberly-Clark's Globe Mill was producing. In 1877, Charles bought Patten's flour mill and started up a new business with John R. Davis Jr., called Howard & Davis. Through the 1880s, Charles's mills were so successful that he emerged as one of Neenah's leading industrialists, building a large, three-story Victorian house sporting gray shingles, three gables on the roof, a porch stretching across the entire front expanse, and enormous picture windows, from which he could see bits of the Fox River peeking out from behind the even more enormous mansions of his neighbors across the street on East Wisconsin Avenue: John A. Kimberly Sr., John A. Kimberly Jr., and perhaps the area's most powerful individual, the lumberman and politician F. J. Sensenbrenner.

Money was the sole arbiter of social standing in this boom town, and if Charles Howard, now known as C.W., could afford a grand home on Park Row, the most fashionable strip of East Wisconsin Avenue, facing the park and lake, he was entitled to it. Nevertheless, C.W. was something of a pariah even among this city's generation of nouveau riche. By one local account, he "was unfavorably known as a braggart, drunkard, and bully. A habitué of the Russell House barroom, C.W. was prone to wild exaggerations and fistfights. On more than one occasion he publicly announced that he had made more than $500,000 buying and selling a single Menasha paper mill. After a trip around the world he also informed the local residents that the world was flat: "This idea that the world is round," he told lumberman Henry Sherry, "is all damn nonsense."

Unlike his more fastidious neighbors, C.W. also had a taste for the stage, and he sometimes starred in local theatricals, where he could bellow away to his heart's content in the most extravagant Victorian-era fashion. His reputation for pulling hoaxes reached its peak in 1883, when "he shattered his office window with a marble, lodged a bullet in the soft plaster of the opposite wall, and then excitedly told the police [his wife's brother, J. W. Brown, was chief of police] that some mysterious assassin had nearly killed him while sitting at his desk, leaving the sleepy little town in a complete uproar for more than a month." (Charles Coburn comes to mind as the actor who most ideally could have played C. W. Howard.)

But his wife tolerated her husband's excesses, and C.W. doted on his daughters Helen, born in 1872, and Bernice, born four years later. A first child had died in infancy, and although it was never discussed, there was almost certainly another daughter, Emily, who died very shortly after her birth in 1873. The tragedy that most marked the family, however, was the accidental death of the couple's only son, Neil. Born in 1879, Neil was just four or five when he drowned in Lake Winnebago.

Helen and Bernice were both smart and curious, and Helen and Theda Clark became best friends very young when they began attending the tiny Point School, the last of the city's one-room country schoolhouses. Still renowned locally because of the outstanding Theda Clark Medical Center and other facilities bearing her name, Theda was Neenah's golden child, a bright, high-minded princess of wealth and refinement whose noble goals were to cultivate her mind and help others. As Theda and Helen hit their teens, they began organizing elaborate socials and dinners, and then decided to attend college together, thus becoming part of the first generation of American women to pursue advanced education rather than "finishing schools."

Henry Wells, who had made his fortune with his Wells Fargo Stagecoach Lines, founded Wells College in 1866 in Aurora, New York, intending it to offer women an Ivy League–level education, on a par with what men received at Harvard, Yale, or Princeton. The school never grew large enough to become a significant force, but in 1888, when Theda and Helen enrolled as freshmen, Wells was still one of the most desirable, exclusive schools young American women could consider. It was also about to enjoy a particular cachet as the alma mater of Mrs. Grover Cleveland, the new First Lady. Their graduating class in June 1892 consisted of seven women, and the commencement address was entitled "Free Individuality, the Goal of Civilization," which promoted "a desire for higher ideals and for characters free from selfishness and contaminating vices which lead to divorce, suicide, and often living death."

For quite some time after graduation, the Wells women traveled to visit one another at their homes around the country. These visits often lasted for several weeks apiece and involved a continuous succession of parties and dinners. Theda and Helen naturally went to stay with their friend Helen Curtenius, who lived in Goshen, Indiana, where they met the young men Will Peters and Frank Hawks. Helen and Frank fell in love and got serious very quickly, while Theda and Billie, a young journalist, took considerably longer to work out their relationship.

Helen was far from the most attractive woman in Neenah, or even in her small class at Wells. With dark curly hair, wide-set eyes, and a prominent jaw, she had an undeniably horsey look that was overcome by her quick intelligence and adventurous enthusiasm. Frank Hawks, on the other hand, was tall and handsome in a distinguished way, and certainly one of the most eligible bachelors in Goshen at that time. With its shady streets and slow, comfortable way of life backed up by reliable industry, Goshen felt very familiar to Helen, and she and Frank pursued their romantic, traditional courtship by mail as well as in extended stays in the each other's hometowns; Frank, for example, spent New Year's Eve that year in Neenah, where Theda and Helen's party was so minutely planned that all the women were dressed so as to present a history of feminine fashion in American history, from colonial days to the present. Compared to the warmth and liveliness to which she was accustomed at home, however, Helen confessed to finding "a little strain of queerness" in the Hawks family, and had to suppress her natural zest and outspokenness to get along with Frank's moody mother. By contrast, C.W. instantly adored the affable Frank and began treating him like the son he had only so briefly had.

For Neenah society at the time, the mere idea of a long-distance romance was decidedly unusual, and for a girl of Helen's standing to marry an out-of-towner caused no end of talk. But everyone agreed that the match of these two wealthy, bright, well-principled young people seemed ideal, and their wedding, at the Howard home in Neenah on June 5, 1895, was the social event of the year, and the account of the event in the *Neenah Daily Times* the next day was placed at the top and center of page 1.

By August, the bride and groom were settled at his mother's home in Goshen. With Frank halfheartedly working at the mill and obliged to look after his mother, Helen agreed to stay there, and almost immediately discovered that she was pregnant. When Howard Winchester Hawks was born, the fact was promptly noted in the newspapers of both Goshen and Neenah. Six weeks later, in mid-August 1896, Helen and Frank brought the baby to Neenah for the first time and, in a letter to Helen Curtenius, Theda Clark provides a unique portrait of Howard Hawks as an infant:

> Helen Howard Hawks and her flock have been home a week; the baby is a dear. If you can imagine Frank reduced to a pygmy, then you can see the child in your mind's eye; they are so alike.
>
> The baby cries much with colic, and Helen is most devoted. I often sit with the lady when she rocks her "little man" to sleep at night. The whole family is wildly devoted and grandmother, mother, father, aunts, uncles, cousins and dogs gather about to watch the miniature breathe.

C. W. Howard lavished attention on his grandson and spoiled him from the very beginning. In every way, Frank, Helen, and little Howard were more comfortable in Neenah than in Goshen, but they kept their primary residence in Indiana. Just before Christmas in 1896, barely six months after Howard was born, an event of some note took place in Goshen: "The first motion picture ever shown in Goshen was brought to town by Frank Irwin. *Kinematographe* was promoted by the Trans-Oceanic Star specialty company and was touted as 'the scientific wonder of the world.' The Irwin Theater was packed Dec. 10, 1896, when the film was shown the first time, but the audience was disappointed and business began to dwindle after the first showing."

Despite the fact that her family came to visit frequently, after three years in Goshen, Helen had had enough of living under the same roof with her mother-in-law. So after Kenneth Neil—his middle name a tribute to Helen's brother, who had died so young—was born on August 12, 1898, Frank moved the family to an apartment in a local hotel. This was just an interim step before the inevitable move to Neenah. C.W. had made a standing offer for Frank to join him in his business, and it was clear that Frank—who had so much money he didn't need to work anyway and was somewhat resented by his cousins Frank E. C. and Edwin for his less-than-total commitment to the family businesses — would never amount to much more than a name on a brass plate at the Goshen Milling Company. So the move was made, beginning in late 1898. By early the next year, the family was finally installed at 437 Wisconsin Avenue East, just up the street from C.W.'s dark, Queen Anne style house at 409, and Frank was named secretary-treasurer of the Howard Paper Company.

By the turn of the century, when Howard Hawks was four years old, Neenah, Wisconsin, was a town dominated by fourteen churches, including the First Presbyterian, to which the Howards belonged. There were more churches than there were paper mills, hotels, and restaurants. There were seven hotels, seven horse shoers, six restaurants, four dentists, four cigar manufacturers, four harness makers, three newspapers, three wagon makers, three hardware stores, three ice cream parlors, two banks, one bowling alley, one telephone company, a flour mill, a brewery, and Sam Wing's laundry. Within the next couple of years, two billiard parlors opened up, as did two gun-and-ammo shops.

From the beginning, the Hawks boys were pampered like American royalty. All their clothes were of the finest material and cuts, their hair was groomed daily and slicked down in the current fashion, and C.W. outdid himself in finding the most elaborate and expensive toys to give them. This wasn't at all surprising, in that by the standards of the day he had also displayed an indulgent attitude toward his daughters, encouraging and delighting in their adventurous streaks. Helen and Bernice were the first girls in town to ride bicycles and, later, to drive automobiles, and when the early aviator C. P. Rogers came through the Fox Valley, Bernice reportedly paid him five hundred dollars to take her up in his rickety early plane. One doesn't have to look far to find the models for what later became known as "the Hawksian women"; they were Howard women.

Two years older than Kenneth, little Howard was close to and protective of his younger brother. But it was a different story when the family's next son, William Bellinger Hawks, arrived in 1902. The oft-repeated family story had it that to get him out of the way, six-year-old Howard was sent to the home of a friend, Judge Cleveland, the day William was born. Resenting his new brother, Howard offered to sell the baby to the judge, sight unseen, for ten cents.

Theda Clark's letters provide a few little snapshots of the young Howard Hawks, including one of a traumatic event he was never heard to speak about as an adult. On June 14, 1900, just after Howard's fourth birthday, Theda wrote that a little playmate of Howard's had drowned in the Fox River right across from his house, and that Howard had apparently witnessed it. With the boy's heavy German mother lumbering in hysterics toward the scene, Howard ran up the sidewalk to Theda and said, "Aunt Theda—Aunt Theda—a little boy drowned!" The tragedy deeply depressed Helen, since her little brother had died the same way.

The following year, after having made a very Henry Jamesian tour of Europe and having begun her very active philanthropic career, Theda finally married Will Peters of Goshen after an up-and-down six-year romance that did not enjoy the unqualified enthusiasm of Theda's mother. The correspondent for the *Chicago Chronicle* couldn't help but mention that "disparity in the conditions, however—an heiress to millions and a comparatively poor newspaperman—engendered complications which prevented the marriage for over six years." In other words, the Clark-Peters romance had the making of a perfect screwball comedy, thirty-five years before Howard Hawks helped pioneer the genre. At the ornate wedding at the Clark home, Frank was the best man, while the bridesmaid "preceded little Howard Hawks, who was dressed all in white and carried a massive bouquet of American beauty roses."

As had Helen, Theda settled initially in Goshen. But since Will, having left his job as managing editor of the *Goshen Times*, was on the road a great deal in his new, better-paid position as a salesman for the Philadelphia wallpaper company Cresswell & Washburn, Theda still spent much of her time in Neenah. She would very often have Howard and Kenneth over for lunch, and she wrote to a friend that "such great, dirty, freckled, rowdy boys you never saw and all out at the knees."

Theda was unstinting in her charity work. Her hero was Jane Addams of Hull House in Chicago, and she donated the land and a great deal of money for the construction of a superb, Roman-style library in Neenah. Theda and Helen each became pregnant at virtually the same time early in 1903. On October 17, Helen gave birth to her fourth child and first girl, Grace. But the very next day, Theda, who had experienced an increasingly difficult pregnancy, was unable to deliver normally, and the baby girl had to be "taken with instruments." But the hemorrhaging could not be stopped, and the next day, with her sister, Will, Helen, and a Dr. Barnett attending her helplessly, she bled to death. Theda, who had just turned thirty-two, had the largest funeral Neenah had seen since her father died. In her will, she had designated a large sum of money for the construction of Neenah-

Menasha's first hospital, which was shortly built and has operated ever since right across the river from her former home.

During his wife's preoccupation with Theda's illness and death, Frank Hawks busied himself with the countless details pertaining to the family's new home. If not quite a mansion, the house—at 433 East Wisconsin Avenue, three lots west of the Howard abode—was certainly grandly imposing, a three-story structure with fifteen rooms, built at a cost of $20,000 (more than $400,000 by 1990s standards). Frank even imported an architect from Boston, the first time an outsider had ever been brought in to Neenah to design a building. A large, rambling house, elegant in brown-gray shingles and fieldstone and exceedingly well built, it had a backyard stretching an entire city block north to Doty Street, a dream for young boys. There were two bay windows on either side of the front door, an east-facing porch, a grand front staircase, and dark wood beams and appointments on the first floor. Four bedrooms, one with a sitting room, took up the second floor, while the third had two bedrooms and a ballroom. Six fireplaces helped heat it. When Howard made *Ball of Fire* years later, he noted the similarity of the professors' home to the one in which he spent part of his youth, saying, "I know what this kind of house is like." Across the street and down a house was a small landing for boats, while 150 yards further east was beautiful Riverside Park, dotted with many trees. About a half mile further east was the shore of Lake Winnebago. It was, in all ways, one of the half dozen most impressive private homes in Neenah, and an idyllic place for children to grow up.

But by the time the family moved in, in 1904–05, the first signs were appearing that the Hawkses wouldn't be staying in Neenah much longer. Already rather debilitated after delivering William and Grace, and devastated by the loss of Theda, Helen was brought to the limit by the birth of a fifth child, and second daughter, also named Helen, in 1906. After having borne so many children, she became "professionally ill," in the opinion of a friend, and needed to find a way to recapture her health. Helen's doctor advised her to leave Wisconsin, particularly during its brutal winters. Frank didn't have to work, so they spent the winter of 1906–07 in Pasadena, California, a town northeast of Los Angeles that had recently caught on as a popular destination for well-to-do families from the East and Midwest. Initially, the Hawkses returned to Wisconsin during the summer, but by 1910 they left Wisconsin behind for good. C.W., who took to wintering in Pasadena himself, said, "It was too damn bad they didn't know this before they built the house," but they shortly rented it to

C. B. Clark Jr., Theda's brother, who later became mayor of Neenah. In 1912, Frank finally sold the house.

In the early 1900s, the ranks were thinning in Goshen as well; Frank's very successful uncle Joel P. Hawks died on April 8, 1905, at the age of eighty-three, while his aunt Sarah died a little more than a year later, at eighty-two.

As for old C. W. Howard, he finally sold, at great profit, his interest in what had become the Island Paper Company; retired from active work; made investments, such as one in a hotel across the river in Menasha; devoted considerable time to the Winnebago Humane Society and the Mason Lodge; traveled extensively in Europe with his wife; and gave his eldest grandson whatever he wanted. When Howard, barely old enough to drive legally, showed an interest in auto racing, C.W. bought him a Mercer race car. And just as he had indulged his daughter Bernice's interest in flying, C.W. arranged for the teenage Howard to take flying lessons in California so that he could qualify as a pilot; Kenneth soon followed suit. Partly because of his family's wealth, but even more because of the way his grandfather catered to his every whim from the earliest age, Howard was accustomed to getting what he wanted. C.W. always told him he was the best, that he could do anything, and why shouldn't the boy believe him? Howard also learned the art of the tall tale from his grandfather: if you told it often enough with a straight face and didn't permit contradiction, it became part of your personal lore, if not simply taken as the truth. America, at that time, was made for an adventurous young boy of privilege like Howard Hawks, and his family's position gave him the means to take advantage of it. At the same time, every man on both sides of the family as far back as anyone could trace had been engaged in very traditional business; they had pioneered, worked hard, been good farmers, fighters, cattlemen, millers, builders, and furniture makers. Except for C.W.'s amateur theatrics and Helen's interest in music, no one in the family had ever shown the slightest inclination toward the arts, for branching away from the practical into the realm of the imagination.

In the early-morning hours of Wednesday, January 5, 1916, the temperature in Neenah reached 12 degrees below zero, a record low for the winter. The west wind bit fiercely, but by that afternoon, as C. W. Howard walked to the Neenah Club downtown for a couple of drinks and some chat with the boys, the thermometer nosed slightly above zero. In the dark of the late afternoon, he boarded the 5:30 P.M. streetcar for the short trip east on Wisconsin Avenue. Euphemia had not been well of late, and C.W. went directly up to his wife's bedroom to check on her. It was there that he suffered a stroke. He was semiconscious at first, with his right side paralyzed, but he "soon lapsed into a stupor from which he never emerged," according to the front-page story in the next day's *Neenah Daily Times*. "Death came quietly and without the least suffering according to those at his bedside." C. W. Howard died at 2:30 A.M. on January 6, 1916, at the age of seventy. The official cause of death was a cerebral hemorrhage, with a secondary cause of arteriosclerosis.

As befitting a man of his stature, C.W. had a large funeral. In ill health already, suffering from cancer of the uterus, Euphemia could not easily absorb the shock of her husband's sudden death. She died just three months later, on April 13, also at seventy.

In the distribution of C.W.'s estate, which finally took place in October 1918, it was revealed that his net worth, after the sale of his home, other property, and stocks, came to $264,090; this would have made him a millionaire many times over in 1990's adjusted dollars. The great bulk of it went to his already very comfortable daughters, with Bernice receiving a lump sum of $115,315 and Helen getting $57,657 immediately and an equal amount to be apportioned out in stages to her monthly. Helen's children each received $5,736 (about $120,000 in current dollars), perhaps not enough to set them up for life, but plenty to send them into their adult lives in high style and without need of mundane employment.

The story of C. W. Howard had a bizarre postscript. Some years later, after his daughter Helen had become a confirmed, perhaps even fanatic, Christian Scientist and adherent of cremation, she returned to Neenah. She had her father, mother, and brother Neil dug up and cremated (in Milwaukee, as no one closer by would do it). After mixing the ashes in an urn, she went out to Riverside Park and threw it in the river, where it was discovered decades later, with the names and dates still legible, by scuba divers. The grave marker, a big red marble ball six feet in diameter that C.W. had bought for himself at the 1896 Columbian Exposition in Chicago, Helen sold to the Abenschein family, whose grave it still marks today.

2

Boy of Privilege

Pasadena in the first decade of the twentieth century was a garden grown of imported privilege and prosperity, an enclave of wealth and immaculate conservatism populated mostly by well-to-do former Midwesterners, like the Hawkses, seeking the year-round comfort of one of the most ideal climates in the country. Vast orange groves surrounded impeccably manicured estates and a prosperous but unhurried downtown on Colorado Boulevard, and to the north and east soaring mountain peaks, which were topped with snow during the winter, formed a spectacular backdrop to the intense green of the city.

During the winter visits, Frank Hawks had installed his family at the ultrafashionable Maryland Hotel, and that is where they lived when they came out to stay in 1906, before renting a house for a short time at 408 Arroyo Terrace. Frank, still only in his early forties, didn't need to work. But he and C.W. made some hotel investments along the West Coast that gave Frank the excuse to travel occasionally, and he bought some orange groves in Glendora, less than twenty miles to the east, that engaged his active interest.

One of the most distinguished academic facilities in southern California at the time was the Throop Polytechnic Institute, which later became the California Institute of Technology. Founded in 1893, the school was just down the street from the large, comfortable house Frank found for the family at 998 San Pasqual, which has long since been torn down. Throop, pronounced "Troop," at the time encompassed all levels of classes, beginning with grade school, and that is where Howard attended the sixth grade. But when the Throop trustees decided to concentrate all their effort on advanced education, the Grammar School Department was reorganized into a separate entity.

The new Polytechnic Elementary School opened on October 10, 1907, and Howard, Kenneth, William, and Grace Hawks were among the 106 pupils enrolled. Frank Hawks soon became a trustee and remained on

34

the board for a decade. The school was, and still is, a coed, nonsectarian establishment that, in addition to the usual grade-school curriculum, gave special attention to industrial arts; this marked the beginning of Howard's lifelong hobby of wood and metal crafting. The average class size was sixteen students, and the school prided itself on the special attention given to the children, who advanced to the next level in each class not according to the calendar but by virtue of their success in the current grade.

Howard Hawks was a thoroughly average student at Poly. His standard courses were English, arithmetic, geography, German, art training, manual arts, penmanship, music, and gymnasium; he later added French and substituted history for geography. Four grades—excellent, good, medium and low—were given, and in his sixth-grade year, Howard received seventeen Ms, thirty Gs, and six Es. In the seventh grade, his grades dipped slightly; he got thirty Gs, twenty-four Ms, and no Es. In the eighth grade, his marks slipped further, with four Ls, including two in arithmetic, only two Es, in English and art training, twenty Gs, and twenty-three Ms. He scored better in German than in French, did not excel at gym, was good in the reading section of his English classes.

School photos of Howard at the time—one of which shows him in a typical pose, holding a tennis racquet and slouching against a building—reveal him to be slim and on the short side compared to most of the other boys, always with a very serious, rather suspicious air that was accentuated by his tight little mouth. Howard was not among the winners in the school's tennis tournaments, nor was he among the many contributors to the yearbook of Poly's first eighth-grade graduating class in 1910. It is likely, however, that he participated in one of the local boys' favorite sports: "coaster" racing, in which large but motorless race cars were piloted downhill on dirt roads in nearby Altadena. Fifteen boys, including Chuck "Roughhouse" Hunt, the son of Myron Hunt by his first marriage, and five girls made up the class, and the inscription beside a portrait of a grim-looking fourteen-year-old boy in a double-breasted suit reads, "Howard Hawks—'Our English descendent.'"

During the same period, three other Hawks kids were following right behind Howard. Despite being two years younger, Kenneth entered Poly in the fifth grade in 1907, and after a rough start he made solid Gs. William, who was three years behind Kenneth, performed similarly well in school, getting Gs all around. Grace entered in 1907 and was by far the best student among the Hawks children, earning many Es and being singled out on her third-grade report card as "A fine worker."

In May 1911, the most horrible of tragedies hit the Hawks family, the first of three to befall the children of Frank and Helen Hawks. On May 4, Helen Bernice, their youngest child, then five years and four months old, ate a bad piece of fruit and suddenly died. The cause of death was officially listed as acute enteritis, but it seems likely that the fruit, described as "unripe" on her death certificate, was actually somehow infected or poisoned. In accordance with her Christian Scientist beliefs, the girl's devastated mother instructed the funeral director to cremate the remains, and the ashes were interred at Mt. View Cemetery two days later. Typically, the family kept its grief subdued and as controlled as possible, and what happened to Helen was rarely spoken about subsequently.

For his freshman, sophomore, and first quarter of his junior years of high school, from September 1910 through December 1912, Howard went to the public Pasadena High; decades later, the facility evolved into Pasadena City College, which currently occupies the same site at Hill and Colorado. Freshman year, he earned "good" marks across the board in English, algebra, wood shop, freehand drawing, mechanical drawing, and gym, though only a "medium" in French. Sophomore year, when the grading system was changed to percentages, he managed a ninety-one in mechanical drawing, an eighty-seven in English, an eighty-five in geometry, an eighty-three in shop, and a seventy-seven in French. During the first term of his junior year, he scored an excellent ninety-six in German, a split ninety/eighty-six in English, a ninety/eighty in algebra, but a failing sixty in chemistry.

In late 1912, the family left Pasadena and moved east to live a much more rural life among Frank's orange groves, at 352 North Los Robles in Glendora. The reasons for the abrupt change are unknown, although they could conceivably have had something to do with a desire to leave behind the house at 998 San Pasqual, where little Helen had died, or might have been connected to either Grace or Helen's health.

When the family moved, Howard transferred schools and finished his junior year, from January through June 1913, at Citrus Union High School in Glendora, in the boondocks compared to the quiet elegance and refinement of Pasadena. He did relatively well there, so that Frank and Helen, hoping to set their eldest son even more firmly on an Ivy League course, decided to send Howard east for the most rigorous formal education available. It remains uncertain exactly how they got him into the Phillips Exeter Academy in New Hampshire, the most prestigious prep school in the United States, although money may have played the decisive role in slipping a West

Coast boy with respectable but hardly distinguished grades into a school in which the vast majority of the 572 students at that time were upper crusters from the northeastern states. Howard Hawks, at age seventeen, was accepted into Phillips Exeter but, inexplicably, only as a lower middleclassman, the equivalent of a sophomore, meaning he was two years older than most of the 165 other boys at his level and two years behind where he was supposed to be. After the long train trip across the country, he arrived in time to start classes on September 15, 1913.

The small town of Exeter, founded by English settlers in 1638, lies ten miles from the Atlantic Ocean about midway along the short stretch of New Hampshire that separates coastal Massachusetts and Maine. The trip to New England marked Howard's first visit to the area his earliest American ancestors lived in, although family and sentimental ties meant little to him then or later. Opened in 1783, Phillips Exeter had long been the most elite of secondary schools; among its alumni at the time were eight senators, twenty state representatives, twelve state governors, one associate justice of the Supreme Court, and hundreds of other successful men of academia, the law, medicine, and religion. The most famous graduate was Daniel Webster. The school prided itself on its adherence to fairness and democratic dealings with all students but insisted "first of all on honest labor. The day's work must be done. Every boy, high or low, rich or poor, must show actual performance. Not to learn one's lesson is a breach of trust."

Although at least half the boys lived in private lodgings off campus, Hawks took student facilities in large Webster Hall, a classical four-story, redbrick building in which he shared room 28 with a senior, Horace Alonzo Quimby, of Springfield, Massachusetts. All the evidence suggests that Hawks in no way entered into the spirit of life at Phillips Exeter, certainly not academically and not even in the expected extracurricular activities. Attendance at chapel was required of all students, and Hawks, as one of only three registered Christian Scientists at the entire school, was assigned to the menial position of church monitor for the Christian Science contingent. He automatically became a member of the California Club, of which there were just nine others. He also joined the Assembly Club, which was in charge of arranging social events and inviting outside speakers. Although Phillips Exeter had become very athletically oriented over the previous decade and boasted first-rate sports fields and facilities, Hawks went out for no sports teams. He did, however, keep a meticulously assembled scrapbook into which he pasted local newspaper articles highlighting the exploits of all the prep school and Ivy League sports teams.

His academic record was grim. In the highly competitive and demanding scholastic environment of Phillips Exeter, Howard Hawks, never a notable student, simply couldn't cut it. The academic year was divided into three terms; in the first of them, Hawks received Cs in mechanical drawing and physics; Ds in math, German, and history; and no grade at all in physical training. During Christmas break, Howard forwent the long trip back to California and, instead, stayed with a family in Brookline, Massachusetts. As the many ticket stubs and playbills obsessively pasted into his scrapbook attest, the young man attended nearly every theatrical production playing in Boston that season. Returning for the winter term in January, he managed a B in mechanical drawing, got Cs in physics and physical training, but earned Es in German and history. Such marks, indicative of a near-total failure to live up to his potential or to apply himself, were fatal at an institution with the standards of Phillips Exeter, and Hawks did not return for a third term to finish the year there. The school was designed for "the boy of good ability, good character, and earnest purpose," and not for "the careless, thoughtless, unambitious boy, who burdens so many schools with his deadening lethargy and lack of worthy ambition." In the view of the administrators, there was no question to which group Howard Hawks belonged.

With his tail between his legs, Howard returned during Easter break to Glendora, where the family was still living and where Kenneth, two years younger than Howard, was in his junior year—officially one class year ahead of his older brother. Through some clever card shuffling, it was arranged for Howard to reenroll in Pasadena High in April 1914 as a senior. Back on home turf, his performance improved immeasurably. He excelled in trigonometry, with a ninety-five, and did reasonably well in physics, with an eighty-five. On his official school records, Fs and Os in German and American history are strangely written over with eighties in both subjects. The meaning of this in unclear, but Howard, in any event, did not graduate with the rest of the students in June. He was forced to take summer school, in which he got a ninety in American history and an eighty-five in German, and he finally graduated on July 31. Conveniently, in May the family had moved back to Pasadena, where William and Grace reentered the Polytechnic School.

Even more mysterious than Hawks's acceptance at Phillips Exeter is precisely what induced Cornell University, one of the leading schools of the Ivy League, to admit a young man with Hawks's thoroughly haphazard and unpromising academic record; Hawks did not even apply to the university until August, a month before classes began. Once again, it can only have been his family's social position in a well-to-do community, financial considerations, and, possibly but untraceably, his parents' connections to old friends with influence back East; Helen, after all, had attended Wells College, the pioneering women's school in central New York, and might well have been able to pull the right strings to have her son taken by Cornell, located in Ithaca, only twenty-five miles away.

In September 1914, Hawks entered Cornell at age eighteen as a mechanical engineering major. Unfortunately, all school academic records for the period Hawks was a student have been destroyed, so his grades and athletic affiliations are unavailable; but all indications point to an indifferent academic career there. In his freshman and sophomore years, he was a member of the Exeter Club, although he had not graduated from that school, and he eventually joined the Delta Kappa Epsilon fraternity. The secretary of Hawks's graduating class, Ray S. Ashbury, reported that Hawks was referred to as Howie by his buddies, and remembered that the Californian spent much of his time shooting craps in Ithaca rather than studying. Little will ever be known about Hawks's college career, but it seems clear that Hawks acquired more of a taste for gambling and liquor during his college days than he did for higher learning. It also appears that Hawks traveled to New York City on occasion and attended the theater, for he was conversant with the playwrights and some actors of the period. He also read a great deal, mostly popular American and English fiction, which came in handy a few years later when he went to work in the scenario department at Paramount. Nothing Hawks ever said suggests that his college years were decisive to him in any way, except for what he did during his summer vacations.

Around this time, shortly before his death, C. W. Howard bought his grandson a Mercer racing car, and the teenager was able to start tinkering with it and racing it, in an occasional, amateur fashion, in California. Auto racing in those days was a rough-and-tumble affair done on dirt tracks in machines that were far from precise in their handling or reliable in performance. The cars kicked up enormous amounts of dirt that made visibility almost nonexistent for the drivers behind them, and if it had rained, the resulting mud made conditions even more dangerous. As Hawks testified, "It wasn't very polite racing." For Hawks, it was rich boy's fun, a form of sport slumming against young men who were mostly grease monkeys, not

Ivy Leaguers. But one of these former auto mechanics, who several years earlier had been an actual barnstorming race-car driver in the days when the fatality rate for professional drivers was about fifty percent, soon became his best friend and a deep influence on his life. This was Victor Fleming, and the way Hawks described their first encounter is not only incredibly self-serving, with him coming out on top, as usual, but has the feel of a scene from a film that either of them could have made. As Hawks told it, they were driving against each other in a race, and "I put him through a fence and wrecked his car. I won the race and saw him coming: I thought I was gonna have a fight with him. Instead of that, he came up with a grin and he said, 'That was pretty good, but don't ever try it again, because I'll just run into you.'"

True, false, or merely exaggerated, the story sets the tone for an enduring friendship that had a strongly competitive edge but that the men never allowed to become endangered by personal or professional jealousy, despite repeated opportunities over the years. Thirteen years older than Hawks and in his early thirties when they met, Fleming long served as an unacknowledged role model for Hawks. Everything Hawks considered himself or was ever known as—film director, macho sportsman, ladies' man, auto racer, flier, tough guy—Fleming did first and, with the exception of directing, better, although many of their contemporaries would have differed even on that point. Fleming was the real thing, the genuine article. Tall, physically powerful, and described by one woman as "a composite between an internal combustion engine hitting on all twelve and a bear cub," Fleming was also deeply, compulsively emotional in a way that Hawks never was, a man who agonized over work, often got himself into binds, and repeatedly pushed himself to the brink, and whose serious drinking, recurring ulcers, and other physical ailments were a direct result of his complicated, demanding, tumultuous life. If Hawks kept all his tension and anxiety wound up tight inside, Fleming let it all out. And if there was a real-life inspiration for the prototypical "love story between two men" that Hawks kept returning to as his ideal subject, beginning with A Girl in Every Port, it was his own relationship with Victor Fleming.

The two grew up very near each other, although too far separated in years for it to have mattered. He lied about his age later on, but Victor Fleming was born in Pasadena on February 23, 1883. His father, W. R. L. Fleming, of English stock, was an engineer in charge of installing Pasadena's first water-supply system, but he died when his son was four. Victor's mother, the former Evelyn Hartman, who was Pennsylvania Dutch, remarried and moved to Los Angeles. As an adult, the handsome, dark-haired Fleming always boasted that he had Cherokee blood, but there is no trace of this in his official lineage. For unknown reasons, Victor was separated and placed with Evelyn's brother Edwin Hartman, who ran a ranch in San Dimas, a small rural community immediately south of Glendora, where Frank Hawks would purchase his orange grove some twenty years later. A "holy terror" at school, Victor quit at fourteen and took a job at a Pasadena bicycle shop. The shop also had agency rights for one of the new cars then gaining popularity, the Oldsmobile, so the teenager quickly turned his attention to automobiles and got to know them inside out. By the turn of the century, Victor Fleming was racing cars at fairground tracks; he rode as Charley Soules's mechanic in the first Vanderbilt Cup race in Santa Monica. Fleming got to know Soules's longtime partner, Barney Oldfield, and worked on Oldfield's famous Blitzen & Peerless Green Dragon racer in addition to continuing to barnstorm on his own on the standard mile-long circular courses, winning plenty of trophies in the process. In addition to having been in on the ground floor of automobile racing, Fleming was the 5,912th American to be certified with a pilot's license, logging fourteen hundred hours in the air long before World War I began.

In Pasadena, Fleming had known a brash kid eight years his junior named Marshall (Mickey) Neilan, who likewise had lost his civil-engineer father at a very young age. A carouser and a vagabond of sorts, Mickey Neilan came into films as D. W. Griffith's chauffeur in 1911, and by the following spring he was acting in Westerns for the American Film Company (or Flying A) in Santa Barbara under director Allan Dwan. In 1912, Dwan bought one of the biggest and most luxurious cars then in existence, the Mitchell Six, which Neilan taught him to drive, but one day it went on the blink. When none of the mechanics in Santa Barbara could fix it, Neilan remembered that Vic Fleming from Pasadena was working as a chauffeur and mechanic for a rich family in Montecito. With some difficulty, they found him at an estate up in the hills, and Fleming supposedly fixed the car, on which the timing was off, in ten minutes. Seeing some photographic equipment in the garage and learning that Fleming was an amateur photographer, Dwan asked if Fleming could repair his old English Williamson camera. Fleming knew nothing about that brand, but after he noticed that the brass aperture plate was scratching the film, he solved the problem by replacing it with a steel plate. The conventional, but incorrect, version of what happened next is that Dwan offered him a job; Dwan did not. Fleming, anxious for work in the fledgling industry, had to beg Flying A owner Samuel

S. Hutchinson for any kind of job. He began by developing negatives, then moved to the set by carrying film and helping with props, all this when he was nearly thirty years old. Impressed by his dedication, Dwan soon made him an assistant cameraman, and Fleming was, by 1916, around the time he met Hawks, the cinematographer of the Douglas Fairbanks films Dwan was directing for producer D. W. Griffith at Triangle.

Fleming was the director of photography on the Fairbanks picture *In Again—Out Again,* directed by John Emerson, the husband of writer Anita Loos and the future director, not coincidentally, of the first screen version of *Gentlemen Prefer Blondes.* Although Hawks never verified it for certain, all the circumstantial evidence points to *In Again—Out Again,* which was a sensation when it was released in April 1917, as the first picture on which Howard Hawks worked. It would also seem that Victor Fleming, as the one person Hawks definitely knew in the film business at that point, was very likely responsible for bringing him in. *In Again—Out Again* was Fairbanks's first foray as a producer and his first film for Artcraft-Paramount. The most Hawks ever said about his motivation for entering the film business was, "I just wanted a job during summer vacation. Somebody I knew at Paramount got me one in the Prop Room." He further explained that an emergency had arisen on the Fairbanks picture—the film needed a modern set built in a hurry at a time when the studio's sole official art director was away. Hawks, with his limited architectural training, volunteered his services—or perhaps was recommended by Fleming. Fairbanks liked the work as well as the young man who did it, which led to further employment at the studio.

For Hawks at first, it was just summer work; he might more plausibly have found a job with an automotive shop or a construction company, the latter a logical choice for someone who was training to be a mechanical engineer. He never claimed to have been a film fan that early in life, to have been dazzled as an impressionable youth by the allure of motion pictures or the recent achievements of D. W. Griffith, Charlie Chaplin, or anyone else. And he certainly didn't need the money. It was even more unusual for a film studio to employ a rich kid like Hawks in such a menial position than it was for an upper-class boy to take such a low-end job for the summer, for there was, as yet, very little glamour associated with an industry that still saw its members shunned from boardinghouses and apartment buildings, not to mention clubs, schools, and respectable institutions of all types. The vast majority of people entering the film business at that time came from distinctly humble origins, and more than a few assumed new names and rewrote their life stories. Allan Dwan compared Hollywood at that time to a circus, populated by "a pleasant gang of gypsy-like people."

At that time, starting at the top meant working for either D. W. Griffith or Cecil B. De Mille; through recommendations from Fairbanks and Mary Pickford, Hawks very quickly found himself working for the latter. Autocratic and a tough taskmaster even then, De Mille, had come out to Hollywood from the East in 1914 and made his great breakthrough with *The Squaw Man*, the first legitimate feature-length American film; by 1916 he had already done more than anyone else to consolidate and promote the idea of Hollywood as a center for motion picture production. In the two years since *The Squaw Man*, he had produced and directed an additional twenty-five pictures and was quickly developing his reputation as the greatest showman in the young industry.

Hawks never specified which De Mille picture he worked on during the summer of 1916; it could have been *Temptation, The Trail of the Lonesome Pine, The Heart of Nora Flynn, Maria Rosa, The Dream Girl,* or *Joan the Woman.* Those who knew the cool, unflappable Hawks of later years would have trouble imagining him as a fumbling, inexperienced underling, but Hawks told Kevin Brownlow that on this early job he was hidden in an adobe house with the responsibility of lighting a flare when he heard a bugle blow once and putting it out when it blew twice. "Well, the first time I lit the flare it caught all the other flares that were in there on fire and when a flare's on fire it travels and I was running around thinking I was going to get burned up, but I'll never forget all of the bugles blowing and blowing and I was saying, 'Oh, shut up!' I couldn't put the flare out, I was trying to keep myself from being burned alive."

Having failed in his attempt to transfer to Stanford University, the closest thing to an Ivy League university on the West Coast, Hawks returned to Cornell in September 1916 for his junior year. But when the United States entered World War I in April 1917, Howard Hawks's academic career effectively ended. The great majority of students, including Hawks, would soon be called up for military service, with the members of Hawks's class plucked out of school with just a year to go. What was done, in the end, was to graduate the servicemen of the class of 1918 in absentia. They received actual degrees, not honorary ones, even though they missed their entire senior years. This, then, is how Howard Hawks came to graduate from Cornell with a degree in mechanical engineering, despite his being far away when diplomas were handed out. But in the buccaneer days of the film industry, formal education counted for nothing; the last thing a producer

or executive ever thought to ask a prospective director was where he went
to college, since hardly anyone had. For Hawks, the prep school and Ivy
League credentials, however undistinguished in achievement, gave him a
certain aura, a polish that few others in his profession at that time possessed,
which set him apart from the crowd in an impressive way. They also added,
like medals, to his intimidation quotient, his forbidding talent to convince
others, particularly those of more humble origins — that is, his bosses — that
he just naturally knew more than they did, that he was smarter, more refined, and in every way more capable. This was an important key to his ability
to so consistently get his way throughout the main part of his career.

Apparently, Hawks took the opportunity of the country's declaring war
to leave Cornell at once, before being called up for service, for in April 1917
he was back in California working for De Mille. *The Little American* was a
big World War I romance in which Mary Pickford played an American girl
whose two suitors, a German and a Frenchman, must return in 1914 to fight
on opposite sides in the conflict. Surviving the sinking of the *Lusitania* on
her way to Europe, Mary ends up in a château with the German when the
French bombard it, which is where Hawks came in. Hawks was working
props in the violent scene in which the château is demolished and, as he
told Brownlow, "they had canvas all over the set and about six pails of flashlight powder that was supposed to go off. Well, nobody told me and I was
up the top and when it went off I was supposed to drop a lot of cement and
things. But all I got was all the fumes from six pails of flashlight powder,
and I couldn't breathe and instead of cement coming down, I fell down in
the middle of the table in the middle of the scene. And when he [De Mille]
saw who it was he just shook his head" — no doubt remembering the lad's
faux pas with the flares the year before. On this picture, which was in production between April 13 and May 22, 1917, Hawks became friendly with
the eighteen-year-old Chinese-American slate boy, Jimmy Wong Howe, who
was just entering the business.

Hawks claimed he and De Mille liked each other and always got along
well, although he also paid him a backhanded compliment, saying that
whatever approach De Mille would take as a director "I would work exactly
the opposite, and do quite well doing it. If I tried to tell people to do some
of the things he did, I'd laugh while I was trying to tell 'em. But he made it
work. I learned an awful lot because I did the opposite." He also made the
far-fetched claim that once, when the famous De Mille temper was unleashed in Hawks's direction, the lowly assistant prop boy promptly "got
him by the front of the coat," said he didn't like to be talked to that way,

and promised to slug him if he ever did it again. In this fairy tale, which is identical to similar stories of how Hawks later manhandled Louis B. Mayer, Humphrey Bogart, and other tough guys, De Mille immediately apologized.

The Little American was well received upon its release in July 1917, and Hawks is known to have worked on two additional pictures before entering the armed forces, one of which gave him his chance to direct for the first time. In 1916, Mickey Neilan largely quit acting to take up directing full-time. Having appeared opposite Mary Pickford in numerous pictures, he became one of her most trusted collaborators. All the same he grew even more devil-may-care with success, and while directing *The Little Princess*, an adaptation of Frances Hodgson Burnett's famous children's book, starring Pickford, Neilan went off on a drunk and simply didn't show up one day. The way Hawks told it, when Pickford despaired of doing any shooting that day, Hawks said, "'Why don't we make some scenes?' She said, 'Can you do it?' and I said, 'Yeah.' I made some, and she liked it very much."

What Hawks and Pickford's regular cinematographer, Charles Rosher, did were basically some trick shots, amusing double exposures that were basically in-camera special effects. The principle was that a shot could be taken of someone, for example, sitting in a chair, whereupon the film was carefully wound back to the same starting place and then run through the camera again, only this time showing the person getting up from the chair and walking across the room, which would effectively convey a dream or fantasy. Pickford said she wanted a scene in which she would, in effect, follow herself into a room, so Hawks and Rosher filmed her once in the room, rewound the film, and then took a shot of her entering the room. "And it happened that they matched," Hawks said. "The cameraman was just sweating because he said it's only one chance in ten that it'll match." They also executed a crude but charming stop-motion scene, the live-action equivalent of animation, in which they rigged a doll so that, by filming it one frame at a time in slightly different positions, it could be made to look as though it was moving of its own accord. These scenes, which rested entirely on cute little tricks, represented Howard Hawks's directorial debut. After *The Little Princess*, Hawks worked on one more Neilan feature, *Amarilly of Clothesline Alley*, one of Mary Pickford's less celebrated outings, in which she played a lower-class girl who comes close to being snatched up by a gilded youth but eventually realizes that happiness for her rests with one of her own.

In addition to becoming good friends with Mickey Neilan, Hawks learned a great deal from the boisterous, irreverent Irishman that was pertinent to his own work later on. "Neilan had a great sense of humor," Hawks noted. "He had a very opposite sense . . . he could get fun out of odd, quick little things, he could get fun out of stress and duress. And he taught me how to do it." It was the cue he got from Neilan that inspired Hawks to always look for a different way of doing something; to try to make any story a comedy if possible; to reverse a situation from what an audience expected; to realize the comic potential in frustration, hazard, and embarrassment; to cast, perhaps, a woman in a man's part; and to maximize the potential of intimacy and compression instead of going, à la De Mille, for broad strokes and general effects. Hawks would work with Neilan again numerous times before beginning his directing career, and Neilan's impact was so strong that he remained a conscious influence on Hawks as late as the 1960s, in *Red Line 7000* and *El Dorado*.

By the summer's end, Hawks, now twenty-one, was obliged to join the armed services. Distressingly, Hawks's military records appear not to exist; it is overwhelmingly likely that they were among the 80 percent of all army personnel records for the years 1912–59 that were destroyed in a fire on the top floor of the St. Louis National Personnel Records Center on July 12, 1973. All there is to go on regarding Hawks's World War I service is his own testimony, which is scant. Hawks began his stint in the Army Air Corps with fifteen weeks of ground training in a special program at the University of California at Berkeley, which prepared him to be a squadron commander even though he didn't yet know how to fly and only got to spend a token amount of time in the air. While Hawks was there, Mary Pickford visited the Bay Area on a war-bonds tour, and Hawks's friendship with her astonished his superiors. He was then sent to Texas, where he was finally taught to fly, although he said, "I think I got about an hour and three-quarters flying, and they made me an instructor." Hawks's army experience appears to have been frustrating and relatively uneventful, since his evident skill at teaching flying amounted to a sentence to continue doing so, which reduced his chances of going overseas to near zero. Hawks said that his time in Texas, which spanned roughly the first half of 1918, was a grindingly dull period "because there were two or three thousand cadets down there and about seven or eight airplanes. They didn't even have enough airplanes to train people. So we applied for almost anything we could do to get out of there." Hawks's application for a transfer was continually held up, but he was finally sent to Fort Monroe, Virginia, where he was briefly trained in spotting big guns and artillery shelters from the air before the Armistice was declared in November 1918. His rank upon his discharge was second lieutenant.

Despite the lackluster character of Hawks's military career, it had an indisputable influence on his life and film career. He continued flying for personal pleasure, for more than a decade, and aviation was the central preoccupation of six of his films, which made it the subject, more than any other, that the public most readily associated with Hawks through the early 1940s. In Texas he met a number of fliers who would later work for him in that capacity in Hollywood, and his limited Army Air Corps experience facilitated his friendship with the future Major General Henry H. (Hap) Arnold, without whom *Air Force* would never have been filmed. And even though he never went overseas, the kinship he developed with many fliers gave him a strong feeling for the World War I Lost Generation characters who populated *The Dawn Patrol* and *Today We Live,* as well as for the intrepid pioneers who figured in *Ceiling Zero* and *Only Angels Have Wings.*

3

Rich Kid in Hollywood

Hawks's activities in the immediate post–World War I period are more difficult to pin down with certainty than those in any other part of his life. Hawks said that he built cars and planes and raced the former, although he did neither on more than an amateur sport basis, never for a living. He indisputably developed a taste for the most expensive automobiles early on. In fact, the first two of the countless lawsuits in which Hawks became embroiled during his life concerned cars. In the first, a man who in 1919 sold a new twelve-cylinder Packard touring car to Howard and Kenneth had to go to court to collect the final five-hundred-dollar payment, forcing the sheriff to attach Howard's bank account after one of his checks bounced. In 1923, Hawks was sued by the Walter M. Murphy Motors Company of Pasadena for nonpayment of $316 he owed for repair work performed on one of his cars, which led the police to seize the car at his home. For similar reasons, the city impounded Howard's Buick the following year.

After his military service, Kenneth returned to Yale, where he had enrolled before the war, and graduated in 1919. Kenneth had become a terrific tennis player, much better than Howard, who didn't continue playing very long into his adult life; even his oldest child, David, doesn't remember ever seeing him play. According to Howard, Kenneth was good enough to beat Bill Tilden a month before the era's greatest player won at Forest Hills, and Howard said that he and his brother would often hustle other guys on local courts, deliberately playing poorly while warming up to sucker some doubles team into a hefty wager, then clobbering them in the actual match. Howard also said that he and Kenneth were the only Los Angeles players who could hold their own with two other top players of the time, Maurie McLoughlin and Tom Bundy. If so, Kenneth must have been an extraordinary player to make up for Howard's more average skills; if Howard had been exceptional at all, he surely would have played in school, and there is no record of this anyplace he attended, making it virtually

48

impossible to believe his boast that he was once national junior champion in the sport. However, Howard did use what sporting talent he possessed for social advancement, securing a place for himself as part of Doug Fairbanks's weekend circle by becoming adept at a rugged sport invented by Fairbanks himself, a particularly strenuous form of badminton played with heavy, oversized racquets.

Kenneth's athletic abilities were attested to by Allan Dwan, the pioneering director, who met the boys in 1919, when they were hanging around the Famous Players–Lasky studio on Vine Street, where Hawks had worked before the war. Dwan's strongest initial memory was that "Kenneth Hawks had the most amazing right arm. He could throw a football further than any man I ever knew. They knew that I was a Notre Dame football player, I'd just come out of Notre Dame shortly before then, and so Kenneth came around one day on the lot and looked me up, and I was a kicker, so I'd kick it back and he'd throw it to me. And he actually could throw a football eighty yards, and I have never seen anybody able to do that." Dwan had not only starred for Notre Dame but coached there briefly after his graduation in 1907. Even in the late 1920s, May McAvoy, who starred in Howard's first film, would see Kenneth heaving a football to anyone he could find on the Fox lot.

"They were all tennis players, all typical society boys from New England," Dwan said of the Hawks brothers. "They lived like New Englanders in Pasadena. The family had that quality—lace trimmings, mahogany furniture, silver—they were quite New Englandy. The old man was sedate and rather stiff. We saw the boys occasionally, we took short motor trips here and there. The sister was floating around, we sort of didn't pay much attention to her, as boys won't."

Even Dwan, one of the few other college graduates in the motion picture world at that time, felt there was something odd about these two upper-class boys from a genteel family trying to break into the knockabout silent film industry. They wanted very badly to get in, Dwan remembered, "and none of us could figure out just why." In Dwan's eyes, Kenneth, never having had a job before, was the more eager and interested of the two, so the director took him on as an assistant. Howard, already seeing himself as a seasoned pro after having worked on a handful of pictures with the likes of De Mille, Fairbanks, and Pickford, had no interest in returning to the property department; more likely, he wasn't welcome back, since Dwan recalled that he developed a reputation for "borrowing" props and never returning them.

But it didn't take Howard long to figure out an angle. The one advantage he had over other newcomers and wannabes was money—his own and access to that of others—so why not buy his way into the business? This way he could enter near the top, control the purse strings, and be his own boss.

It was an aristocratic, foolhardy way to approach things, but he was only twenty-three and ready to jump in, and it wouldn't matter all that much if he had to learn the hard way for a while at his own expense. Although it is unknown how they met, Hawks's first, and fortuitous, plunge into the Hollywood financial arena was to loan some money to Jack Warner. Four years older than Hawks, Warner and his brothers had been variously involved in the movie business since 1903, but it was only in 1918 that they had had their first significant success, with a picture called *My Four Years in Germany,* a propaganda piece designed to rally American support for the war effort by spotlighting the conniving, duplicitous ways of Kaiser Wilhelm. The next year, however, Jack Warner was in a pinch again and Hawks was in a position to bail him out. So, in exchange for a loan, which Warner paid back shortly thereafter, Hawks was assigned to oversee a new series for Warner called the Welcome Comedies, one-reelers starring an Italian comic dancer named Mario Bianchi who had come to notice playing small parts in Fatty Arbuckle shorts under the name Monty Banks. A former Mack Sennett director, Frank Griffin, was hired to make a comic star out of Banks, but he didn't last long, leaving it to Hawks and Banks himself to make the films. The first of these was *His Night Out,* which was distributed by CBC Distributing Company. The scant scholarship devoted to Banks includes no record of who directed his early one-reelers, which no longer exist and probably ran no directorial credits anyway, so it is impossible to verify or deny Hawks's contention that he directed three or four of them after Griffin's departure. Hawks's rather disparaging remarks about Banks, saying that the comic "began to feel as though he was kingpin" after just a couple of pictures, suggest discord between the two men, and his claim that he fired Banks over his temperamental behavior and that the actor "got down on his knees and begged to be allowed to come back" smacks of the usual Hawks one-upsmanship. His too-big-for-his-britches characterization of Banks also seems unfair, in that Banks was soon successfully directing himself in comic shorts before moving on to a directorial career that embraced twenty-three features, suggesting at least some competence. Hawks said he quickly got bored with the series and left with a handsome profit, but he also had the audacity to suggest that his ever-so-brief stint in short-form, gag-oriented comedy gave him "thorough comedy training" on a par with that earned by the likes of Frank Capra and George Stevens, each of whom put in years in silent comedy.

Emboldened by his success as a financier in his first time up to the plate, Hawks hatched a grander scheme to finance feature-length films with first-rate directors and important actors. Working quickly and cleverly, Hawks got together Allan Dwan, Mickey Neilan, and Allen Holubar, the latter an up-and-coming director then working at Universal with his wife, the actress Dorothy Phillips, and told them that he could raise the financing for pictures that each man would direct, produce. and, if he so chose, write himself. The films would be distributed by First National, a company formed two years before by several exhibitors fed up with the monolithic block-booking practices of some of the major companies. The business arrangement represented an early form of a negative pickup deal, with First National reimbursing the new company, called Associated Producers, upon delivery of the negative, then sharing a portion of the revenues when they came in. One of Hawks's schemes for making immediate profits was to try to come in under budget; if there was an agreed-upon cost of, say, $200,000, the company would try to bring it in for $20,000 to $30,000 less than that and keep the difference when First National paid the $200,000.

Dwan recalled that Hawks obtained the money to get Associated Producers off the ground from a man in Pasadena. "He was quite wealthy, and quite interested in films. The first time I met him, it was in his house, and he wanted to talk about films." Dwan's ulterior motive in meeting him was to use his lavish house as a location for a picture, "and that was shocking to them, and to the man's wife. But we learned that he wanted to be an actor, of all things. I immediately employed him, I employed him as an actor, and I got his house. And after we had done that a couple of times, he signed up with Universal and got himself a job."

Hawks also arranged for some bank loans to cover production costs before First National paid him back, and it was Dwan's impression that Hawks didn't use his own money. "He never put a nickel up," said Dwan. "They weren't wealthy. They were well-fixed, but not wealthy by any means. As a matter of fact, I know they weren't, because knowing the old man, he used to ask me very pointed questions about what guarantee there was in getting a nickel out if you put a nickel into motion pictures. He didn't act like a financier. . . . They knew percentages, but this fellow was blind as a bat, and I think Howard was, too. He'd just keep his head in the sand and spend."

Early on, Hawks and Dwan went to Honolulu, partly for vacation and partly to size up the possibility of shooting a picture in Hawaii, something no one was yet doing. When word got out, Dwan recollected, "We were invited to the Chamber of Commerce, to a luncheon they gave in our honor. And Howard is peering into the pockets of every guy there, to see if he can try to make a picture. I don't remember whether he got anything out of Honolulu or not, but I know we came back home very shortly after that and he found money someplace and we were making a picture." Hawks's role in Associated Producers was strictly financial. At the time, Dwan said, Hawks "thought that's the good end of pictures. He wasn't thinking story. . . . He never got down to that for years."

Hawks and Dwan took another trip together, this time also with each man's brother: Kenneth, of course, and Leon Dwan, a Chicago lawyer who came out to handle Allan's business affairs. Ostensibly scouting locations for a picture, the four self-styled sportsmen, Dwan recalled, really just went off on a lark to see the Grand Canyon, "and if a fella was there in a Rolls-Royce we'd see if he had any money he wanted to put in pictures." Dwan joked, "With my brother and me, we made a pretty good foursome. We could go out all day long and nobody would say a word. Can you imagine four people together, all silent? I'd generally break it up, I'd start blabbing and there'd be an argument. I could always start an argument. It didn't matter. I'd say, 'I think it will rain later.' 'Now why would it rain? It isn't rainy season.' And that starts the day's conversation, and it could go all day long. Then, at dinner, at night, they'd say, 'Well, I thought it was gonna rain, wise guy.' Then the next day they'd say, 'Well, you were right about the rain. I suppose it's going to avalanche today.' 'Oh, sure.'" Surprisingly, Dwan said, "I don't think we paid a damn bit of attention to women. We were doing sports, we were exploring, we were adventuring. We were look-ing for locations most of the time." Neither of the Hawks boys were big drinkers then, and Dwan remembered noting in particular that "Howard was very slow-spoken. He always had that slow-drawl way of speaking. He always had that, as if he were thinking the next word he'd say."

There are no official production records for Associated Producers, but the best evidence suggests that the company was responsible for fourteen pictures between 1920 and 1923: eight by Neilan, and three apiece from Dwan and Holubar. Things got off to a promising start the first year with two big hits by Neilan. *Go and Get It* was an offbeat newspaper story highlighted by some daring aviation stunts and a notable appearance by a child actor named Wesley Barry in a secondary role as Dinty. Neilan, well known for his skill directing kids, immediately came up with a starring vehicle for Barry called, plausibly enough, *Dinty*, a heartrending rags-to-riches melodrama about an orphaned Irish kid on the streets of San Francisco. The company's final entry for the year was Dwan's warm melodrama *The Forbidden Thing*, about Portuguese fishermen and their women in Provincetown.

Dwan followed up with a commercially and artistically attractive entry for early 1921, *A Perfect Crime*, a sort of Jekyll & Hyde fantasy about a "pinhead" bank clerk played by Monte Blue who, at night, upon removing his glasses and straightening up his posture, becomes the dashing spinner of Münchhausenesque stories. The picture marked the screen debut, in a small part, of a twelve-year-old distant cousin of Hawks's named Jane Peters, whom Dwan spotted playing baseball in the street. When she resumed her screen career several years later, it was under the name of Carole Lombard.

With their next productions, however, Associated Producers got rather carried away. For his first contribution to the company, Allen Holubar made a pretentious spectacular entitled *Man-Woman-Marriage*, a study of man's treatment of woman through the ages. Expensively appointed, it was not a hit.

This was nothing, however, compared to Neilan's superproduction *Bob Hampton of Placer*, an epic of the Old West that climaxes at Little Big Horn. Based on a 1910 novel, the film was confusing and misguided in the telling and was a mess both in production and on the screen. Hawks admitted that they used trip wires in the cavalry scenes, which made many horses fall onto their heads and necks, a practice that was later outlawed. Hawks was in charge of the second unit and, after two failed attempts to film Custer's Last Stand, one in Montana and another in Arizona, the company announced that the battle would be filmed from a blimp. But when the blimp refused to leave the ground, Hawks had the brainstorm of shooting the sequence in the Arroyo Seco, a large ravine along the western edge of Pasadena very near the Green & Green house at 408 Arroyo Terrace, where the Hawks family had lived some years before. Not wanting to lose the publicity benefits of the blimp story, Hawks had a window washer–style platform dangled off the Colorado Street Bridge over the ravine; he then had the platform jostled so that it would still look as though the cameras were on an airship. In an unusually vicious review, *Variety* attacked the film mercilessly, advising that "What might save [Neilan] would be action on the part of his backers. Hand him $35,000 and no more. Tell him to make a picture with it. Then he would have to use his brains, not money. Then possibly we would get something again."

Due to all the mishaps and lack of organization, the film went wildly over budget, and the problem fell directly into Hawks's lap. In fact, the situation became so bad, and relations between Neilan and Hawks so strained, that it resulted in a major lawsuit, which revealed that, contrary to Dwan's impression, Hawks was directly involved in the financing of at least some of Associated Producers' films and may have been wealthier than Dwan thought. Hawks's complaint against Neilan, filed in June 1923, stated that Hawks had loaned Neilan a total of $95,490 (roughly $2 million by today's standards) toward production costs on *Bob Hampton*. To cover the rest of the budget, Hawks arranged a bank loan of $125,000. However, as the costs grew, Neilan, supposedly without telling Hawks, borrowed an additional $50,000. When Neilan delivered the picture to First National in February 1921, he was reimbursed for the agreed-upon budget $200,000, but this still left a large gap, since the actual costs came to $287,066.

After much equivocation, in 1924 both sides met and agreed upon a settlement by which Neilan would pay Hawks everything he owed plus interest; but shortly thereafter Neilan reneged and denied that he had ever agreed to pay interest. At the end of the year, the case was finally dismissed with prejudice against the defendant, suggesting that Hawks was reasonably treated in an out-of-court settlement. Allan Dwan said that Neilan also owed him a great deal of money during this period, although it apparently never led to a lawsuit.

Hawks, in turn, was sued by one of his lenders, William Shea, for failing to pay back five hundred dollars he'd borrowed in January 1923. When Hawks did not respond to a summons, a writ of attachment was issued for Hawks's bank account as well as for that of a company called Hawks-Morosco Productions, in which Hawks was partnered with Walter Mitchell, also known as Walter Morosco, presumably to help finance the Associated Producers features. It took two years, but the court finally removed $531 from Hawks's bank account to satisfy Shea.

Once the company took this costly wrong turn in 1921, it was never the same again, although, remarkably, Hawks and Neilan continued working together on five more pictures. On the heels of *Bob Hampton*, Dwan contributed *A Broken Doll*, a contrived, sentimental tale about the far-fetched misadventures of a ranch hand (Monte Blue again) who tries to replace the favorite doll of the owner's crippled daughter. For his part, Neilan followed up with another commercial disaster but a film Hawks actually liked a great deal, *Bits of Life*, featuring Wesley Barry and Lon Chaney, an ambitious attempt to tell four unrelated stories in a single feature. As a group, they were remarkably grim and depressing, following seedy characters to gloomy conclusions. This is precisely what impressed Hawks, who found it "a very good picture — very bitter, downbeat." Still, he admitted that it had no chance of success because "it left you feeling very bad."

But despite the film's failure, Hawks remained highly intrigued by the challenge of telling multiple stories in the same picture and was directly inspired by *Bits of Life* when he was preparing *Red Line 7000* more than forty years later. The results then, however, proved no more popular than they were in 1921, leading Hawks to conclude that the problem with such a film was that "just when you get people interested, you have to drop one story line to go on to start another."

Remarkably, Neilan was able to finish yet another picture for the company that year, *The Lotus Eater,* a curious story in which John Barrymore played a young man who stumbles upon a deserted island inhabited by some shipwrecked folks who have fashioned a free-thinking society far from civilization. Despite the dashingly romantic figure cut by Barrymore, the film was not one of his more popular attractions. It is doubtful that at the time Hawks even met the actor, then at the virtual pinnacle of his celebrity, since the picture was shot off Miami and in New York.

In 1922, Allan Dwan moved on to make the enormous and enormously successful *Robin Hood* with Douglas Fairbanks, which launched the most important phase of the director's long career. But Neilan kept on with three more pictures for Associated Producers and First National. *Penrod,* an adaptation of Booth Tarkington's novel and play, relied heavily on the antics of Wesley Barry and other child actors. Much more interesting was *Fools First,* a prime example of what Hawks described as Neilan's rare ability to switch moods, lay in unexpected business, and subvert audience expectations. Co-starring Richard Dix and Raymond Griffith, the latter to become a friend and favorite of Hawks, it was fundamentally a Hell's Kitchen story and an account of a bank robbery, but one elaborated with unusual character motivations, themes of redemption, and plot twists. Neilan paused, for example, to show the human side of the gang leader by having him sensitively tend to a lost child. Neilan also laced the more grisly elements of the story with black, macabre humor. Hawks, who was making a point of studying his directors very carefully, was impressed most of all by Neilan's approach. "He always had a good foundation for a story," he told Peter Bogdanovich, "but his method of treating it lightly crept in, or of stopping in the middle of something very dramatic to get a laugh. He always worked that way and it looked like a good idea to me."

Neilan's final contribution to the company was a picture he directed with Frank Urson for early 1923 release. A rather standard romantic comedy, *Minnie* is about an ugly girl who pretends to have a secret admirer but then not only wins the heart of a newspaper reporter but is transformed into a beauty at the end through plastic surgery.

Allen Holubar weighed in with two further pictures, beginning with *Hurricane's Gal*, a large-scale adventure in which his wife, Dorothy Phillips, played the orphaned daughter of a high-seas smuggler who tries to continue his rough, illegal dealings, only to see the error of her ways. The 1922 film concluded with a spectacular sea battle that attracted considerable attention. Associated Producers' last venture, which came out in the spring of 1923, was Holubar's *Slander the Woman*, a melodrama in which Phillips reappeared as a Montreal society girl who is branded the "other woman" in a murder case and retreats to her father's hunting lodge near Hudson Bay, where she becomes involved in further intrigue before her name is cleared. It was, from all accounts, a real dog, an ignominious end to a company that started out strongly but had, at best, an erratic artistic and commercial track record. Hawks simplistically blamed the failure of the company on the fact that all three of his directors were led astray by women, which in his mind somehow clouded their judgment and prevented them from making any more good pictures. He told Kevin Brownlow that "each one of them ran into some girl he thought was Sarah Bernhardt. And they started to make pictures and that was the end of us. Oh, brother, we made some stinkers. I decided no more other directors, I was going to direct myself. And that I was never going to get mixed up with any girl — that can be done outside of office hours. Because it was very strange. All three of them went the same way. Just that quick. . . . Mickey Neilan was by far the better of the three of those, but he went the fastest." Holubar died on November 20, 1925, of an internal disorder and gallstones, while Dwan and the Hawks boys drifted apart, their careers taking them in separate directions, although Hawks retained his admiration for Dwan. "He was a pro — tough and hard with a good touch," Hawks later said. "He didn't dwell on things — he just hit 'em and went on."

Once he had decided he wanted to direct himself, Hawks began seeing as many movies as he could, often two or three a day. When he saw a picture he particularly admired, he would sit through it a second time to study the storytelling techniques and the director's approach to the camera and actors. Above all, he appreciated the work of John Ford, who, in 1923 was still Jack Ford, a director of Westerns, but was on the verge of breaking through with the monumental production *The Iron Horse*.

But wanting to direct and actually doing so were far different things, so Hawks had little choice in the short term but to continue as a producer, although this time with the added creative role of screenwriter. He came up with an efficient story for a modern Western, about a young army officer posted along the U.S.–Mexico border to crack a major drug-smuggling ring. The officer falls in love with the daughter of one of the U.S. Customs Service investigators but comes to suspect that she is in league with the gangsters. It turns out that she is an undercover agent, and when the father, daughter, and officer are captured by the smugglers, the U.S. Cavalry must ride to the rescue.

Hawks said he made *Quicksands* because a colonel he knew, presumably from shared army days, offered him the use of the Tenth Cavalry, "a Negro cavalry that chased Pancho Villa," along with food and lodging in Texas. In exchange, Hawks made a short filmed history of the Tenth, including a reenactment of its pursuit of the outlaw Mexican leader who would serve as the subject of one of Hawks's feature films twelve years later. Financing the production himself, Hawks cut every corner, arranging that his stars, Richard Dix and Helene Chadwick, could finish their scenes in the minimum amount of time to keep costs down; pulling in favors; and generally paying everyone next to nothing. It remains difficult to believe that he brought it in for eighteen thousand dollars, but it may not have been much more. The director was Jack Conway, another member of the rugged circle to which Hawks was drawing closer, which included Vic Fleming, Eddie Sutherland, and Harold, Richard, and Art Rosson. Conway, nine years older than Hawks, had previously been an actor and an assistant to D. W. Griffith, who had already proven himself, through a decade of experience, to be a versatile director. Sutherland, an actor and production assistant who was a year Hawks's senior, shared Hawks's Eastern prep school background, and the two became frequent golf companions. Sutherland, who in the mid-1920s became a very busy director, was also an amusing bon vivant whose home at the Bachelor Lodge in back of some buildings on Hollywood Boulevard was the scene of a constant party in the postwar years. Subsequently, he and Jack Conway shared a penthouse at the Hollywood Hotel, where the carousing was only partly interrupted by Sutherland's marriage to Louise Brooks between 1926 and 1928. On *Quicksands*, Sutherland was one of two stuntmen, along with Richard Arlen, a sportsman and pilot who began acting the following year and would later costar for Hawks in *Tiger Shark*. Shot in late 1922, the film was made hectically and very quickly. When it was finished early the following year, the American Releasing Corporation picked up distribution rights, but despite a solid cast and good reviews, the picture did only fair business. In 1927, it was bought by Paramount Famous Lasky, cut from seventy minutes down to an hour, and briefly rereleased. No print is known to survive today.

After living in Pasadena for some time after the war, in the early 1920s, Howard and Kenneth rented a house at 7125 Hillside Avenue, a tiny street just off upper La Brea north of Franklin. Hawks said that Victor Fleming once asked if he could put up at his place for a short time and ended up staying five years; while the length of time seems unlikely, it was definitely during this period. In early 1924, the two Hawkses moved to a house at 6626 Franklin Avenue, just two blocks up from Musso & Frank's restaurant, on the spot where the celebrated show-business apartment building the Château des Fleurs would be built in 1927. Living with them for a good deal of this time was Jack Conway.

A man who came into Hawks's world in the early 1920s and had a profound effect on both his personal and professional life was Irving Thalberg. It is unknown who might have brought Thalberg (who shared Hawks's May 30 birthday but was three years younger) into the group, but occasionally Hawks would find this "little red-cheeked Jewish boy, very bright guy," at his home or at one of his friend's. Although Hawks admitted that he wasn't initially sure of the identity of this fellow, whose frailness and retiring nature contrasted markedly with the exuberant, macho personalities of most of the others, he endlessly told stories about him. Thalberg, of course, was Hollywood's boy wonder, the fellow who had commandeered production at Universal at age twenty, wrestled Erich von Stroheim to the mat over the director's prodigious excesses, and, in early 1923, left Universal to join Louis B. Mayer in a partnership that bloomed at MGM the following year. A very protected mama's boy who was forced to leave Universal when he decided he didn't want to marry boss Carl Laemmle's daughter, Thalberg was earnestly trying to be one of the boys by hanging out with the likes of Fleming, Conway, Sutherland, and the Hawkses, all of whom Mother Thalberg considered wayward young men whose wild ways could only have a pernicious influence on her sensitive child.

In fact, the influence worked much more in the opposite direction. Fleming and Conway became two of the most important directors at MGM under Thalberg, while Hawks entered a significant new phase of his career thanks to the young executive. Early in 1923, Hawks got a call out of the blue from Jesse Lasky, vice president in charge of production at Paramount Famous Lasky. Of course, Hawks had worked at the studio some years before, but he was a lowly prop boy then and scarcely had a nodding acquaintance with the boss. The way Hawks magnified it in later years, Lasky started by flattering him, saying that, "Thalberg says you know more about stories than anybody else that he knows, so I'd like to have you." Offering him, according to Hawks, unlimited funds and direct access to his office, Lasky asked him to take charge of the production of a slate of forty pictures, to be responsible for literary purchases; choosing directors, writers, and cast; and cutting and titling the films. Hawks added that he didn't have an official title at the company by his own request and boasted, finally, that his office was "really doing all the producing."

The truth, not surprisingly, was rather more prosaic. Hawks was hired, at a cushy salary of about five hundred dollars a month, as one of the scenario department's four production editors. (The other three were Lucien Hubbard, Hector Turnbull and Walter Woods.) The production slate under way when Hawks came onboard was publicized in the trade as Paramount's *Super Thirty-Nine*, the second half of its lineup for the current year. Hawks later claimed that he bought about thirty stories for the studio—two Joseph Conrads, two Rex Beaches, two Jack Londons, two Zane Greys—as if no one had ever adapted these writers' works for the screen before. Tossing it off as if it were nothing, he said that, "In two weeks' time, I had forty pictures and had 'em cast. Then all I had to do was to get people to write 'em. That was the most successful year Paramount ever had."

But Hawks shared these duties with three others and was worked fiercely by Lasky, one of the more benevolent bosses as Hollywood executives went and a man who appreciated Hawks's intuitive smarts and mainstream literary tastes. Hawks claimed that Lasky agreed to give him Wednesday afternoons off to play golf, and that he was sometimes able to persuade his boss to go with him so they could talk about work while enjoying themselves; if true, it was a clever ploy on Hawks's part, not only for selfish reasons but as a way to get Lasky's ear for a prolonged period, apart from everyday distractions. With only two title writers on staff, Hawks was able to persuade Lasky to hire two more, Malcolm Stuart Boylan and sportswriter Beanie Walker, both of whom became top names in the field. Hawks even insisted that he saved Cecil B. De Mille's contrived 1925 melodrama *The Road to Yesterday* by rewriting its titles. The picture, according to Hawks, had turned out badly, with the director having approached the story "very,

very heavily," so Hawks told De Mille he could improve it. "I made, not a comedy out of it, but at least in a lighter vein," he bragged to Kevin Brownlow. "I changed the whole tenor of the story. So it didn't take itself seriously, it took itself in a semi-humorous way. He took it out and previewed it and he was very pleased with himself that he'd gotten laughs and he decided he was going to make comedies." Hawks also admitted, "I started the evil of the 'associate producer' because I had so much to do I had to hire a couple of fellows to help me."

Because of Hawks's shared responsibilities on the *Super Thirty-Nine* slate, it is difficult to say with certainty which properties he bought and which projects he supervised. He himself took credit for several. Among the ones to come out in 1924 were George Melford's adaptation of a Frances Hodgson Burnett play, the crime drama *The Dawn of a Tomorrow*, featuring Hawks's friend Raymond Griffith; two Westerns by Irvin Willat, a Zane Grey story called *The Heritage of the Desert* and *North of 36*; and *Open All Night*, also with Griffith, a sophisticated romantic comedy that was writer Paul Bern's second film as a solo director. That first year Hawks himself received a writing credit on a George Melford film, *Tiger Love*. Based on an opera called *El Gato Montes*, it was a Robin Hood–like tale of romantic intrigue and derring-do in Old Spain. It starred Antonio Moreno and Estelle Taylor and was judged good, if formulaic, fun.

Then there were the films directed by Victor Fleming. Hawks actually claimed that he was responsible for Fleming's directing career, telling Peter Bogdanovich, "Then he became a cameraman, which he was until I became a producer at Paramount and made him a director." This is one of Hawks's most blatant pieces of one-upmanship on his more experienced friend, simply because it is so outrageously false, a weak attempt at building himself up when, in fact, his friend was way out in front of him, doing what Hawks really wanted to be doing. After spending the war in the Army Signal Corps, Fleming had sailed with President Wilson in December 1918 to attend the Versailles Peace Conference, where, as chief cameraman for the American delegation, he had filmed the assembled world leaders. He had shortly thereafter become the first American to shoot movie film inside the Vatican, when Wilson visited St. Peter's. Upon his discharge in 1919, he had begun his directorial career at once at the behest of Douglas Fairbanks, his roistering buddy. He'd arrived at Paramount in 1922, and had already directed five films there when Hawks joined the studio.

The first picture on which Hawks and Fleming were jointly associated was *Empty Hands*, the story of a scandalous flapper who is swept down some rapids in a canoe while visiting the Canadian Rockies and survives in the wilderness thanks to her father's brawny engineer. Jack Holt portrayed the man, while the flighty girl was played by Norma Shearer, a Canadian actress whose career had slowly been taking shape for several years. A former advertising model in New York, Shearer left her married sister, Athole, behind and traveled with her mother, Edith, to Hollywood. Shearer was charming and pretty, if slightly wall-eyed and horsey, and also very proper; and she was now, after a period of struggle, seemingly on her way up the ladder to stardom.

The mountain portions of the film were shot at Lake Arrowhead, a couple of hours east of Los Angeles, and Shearer immediately fell hard for her director, to the distinct disapproval of her ever-hovering mother, Edie. In her unpublished autobiography, which tends to put a polite finish on the events of her life, Shearer as much as admits that Fleming was her first lover. "His few silver hairs and kind gentle ways attracted me enormously," she wrote. "I suppose psychiatrists would have said my love for my father, whom I was missing so much, expressed itself in my romantic yearning for this mature man—this undoubtedly was the basis for my tender affection which must have overwhelmed me one moonlit night as we sat in a hammock on the terrace of the hotel overlooking the beautiful lake. I found myself saying, for no reason at all, 'Mr. Fleming, would you kiss me?' And to my surprise he did and I loved it.'" Enthusing about "his amazing hands" and his talent for little endearments, Shearer revealed that, "I had a lovely time courting this mature man—the first I had known." She added that, "Sport cars were his passion and he drove a beautiful dark grey Dusenberg too fast—except when Edie was in the backseat—because she would scream 'Victor' and hit him on the back and he would pretend she had knocked him off the seat onto the floor."

As it happened, Howard Hawks was also quite taken with Norma Shearer, but not in a romantic way. Hawks first noticed her in a picture Jack Conway made at Warner Bros. in 1923 called *Lucretia Lombard*, which he claimed to have improved by retitling it to favor Shearer, who played the second female part, over the leading lady, Irene Rich. Hawks took credit for signing her for *Empty Hands* over the objections of Jesse Lasky, who found her unattractive. After he saw the finished picture, Lasky realized his mistake and wanted to sign her for further films, but she was already under contract to MGM. Thalberg had had his eye on her for three years and, by 1925 Shearer was a star at MGM. In 1927, she married Thalberg.

But the romance with Thalberg was slow to catch fire, and for some time Shearer continued to see Victor Fleming while he made three more pictures that Hawks supervised: *The Devil's Cargo,* a dubious story of sinners and redeemers during California Gold Rush days; *Adventure,* an action-and-romance-packed adaptation of a Jack London novel set in the Solomon Islands; and *Lord Jim,* a superficial but impressively physical telling of the Joseph Conrad tale.

Among Hawks's other projects were two more Zane Grey Westerns, *The Code of the West* and *The Light of Western Stars,* both directed by William K. Howard, as well as a picture on which Hawks shared a story credit with Adelaide Heilbron, *The Dressmaker from Paris.* The picture, directed by Hawks's friend Paul Bern, tells of an American soldier, played by Allan Forrest, and a French maiden, portrayed by Leatrice Joy, in a comeback role after time off for motherhood, whose romance is thwarted when the Yanks go home. Some years later, the young man, stuck managing an old-fashioned clothing store in a sleepy Midwestern town, decides to shake things up by inviting a famous Parisian designer to put on a fashion show at the store. It turns out, of course, that the couturiere is none other than his long-ago love, and the two surmount the shocked protests of local prudes by putting on a successful show and heading for the altar. Although the predictability of the story was criticized, the fashion show sequence was incredibly lavish, loaded with beautiful models and an endless succession of gowns, furs, and revealing outfits. Despite his credit, Hawks absolved any real creative input on this film, telling Joseph McBride, "I just thought of the title and gave a writer the idea for a story, and she wrote it." Hawks liked Leatrice Joy, however, and through her met her husband, John Gilbert, whom Hawks also liked a great deal. The actor's contract with Fox was up, and Hawks pushed both Lasky and Cecil B. De Mille to sign him up at Paramount. But Lasky missed the boat, and Gilbert shortly became Hollywood's most romantic leading man at MGM.

As it turned out, Hawks's stint at Paramount was also near an end. On September 1, 1924, he signed a contract to work for one more year as a production editor at the studio, at $650 per month for the first six months and $750 per month for the remainder. Within a matter of weeks, however, he abruptly quit and took a similar position with Thalberg at MGM. Although he felt he was overworked, Hawks's ostensible reason for leaving was that Lasky offered him no prospect of moving out of the scenario department and into directing. Thalberg, on the other hand, promised that if Hawks spent a year as a story executive, he would then let him direct. It was a promise not kept, however, and a year wasted as far as Hawks was concerned. Granted, Hawks admired Thalberg and learned a great deal watching him analyze scripts and first cuts of films, figure out what was wrong with them, and then create new scenes that would sometimes dramatically improve the pictures. Hawks worked with dozens of writers, met many of the stars, and had an affair with at least one of them, the newly arrived Joan Crawford. But by late 1925, he could tell nothing was about to change for him at the thriving studio. When Hawks complained to Thalberg about it, he remembered the executive saying, "'Howard, Christ, we can get all the directors we need. I can't get anybody to do your work.' I said, 'I just quit this morning.' He and I were very good friends, and he said, 'Nothing could change your mind?' I said, 'Nothing can change it.' 'Well,' he said, 'I could let you direct.' I said, 'No, I don't want you to do that. You can let me direct some time after I show you what I can do.' And I went off to play golf."

4

Showtime

It took balls for Howard Hawks to walk out on Irving Thalberg, but it wasn't the first and it was far from the last time Hawks would tell a boss what he could do with his job; it got to be one of his most endearing habits. Every day he spent at MGM represented an additional day of frustration and treading water, to the point where he was beginning to get depressed. Still, the way he told it, Hawks left MGM one morning and was all set to direct a picture at Fox the same afternoon. According to him, when he went to play golf after kissing off Thalberg, he ran into Fox's general studio superintendent, Sol Wurtzel, who, when apprised of Hawks's availability, invited him to write and direct a picture on the spot. There is no way to confirm or refute the story, of course, but it is true that Hawks was launched on his directorial career with incredible speed; he was signed by Fox at the end of October 1925, and his first film was finished by February.

Hawks joined Fox at a time when the studio, under the stewardship of its vice president, Winfield Sheehan, a longtime associate of William Fox's, was gearing the company up to unprecedented levels of production in a determined effort to become a dominant force in the industry; its enormous 1926–27 program called for spending $10 million on at least forty-nine features and fifty-two comedy shorts. Part of this surge involved beefing up the studio's directorial roster, and Hawks signed his contract on October 28, 1925, at the same time as Harry Beaumont and Irving Cummings. Among the other top directors on the lot at the time were John Ford, Frank Borzage, Raoul Walsh, Allan Dwan, Alfred E. Green, Roy William Neill, and John G. Blystone. Hawks's deal called for him to receive $5,000 for his original story, $7,500 to direct, and an option on his services for three more pictures to be produced within nine months, the first of which would pay him $10,000, the next two $12,500. Fox included a further option for four more films to be made during a one-year period. Hawks celebrated the attainment of his long-elusive goal by taking an ad in the year-end issue of

Variety that stated, "Happy New Year—Howard Hawks—Now Directing for William Fox." Early in the new year, his brother Kenneth, who had been working steadily as an assistant director for Clarence Badger at Paramount, followed him to Fox, where he quickly became one of the studio's top production supervisors.

Fox needed product immediately, which put Hawks on the spot to come up with a story that could be written, cast, and put before the cameras within a matter of weeks. The inspiration for his proposed picture, drawn from real life, was exceedingly poignant. As he told Joseph McBride, "It was taken from a little incident that happened once where a beautiful girl went blind from drinking bootleg liquor at my house. While we were waiting for the doctor, she said, 'Just because I'm blind it doesn't mean I can't perform pretty good in bed.'" Hawks said he "loved the attitude she had," as most men would.

Unfortunately, the story Hawks wrote had nothing to do with this episode except for the blindness. *The Road to Glory*, which was also tentatively titled *The Chariot of the Gods* during production, is one of two films Hawks directed that are not known to exist. As his first film, and one basically written by him as well, it is worth delving into the story and its development in some detail, since its inspirational, religious theme and gravely serious treatment stand at such odds with the majority of his later work.

Hawks did very few extended pieces of writing of any kind during his life, and one of the longest is the thirty-five-page treatment he wrote for *The Road to Glory*. Although it doesn't solve the question of what motivated him to create a story so squarely founded upon the importance of a devout belief in God, just as it doesn't provide any sort of cogent summation of his philosophy or attitudes, it is pure Hawks at age twenty-nine, unfiltered by anyone else's input or even, so it would seem, by commercial considerations, until the staggeringly unrealistic and unbelievable happy ending.

The treatment's first paragraph is the closest the work comes to expressing an outlook on life: "Chance brings a man and woman together. By chance they fall in love. A new element enters and thrusts them apart. Then comes coincidence to reunite them. Without coincidence, life would move in a preordained groove destroying genius and blasting ambition. The greatest coincidence is life itself."

The opening scenes shows two Jazz Age hedonists, Judith, "a speed-mad nymph," and David Hale, of "muscular body and steady nerves," racing at more than seventy miles per hour down a country road. When they suddenly come upon a wagon, David runs the car into a ditch and through a rail fence, throwing them both clear, although Judith suffers a bruise over her right eye.

Judith shortly goes home, to a large suburban estate she shares with her father, Jim, a "big, youngish looking man" whom she loves "with a fierce passion" and calls "boy-friend," as in "You're late, boy-friend!" and "Not mad at me, are you—boy-friend?" Despite Judith's blurred feelings for her father, Jim and David get along pretty well, although, on a walk with her, David admits, "Sometimes I'm almost jealous of him. I wonder if you'll ever love anyone as much as you love 'the boy-friend'?" "It depends," Judith responds. "On what?" David asks. "On whether or not this other person loves me as much as 'the boy-friend' does."

Also living at the house is a fanatically religious Negro cook named Aunt Salina, a role written in thick black dialect. Judith feels increasingly severe head pains, and when Jim is abruptly killed by a falling brick on his way to his office, Salina laments that, "De good Lawd sho' done sent perversity to dis house. Fust He took Mistuh Jim an' den Miss Judy gits a complaint wid her haid." But the news is worse still: a doctor who would rather be out playing golf informs Judith that her injury is going to make her gradually go blind.

Deciding at once not to inflict this "pitiful curse" upon David, she rejects David's marriage proposal, cuts off their relationship, becomes totally bitter, and comes to hate God. David decides to bury his grief in manual labor in a mine, while Judith, her sight ebbing away, cares about nothing anymore and accepts a invitation from her father's old business partner, the fat, lecherous Del Cole, to a mountain lodge that happens to be near the mine.

In a breathlessly melodramatic final section, David is seriously injured in a mine explosion and is brought, of course, to the lodge as a train is arranged to take him to a hospital. Judith forces her way onboard, but the trains loses its brakes and careens out of control down the mountain. Everyone jumps off except for the immobile David and an ecstatic Judith, who, knowing they are about to crash, at last tells David about her blindness and exults, "Soon it will all be over."

After the crash, Judith is seen, "miraculously unhurt," in a hospital. Informing her that David's condition is grave, the doctor urges Judith to "ask the Only One who can help." Attempting to overcome her resentment of God and trying to remember how to pray, Judith recalls what a kindly old man told her once in a park: "God is Love." Suddenly, David makes a remarkable recovery and, to top it off, Judith's sight is fully restored, where-upon the medic says, "A doctor can only help a little. It is God who cures," before heading off to play golf.

A final scene repeats the circumstances of the opening sequence, with Judith and David zooming in their car along the same road. This time, however, they miss the wagon and continue uneventfully on. "Gee, that was a close call," says David. "What was it?" asks Judith.

To quickly flesh the story out into a full screenplay, Hawks suggested L. G. Rigby, the cowriter of Fleming's Jack London adaptation *Adventure* at Paramount. The script went through three drafts in November, with shoot-ing beginning in December and extending into the new year. The first change was to remove Aunt Salina and replace her with Graves, "a fat and amiable butler" whose main function is to comically hide and provide Judith's bottle of Scotch. Diary entries from Judith were introduced to con-vey some of her inner thoughts. To emphasize the competitiveness between David and Jim, there was a scene at home in which the two youngsters dance the Charleston and Jim, unable to keep up, is forced to realize that he will soon be losing his daughter; later, at his office, Jim practices the dance so the kids won't be able to make fun of him again. After she is informed of her oncoming blindness, Judith is overcome with horror as she passes a sightless soldier stumbling through a park, led by a small dog on a leash. Finding a pamphlet entitled *God Is Love*, she throws it in the fireplace; subsequently, she goes to a bookstore and furtively requests a book in Braille. When she discovers the shopkeeper has given her a copy of the Bible, she violently throws it across the room.

Now feeling desperate and reckless, Judith accepts Del Cole's invita-tion to a wild party at a club, where she runs into David. Judith's vision is virtually gone, but neither man knows what the problem is, and David takes her erratic behavior as proof that she isn't the angel he thought she was. Cole takes her home and puts the make on her but backs off upon discov-ering she's blind. She responds by mocking him for no longer wanting her, and, expressing in a banal way the fears implicit in the remark of the real-life girl who inspired Hawks's story, she says, "Nobody would want me!"

The ending in Rigby's adaptation becomes, if anything, infinitely more melodramatic than Hawks's original, although he approved the changes. Judith installs herself at the lodge with Graves and his wife, while David, not a mine worker in this version, races up the mountain through a storm to assert his love for her. The moment he does so, lightning strikes a huge tree, which crushes the cabin and knocks David out. The next day, the grim attending doctor issues the same religious imperatives to Judith, who, overcoming her qualms, takes to her knees, clasps her hands together, and prays for David's survival. Before she's even done, a ray of sun breaks through to fall upon her face, and not only does David instantly recover, but Judith can see again. The doctor tells her that even though the shock of the storm might have restored her sight, she should be thankful to God, whereupon she says, "Thank you, God—Thanks awfully."

The coda this time has the couple driving along in their car cautiously, at just ten to fifteen miles per hour, and the final shot shows the back of their car to reveal them as newlyweds.

Contemporaneous reviews indicate that the finished film hewed very closely to the storyline as described, and Hawks's suggestion to Peter Bogdanovich that he and former Mack Sennett comic Ford Sterling, who played the father, improvised the idea of his character being killed by a falling brick is completely contradicted by the incident's full description in Hawks's original treatment. Upon the film's unveiling in April 1926, in both the United States and Britain, the critics' comments were reasonably good, unanimous in praising May McAvoy's performance as Judith as well as the film's technical aspects. The London *Bioscope* found that "the story is a little bit morbid," and *Variety* sarcastically suggested that the film might as readily be booked by church organizations as movie theaters, "since a half dozen or more morals and lessons are neatly sugar-coated."

The most extended commentary on the now unviewable results of Hawks's first full-length piece of direction came from the British *Kinematograph Weekly*, which felt that Hawks "has achieved a notable picture very much ahead of its prototypes. Emotional to a degree almost too poignant at times, the overpowering pathos avoids 'mush' and is treated with ingenuity that is never laboured; the early reels have a delightful light touch in well-devised contrast to the double tragedy that swoops like a cataclysm and will grip even those who hate having their withers rung. Concessions to hackneyed banality—the super-dog, the cabaret, and the prayer—are mercifully restrained, and smooth treatment is very effective."

Years later, Hawks assessed it by saying, "It didn't have any fun in it. It was pretty bad. I don't think anybody enjoyed it except a few critics." He was, he said, under the delusion that "the thing to do was to be dramatic." He was quickly disabused of this notion by Sol Wurtzel, whom Hawks greatly respected and who issued him the following directive: "Look, you've shown you can make a picture, but for God's sake, go out and make entertainment."

It was advice Hawks took to heart and that he heeded, not only on his next picture, but for the rest of his career.

Directing three films in a year and writing the story to a fourth, as Hawks did in 1926, was nothing unusual during the silent era. Most pictures ran little more than an hour, directors were often assigned to projects literally moments in advance of shooting, and postproduction time was minimal, given the absence of a soundtrack, meaning that pictures could be in theaters very soon after filming was completed. The way Hawks remembered it, he had no sooner finished shooting *The Road to Glory* than he went home and wrote something intended to be entertaining and commercial. On January 28, he submitted a five-page outline for *Fig Leaves* which he divided into eight sequences. A sex comedy about the early tests and trials of a marriage, the story begins in the Garden of Eden, where the couple goes through their morning routine: they are awakened by a coconut-and-sand alarm clock; Adam breaks the morning newspaper, a stone tablet, into two halves—whereupon Eve complains, "I have nothing to wear"; Adam leaves for work in a brontosaurus-drawn conveyance; and Eve is visited by a friendly snake.

As the film leaps ahead thousands of years to contemporary New York City, the serpent transforms into Eve's next-door neighbor Alice, a flapper who insists, "It is every woman's right to have pretty things to wear." Hawks has his heroine secretly become a model for fashion designer André, who, despite his effeminacy, tries to seduce Eve, who wants no part of him but likes wearing beautiful clothes. When Adam and his buddy Eddie coincidentally arrive at the shop to fix the plumbing during an elaborate fashion show and see Eve parading around in very skimpy garb, Adam says he doesn't want to see her again. But when Eve gets back to the apartment and finds Alice wearing her fur coat from the shop, the two women begin fighting, to Adam's vast amusement, and Eve kicks her conniving neighbor out. Back in the Garden of Eden, Eve is seen shooing the serpent out with a broom; she and Adam make up, and "Adam suggests that Cain and Abel are holding a sale and Eve may find just what she wants."

It was a slight, clothesline of a premise with very little story, very likely inspired in part by the successful sex comedies De Mille and Neilan had done, but with sufficient opportunity for amusing scenes, energetic spats, and visual distractions. Appeal to the female audience was considered particularly important by executives at the time, and *Fig Leaves* had that in abundance. Writers Hope Loring and Louis D. Lighton quickly elaborated Hawks's rough story into a full screenplay without changing any essential elements; George O'Brien and Olive Borden, Western stalwarts who had just acted for John Ford in *Three Bad Men*, were cast as Adam and Eve; and Hawks was shooting his second picture by March.

The sexual sparring and light comedy was handled buoyantly enough, and while the film is a perfectly agreeable example of silent-era romantic comedy, it is more interesting in the way it plants the seeds for various Hawks motifs that would flower in his sound comedies. There is the woman-animal connection that would reappear in *Bringing Up Baby, Monkey Business*, and *Hatari!*; the first of many instances of female impersonation in Hawks's films; the introduction of the sort of "theatrical" behavior, in André's extravagant gestures, which would later be seen in John Barrymore's Oscar Jaffe in *Twentieth Century* and often in the later comedies; and sexual role-playing and, by extension, playacting, which would become a principal way for men and women to define and redefine their relationships, perhaps nowhere so much as in *His Girl Friday* and *Monkey Business* but also in *Ball of Fire, I Was a Male War Bride*, and elsewhere. In a broader sense, *Fig Leaves* gives the first taste of the sort of physical expressiveness Hawks liked in performances and of the lively, good-humored give-and-take between men and women that became a hallmark of his work.

At the time of its release, however, the picture was most noted for the splashily striking production values of the prehistoric and fashion show sequences. The Rube Goldberg devices concocted to adorn the Garden of Eden are disarmingly clever, and the exaggerated animals—dinosaurs, the snake, and a giant ape—seem so homemade as to be endearing. Hawks said he and the cinematographer, Joseph August, had fun devising a way to dissolve between the story's two time periods, at a time when lap dissolves hadn't yet become commonplace: they took a beer bottle with a flaw in it, began by shooting through the clear portion, then turned it so the flaw would blur the image.

But what most reviewers commented upon were the fashion sequences. With extravagant sets by William S. Darling and William Cameron Menzies and costume designs by Adrian, who would shortly become one of the most celebrated practitioners in his field, the fashion parades, which were shot in two-color Technicolor, were spectacles without precedent in pictures, a cinematic equivalent to Ziegfeld's stage revues. Fox publicity boasted that Borden's costumes alone cost fifty thousand dollars, and *Variety* noted that the salon setting "gives opportunity for the display of a group of lingerie models which comes within an ace of having the sex kick of a nightclub show."

It is impossible to ascertain precise box-office figures for films released in the 1920s, but it is clear that *Fig Leaves*, which opened in July, was a hit—Hawks fantasized that "It got its cost back in one theater"—thereby assuring its director's career in silent pictures. In his late-in-life interviews, Hawks had a tendency to downplay and even dismiss his silent work, but he did like *Fig Leaves*. When he saw it in France in the early 1970s, his first viewing since he'd made it, he found it "amazingly modern."

In August 1926, another film opened that had Hawks's name on it, but only as the author of the original story. In fact, the finished film *Honesty—the Best Policy*, directed by Chester Bennett from a scenario by L. G. Rigby, Hawks's collaborator on *The Road to Glory*, seems to have borne only a partial resemblance to the idea Hawks himself submitted, since it was considerably reworked in the interim. Since the picture apparently no longer exists, it is impossible to say for sure, but on the basis of the few contemporaneous assessments of it, it seems to have been something of a mishmash. Certainly, what Hawks and Rigby cooked up together is even more contrived than *The Road to Glory*, one of the least promising pieces of material ever to have carried Hawks's name.

Dangers of a Great City, which the two men developed virtually simultaneously with *The Road to Glory*, between October and early December 1925, is a crime story about Bob Dare and Nancy Kay, a pair of robbers evading police captain Randall in San Francisco. Surprisingly, the two are not romantically involved, for, Nancy insists crime for her is strictly business.

The police almost nab them at a glamorous masquerade ball, but the two manage to escape. Leaving Bob behind, Nancy makes a getaway and, after a long chase, Nancy and Randall both crack up their cars. A suddenly considerate Nancy then drags the badly injured cop out of danger, and incredibly, Randall now declares his love for Nancy. When Nancy tells him that he's got to do his duty and take her in, Randall weakens and says she can go free anyway.

Back in San Francisco some time later, Bob has managed to capture Randall and is about to shoot him when Nancy convinces him to spare the detective. Randall tells Bob that if he really loves Nancy, he'd better take her away and settle down.

The story becomes increasingly unbelievable as it unfolds, and there is the major problem of which characters, if any, merit sympathy or interest. Fox wasn't happy with the material, and Hawks dropped off the project after three drafts. The picture was shot in early spring 1926, with Rockliffe

Fellowes as Randall, Pauline Starke as Nancy, and Johnnie Walker as Bob, and was released that August with a framing story, directed by Albert Ray, about a young author who is trying to win publication for his story from a publisher's "jury" of office stenographers. The crime story is intercut with brief comedic scenes of the attractive listeners reacting to the suspense-filled tale.

The patch job, devised long after Hawks left the project, appears not to have been terribly successful. Describing it as "a picture of strangely mixed purpose," *Variety* complained that just as serious excitement was being built up by the central narrative, the film undercut itself by returning to the "short-skirted girls [tying] their legs around chairs." The film was not one of Fox's big attractions of the year.

Thus far, Hawks had only worked on pictures for which he himself wrote the stories. However, Fox's commitment to its steady grind of productions meant it didn't have time to wait around for directors to come up with their own ideas, so Hawks was assigned to a script he always said he never would have chosen to do himself. In good measure because of Hawks's own exaggerated descriptions of it, *Paid to Love*, which is little-seen even among Hawks aficionados, is one of the director's most misrepresented works, in that it is thought of as the director's one, failed stab at an art film. Although beautifully crafted, it is nothing of the kind, resting instead firmly in the tradition of comic Ruritanian romances that stemmed from operettas and were so popular in Hollywood in the 1920s and early 1930s. It also introduced some major motifs that became hallmarks of Hawks's work for the rest of his career.

Paid to Love originated at Fox as a thirty-two-page treatment written early in 1926 by Harry Carr, a longtime *Los Angeles Times* columnist. A second approach, by Benjamin Glazer, turned the French leading lady into an American. But the decisive treatment was developed by writer Seton I. Miller. A smart, well-read twenty-four-year-old from rural Washington State and fresh out of Yale, Miller had just arrived in Hollywood earlier in the year to work as a technical adviser and actor on MGM's feature *Brown of Harvard*, which incidentally dealt with rival Yale. He then joined the screenwriting staff at Fox, where *Paid to Love* was his first assignment. At least superficially, Miller and Hawks were a good match because of their mutual West Coast–Ivy League backgrounds, a similar literary bent, and a shared taste for racy, modern, hard-surfaced stories, and the fledgling writer became the rising director's most frequent early collaborator. Miller would work on eight of the next ten films Hawks made, through 1932.

On *Paid to Love*, Miller came up with the character of an American diplomat-financier who takes the king of a small nation to a bawdy Paris nightclub to find the introverted crown prince Michael "a real hotsy totsy wild woman." Miller also introduced another character, Prince Eric, Michael's playboy cousin, whom the public prefers, and generally made the story far more mischievous, sophisticated, and fun. The young former newspaperman and titles writer William M. Conselman was brought in to add further polish and provide a less contrived ending, and a top cast was assembled that included George O'Brien as Crown Prince Michael, the beautiful Virginia Valli as Dolores, and William Powell as Prince Eric.

Paid to Love has always had a reputation as Hawks's most stylistically atypical film, the one time he experimented with elaborate tracking shots, expressionistic lighting, and fancy cutting. This impression was particularly furthered by Hawks himself, who admitted allowing himself to be influenced by the German expressionist master F. W. Murnau. "It isn't my type of stuff," Hawks said, adding that, as far as artsiness was concerned, "at least I got it over in a hurry. You know, the idea of wanting the camera to do those things. Now the camera's somebody's eyes."

One of the most influential European films of the time for Hollywood filmmakers, including Hawks, E. A. Dupont's *Variety*, opened in the United States in late June; so impressed were the executives at Paramount, for example, that they not only bought the American rights to the picture but showed it to employees as an example of how movies should be made. Murnau, whose *The Last Laugh* had earlier impressed film professionals with its supple camerawork and seamless storytelling, arrived in Hollywood with great fanfare at the end of July to commence his celebrated Fox contract with *Sunrise*. His presence on the lot was greatly felt, and his influence is difficult to overestimate. The awe in which the German directors were held was at its peak at the very moment Hawks started shooting *Paid to Love* at the beginning of August 1926, and it may be this atmosphere that Hawks was thinking of when he said that he tried to out-Murnau Murnau on the picture.

The irony is that, while this may be Hawks's most visually stylish picture, graced with lovely shots and very impressive production values, it is far from radical or even the least bit extreme in its technique; the camerawork of L. W. O'Connell, who, the following year, would shoot Murnau's *Four Devils*, merely seems to have a bit more range and appear less locked down than in Hawks's subsequent work. Although not an important film, *Paid to Love* is amusingly suggestive romantic fluff, entertaining in precisely the way it intends to be. The story is rife with role-playing—the entire plot, in fact, pivots on the idea that the two leads initially present identities other than their true selves. In terms of Hawks's career, as the title itself would indicate, it is significant as the vehicle that introduced a prototype of one category of the Hawksian woman, the vagabond showgirl–quasi-prostitute—kept woman who would appear in any number of pictures, from *Barbary Coast*, *Come and Get It*, and *Only Angels Have Wings* to *Ball of Fire*, *To Have and Have Not*, and *Rio Bravo*. In *Paid to Love*, this character, Dolores, is first seen performing at the exotic Café des Apaches in Paris, where she is engaged to "make love" to Michael in order to "arouse his interest" in women, a development that will inspire the confidence of the American financier who will make no further loans to the small Mediterranean country of San Savona unless a line of succession is assured.

Hawks has fun portraying American discomfort with formal European traditions, and his purely visual presentation of Prince Michael's lack of interest in the opposite sex is as superbly simple as it is uncharacteristic: a floor-level tracking shot follows the shapely legs of a maid; the lecherous Prince Eric turns to appreciatively stare at them, but after the legs are shown again, an oblivious Michael doesn't bother even to glance at them. This sort of male character, who ultimately succeeds with women despite either apparent lack of interest or simple awkwardness, always amused Hawks, and it was a characteristic he pushed on occasion in his work with Cary Grant and particularly with John Wayne in his late films. The connection between the old king and Dolores is initiated by her taking a lit cigarette from him, apparently the first of countless such exchanges in Hawks's films, and there is further cigarette play later in the picture. Given the director's keen interest in automobiles, the sight of Michael working on an engine block in the middle of his huge, elegant living room registers as a humorously personal touch. There is also a highly erotic close-up of Valli's Dolores after she has kissed Michael, a shot more akin to the way William Daniels would shortly be shooting Garbo for Clarence Brown or Sternberg would one day film Dietrich than to anything else in Hawks's canon. With her hair cut short and combed wet and back, Valli looks rather like a boy with a woman's body. The most outrageous moment of all comes when the leering Prince Eric slowly peels a banana while watching an oblivious Dolores getting undressed. Overall, there is a lovely pictorialism to the film that is impossible not to enjoy, although its self-consciousness may be what felt alien to Hawks.

Hawks completed *Paid to Love* in mid-September. Normally, it would have been expected to come out before the end of the year. For unknown reasons, however, Fox sat on the film for nearly a year, by which time Hawks had directed two more features. Hawks said that the studio held it back "because they thought it was so interesting" but also maintained that by the time it came out, in late July 1927, "everybody had done everything we had done in the picture," resulting in a flop. This makes little sense as an explanation, but there is really no reason that can account for such a protracted delay, except, perhaps, an overabundance of George O'Brien titles on the release schedule. The reviews were on the mixed-to-positive side, with special kudos reserved for Valli and the visual qualities, but the director's perennial derision of the film was no doubt prodded by its relative commercial failure.

Hawks's protests years later that sophisticated, European-style sex dramas were not his cup of tea perhaps should not be taken too seriously, for there is further evidence that he was enormously influenced by the likes of Murnau, Lubitsch, Dupont, and the entire Continental wave then washing over Hollywood. As soon as he finished making *Paid to Love*, Hawks undertook one of the most surprising and overtly emotional projects of his career, *Budapest*. Written by Hawks, the story was fleshed out by Seton Miller into a very detailed, scene-by-scene, forty-six-page adaptation dated January 12, 1927, that bears the intriguing alternate title *The Satyr*. It is, in fact, the commanding story of a big man brought low, a tale of war and sacrifice, a study of how the toughest and most egotistical of men is transformed by love. It contains several prominent motifs that would surface in later Hawks films: the leading character literally becomes crippled, the central female character is a beautiful entertainer who inspires a rivalry among three men, and one man willingly sacrifices his life to save another man, a gesture that recurs in Hawks's early work. But it also possesses an emotionally sincere, deeply felt quality that is unusual for him, as well as a vivid illustration of how a man can possess both an exceedingly hard outward personality and a heart capable of infinite tenderness and generosity.

Set in pre-war Budapest, the story contains such startling elements as the sadistic hero's seduction of a beautiful dancer while she is strapped into his prize possession, a torture chair from the Spanish Inquisition.

But after a very strong start, Hawks's and Miller's treatment becomes overly melodramatic and contrived, lacking the irony, the intellectual distance on human behavior that made the dramatization of similar stories by Stroheim, Sternberg, and others so distinctive. Fox didn't bite on the project in 1927, nor did it when Hawks and Miller resubmitted it for consideration in May 1928. Later that year, however, the studio assigned eight different writers to take a stab at it, asking them to keep the title but jettison Hawks's and Miller's characters and story line; none of the subsequent outlines or treatments, including one in late 1929 that was intended as a musical, bore any relation to the original idea.

Hawks often claimed that he had everything to do with one of the most famous pictures to come out of the late silent period, Josef von Sternberg's *Underworld*, which was heralded as the first real gangster film. He told Joseph McBride, "Ben Hecht sold a story to me. Ben and I worked on the story, and a friend [Art Rosson] was to be the director. He went up to San Francisco, as I remember, to go to the prison there, but unfortunately got tight, so they had to fire him. We had sketches made of every scene. We had sets built, and we had a cast. It was beautifully written. Then we got Joe von Sternberg to direct the picture, and out came this really good picture." When Kevin Brownlow asked Hawks about Sternberg, he said, "We needed another director and I'd seen a little quickie that he'd made and said let's give this guy a chance. And they said, if you watch him. And I said, sure, I'll watch him." The only problem with these stories is that *Underworld*, a Paramount production, was prepared with Rosson in late 1926 and shot by Sternberg beginning in late March 1927, when Hawks had already been directing pictures at Fox for a year and a half and hadn't been employed at Paramount for three years. To be generous, it is entirely possible that Hawks might have consulted with his friend Art Rosson about the project, may have first met Ben Hecht through him, and could easily, once Rosson was fired, put in a good word with Jesse Lasky and others at Paramount on behalf of Sternberg, whom he liked a great deal. But whatever he may have done, he did it privately, as a friend or adviser, not in any official capacity. And under no circumstances did Hawks "watch" Sternberg as anything other than a friendly spectator, since he was busy at Fox preparing *Fazil* at the time. This is not only a case of Hawks once again taking credit for making an important filmmaker's career, but an instance of inverted influence: there is no question that Sternberg, Hecht, and a couple of the other writers on *Underworld*, the credited Charles Furthman and the uncredited Jules Furthman, had more influence on Hawks than he did on them.

When *Budapest* didn't proceed, Hawks suddenly inherited one of the studio's most promising commercial projects. Fox had bought one of the most popular Broadway plays of the era, Russell G. Medcraft and Norma Mitchell's *The Cradle Snatchers*, a farce about three wives who combat their husbands' philandering by pursuing some college students. The play was the big comedy hit of the 1925–26 season, running for fifty-nine weeks beginning September 7, 1925. The playwrights were engaged to write an initial treatment, but the real screenwriting chore was turned over to thirty-year-old Sarah Y. Mason, whose husband, writer-director Victor Heerman, was an old collaborator of Mickey Neilan's. At first, Allan Dwan was assigned the directing job, but abruptly, at the end of November, Dwan was off and Hawks, the older man's money man just a few years before, replaced him.

Fox and Hawks felt considerable pressure to make sure the film version lived up to the often hilarious play. It is very doubtful that Hawks ever saw the stage production, and even though the basic three-act structure was not toyed with, silent films often proved ill-equipped to deliver the virtues of dialogue-rich stage plays. It was an assignment unlike any Hawks had yet faced in his short career, in which comic timing and theatrical technique would be critical. But Hawks was up to the challenge, turning out another audience-pleasing comedy that met the approval even of critics who held it directly up against the play.

Hawks shot the picture between January 17 and February 15, 1927, and it opened at the giant Roxy in New York City on May 28, nearly two months before *Paid to Love* debuted at the same theater. Joseph Striker's Joe is the campus "sheik," and Nick Stuart's Henry Winton is stuck on one girl, while Arthur Lake's Oscar, the "Swede," is another of Hawks's comic leads who is desperately afraid of women. The fortyish women played by Louise Fazenda, Dorothy Phillips, and Ethel Wales are seen dealing with their errant husbands in different ways, and Hawks gets in a personal joke when an insert of a business card for an establishment called The Club 400 reveals the name "Victor Flemen" scribbled on it.

Part of reel three and all of reel four of the seven-reel picture are missing from the print Peter Bogdanovich salvaged some years ago from Fox, this after years of the film having been thought lost. But it all builds to a climax in which the society women decide to punish their husbands by consorting with the spiffy college boys, in the hopes of teaching them a lesson. It is a boisterous, energetic Jazz Age film, sprightly paced and fresh-feeling despite its obvious theatrical origins. Like Hawks's other early work, it hardly stands as a major silent film, but it did just what it set out to do and certainly bolstered Hawks's confidence in his ability to direct comedy and achieve desired effects. As Leland A. Poague points out in his critical book on the director, *The Cradle Snatchers* can be seen "as a paradigm instance of role reversals and role playing in Hawks," and while it may indeed forecast more of the same in his films over the years, the overtly theatrical origins of the piece have more than a lot to do with this. At this point, Fox had every reason to believe that its new director, after a year and a half on the job, had found his niche in comedy.

All through this time, Kenneth Hawks was quickly establishing a great deal of credit for himself at the studio as a supervisor, the equivalent of a contemporary line producer, or the studio's administrator and organizer on a particular production. Kenneth's intelligence and amiability stood him well in this job, which he performed on Albert Ray's *More Pay — Less Work* and John G. Blystone's *Ankles Preferred* before dabbling in editing on Sydney and H. A. Snow's Arctic documentary *The Great White North,* in story writing on Albert Ray's *A Thief in the Dark,* and even, it seems, in cinematography on Richard Rosson's bootlegging melodrama, *The Escape,* although his shared camera credit is somewhat questionable. In any event, Kenneth received a very well-rounded education in the various aspects of filmmaking in a very short time, and soon went back to supervising.

From the second half of 1926 through 1927, romance bloomed for all three Hawks boys. The Mayfair Society was an elite social institution that held formal white-tie dinner dances once a month at the Ambassador Hotel. Several friends of the Hawkses, most notably Mary Pickford, were among the frankly snobbish group's prime movers, and it was at one of these elegant affairs that both Howard and Kenneth Hawks had their first dates with the women they would marry.

Victor Fleming was still seeing Norma Shearer sporadically in 1926, and when she agreed to accompany him to a Mayfair ball that summer, she asked if he knew anyone who might escort her younger sister, Athole. Howard Hawks, always quite fond of Norma, readily agreed to fill out the foursome. According to their daughter Barbara, it was "romantic love at first sight" between Howard and Athole. Physically, there was no mistaking that Athole was Norma's sister; both were pale-skinned brunettes with very English good looks, but most people considered Athole the greater beauty of the two. Even Norma admitted as much in her unpublished autobiography: "I wasn't nearly as popular with the boys as my sister — she was two years older and much prettier." Norma, who had the bluest of eyes, added that Athole had "an unusual pair of brown eyes that caught all the beaux"; Norma, in her pre-Hollywood days, got only the hand-me-downs. Athole was not driven professionally the way her sister was, and she had impeccable grace and manners that appealed greatly to Howard's sense of propriety and good breeding.

Born on November 20, 1900, Athole Dane Shearer was at a curious stage in her life when she met Howard Hawks. Athole, Norma and their brother Douglas had enjoyed a spoiled upbringing in suburban Montreal, with Athole often tutoring her younger sister, who rarely attended school. But their pampered lives began to be threatened when their father Andrew's lumber company and investments went bad during World War I. In reduced circumstances, they had to sell their large house in fashionable Westmount and move into a modest apartment, and family life was strained further by the constant philandering of Andy, a "sport," as Norma put it, who "was a gay blade and had sown plenty of wild oats."

In the winter of 1917–18, Athole showed disturbing signs of some sort of emotional or psychological imbalance. As Norma described it, "my beautiful sister Athole became desperately ill—apparently the psychological effects of the war during our adolescence." Athole had dated several young men who had gone off to war, and many schoolmates she knew more casually were in the trenches as well. Canadian casualties were proportionately high, and when the inevitable word came back that some of her friends had been killed, the news hit Athole hard. The sisters' bedroom was plastered with patriotic posters, and Norma remembered that Athole "began to look at them strangely one day—then she said quietly with frightened eyes, 'I can hear them—they're coming—up in the sky!' We thought she was out of her mind!" Despite the fact that "screams from the upper window each morning turned my steps back from school," no professional treatment was sought for Athole because of the embarrassing stigma attached to mental illness. "But she recovered one day, after three months, as suddenly as she became ill. We never knew how or why! Everyone was elated and breathed and ate and slept once more!"

That was the way Norma remembered things. In fact, Athole withdrew gradually into her intense depression, becoming progressively worse whenever she learned of further deaths among her friends, until she finally stopped speaking. With this, the family physician ordered her confined to her bed, and she was sedated for a month, after which she suddenly returned to something resembling normal. The teenager suffered another attack of acute melancholia some months later, but by then doctors, who had seen numerous cases of similar female misery, had decided that the condition was specifically war-related and would disappear as soon as the conflict ended. For the moment, then, Athole's problems were conveniently swept under the carpet.

After the war, the family fell on hard times. Andy's plant closed entirely, young Douglas became a chauffeur, Norma stayed on a friend's couch, and Athole, who knitted sweaters for four dollars apiece, and her mother, Edith, moved into La Corona Hotel, where they could stay for very little since it was owned by a family friend. Soon Edith sold everything and, with four hundred dollars, took the girls to New York City with the intention that they would conquer Broadway. Living in a dump of a building, refused as showgirls by Ziegfeld but able to get representation with the Edward Small Agency, the two sisters found minor movie work with the Transatlantic Picture Corporation in Mount Vernon, in a two-reel comedy about a girls' finishing school, and were extras in D. W. Griffith's *Way Down East* and the Marion Davies film *The Restless Sex,* both released in 1920. But after a year they ran out of money and retreated to Montreal, where the girls became models for the city's leading portrait photographer, Jimmy Rice. With a bit of experience under their belts, they were able to return to New York City, where Norma found regular work as a model for illustrators and photographers and had a little romance with Ben Lyon, an aspiring actor who would go on to star in Howard Hughes's *Hell's Angels.* Edith took a job in the blouse department of Franklin Simon's on Fifth Avenue.

For her part, Athole was happy to return to New York so she could see what might develop between her and a young man named John Ward. The son of a prosperous New Jersey textile manufacturer, Ward had left the security of the family business behind to pursue a career writing for radio but picked up money wherever he could. He and the Shearers had met the year before, when they were all extras in *The Restless Sex.* Eventually, John and Athole began seeing each other, and he abruptly proposed marriage. Edith was against the match, correctly sensing that Ward was a questionable prospect since, as Norma snootily put it, he "chose not to share in his father's fortune." Evidently, the Ward family's feelings about the Shearers and their show-business orientation was mutual, for the two families met for the only time at the civil ceremony in New York City in early April 1923. The couple honeymooned in the Adirondacks and moved into a modest Greenwich Village apartment with, in Norma's view, "not much money and a rather uncertain future."

During this time, Norma, with Eddie Small as her agent, had begun appearing regularly in films made on the East Coast, and shortly after her sister's wedding she signed an MGM contract and moved with her mother to Hollywood, where she made eight films within a year. The following year she was loaned to Paramount and began her serious romance with Victor

Fleming, just as she was being admired from afar by Irving Thalberg. On July 31, 1924, in New York City, Athole gave birth to a son, Peter John Ward, but this by no means indicated a happy marriage. According to Norma, her sister's "life seemed somewhat dismal at this moment," and about eighteen months later, feeling Athole needed both emotional and financial help, Norma and Edith brought Athole and little Peter out to Los Angeles, where she moved into the Shearer bungalow on Franklin at Whitley Heights, just a block from where Howard and Kenneth Hawks lived.

Norma echoed Barbara Hawks's sentiments about the romance between Howard and Athole, at least as far as Athole was concerned. Hawks was "more fascinating than any man she had ever met," Norma claimed. "My sister, to make the story simple, fell in love with him so deeply that it was to last a lifetime, although not their marriage." Athole had her son to take care of and was with her mother and sister, but she was still quite lonely in Los Angeles when Hawks entered her life, and there can be little doubt that Howard, in addition to seeming like a terribly dashing and accomplished figure, benefited from reminding Athole of the father who had been so absent from her life. Like Hawks, Andy Shearer had gray hair and blue eyes. Very athletic, he loved horses and was a member of the Montreal Hunt Club. Raised in a very sporting environment, Athole was a fine horseback rider, swimmer, ice skater, skier, and sailor, better than Hawks in just about all these areas. She and Howard saw each other constantly through 1927, playing golf and making the fashionable social rounds, and Hawks didn't take long to push the idea of marriage. But the acutely sensitive Athole was increasingly distraught over the prospect of telling Johnny Ward that she wanted to leave him, and it took months for her to work up the nerve to ask for a divorce.

During precisely the same period, Kenneth Hawks saw his own love life take off. In the late summer of 1926, at the canteen at the Fox studios, Kenneth was introduced to the actress Mary Astor. Only twenty, this patrician beauty, also a Midwesterner by birth, had already acted in more than two dozen films and had been something of a star since appearing in *Beau Brummel* in 1924, opposite John Barrymore, with whom she had had a wild affair. For their first date, Kenneth asked her to the Mayfair Society ball, and by that fall they were dating regularly. She described their early time together in her autobiography, *My Story*: "I liked being with him; it was never hectically romantic, with the emphasis on sex. I liked his quiet good manners and his good taste. He had prematurely grey hair, very twinkling blue eyes behind horn-rimmed glasses, and a grin a mile wide."

Mary was working constantly, and when she went away on location, Kenneth visited her as often as possible. He fell hard very quickly, and when she stunned him by confessing her recent passionate involvements with Barrymore and another man, he decided that her honesty made him think even more of her. When he proposed, she gently put him off for a while, uncertain as to whether she was ready for marriage, but Kenneth persisted. She liked Frank and Helen Hawks, her parents liked him, and by February 1927, Mary decided she would marry Kenneth. As she explained, "We had built a wonderful companionship. He was a very real, substantial person, comfortable to be with. Wherever we went together we had good times. We worked hard, both of us, but we also found time for fun." They played golf and attended sporting events and premieres, and she was very impressed with his thorough knowledge of the moviemaking process. Distressed at how little money he was earning compared to the star salaries Mary was raking in, Ken refused to set a date until his new Fox contract was approved, but Mary, realizing what a "fair-haired boy" Ken was at Fox, had no doubt that her fiancé was a young man with a decidedly bright future.

The couple spent a good deal of time at the Hawks family home in Pasadena, which she found warm but clouded by the dire illness of Grace Hawks, who, at twenty-four, was suffering from severe tuberculosis. Despite the intense objections of her three brothers, Helen Hawks's staunch Christian Scientist beliefs prevailed, and Grace was not sent to a sanitarium. Grace slowly deteriorated, and the boys privately blamed their mother for what they saw as their sister's unnecessary death, which came on December 23, 1927. The funeral was held two days after Christmas.

In the spring of 1927, as Mary was starring in Lewis Milestone's *Two Arabian Knights*, the first major film produced by Howard Hughes, she and Kenneth matched up the latter's younger brother, Bill, with Mary's friend the actress Bessie Love, setting another betrothal in motion. During this time, Mary and Kenneth decided to abstain from sex until they got married, even though the date still lay vaguely in the future. Although Mary agreed to the arrangement, it came to bother her as the weeks and months wore on. By contrast, "Ken seemed not to mind," she allowed; "he was not a sensual person at all. He had none of the deep, fierce passion that I had known. He was very affectionate and demonstrative; often we sat in a big chair, with me curled in his lap, and read from the same book."

There were numerous joint outings with Howard and Athole. On the weekend beginning Thursday evening, August 11, 1927, they all attended a dinner party at the Biltmore Hotel at which Irving Thalberg and Norma Shearer announced their engagement. On Friday night, the entire Hawks family assembled to celebrate Kenneth's twenty-ninth birthday, and on Saturday, the quartet joined Victor Fleming and Arthur Rosson and the latter's wife, Lou, for a weekend excursion to Santa Barbara, where Howard gave rides on his new Chris-Craft. On September 29, they all attended the Thalberg-Shearer garden wedding, where Kenneth uncharacteristically made a fool of himself by shouting, "Yea-a-ay!" when Herman Mankiewicz ceremoniously carried out the Cup of Life, which Kenneth took to be a giant champagne goblet.

Finally, at the beginning of December, Kenneth received his new contract, at one thousand dollars per week, and set the wedding date for February 24. Kenneth and Mary rented a small house on Alcyona Drive on the hill above Vine Street and Franklin, not far from where Kenneth and Howard had lived together; furnished it beautifully; and left the evening of the wedding on the train for New York. Mary Astor loved Kenneth, but she knew something was amiss when her husband, on their wedding night, simply kissed her good night and repaired to his own berth to go to sleep. But the whole matter was, she said, "not a subject Ken and I could discuss freely. He possessed a kind of natural delicacy that seemed inviolable. In our own relationship we were happily comfortable, but I clearly sensed the existence of an intangible line that I could not, and did not want to, cross over."

During their honeymoon, they saw a play at nearly every performance time in New York; visited Ken's alma mater, Yale; took the train to Florida and a plane to Havana; then sailed back to Los Angeles via Panama. During their monthlong trip, they never once had sex. In the coming months, Mary acknowledged, her "marital relations with Ken were, in effect, nonexistent; their infrequent occurrences were brief and unsatisfactory. Total abstinence was easier than this; but either solution caused me to be nervous and upset." Mary eventually sought refuge in the eager attentions of a Fox executive, Russell Bradbury, who convinced her that Ken was more interested in making movies and playing golf than in developing any sex life. Although tortured from the beginning by her betrayal, the frustrated Mary finally gave in and started an affair. But she soon became pregnant— definitely not by Kenneth—and had an illicit abortion, which she somehow managed to hide from her husband. Mary's mother finally told Ken what his wife was up to, and the couple was finally forced to clear the air about things, which in the end helped the relationship. The marriage became stronger, and they took a new, larger house on Appian Way at the top of Lookout Mountain and entertained quite a bit, although Mary Astor never did say if their sexual relations ever markedly improved.

In March 1927, just after *The Cradle Snatchers* was finished, Fox extended Howard Hawks's contract for a second year. He was to make three more films, for thirty thousand dollars per picture, and the studio included options for two years beyond that at a salary that stepped up by ten thousand dollars per picture per year. At once, Hawks was assigned to another exotic romance to which he felt he had little to contribute. *Fazil* was based on Pierre Frondaie's 1922 French play *L'Insoumise*, which had been a particular hit on the London stage under the title *Prince Fazil*. The piece concerned an Arab prince's disastrous marriage to a free-willed Parisienne and was adapted by Philip Klein, a World War I veteran whose father was the playwright Charles Klein, and written by Seton Miller. With its emphasis on decor, costumes, heavy breathing, and fatalistic romanticism, this was decidedly not Hawks's cup of tea; nor did the director ever find Fox's all-American star, Charles Farrell, remotely credible as a volatile sheik. But Hawks still found many ways to make the best of a questionable situation, and while the film is indisputably artificial in the extreme, its sexual charge and numerous deft directorial touches make it a perfectly reasonable exercise in *Romeo and Juliet*–style tragedy.

The film begins by contrasting the old ways of the Arab world with the new customs gaining wide currency in Europe. In a scene found terribly gruesome by some at the time, Hadji Fazil is seen ordering the execution of a runaway servant. Just before the huge sword is about to come down, it is time for prayers; but as soon as devotion to Allah is paid, the blade is raised again to complete the job. In vivid relief, Fabienne, played by the blond Norwegian star Greta Nissen, is seen "glorying in the freedom of the modern world" in Europe. At the outset, Fazil is a member of a particular Hawksian club: "Women do not interest me," he says, upon being encouraged to continue his lineage.

While on a business trip to Venice, however, Fazil finds his interest aroused when he spots Fabienne. In one of Hawks's most arresting inventions, the two future lovers see each other in big open windows across a canal, and the remainder of the scene is shot from the point of view of a gondolier. The comic undertones here and elsewhere demonstrate the strong influence Lubitsch had on Hawks at this stage, as he did on so many other directors. Fabienne, displaying her modern temperament, readily sleeps with the prince, and the morning-after scene is particularly lovely: beautiful shots of Fabienne awakening and smiling rapturously, while Fazil is seen bowing in prayer toward Mecca. To keep himself amused, before one of the lovemaking scenes Hawks told both Farrell and Nissen privately that the other performer was very shy and that they would have to do something provocative to bring the scene alive. "Well, they were two of the busiest beavers you've ever seen in all your life," Hawks chuckled, and it is true that no Hawks film ever again featured nearly so much heavy kissing, touching, holding, and general overt physical sex as this one.

But the East-West rift soon asserts itself. Fabienne can't bear the traditional role she is expected to play, and Fazil is so miserable that he considers killing himself. Instead, however, he takes a harem, and when Fabienne visits it there are some imaginative shots, courtesy of cinematographer L. W. O'Connell — of one concubine, for instance, shaving her armpits, as well as some silhouetted nudity — that foreshadow the fetishism of Sternberg, although with Hawks it is less extreme. Fazil shuts down the harem, save for the sexiest member of it, who is kept on as Fabienne's servant, but Fabienne quickly becomes miserable being cooped up at her husband's compound. As with *Romeo and Juliet*, there is no way out except death. Mortally wounded, Fazil uses his suicide ring on Fabienne so they will be together always and, after being unable to utter the crucial words throughout their entire relationship, finally says "I love you" just before she dies. He follows quickly, to join her in another, better world.

On the one hand, this is the sort of melodramatic Hollywood hokum that Hawks saw fit to avoid for the remainder of his career, the end of his flirtation with the sort of sophisticated, European romance that was in vogue at the time but was never something he could make his own. On a more personal, psychological level, *Fazil*, coincidentally or not, dealt directly with issues Hawks was facing in life at that very moment. As Fabienne says, "I am afraid of marriage, afraid of anything that might take away the freedom I love." One needn't take it too seriously, but *Fazil* is a worst-case scenario about marriage, a horror story about the fearsome consequences of taking the plunge, something that was very much on Hawks's mind when he was making the film. Faced with this story later in life, Hawks would undoubtedly have made a comedy out of it rather than such a serious piece. On the other hand, throughout the rest of his career, he chose to virtually never make any more films about marriage at all.

Hawks provoked studio executives by going seriously over schedule and budget on *Fazil*, shooting from June 5 through August 3, 1927, about double the time it usually took to film a normal silent picture, and spending a great deal more than the allotted $125,000. Sol Wurtzel, who had already been irritated by what he saw as Hawks's poky work habits, even considered shutting the production down at one point rather than squandering more money. Hawks's extravagance on *Fazil* put a black mark next to his name in Wurtzel's book, which made the studio keep a close eye on him from then on and represented the beginning of the director's lifelong adversarial relationship with his bosses.

Inexplicably, *Fazil* wasn't released until June 4, 1928, long after the picture Hawks would make next. That film, *A Girl in Every Port* stands as the first defining work of Hawks's career, the first that announced a great deal of what its director was all about. It is not a great film, or even one of the most significant American pictures of the silent period, but it is the Hawks silent that connects in the most crucial ways to the work he would do later.

Hawks himself wrote the original story, in late summer or early fall of 1927. The immediate instigation was Fox's desire for some sort of follow-up to its smash hit *What Price Glory?*, Raoul Walsh's adaptation of Laurence Stallings and Maxwell Anderson's World War I play about two soldiers who are great friends as well as romantic rivals. The film, which heavily played up the comedy, opened in December 1926 and made a star of Victor McLaglen, the brawny English former boxer and soldier. Hawks's story simply made the characters merchant seamen and dispensed with the war, allowing the characters to concentrate full-time on boozing, brawling, and womanizing.

Humorously emphasizing the phallic from the outset, Hawks named his characters Spike (McLaglen) and Salami (to be played by Robert Armstrong, a future screen tough guy who had appeared in only a couple of films previously). Hawks's initial nine-page treatment has the men putting into seven different ports of call—Amsterdam, Buenos Aires, Panama, Fiji, Cavite, Bombay, and Hong Kong—and is based on the premise that everywhere Spike goes, the girls he encounters have all been tattooed with "The Mark," a heart-and-anchor insignia that tells him that somebody is consistently beating him to the clinch. In Panama, the men finally meet and come to blows, but, faced with a common foe in the police, join forces to fight the cops, which lands the duo in jail. Once released, they resume their battle, but when they fall into the sea and Salami realizes Spike can't swim, he must rescue his rival, and the two become friends over a smoke.

In Hong Kong (or Singapore in an alternate version—it didn't matter), Spike genuinely falls for a café entertainer. But when he finds out that she's got Salami's mark on her too, Spike takes pleasure in watching Salami get beaten to a pulp in a saloon brawl. He ultimately takes pity on him and mothers his pulverized pal, and when the cops arrive, they join forces again before fleeing. Hawks's final scene has the buddies meeting two attractive girls; before they all go off together, Spike checks to make sure that his choice doesn't have Salami's mark on her.

The first writer brought aboard was James Kevin McGuinness, who had just that year arrived in Hollywood as a Fox contract writer on the basis of his considerable reputation as a sportswriter for the *New York Telegram*, a columnist for the *New York Sun*, and a contributor to "Talk of the Town" in the *New Yorker*; much later, he became an MGM executive, a writer for John Ford, and one of Hollywood's most virulent anti-Communists. McGuinness, who was ultimately credited for the adaptation, added the plot business of treachery on the part of the girl Spike falls for, with her trying to set the two men against each other as she double-crosses Spike and robs Salami of his cash. He also wrote a credo for the two men that could stand as a definition of Hawks's ideal for a love story between two men throughout his career: "If they occasionally outwit each other to gain a private assignation with some particularly appealing girl, all that follows between them is the broad humor of triumph on one's part, and the unconcealed chagrin of defeat on the other's. No bitterness remains when the affair is over, never a smouldering resentment."

McGuinness also came up with a clever final scene in which the men, after escaping overwhelmingly poor odds in an enormous brawl, stumble into the street and find two girls, one very pretty and the other "terrible looking." After each one offers the other the attractive one, they flip a coin. From this point on, we see the women only from the waist down: one male arm moves around the pretty girl's waist, another arm surrounds the ugly one; then the arm around the cute girl moves down a bit, while the arm around the unsightly one tries to move down but can't go through with it. That's the last we see of the sailors. "Who got the pretty girl and who the ugly one, we never know. But we do know that the two men went off together . . . friends."

Several uncredited writers, including the well-known Mack Sennett gag man Reginald Morris, Marion Orth, and Philip Klein, did further work on the story, but Hawks called upon Seton Miller to write the actual scenario. To streamline the action and meet Fox's demands to cut down on sets, the number of ports was reduced to five and, perhaps in deference to the influence of Dupont's *Variety*, the girl Spike falls for was transformed into a circus high diver. When Spike announces that he won't be sailing any further because he's in love, Salami replies, "You're not in love — you're just broke out all over with monkey bites," a line ace title writer Malcolm Stuart Boylan came up with and which Hawks attributed to Ben Hecht on *Twentieth Century*.

The actress Hawks cast in the film's largest female part had attracted attention for her beauty in the dozen or so pictures she had made since changing professions from showgirl to actress two years before, but she was by no means considered a serious actress. Louise Brooks was married to Hawks's friend Eddie Sutherland, and Hawks, liking her direct, irreverent manner as well as her striking looks, asked Fox to borrow her from Paramount to play the high-diving Marie. Brooks's boyish figure is shown to maximum advantage in her tight-fitting swimsuit, and Hawks resorted to a fancy shot from beneath to highlight her dramatic dive from a tower into a small tank. With her black hair worn in her distinctively sharp bob and her bangs trimmed just above her eyebrows, Brooks stood out in her brief appearance as the double-dealing conniver who tries to take Spike for his money and two-time him with her old beau Salami.

Forty years later, Hawks told Kevin Brownlow why he chose Brooks: "I wanted a different type of girl. . . . I hired Louise Brooks because . . . she's very sure of herself, she's very analytical, she's very feminine, but she's damn good and sure she's going to do what she wants to do. I could use her today. She was way ahead of her time, with that hairdress. And she's a rebel. I like her, you know. I like rebels. . . . What I don't like are these little curled-up things that all look alike, who are trying to be pretty and are not interested in being chic and smart and different." Looking with Brownlow at a photo of Brooks, the director said, "Just think of how modern she looks. Oh, God, she was a good-looking girl."

Brooks was nothing if not brutally direct and honest in her assessments of her friends and coworkers, and she returned the compliment. "Howard Hawks admired me," she told John Kobal. "He was the perfect director. He didn't do anything at all. He would sit, look very, very beautiful, tall and graceful, leaning against anything he could lean against, and watch the scene; and the person who did all the directing was that big ham Victor McLaglen. I mean, when we were shooting, diving into the tank, it was a freezing cold night on the Fox lot, and Howard was walking around in a very smart tweed jacket, and I was shivering with the cold coming out of this damn greasy tank, and he smiled at me and he said, 'Is it cold?' He was just someone who had wandered on the set and was being sympathetic, but I liked him very much as a man and as a director." On the basis of her appearance in *A Girl in Every Port,* Brooks was chosen by the German director G. W. Pabst to star as Lulu in *Pandora's Box,* a role coveted by nearly every actress in Europe, including Marlene Dietrich. It was the film that would make Brooks a cult legend.

A Girl in Every Port was shot entirely on the Fox lot from the end of October through December 21, 1927, with L. W. O'Connell, once again, and Rudolph Berquist manning the cameras. The future star Myrna Loy and the fan dancer Sally Rand appeared briefly as two of the many girls, and even though Fox executives were nervous about Hawks's tendency to take his time, and with it their money, they kept their distance because they smelled a winner, and the director appreciated it.

It was on this film, his sixth, that Hawks finally felt that he got in the groove as a director and began to recognize what he could do and what he was good at. One of his talents was turning toward comedy with material that a routine director might just play straight or for melodrama. Given the importance of the female audience, many questioned the idea that a film would put male friendship above a traditional romantic attachment, but Hawks proved not only to others but to himself that such a theme could carry a film, and he continued to use it throughout his career; his last serious project, in the 1970s, was ostensibly a remake of *A Girl in Every Port.* This film was also, Hawks told Peter Bogdanovich, "the first time I had a chance to use the kind of people I knew. Up till that time, I was working with characters who were figments of other people's imaginations. But on this film, the Westerns, the pictures with race drivers and things like that, I felt I was on familiar ground because I knew the people." This doesn't quite square with his having written the original stories to two of his previous films, but it is easy to see what Hawks meant, and easier still to observe how Spike and Salami link up with the competitive but friendly men in so many of the director's subsequent pictures.

The "love story between two men" motif appears in its crudest, most elemental form in *A Girl in Every Port,* and Hawks scholars have long argued over what one is to make of Hawks's apparent approval of male camaraderie coming before heterosexual romance. A conventional reading finds Hawks's insistence on positioning the women here as either disposable, interchangeable prey or threats to the men's convivial status quo to show simple misogyny. Those tracing the homosexual subtext in Hawks's work need only begin here, with the outrageous running gag, introduced by Hawks himself in the original outline, of Salami's repeatedly asking Spike to pull his middle finger when it gets out of joint during a brawl. Robin Wood, a leading champion of Hawks, finds this picture hopelessly adolescent and unsatisfying because the resolution, "in which the characters remain arrested at an immature stage of development," is offered up as a "happy ending." Leland A. Poague, in his book on the director, sees it very differently, as a sort of ironic tragedy in which the men "are trapped, quite literally, in and by their own plans and values." It is entirely likely that Hawks might have agreed with Wood's conclusion about the characters' arrested development, since, as he grew older, he gravitated toward more varied and complex resolutions of the tensions implicit between male friendships and heterosexual couplings, most maturely in *The Big Sky*.

A psychobiographical analysis of *A Girl in Every Port* would point out that along with *Fazil*, it displays a paralyzing fear of commitment and marriage. The choice for men in both films is explicitly seen to be a wife, on the one hand, and literally a harem, or endless string of available women, on the other. The first scene of Spike going ashore in Amsterdam to look up an old flame shows him fleeing when he discovers that she now has a husband and three kids. The other family unit, of a widow and her son (possibly by Spike) in San Pedro, is depressingly down-and-out, and as soon as Marie inspires thoughts of domesticity in Spike, they are rubbed out by her calculating behavior. Whether or not Hawks was inwardly agonizing over giving up his bachelor ways for marriage cannot be known, but the two films he made in the year before his wedding certainly lend artistic evidence to such a possibility.

Hawks finished shooting *A Girl in Every Port* just before Christmas 1927, but, despite the good commercial showings of *Fig Leaves* and *The Cradle Snatchers* and the evident promise of the new picture, Hawks was in hot water with his bosses. Costs were cut on the latest production by eliminating some of the ports of call (the picture runs only sixty-four minutes) and by dressing existing sets in the most minimal ways to give them their requisite foreignness. But Hawks had already established a reputation as an overspender and as a director prone to "dilly dallying around," in Sol Wurtzel's opinion. Even more crucially, Hawks kept turning down stories the studio wanted him to do, with the result that by January, seven weeks from the conclusion of his year's contract that started in March 1927, he had made only two of the three films he was obliged to deliver. As of that moment, Hawks had drawn more than ten thousand dollars on his third picture, even though he hadn't decided on a script, and Wurtzel was not only in a mood to stop any further payments to Hawks until he got cracking on another film but was seriously considering not exercising the studio's option on Hawks's services when the current contract expired in March.

Fed up with what he considered Hawks's "procrastinating methods" and his "slowness and dilatory method of working," Wurtzel gave Hawks an ultimatum: he must choose at once from between two stories, "The Richest Man in the World" and "Part Time Marriage," and then make the film for $125,000 and not a penny more. Two days later, Hawks replied flatly that any delays or overages on his picture were "not due to any fault of mine." He insisted, "If your budget has been exceeded, it has only been because of my earnest desire to complete a satisfactory production, and one of which you might be proud." Claiming that he was "more than anxious to cooperate with you in any way," Hawks said that while he didn't like either of the scripts Wurtzel was proposing, he would choose "Part Time Marriage." Ironically, the property Hawks turned down, "The Richest Man in the World," a contrived reworking of the story of the late European tycoon Alfred Loewenstein, was fatefully taken on the following year by his brother Kenneth.

Hawks had recently taken a house at 705 Rexford Drive in Beverly Hills in anticipation of getting married, and he certainly did not want to lose the $120,000 he expected to make in 1928. Fox was not about to indulge Hawks by making *Budapest*, which promised to be expensive, and Hawks inadvertently dug himself deeper into a hole with management thanks to a prominent story element in *A Girl in Every Port*. Unbeknownst to Hawks, studio head Winfield Sheehan had been, in the early 1910s, the secretary to the police commissioner of New York City, and he counted many cops among his close friends. Spike and Salami's hatred for cops is one of the most prominent running themes of *A Girl in Every Port*, and Sheehan blew his top when he saw the finished picture. "We went to the preview and I've never seen a more responsive audience," Hawks recalled. "But when we came out, he said, 'This is the worst picture Fox has made in years.' I said, 'You're just a damned fool.' Well, from that time on, he didn't like me very well." One hitch that came up just before release was that the name Salami simply proved too much for the New York censor board, which insisted that it be changed. On American prints, at least, the character's name was changed to Bill in the intertitles, although British reviews that appeared in March 1928, shortly after the film's American debut, still refer to the character under his original nickname. The picture performed well in its native land but was ecstatically received in Europe, particularly in France, where, during the ascendancy of surrealism and the waning days of expressionism, its straightforward functionalism was seen as the height of modernity and Louise Brooks was considered a revelation. Henri Langlois

crowned Hawks as the Gropius of the cinema and reported that Blaise
Cendrars thought that the film "definitely marked the first appearance of
contemporary cinema."

Acting quickly, Hawks got out of making "Part Time Marriage" (Fox
must not have thought much of the property, since they didn't force anyone else to make it either) by coming up with a story of his own that seemed
commercially promising to the studio. Hawks proposed a modest little contemporary story that almost seemed like a milder offshoot of *A Girl in Every
Port*, an account of how two young men learn to become pilots at flight
school while competing for the same girl. Flying as a subject could not have
been hotter: since Lindbergh had made his successful solo flight in May
1927, seemingly every kid in the country had caught the flying bug, and
after the release of William Wellman's *Wings* three months later, the demand for places in flight schools had skyrocketed. *The Air Circus*, Hawks's
proposed film, would feed off of all this, and it seemed like a natural, since
the director himself had been flying for ten years. Anxious to get Hawks
moving on a project, Fox approved it in early March for an almost immediate start.

The writing credits on the finished film are at variance with the way
the names appear on the assorted successive script documents. While the
film's official credits cite Graham Baker and Andrew Bennison as the authors of the original story and Seton Miller and Norman Z. McLeod as the
scenario writers, the first-draft screenplay names Hawks and Bennison as
the story men, and Miller and Baker as the screenwriters. McLeod, an
American who had flown in Europe with the Royal Canadian Air Force
and was Wellman's assistant director on *Wings*, came on afterward to beef
up the flying material; later in 1928, he would launch a successful directing career of his own.

Miller's first synopsis, written with Hawks's supervision, was composed
quickly, with the actors already set for their parts. David Rollins, a new Fox
contract player who had appeared in just one previous film, would star as
Buddy, an overly sensitive mama's boy who is motivated to overcome his
fear of flying by the memory of his brother Bill, a World War I flying ace
who was killed in action. He heads off for flight school with his boisterous
chum Speed, to be played by Arthur Lake, the former vaudevillian who had
worked for Hawks in *The Cradle Snatchers*. Arriving at the Pacific School
of Aviation in Santa Monica, the two pals meet the school's operator, who
was to have been played by Robert Armstrong and was Buddy's brother Bill's

close friend during the war; they are instantly taken with the boss's sister Sue, a role destined for Sue Carol.

As Hawks admitted, the film was "full of anecdotes—very little story. It was just about how boys of that particular period would learn to fly. Some of them got frightened and some of them were kind of crazy." Speed goes up with Sue to learn how to control a plane but pulls a bunch of pranks, which prompts her to parachute out as a rebuke. Speed rises to the challenge and executes a perfect landing on his own, prompting everyone to admit that he's a natural even if he's also a reckless wildman. Buddy, on the other hand, feels his fear growing daily; after falling out of bed during a nightmare in which he crashes, he is grounded when he puts a plane on its nose while taxiing. At an exhibition called Field Day, Speed wins a race. But later, when the small airport is deserted, Speed unknowingly tears off his landing gear while taking off. Only Buddy sees it and, screwing up his courage, he sets out in another plane to warn Speed that he has no wheels. Speed misinterprets his friend's hand signals as instructions to land, which Buddy must then prevent him from doing by daringly diving under his plane. Finally, Speed parachutes down, and Buddy is knocked unconscious in his first attempt at a solo landing. But in a cornball ending, Buddy is deemed the real hero, Sue declares that she loves him, and Buddy can now feel that he is worthy of his brother's memory.

The first draft script added more hokey elements as well as more typically Hawksian incidents and attitudes. Among the former: the full script gave more weight to the misgivings of Buddy's mother, to be played by theater veteran Louise Dresser, about the aviation aspirations of her only remaining son. Also, the school's owner was not only an old friend of Buddy's late brother, but a rare Hawks flashback shows how Bill gave up his life by crashing his plane into a German one that was right on his friend's tail. Among the improvements: Sue becomes something closer to a Hawksian woman, surprising both men upon meeting them by offering, "I'll take you both up"; a comic character is added, that of Jerry the mechanic, played by Heinie Conklin in the first Walter Brennan–like role in a Hawks film; and there is considerably more documentary-style detail about learning to fly.

Also added was a big dance sequence designed principally to exploit the comic frustration of the boys' having only one tuxedo between them. By arrangement, Buddy takes Sue to the dance; then Speed sneaks through a window into a back room, where they are to swap clothes for a while, giving Speed some time with Sue at the dance. Naturally, things go awry, but the entire scene seems distended and silly. A more curious scene was a digression dropped into a lecture the instructor gives about the unlimited opportunities awaiting the students in aviation; visually backdropping this was intended to be a "Jules Verne" sequence showing future designs for planes, airports, air traffic systems, and so on.

The Air Circus was shot in a spirit of fun from April through June 9, 1928. Hawks said that Arthur Lake, who played the daredevil Speed, in fact soloed for the first time during the filming, and the director was pleased with the result. Ironically, three days later, Fazil finally had its Los Angeles premiere at the Carthay Circle. But now The Air Circus would be held up as well. Since the sensational debut of The Jazz Singer the previous October, the studios had begun gearing up for the inevitable changeover to sound pictures. Part-talkies were now appearing with some regularity, and this strange transitional period is marked by quite a few pictures that were begun or, as in the case of The Air Circus, actually finished as silents but that had one or more dialogue sequences added.

It is not entirely clear if Fox asked Hawks to work on the dialogue passages with Lewis Seiler, a director of comedies and Westerns with eight films to his credit at that time, or if the studio simply replaced him; even Hawks fudged the point somewhat. In any event, Hawks, who hated the dialogue prepared by Hugh Herbert because he felt that "nobody talks that way," had nothing to do with them. Given that the film is lost, it is not even certain how many new scenes were added. Several sources and Hawks himself referred generally to "talking sequences," but the Variety review specifically timed the dialogue episode at fifteen minutes (out of eighty-eight total) and identified it as "a sentimental session" between a blubbering Buddy and his mother that "reduces the hero of the film to the status of a big baby"; Hawks called the result "mawkish" and said, "You have never known such bad dialogue."

It was a dangerous period for artists who had worked only in movies and never in the theater. The knee-jerk reaction of executives and producers was to find actors, directors, and writers with stage experience and throw them into films. No one who had been working in films was safe; everyone had to prove themselves. Hawks was in double jeopardy because he had alienated both Winnie Sheehan and Sol Wurtzel, but his track record was just good enough to keep himself on the studio roster, at least, it seemed, until his contract was up the following March.

Hawks needed his job because his life was radically changing, his responsibilities growing. He and Athole had originally hoped to marry on

February 8, two weeks before Ken and Mary Astor. In early 1928, however, Athole sank into another deep depression. The recurrence of her psychological problem, which had first manifested itself a decade before, came very soon after she returned from Reno to finalize her divorce from John Ward. Norma assumed that Athole had suffered a nervous breakdown and bizarrely attributed it to her sister's severe disapproval of their mother's new involvement with her very young, guitar-playing chauffeur who, she hastened to add, "was no monk." According to Norma, Athole's behavior was as disturbing as ever, as "she sat up in bed and began to say strange things — that the clock was making too much noise and by her expression I knew it had happened again and I was very frightened but couldn't let her know." Doctors passed her condition off as "nervous exhaustion," while Irving Thalberg simplistically supposed that once Athole was married to Hawks, she would be fine. As before, the Shearer family covered up any and all hints of unsavory, negative information and merely waited until Athole started feeling better, which she finally did.

It is not known how much Hawks really knew of Athole's problems; in his biography of Norma Shearer, Gavin Lambert suggests that the Shearers so successfully kept Athole's illness a secret that "Hawks heard only that she had suffered another bad attack of the flu." Everything else about Hawks's character would indicate that he was too sharp to be so completely hoodwinked. But what is indisputable is that Hawks exhibited the patience of a saint for months, waiting devotedly until Athole was improved and then resetting the wedding date for May 28, two days before his thirty-second birthday. Norma was the matron of honor, and Athole looked beautiful and thoroughly happy. *The Air Circus* still had two weeks of shooting left, and it is possible that Hawks had nothing to do with the added dialogue footage for the simple reason that he was gone on his honeymoon when they were done. Once Hawks was finished with the picture, he and Athole sailed for Hawaii; unlike Ken's honeymoon, there are no reports of Howard's performance during it. Rather, 16mm. color home movies of their trip show the couple appearing to enjoy a fun-filled, adventurous time, learning to surf with skilled young men on Waikiki Beach in front of the Royal Hawaiian Hotel, where they stayed, traipsing through rocky, rugged terrain on a hunting expedition in a mountainous region, where Athole shot a mountain goat, and being instructed by local guides on the fine points of killing an octopus, an act involving biting down on the brain sac and spitting it out. Athole looks spirited and happy in the footage, and Hawks appears in the peak of manhood, lean and trim in a bathing suit, not an ounce of fat on him.

Unfortunately, when Hawks returned to the Fox lot after his honey-moon, not only did he find *The Air Circus* ruined, in his opinion, but the studio insisted that he get moving on another script he found worthless, a romantic comedy-drama called *Life's a Gamble*. Hawks procrastinated on this for the rest of the year, driving Wurtzel crazy with protestations and excuses about why he didn't think it was worth doing, drawing salary all the while but falling way behind on his contractual obligation to deliver three pictures a year. Finally, at the end of the year, after spending nearly $45,000 going nowhere with *Life's a Gamble*, Fox assigned Hawks "as a last resort" to direct an adaptation of the popular English mystery novel *Trent's Last Case*. The way it turned out, it easily could have been Hawks's last film — and was, for a while.

5

The Sound Barrier

*They thought my career was finished. They thought
John Ford's career was finished. They said, What do you
know about dialogue? —Howard Hawks*

As it was for Hollywood and the nation, 1929 was a pivotal year for Howard
Hawks; once he got through it, his career would never be in doubt again.
The year would bring him his first child but would also lead his family to
the brink of its greatest tragedy.

The Air Circus had been reasonably successful, with Hawks's flying
footage particularly praised, but his refusal to have anything to do with the
hastily added talkie sequences did little to persuade Fox that he could handle
dialogue. Nevertheless, Hawks was still one of the studio's most reliable
young directors, and he jumped at the chance to tackle the adaptation of
E. C Bentley's 1913 British mystery, *Trent's Last Case*, which had faithfully
been filmed in England in 1921.

Hawks considered the book "one of the great detective stories of all
time" and enthusiastically embarked upon what was meant to be his first
all-talking picture, with the shooting title of *Murder Will Out*. Set in an
imposing English mansion, the story tells of a disagreeable, clubfooted man,
Sigsbee Manderson, who resolves to commit suicide through circumstances
that will make it look as though he were murdered by his male secretary,
who is in love with his wife. After the authorities have bungled the case,
the amateur criminologist Philip Trent enters the scene to sort things out
in typical murder-mystery fashion, with the butler and maid both having
their moments, only to retire after his deductions prove inaccurate.

Fox originally bought the novel with the expectation of producing it
as a silent, but with the advent of sound, a dialogued script was quickly
prepared by Scott Darling and adapted by Beulah Marie Dix. It was a moment for which Hawks was well prepared. Late in 1928, rightly concerned
that his lack of stage experience might endanger his livelihood, he conducted extensive tests to figure out how much dialogue a sound feature
would accommodate. From a standard-sized book Hawks took five pages
consisting of dialogue passages, which he had actors read at a relatively fast

pace. The reading took a bit more than six minutes and ran 560 feet of film. He could thereby calculate that fifty pages of straight dialogue from a book would occupy about an hour of screen time, without allowing for any action or pauses. In the test, Hawks's crew had trouble keeping the microphone both at a consistent distance from the actors while they moved around and out of view of the camera. The test was viewed as helpful for Fox in determining how much dialogue could safely be included in a picture, and it taught Hawks that picture dialogue could be delivered quickly, despite early conventional wisdom to the contrary.

However, no sooner had Hawks shot the first couple of scenes of *Murder Will Out* than he was told to stop and go back to filming it as a silent. Starring as Trent was a good friend of Hawks's, silent star Raymond Griffith, whose vocal chords had been severely damaged by poison gas in World War I and who couldn't speak above a hoarse whisper. Later on, Hawks unconvincingly blamed the change on Fox's belief that Griffith's muted voice was unsuitable for sound pictures (he said, "I thought he ought to be great in talking pictures *because* of that voice," but the coming of sound did bring Griffith's career to an end). Had this been the case, with the film just starting, Griffith's part could easily have been recast. The truth, in fact, was much more damning of Fox: in purchasing the property, the studio's legal department had bungled by only securing silent-picture rights; sound rights would have to be separately negotiated, at considerable further expense.

This effectively sabotaged the picture, since the market for purely silent pictures was rapidly vanishing. One can only wonder why the studio went ahead with the project at all at this point, since it was obvious that the film would be a commercial lame duck. "By that time we knew nobody was going to look at it," said Hawks. "We just kidded the thing . . . we just had fun with it. I don't know anyone who ever saw it, because talking pictures took over right then and there." In response to the dramatic rug having been pulled out from under him, and always tickled by Griffith's droll, very particular sense of humor, Hawks pushed the Edwardian-era material toward comedy whenever possible—even while cinematographer Hal Rosson retained a moody, melodramatic look spiked by some elegant camera moves, low angles, and macabre special lighting effects, notably in a shot of the evil Manderson silhouetted in black in the foreground and the maid screaming when she sees him. Still, the tone is wildly uneven, with broad, arched-eyebrow acting (especially from a very hammy Donald Crisp as Manderson) conflicting with the very upper-class setting and a campy tone prevailing in the midst of ostensibly serious doings. Griffith plays Trent as a conceited dandy, and the film is riddled with disruptive flashbacks from different characters' points of view. It could well be that the desultory result here is what set Hawks so resolutely against flashbacks, for he never again used them—and he spoke out against them—during the remainder of his career.

Perhaps not even Hawks could have predicted how few people would end up seeing *Trent's Last Case,* since it was never released at all in the United States and was not even shown to the trade press. Having finished its monthlong shoot on February 15, 1929, the ill-fated picture opened for brief runs in Great Britain on September 23, with one critic rightly stating, "It is a thousand pities that Fox has altered this classic detective novel by reducing it to the level of farce and melodrama. If I were E. C. Bentley, I should not feel flattered."

The film understandably vanished from sight and for decades was considered lost, until in the early 1970s a print was found among a large cache of early Fox films in Alaska (among the other titles found at the same time were Hawks's *The Cradle Snatchers* and *Paid to Love*). Therefore, the film apparently had its American premiere on April 24, 1974, as part of a Hawks retrospective at the Pacific Film Archive. Hawks went up to Berkeley for a few days in connection with the event, but when the archive director, Tom Luddy, excitedly told him about the *Trent* screening, Hawks was dismayed. "You're not going to show that, are you?" Hawks asked disdainfully. Unable to thwart the screening, Hawks sat in to see this runt of his cinematic litter for the first time, but midway through he couldn't take it any longer and charged up to the projection booth, where he demanded that the projectionist destroy this one and only copy immediately after the screening. Naturally, his wish was not granted, but the experience was enough to reaffirm to Hawks that *Trent's Last Case* was his worst film, an opinion with which it is impossible to argue.

With *Trent* a total loss and Winnie Sheehan still offended by the director's uppity attitude, Hawks's position at Fox was extremely tenuous by the spring of 1929. Still, he balked at being reassigned to the *Life's a Gamble* project that he had resisted directing the year before. Putting Hawks back on the film may have been Sheehan's way of forcing Hawks's hand, and for two and a half months, despite having been paid more than $23,000 for the time he was supposed to have put in on the film, Hawks did little or no work on it. Then, for a short time, he was in line to direct *Big Time,* a vaudeville romance cowritten by the future Astaire-Rogers director Sidney

Lanfield. Although snappy and funny in a way that anticipated the kind of lightning direction Hawks would supply for his later comedies, the script was too sentimental for his taste, and he deflected this project as well.

Finally, on May 14, Hawks was fired, for having "willfully neglected to perform his services in the manner agreed upon." Hawks later turned the story around, claiming that his contract kept him at Fox, but inactive, for a year and a half. In 1932, he sued Fox for wrongful dismissal, whereupon the studio countersued over Hawks's failure to fulfill the terms of his contract. Hawks later bragged to Peter Bogdanovich that Fox's ploy backfired and that the studio was forced to pay him $120,000. But court records indicate that the suits were dismissed with prejudice, with each side required to pay its own legal fees. (Hawks also told Bogdanovich that he never again signed a contract with any studio, a claim that can be disproved time and again by the records of the subsequent years of Hawks's career.)

Four days after his ouster from Fox after more than four and a half years on the lot, an unsettled Hawks hired a new agent, Ruth Collier, who later testified to Hawks's troubled position during that summer: "During the months of June, July, August and September, I made every possible and reasonable effort to secure employment for Howard Hawks as a motion picture director, and in particular, I negotiated with First National Pictures Corporation, Universal Pictures, Pathé, Warner Brothers, United Artists, Metro-Goldwyn-Mayer, Columbia Pictures Corporation and R.K.O.; . . . during all of this time, and in each of the instances above set forth, I was unable to place Howard Hawks with any or either of the aforesaid companies, and was unable to secure any employment for him."

By contrast, Kenneth's career was very much on the upswing. After having supervised several films at Fox and worked as an editor and story writer as well, Kenneth was promoted to director early in 1929. When David Butler, the original director of *Masked Emotions,* was needed on another picture, Kenneth was asked to finish the film. A silent George O'Brien melodrama about the apprehension of Chinese smugglers along the California coast, it opened to decent response that July. Then, with his brother having bowed out, Kenneth was given *Big Time* as his solo directorial debut, to shoot in June, and he did a fine job with it. Lee Tracy and Mae Clarke played young New York vaudevillians looking for their break. The talented pair are on their way up to headliner status when she becomes pregnant, which leads the otherwise thoughtful husband to introduce another woman into the act. Clarke dutifully instructs the newcomer, portrayed by Daphne Pollard, in the required routines, and before long Pollard begins trying to seduce Tracy. The fateful moment arrives in the form of an invitation to play the Palace: Pollard manages to convince Tracy to squeeze his wife out of the act in order to take the coveted gig. But Tracy is soon sorry, as Clarke walks out on him, leaving him desolate despite having, ever so briefly, made the big time. Soon reduced to working as a waiter in a slophouse, Tracy learns from faithful vaudeville janitor Stepin Fetchit that Clarke has gone to Hollywood. So Tracy rides the rails out west and manages to land a job as an extra in a film in which both Clarke and their precocious kid are starring. He collapses from hunger after they meet on the set, but she finally says, "Come back to me" and sings "Nobody Loves You like I Do" to bring things to a happy close.

It is easy to see that Howard would have considered the story too sappy for him, but Kenneth made breezy, generally heartwarming fun out of it, thanks in no small measure to the crackling performances of Clarke and, especially, Tracy. Some pretty decent vaudeville routines are presented at length, and although some of the acting is on the theatrical side, it can certainly be said that Howard Hawks did not invent fast dialogue direction, as his brother proved quite accomplished at it here, several months before Howard had ever directed a talking picture.

There are some distinctive, even memorable humorous scenes: Tracy squealing, spinning, and crowing, "Am I a man!" when his wife informs him she's pregnant; a lovely camera move in on Clarke's disturbed face as she teaches Pollard some dance steps; the weird collision of comic styles in a scene between Tracy, who may have been the fastest talker in movies, and Fetchit, who was probably the slowest; a cameo by John Ford as himself; and Tracy's resourcefulness upon facing his toughest audience, a farmer in a mule-filled freight car who says, "Make me laugh." Although the film may not be particularly strong on visual style, it boasts a pleasing feel for backstage life and stands as a very creditable thematic precursor to *A Star Is Born*. It is a fine example of early sound filmmaking not overtly hampered by technical constraints or lack of know-how, and it is solid proof that Kenneth Hawks had talent. Upon its successful release at the Roxy in New York on September 7, Kenneth began preparing his next project, a melodrama called *Such Men Are Dangerous*, which would go into production toward year's end.

6

A New Dawn

One cup to the dead already—
Hurrah for the next that dies!
—Bartholomew Dowling

With producers and the studios convinced that legitimate stage directors were far more qualified to direct sound pictures than most silent filmmakers, Hawks realized over the summer of 1929 that extraordinary measures might be needed to put himself over in this new era of film production. Not that he had any doubts about his ability; it was almost immediately apparent that his natural inclination to underplay, to cut across obvious and conventional effects, and to allow the natural personalities of his performers full reign would serve Hawks even better in sound than they had in silents. Nonetheless, he had to get his shot, and by August he was arranging to do this through a bit of subterfuge.

At the time, John Monk Saunders was one of the most respected, sought-after writers in the business. A World War I flying instructor who, like Hawks, hadn't gone overseas, he had heard a lot of war stories from British, Canadian, and French fliers while at Oxford as a Rhodes scholar in 1919–20, as well as from Yanks when he lodged at the American Flying Club in New York upon his return. After taking up newspaper and magazine work, he wrote a story in 1923 that became *Wings*, the first Hollywood picture to depict the war in the air and an enormous commercial success that, in 1927, became the first picture to win the Academy Award. Married in 1928 to the actress Fay Wray, Saunders was a full-fledged member of the Lost Generation, a glamorous, good-looking young man of refined breeding and excellent education who drank a lot and had a strong self-destructive streak. In the summer of 1929, when he was thirty-one, he was just finishing a novel called *Single Lady*, inspired by a decadent affair he had had that spring with a young heiress named Nikki he met at the Ritz Bar in Paris. In 1931 the novel was produced on Broadway as a musical, *Nikki*, with Wray as the heiress. Saunders later wrote a screen adaptation of the same material, *The Last Flight*. This film, directed by William Dieterle in 1931, represents a fascinating treatment of former World War I fliers living in dissolute glamour in 1920s Paris, and its story, spirit, and tone make it the closest cinematic equivalent to *The Sun Also Rises,* Saunders's favorite novel. It also made Saunders an obvious choice for Hawks's next project.

The idea behind *The Dawn Patrol* concerned a small group of British fliers continually faced with near-suicidal bombing missions on German targets; the men bear up under the tension through an intense bonhomie and the constant intake of liquor. In later years, Hawks claimed to have come up with the story himself, telling Kevin Brownlow that he paid Saunders "$10,000 to put his name on it because I knew they wouldn't accept me as a writer of dialogue because I'd never been backstage. And Dick Barthelmess read it and I was assigned to make it with Barthelmess, and it was the biggest grossing picture of the year — *Dawn Patrol.* After that everything was easy."

Hawks recalled things in more detail to Peter Bogdanovich: "I got the idea from a story — I think it was by Irvin Cobb — about an evening with a British squadron that was being hit hard. . . . David Selznick went to John Monk Saunders to try to buy it. He wanted to give it to Billy Wellman [a former war pilot who had directed *Wings*], not me, and then when he couldn't do that, he came to me to see if I'd do it, and I told him I didn't think he was any kind of guy I'd want to work with because he'd gone behind my back. I said, 'Didn't you know I wrote that story?' And he said, 'No.' 'Well,' I said, 'I wouldn't do it with *you* if I never make the picture.' So I made it with Barthelmess at Warners. Funny thing — I almost made it with Jack Gilbert. Gilbert hadn't made a talking picture, but he was the biggest star we ever had in silent pictures and Louis B. Mayer got me to bring Gilbert in and talk to him. Well, Gilbert went back and told Mayer he'd make the picture without any salary and that's all Mayer wanted, because he told Gilbert he wouldn't let him do it if he *paid* to make the picture. He wanted to humiliate him. I got Mayer by the front of the coat and bumped his head up against the wall and said, 'Don't ever make me part of your dirty little schemes again.' I didn't stand too well with Mayer for a while."

As Fay Wray recalled it, Hawks turned up at their house on Selma just west of Fairfax one Sunday morning that summer with a story idea "that he wanted John to sell because John was most successful with scripts about aviation." The two men, she felt, would properly share story credit, but Hawks "wanted no authorship credit for himself on the screen or in advertising; he instructed the studio of that choice in writing." Both Wray and the film's costar, Douglas Fairbanks Jr., remembered Saunders working on the script at the studio and, subsequently, rewriting dialogue on the set, so Wray was always astonished decades later when she heard Hawks immodestly assume total responsibility for both the story and script. When they ran into each other at the 1966 Montreal Film Festival, she asked him about this, and she was even more amazed at his casual attitude toward giving Saunders screen credit—"I told him to go ahead and take it"—when it had cost him a share of an Academy Award.

Having accompanied her husband to the Oscar ceremonies in 1931, when *The Dawn Patrol* won the award for best original story, Wray noted that Saunders's acceptance speech acknowledged a degree of ambiguity concerning the extent to which he deserved exclusive credit for the film, as it questioned "which came first, the chicken or the egg." As Wray remarked, "He might have said the chicken *hawk* or the chicken *hawk's* egg. Howard Hawks had been involved with the story, as well as the direction of that film."

Nonetheless, Saunders remembered it differently. In a sworn deposition given in August 1930, in connection with Howard Hughes's lawsuit over material allegedly stolen by the creator of *The Dawn Patrol* from his film *Hell's Angels*, Saunders stated that he had dined with former war journalist Irvin S. Cobb at the latter's Park Avenue apartment in 1919 and had that night heard the story of "young British pilots in a combat squadron in an airdrome at the front. [Cobb] was impressed by the gallant manner in which each of these young inexperienced and untrained pilots flew out in the morning to face almost certain death in aerial combat with veteran German air fighters. Between themselves and death these young British fliers hung up an alcoholic curtain of laughter, song and card playing. Mr. Cobb said that he would never forget the magnificent courage and spirit which those young Englishmen displayed." Saunders added that while at Oxford, he had quizzed such pilots specifically about the situation Cobb had described.

The writer mentioned that Hawks had approached him a year before, saying that "he would like to obtain an air story with a war atmosphere as a starring vehicle for the well-known actor Ronald Colman. He stated that Samuel Goldwyn would buy such a story for the purpose of starring Mr. Colman and would employ Howard Hawks to direct it. . . . I then told Hawks the idea Mr. Cobb had given me . . . that I had in mind a story involving that tragic atmosphere of which Mr. Cobb had spoken, that to my knowledge the subject of a British airdrome at the front and the comradeship and attitude of mind of the British pilots had never been shown on the screen and that we had therefore a story which was in background and atmosphere altogether original. . . . I then gave Mr. Hawks a synopsis of the story which I had in mind ["The Flight Commander"] and which was later produced on the screen under the title of *The Dawn Patrol*.

Saunders claimed that his original story outline went largely unchanged, save for "minor suggestions, revisions and pieces of business," and
that the climactic episode of a pilot on a solo mission to blow up a German
munitions dump under heavy artillery fire [which is what Hughes felt was
plagiarized] "was original with me."

Goldwyn eventually passed on the package, however. Instead, First
National, a company owned and controlled by Warner Bros., agreed in
October to produce *The Dawn Patrol*, with Hawks directing for a flat salary
of eighteen thousand dollars. In Saunders's original eighteen-page treatment,
there was a prominent plot element that might easily have represented a
Hawks contribution, since it turns up in films from *A Girl in Every Port* all
the way through *El Dorado* and beyond. A veteran ace newly arrived at
Camel Squadron 31 during the winter of 1916, Captain Guy Courtney is a
wild loner who has been jilted by a beautiful peeress before the war and
quickly moves in on Céleste, "the spirited little French godmother of the
squadron." After Courtney and the green Lieutenant Warwick Scott become
close, they carouse together with Céleste, until Courtney learns that Lieutenant Scott is the man for whom Lady Mary Cambridge left him. When
Courtney then loses Céleste to him as well, the men become estranged and
Courtney heartily approves of sending Scott out on an almost certainly fatal
mission. All women were eliminated from the final script, one factor that
made the film so unusual at the time and so questionable to many executives. Hawks purchased the rights to Saunders's "Flight Commander" story
for ten thousand dollars, then promptly sold it to First National for the same
amount while waiving all rights and credit for himself (thus cheating himself out of not only an Oscar but a substantial sum nine years hence when
Warner Bros. remade the picture).

Saunders piled up quite a few more credits over the next few years,
but by the mid-1930s his career was essentially finished. He and Fay Wray
had a daughter scarcely a year before they were divorced, in 1938, and two
years later Saunders was found dead, a suicide by hanging, in his beach
cottage in Fort Myers, Florida. He was forty-two. No notes were found, although he had recently been under care at Johns Hopkins for a nervous
disorder.

The fall of 1929 was an extremely eventful time for all three Hawks
boys. On the domestic front, Howard and Athole's first child, David Winchester Hawks, was born on October 9 at 10:30 P.M. at Good Samaritan
Hospital; Howard was thirty-three, his wife twenty-eight. Athole delighted
in her second son at the Linden Drive house while Howard worked six days

a week at the studio. The entire family also busily anticipated William's wedding to the actress Bessie Love, planned for December 27. At the time, William was working in a Pasadena stockbroker's office, and it is impossible not to notice that all three Hawks boys, whether by design or coincidence, had married actresses—or, in Howard's case, Hollywood royalty —better known than they were, women whose status could only improve the men's standing in the industry.

A petite, very attractive Texas girl, Bessie Love, then thirty-one and never before married, had debuted in *Intolerance* in 1916 and had made some seventy silent pictures, including films directed by such Hawks family pals as Marshall Neilan, Victor Fleming, John Ford, and Frank Capra. By 1929, after several ups and downs, her career was in transition again, as she had just emerged as a potential musical star at MGM in *Broadway Melody, The Girl in the Show, Hollywood Revue,* and *Chasing Rainbows.*

The wedding was an elaborate High Episcopal affair. Marshall Neilan's wife, Blanche Sweet, was the matron of honor, and the bridesmaids were Athole and Norma, Irene and Edith Mayer, and Bebe Daniels and Carmel Myers. A grand party followed that evening at the Biltmore Hotel.

Meanwhile, Ken and Mary Astor's relationship seemed improved, although Ken was keeping her in the dark about his financial difficulties. Despite making a thousand dollars per week at Fox, where his star was quickly rising, Ken had lost all his money in the stock-market crash. He was also behind on his house payments and, without informing his wife, had been forced to discontinue his substantial life-insurance policy. On New Year's Day, as usual, the younger Hawkses and their wives attended the Rose Bowl Game, followed by an early dinner at Frank and Helen's home, within easy walking distance of the stadium. Ken then drove his wife downtown to the Majestic Theater, where she was working onstage for the first time, co-starring with Florence Eldridge and Edward Everett Horton in Vincent Lawrence's comedy-drama *Among the Married.*

Ken was then shooting *Such Men Are Dangerous,* a melodrama based on the life of the late Captain Alfred Loewenstein, who either fell or jumped to his death from his private plane while crossing the English Channel on July 5, 1928. On January 2, Ken left the house early to drive across town to do some special shooting at Santa Monica's Clover Field (named after a one-time roommate of Ken's, Greer Clover, who had been killed flying). Ken asked Howard, a more experienced pilot, to come to the airport to help check things out and watch the parachute jump they planned to film off the coast. Normally, Howard would have gone, but Athole, who felt her husband saw little enough of her and their nearly three-month-old son as it was, prevailed upon him to stay home. The job at hand was pretty straightforward, but not without risk: in order to film a scene representing Warner Baxter's Loewenstein character making a parachute jump into the sea near the coast of England, two planes carrying camera crews would fly close together, one slightly above the other, and capture the action as a stunt man jumped from a third plane. One crew would film close-ups, the other long shots. Ken had told his concerned wife, "If it looks as though there's going to be anything dangerous about it, I won't do it." Everyone felt that the only person to worry about was the stuntman who would be making the jump into the ocean.

Howard, however, was not so sure. "Ken wasn't much of a flyer, and I said, 'You'd better look out, you're liable to run into one another. Take care about it, and especially the man you're flying with isn't much good.' When they called me and said there'd been an accident, I said, 'Did they run into each other?' and they said, 'Yes.'"

Howard was at home when he received the news, as were his parents. Mary Astor had just completed the matinee performance of *Among the Married* and was relaxing on a couch on the Majestic stage when Florence Eldridge sat down beside her and said she needed to speak with her. "There's been an accident, Mary," Eldridge told her. "The planes—we've only just heard—they're not sure about anything yet—we've just got to wait."

Encouraged with false hope, Mary was advised by Horton to skip the evening performance no matter what happened, and understudy Doris Lloyd was quickly called in. Mary Astor was in her dressing room removing her makeup when a Fox producer arrived at her door. "He was fighting back tears," she remembered, "and when he started to talk he couldn't; he just choked up. But he didn't have to say anything. I looked at him, and I knew. 'He's dead, isn't he,' I said, and he could only nod."

The two camera planes had collided in clear weather during a test run over Santa Monica Bay, killing all ten crew members. After Lieutenant Colonel Roscoe Turner, the pilot and a close friend of Kenneth's, took off with the parachutist, Jacob Triebwasser, and crew members Fred Osborne and Bert White, the two camera planes—large, closed cabin, single-engine Stinson-Detroiter high-winged monoplanes carrying five men apiece—followed in V-formation, heading out over the bay into the sun and rising to three thousand feet. At 4:30 P.M. they were about three miles offshore and two miles south of Redondo Beach, above the spot where lead cinematographer L. William O'Connell and other crew members were waiting in several small boats to photograph the parachutist and then fish him out of the water. O'Connell was a flier himself, but his wife had asked him not to shoot any flying pictures, which is why he was not aloft. With the planes flying at virtually the same level, they were attempting to make quarter turns when one of the planes veered toward the other. The wings touched; then one plane lurched around and smashed head-on into the other at a forty-five-degree angle. There was an explosion, and the planes went down together, nose-locked and burning. Flying a bit ahead and beneath, Turner, the lead plane's pilot, did not actually witness the crash, but Osborne saw it and said, "Look, they have hit each other!" At that, Turner said, "I winged over and turned around to get a look at them. They were tangled together, both afire, and plunging toward the ocean. Just as they were about to hit, two or three of the men either jumped or were thrown out of the burning planes. I saw the bodies splash into the ocean a little distance away from the point where the planes hit the sea."

The crash and the aftermath were also seen by thousands of motorists along the Pacific Coast Highway, by fishermen and sailors in boats, and by passengers on the cruise liner *Ruth Alexander*, which was steaming off Point Vicente at the time. Speedboats and launches rushed out to join the camera boats, but the planes sank immediately, leaving in their wake gasoline and minor debris that blazed for two or three minutes on the surface of the water.

Three bodies were recovered quickly, those of assistant director Max Gold, cameraman Conrad Wells and assistant cameraman Ben Frankel, all of whom had gone out the open door of their plane on the way down and hit the water apart from the aircraft. Gold was still alive when picked up, but he died on the speedboat heading back to shore, his bones, like those of the other two, badly broken in many places. O'Connell recalled that "the bodies had burned in the explosion before hitting the water. The assistant director's body came up first because he had zipped his jacket all the way up."

Back at Clover Field, pilot Roscoe Turner told reporters, "I don't know how it could have happened unless the sun got in the eyes of the other two pilots. They were probably jockeying to get in position and one swung into the glare of the sun, hitting the other head on before he knew it." Turner was so devastated by the tragedy that he broke down and went into seclusion at home. Other pilots at the airport agreed that blinding sunlight could be the only explanation for what had happened. After darkness settled in, a

Coast Guard cutter flashing its searchlights cruised the area all night in the hopes of finding more bodies.

The accident was big news both in Hollywood and around the nation. Nothing like this had ever occurred in connection with the shooting of a motion picture. Three pilots had died filming aerial stunts for Howard Hughes' *Hell's Angels*, but this was something altogether different, ten men lost while flying on what should have been a routine, straightforward job. Gold, Wells, Frankel, and property man Henry Johannes were piloted by Ross Cooke, while Hallock Rouse flew the plane in which Kenneth Hawks, cameraman George Eastman, assistant cameraman Otto Jordan, and property man Thomas Harris died. Seven of the ten men were married, and six children were left fatherless. Captain Ross Cooke had flown in aviation camps in Texas during the war and had flown for movies, including *Wings* and *Hell's Angels*, for more than ten years, while the other pilot, Hallock Rouse, was a former flight instructor who had also done a great deal of film work; it is unclear which one Howard did not trust, as he undoubtedly knew both of them.

As soon as he heard, Howard went out to the search site, but there was nothing he could do as night had arrived. While being driven from the theater, Mary Astor was subjected to the agony of having to listen, at intersections, to newsboys yelling, "Ten die in film accident. Mary Astor's husband killed." Edward Everett Horton went onstage before the evening performance of *Among the Married* to explain his costar's absence to a subdued crowd, and Fredric March and Florence Eldridge cared for her at their home for more than a week. William Hawks and Bessie Love returned early from their honeymoon to be with the family in Pasadena.

The morning after the accident, with two minesweepers, eighteen Navy planes, five commercial aircraft, two speedboats, and three Coast Guard cutters participating in the search, the wreckage was found by the Navy minesweepers at fifty-three fathoms, or three hundred and eighteen feet down. Because of a winter storm, it was not until January 6 that a diver, Charles E. Smale, was able to get into one of the planes, where he recovered the bodies of Kenneth Hawks and Thomas Harris, which had been rammed against the instrument panel.

The bodies were taken to the Nolan Undertaking Company in Venice, California, where Howard identified the remains of his brother. Technically, the inquest concerning the case was conducted over the body of Kenneth Hawks, but it was extended to cover all the other victims. The coroner's jury found no specific person or company responsible for the accident but criticized the way the job was approached. "We find that the collision was caused by the airplanes flying in too close formation, one of the planes turning at too short radius and possibility of sun glare. We believe that flying of such a nature is too hazardous and it in no way encourages commercial aviation and in too many instances seems unnecessary." Sol Wurtzel made all the appropriate remarks of remorse and condolence on the part of Fox, which was completely insured for such a mishap, although it is unknown to what extent the victims' survivors were compensated.

Kenneth's funeral on January 8 at the Little Church of the Flowers at Forest Lawn Cemetery was conducted by the same Episcopalian minister who had married him and Mary Astor two years earlier. But while the service was attended by many prominent members of the film industry, Mary was conspicuous by her absence. Ken's ashes were scattered into the Pacific off Point Vicente, close to where he died. Only after the funeral did Mary learn that Ken was virtually destitute: the sale price of their home would barely pay for back taxes; his $200,000 insurance policy had lapsed; Fox was declared, in a suit brought by some widows of the victims, not to have been negligent in the accident; and the stock-market crash had wiped out her husband's cash assets. He even owed money on some gambling debts. Quickly deciding that it would be best for her to put her past behind her, Mary had little contact with the Hawks family from then on.

Hardest hit, however, were Frank and Helen. Now three of their five children were gone, and they can only have worried about Howard, who was about to make a dangerous aviation picture himself.

Always closer to Kenneth than to anyone else, Howard was unquestionably as affected by his brother's death as by any other event in his life. Already prematurely graying at thirty-three, his hair turned entirely gray thereafter. Publicly, however, he kept his own counsel, never even speaking about Kenneth to his wives and children. In later years he was only known to comment about his brother unsentimentally, in the manner of a professional evaluation. "I thought he had a good deal of promise," he told Kevin Brownlow. "He had a great deal of warmth, much more than I have. I don't think he knew as much about story as I do but he had his own little way, he had a very good sense of humor and he showed that in his first picture and they definitely thought he had talent." *Such Men Are Dangerous* opened to tepid response at the Roxy in New York on March 7, 1930, with the *Variety* review carrying the credit "Directed by the late Kenneth Hawks."

The Dawn Patrol provided vivid and daily reminders of Kenneth's violent death, not only for Howard but for everyone on the production. Still, the temperament of the piece, with its projection of stoicism, bravado, and steel nerves under the constant threat of sudden extinction, as well as the breezy professionalism of the crew and many fliers employed on the show, created an atmosphere that encouraged setting aside cautious, sentimental considerations. Howard himself put up a philosophically pragmatic front. Of his group of six best friends who had enlisted in the Air Corps together in 1917, two had been killed on the airfield at Issoudun in France, two had crashed into each other pursuing a balloon in Italy, and now his brother was dead—all killed in planes. "So I was the only one left," he realized. "I always thought of it as just the luck of things, you know. It never frightened me about flying."

The Dawn Patrol represented a late entry in a cycle of phenomenally popular World War I films, which began in the silent era with *The Big Parade* and continued through *Wings, What Price Glory?, All Quiet on the Western Front,* and *Hell's Angels,* which Howard Hughes had been making since 1927.

As *The Dawn Patrol* neared production, the main challenges were refining the script, casting, and securing sufficient airplanes to enact the aerial missions. Officially produced by the cultivated Robert North, the film was overseen by Hal Wallis, then just a year into his job as general manager of First National under the overall stewardship of Jack Warner. Wallis and Hawks took an immediate dislike to each other, and the mutual antagonism grew into a barely manageable stormy relationship that nevertheless produced eight mostly outstanding films over a period of seventeen years. Just as Hawks had no tolerance for overbearing executives who meddled in his business, Wallis had little patience for egotistical directors who fiddled with the script on the set and went over schedule. There was never any common ground between them except for the needs of the project at hand, and all their dealings over the years were marked by exasperation and mistrust on both sides.

As far as *The Dawn Patrol* was concerned, Wallis liked John Monk Saunders, whom he considered "a very interesting man . . . a fine writer in the Scott Fitzgerald mode. Saunders, like the people he wrote about, was never completely at ease in civilian life." With *The Dawn Patrol,* Wallis felt, Saunders had written "a beautiful screenplay, authentic in every detail. His only weakness was a tendency to overwrite. We worked together, trimming and tightening, until we had a lean, workable script." In this regard, Wallis ignored the contributions of two more writers. From Fox, Hawks brought over Seton I. Miller, the blond, facile scenarist of four of the director's silents, including *The Air Circus*. Hawks wanted Miller to help him flesh out the original into a detailed screenplay. Dan Totheroh, who had seen combat in France and had just finished working for Victor Fleming on *The Virginian*, was later brought in to work on dialogue through the shoot.

With Hawks's original choice of Ronald Colman now out of the picture, there was no question but that Richard Barthelmess, the star of *Wings* and one of the biggest names of the silent era, would play the ace, Captain Courtney. The other important role was that of his younger charge, Lieutenant Scott. Barthelmess recalled that Hawks "wanted very much to have Doug [Fairbanks Jr.] in this part. I'd known him since he was in short trousers and always thought of him as 'Little Doug' because his father was one of my great friends. I went to Doug and said, 'Look, you must do this part, it's going to be good for you.' He said, 'But Jack Barrymore wants me for a picture of his.' I said, 'Look, go to Jack and put it up to him, see if he won't release you.'

"Well, Jack being the great fellow he was said, 'Well, if the part is better than the one in mine, certainly, for goodness sakes take it.' Doug did, and he was such a howling success in it that it established him as a star."

The experienced stage actor Neil Hamilton was selected for another principal role, Major Brand, whose command Courtney relieves. In search of a cameraman, Hawks talked to Harry F. Perry, who had done considerable shooting on *Wings*, *Now We're in the Air*, and *Hell's Angels*, but Barthelmess insisted upon "his own personal cameraman," Ernest Haller, a polished studio craftsman who was inarguably more experienced.

By February 28, 1930, when *The Dawn Patrol* started shooting, Howard Hughes was in the final stages of converting his air epic, *Hell's Angels*, into a talking picture. The film had begun shooting in September 1927 under the direction of Marshall Neilan. Luther Reed had later taken over before Hughes himself assumed the director's chair in April 1928. When talkies hit, Hughes rightly judged that he couldn't risk sending out his nearly three-million-dollar investment as a silent, so he began reshooting it with dialogue, with a partly new cast that included Jean Harlow, under the direction of James Whale; the film finally wrapped in November 1929.

In a move that was both shrewd and shameless, Hawks began interviewing and hiring many of the experts who had just finished working on *Hell's Angels*. Among them were Elmer Dyer, the chief aerial cameraman on the Hughes film, who would become a good friend of Hawks's and shoot the airborne footage in *Only Angels Have Wings* and *Air Force;* Harry Reynolds, a mechanical engineer and aviation technician; and Ira Reed, a pilot-actor. There was nothing Hughes could do about this, but when he learned what the *Dawn Patrol* company was up to, he tried to buy up all the World War I fighter planes he didn't already own, even though his picture was finished. In Wallis's view, Hughes, "furious that we dared make a rival picture . . . raised competitiveness to the level of mania," sparking a run on the market for old Spads and Camels.

Having heard that *The Dawn Patrol* contained dramatic incidents that seemed suspiciously similar to some in his picture, Hughes tried various other ploys to thwart the production. According to Hawks, the first time he met Hughes was when the young tycoon turned up unannounced at Hawks's house one Sunday morning. Hughes, he said, objected to a scene from *The Dawn Patrol* that resembled one in his film, in which a fighter pilot is shot in the chest and coughs up blood before his plane explodes, and tried to talk the director out of using it. In one account, Hawks said that he replied, "Howard, I make pictures for a living, you make them for fun. I got a hangover. I'm not interested in talking about it." In a legal deposition, Hawks declared that he told Hughes, "'Hell, anybody in a war, when they get shot in an airplane, the chest is the biggest target. That's just the usual thing.' . . . I think I used some harsh words about it. Anyway, I refused to do it."

After this acrimonious initial meeting with Hawks, Hughes plotted to ground the First National project by legal means, but through an illegal maneuver. Hughes induced one of his writers to bribe Hawks's secretary into giving him a copy of the script of *The Dawn Patrol*. She informed Hawks, whereupon the studio had two detectives waiting, and they arrested Hughes's man for theft.

Hawks said that "Hughes called me up and said, 'Hey, you've got my writer in jail.' And I said, 'That's where the so-and-so belongs.' I said, 'Why did you try to corrupt a perfectly nice girl by bribing her? If you wanted a script, I'd have given you one. Now I don't give a damn about it.'"

First National filed for a restraining order to prevent Hughes from any further interference with their production, while Hughes sued for plagiarism in a desperate attempt to postpone the opening of *The Dawn Patrol* to a time well after *Hell's Angels* had played out. Hughes testified that he had had a long meeting with John Monk Saunders at the Wilshire Country Club early in 1929, at which he had described *Hell's Angels* to his fellow flier at length, including his ideas for the "munitions bombing" climax. He added that he knew that Howard Hawks "was informed in full detail concerning the motion picture 'Hell's Angels' and the various scenes and maneuvers portrayed in the air sequences and the unusual methods of photography used therein." In a sworn affidavit, Hughes went on for ten court manuscript pages about how *The Dawn Patrol* had "copied every detail portrayed in the picture 'Hell's Angels,' in addition to copying the dramatic characterization, sequences, motivation and the greater part of the dramatic incidents connected with the final bombing sequence."

In March, the company began shooting the English airdrome scenes at Triumfo, off Ventura Boulevard, forty miles west of Burbank, although heavy rainstorms disrupted filming and stretched the stay there to three weeks. The German airdrome sequence, shot at Newhall, took an additional four days. But as the arduous shooting of *The Dawn Patrol* reached late May, the climax had yet to be filmed. Hughes claimed that late in the month, when he learned that his rivals were preparing to shoot their dramatic finish, the daring raid on a German ammo dump, he objected to the sequence to Hawks, given its similarity to a crucial episode in *Hell's Angels*. Hawks, Hughes said, told him that he could change the scene "without affecting the value of the picture . . . and that he would make the change as the photographing of that sequence had not been commenced." The next day, however, Hawks told Hughes that Hal Wallis had refused to make any changes, thus taking the onus off Hawks. Furthermore, Hughes complained, the bombing sequence wasn't even shot until after May 27, 1930, "when Howard Hawks and other First National executives attended the opening of 'Hell's Angels.'"

In fact, upon wrapping the picture within days thereafter, Warner Bros., which released all First National products, rushed *The Dawn Patrol* through final editing and into release. The film premiered on July 10 at the Winter Garden in New York to excellent reviews and even better business; it was standing room only for the entire first week, smashing the house record with a take of $51,200. Reliable figures on its eventual earnings don't exist, but the film was a tremendous success, one of the biggest hits of the year. After the tremendous hoopla of his *Hell's Angels* premiere at Grauman's Chinese in Hollywood, Hughes returned to the cutting room to make some refinements on his film. Its second engagement, in a tighter version, didn't begin until July 18, in Seattle, head-to-head with *The Dawn Patrol*, after which it fanned out across the country to strong public response. Still, the weighty $2,500,000 gross fell at least $1.3 million short of what

Hughes had spent on his pet project over nearly three years; however, Hughes expected to make a profit from foreign revenues.

As far as the court case was concerned, Hawks's later self-serving explanation was that Hughes reached him by phone at a golf course, saying he wanted to play with him, a proposal Hawks refused because of the lawsuit. "I'll call it off," Hawks claimed Hughes said, whereupon Hawks supposedly beat Hughes on the links with a 71 to Hughes's 72. In fact, the matter was resolved by a single judge at one sitting. Wallis recalled, "I sat with Jack Warner in Judge Cosgrove's chambers, U.S. District Court, while he ran *Dawn Patrol* and *Hell's Angels*. His judgment was unequivocal. No plagiarism was involved. As it turned out, both pictures did extremely well and probably helped each other out." Nonetheless, Hughes and Hawks had managed to break the ice, and they soon realized they had more than a few things in common: golf, women, pictures, and a well-developed contempt for the Hollywood establishment and conventional rules. It wouldn't take long for these two lanky, taciturn men to start talking about working together.

Convinced on the eve of *The Dawn Patrol*'s opening that it had a success on its hands, on July 8 First National signed Hawks to a three-picture deal at $25,000 per film. (For good measure, John Monk Saunders was simultaneously signed to a contract.) During the shooting, however, studio executives, and Wallis in particular, hadn't been so sure that Hawks knew what he was doing. Yes, the aerial footage was excitingly effective, but Hawks had kept his actors on a very tight leash, directing them to speak their often bitter, ironic, clipped dialogue in a very stylized way, without the heightened histrionics customary in the earliest sound films. Hawks later said, "Actually, *The Dawn Patrol* was the first dramatic talkie made without a lot of overacting. It was very quiet. During the shooting I had thirty or forty communications from the front office saying I had a marvelous chance to make a good scene and didn't do anything with it. It was just a different way of playing it, you see. I was saying that they had been emoting too much and by underplaying we got away from that. . . . After that it was easy. Nobody asked me if I knew it. It was just a new form of acting, and that doesn't happen very much. People liked the scenes because they were underdone, because they were thrown away. Nobody emoted in the pictures that I made."

Hawks admitted that, of his three leads, Hamilton was the least willing to toe the line, and that he "was probably a little 'on stage.'" Barthelmess fell into the method easily, and Fairbanks wasn't a problem because, being young and relatively new to acting, "You could control him." In terms of its dialogue delivery, *The Dawn Patrol* does stand apart from the majority of films made in the 1929–30 period, but so do a few others, most notably Rouben Mamoulian's *Applause* and Josef von Sternberg's *Morocco*, in which the dialogue, if not at all naturalistic, did not sound projected as if from a theater stage. Today, the dialogue in these films, including *The Dawn Patrol*, sounds just as artificial as drawing-room chatter, but in a different way, a way more comfortable because it points in the direction that the best screen dialogue of the coming decade would take—fast, terse, hard-bitten, and unfancy.

In terms of its expression of what would become known as the Hawksian world, *The Dawn Patrol* is far from fully elaborated, but it did introduce any number of themes and motifs that the director would develop in subsequent years. The pressure-cooker principle set is something that would appear again in many films, from *Ceiling Zero, Only Angels Have Wings,* and *To Have and Have Not* to *Rio Bravo* and *Hatari!,* from which the characters venture out on hazardous missions into an unpredictable and hostile world; there is also the pronounced feeling of living for the present alone, an attitude made explicit here by Barthelmess's statement that the past "seems like it never happened"; the sense of camaraderie among a group of men brought together for a single purpose, a bond furthered by off-hours drinking and singing (the parallel between Hugh Herbert's drunken braying in the motorcycle sidecar and a scene in *Hatari!* is striking); the preference for individual initiative over official orders as a means of achieving a desired goal, best expressed here by Barthelmess and Fairbanks's daring dawn attack on the German camp, the film's most exciting and impressive sequence; the quasisuicidal mission, something that would appear repeatedly in Hawks's films through the mid-1930s; and the mutual respect of fellow professionals, even if life has pitted them as enemies, signaled here in Barthelmess's gallant salute of recognition to the German pilot who shoots him down (played by Hawks himself) and summed up most explicitly some thirty-five years later when John Wayne, in *El Dorado,* tells his nemesis, Christopher George, after shooting him, "You're too good to give a chance to." Between the writing of the initial treatment and the final screenplay, Hawks toned down the element of rivalry over women between Courtney and Scott, diminishing it from the *Girl in Every Port* I-got-there-first motif to a passing reference to how the two men had competed for the same girl in Paris. And on a very personal, less thematic note, one can hardly miss the arrival of Scott's kid brother, a less expert flier who, despite his older brother's efforts to warn and protect him, gets himself killed in a plane.

Even though Hawks never fought in the European war, his film caught the fatalism and waste of a generation as strongly as did *Journey's End, The Last Flight,* or any other film on the subject. Although no one mentioned it at the time, it also positioned him as the closest thing to a Hemingway of the cinema, in the way he eloquently and poetically defined his characters through their attitude toward what they did. Instinctively, Hawks expressed the novelist's famous maxim of grace under pressure; he would continue to do so, with increasing skill and complexity, for several decades.

7

The Criminal Code

Hawks's new First National deal provided for him to be loaned out to other studios. Right after *The Dawn Patrol* opened, Universal crowed about how it had snared the town's newest hot director to make an aviation picture. But Harry Cohn had already approached Hawks about doing a picture for his low-rent studio, Columbia. In terms of financing and prestige, Columbia was a significant cut below the true major studios, such as MGM and Paramount, but above some of the thinly capitalized companies that wouldn't survive the Depression. Columbia couldn't afford to sign major stars to long-term contracts, so Cohn instead sometimes placed his chips on directors he thought might bring in a good picture. He'd recently used Victor Fleming, who may well have recommended Hawks to him and did tell Hawks that Cohn was someone he might want to talk with. After initially trying to snare Lewis Milestone, at the moment one of the two or three most sought-after directors in town, something told Cohn that Hawks might be worth the gamble.

Urgently searching for material that would be appropriate for sound pictures, Columbia bought the rights to Martin Flavin's stage play *The Criminal Code*, which opened on Broadway on October 2, 1929. The grimly bitter drama, which was well received critically and ran for a respectable twenty-two weeks, was part of a new movement in theater and films keyed to exposing prison conditions and advocating penal reform. Centered on a reform-minded new warden and a young man doing time for an accidental killing, the play was designed to demonstrate how abhorrent conditions, along with a "code" that demanded prisoners not rat on each other, could drive an essentially decent man over the edge to become a killer. Hawks knew that the character of the warden "was based on a district attorney in California who was sentenced to prison, and they had to put him in the prison hospital to protect him because the place was full of men he had sent up—and I'm quite sure he'd framed a lot of them. Finally he said, 'I can't take this any longer. I want to go out into the yard.' He went out into the yard, and the scene we did in the picture was just what had happened, except that [the actor Walter] Huston was the warden. He walked right out among them, daring them, and no one made a move."

Flavin made four unsuccessful attempts to adapt his work to the screen for Columbia, but as soon as Hawks was signed (for thirty thousand dollars, compared to Walter Huston's forty thousand), the director brought in his frequent collaborator Seton I. Miller, who helped Hawks turn the property around in less than a month. (Fred Niblo Jr. also received screenplay credit, but there is no record of his specific contributions to the picture.) Hawks and Miller felt that the play's first two acts worked well but that the third act fell completely flat. For starters, they removed the prominent character of a prison doctor who becomes taken with the young prisoner's case and argues for an improvement in his big-house job and conditions. But the most crucial change they made involved taking the murder weapon out of the hands of the young man (Phillips Holmes) and putting it into those of another prisoner, Galloway (played by Boris Karloff), thereby allowing for a happy ending (the young man is able to pursue his romance with the warden's beautiful young daughter) but also effectively removing the pre–New Deal left-wing social determinism from the piece. This change, Hawks said, was not invented by him or his writers but by some actual convicts whom the director asked for advice; similarly, numerous ex-cons helped populate the prison for the movie. Hawks also strengthened the camaraderie of the prisoners, especially in his emphasis on "the convicts' code of not squealing" and built up the comic elements. "I loved the scene with Walter in the barber chair staring at the fellow shaving him. 'Don't I know you?' And the man said, 'You do.' 'I sent you up, didn't I?' He said, 'You did.' Walter said, 'I don't remember what for.' And as he lifted Walter's chin, he said, 'For cutting a guy's throat.' I liked that. I let the scene run a hundred feet—just watching Walter's eyes. It was the first time I discovered almost any tragedy can also be very amusing."

For Hawks, the greatest pleasure of making *The Criminal Code* was collaborating with Walter Huston, whom he said was "the greatest actor I ever worked with." Constance Cummings, who was cast as his daughter at the last minute and was also terribly impressed with her costar, remembered Hawks spending most of his time with Huston, to the point where she felt left out of the otherwise virtually all-male cast and crew. Phillips Holmes, a young pretty boy who enjoyed a brief vogue in the early 1930s before vanishing from the scene, was as bland and ineffectual as ever, one of the few painfully sincere performances to have been allowed through in a Hawks film.

Beginning September 23, 1930, the film shot largely in sequence on six- and sometimes seven-day weeks through November 8. With rewrites continuing apace, Hawks worked for the first time with cinematographer James Wong Howe for the first three weeks, mostly on the early scenes in the warden's and the D.A.'s offices, the police station, and Spelvin's Café, a big scene shot on the Universal lot. When Howe left to shoot another picture, Ted Tetzlaff came in for the remaining four weeks to photograph all the prison scenes, including the five days spent on the spectacular prison-yard set, where Huston wades in amongst the convicts.

These scenes, which involved as many as eight hundred extras, were shot on the huge set on the MGM lot used just a few months before for the first major studio prison picture, George Hill's *The Big House*, cowritten by Flavin, which had been released in June and to which *The Criminal Code* has always been compared. An exciting film until its cop-out ending, *The Big House* is impressive for its size and near-architectural qualities, but scenes from *The Criminal Code* stick in the mind more indelibly: Huston's repeated displays of arrogant confidence as he faces the prisoners in the yard, yells back at them in their own crude manner, and defiantly lights his cigar and stares down their hate for him; Karloff's implacable stalk as he corners the sadistic guard for the kill while the other prisoners cover the act with their shouting, and the surprising humor Hawks draws from grim surroundings and characters. Hawks also dabbles in overlapping dialogue for the first time, in the opening scene in the police station, where one cop is on the phone while two other men are playing cards. *The Criminal Code* doesn't seem as timeless or congenial as many of Hawks's later films, and it is damaged by an uncharacteristic sappiness in the scenes with the romantic youngsters. Even here, however, Hawks softened the blow with his determinedly unsentimental treatment of a potentially predictable moment: when a cable arrives with the news that Phillips Holmes's mother has died, he is playing checkers in his cell; the cable is passed around among the cons in silence, but before the expected reaction can set in, Holmes's cellmate says, "Your move, kid," nipping any overt emotionalism in the bud.

The Criminal Code opened in New York on January 3, 1931, less than two months after it wrapped, and did very good business, especially for a Columbia release. The film did encounter some problems because of its violent and potentially volatile content, particularly in Chicago, where its bookings were canceled after the local censor board demanded heavy cuts.

By the time Hawks finished up retakes and final work on *The Crimi-nal Code* in mid-November, Howard Hughes's relationship with Hawks had warmed considerably. Hughes's next production was to be a gangster epic, and Hawks's expression of interest in directing it had developed into a firm intention. Aside from liking the idea of making the ultimate gangster film, Hawks enjoyed the fact that everything the young Texan did represented a snub at the powers that be of the Hollywood establishment. To Hawks, align-ing with the wealthy Hughes meant the possibility of real independence from the ruling nabobs. The only problem was his freshly minted contract to direct three pictures for First National, which had been patiently wait-ing since August for him to finish *The Criminal Code*. Determined not to miss his chance with Hughes, Hawks had to figure out a way to slither out of First National's grasp in order to make the most explosive picture of gang-land the world had ever seen.

8

Tough Guys: Hughes, Hecht, Hays and *Scarface*

On November 28, 1930, when Hawks reported for work at First National, Hal Wallis immediately teamed him up with the writer Waldemar Young to prepare an adaptation of A. Hamilton Gibbs's popular novel *Chances*. Hawks's assignment to this project was a typical example of studio thinking: since the director had handled *The Dawn Patrol* so effectively, let's give him another tragic World War I story, albeit one dominated by a triangular love story. Almost immediately, Hawks objected, deriding the material at story meetings and telling Wallis and Jack Warner in no uncertain terms that the book was lousy and could only make for an equally poor picture. Soon realizing that Hawks's attitude made further insistence futile, the studio proposed several other projects to the director, all of which he rejected out of hand. Finally, on December 11, figuring he'd show his obstinate employee who's boss, Wallis yanked Hawks off *Chances* but also put a hold on any salary payments until such time as Hawks came around. Five days later, Hawks strolled over to the cashier's office to collect the three thousand dollars he was contractually owed for his work since November 28 but was told there was no check for him. The next day he returned and was again rebuffed. He thereupon informed First National that he considered the studio in breach of contract and that he was therefore free to sign another deal, which he did with Howard Hughes on January 16.

Understandably, First National saw things a little differently. No other director treated them so rudely—not Bill Wellman, not Mike Curtiz, not Mervyn LeRoy—and a contract worker was a contract worker, expected to do what he was told. Still, Jack Warner liked Hawks, so he deigned to sit down with the upstart Howard Hughes three times in February, the final time at the Lakeside Country Club, to try to resolve "the Howard Hawks problem." No solution could be found, however, so, on March 6, 1931, First National filed suit against Hawks and Hughes's The Caddo Company for breach of contract. The studio asked, among other things, that Caddo be restrained from employing Hawks, who was then in the thick of preparing *Scarface*, until the matter could be settled.

Although Hawks might not have expected the case to go as far as it did into a lawsuit and a public airing of his terms of employment, he certainly didn't mind, since it asserted his will and, in his view, his right to operate independently of the studio harness. Upon a closer examination of the case, there can be little doubt that Hawks orchestrated it to unfold almost precisely as it did, completely in his favor and on his terms. That he lied and behaved disdainfully toward his employer was of no consequence to him, since it enabled him to direct the film he wanted to make at that moment. More than that, the case established, for the first time, Hawks's position that he needed the studio chiefs less than they needed him. If they wanted to deal with him, it would be on his terms, not theirs. He had money, he had talent, he could say no and walk away. Very few other directors in the nascent studio system dared behave this way, or were in a position to. It took nerve, but Hawks got away with it, and he set the terms under which he was able to pursue the extraordinary career he did, one that was virtually unique in Hollywood at the time.

It seemed like the sort of squabble that could have easily been settled by a gentlemen's agreement: sure, we'll let Hawks direct *Scarface*, but then he's got to come back right away and make the three pictures for us that he's contracted to do, and no more loan-outs and no money from us until he makes them. But there were two factors mitigating against this. First, the Hollywood moguls, as competitive as they were with one another, were united in one thing: they hated Howard Hughes. This maverick with money of his own who could spend three years monkeying with a movie, a good-looking, high-flying thirty-one-year-old bachelor with no respect for the way things were done in Hollywood, rubbed the big bosses the wrong way on every count. What's more, at this moment before the rise of Darryl F. Zanuck, when literally all the studio heads—Mayer, Zukor, Schulberg, Cohn, Warner, Goldwyn, Laemmle, Fox, Schenck—were Jewish, Hughes was clearly not destined for membership in The Club; it was noticed that Hughes hired virtually no Jews and that one of his pet projects was an adaptation of the scathing Hollywood satire *Queer People*, whose virulent attacks on the industry's power brokers were widely perceived to be anti-Semitic. Therefore, the establishment bigwigs would happily go out of their way to do anything they could to deal Hughes a setback.

Second, the studio executives, having effectively wrested control of the business over the past five or six years and now in the process of consolidating their power, needed to assert their absolute authority over "talent." The whole studio system was being structured and continually refined to keep actors, directors, writers, and all other personnel in their place; Hollywood unions were still pie in the sky and would be created over the dead bodies of the bosses. It was their money, they called the shots, and if some actor or director didn't like what they were told to do, he could just sit out on suspension until he came to his senses. It was therefore only logical to sue Hawks to bring him into line and to prevent him and Hughes from showing the world that two rebels, answerable to no one else, could make a film as well as—or even better than—they could.

In essence, both sides in the suit alleged breach of contract, First National accusing Hawks of not fulfilling the terms of his contract, to direct three films during the 1931 calendar year, and Hawks claiming that the contract had not been effect since December 17, when the studio had refused to pay him, thereby freeing him to seek employment elsewhere.

In his account of the events leading up to the break, Hal Wallis stated that Hawks was recalcitrant about the *Chances* project from the outset. "I discussed Hawks's objections with him, but Hawks made no criticisms of the story other than a general statement that it was poor or weak. He offered no suggestions as to how to change or improve the story. I told Hawks to attempt to work the matter out with [Waldemar] Young. Several conferences were held in which Hawks, Young, Charles Graham Baker, one of First National's production executives, and I participated, for the purpose of discussing the adaptation. . . . Hawks persisted, in all of these conferences, in his attitude that he would not make any photoplay based on this novel. He disagreed with and dissented from every suggestion made for improving the story, but made or offered no suggestion of his own. . . .

"Finally, Hawks refused absolutely to make *Chances* and also refused to make any of several other stories which were suggested to him. Hawks was then instructed, about December 11, 1930, that he would be paid no further compensation until he complied with his contract by beginning work upon a story assigned to him."

To build the case for Hawks's uniqueness and consequent value to the studio, Wallis was forced to add an evaluation that can only have made him choke on his words: "In my opinion, Hawks is a motion picture director of unusual and extraordinary ability. . . . He commands and has commanded, by reason of his reputation and ability, a compensation which is large as compared with the salaries of ordinary motion picture directors."

Waldemar Young, who had no particular ax to grind with Hawks, added: "I had several meetings with Hawks lasting until about December 10, 1930. At no time did he confer or work with me for more than one or two hours per day. During these conferences Hawks's suggestions were consistently destructive and not constructive to the adaptation of the novel." Young also noted that, after December 17, he continued on without Hawks and polished off the adaptation within two weeks' time.

Most revealing, however, is Jack Warner's commentary. Although Warner held no title at First National, Warner Bros. owned First National and they essentially functioned as the same company. Warner commenced by proclaiming that "Hawks's reputation as a director is now such that he has 'box office value,' that is, his name, advertised as the director of a picture, attracts persons to see such picture. I do not believe that it would be easy to replace Hawks's services, nor do I believe that there are many, if any, directors whose services and ability duplicate or excel those of Hawks." He thereupon set out his complaint that Hawks had spent very little time at the studio since initiating his contract. Noting that Hawks had come to him in person and refused to make *Chances*, Warner added that, on December 10, Hawks "also stated that he could not and would not work with Harold B. Wallis. . . . I pointed out to Hawks that under his contract he did not have any right to select or approve the stories upon which he was to work, but that I was willing to attempt to please him if possible. Therefore, I gave him several other stories—*As Good as New, The Noose* and *Ambush*—all successful and well-known novels or plays, as well as John Monk Saunders's original story 'The Finger Points.' About December 11, 1930, Hawks returned to my office, threw the above-named books on my desk, and stated that he would not make any of them, that they were all poor. He then asked me to release him from his contract entirely and to enter into an arrangement whereby he could make one picture a year for First National based on some of his own stories. This I refused to do. I again pointed out to him that under his contract he had no choice of stories, and no right to dictate the particular story upon which he was to work."

Hawks nevertheless plunged ahead to propose to Warner two stories he claimed he'd written. The first was "based to some extent upon the life of a well-known Los Angeles evangelist," and Hawks offered to let Warner have it for ten thousand dollars. The second was an original submarine story that Hawks was willing to part with for twenty thousand dollars. Just as Hawks surely knew they would be, both were rejected, and Hawks left Warner's office knowing that his next move would be a call to Howard Hughes telling him the coast was clear.

By the time the suit was filed in March, First National had collected a truly extraordinary set of affidavits from many of the top bosses in Hollywood. Assembled to help First National bolster its case, they also made for an array of quotes that any director would have been thrilled to put on his résumé. Samuel Goldwyn asserted, "Hawks possesses the requisite essentials of a first-class director. His abilities are such that a producer securing his services, rendered in good faith, is assured of ability which few other directors possess. His services, in my opinion, are of a special, unique and extraordinary character." Joseph M. Schenck and Louis B. Mayer also gave ringing endorsements.

A less enthusiastic assessment came from the leading agent Myron Selznick, the brother of one of Hawks's least favorite Hollywood executives, David O. Selznick: "Mr. Hawks has directed several good motion pictures, and in my opinion is a good director, but . . . in my opinion there are many directors who could satisfactorily and artistically perform services of the kind and character performed by Howard Hawks."

Amazingly, the most halfhearted endorsement came from Hawks's own agent, Ruth Collier, who had spent the previous summer unsuccessfully attempting to find Hawks work with some of these same moguls who now found the director's talents so extraordinary. "Based on my efforts to secure employment for Howard Hawks as a motion picture director," she remarked, "I am of the opinion that he is a good director but that it is reasonably possible for his services to be satisfactorily replaced by other motion picture directors."

Douglas Fairbanks Jr. contributed his view about *Chances*, which by March he had already finished starring in, under the direction of Allan Dwan: "I was personally present when Howard Hawks made several suggestions for changes in connection with the adaptation of said story, and I personally know that several of the suggestions made by Howard Hawks were actually used in filming said motion picture. . . . In my opinion . . . the suggestions of Howard Hawks strengthened and improved said motion picture."

Hawks responded to First National's charges by issuing a total denial of everything the studio claimed: no, he did not refuse to work on *Chances*; no, it was not true that in Warner's office he "threw on his desk the books mentioned in his affidavit, or any other books, or that I stated I would not make any of them"; no, he had not asked Warner to enter into a separate agreement to make one film per year of his own choosing; no, "it is not true that my services cannot be replaced, but on the contrary it is true that First National secured the services of another director to direct . . . *Chances*"; yes, it was true that he participated in one story conference concerning the film, "but it is not true that in said conference I made or offered no suggestions of my own. On the contrary, I talked in extenso . . . and I now state that a great many of the suggestions that I made were actually used"; but no, "it is not true that I refused to work."

A succession of demurrers, delays, and broken trial dates, and requests for restraining orders was paraded through the court all spring. By far the most extraordinary document filed during the entire proceedings was a statement by Hawks denying everything First National and their high-powered allies stated was special about him. A blanket admission that he possessed no special skills whatsoever, it may be the biggest lie Hawks ever uttered, and is worth printing nearly in its entirety for its full astonishment value:

> This defendant denies that he has developed or has a method or technique of directing motion pictures, and/or of doing and/or performing the other duties of a motion picture director which were or are peculiar or unique to himself alone, or which cannot be or are not duplicated by any other motion picture director. Said defendant denies that he has or is possessed of the ability to do or perform all of the special duties of a motion picture director . . . or in an unusual or extraordinarily able manner, and/or as a result thereof, to produce or direct high-class or exceptionally successful motion pictures. Defendant admits that he has directed and produced in the last past several years a total of nine motion pictures, some of which motion pictures have been and are financially and artistically successful to a certain degree, and alleges that other of said motion pictures which he has directed and produced are motion pictures which have not been financially or artistically successful. Defendant admits that he directed the motion pictures entitled *The Dawn Patrol* and *The Criminal Code*; the defendant has no information or belief upon the subject, and basing his denial upon said ground, denies that each of said motion pictures has been or is highly successful, or that each of said motion pictures is or has been declared by motion picture critics and reviewers to be among the best motion pictures produced; defendant denies that by reason of his ability . . . or by reason of the successful character of motion pictures directed or produced by him, he has acquired

or has a nationwide reputation as an outstanding and/or unusually able
motion picture director, and denies that the defendant commands or
has commanded a high salary.

Hawks concluded by confessing that when he signed the First National
contract, he "had been unable to obtain work for a great many months,"
and therefore "was compelled to and did accept such provision in said contract" that he might not have otherwise.

Already irritated with Jack Warner and Hal Wallis for refusing to make
a court appearance on the specious grounds that neither was actually an
officer of First National, the judge in April denied the company's application for a temporary injunction against Hawks and Caddo. Two months later,
with *Scarface* about to roll and a trial date yet to be set, the matter was suddenly dropped. The big boys had failed to stop Hughes and Hawks from
proceeding with their reckless, independent film, but there would be other
places to ambush them down the road. In the meantime, what might have
seemed like a logical solution before all the legal huffing and puffing began
was agreed to out of court: Hawks's old First National contract was torn up
and a new one was signed, stipulating that immediately upon completing
Scarface, Hawks would return to First National to make one film a year for
two years. With First National pleased to be saving a degree of face, the
deal was signed June 22. The next day, Hawks, having got what he wanted,
started shooting what would always remain his favorite film.

As usual, the family passed the 1930–31 holidays at Frank and Helen's
in Pasadena, and so much had changed from the previous Christmas. Little
David, their first real grandchild, was over a year old, while Peter was now
five. Athole was feeling well, not having had the slightest sign of a relapse
since her son was born. Howard, thanks to his break with Warner Bros.,
was officially out of a job, even though he had directed one of the biggest
hits of the year. Bill, celebrating the first anniversary of his marriage to Bessie
Love, who had appeared in five pictures that year, told the family that he
would soon be starting his own finance-management company, with show-
business personalities as his prospective clients. All in all, the Depression
had not hit them particularly hard, compared to most families in America;
Frank's investments and orange groves were solid, and Howard was thriving and building a big house in Beverly Hills. But none of this could make
up for the void that was all too obvious and still painfully felt, the absence
of Kenneth at Christmas dinner for the first time.

The day after New Year's, Hawks bid farewell to Victor Fleming, who, with buddies Douglas Fairbanks Sr. and John Monk Saunders, set sail for Japan on the first leg of a ten-month journey that would result in a larky semidocumentary film, *Around the World in Eighty Minutes*. *The Criminal Code* opened the next day, and in the middle of January, just as Warner Bros.' *Little Caesar* was opening like gangbusters around the nation, Hawks signed his deal with Hughes to direct *Scarface* for $25,000.

The two recent adversaries and new partners had quite a bit in common. Tall and rangy, with somewhat drawling ways of speaking and a craftiness lurking behind their reserve, the two Howards loved planes, golf, and dazzling women, although Hawks's taste in the women tended toward the classy and well-bred, whereas Hughes preferred brassy starlets. Although more of a Hollywood insider than Hughes, Hawks privately viewed most of the town's potentates as fools or clowns and could easily play into Hughes's own contempt for the studio bosses from a more informed and experienced vantage point.

At the time they teamed up, Hughes had already produced seven movies in just four years. In 1926, two years after inheriting a vast fortune, the twenty-year-old Hughes had come to Hollywood thinking it would be fun to make pictures. To the town's amazement, he started off with a surprise hit, *Everybody's Acting,* which went out through Famous Players–Lasky. Aligning himself with United Artists, Hughes next made *Two Arabian Knights*, a buddy comedy not unlike *A Girl in Every Port* that also scored big and won Lewis Milestone an Oscar for direction. While immersing himself in his three-year labor of love, the aviation epic *Hell's Angels*, much of which he directed himself, Hughes also produced the comedy *The Mating Call*, the early gangster melodrama *The Racket* (which contained some seeds of *Scarface*), and three appallingly silly flops—*Cock of the Air, Sky Devils*, and *Age for Love*, the last two starring the petite former Broadway showgirl Billie Dove, whom Hughes was trying to make into a star and who most people felt would become his wife. Having lost money overall in the motion picture business, Hughes decided that gangster pictures provided the nearest thing to a guaranteed profit. He figured that if he made the greatest underworld saga the public had yet seen, it would stand a good chance to be a smash. To this end, he put his own directorial aspirations to the side, swallowed his pride, and pursued the man he had decided was the best director in Hollywood.

The erroneous assertions of Ben Hecht's biographer to the contrary, Hawks preceded the writer onto *Scarface*. Both Hawks and Hughes had

had prior dealings with the cynical, prodigiously talented former Chicago newspaperman. Hawks and the writer had hit it off when they met in connection with *Underworld* four years earlier, and Hecht, not known for his generous opinions of movie folk, had fond feelings for Hawks: "I like him," he wrote to his wife. "He is one of the few half humans—to whom movies are a pleasant sideline, a thing to be done as work, not to be lived as a career." For his part, Hughes bought Hecht and Charles MacArthur's great 1928 play *The Front Page* in the fall of 1930 for $125,000, and had Lewis Milestone filming it by late January of the following year, when the team for *Scarface* was just coming together.

Just after the holidays, Hecht and MacArthur boarded the train from New York to Los Angeles, bringing with them a clean-cut young Midwesterner named John Lee Mahin, a Harvard graduate and former reporter who had just quit his job as an advertising copywriter on the strength of Hecht's promise to add him to his writing stable at two hundred dollars a week and find him a job in Hollywood. Ostensibly, Hecht and MacArthur were headed west to write the third act of *Twentieth Century*, the play they had started in the fall, and Hecht hoped Mahin would prove up to performing as ghostwriter on *The Unholy Garden*, which Hecht had recklessly agreed to write for Sam Goldwyn on the basis of $10,000 for the story and the lure of $125,000, an unheard-of sum, for the finished script. Paying rent of $1,200 per month, Hecht and MacArthur installed themselves at the sprawling Youngworth Ranch, a seventy-five-acre avocado ranch in the hills of Culver City overlooking MGM, where they hosted brawling parties and became easily distracted from the task of finishing *Twentieth Century*.

In mid-January, with Hecht recently arrived on the Goldwyn lot to cope with the unwanted *Unholy Garden* and Hawks just installed in offices Hughes had rented from the producer, Hawks bumped into the writer and called him into his office. The way Hawks told it, "I wanted Ben Hecht to write on [*Scarface*], and he said, 'Sure, what are you going to make?' I said, 'A gangster picture.' He said, 'Hell, you don't want to make one of those things.' I said, 'Well, Ben, I've got an idea that the Borgia family is living in Chicago today. See, our Borgia is Al Capone, and his sister does the same incest thing as Lucretia Borgia.' And he said, 'Well, let's start tomorrow morning.' We did the script in eleven days."

Hecht remembered the encounter quite similarly, admitting he didn't like the idea of writing another gangster film, but that he was talked into it by Hawks. There was no mention of the Borgias, however, and Mahin adamantly insisted that "*Ben* said that to *Hawks*. I heard him say that. The

Borgias have always been Ben's favorite characters. Howard, bless his heart, probably knew who they were, but I think he looked them up in the encyclopedia. Howard was such a liar! That's a typical example."

Hecht said that when he jumped off *The Unholy Garden* Goldwyn "was in a state of epilepsy for about two days." He also recalled, "I met with Mr. Hughes, who told me the story he had bought and I didn't think it was any good. It was about two brothers, one turns out to be Capone and the other's the Chief of Police, and they have a great struggle. So I didn't trust Mr. Hughes, because he looked kind of goofy. He had a very weak face. He was deaf, couldn't hear anything you said, and he couldn't talk, and he was lanky, and he seemed to be a messy-looking fellow all around. So I couldn't imagine he had any money, so I made him pay me every night at 6 o'clock a thousand dollars, and then I would work the next day. I told Hughes I would make up a different story, and he said 'What's the plot?'

"I said, 'I haven't got any plot, but there have been several gangster pictures made, and I will double the casualty list of any picture to date, and we'll have twice as good a picture. *The Secret Six* killed off about eight people. I will kill off twenty, and we'll have the audience right in our hands.'"

Prior to Hecht's arrival, several other writers had tried to knock out a screenplay for *Scarface*. None had succeeded in pleasing Hughes, although two of the initial scenarists, Fred Pasley, a former Chicago reporter and crimeland expert, and W. R. Burnett, ultimately received screen credit. Burnett, a hard-boiled fiction writer hired because of his 1929 mob novel *Little Caesar*, was paid two thousand dollars a week for five weeks to write a script for *Scarface*. "I don't say my script was very good. I don't say anybody could write a good script under those circumstances. It was a mess. Nobody really knew what the hell they were doing—except for Howard Hawks apparently. But I never got along with Hawks, and I didn't work for Hawks when I was working for Hughes. I went in and talked to Hughes, and he gave me an office down the hall, and they started bringing in scripts. Pretty soon I had twelve scripts piled on my desk, until I said, 'What the hell's all this?'

"Hughes had the book as a sort of skeleton—with an incest theme. I didn't know what it was with Hughes and incest. So I wrote a whole script, and after I finished it, Hughes set a starting date. But Hawks didn't like my script. So they brought Ben Hecht in ten days before shooting. . . . I think Hecht was responsible for getting that picture made. He tightened it all up. He was an absolute pro, when he wanted to be. And he managed to tell the story, such as it was."

Burnett's figures of twelve scripts and ten days before shooting are exaggerations. But when Hawks and Hecht went to work they set about altering the basic story line, dropping the two brothers angle, working in the Borgias approach, borrowing liberally from *Underworld* (especially the triangular relationship and the trapped couple gunning it out with police at the end), and generally patterning the rise of their hero, Tony "Scarface" Camonte, on the most famous man in America, Al Capone. Hecht had met Capone and, as Hawks pointed out, "he knew a lot about Chicago so he didn't do any research." Mahin added that, despite all the other names on the screenplay, "the basic story was Ben's. Without his material there was nothing because I saw some of the stuff Hughes had."

During this intense period, Hecht wrote to his wife back East of *Scarface* that, "I'm doing it as homework when I'm not with Goldwyn. . . . Hughes is out of his mind with delight over my first days work on *Scarface*. Says it is more than four authors did for him in two months time. Hawks, the director and a charming gent, a hero aviator is pleased." As for the payment in daily, messengered thousand-dollar bills, it was carried out as advertised, although Hecht, having received a great deal from the young tycoon for *The Front Page*, knew better than to suspect that Hughes wouldn't be good for the money due him. Rather, the whole thing was a publicity stunt concocted by Hecht and his film agent, Myron Selznick, to further Hecht's legend as the most prolific and highest-paid writer in Hollywood.

Hawks always boasted of having consulted with real mobsters while preparing the film, although his claims on this score are suspect because of his dubious insistence that Capone himself loved the film and owned a personal print; by the time the picture was released, the gangster was behind bars. More believable is Hecht's story of having been visited by a couple of Capone goons who threateningly demanded to know who this Howard Hughes was who thought he could make a film about their boss. Hughes, Hecht assured them, was "just the sucker with the money" and in no way posed a danger to their boss.

Still, even Ben Hecht couldn't write a brilliant and fully dialogued screenplay in just eleven days, which is how long Hawks said it took. (Mahin claimed it was fourteen days, but the discrepancy might have stemmed from the conditions of Hecht's contract with Hughes, which stipulated that the writer was to receive a thousand dollars a day for a maximum of fourteen days; if he worked any period beyond that, he had a salary ceiling of fifteen thousand dollars, which answers the critics who have always wondered why he didn't drag out his writing schedule.) What Hecht produced during this period was a detailed sixty-page treatment, whereupon he booked his return trip to New York, telling Mahin, "Now you've got to fix it up." The novice Mahin felt the text was great as it was, but Hecht said, "It's so full of holes, this thing, John. There's hardly any dialogue. This isn't a script, this is a full treatment. You're going to have trouble, but this is your job that we promised you."

Finding Hecht's work "brilliant" but knowing better than Mahin how much work remained to be done on the script, Hawks hired his trusted collaborator and fix-it man, Seton Miller, to help Mahin out during the month of March for six hundred dollars a week. "Seton put all the numbers down, and I just redid the dialogue," Mahin recalled. "We did the final script with Hawks. We started from page one, redoing the dialogue." Miller and Mahin would work in intense sessions with Hawks, hammering out ideas for dialogue based on Hecht's scene structure, then set it down on paper on their own.

Even this wasn't enough, however. Angry, according to Hawks, that he hadn't milked as much as he might have from Hughes, Hecht, after his next trip to the Coast, arranged to travel with Hawks back to New York, where the director was headed to search for actors. The writer spent much of the trip honing and polishing the script in league with the director, the work interspersed with sessions of backgammon, which Hawks didn't yet really know how to play. In the end, according to Hawks, Hecht put twenty days into the writing of *Scarface* and received his deserved amount of money, although it's unclear whether the remainder was paid legitimately or by Hawks as a gambling debt.

As a rule, the major studios were unwilling to loan any of their important players to the upstart Hughes, which limited the field considerably. Although Hawks said that his friend Irving Thalberg tried to push a young MGM contract player named Clark Gable on him for the title role, Hawks didn't think he would do. "I'd seen his first picture, and I turned him down. We needed a fantastic *actor*, not just a personality. Nothing wrong with a personality; the camera likes certain people and turns them into something special and wonderful. But we needed *actor* actors, and I told Hughes I'd go to New York and look for some."

Given Hecht's vast knowledge of the New York theater scene, it is highly probable that he gave Hawks plenty of suggestions on who and what to see while in town. He undoubtedly recommended that Hawks look up Osgood Perkins (Tony's father), since the actor had originated the role of Walter Burns in *The Front Page*. Hawks felt immediately that he would be good as the selfish but ultimately weak gang leader Johnny Lovo, who gets rubbed out by his lieutenant, Scarface. "I always had the theory that heavies had beady eyes," Hawks remarked, "and Osgood certainly had them."

As for Paul Muni, Hawks was hardly an aficionado of the Yiddish theater scene, and Hecht's claims that he was responsible for Muni winning the lead seem plausible. At the very least, he probably brought him to Hawks's attention. At the time, Muni was back in New York after a disappointing first stab at Hollywood in *The Valiant* and *Seven Faces* in 1929, convinced that his future lay on the stage, not in pictures. Hawks claimed, "I remembered seeing him in the Yiddish theater in a fine scene with his back to the camera [sic], where he was such a purist he'd even made up his hands to fit the character." Another time Hawks said, "I saw Muni in a Jewish theater on 39th Street playing an old, old man." As it happens, Muni was not appearing on any stage at the time of Hawks's visit, but the director paid a call on him anyway. "He was very pleasant and smiled but said he couldn't play that kind of man, he wasn't that kind of person, he wasn't physically strong enough," Hawks explained. "Besides he protested that Cagney had made *Public Enemy*, and Robinson had made *Little Caesar*. What more could be done in *Scarface* that hadn't already been done?"

Hawks challenged Muni to make a test, and Muni's wife, Bella, who found Hawks "charming and persuasive" and had great influence over her husband, helped talk him into it. While Hecht brought the actor up to his home in Nyack, where he "taught him how to throw a right hook punch to the belly, so he would seem like a fighter," Hawks prepared to shoot the test in late April. He rented a tiny studio, designed a padded suit that would give the actor more bulk, hired other actors who were shorter than Muni, and even decided to put him on raised boards to increase his stature.

The results of the silent test, in addition to his favorable opinion of the script and his faith in Hawks, convinced Muni to take the part. Hughes requested further tests, and while Jerome Lawrence, in his biography of Muni, stated that no further tests were done, *Variety* reported on May 17 that Hawks was finally leaving New York "after making further Muni tests." As for salary, Hughes offered the actor $20,000, but Muni held out for $27,500 and began reading and learning everything he could about Capone.

Once back in Los Angeles, Hawks quickly cast the other important roles. The story goes that Hawks noticed George Raft in the audience at a prizefight at a time when "he was carrying a gun for the gangs." Actually, the former New York dancer and gigolo had already appeared in three films, including Rowland V. Lee's excellent *Quick Millions* at Fox, which Hawks had seen. Raft said that Jules Furthman sent him to see Hawks. At the time, Raft was due to go to Florida to join his former boss, the gangster Owney Madden, on tour with the Primo Carnera boxing carnival, so Hawks, who sensed that Raft's "unique look" and "marvelous impassive quality" would make him ideal as Scarface's bodyguard and best friend, Gino Rinaldi, a role modeled on Capone's bodyguard Frank Rio, signed him up at once, with Raft proposing to do it for a mere five hundred dollars. Hawks later hiked the amount when Raft ended up working more than fifty days.

To celebrate, Raft went to a popular industry restaurant where Paul Muni happened to be dining. Muni noticed Raft, asked him to join him at his table, and soon told him he'd be perfect for a role in the new gangster picture he'd come out to do. "That's really funny of you to say that," Raft replied. "I just saw Mr. Hawks and got the job." Muni and Raft became close during the shoot, with the highly trained thespian giving the novice more than a few acting tips.

Raft was responsible for bringing Ann Dvorak into the picture. Raft brought the slender, eighteen-year-old chorus girl to an elegant party at Hawks's home. Hawks recalled that "Ann asked [Raft] to dance with her but he said he'd rather not. She was a little high and right in front of him starts to do this sexy undulating dance, sort of trying to lure him on to dance with her. She was a knockout. She wore a black silk gown almost cut down to her hips. I'm sure that's all she had on. After a while George couldn't resist her suggestive dance and in no time they were doing a sensational number which stopped the party."

The evening proved fateful on a number of fronts. The next day, Hawks called Dvorak in to see him, and after working out a deal with Eddie Mannix to release her from her contract at MGM, where she was languishing on the vine, he cast her in the key role of Cesca, the sister Scarface loves who becomes involved with Raft's Gino. So big an impression had Dvorak's dance made on Hawks that he had her repeat it in the film, in the key night-club scene in which Cesca tempts Gino onto the dance floor, marking the beginning of their passionate but doomed romance. For Hawks, "the scene played like a million dollars because it was something that really happened between George and Ann."

It was also the beginning of something happening between Howard and Ann. Lean and sharp-featured, very much to Hawks's taste, Dvorak soon became the director's after-hours companion in a liaison that lasted through *Scarface* and into their next picture together, *The Crowd Roars*. Hawks liked

Dvorak's sprightly, direct, unbashful manner, and she was one of the few actresses he ever used in two films.

The other sexual crosscurrent on the *Scarface* company was an uncomfortable one involving Raft and Hughes. Raft had known Billie Dove in the late 1920s, when she was going out with New York Mayor Jimmy Walker. They met again during the *Scarface* shoot, and Raft, who claimed ignorance of Dove's involvement with his boss, decided to push the relationship to a new level. Suspicious of what was going on, Hughes traced the couple to the Ambassador Hotel. A hoodlum pal of Raft's noticed Hughes in the lobby and called the actor upstairs, who was right in the middle of things with Billie Dove at that moment. "She was pretty upset when I told her what was happening, since the last guy in the world either of us wanted to cross was Howard Hughes. So, as gracefully as I could, I said my good-byes to Billie, slipped down the service elevator, and beat it home."

Karen Morley won the role of Johnny Lovo's blond moll whose choice in men shifts with the winds of power. Boris Karloff, the big-house killer in *The Criminal Code*, pressed Hawks for a role and got the similarly sinister part of Scarface's crosstown rival, Gaffney. To play Scarface's goofy personal secretary, Hawks resourcefully selected Vince Barnett, who had played a few bits before but who, along with his father, also worked as a professional ribber, or cutup, at parties and official functions. Expert at posing as a waiter and spilling things on people, or getting up and insulting bigwigs in front of their peers, Barnett, with his bald pate, out-turned ears, and childlike expression, had become too familiar a face to get away with this stuff anymore. So Hawks, by giving him his first important role, launched his career as a successful character actor. In all, the cast was a bargain, with only stage veterans Muni and Perkins earning anything resembling real money and everyone grateful for the break.

By the time Ben Hecht was finished with his contributions to the script of *Scarface*, the story was much harsher, more cynical about human motivations and behavior, more jaundiced about political realities, and more forthright than the finished film would be. *Scarface* would still emerge as the most potent film about organized crime Hollywood would produce for decades, and even the diluted version went well beyond the contemporary norm in violence. The story of what happened to the content of *Scarface* between June 1, 1931, a month before shooting started, and its openings—in different versions in various parts of the country—the following April and May illustrates the vagaries of censorship laws in the U.S. at the time and specifically demonstrates how pressures could be brought to bear on producers during what is now considered the racy pre-Code era in Hollywood. The tale plays out as a pitched battle among the wills of some fiercely independent filmmakers, the financial priorities of businessmen, the righteous dander of the press, and the intrigues of politicians and officials with personal agendas of their own, which in some cases involved the neutralizing of Howard Hughes as a force in Hollywood.

As reworked by Hecht, with Hawks's enthusiastic participation, the resemblance of *Scarface* to the career of Al Capone became a great deal closer than the pronounced facial feature that, in the real gangster's case, extended along his jaw and across his neck, the result of an unsuccessful attempt to slit his throat. The film's magnificent opening scene, in which fat-cat mobster "Big Louie" Costillo is rubbed out in a phone booth after an all-night party, was based on the killing of Chicago racketeer "Big Jim" Colosimo by Capone and Johnny Torrio in an effort to take over the Chicago underworld. The next to go is the unseen O'Hara, an obvious stand-in for Deanie O'Banion, "the last of the first-class killers," whom Hecht and, especially, MacArthur had known well. His death prompted a retaliatory raid on Capone's headquarters—reproduced in the film almost exactly in the attack on a restaurant that Scarface survives by lying flat on the floor, just as Capone had done. The St. Valentine's Day Massacre, while not reenacted, is depicted in its bloody aftermath, and Hecht slipped in innumerable other details based on his knowledge of how things actually happened in Chicago.

As the story progresses, pure fiction increasingly dominates. Tony, sensing that his boss, Johnny Lovo, is weak, guns him down and takes over the town and his girl. Protective and jealous of his sister Cesca in a way that seems unnatural, he shoots his best friend, Gino, when he discovers him in his sister's apartment, not knowing they've married. This one "unprofessional" killing triggers his downfall, which climaxes when he and his sister are cornered in his private armored hideaway by an army of cops.

In 1931, the watchdog Hays Office, headed by the puritanical former Republican Party national chairman Will H. Hays, enforced general rules of behavioral decency in movies: bad guys had to be punished, pre- or extramarital affairs could not be explicitly shown, religions and other respected institutions could not be insulted, and so forth. (The immeasurably more restrictive rules, such as married couples not being allowed in the same bed and kisses limited to three seconds, were still more than two years away.)

Employed by the major studios, Hays made sure that their films toed the line, but he also did the bidding of the moguls, and he was particularly close to the most powerful boss of all, Louis B. Mayer, a friend and big supporter of President Herbert Hoover. No film could be released without a Production Seal issued by the Motion Picture Producers and Distributors of America, and Hays, along with his deputy, Colonel Jason Joy, and industrious foot soldier Lamar Trotti, was in charge of dispensing the seals. The Hays Office generally began its surveillance of films at the script stage, advising producers of suitability and indicating dialogue and other business that might fail to meet not only its own standards but those of the myriad state and municipal censor boards that then existed around the country. In this capacity, the Hays Office saw itself not strictly as a censorship organization but as a helpful entity standing between filmmakers, who often tried to get away with as much as they could, and local censorship panels, which could be truly irrational, unpredictable, and inconsistent in their judgments.

A script of *Scarface* was duly delivered to the Hays Office, and on June 1, 1931, came back the rather alarmed response. Not surprisingly, the first objection concerned the character of Tony Camonte's mother. Hays was incensed at the negative depiction of the mother "as a grasping virago, distinctly an Italian criminal type mother" and insisted that the character be changed and that she "present to the son a dialogue telling him what the Italian race has done for posterity and that he, Scarface, was bringing odium and shame upon his entire race.

"For the same general reason," Hays continued, "the lawyer, Epstein, should not be so pronouncedly Jewish, if at all, as it will react at least racially against the picture."

Also ordered out was a character named Benson, a state's attorney shown to be friendly with Camonte but prone to pompous public pronouncements, such as, "The gangs must go. Prohibition must be enforced." Hays also advised that all action showing "judges issuing habeas corpus ought to be eliminated as tending to show a breakdown in the forces of law and a connivance with criminals."

The original script had Gino Rinaldi and Scarface's sister Cesca shacking up together out of wedlock when her brother finds them, and it even made his mother the one who brings the relationship to Scarface's attention. This is another significant plot point upon which Hays's advice had direct effect: "Instead of having his 'pal' live with his sister and meet death at his hands, this should be changed as if he had been secretly married to her. Dramatic effect would be better and moral effect upon audience would be better."

A major scene—also inspired by Capone—involved Scarface and Lovo's former moll, Poppy, vacationing in Florida onboard Scarface's yacht in the company of many social bigwigs and artistic types, including a woman writer of dirty books. The sequence was objected to on the basis that it glamorized the sweet desserts of the criminal life, and was never shot.

But the most troublesome aspect of *Scarface*, from the first reading of the script to even after its release, was its ending. In the original draft, Tony Camonte, retreating to his metal-shuttered refuge with his beloved sister, shoots it out with the police while showering them with contemptuous verbal abuse. After exchanging charged expressions of filial love and eternal devotion, Cesca is shot and Tony is driven out by tear gas and an engulfing fire. Like a mad animal, Scarface charges down the stairs to receive a relentless torrent of police bullets, which somehow fails to stop him. Still on his feet, he lurches toward the cop Guarino (upon whose badge he had lit a match early in the story), aims his gun at his face, and fires at point-blank range. But the pistol just clicks; the chamber is empty. Guarino then seizes his opportunity and shoots Scarface, who crumbles to the pavement but still keeps pulling the trigger of his gun as he falls, expressing murderous defiance and insolence to the end.

Hays would have none of this. "In the closing episode of this story," he objected, "Scarface is endowed with humane kindly qualities especially as applied to the welfare of his sister. He is also given super-human power in escaping a barrage of bullets. This should all be readjusted, otherwise it . . . would readily lend itself to the charge of so-called 'glorification' of the criminal."

Three days later, Colonel Joy followed up with an official letter expressing great concern that Scarface would appear too heroic, suggesting, for the first time, that the character become "a cringing coward" at the end and that the character of the police detective Guarino be built up to be the brave one sent into the blazing inferno to capture the gangster singlehandedly.

With Mahin the lead writer now, revisions were quickly initiated in an attempt to placate the Hays Office. By mid-June, Hawks and Hughes's executive E. B. Derr were involved in nearly daily meetings with Colonel Joy "in a last endeavor to salvage as much as possible of the story." In the midst of the negotiations and rewrites, Joy reported to Hays that though "the treatment of the story is becoming more satisfactory, there still remains the most harsh and frank gangster picture we ever had. We told [Hawks] that we did not expect it to pass any of the censor boards, and that it would probably have the effect of closing the door for any further possibilities in that direction."

Finally, with the picture ready to roll and Hughes and Hawks both fed up with being told what they could and could not do, they received a stern warning from Colonel Joy: "Under no circumstances is this film to be made. The American public and all conscientious State Boards of Censorship find mobster and hoodlums repugnant. Gangsterism must not be mentioned in the cinema. If you should be foolhardy enough to make *Scarface*, this office will make certain it is never released."

Enraged at the hypocrisy of an organization that had approved dozens of gangster films for release and sure that this was just another sign that the industry leaders wanted to chase him out of town, Hughes sent Hawks a note: "Screw the Hays Office. Start the picture and make it as realistic, as exciting, as grisly as possible."

The shooting of *Scarface* began on June 23, 1931. Most of the studio work was done at the Metropolitan Studios, at Formosa and Santa Monica Boulevard, which later became the Samuel Goldwyn Studios, while some additional filming was done at the Harold Lloyd Studios, at a small, ramshackle studio in Westwood, and at the Mayan Theater in downtown Los Angeles. Emboldened by Hughes's command, Hawks played the toughness of the characters and the violence of the action to the hilt. He was also inspired to new heights artistically. For a director who had rejected fancy camera movements and stylistic frills after what he considered the failed experimentation of *Paid to Love*, Hawks's opening shot was like a glorious throwback to the silent cinema and a bouquet tossed to the influence of Expressionism. For three minutes, the camera drifts weightlessly amid the remnants of what has obviously been a bacchanalian gangster party. Beginning with a streetlamp going out, the camera moves down to show milk being delivered outside what had been a First Ward stag party. A cleaning man clears some confetti off the potted palms and finds a brassiere on the floor, while the host, "Big Louie" Costillo, is well satisfied with himself, admitting to his two drunken buddies that his former partner Johnny Lovo is bound to cause trouble but boasting that he, Louie, is "on top of the world." After Louie heads over to make a phone call, the camera continues right to pick up a shadow moving in from the right, quietly whistling a theme from Donizetti's opera *Lucia di Lammermoor*. The figure moves resolutely onward toward the phone booth. Standing in silhouette, the figure draws a gun, says, "Hello, Louie," and fires, shattering the elegant relaxation of the scene, launching a gang war, and getting *Scarface* off to a shocking start.

All through preproduction, Hawks's right-hand man was Richard Rosson, the brother of Arthur, who was to have directed *Underworld*, and Harold, Hawks's cinematographer on *Trent's Last Case*. As the film's official "codirector," Rosson not only helped with script matters and conceptualizing sequences, but would also shoot most of the action scenes (or second-unit sequences, as they would come to be called), notably the car crashes, machine gunning, and many insert shots. Behind the camera, Hawks had Lee Garmes, "a great cameraman" who used half the light of an ordinary cinematographer. "We had more light in the houselights than we did on the set. We had just got some faster film too." The other cinematographer was Hawks's reliable collaborator from his silent pictures, L. William O'Connell, who shot with Rosson as well as with Hawks on numerous scenes. "Garmes was the self-styled artist of Hollywood," O'Connell explained. "He was a very daring cameraman, and he was the big shot of all the camera departments. He made himself important. He initiated contrast photography. . . . I did all the stunts. I wasn't just a stooge to Lee Garmes on *Scarface*. We were scheduled out for different types of scenes."

Garmes's work is unusually sculpted and hard-edged for the time, increasing the film's tough, brutal quality. Hecht was so impressed with him that he made him cinematographer and codirector of his later independent New York pictures. He felt that Garmes was "one of the unsung heroes of Hollywood, who possibly knows more about direction than any five directors." For his part, O'Connell's proudest contribution was devising the memorable shot in which, after Boris Karloff's Gaffney is gunned down in a bowling alley, the final bowling pin spins and spins before falling down, giving the dead man a strike; O'Connell said that he rigged the pin with a wire to control its movements, but that the shot still took many takes to get right. He was impressed that "Hawks was full of symbolism."

Carrying on a tradition of the silent cinema, Hawks had live music played on the set to put his actors in the proper mood. However, his directorial ingenuity and tact were put to the test by the diametrically opposed problems presented by Muni and Raft, the technique-laden theatrical veteran and the rank amateur. When he started, Muni laid on both the Italian accent and the editorializing about his character far too thick. Hawks had him cut down his accent by half, then by half again because, "we just want the *suggestion* that you're Italian. It's more in the inflection than in the accent. Besides, we want to understand you." Some viewers even pick up that Muni's accent becomes less distinct as the picture progresses, as Tony Camonte grows more "American" and moves further away from his roots. Hawks also told Muni that he was initially attacking his character too heavily and suggested that he lighten up his characterization by adding a playful veneer over Camonte's innate viciousness. By way of example, he cited the famous story in which Capone hosted a banquet for a rival mobster, sang his praises, told some jokes, toasted him, then grew more serious and sarcastic until he pulled out a baseball bat and clubbed the man to death. This scene was not included in *Scarface* but appeared nearly thirty years later in both *Party Girl* and *Some Like It Hot,* in which it was enacted by none other than George Raft himself. In 1987, Robert De Niro performed another version of it in *The Untouchables.* Muni threw himself into the role with the absorption and attention to detail for which he would become famous, arriving at the studio at 5:30 A.M. to go over his scenes, practicing in front of a full-length mirror in his dressing room, and reciting his lines into a dictaphone so he could play them back and find the proper gestures to accompany them.

Raft required an entirely different sort of guidance. Hawks hired him for his look and personality and knew that his clothes, eyes, and mannerisms would be primarily responsible for his effectiveness on-screen. Raft looked great in good clothes, and Hawks often inserted him into scenes where he actually had nothing to do, just to add to the mood and to give Gino Rinaldi weight and authority. As for Raft's celebrated bit of flipping a coin, which Hawks believed "probably helped make him a star," credit for it is once again disputed between the director and writer. Raft always maintained that Hawks thought it up, and said that "I spent most of my time on the set practicing flipping the nickel." Glad to accept responsibility, Hawks said that he got the idea from an old mob story about a killer who, as a sign of disrespect, left a measly nickel in the fist of his victim. John Lee Mahin, on the other hand, swore that Hecht wrote the bit of business into the script, which he suspected Raft never even read.

Whoever invented it, Hawks recognized that giving Raft something to do would go a long way to cover his awkwardness and inexperience. "Having George flip the coin made him a character," Hawks said. "The coin represented a hidden attitude—a kind of defiance, a held-back hostility, a coolness—which hadn't been found in pictures up to that time; and it made George stand out." Raft, who acknowledged that cheap hoodlums across the country began imitating him as soon as the film came out, admitted that flipping the coin helped him with the stress of repeated takes. "I had to flip the nickel so that my hand was steady and firm, and I even managed to do it while staring at someone."

Raft even managed to do it during his death scene. When Muni played the scene of Scarface coming to his sister's apartment and gunning down his best friend, Raft, who was tossing a coin on Hawks's instructions, fell back and accidentally hit his head on the door. "When I slid down the door," Raft recalled, "I was slightly unconscious and landed in a small pool of my own blood. My eyes sort of rolled up in my head, like people's do when they are dying. The coin I had been tossing fell out of my hand. I heard Hawks say, 'Print.' Everyone there said this was the greatest movie death scene they ever saw. Hawks filmed the coin rolling along the floor until it lost its motion, and fell flat. Hawks told me later, 'The roll of the coin and then its falling still told the story of Gino's death.'" None of this ended up in the finished film, however; Raft simply slumps down in the doorframe upon being shot, shaking his head in stunned disbelief, his hand now empty of the coin it had been flipping.

Raft loved Hawks, saying he was "wonderful, wonderful" and that "he never bawled anybody out, in contrast to other directors, who'd always scream. He never talked above a whisper, and got the best out of everybody by being quiet." Hawks later remarked, "Raft is one of the few actors who is grateful for the start I gave him. For ten years after we made *Scarface*, Raft would write me every year saying he'd do any story, anytime, anywhere — for half his normal price."

Working seven-day weeks when the industry norm was six, Hawks pushed ahead with shooting, with Mahin revising dialogue daily. When Hughes, whom Hawks had audaciously banned from the set, saw dailies of the first car wreck caused by machine guns, he loved it so much he ordered Hawks to film several more of them, which depicted Scarface's Reign of Terror. Inspired by newspapers' habit of marking crime photographs with an X in the spot where bodies were found, Hawks wanted to use a running gag of a visual X in every scene involving a murder. He offered crew members first fifty dollars, then one hundred for any clever suggestion that made it into the film, and there are several good ones: the cross of an undertaker's sign above a crime scene on a sidewalk; the roof supports in the garage setting of the St. Valentine's Day Massacre; the Roman numeral X on the apartment where Tony comes to kill Rinaldi; and, most memorably, the X mark for strike on Gaffney's bowling line score. As usual, Hawks injected sly humor whenever possible, such as in the scene where Vince Barnett's secretary survives a raid on his boss's headquarters while on the telephone, but he also made the violence as realistic as possible, even down to using real bullets to tear up the place in the same sequence. The director filmed the destruction once without actors, then had the actors play before rear projection of the violence to heighten the realism. The use of live ammunition did have tragic consequences, however, on the night of July 16. Gaylord Lloyd, the brother of the celebrated comic star Harold Lloyd, was visiting during the filming of one of the big action set pieces. Against instructions, he changed position to get a better view and was hit in the eye by a ricocheting bullet. Despite prolonged efforts by doctors, he lost the eye permanently.

Hughes and Hawks had taken the attitude that they were going to shoot the picture they wanted to make, but they still had to play ball with the Hays Office if they hoped to show *Scarface* to the general public. On July 8, a test scene was submitted to Hays as an indication of "the atmosphere" of the picture. Three days later, however, Colonel Joy indicated to his boss that "inasmuch as they have everything in the story, including the inferences of incest, the picture is beginning to look worse and worse to us, from a censorship point of view."

On July 22, Colonel Joy looked at rushes representing about a third of the picture and had lunch with Hawks and E. B. Derr, during which they "went over the shooting script with a fine tooth comb." Joy told Hays that "they agreed to eliminate or change the countless things which render the script a violation of the Code." However, the filmmakers still hadn't agreed to three things requested by Hays: making a suitable "foreword" that condemned gangsterdom, writing "a strong speech by a suitable character," and making the title character "yellow at the end."

Joy looked at more footage on July 29 and again on August 20, but he felt that "radical" revisions would still be necessary; as things stood, he believed, only fifty percent of theaters in the United States would play the picture.

During July, Los Angeles experienced one of its worst heat waves on record, which could conceivably have contributed to Hughes's frayed nerves and severe strain over the progress of production. Although thrilled with the results Hawks was getting, by midmonth he began putting heavy pressure on his director to pick up the pace; his original estimate of twenty-eight shooting days had already been reached and Hawks wasn't even half done. For Hawks, there was also tremendous pressure at home, as Athole suffered one of her periodic attacks and had to be hospitalized. Under the circumstances, her husband scarcely had time to visit, much less care for her. On the job, Hawks tried to reassure his producer that he needed the extra time to make the film they both wanted, and Hughes had no choice but to wait until Hawks finished the picture to his own satisfaction. He finally did so at the end of August after a sixty-day shoot, and Hughes announced a November 28 release date through United Artists.

On September 8, Colonel Joy informed Will Hays about the film's progress: "With Mr. Trotti we sat in with the executives of Caddo while the first rough-cut version of *Scarface* was screened, after which we argued for an hour for a complete revision of the ending of the story. If this suggestion is accepted, it will involve another five days' shooting and will greatly weaken the value of the picture, *but* it will relieve the picture of any nonconformance to the Code."

Endless conferences, discussions, and negotiations dragged on through September, with Trotti suggesting that "the ending be changed to show Scarface going yellow and being taken by police. An entirely new thread will be run through the picture shifting its meaning as follows: The gangster is a great man as long as he has a gun; once without a gun, he is a yellow rat. The final message of the picture will be—not to let criminals get possession of guns. Mr. Hawks was enthusiastic about the suggestion and will attempt to develop it and then sell the idea to Mr. Hughes."

At the time, New York Governor Franklin D. Roosevelt, then a hopeful for the 1932 Democratic presidential nomination, was undertaking major legislation against the private ownership of machine guns; there was much hue and cry about the issue of violence, and agitation to repeal Prohibition was reaching a peak. In mid-September, Joy and Trotti spent many hours with Hawks and Derr going over the antigun scenes as well as the new ending, which would take four days and $25,000 to shoot and "would be essential" if the picture were to be passed. "Mr. Hawks has a splendid conception of the whole plan and a dramatic finish which ought to make the picture acceptable."

This "dramatic finish" was the climax seen on most prints of the picture, the one commonly accepted as the "official" ending, but one that was made only in an attempt to placate the Hays Office. Hawks, of course, regretted being forced into the compromise, and it seems probable that he recalled the never-seen original ending of *Scarface* when he (and an uncredited Ben Hecht) devised the violent conclusion to *The Thing* 20 years later, in which the monster is shot to smithereens and still won't go down. Unable to use Hecht's original ending, Hawks came up with a way to meet the censors' insistence that Scarface turn "yellow" and be shown to be nothing without a gun. He began with the scene in Scarface's armored lair by changing the tenor of Tony and Cesca's final moments together. When his sister is shot, Tony becomes hysterical, cries "I'm no good by myself," and insists that she mustn't die, making her realize that he's actually afraid. This was designed to prepare the audience for the sniveling cowardice with which he ends his life. Police tear gas drives him out and onto the stairway, where his gun is shot out of his hand. He asks to be given a break, then makes a run for it, whereupon he's brought down by a few shots from the surrounding police, coming to rest beneath the sign announcing "The World Is Yours," an echo of the beckoning "The City Is Yours" billboard in *Underworld* four years before.

This ending was shot at the end of September, with the Hughes team under the impression that it would win *Scarface* a Production Code seal and that the film would meet its newly advanced release date of November 12. Paul Muni caught the train back to New York the day after finishing these retakes in order to rush into rehearsal for Elmer Rice's new play, *Counsellor-at-Law*. First National had been chomping at the bit waiting for Hawks to finish so he could return to direct a picture for them. The prolonged *Scarface* schedule had already forced him to yield the directing job on *Environment* (released as *Alias the Doctor*), starring Richard Barthelmess, to Michael Curtiz, and James Cagney and Douglas Fairbanks Jr. couldn't wait much longer if they were going to team up in a boat-racing picture Hawks had proposed doing with them that fall. For his part, Hughes was anxious to begin recouping some money from his heavy film investments; his latest attempt to make Billie Dove a star, *The Age of Love*, was a bomb, and in August, after having spent more than $100,000 developing it, he had finally thrown in the towel on *Queer People* because of the strenuous opposition to it and a not entirely unrelated inability to find actors who would appear in it.

In the first week of October 1931, after nine months of work, Hawks departed *Scarface* and Howard Hughes's employ and reported back to First National. Arguably, *Scarface* was entering the most difficult period of its birth pangs; additional scenes would be ordered shot, new titles would come and go, and tremendous battles would be waged between the Hughes side and the Hays Office, in particular, and various censorship forces, in general. Hawks, off directing *The Crowd Roars*, was around for none of it, and even Hughes, although deeply involved and kept informed by constant telegrams, letters, and phone calls, was away on his yacht during most of the struggle to keep *Scarface* from being dismembered or banned altogether.

In their absence, the standard bearer in the crusade on behalf of *Scarface* was Hughes's publicity director, Lincoln (Link) Quarberg. A former newspaperman who knew key editors and writers on papers throughout the country and was known in town as the man who had dubbed Jean Harlow the "platinum blonde," Link worked passionately and tirelessly to try to keep the film as undiluted as possible and was dead set against any compromise with the organs of censorship everywhere. Brash and extreme, he was prone to conspiracy theories when it came to the machinations of Hays, the studio heads, and government officials, but most of the time he was right. He eventually realized that Hays, having promised various censor boards a year earlier that he would rid the nation's screens of gangster films, was dilly-dallying in order to keep *Scarface* away from the public indefinitely. Quarberg felt that the press and public would rally en masse behind Hughes, however unlikely the role of crusading civil libertarian might appear for the freewheeling millionaire. He also felt that "Elder Hays" and his ilk would ultimately do themselves in with their hypocritical self-righteousness, to the ultimate benefit of *Scarface*, if only Hughes would hang tough.

In mid-October, Colonel Joy, at Hughes's expense, personally took a print of *Scarface*, as revised per the instructions of the Hays Office, to New York to show Will Hays and the New York Board of Review, which had to pass on all films to be shown in the state. At that time, the states with the most stringent cinematic morality standards were New York, Pennsylvania, and Ohio, which accounted for 40 percent of the nation's moviegoing public. Many cities, notably Chicago and Dallas, had even tougher censor boards, and individual states could sometimes do surprising things; some months earlier, Maryland, one of the many states then considering a ban on gangster films, had cut the James Cagney smash *The Public Enemy* by about a half hour. It was this sort of haphazard, chaotic censoring that the Hays organization hoped to forestall, which was why Hughes felt at least halfway compelled to cooperate with him, in the hopes that clearance by Hays, especially in New York, would circumvent further censorship and open the doors to *Scarface* playing everywhere.

Joy showed *Scarface* to Hays and to Police Commissioner Mulrooney, who endorsed the picture. During his three weeks in the city, however, he insidiously refrained from screening it for the New York censors, because he and Hays feared that they might pass it. Instead, Joy returned to Hollywood to inform Hughes that more cuts would be needed, along with a new ending that would force Scarface to pay for his crimes. As Quarberg sarcastically remarked, "The Hays ending was a creative masterpiece. Although no gangster in real life has ever been hanged, they proposed to do just that with *Scarface*. And for fully four minutes after the picture, unmatched for realism, has logically ended, and the audience is walking out of the theatre, you are shown what happens to a bold, bad gunman—the trial, the conviction, the speech by the judge when he pronounces sentence, and all the other details of the hanging process, including the reading of the final death-warrant to the hangee, testing of the scaffold, dragging the condemned man to the noose, and finally the actual neck-stretching."

At Hays's instructions, this artistic death sentence was carried out, but without the participation of either Howard Hawks or Paul Muni. Using a double for Muni in long shots and relying on close-ups of cuffed hands, manacled feet, and the prisoner's back most of the time, Richard Rosson patched together this turgid, utterly unrealistic ending that satisfied only one man, Will Hays.

Through the fall, Quarberg did what he could to generate favorable word of mouth about *Scarface* in Hollywood, showing the original version to the *Hollywood Reporter* publisher Billy Wilkerson, who wrote a front-page editorial raving about the film and urging that it be approved and released at once. Quarberg also argued to Hughes that the best parry to Hays's delaying tactics would be to open the film immediately in all territories that did not have local censorship panels and let critical acclaim and public enthusiasm take care of the rest. Hughes was reluctant, however, feeling that too much of the country would remain off-limits for him to recoup what was now a $700,000 investment, a sentiment seconded by Joe Schenck and United Artists, who would be releasing it.

Still dragging his feet despite Hughes's compliance in making the hanging ending, Hays, by November, was insisting upon a new title that would reflect an anti-gangster stance. United Artists proposed *The Menace* and *An American Menace*, while Hays himself came up with *Shame of the Nation*. Hughes was ready to go along with *The Scar on the Nation*, even though Quarberg told him it sounded like a gag, as long as the ads bore the prominent credit line "from the book SCARFACE by Armitage Trail."

In further compliance with Hays's dictates, Hughes agreed to finance the shooting of yet another sequence, one showing indignant civic leaders in the office of a Hearst-like newspaper publisher, accusing him of glamorizing gangsters in print. In response, the publisher fulminates against guns and lack of legal action against these public menaces. The most notorious addition to the picture, the sequence was polished up by Seton I. Miller from material prepared by Colonel Joy and Caddo's E. R. Derr and directed by Richard Rosson at the beginning of December. The scene is so badly directed and acted, that Hawks, who had nothing to do with it, calmly told Hughes, "It can't hurt the picture. Everybody will know it wasn't part of the picture."

Hughes spent nearly all of January 1932 in New York City, cooperating with the Hays Office with an eye to getting the film approved quickly and into general release on March 26. Aside from using the hanging ending, essentially eliminating the incest theme, and accepting the *Shame of the Nation* title, Hughes agreed to tack on a special prologue for New York, delivered by Police Commissioner Mulrooney, who had approved the film's original version months before. This would replace the written broadside against gangsterdom and public apathy previously prepared at Hays's behest. On January 21, Hughes cabled Quarberg the following message:

> Naturally all of us would like to be able to make and release our pictures just as we wish however unfortunately I don't own my own releasing company and when United Artists tells me they won't release the picture unless passed by Hays and when the Publix Loews Fox and Warner chains of theatres state they will not play the picture unless passed by Hays there is only one thing I can do and that is to get the picture passed by Hays and that I have done with as little damage as possible. The Mulrooney foreword will be used only in New York State. For general distribution the picture will carry the foreword which was on it when shipped to New York the last time which, it might interest you to know, was written by Mr. Hays personally. Furthermore, most of the last changes were suggestions Mr. Hays was kind enough to give me. I showed him the picture and he thinks it vastly improved.

Hughes may have thought that kowtowing to Hays on all these points would automatically give him both the Production Seal and New York censor approval, but he was dead wrong. To his shock, when Hays, after a four-month delay, finally got around to showing the most watered-down version of *Scarface* to the Board of Review, it was rejected in its entirety. "So much for the alleged 'cooperation,'" hooted Quarberg, "which you see has all been . . . just a plain scheme to delay the release of *Scarface* as long as possible, if not indefinitely." In a confidential letter to Hughes, he wrote, "As you undoubtedly realize by now, the men who are actually running the picture business, including Will Hays and the Big-Shot Jews, particularly the MGM moguls, are secretly hoping you have made your last picture. They are jealous of your successful pictures, and have resented your independence, and your entrance into the industry from the start. On top of all this, they are inwardly incensed, and further aggravated, because you purchased the film rights to *Queer People*." He suggested that his boss release *Scarface* instantly wherever possible, including California, and quit the Hays Association "with a grand public gesture."

Furious with Hays after having been strung along by him for so long with no results, Hughes left New York on February 11 amid rumors that he was quitting the picture business; it didn't help matters that for long periods over the next two months Hughes would be incommunicado aboard his yacht. At this point, Quarberg felt that his best bet would be to drum up so much press and public outrage against Hays and the suppression of the picture that the pressure would force it out. He started by trying to arrange for Senators La Follette and Brookhart, two personal friends, to introduce a resolution in the United States Senate calling for nationwide investigation of motion picture censorship. On February 29, he screened the original version of *Scarface* at Grauman's Chinese Theatre in Hollywood for two hundred members of the press, who gave the film the "greatest ovation ever accorded any motion picture at any preview. Broke into spontaneous applause at finish. All singing praises of picture. *Scarface* talk of Hollywood." Three days later, the *Los Angeles Times* published a column of unrestrained support for the film, calling it "the best, most incisive gangster film ever done" and stating, "Had *Scarface* been produced at the height of the gangster epidemic it would have been an enormous sensation." Calling the film a "masterpiece," Billy Wilkerson of the *Hollywood Reporter* charged Will Hays with "hysterical gestures" in regard to *Scarface*. Quarberg arranged to show the picture in New York to Robert E. Sherwood, a writer whose film column was syndicated in hundreds of papers nationally. Sherwood was also a screenwriter, and no one at the time seemed to notice that he had recently written a film for Howard Hughes, *Cock of the Air*. United Artists confirmed Quarberg's suspicions that it was working at cross-purposes with Hughes when, directly contrary to Quarberg's instructions, it showed Sherwood the Hays version with the hanging ending rather than the original, thus inadvertently giving Sherwood the chance not only to praise the picture but to "give the Hays office the verbal lacing of their lives." Revving up his campaign even further, Quarberg suggested that Hughes file suit in New York, "applying for a restraining order to prevent the state censor board from interfering with the showing of *Scarface*."

Finally convinced that Quarberg was right about Hays fronting a covert industry-wide campaign against *Scarface* and himself, Hughes decided to take his earlier advice and launch the picture in a market where there were no censorship concerns. United Artists booked the film into the Loews State Theatre in New Orleans, where it had its world premiere on March 31, 1932. Seizing the opportunity he had long sought, Quarberg surrounded the opening with all attendant hoopla, including having the print delivered by an armored truck driven down the entire length of Canal Street to the theater, flanked by two police motorcycles with sirens blaring. Not surprisingly, *Scarface* became the hit of the season, doubling the grosses of the year's biggest opening up to then.

Emboldened, Hughes and United Artists planned a general release for April 22 in the same "original version"—that is, with the "yellow" ending in which a fleeing Scarface is shot by police—presented in New Orleans. Sensing the tide turning after the Los Angeles screening, the Hays Office had begun dissembling and releasing disinformation, most of which was designed to make it look as though it had been responsible for a version of *Scarface* that was presentable to the public, rather than the cause of its long delay. Three days before the New Orleans opening, the Hays Office stated that "the picture has been completely remade by [Lewis] Milestone, and that it is the new Milestone version which is to be released," adding that, "it was the Howard Hawks version, now discarded, which had been rejected by the N.Y. censors." At one time, Hughes had considered letting Milestone take a crack at recutting *Scarface* for the benefit of the New York board, but this was never done. After the successful Los Angeles press screening, the Hays Office had also tried to claim that the cut shown there "was their revised version of the picture," all of which begins to explain the confusion about the different versions of *Scarface* that have come down through the years.

To ensure that his preferred version of the film be shown in all situations possible, Hughes put out the word that all prints with the "hanging" ending were to be rounded up and sequestered. The producer also finally resurfaced in the United States, turning up with Billie Dove at the opening of *Scarface* in his hometown of Houston on April 22. Hawks and Ann Dvorak, who had recently finished *The Crowd Roars*, also came in at Hughes's request, and *Scarface* broke the opening-day house record at the

Metropolitan Theater. Initial box-office results from other cities were strong as well, the tough Ohio censor board had just passed the picture without cuts, and it seemed that Quarberg's persistence would pay off.

Ironically, it was just at this moment of apparent victory that the tension that had long been felt between the Hughes organization and United Artists erupted into open fissures. In early April, without authorization from Hughes, Joe Schenck "had a print of *Scarface* cut and edited in New York to conform to all the latest censorship demands" in an attempt to get the picture out before Hughes filed legal action. A Hays-inspired attack on *Scarface* in the trade journal *Film Daily* provoked Hughes to withdraw all advertising from the publication, a move he forced a reluctant United Artists to make as well, and Schenck, who was still beholden to Hays even if Hughes wasn't, became so embarrassed by Quarberg's merciless attacks on "Elder Hays" that he demanded that Hughes restrain and, finally, fire the "meddlesome incompetent fool." Hughes refused.

Hughes's response was to send telegrams to the eleven New York dailies, attacking the "politically controlled censor boards" and announcing immediate legal action to get the film shown in New York, Chicago, and elsewhere. In a last-ditch attempt to prevent such a move, Schenck submitted to the New York censors a "special print" including the Mulrooney antigun foreword and the hanging ending. In mid-May, *Scarface* was cleared for exhibition in New York State.

Quarberg immediately put out a gloating press release declaring a "knockout victory over New York Board censors," who placed their "stamp of approval on the original version of the picture." In fact, the film had been approved "with eliminations," but Hughes instructed United Artists not to publicize the fact that the New York version "is not original and unchanged version as of course picture will draw more customers if public told they will not see any censored version but will see the real thing and thus capitalize on the publicity we have already had on the controversy over censorship." Personally, Quarberg was disappointed in Hughes for accepting the cuts in order to release the film quickly, rather than fighting it out, in court if necessary, for the original version. But financially, Hughes's tactics paid off. *Scarface* finally opened in New York City on May 19, 1932. With local boy George Raft in town to boost interest further, the film played at the Rialto Theater for seventy-two hours straight at the start of its run and, as *Variety* put it, "opened like a machine gun in action," grossing a tremendous $57,200 in its first week. As the trade paper described the patronage, "Picture is drawing a preponderance of male trade. Women represent only around 10% while the men represent everything from First to 10th Avenues. Femmes appear mostly to be of the carriage trade." The film went on to gross $161,600 in seven weeks at the Rialto alone before heading out into neighborhood runs.

Variety waited to review the hanging version at the film's New York release. "Presumably the last of the gangster films, on a promise, it is going to make people sorry that there won't be any more," it predicted. Confirming that Hughes and Hawks had fulfilled their original intentions, the review stated that *Scarface* "bumps off more guys and mixes more blood with rum than most of the past gangster offerings combined. The blows are always softened by judicial preachments and sad endings for the sinners. But the punch is in the violence, the killings, the motives and the success of the cast in giving the director what he wants." Word got out among the cognoscenti that, United Artists' claims notwithstanding, the version on display in New York was not the one to see, so discerning New York critics and viewers wanting to see the unexpurgated version merely crossed the Hudson River into New Jersey.

There were still some battles to be fought. It took the Pennsylvania Censor Board another two months to reverse its original decision and pass *Scarface*, and some cities, such as Dallas, insisted on the hanging ending. In Chicago, where Hughes's previous gangster saga, *The Racket*, had never been permitted to play, the showing of *Scarface* was similarly blocked indefinitely. Ultimately, the censorship battle over *Scarface* held up the film's release for just five to six months, not the two years often claimed by Hawks and many film historians.

Overall, *Scarface* did very well at the box office, but it did not clean up as it might have had it been released at the height of the gangster craze, or had it enjoyed unlimited access to the nation's markets. Between its first wave of bookings in 1932 and its final run in 1935, *Scarface* grossed $905,298 for United Artists, a healthy figure but well under half, for instance, of the $2,361,125 grossed by Hughes's biggest hit, *Hell's Angels*. Hughes's deal gave him 75 percent of the gross. The original budget of *Scarface* was $600,000, but all the additional shooting and editing demanded by Hays had run costs well over $700,000. After all accounts were in, Hughes earned just a small profit on *Scarface* based upon domestic returns alone, although he received additional revenues from other territories, including Great Britain, where the film did well.

Between 1936, when domestic distribution rights to Hughes's productions were taken over by Astor Films, and 1947, when they were all reissued, *Scarface* grossed an additional $297,934, giving the picture a total U.S. gross of $1,203,233 before it was withdrawn from circulation. Thereafter, based on its reputation and almost utter unavailability, it became one of the most sought after films among buffs and scholars, viewable only overseas or at clandestine screenings, where the prints shown were almost invariably awful 16mm bootleg dupes of who knew what version of the film. Not until 1980, when most of the Hughes titles were bought by Universal, could *Scarface* once again be properly seen. Its return was heralded by a special showing at the New York Film Festival—marking the official Manhattan premiere of the original version, never before allowed into the city—and a screening at the Directors Guild of America in Los Angeles. Following were limited theatrical and video release, as well as Brian De Palma's popular 1983 remake for Universal; the excess and carnage in this version should have been enough to set Will Hays spinning in his grave.

Persuaded by Schenck not to make *Queer People*, frustrated over the enormous effort he'd put into films for marginal returns, and increasingly enamored of aviation, Howard Hughes, to the undoubted relief of the moguls, left the film business for nearly a decade. (When he returned, the censorship battle over Jane Russell's appearance in *The Outlaw* would make the fight over *Scarface* look like a schoolyard squabble.) Often scornful of his Hollywood work-for-hire, Ben Hecht in later years denigrated *Scarface*: "I didn't look at it," he lied. "I thought it was a cheapy film. Just cheap stuff." In fact, Hecht was deeply impressed with the film as it took shape on-screen, saying after he first saw it that, "It is the best-directed picture I have seen." However, he did offer an interesting critique of Muni's performance: "He didn't use any of his talents in *Scarface*. He was a lyric actor with a great deal of emotion. He was a make-believe tough guy. You think he's a menace, but he doesn't do anything. You write the part for him, you say he's tough, he's ruthless, but . . . he just stares. He's intelligent enough not to do the wrong thing." He also remarked, "I knew Capone. But as Muni played it, Capone was a silent, moody fellow who was a little like Hitler."

As for Hawks, whenever he was asked about his favorites among his own pictures, even as he shuffled the titles of the others, *Scarface* always remained at the top of the list. At least part of the reason was his fondness for the circumstances under which it was made. It was his favorite, he said in the 1970s, because, like high fliers and gamblers, "we were completely alone, Hughes and I." Speaking like John Wayne in *Rio Bravo*, he said he was proud that "we didn't get any help from anybody. And that's why I think I liked it best."

Scarface is far from a typical Hawks film. Few of his other films have a "rise and fall" structure (perhaps *Land of the Pharaohs* comes closest), and rarely again would overt stylistic flourishes assert themselves so prominently. Only a few more times would he work with "actors" rather "personalities," and only in his World War II films would contemporary "issues" again play a role in his work. Certainly, it would be wonderful to see the true "original" version of *Scarface*, before the Hays Office became an artistic collaborator on it; at the same time, even the tampering that was done to the picture couldn't eviscerate it, since Hecht and Hawks's cynical, playful, irreverent, defiant attitude comes through in nearly every scene. Muni's characterization may, in essence, be an artificial contrivance, but Hawks's direction to lighten his approach, to give Tony a childlike glee, was crucial and allows the performance to work anyway. Karen Morley is overly sullen as Poppy, the wafting moll, lacking the sassy vibrance that practically any Warner Bros. contract actress could have brought to the role, and even Osgood Perkins is perhaps a bit too cultured and refined as the boss Scarface must mow down to take over the town. The only significant flaw, however, is the characterization of the police as one-dimensional boobs. It would seem that Hecht and Hawks missed a beat in not at least making the lead cop on the case, Guarino, someone formidable or at least interesting to watch. C. Henry Gordon, however, comes off like a mediocre member of a stock company, rushing to and fro in almost mock-earnest fashion in his futile effort to get the upper hand on Scarface. The scenes with Tony's mother, which would have given the picture's cynicism an added layer of depth had they been done Hecht's way, also lend an air of creakiness to film as seen today. But *Scarface* remains, as it was in 1932, the last word on Chicago gangsterdom of the 1920s, the smartest, cleverest, punchiest portrait of an individual mobster's rise and fall. As would repeatedly happen throughout his career, Hawks didn't make the first entry in a given genre, but he made one of the best.

9

Back to Warners:
The Crowd Roars

Hawks came out of the *Scarface* experience not only liking the film but quite liking his producer. Judging that he and Hughes had become "very good friends," Hawks and the multimillionaire played golf together numerous times at various country clubs. At the time, Hawks had a four handicap, while Hughes had a five or six, and Hawks was amused that Hughes would never bet more than a dollar. He was also impressed by Hughes's "amazing stick-to-it-ive-ness" in improving his game. Hawks went for dinner several times to Hughes's Muirfield Drive home even though he tried to avoid it "because we were so badly fed. I'd get there for dinner and the butler would say, 'I don't know where he is.' And I'd say, 'Well, I'll find him.' And I'd go out and down to the garage and find him underneath the car, and he didn't know what time it was."

Hawks felt that they had one major thing in common: "He was not a communicative man . . . and neither am I." But in addition to films, the men's relationship seemed based more than anything on their mutual fixation on cars and planes: Hughes drove and admired Hawks's Dusenberg and decided he wanted one himself, although he continued to drive his beat-up Chevy when out by himself. "Many times he would call me and take that funny little Chevrolet that he had, and we'd go out in the desert and talk where—heck, I could yell and he wasn't afraid of being overheard, because he was extremely sensitive about that."

Given that Hughes was well on his way to becoming one of the three or four most famous aviators in America, Hawks still needed in his own mind to place himself above his friend, saying that Hughes asked him frequently about planes he was building "because I'd been flying for a lot longer than he had." Hawks never flew any of his friend's planes, since Hughes never labeled any of his control-panel dials—"That's kind of a quirk that he had," Hawks said admiringly—nor was Hawks terribly fond of riding as a passenger in planes piloted by Hughes, "because I didn't think he was a great flyer by any manner or means." In the end, despite the tycoon's eccentricities, Hawks found Hughes's outlook on things very compatible to his own. "I liked the way he did things. He would argue like the devil over ten cents and go out and spend three or four thousand dollars. And it never took me any time to get a decision from him. I was a great admirer of his aeronautical world, of the things he did. He built a pursuit plane that was far better than any the combined army and navy have . . . so that has to be pretty damn good engineering." Hawks said, "As far as I'm concerned, my type of man, Hughes was that type."

Hawks's passion for cars was at the root of his next film. As the sorry changes were being wrought on *Scarface*, Hawks was plotting to make his return to First National very much on his own terms. *The Barker: A Play of Carnival Life*, by Kenyon Nicholson, had been produced on Broadway in 1917 starring Walter Huston as a barker who is living with a younger woman. When his son comes to visit, the father doesn't want him to discover the arrangement, so the older man has his girlfriend recruit a friend of hers to seduce the son. Hawks liked this basic situation and decided to fold it into the sort of competitive story between two men that he instinctively favored.

More involved in yachting and boating of late, thanks to Athole, than in auto racing, Hawks initially considered setting the story in the milieu of speedboat racing, with James Cagney and Douglas Fairbanks Jr. as the leads, but he soon returned to the sport he knew better. As the resulting film, *The Crowd Roars*, eventually turned out, the story concerned an older, experienced race-car driver who takes his green-but-avid younger brother under his wing. The change from father-son to brother-brother could easily be interpreted as an autobiographical move on Hawks's part, a way of portraying his relationship with Kenneth on-screen. However, Hawks's original workup of the story, in which the characters are unrelated, shows that there's nothing to this analysis; the story is more an expression of how women can disrupt the close relationship between close male friends. Joe Greer, a "hard-boiled veteran of the racing game; four-time winner at Indianapolis," arrives with his buddy Spud Smith in Wichita, home of racing hopeful Eddie Murphy. After Eddie impresses him with his skills, Joe asks the kid to drive his number-two car in a race the next day. When Eddie wins, Joe invites him on the remainder of the tour, which ends in Los Angeles with the winter racing season.

Back in L.A., Joe's mistress, Lee, quickly comes to resent Joe's preoccupation with Eddie, whom Joe now feels is a potential champion. When Joe and Lee split up, Lee goes to stay with her friend Anne Morton—"a pretty girl, no virgin"—to persuade her to hook Eddie, then sink him. Instead, after a wild party, Anne falls in love with Eddie after sleeping with him, which finishes off Joe and Eddie's friendship. In the next race, Eddie races against Joe furiously; trying to avoid Eddie, Joe's buddy Spud crashes and dies, whereupon the guilt-ridden Eddie disappears.

Suddenly, it's Indy 500 time, and everyone converges there. Eddie and Anne meet again. During the race, Joe breaks an arm but keeps driving, but after Eddie, Anne, and Lee meet him during a pit stop, Eddie takes over in Joe's car. Haunted by the black smoke of an accident he is forced to pass through again and again, as he did when Spud died, Eddie spins out, but he's okay, and the foursome, reunited and grinning, head off "already planning next year's race."

In October 1931, shortly before he reported back to Hughes to rewrite material for *Scarface* retakes, Seton Miller was paged by Hawks to help him with the story; this would be their eighth, and final, collaboration. At once, the character relationships changed: Joe Greer and Eddie became brothers, and Lee is introduced at the outset, traveling with Joe and Spud. With his initial success, Eddie quickly becomes so cocky and obnoxious that Lee comes to hate him, and she isn't pleased when her friend Anne falls in love with him rather than getting him out of the picture. Instead of being Eddie's fault, Spud's death is laid at Joe's feet, and Joe then becomes a derelict. Wandering into Indianapolis, he runs into Lee in a hash house, and Joe watches his brother doing well in the race until Eddie breaks his arm. Joe jumps in to drive while Eddie takes the mechanic's seat, and as they spin out, the upbeat "wait 'til next year" ending remains.

Ever since seeing him for the first time, Hawks had wanted to work with Cagney, whose electric performance in *The Public Enemy* had shot him to stardom. With gangster films now out and Warner Bros. wanting to modify the star's image somewhat from the bantam tough guys he'd been playing, *The Roar of the Crowd*, as it was known during production, seemed like a good fit. To turn the Hawks-Miller story into a full screenplay, the studio's new production chief, Darryl F. Zanuck, turned to the lot's star writers, Kubec Glasmon and John Bright, who had written the previous four Cagney films. Hawks was about to leave for Indiana with cameraman Hans F. Koenekamp to shoot some background racing footage in Indianapolis, so Glasmon and Bright joined them, stopping in South Bend on the way to attend the Notre Dame–University of Southern California football game, soak up some atmosphere, and meet some actual race drivers.

Older and more conservative Glasmon was a mentor to Bright, a brash young left-winger who was responsible for a fair share of the proletarian fire that ripped through Warner Bros. films of the early 1930s. Unsurprisingly, Hawks took an immediate dislike to him, and Bright returned the compliment. While in Indianapolis, Glasmon and Bright stayed at a fleapit they called the "Hotel Cesspool" in order to hang out with the drivers, while Hawks stayed at the mansion of Fred Dusenberg, the maker, with his brother Augie, of the most elegant new car in the country. Dusenberg readily agreed to loan quite a few racing cars for use in the picture, and Hawks slyly managed to induce him to throw in a new Dusenberg for himself in exchange for the publicity.

Bright heard a true story from a racer about how a jealous driver had caused the death of a friend during a race and related it to Hawks, who was unresponsive. Bright was later amused to learn that Hawks had told the story to Zanuck as if it were his own, whereupon Zanuck recounted it back to Glasmon and Bright as if *he* had thought it up. This would be a typical example of Hawksian credit-taking if such an incident had not already been present in the treatments originally written by Hawks and then Miller.

While Hawks and Koenekamp remained in Indianapolis to shoot some racing footage, Glasmon and Bright were ordered home to knock out a draft. In their presence, Zanuck dictated a nine-page, single-spaced letter to Hawks that contained all their combined ideas about the script, a document that reveals Zanuck's leading role in making Warner Bros. films the sharpest, most vibrant, and fastest-paced of the early 1930s. Zanuck posited that although the story "may be lacking in plot twists, such twists are not essential with so colorful a background and such a sound foundation for a dramatic, human story." He also insisted that the script be cut down by a third, to no more than one hundred pages. The dialogue, he felt, "is lacking in the sparkle and the quick wit of the modern picture . . . we should tell our story in the modern manner of compressed drama. . . . What we want to achieve is the rapid story progression that we had in *The Public Enemy* and you had in *The Dawn Patrol*." To this end, he made dozens of specific points and suggestions and was vigilant about discarding clichés. He also felt that Anne shouldn't fall in love with Eddie after spending just one night with him. "The next sequence is after a lapse of time, and gives her time to fall in love with him. Otherwise he would have to have a terrifically long donniker to have her fall in love with him overnight." He also expressed alarm over the budget, pointing out that even *The Dawn Patrol*, one of Warners' biggest hits of the previous year, "made a net profit of less than $200,000—and pictures are not making anywhere near as much as they were when *The Dawn Patrol* was released."

After doing one rewrite of the first draft, Glasmon and Bright were ushered off the picture. Niven Busch, a twenty-eight-year-old writer just in from New York, where he had written for *Time* and the *New Yorker,* was brought in to rewrite during the shoot. For some reason, Zanuck believed Busch was supposed to be great with dialogue, although Busch had never written any in his life. Every evening after shooting, Busch would go to Hawks's Bedford Drive house, where "with unerring accuracy [Hawks] would describe how the [next day's] scene should go. I'd make rough notes, and then I'd go back to my apartment in Hollywood, with my memory fresh, [and] I'd write the scene, which would take me till after midnight." The next morning, Busch would be on the set with the fresh pages. Aside from the dialogue Cagney changed (and, in Busch's opinion, mostly improved) to suit his style, Busch claimed that all the dialogue in the picture was his. Busch, who went on to write such Western landmarks as *The Westerner, Duel in the Sun, Pursued,* and *The Furies,* also appeared in the film briefly as a gambler, ad-libbing a scene with Cagney.

Although he admired Hawks's talent, Busch admitted that he was hardly awestruck and "sort of felt [Hawks] was covering up something." Later on into the shoot, when he was feeling more confident, Busch dared to suggest that a scene ought to be written differently than the director was advising. Hawks stopped him with "his reptilian glare. The man had ice-cold blue eyes and the coldest of manners." As Busch recalled it, Hawks then said, "'Niven, we have no time to waste. I want to explain something to you. What we're writing and shooting is my adaptation of a play by Kenyon Nicholson called *The Barker.* It played on Broadway for two years. I have taken it out of a carnival setting and put it on the racetrack. It's working very well. Nobody is going to understand its source. Now, here is *The Barker.*' And he pulls out of his back pocket a tattered, coverless Samuel French play edition. He opens it and he says, 'Here is the scene we're shooting tomorrow. Write it the way it is here, but don't use the same words!'" Busch later asked him if he wasn't worried about a plagiarism suit, but Hawks replied that there was nothing to worry about since Warner Bros. already owned *The Barker.*

The first day of production was a night shoot on December 7 at Ascot Motor Speedway that lasted from 6:30 P.M. until 4:30 A.M. Thirteen race cars were photographed in action at what was known on the circuit as the "killer track" because, since its construction in 1924, it had claimed the lives of twenty-four drivers, more than any other track in the nation during the same period. Two additional outings were made to Ascot, and the worst mishap occurred when the car driven by Leo Nomis turned over and injured him. On the weekend before Christmas, Hawks and the crew also traveled to Ventura Race Track up the coast, although fog, low clouds, and wet conditions severely limited what could be shot there.

Originally, the sexy Warner Bros. contract player Dorothy Mackaill was cast as Lee, Cagney's mistress, with Hawks's playmate Ann Dvorak onboard as the temptress Anne. Just before shooting, however, Hawks decided he didn't care for Mackaill and brought in one of the studio's busiest young actresses, the spunky Joan Blondell, who had appeared repeatedly opposite Cagney of late. Once they got down to work, however, Blondell announced, "I can't play a neurotic," and Dvorak decided, "I can't play an ingenue," so, with Hawks's agreement, they swapped roles without even telling the studio.

Shooting six-day weeks right through the holidays, with only Christmas and New Year's Day off, and wrapping February 1 after twenty-six days of filming, longish for a Warners film of the time, Hawks enjoyed himself thoroughly, mostly because of the cars and Cagney. His adolescent interest in cars revived, Hawks recruited a dozen professional racers, including 1930 Indy winner Billy Arnold, to appear in the picture, and nothing like the wild action they created had ever been seen in feature films before. Both Dusenberg brothers came to the shoot to see what Hawks was up to with their cars, and Augie created a special tow bar that allowed one car to pull another and then release it automatically at a desired moment. In one scene, the dust becomes so thick that it's obvious the drivers can't see through it, creating considerable suspense, although no one got hurt filming it. For another sequence, gasoline was poured over a section of the track, and the resultant fire made for an equally exciting spectacle. The racing scenes are decidedly the highlights of the film, and so intense did they seem in their time that at the opening-night show caught by the New York press, several women became hysterical when Frank McHugh was burned and killed. "This is no movie for weak-hearted people," the *New York Graphic* advised.

Hawks adored working with Cagney because the actor was always coming up with things that surprised him on the set. Most "personality" actors, like Cary Grant, Gary Cooper, and John Wayne, delivered pretty much what their director knew they would. But Cagney "had these funny little attitudes, you know, the way he held his hands and things like that. I tried to make the most of them, and I think we did pretty well even though I didn't know how he worked."

Even though Cagney's Joe Greer is a hard-living, fast-talking guy in the manner of his earlier characterizations, this was generally considered a "reformed" role for the actor, after his portraits of bootleggers and killers. But while the racing footage was widely admired as exciting, the scenes in between were found rather routine, even dull by many reviewers. Today, the premise of an older brother having to hide his girlfriend from his younger brother seems like a bit of a stretch, and as Eddie, Eric Linden, like Phillips Holmes in *The Criminal Code* the year before, gives one of the rare bland "ingenue" performances in a Hawks film.

What's more, it is clear here that Hawks hasn't yet found his own formula for presenting women on the screen. Ann Dvorak, while good at what her cast-off lover role demands, plays a complainer, a woman who mopes about her sad predicament after being dumped by Joe. As such, she is highly atypical for a Hawks character; her type, like Eddie's, will quickly be banished from his world. The level on which *The Crowd Roars* promises to be most interesting, that of the rivalry between two adventurous brothers, also proves pretty much of a washout; the older brother is so dominant, and the relationship so unequal, that there is nothing particularly interesting or complex about it.

10
Tiger Shark

A Midwesterner, Howard Hawks never felt the call of the sea. However, he did heed the call of fashion, and as sailing became the rage among picture folk, Hawks yielded to the urgings of his wife and bought a yacht. Athole had done considerable sailing off Long Island before coming to California, and after Hawks bought a sixty-foot Norwegian sloop (which he named, naturally enough, the *Sea Hawk*), Athole became a very good sailor. With a good deal more time to devote to it than her husband, who in any event preferred golfing, flying, and hunting, Athole even took up boat racing. On one occasion during a race around Catalina Island, Athole's brother Doug fell overboard, and witnesses credited Athole with saving Doug's life, as she expertly brought the boat back around and fished him out before it was too late. Docked at San Pedro, the *Sea Hawk* was often taken on family outings to Catalina on weekends. Hawks was game for a while, learning the rudiments of sailing and enjoying the social side of it. But he would often get seasick and "never took to it too much," in their son David's view. Finally, taking the helm one day, Hawks made a navigational error and Athole corrected him. Furious at being faulted by his wife, Hawks never went sailing again.

Nevertheless, Hawks was to spend a good deal of time shipboard through the first half of 1932. On February 1, immediately upon wrapping *The Crowd Roars*, First National announced that Hawks would make "a fish story" called *Tuna*. First, however, Hawks and Athole would take a much-needed vacation together. After the breakneck schedule that saw him complete *The Dawn Patrol, The Criminal Code, Scarface*, and *The Crowd Roars* within two years' time, Hawks needed a breather. Their marriage also needed some attention. Although raising Peter, now seven, and David, now two, was gratifying and more than filled her time, Athole felt seriously neglected by her always-busy husband. "She would get upset if he wouldn't be home at 6 P.M., even if it was just because of late work at the studio," their daughter Barbara later said, and Hawks was rarely home by 6 P.M. Athole had basi-

cally recovered from the serious breakdown she had had the summer before, and at least she could be reassured that Howard's fling with Ann Dvorak
was over, presuming she knew about it at all, since the actress was engaged
to the British-born actor Leslie Fenton and would marry him in March.

Within a week of his finishing *The Crowd Roars*, Howard proudly
packed up his new brand-new kelly green, four-door, dual-cowl, soft-top
convertible Phaeton Dusenberg—very possibly the most beautiful automobile in America at that time—whereupon he and Athole set out up the coast
for San Francisco. There, they boarded the U.S.S. *President Lincoln* for the
four-day voyage to Honolulu.

Ensconced with his wife in a lanai at the Royal Hawaiian, the last word
in luxury on Waikiki Beach, Hawks was in a mood simply to relax under
the sun, swim, and have a few drinks. He had brought along Houston
Branch's twenty-three-page story outline for *Tuna*, as his hefty expense
account was predicated upon his promise to Zanuck that he would work
on it while he was gone, but Hawks was of no mind to worry about it. If
Hawks thought, however, that he'd be getting away from it all, he was in for
a surprise, as Hollywood was a lot closer than he could have imagined.

Who should suddenly turn up at the bar of the Royal Hawaiian but
King Vidor, Myron Selznick, Joel McCrea, Dolores Del Rio, and Clyde
De Vinna? RKO's big, exotic romance *Bird of Paradise* was intended to
shoot in Hawaii, but the local authorities were on a morality kick, and if,
where, and for how long the company could film was open to question.
Among the *Bird of Paradise* contingent was the thirty-one-year-old screenwriter Wells Root, a Yale man and former *Time* magazine drama critic who
had been brought along to polish the dialogue. Selznick introduced Root
to Hawks, who mentioned his own script predicament to the writer. The
next morning, Selznick was on the phone to Zanuck, and suddenly Root
had a new job.

As Vidor's demands on Root's time were minimal, the writer put himself at Hawks's disposal. "Howard said, 'Meet me on the beach and we'll
talk about the story.' But Howard didn't want to talk about the story. He'd
say, 'I don't feel like thinking about it today,' and that would be that. Really,
he felt he was there on vacation, and he didn't intend to work on a screenplay. Four weeks went by and we didn't have a single line. I was getting
nervous, because I was just a young writer, but he was so smooth and so
pleasant about the whole thing." Observing the Hawkses as a couple, Root
found Athole "very quiet, reserved and composed. . . . She was a perfect
lady, and a good complement to Howard in that respect."

Toward the end of March, Hawks and Athole and Wells Root and his wife boarded the *President Lincoln* for the trip home. "Howard said, 'We'll work on it on the ship,' but then he didn't want to work on the ship either. We got back to San Francisco and we still hadn't done anything.

"I said, 'I can't go back to Zanuck and say that nothing's been done.' Howard had this big, marvelous Dusenberg that he had driven to San Francisco, and he proposed putting our wives in back and discussing the script on the drive back to Los Angeles. So when we got to the car, he asked Athole to get in front. We got all the way back to L.A. and still hadn't done anything. We had a date to see Zanuck the next morning, and Howard said, 'I'm going to call Zanuck and tell him we have the story but we had a new idea on the boat and we haven't had time to write it up yet.' He managed to put off Zanuck for about a week, and I went to Howard's house and we worked like slaves."

During this compressed time, Root and Hawks "came up with basically an original story," the only similarities to Houston Branch's outline being the "Little Portugal" setting in San Pedro and the romantic triangle among the immigrant fisherman Miguel "Mike" Mascarenas, a woman, and a younger, better-looking man. What Branch had written was a vivid example of the sort of Depression era, proletariat-versus-exploitative-capitalist-owners story to which Warner Bros., far more than any other studio, was partial at that time. Inspired by a real dispute in the tuna industry at the time, the tale centered on a "fish war" in California between the fish canneries, with their big fishing boats, and the traditional, independent Portuguese fishermen who struggled just to make a living. His own boat sunk, Mike accepts a job from a local big shot and helps him bring in a record catch, but he can only stand by as the Portuguese crew members are screwed out of much of the money they've earned. The workers then decide to buy their own big boat, but must recruit an American citizen, Cardan, to purchase it. The wireless operator on the boat, the *San Christofero*, is a clean-cut fellow named Sparks, whom Mike subsequently saves from drowning. Still up against the cannery interests, Mike decides to become a U.S. citizen. When Mike correctly predicts that Cardan, too, will incite a disturbance to justify cheating the poor fishermen out of their share, he locks Cardan in the freezer, but the workers are shortchanged anyway. Finally, when Mike becomes a citizen and the captain of his own boat, he throws a party and "buys" the permanent companionship of Bobbie, an L.A. taxi dancer.

Unfortunately, it doesn't take long for Bobbie to fall for Sparks, whom the trusting Mike has made captain of his supply boat, nor for Cardan to inform Mike of his girl's affair. Enraged, Mike gives Cardan a time bomb to place aboard the supply boat. In the meantime, however, Mike's boat is split in two by a passenger liner in the fog and Mike is forced aboard the supply boat. Revealing what he's done, Mike sets out full throttle for home and throws everything overboard, attracting a swarm of sharks. After Mike himself ends up in the water and one shark is shot, the men all madly swim for shore, with Sparks helping Mike make it. Mike relinquishes his claim to Bobbie and, discredited among the other Portuguese, leaves town. The final scene finds him at the end of Santa Monica Pier, where he borrows a line to catch a fish. He sells it for a dime and buys a dance ticket, saying to a little blonde, "Didn't I tell you I'd be right back?"

Clearly, Hawks and Root had a lot of work to do if they were to make anything worthwhile out of all this. While his friend Bill Wellman might have been attracted to a hard-hitting attack on the ruthless cannery- and fishing-industry bosses, Hawks could never credit that sort of simplistic, ideological thinking; outside of the pro forma propaganda of his World War II pictures, there are virtually no overt politics, polemics, or even politically aligned characters in any Hawks film, except in incidental cases where the object is satiric, as in *I Was a Male War Bride,* or when the characters are soldiers or Western lawmen. His films are positively brimming with a *philosophy* of living and behavior, but this is never placed in a context that could be called political except in the most general of senses. Root said that not once during their several months together did Hawks ever mention politics. "I guess he just didn't have any," he surmised.

After a week during which Hawks and Root hammered out a new story line but put nothing down on paper, Zanuck would be denied no longer. "Hawks realized the spot I was in, and he was absolutely wonderful. First off, Hawks gave Zanuck the title *Tiger Shark,* which was the first time I heard it. He then proceeded in that quiet, convincing style of his to tell Zanuck the story, managing to fill in the holes, and he made it sound absolutely wonderful. He finished by apologizing for not having it all down on paper, saying we didn't think we could do the picture justice because some of the ideas we'd just had in the last couple of days."

Awestruck by Hawks's performance, Root promised to have the first draft ready within four weeks, a necessity because of the heavily committed schedule of Edward G. Robinson, who was set to star as Mike. "We hired two secretaries and I dictated to one in the morning and one in the afternoon. I had never worked that way before and never did again," recalled Root. "Howard would come in and read every day, he worked right along with it." Root hung around San Pedro to pick up dialect, and Hawks later enlisted a Portuguese fishing captain for the duration of the shoot to guarantee the authenticity of the dialogue.

Root wasn't the only one to notice a similarity in the story, as Hawks developed it, to Sidney Howard's 1924 Pulitzer Prize–winning play, *They Knew What They Wanted*, about a homely middle-aged wine grower in Napa Valley whose mail order bride runs off with a younger, good-looking worker. Neither Root nor anyone else said anything about it, however, a tribute to Hawks's stealthiness in his thievery. Years later, Hawks admitted that even while he was still in Hawaii, he "had figured on stealing *They Knew What They Wanted*." He was smart enough to know that "you don't just take a scene and paraphrase the dialogue. I doubt if you could find a *scene* in *They Knew What They Wanted* that was like one in *Tiger Shark*. It's only a basis." Picking up on Hawks's methods over the weeks, Root felt that a particular kind of brinksmanship represented a "strange key to his character. He was, in a sense, so heartless about risking this whole thing for his vacation. We were right on the edge almost all the time. But he cared enough to see that we got it done when it mattered, so we didn't really get in any trouble."

One of the key decisions Hawks and Root made, one derived rather obviously from *Moby Dick*, was to have, in the opening scene, a shark bite off Mike's hand, which is then replaced by a hook. "Giving him a hook on his arm was a lot of help to the character," Hawks maintained. "It removed him further from the girl, and it made him dangerous in an interesting way." At first, Robinson challenged his director about the need for the device, but he quickly came around, as he did when Hawks suggested he wear an earring. Most crucial of all, however, was the advice Hawks gave Robinson on the first day of shooting. "We started the picture with a dour man, thinking it'd have more drama and chance of violence when he found out about his wife's unfaithfulness. We shot until about three in the afternoon the first day, and I stopped things and said to Robinson, 'Eddie, this is going to be the dullest picture in the world. We have nothing to relieve it. All we've got is a dour, unpleasant man.'" Hawks told the actor about a man he knew who talked quickly and constantly to cover up his shyness, and suggested Robinson make Mike a blustering, happy-go-lucky fellow whom "you felt kind of sorry for and who could also be pretty tough." For Hawks, "the whole tenor of the picture changed" due to the alteration, much for the better, and it also made Mike something of a brother to Muni's Scarface—brutal, insensitive, but also somewhat innocent.

Robinson was initially wary of Hawks, who had all the Waspy qualities he frankly admitted made him feel insecure. "Howard seemed to be patrician, aristocratic, and I sensed he was looking down his nose at me," the actor revealed. But he soon came around to like and admire the director, paying him high praise indeed when he said that, as a Broadway actor, he didn't know anything about the difference between stage and screen acting until he worked with Hawks. "He instinctively knew that a movie had to tell its story pictorially. Screenplays in those days, particularly a Hawks screenplay, were very sketchy and vague scenarios rather than screenplays as we know them today. But in the abstract, Hawks had a good basic story. Hawks would describe what he wanted and rely on my stage experience to ad-lib and convey the feeling of a scene to the audience with more action than dialogue. Hawks's development of a story was not unlike improvisation." The latter was a term Hawks always scorned when it came into fashion years later. "They talk about 'improvisation.' That's one of the silliest words that's used in the motion picture industry. What the hell do they think a director *does*?" he asked sarcastically. "How do you expect that we can go out with a story that's written up in a room, go out to the location, and do it verbatim? I have never found a writer who could imagine a thing so that you can do it like that."

To film the extensive fishing sequences, Hawks once again enlisted Richard Rosson, who, with cameraman Byron Haskin and a sixteen-man crew, sailed between Ensenada, Magdalena Bay, the Socorro Islands, and Mazatlán on Mexico's Pacific Coast throughout most of April and May. Suffering just one minor casualty when a deckhand broke his ankle in an anchor line, this action unit filmed wonderfully evocative material, including the capture of sharks as well as nets full of tuna. They used a diving bell for some shots and were helped in other instances by an old flying squadron friend of Hawks's equipped with an airplane that was used to fly out to look for schools of tuna. In the early 1930s it was rare for any director, let alone one of Hawks's stature, to entrust someone else to film key sequences for him, but Hawks thought so much of Rosson that he gave him such authority and was confident that the material "would come back just as though I'd made it." It was with work like this, which generated considerable comment upon the film's release, that Dick Rosson almost single-handedly invented the job of second-unit director.

By early April, Hawks and Root had revamped the story line to something quite close to what appeared in the finished film. In the initial script, which Zanuck liked for its story and atmosphere but criticized for having too much melodrama and action and not enough detailing of Mike's "strange character and strange psychology of life," numerous motifs favored by Hawks suddenly appeared: mutilation (Mike receives a facial scar, à la Scarface, in the opening scene, before his hand is bitten off by a shark), a painful extraction (Mike must pull a fish hook out of his buddy's neck, prefiguring a similar scene nearly twenty years later in *The Big Sky*), and a near suicide (Quita — formerly Bobbie — is about to kill herself over having been deserted by a married man when Mike arrives just in time). A song used to parallel Mike's being cuckolded recalled the effective device from *Scarface* of Tony whistling the operatic tune just prior to committing a murder. Any mention of politics was now gone, and a final tag scene was written to give the film some uplift at the end, but it ultimately was not used.

Root was hurriedly finishing the script, and trying out three different endings, when Hawks began shooting on April 28. Hawks was receiving his highest directing fee yet, $50,000, while star Edward G. Robinson drew $46,666. Feeling that a glamorous movie-star type would be all wrong for the troubled, working-class girl Quita, Hawks remembered Zita Johann, a Hungarian-born actress whom he had seen onstage in New York and who had an odd, off-center, interestingly ethnic quality, and borrowed her from RKO, where she had just signed, for fifteen hundred dollars a week. Paramount loaned Richard Arlen at the same price to play Pipes, and Hawks brought back Vince Barnett for a little pre–Walter Brennan comic relief. Zanuck had made Hawks's whispery-voiced pal Raymond Griffith an associate producer at the studio as a payback for favors Griffith had done for him when Zanuck was struggling to find a toehold in the industry, and Hawks was glad to have him onboard as the production supervisor. The affable Bryan Foy, whom the director also liked, repeated as nominal producer for Zanuck, as he had done on *The Crowd Roars*.

The first scenes shot were those between Robinson and Johann in Quita's boardinghouse, and from the outset, it was clear Hawks's pace was about half of what the studio expected. Zanuck respected Hawks immensely and tolerated the overages, but his measured manner of working infuriated nearly every other studio executive Hawks ever worked for, as did Hawks's high-handed disregard for matters of schedule and budget and his refusal to work if a producer or executive so much as set foot on a set. Hawks virtually institutionalized rewriting and trying new things on the set, saying, "You're not trying to photograph a budget or a cost sheet. You're trying to make a scene that's going to be good, the best you know how." On the other hand, Niven Busch felt that "the reason he was slow was he didn't want to make any mistakes."

Wells Root was on the set every day trying to fine-tune the dialogue, and his proudest impromptu contribution came when Hawks needed a better comeback line for Quita after Mike challenges her with, "So you think you're better than I am?" "So far," Root had her say, which Hawks heartily approved. Nevertheless, the director still felt the dialogue overall left something to be desired and turned to his *Scarface* collaborator John Lee Mahin, who had since signed a two-hundred-dollar-a-week contract with MGM on the basis of recommendations from Hawks and Charles MacArthur. Mahin moonlighted on *Tiger Shark*, noting, "I'm sure Howard told Warner Brothers that he had rewritten it, you know. But that's all right, I don't mind, it's just one of Howard's charms." All the scenes were set, so Mahin, who found the existing dialogue "very pedestrian," felt that his main job was to "lighten it up," mostly for Robinson's speeches.

Robinson no doubt believed that the modest dialogue changes he was getting were indeed coming from Hawks, while Root was unaware that Hawks had engaged another writer sub rosa to polish up his stuff. "There were no hunks of dialogue coming in from left field while I was on set," Root maintained. "And when I saw the finished picture, I would have noticed if there were any major changes." Root found that Hawks "was a man who favored great economy of dialogue," and he figured that the director was always looking for ways to whittle scenes to their essence, especially in a script that, at 125 pages, was far too long for a film that shouldn't run more than ninety minutes.

After three weeks of studio work, in mid-May the company moved down the coast to San Diego to do seven days' work on the wharf, where they ran into constant delays because of noise from boats, planes, and whistles. After a couple of more days back at the studio, on May 28 the crew moved to Catalina Island off Los Angeles for the duration of the shoot. Joined by Rosson's outfit, Hawks then shot all the shipboard sequences with the principals. Hawks arrived at the Isthmus of Catalina on his own yacht and took to directing wearing a blue pea coat and captain's hat. By chance, the film version of Somerset Maugham's *Rain* (ironically, the play Tony and his henchmen go to see in *Scarface*), directed by Hawks's friend Lewis Milestone and starring Walter Huston and Hawks's old flame Joan Crawford, was being shot at the Isthmus at the same time. Every evening there were cocktails and lively parties onboard the yachts of the combined companies.

Ray Griffith was on hand to represent the studio and engaged Hawks in almost daily conferences regarding the script, which was continually in flux. Root was still around to contribute his ideas, especially for the ending, which remained unsettled, and he initiated what became a lifelong friendship with Zita Johann's husband, the future producer John Houseman, who stayed close to the production to be with his wife as well as to learn everything he could about the filmmaking process. Houseman claimed that for a short time, thanks to his wife's agent, Leland Hayward, he "became one of the five writers whom Hawks kept in various hotel rooms writing different versions of the script, from which he would, each morning on the set, extract the lines that took his fancy. Not one word of mine was ever used and I soon stopped trying and spent all day on the pier watching him shoot." (Who the other two writers might have been, if they existed at all, cannot be fathomed.)

Shooting of the climactic shark attack involved using two giant sharks Rosson's crew had caught and then frozen, which were subsequently wired to "perform" violent actions for the scenes. Finally, on Saturday, June 11, a day that stretched until 4 A.M. Sunday, when Hawks filmed Richard Arlen getting hooked in the neck, the production wrapped after forty-one days, seventeen days over schedule. Two weeks later, one more day of filming was required to enact the beach campfire scene among the three principals.

Watching Hawks throughout the shoot, Root came away exceedingly impressed with his boss's "supreme ego and self-confidence that, in a jam, he could pull it off. . . . He was magnificent in a pinch." At the same time, "He didn't play God or fling his ego about like some others. As a director, he was the ultimate pragmatist, who'd found out that certain things worked and others didn't, which resulted in a simplicity that was impressive." In other ways, the writer found Hawks a curious case. "He seemed to be more an observer as a director, more than the one who was making it happen. . . . He didn't seem to give the actors much direction. He let the actors bring the scenes to life. He let the actors do it first their way, and he knew when he didn't like something. . . . On the stage or story, you always knew where he was coming from, you always knew what he thought of something. This was certainly not true in his private life."

On June 28, four days after the completion of *Tiger Shark* and two other pictures, Warner Bros. closed its gates until August to consolidate and cut costs during a difficult period. Hawks's films only helped the studio, however, as both of his 1932 films for the studio did very well at the box office. *The Crowd Roars* had opened in March to great figures at the Winter Garden in New York, and in May, just as *Scarface* was beginning to fan out across the country, the racing picture debuted in Los Angeles with strong results, which were repeated throughout the country.

Tiger Shark, which opened a very big four-week run at the Winter Garden in New York on September 22 and was a strong attraction for the studio, stands as a fine example of Hawks's talent for injecting unexpected comedy into inherently dramatic, even tragic, material. At least one critic felt that the milieu and narrative trajectory of *Tiger Shark* suggested Eugene O'Neill, and it's easy to imagine the story played for heavy, somber effect. If less profound, Hawks's approach of mixing moods and blending tones seems more modern and invigorating. It also planted a thematic seed that would be taken up in another, massively successful shark tale more than forty years later.

11

Sidetracked at MGM: Faulkner, Thalberg and *Today We Live*

Everything except common sense dictated that Hawks should join Metro-Goldwyn-Mayer. The one studio that was sailing through the worst of the Depression with its head above water, MGM had, in a few short years, unquestionably established itself as the classiest shop in town, the studio with the biggest stars, the largest reserves of money, and the most glamour, power, and prestige. Although he still had to answer to Nicholas Schenck, Joseph's brother and the head of MGM's parent company, Loews, in New York, Louis B. Mayer was widely regarded as the most powerful man in the motion picture business. What other studio chief had spent a night in the White House, even if the president he had so avidly supported, Herbert Hoover, was almost certainly about to be voted out of office in November? Mayer still had the clout to turn the tide against the California gubernatorial candidate Upton Sinclair by flooding movie theaters with scare-mongering propaganda shorts about what would happen to the state if the socialist-minded author actually gained power.

None of this concerned Hawks so much as the fact that he knew Mayer, from his previous tenure at the studio seven years earlier, to be a blow-hard, a phony, overemotional, hypocritical, unrefined tyrant whose taste in films—sentimental, gilded, weepy, family-and-country-oriented—couldn't have been more antithetical to his own approach.

Tipping the scales in the other direction was the best motivation of all in Hollywood: nepotism. With Hawks's stock so dramatically increased over the past two years, Irving Thalberg was more anxious than ever to have his brother-in-law on his roster of directors, and it seemed only logical to him that bringing Hawks in would keep the family closer together. Knowing Hawks's literary values, Thalberg also felt that Hawks could only benefit from MGM's superior lineup of writers and vast trove of source materials, the most extensive in the industry. After his trip around the world, Vic Fleming had rejoined MGM, and his best friend's presence on the lot was something they would both enjoy. For Hawks, it would also mean ultimate prestige after his pairings with the maverick Howard Hughes, the crude Harry Cohn and Jack Warner, and the rough-and-tumble Darryl Zanuck. But most of all, it would mean big, and much needed, money.

Although he spoke of it to no one except Fleming, Hawks was often in debt and in constant need of cash. Because he was born to it, inherited more, married into Hollywood aristocracy, and was now making more than most directors in town, Hawks had little sense of the value of earned money. His sporting hobbies and taste for planes, cars, the yacht, guns, country clubs, fine clothes, parties, and more were par for the course in Hollywood and within reason considering his position. His decisions to build beautiful homes in the best parts of town were astute, but he never kept an eye on his earnings and, increasingly, he tossed away money gambling. Just as Hawks acted as though he were oblivious to his producers' money during production, so he was with his own cash. "Howard borrowed large sums from Victor Fleming at various times," Wells Root said, most often to cover gambling debts to shady characters that could have walked straight out of *Scarface.* "He was a man of extraordinary courage because he wouldn't let the underworld or anyone else phase him."

Men express and play out their need for excitement and adventure in innumerable ways; for Hawks, it came in the thrill of the contest, of placing himself at risk and on the brink of losing, but knowing that he was "good enough" to pull himself out and prevail. There was nothing more consistent than this in Hawks's character; it was true in the way he directed films, for the characters in his films, and in the way he conducted his personal life. Unlike some of his friends and colleagues, such as Bill Wellman and John Huston, who were wild and often irresponsible, Hawks was reckless but within a conservative shell. No one has ever claimed to have seen Howard Hawks lose his composure, his calm demeanor, or his sense of control, even when drunk, angry, or under severe pressure. By the same token, no one saw him deliriously happy or celebratory. "I suppose that, beneath that granite exterior, he must have had the same insecurities as other people," Root speculated. But none that he ever showed.

Moving from Warner Bros. to MGM, which Hawks did in July 1932, just after finishing *Tiger Shark,* was like writing his own prescription for frustration. He could convince himself that his relationship with Thalberg would accord him a privileged position, protection from the whims and dictates of Mayer. But Thalberg was no more a believer in the cinema of the director than his boss, and he had, in fact, been the instigator of the movement by producers and executives to retake control of the production process when he fired Erich von Stroheim from *Merry-Go-Round* at Universal in 1922. Since their bachelor days, when they had endlessly swapped film story ideas, Hawks, like so many others in Hollywood, had felt that Thalberg "was the great genius in the picture business." But in the end, the forces of studio policy, the star system, and sheer accident proved far stronger than Hawks, Thalberg, or their friendship, and Hawks's spell at MGM turned into one of the most unproductive detours of his career. Even so, it provided the beginnings of two of the most enduring professional and personal relationships of his life, those with William Faulkner and Gary Cooper.

Hawks's contractual obligations to various parties at the time he finished *Tiger Shark* were a bit fuzzy, even to the attorneys representing the companies he'd been working for. Technically, Hawks was still under contract to Howard Hughes's Caddo Company under the terms of the multipicture deal he'd signed in order to make *Scarface*. Though Hughes had decided to leave the film business, at least temporarily, his attorney Neil McCarthy wasn't ready to just tear up Hawks's contract, but he did agree that the director was free to work for others. As for First National, even though Hawks had directed *The Crowd Roars* and *Tiger Shark* under a new two-picture deal, the studio still took the position that Hawks owed it another film from his previous deal. In mid-June, upon finishing *Tiger Shark*, Hawks met with Hal Wallis to discuss possible story ideas, and the same old cycle started up again. Wallis proposed that Hawks direct Richard Barthelmess in something called *Shanghai Orchids*. Upon reading it, Hawks refused, whereupon Wallis, feeling it was within his rights, obstinately demanded that Hawks do as he was told. Whatever doubts, if any, Hawks had about absconding for MGM vanished in the face of Wallis's intransigence, and it was arranged that First National would simply turn over Hawks's contract to Metro, on the condition that Hawks return to First National to fulfill his contract there by directing one more picture by the following April. As it happened, it would be two years beyond that before Hawks would return to the house of Jack Warner and Hal Wallis.

The precariousness of Hawks's finances can be glimpsed in a lawsuit he filed at the beginning of 1932, which prompted a retaliatory countersuit. One of the low points of his career had been his firing by Fox after he had finished the unreleasable *Trent's Last Case*. From any reasonable standpoint, what happened on that forlorn picture was far from being entirely the director's fault. But Hawks's renegotiated salary had just kicked in at $50,000 per picture, so rather than continue to pay him, Fox decided to dump Hawks, even though the director owed the studio one more picture. Hawks did nothing about this for nearly three years. Finally, however, in need of more funds, he decided to sue Fox for the $65,000 he believed he was still owed under his contract, since he claimed he was "wrongfully discharged" by Fox.

Insulted and annoyed, Fox fired back in May with a suit of its own, which stated that while in its employ in December 1928, Hawks had received a five-thousand-dollar loan from the studio, to be paid back on demand, or with the sum taken out of his salary if necessary. By the time of his firing in May 1929, Hawks had paid back just one thousand dollars and therefore still owed Fox four thousand. Deposed in the case on June 7 while still on Catalina shooting the final scenes of *Tiger Shark*, Hawks claimed that the five thousand was an advance on salary at Fox and denied that he owed it. In the end, both cases came to naught.

Early in July, when an economically depressed Los Angeles was becoming swept up in the excitement of staging the 1932 Olympic Games, Hawks checked into his new offices on the MGM lot in Culver City. By chance, the six-week, five-hundred-dollars-a-week contract of a writer Hawks greatly admired was coming to an end. The writer was William Faulkner, and from a dry, businesslike meeting that apparently ended in a drunken bender grew a friendship that was central to the lives of both men.

In fact, Hawks had been one of William Faulkner's earliest American champions. Hawks was one of the few to have read the author's 1926 novel *Soldier's Pay*, which a few years later he recommended to some assembled literati at Ben Hecht's home in Nyack. In the interim, the Mississippian had developed an ardent following within small circles for *The Sound and the Fury* and *As I Lay Dying* but was known mainly for his notorious 1931 novel *Sanctuary*. This had made him something of a literary commodity, at least enough for Leland Hayward, then an agent with the American Play Company, to take him on for Hollywood representation. That winter, Sam Marx, the erudite head of MGM's story department, inquired as to Faulkner's availability, but the writer, expecting royalties from the unexpectedly popular *Sanctuary*, declined the offer. However, when his publisher, Harrison Smith, went bankrupt early the following year, Faulkner, on the hook financially for the new home he had just bought in Oxford, Mississippi, felt he had no choice but to undertake a quick mercenary expedition to Hollywood, where he arrived for the first time in May 1932.

Literary lore is rife with stories—some true, some no doubt apocryphal or greatly exaggerated—of Faulkner's initial misadventures in Hollywood: how his long, reserved silences and—when he did talk—often indecipherable Southern drawl put people off; his abrupt disappearance to wander around Death Valley; his legendary boozing; his suggestion that he would be best writing cartoons or newsreels; his disdain for most Hollywood films; and, most famously of all, his proposal that he be allowed to write at home, with the agreeable studio not realizing that what he meant by home was Mississippi, not his Los Angeles residence. Faulkner was hired at a time when the studios, still settling into the sound era, were eagerly looking for anyone who could write good, pungent dialogue, and while Faulkner's loquacious tendencies and rural subjects ran basically counter to the sort of fast talk and urban material favored in films at the time, his reputation, however marginal and vaguely lurid, made him a plausible bet for a short-term tryout.

On his initial tour of duty at MGM, Faulkner wrote four short treatments, none of which came to anything. After six weeks, the studio decided not to renew his option, then hesitated and offered an extension at $250 per week, half of what he had been getting. It was an offer the writer could refuse, since Paramount had just given Leland Hayward $750 for a four-month option on *Sanctuary*, at the end of which it paid almost seven thousand dollars to buy it (it was subsequently filmed as *The Story of Temple Drake*). On top of that, MGM had paid three thousand dollars for the rights to Faulkner's short story "Turn About," published in the *Saturday Evening Post* on March 5 of that year. By Faulkner's standards, he was flush, with no need for a workaday job at a time when he was about to read galleys on his latest novel, *Light in August*. But he got a call from Howard Hawks, at whose request the studio had bought his story (Bill Hawks handled the transaction), and agreed to meet with him.

Physically, the men were a study in contrasts, Hawks long and lean, his prematurely gray-white hair clipped almost to the skull, Faulkner a full foot shorter, compact, his dark hair a bit unruly, with an odd way of walking while seeming to lean backward. But people couldn't help but note the far greater number of similarities. Just a year apart in age, with Hawks the senior, both were reserved to the point of noncommunicativeness; Nunnally Johnson was astonished by the sight of the two of them just sitting together not saying a word. When they did talk, they did so slowly, in a drawling manner. While very much of their respective regions, they were both Anglophiles, favored comfortable tweeds, and smoked pipes as well as cigarettes.

The two had both served in World War I but had not gotten overseas, although this didn't stop them from basing much of their work on the conflict, particularly the air war. Each was the oldest of three brothers, had stepchildren, and was in a marriage that already showed signs of fissure. They hunted and fished, and both liked to drink, although one rather more than the other.

In Hawks's account of their first meeting, when he introduced himself upon the writer's arrival in his office, Faulkner replied, "I've seen your name on a check." "I remember that very well," Hawks said, "because I wanted to kill him. And he didn't say anything else. He just sat there, and the more he sat there, the madder I got and the more I talked." Hawks basically told Faulkner that he wanted him to write the screen adaptation of "Turn About," and that he wished him to follow the original story as closely as possible. "'Well,' I said, 'that's all.' 'O.K.,' he said, 'I'll go.' I said, 'Well, wait a minute. What are you going to do? When am I going to see you again?' He said, 'Four or five days.' I said, 'Oh, Mr. Faulkner, it shouldn't take four or five days to digest what I've just told you.' He said, 'No, to write it.' I said, 'Are you serious?' and he said, 'Yes. You made it very clear what you wanted. I can remember it all. It won't take me more than five days.' 'Well,' I said, 'I was looking forward to meeting you. Would you like a drink?' He said, 'I'd love one.'"

In one account of what happened next, the two men went on a giant drinking tear that ended the following morning in a Culver City motel room with "Faulkner groping for cigarette stubs in a mint julep glass." Hawks merely said, "By the time we'd killed a couple of quarts of whiskey, I took a real drunk man home and he got up the next morning and started to work, and in five or six days he had a script." Hawks gave the novice screenwriter some basic guidelines, the most important being, "The first thing I want is a story; the next thing I want is character." Stunned at the high quality of his new friend's work, Hawks took the scenario to Thalberg and insisted that he read it at once. Thalberg concurred with Hawks's assessment and directed, "Shoot it as it is. I feel as if I'd make tracks all over it if I touched it."

As originally written, "Turn About" stood a good chance of becoming a formidable companion piece to *The Dawn Patrol*, a terse, compelling look at young soldiers daily risking their lives on highly perilous missions during World War I, complete with a suicidal ending. Faulkner's tale centered on an American pilot, Captain Bogard, who becomes involved with two British best friends, Claude Hope and Ronnie Boyce Smith, who run a small torpedo boat. To show them some real combat thrills, Bogard takes the boys up on a bombing mission, whereupon they take him out on one of their torpedo runs, which are highly dangerous as the torpedoes are released from the rear, requiring the speedboat to turn quickly to get out of the way. In the one significant change requested by Hawks, Claude is blinded by head injuries sustained in the attack (yet another instance of mutilation or blindness in his films). In a subsequent attack on a German cruiser, the torpedo-release mechanism jams, so Ronnie, with the sightless Claude on-board, decides to ram the vessel. When he hears of his friends' deaths, Bogard, in a rerun of the *Dawn Patrol* finale, undertakes a solo raid on an ammunition depot, then furiously continues on to bomb enemy headquarters, exclaiming, "God! God! If they were all there—all the generals, the admirals, the presidents and the kings—theirs, ours—all of them."

Fatalistic and enshrouded in a doom lightened only by booze and the camaraderie of beautiful young men, "Turn About" might well have become a noteworthy addition to the Lost Generation cycle of film and literature, and its streamlined structure and clipped dialogue are strong enough to make very clear what Hawks would have done with it. However, what happened to "Turn About" stands as an almost grotesque illustration of the studio system at its worst. It is also an exceedingly rare example of the fiercely independent Hawks accepting without complaint a demand that he had to know would ruin his film. He complied because he knew he had no choice, and because he was working for Thalberg now and wasn't about to treat his brother-in-law in the high-handed manner he treated Jack Warner or Hal Wallis.

Scarcely a week after Thalberg had told Hawks to shoot the script as it was, studio vice president Eddie Mannix, a tough Irishman with whom Hawks got along famously, informed the director that his all-male picture was now to be a vehicle for Joan Crawford. It was common practice at the studio to quickly revamp projects to tailor them for stars who suddenly became available, and Hawks knew that he had nothing to say about the matter. Hawks, who liked Crawford a good deal personally and, as he enigmatically put it, "used to go around with her," went to talk to the actress and said he found her "sitting there with tears dribbling into her coffee cup." She said, "'Are they kidding, Howard?' and I said, 'No.' Oh, she started to cry, and I said, 'Now, look—you have to do it and I have to do it. If you're gonna make drama out of it, it'll all be hell. If we decide to have fun and do it, we'll have a nice time. What do you want to do?' She said, 'We'll have fun.' I said, 'O.K.'"

Hawks broke the news to Faulkner by saying, "That's the picture business, Bill," and Faulkner quickly determined that the best way to shoehorn Crawford into the story was to make her an ambulance nurse. On August 6, however, Faulkner's father, Murry, died, at the age of sixty-two. Returning to Oxford, the writer promised Hawks he'd finish the rewrite at home, which he did, delivering it within a week. Crawford would play Ann, Ronnie's sister. Upper-class children, they had grown up like siblings to Claude, their closest friend, who always thought he would marry Ann. Ronnie and Ann also seem so close as to recall the incestuous feelings of *Scarface*, so the arrival of the dominant American, Bogard, into this mix takes on the dimension of a major disruption of apparent destiny among these altruistic English kids. At Crawford's request, Faulkner gave Ann the same sort of exaggeratedly clipped, low-on-pronouns style of speech that the two English male characters had, hoping to reduce the sentimentality MGM would invariably want to emphasize. To build up the special friendship of Ann, Ronnie, and Claude, he also wrote a childhood prologue, and later a section showing how Bogard and Ronnie had been classmates at Oxford.

In a very short time, and under the terribly adverse conditions of family tragedy, Faulkner did a remarkable job in reconfiguring "Turn About" to the studio's specifications. Still, it was felt that the script needed more work, and there were unresolved casting questions. MGM wanted to use Phillips Holmes as Claude, a choice Hawks, after *The Criminal Code*, was not crazy about. But the main concern was who would play Bogard. Currently shooting *Red Dust* with Vic Fleming, Clark Gable was on the verge of becoming MGM's biggest male star, and the studio had any number of properties waiting for him. First up, as it happened, was a goofy little story Hawks had had a hand in writing, *The Prizefighter and the Lady*, which was designed as a follow-up pairing of Gable and Jean Harlow after *Red Dust*. However, the suicide of Harlow's new husband — and Hawks's friend — Paul Bern in early September put an end to that idea. At one point, MGM even considered "doubling" Gable, working out his schedule so that he could act in two films at once. But Hawks, although friendly with Gable, had his eye on Gary Cooper, whom he had found so effective in Sternberg's *Morocco*. Cooper, who was currently starring in *A Farewell to Arms*, was under contract at Paramount but might be available at the right price. Waiting for Cooper would mean waiting until December, however, and in the meantime, MGM had some other ideas about how they might employ Howard Hawks.

Even if MGM was having an easier ride through the Depression than the other studios, there was still a sense of foreboding. The threats of strikes and the organizing of Hollywood labor were gaining force, and no one was more opposed to these left-wing notions than Mayer and Thalberg. Barring some miracle, it seemed certain that Mayer's friend Herbert Hoover would be out of the White House come January, replaced by the dreaded Franklin D. Roosevelt. Within the studio, Thalberg's always-frail health had taken a turn for the worse; under doctor's orders to rest and cut back his schedule, Thalberg had no option but to look for some people he could trust to help him do his job, and for him, Hawks was a natural choice. In Thalberg's view, just about anyone could direct, but it took a special talent to recognize stories that had real screen potential, as well as to the work with writers and directors to help realize that potential. Thalberg had always felt that Hawks possessed the talent to cut through to the most fertile dramatic essence of a story, and Hawks definitely knew both how to communicate with writers and how to get them to produce. Toward the end of September, with "Turn About" on hold, Thalberg asked Hawks and another director, Sidney Franklin, to become his lieutenants. Franklin wound up going on to a very comfortable career at the studio for another twenty-five years, but for Hawks, the whole thing, a disagreeable reminder of his short stint at MGM eight years earlier, represented a step in precisely the opposite direction from where his career had been building ever since. Nonetheless, Hawks felt obliged to accept, with the proviso that he still be allowed to direct, and the appointments were reported in *Variety*: "In realigning the production forces at Metro, and to relieve himself of considerable burden, Irving Thalberg is assigning Howard Hawks and Sidney Franklin, directors, to supervisory powers. Both men will continue to direct pictures in addition to handling four productions a year. At the time Hawks, who is Thalberg's brother-in-law, joined Metro it was figured that he would become the latter's chief aid. His new duties may shortly bring him to that position."

In short, Hawks had a golden opportunity for a career countless others in Hollywood might have killed for: to become, if he wanted, the third most powerful executive at the world's most eminent film studio. But he had backed away from such a position twice before, at MGM and Paramount, and he would back away from it again now. He knew a full-time office job wouldn't suit him temperamentally: he liked the breaks between pictures to pursue his sporting interests, and he was loathe to give up a schedule that, when he wasn't shooting, left his Wednesdays free for golf. He certainly didn't want to have to report to Louis B. Mayer and deal with him daily. But most of all, even if he never said it in so many words, he was an artist; he needed to create, he needed the thrill that came from working with actors and writers on the set, of being out on a limb and cleverly working out how to get down. Even if Hawks agreed to his brother-in-law's plan, he would simply continue with his directing projects. Sooner, rather than later, the impracticability of his double role would certainly become apparent.

One of the reasons that coming to MGM had looked appealing to Hawks was that Vic Fleming was there. But such close proximity also made the competition between them very direct and apparent for all to see. Therefore, Hawks's own vicissitudes at the studio stood out in even greater relief against Fleming's terrific career upswing. Fleming had just directed Clark Gable and Jean Harlow in *Red Dust*, and the chemistry was in place for one of the more scorching box-office blockbusters MGM had during that period. The first preview took place at the Alexandria Theater in Glendale, and John Lee Mahin, who wrote *Red Dust*, vividly remembered how tremendously its reception bothered Hawks. "Howard was always very jealous of Victor. He went to the preview of *Red Dust* with us. I rode home with him to Vic's house, and Vic drove with somebody else. It had gone over very well. Howard was silent for a long while; then he said, 'I wonder where Vic got that story.' I said, 'What do you mean, where did Vic get that story?' Howard said, 'Where'd he steal it?' I said, 'It came in a fifteen-page treatment of a story to MGM called *Red Dust*, and it was a very purple melodrama about a poor little slaving whore—she got whipped by the heavy, fell in love with Gable from afar, and that's all that happened. So, we decided to turn it into a comedy-drama.' He said, 'Well, I don't know. I think I've heard that story somewhere.' He just couldn't face the fact."

With nearly three months to go before "Turn About" would be ready for the cameras, Mayer saw no reason why Hawks shouldn't direct a film in the interim, so he was assigned to take over *The Prizefighter and the Lady*. When he was at the studio briefly in 1925, Hawks had written a story called "The Roughneck and the Lady," which was earmarked for Norma Shearer but never used. Although the credits of *Prizefighter* attribute the "original story" to Frances Marion, the film bears a strong resemblance to Hawks's earlier yarn, which concerned a lowlife woman who transforms herself into a "lady," only to take up with a boxer while hiding from the police after her gambling establishment has been raided.

Hawks claimed that he developed the story with Josef von Sternberg as a kind of lark. As it emerged years later, it was a silly but workable story about a boxer who becomes involved with a big gangster's lady, and it might have amounted to something with the original Gable-Harlow pairing. But then the studio had the idea of casting real boxers, starting with Max Baer in the Gable role and supported by Primo Carnera and Jack Dempsey. As the moll, the irrepressibly classy Myrna Loy was as implausible a choice as Norma Shearer would have been. This was definitely not the sort of film Hawks came to MGM to make, and he tried to refuse. But Hawks couldn't play games with Mayer the way he had with Warner and Wallis, so, for the second time in three months, he had no choice.

Recasting the experience in retrospect to his own advantage, Hawks claimed that he began directing the film only as a favor, to "do a couple of weeks' work" with Baer to "teach him a little about acting." Hawks said he "made two or three good opening scenes and then [W. S. (Woody)] Van Dyke stepped in and shot the rest." John Lee Mahin, who wrote the film with John Meehan and Frances Marion, remembered things a bit differently, stating that Hawks "was two days on that, and he was six days behind schedule. He probably thought he could get away with it at Metro. But Mayer just put his foot down and said, 'This has got to stop.'" In Mahin's view Hawks didn't fit in at MGM because "he wouldn't take the regimen. He wasn't used to it. You know, he wouldn't allow Hughes on the set. . . . Even at Warners, I think he got away with it. And that's pretty tough to do when you're talking about Jack Warner. But he couldn't get away with it at MGM." Of course, it is entirely possible that Hawks deliberately slowed down to the point where he knew he would be replaced, all the better to go hunting with Faulkner, who was now back in town, and return their attention to "Turn About."

A hunting trip that fall gave birth to one of Hawks's favorite stories. It is impossible to verify, of course, but definitely belongs to the "print the legend" category. Hawks: "Faulkner and I were going dove hunting down in Imperial Valley. Gable called up and said, 'What are you doing?' I told him. He said, 'Can I go?' I said, 'Sure, if you get over here in a hurry.' So we hired a station wagon, and we started down with a couple of bottles of bourbon. We were coming through Palm Springs, and the talk was about writing. Gable asked Faulkner who the good writers were. And Faulkner said, 'Thomas Mann, Willa Cather, John Dos Passos, Ernest Hemingway, and myself.' Gable looked at him and said, 'Oh, do you write, Mr. Faulkner?' And Faulkner said, 'Yeah. What do you do, Mr. Gable?' I don't think Gable ever read a book, and I don't think Faulkner ever went to see a movie. So they might have been on the level."

Still working for $250 per week, Faulkner completed writing several new scenes for "Turn About" in October, notably the stilted opening interludes in which Bogard comes to rent Ann's opulent home and stays for an awkward tea. Toward the end, Faulkner was joined by the young screenwriter Dwight Taylor in making revisions. Although both Howard and Bill Hawks urged the writer to stay in Hollywood, Faulkner had done all he could on "Turn About." Beyond that, his wife was pregnant, his mother wanted to go home, and Paramount had just picked up its option on *Sanctuary* and was about to move into production of the film. This meant more than six thousand dollars for Faulkner, more than he had ever had in his life. Although he was typically dubious about its prospects, *Light in August* was published to ecstatic reviews. Sam Marx asked the writer about the book's motion picture possibilities, but Faulkner doubted its potential. "I told him I didn't think they could use it. It would make a good Mickey Mouse picture, though Popeye is the part for Mickey Mouse. The frog could play Clarence Snopes." Instead, he worked out an arrangement with MGM to continue working from Oxford, which he did until the following August.

With "Turn About" now on track to start by mid-December, the script still needed some improvement in the writing of Ann's character, so the studio assigned Anne Cunningham to write a treatment charting the drama from the woman's point of view. Her sentimental suggestions were rejected out of hand, and the veteran writer Edith Fitzgerald was brought in to strengthen Ann's character, which she did in part by creating more scenes of her working as a nurse. She also did some emergency surgery when the youthful actors engaged to play the leading roles in the childhood scenes couldn't master British accents, making Hawks decide to eliminate the sequences entirely and work references to their childhood into the dialogue.

Retitled *Today We Live*, the film went into production in December without a leading man. Gable wouldn't take on two films at once. MGM offered Gary Cooper a thirteen-thousand-dollar bonus but with *A Farewell to Arms* about to open and promising to further boost the actor's standing, he held out for twenty thousand and got it.

Shooting through the new year until February, Hawks tried to make the best of a bad situation, but by now the film was hopelessly removed from what he and Faulkner had started out with six months before. Faulkner made a valiant effort to position Ann (now renamed Diana) at the center of a story of which she originally was not a part. But this resulted in opening sequences so laboriously expositional that after twenty minutes the film was in a hole so deep it had no hope of climbing out. Hawks and his actors seem so ill at ease in the early drawing-room and church scenes that these emerge as among the worst scenes he ever directed, and though the child actors were let go because they couldn't get the hang of British accents, the professionals do no better. Hawks pushes the stylized, repressed line readings of *The Dawn Patrol* into the realm of parody, with Franchot Tone, cast as Crawford's brother, Ronnie, almost never uttering a first-person pronoun and delivering stiff-upper-lip dialogue such as, "Glad. Been waiting," and, to his sister, "Stout fella" and "Can't help feelings." This seems to rub off on almost everyone else, and rather hilariously led some observers to label Faulkner's dialogue "Hemingwayesque." Then there are the outrageous Crawford gowns by Adrian, one of which had an enormous pointed collar that Hawks said "stuck in everybody's eye." Perhaps topping all was the heavy irony that one of the best scenes in the picture, Bogard's initial bombing raid, used a liberal amount of background airplane dogfight footage from Howard Hughes's *Hell's Angels*, the very film Hughes had accused Hawks of stealing from just two years earlier. As *Variety* sarcastically noted, on this film Hawks was only "in the air again by proxy."

The picture admittedly improves in its second half, which is where, not at all coincidentally, it converges most snugly with Faulkner's original. But it must also be noted that, aside from the air battle, the only memorable scenes in the film, the two torpedo boat attacks, were actually shot by Hawks's ever-reliable codirector, Richard Rosson. Despite the thematic familiarity of the final suicidal run, these scenes offered something visually new and were quite convincingly done, furthering Hawks's reputation as an action director when, in fact, he never stepped off the Culver City lot during the shooting of this picture.

Metro previewed *Today We Live* in Pasadena on March 16, 1933, at the then unheard-of length of 135 minutes. Although *Variety* gave it an upbeat advance review at the time, it was obvious that considerable footage had to come out. The film was cut to 110 minutes, still rather long, and William Faulkner traveled up to Memphis for the local premiere of the film on April 12 and saw his name on the screen for the first time. He never recorded what he thought, but his old interest in flying had been spurred by Hawks. *Today We Live* opened in New York on April 14 at the Capitol, and its big opening followed by a quick decline in business became the pattern around the country. The critical reception overall was lukewarm, with special ridicule reserved for Crawford and her costumes. The big winner on all counts was Franchot Tone, a stage actor in his first film. Tone was rightly singled out as the one actor in the cast who delivered the oddly clipped dialogue with authority. In real life, Tone also won the affections of Joan Crawford, who was married to Douglas Fairbanks Jr. at the time, and public interest in their romance was viewed as a possible boon to the film's commercial chances. In the end, the film did just average business for an attraction with such big stars. Years later, Hawks acknowledged, "I thought some of it wasn't bad," but admitted that Crawford "had her limitations. She was a personality more than an actress, and there were things she just couldn't do. How are you going to explain to these people that the addition of the biggest star in pictures is going to *spoil* your movie?"

Despite the muddled results of their first collaboration, Hawks enjoyed working with Faulkner so much that he was eager to continue their collaboration without interruption. Settled back in Oxford for the winter, Faulkner went to work on an adaptation of John McGavock Grider's novel *Diary of an Unknown Aviator*. It developed into a highly personal effort intimately related to his fiction, possessing some of the same characters, concerns, themes, and complex narrative devices of his major novels. "War Birds" deals with the tarnished, corrupted nobility of several World War I veterans now living in America's South and, during its war flashbacks, focuses on the fatalistic recklessness of the youthful soldiers as well as the erosion of the Old World aristocracy. Despite the strong echoes of *The Dawn Patrol* and even *Today We Live*, the script, which he delivered to Hawks in mid-January 1933, reads as the most thoroughly Faulknerian script the writer ever prepared, and it is probably his best. But the time-jumping narrative and complicated personal relationships were enough to make it uncongenial as material for the straightforward Hawks, so it is not surprising that he let it drop.

Part of what may have put Hawks off of "War Birds," were the "hillbilly" Southern characters Faulkner so often wrote about. With the prominent exception of *Sergeant York*, in his films set in the twentieth century, Hawks never gravitated to Southern or rural characters. "I got mad at him one day and told him I got so sick and tired of the goddamn inbred people he was writing about. I said, 'Why don't you write about some decent people, for goodness' sake?' 'Like who?' I said, 'Well, you fly around, don't you know some pilots or something that you can write about?'"

As it happened, Faulkner had attended an air show and met some fliers and wing-walkers who intrigued him, and he'd centered his short story "Honor" around them. Early in 1933, Harry Behn wrote a treatment of it for MGM, and by March Faulkner had turned it into a screenplay, with dialogue contributions from Behn and, later, Jules Furthman. A tart look at a group of daredevil aerialists and their equally risky amorous flings, it is a wonderful script, permeated by the full-blown Hawksian code applied to professionals performing a dangerous job. The leading character, a wing-walker named Mildred Churchill, is exceedingly well drawn; her need for thrills, in her work as well as in her men, is strongly etched.

There is more than a trace of Furthman in the script, particularly in the characters' sexual gumption and the sense of compressed lifespans. One is left aching to see the film as directed by Hawks at his best (that is, not at MGM) with a terrific, sexy actress (Carole Lombard, perhaps Stanwyck) as the spunky Mildred. Regrettably, it was never made. Faulkner's eventual novel based on the material, *Pylon*, published in 1935, has never been considered one of his major achievements. For Hawks, its central character of an alcoholic newspaperman who becomes intrigued with these danger-loving flyers stemmed from a time when Faulkner "got drunk when he went down to an air show to see what it was like. He had kind of a hazy idea of it." The result, he felt, "wasn't an awful good book" The film made of it twenty-five years later, *The Tarnished Angels,* is impressive in its own right but certainly lacks the juice and hopping hormones of the original script, no traces of which were used.

12

Viva Villa!

One more, even racier project Hawks was considering in the wake of *Today We Live* was a potentially wild comedy called "Moll." Late in 1932, Ben Hecht and Gene Fowler sent Hawks a twenty-five-page treatment of this goofy gangster-themed comedy about a gun moll hiding out in Normandy who marries an ingenuous fellow expatriate. At the close of the story, he insists that she needn't have concealed her past. "You shouldn't have worried about my being upset about a gun-moll," he declares. "I don't want to brag but I killed about a hundred people in the war!" The story is casually amoral at the very least and written complete with nude scenes on the beach.

Unsurprisingly, "Moll" was never made, but it did put Hawks back in touch with Hecht at a time when high drama was enveloping MGM. In December, Thalberg suffered his first heart attack. At the same time, David O. Selznick, Louis B. Mayer's son-in-law, quit his top production job at RKO, after a string of successful pictures, because of disputes over his forthcoming production slate. Baldly taking advantage of Thalberg's illness to reduce the younger man's power and consolidate his own, Mayer offered Selznick his own production unit at MGM, and Selznick installed himself at the studio on February 5, 1933, just after Thalberg had embarked on a long recuperative trip to Europe.

Among the first projects Selznick took on was one about the Mexican peasant revolutionary Pancho Villa. Officially but loosely based on the book *Viva Villa: A Recovery of the Real Pancho Villa—Peon . . . Bandit . . . Soldier . . . Patriot*, by Edgcumb Pinchon and O. B. Stade, the picture was at one point envisioned as a two-part epic encompassing Villa's rise and fall, until the executives realized that his nearly decade-long "fall" had been staggeringly dull and anticlimactic. Upon joining MGM, Selznick called Hecht to Culver City to do a major rewrite on the Garbo picture *Queen Christina*, then teamed him with playwright Edgar Selwyn on the comedy

Turn Back the Clock, which starred Lee Tracy. The prodigiously prolific writer skipped over to Paramount to write *Design for Living* for Ernst Lubitsch, completely rewriting Noël Coward in the process, before returning for what was to have been a short stay in New York. However, while his wife, Rose, and Selznick were waiting for him in Los Angeles, Hecht became involved with another woman and in July impulsively left on a lengthy trip to South America with her and the future writer Ian McLellan Hunter, turning up at MGM only in late August, a month after Thalberg had returned from Europe. Even at that, Selznick put Hecht on a couple of other quick jobs before turning him loose on *Viva Villa!*

During this period, Hawks was weighing his next project, deciding against the two Faulkner World War I stories, nominally filling in for Thalberg by reading material, digging his financial hole considerably deeper by betting ever-larger sums on horses, and supervising the construction of his new home in Benedict Canyon. It was around this time as well that he had his one-night stand with Jean Harlow, an event that didn't do his reputation any good with Vic Fleming or the many others around MGM who heard about it. Hawks always maintained that Harlow's problem was that she was always being bothered by crude, vulgar men. Therefore, she was particularly responsive when a man was nice and considerate with her, an insight he said he used to his advantage. According to his version, Hawks bided his time, becoming friendly with the actress so that she'd feel comfortable with him before he jumped her. He made it sound like a clever conquest, at a time in between the suicide of her husband, Paul Bern, and her marriage to cinematographer Harold Rosson, both of whom were good friends and former collaborators of Hawks's.

John Lee Mahin, who wrote *Red Dust* and *Bombshell* for the star, told the story rather differently. "I was good friends with Jean by the time Howard turned up at Metro. She used to see him around the lot but didn't know him, and she asked me, 'Who's that good-looking man?' 'Oh, that's Howard Hawks.' 'Oh, really, do you know him?' I said, 'Sure, I know him pretty well. Why, are you interested?' She said she'd been in mourning for her husband for, I don't know how long, three months or six months or some such, and she was beginning to get a little itch. So I arranged to bring him around on a Saturday afternoon. We swam and played and had a few drinks, and it seemed like they were getting along pretty well, so after awhile I made a discreet exit. On Monday morning it was pouring rain. I was just parking my car on the lot and I saw Jean holding an umbrella and stomping through the puddles. So I rolled down my window and yelled out, 'Hey, Jean, how did it go with Howard?' She just kept stomping ahead, turned and looked at me, squeezed her nose with her fingers and made the most awful face. I understood he made pretty quick work of it."

With Thalberg convalescing and Mayer's son-in-law rising at the studio, Hawks was suddenly answerable to two of his least favorite people, Louis B. Mayer and David O. Selznick. The latter, however, worked to patch things up by admitting that he had made a mistake in assessing Hawks's talents three years earlier when he tried to steal *The Dawn Patrol* from him, and decided to make it up by offering him *Viva Villa!* to direct. From a producer's point of view, it was a shrewd move, reuniting two of the makers of *Scarface* on a project centered on another brash, sometimes childlike, but powerful figure of recent history. Biography was something Hawks had never before tried (and would only do so once again, with *Sergeant York*), but the prospect of tackling it with Hecht was too tantalizing to pass up. Another plus was that shooting in Mexico would mean that the always-vigilant Selznick would at least be nineteen hundred miles away, so Hawks considered it a good bet that he would be able to operate largely unsupervised, unlike all of his experiences at MGM thus far.

Selznick offered Hecht ten thousand dollars to write the script, with the lure of a five-thousand-dollar bonus if he finished it within fifteen days. Hecht readily agreed, anxious to further his reputation as the quickest writer in screendom. Mayer was less sanguine about the deal but was placated by a memo from Selznick: "I do not think we should take into consideration the fact that we are paying him a seemingly large amount of money for two weeks' work . . . as this would be merely penalizing him for doing what would take a lesser man at least six or eight weeks, with infinitely poorer results."

Pancho Villa was, and remains, an equivocal historical figure, a man of the people who fought a corrupt dictatorship on behalf of the dispossessed but was also a dissolute, unreliable drunkard who constantly cheated on his wife, could not solidify his gains and led an ill-advised attack on the United States in 1915 (something not mentioned in the film). What Villa stories Hecht knew mostly came from Charles MacArthur, who had been part of the American Expeditionary Forces that pursued Villa down through Mexico after his assault on New Mexico. Hecht also brought aboard Wallace Smith, who had ridden with Villa and covered him for the Hearst papers, as a consultant.

Selznick was intent upon obtaining official approval of the script from Mexican authorities before shooting, both to pave the way for location work and to generate favorable publicity. The problem was that there were at least three powerful politicians whose consent was critical: Plutarco Elías Calles, who had fought against Villa and was interested in a movie that showed the rebel as a spineless fool; President Abelardo Rodríguez, of course; and Army General and Michoacán state governor Lázaro Cárdenas, who looked as though he would unseat Rodríguez in the forthcoming election, which would take place while the film was in production. Selznick instructed Hecht to revise the script with an eye toward pleasing (or at least not offending) friend and foe alike, and Joe Schenck acted as an official intermediary. In addition, film star Ramon Novarro's brother, Carlos Samaniegos, who had connections to the Mexican political elite, personally took the revised script to Mexico City, where it was approved by all three key figures. Villa's widow, brought to Hollywood by Selznick, even came onboard, although the script made no bones about Villa's constantly roving eye and the fact that "he gets married all the time." What MGM might have had to pay out to obtain all this cooperation is not recorded.

The challenge of avoiding any ruffled feathers on both sides of the border led Hecht to a sort of ahistorical approach to Villa's career as seen through the eyes of a drunken American newspaperman whose dispatches about ongoing events in Mexico may or not be reliable. It was a view of history as seen and shaped by the media, as well as a glamorization and magnification of the journalist's role in world affairs (and of American influence on internal Mexican politics). Villa is made to fight one battle simply because the journalist has, on a drunk, already reported that it had taken place. That Villa's buffoonish aspect would be emphasized was guaranteed by the casting of Wallace Beery, while Lee Tracy was an ideal choice as the tough-talking scribe Johnny Sykes, who could match Villa drink for drink.

Utterly unconcerned with factual integrity or the actual politics of the period, Hawks saw *Viva Villa!* as an opportunity to make a rugged, boisterous adventure with the sort of irreverent, bizarre scenes rarely seen in a historical piece. Hawks left Los Angeles on September 25, 1933, and in Mexico City worked further with Hecht on refining the script. What tickled Hawks's fancy were blackly comic scenes that underlined the absurd and emphasized the startlingly incongruous. He and Hecht wanted to introduce Villa cutting down dead bodies from a scaffold. As Hawks described it, "And we dissolve, and he's talking with the mayor of a town and he says, 'Speak louder, they don't hear so good.' And all the dead forms were up in a jury box and he was trying the man who sentenced them to death." A variation on this scene remains in the picture, although a similar scene he cherished went unfilmed, depicting female army camp followers scouring a battlefield to find their slaughtered men, then propping them up against trees, drinks and cigarettes in hand, in order to spend one last evening with them. Villa's memorable death scene began as another such sequence, but was highly modified and sentimentalized in the final version. After being shot and mortally wounded, Villa is joined by Johnny, the reporter, and he slowly dies with his head resting on a side of meat outside a butcher shop. "Villa said to him, 'Johnny, I've been reading about what great men said when they died. What am I going to say, Johnny?' And Johnny says, 'I'll think of something.' Villa says, 'No, I want to hear it now, Johnny.' So Johnny went into a spiel about a great man shot and dying, faithful followers coming from far and near. The last thing he says is, 'Forgive me, my Mexico! If I have harmed you it was because I loved you.'" At that, Villa says, "'That's pretty good, Johnny. That's pretty good. Look, don't tell my wife that I was buying pork chops for Rosita, will you?' And he died with that." In the reshot version (not directed by Hawks) Johnny tells him how all the peons will gather to sing "La Cucaracha"; then Villa delivers the final line, "Johnny, what I done wrong?," and the film ends with a close-up of the medal he received for his achievements.

The scene Hecht originally wrote could even have been inspired by some extramarital shenanigans he was pulling at the very moment of the writing. In Mexico City, Hecht had shacked up again with his companion from the South American trip. Suddenly, however, Hecht's wife, Rose, showed up unannounced and the panicked writer turned to Hawks for advice. "I said, 'You'd better be perfectly honest. Be a reporter and tell her the story of her husband who's down here with another woman and what's she going to do about it?' And he did and by God he got away with it. Rose said plenty to him, I don't think she liked it a bit, but God knows she must have known what he was. I think Ben amused me most when he got into a real bind. He enjoyed being the brunt of trouble, it kept him very busy thinking how to get out of it."

Harold Rosson was originally set to photograph *Viva Villa!*, but with his marriage to Jean Harlow in the works (they would elope on October 20), he pulled out and was replaced by James Wong Howe. Mostly in Howe's company, Hawks took little plane trips far into rural and mountainous areas looking for locations. Although he never specified it, it seems certain that it was during these jaunts that Hawks met some of the expatriates and maverick fliers who helped inspire his story for *Only Angels Have Wings*.

The actual shooting of *Viva Villa!* was wild and woolly from start to finish. Very few Hollywood films had undertaken prolonged, full-scale, first-unit location expeditions to foreign lands prior to this. Even if California was only a few hours away, the company was still worlds apart in the hinterlands of Mexico. Posted two hundred miles outside of Mexico City with nothing to eat, the crew subsisted on oranges and brandy. Fed up with the lack of amenities and diversions, Wallace Beery rented a plane and regularly flew up to El Paso for good times, while Lee Tracy boozed even more heavily than usual. Hawks had run-ins with "gangsters," tough guys who knew he'd made *Scarface* and were intent upon showing him how they killed people in Mexico. The crew was large and some scenes required hundreds of extras, which included both army regulars and peons. "There were people shot every day when we were making the movie," Hawks testified. "It was crazy in those days."

Hawks may even have inadvertently killed a man himself. At one location, "a fellow came out and shoved a gun at me and started to yell something. I just turned and hit him, and he went over and hit on his head on the railroad track. I never heard whether he died, or what happened. I said, 'What the hell was he yelling?' They told me that he said, 'This is for the revolution!'" Another man supposedly "blew his brains out" in front of everyone. Hawks's bemused comment on all this turmoil was simply, "It was nutty."

All this was nothing, however, compared to the international incident perpetrated by Lee Tracy on Sunday, November 19, the anniversary of the revolution. The Mexican part of the shoot had just been completed; Hawks claimed, in an outright lie, that he had left by then for Los Angeles and that when his train arrived at the border he was besieged by reporters quizzing him about an event he knew nothing about.

Tracy's outrageous behavior has been reported in many ways, and never so bluntly as by Hawks. He said that even though he had placed Tracy in the hands of a Mexican major to make sure he didn't get in any trouble, the high-strung actor got drunk anyway and, from his hotel balcony, "peed on the Chapultepec Cadets during the Independence Day parade in Mexico City and got put in the can."

U.S. Ambassador to Mexico Josephus Daniels reported more fully to the State Department:

> Tracy appeared on a balcony of the Hotel Regis, unclad and
> using very profane and insulting language at the moment when the

military cadets marching in the parade of November 19th were passing in front of the hotel. He was immediately arrested and . . . was
released at 1:00 o'clock on the morning of the November 20th and
left the capital by plane at 6:00 A.M. that day. His arrival at El Paso,
Texas, was reported in press dispatches from there the following day,
November 21st.

From November 22nd to November 24th the Mexico City press
gave considerable publicity to the Tracy incident, as well as to the
filming of the picture, *Viva Villa!* On November 23rd prominence
was given to a telegram which Mr. Louis B. Mayer sent to President
Rodríguez apologizing for the conduct of Lee Tracy and announcing
his dismissal and the cancellation of his contract with the company.

Prior to the arrest of Lee Tracy, considerable newspaper publicity had been given to alleged complaints against the filming of the
picture *Viva Villa!*, which was said to picture the former revolutionary leader of Mexico, General Francisco Villa, in a manner defamatory
to Mexico.

There was no mention of urination in the ambassador's summary, nor
was there in a more detailed account prepared by the embassy's third secretary, John Aguirre. Frantic skirmishing was necessary on the part of embassy officials and MGM representatives to prevent Tracy from being fined
and deported, which is what the Mexican government wanted to do; in fact,
officials held the train to Juárez for twenty minutes on the night of the 19th,
with the intention of putting him on it. On the 20th, Hawks, who in his
own memory of events had left before any of this started, arrived at the U.S.
Embassy for a meeting, at which he requested that the consulate general
handle the case from here on, which was done. After much bowing and
scraping by MGM; Wallace Beery, who offered to make a public apology;
and Ramon Novarro's well-placed brother, Tracy was allowed to leave, only
to be fired from the picture and banished from MGM forever by a furious
Louis B. Mayer. Tracy, whose star had risen so quickly in Hollywood over
the past four years, continued acting in films for several more years but
increasingly turned back to the Broadway stage. He never worked for MGM
again.

Tracy, of course, tried to put a good face on things, telling reporters
back in Los Angeles, "After some strenuous weeks making *Viva Villa!*, I was
just relaxing—feeling high. I had my pajamas and a bathrobe on. I was in
my own hotel room—not on a balcony. Somebody yelled—I yelled back,

in the customary Tracy manner. There didn't seem to be anything vulgar nor offensive."

He added that there were three other members of the *Viva Villa!* company with him at the window, and they all started cheering when the parade went by. "Somebody shouted back at us. Well, you know how those things are. We shouted back at 'em—'Go to———, ha hah!' or something like that. Anyway, it was all a big joke with us."

When Hawks got back to Los Angeles on November 22, he was immediately called on the carpet by Mayer, who insisted that the director state publicly that Tracy had been impossible to control. What happened next depends on whom you want to believe. The most extreme, and unbelievable, version—Hawks's, of course—is that the director grabbed Mayer, pushed him up against a wall, told him "to go to hell" and quit. The always well-informed John Lee Mahin contrarily claimed that Mayer, upset that the film was going slowly and that retakes would push the budget well over one million dollars, fired Hawks to cut his losses. Whether he quit or was fired, the fact is that Hawks remained on the lot for some time after departing *Viva Villa!*, which would not have happened if he had manhandled Mayer. Having deduced some time ago that his future didn't lie at MGM but tied down by a long contract, Hawks decided to transform this apparent setback into an opportunity to escape. Hawks informed studio vice president Eddie Mannix that Mayer "rubs me the wrong way" and that he wouldn't work for him anymore. Then, Hawks said, he stayed in his office for ten weeks, writing useless material he knew the studio would reject, until they finally agreed to let him go.

As for *Viva Villa!*, Hawks naturally said that when he departed, "they had everybody call me to go back and I wouldn't do it. I said, 'I don't want any more of 'em.'" When his old friend Jack Conway was assigned to replace him, Hawks claimed, Conway "would call me up and say, 'What do I do about this?' and I'd tell him the best I could on the telephone." Conway received solo directorial credit. For his part, Beery piloted his own plane home, refused to answer questions about what had happened, and demanded a hefty bonus for having to replay his scenes with the new actor cast in Tracy's role, Stuart Erwin. Mona Maris, who had been playing an aristocrat who takes a fancy to Villa, only to be brutalized by him, was summarily dismissed and replaced by Fay Wray, and Selznick badgered Ben Hecht, now back in Nyack, into extensive rewriting of the film's second half to cut the reporter's importance way back. The remaining scenes were shot in the mountains outside of Los Angeles and on the Culver City lot. In the finished film, what Hawks and Howe shot in Mexico is pretty easy to spot: the clearly location-made opening scene of the child Pancho watching his father being whipped to death for speaking out against injustice, the enormous crowd scenes, the impassive but noble peasant faces, the many shots of riders moving against stunning backdrops all have a starkness and brute strength missing in the softer, sculpted images Charles G. Clarke created for Conway. Some scenes, notably Villa's farewell speech to his people midway through, intercut between Conway and Hawks, with the former's interior close-ups of Beery appearing utterly isolated from the seeming thousands of cheering, rifle-toting men earlier captured by the latter. But there is less of Hawks and Howe than there might have been due to a highly suspicious accident at El Paso in which a plane carrying twenty thousand feet of negatives crashed and burned after the pilot bailed out.

Although it was nominated for best picture and best screenplay Oscars in 1934, *Viva Villa!* ultimately emerged as something closer to a cartoon biography than a subversively funny look at early-twentieth-century mythmaking, as Hawks and Hecht had intended. "It really could have been one hell of a picture," Hawks believed. "I tried to make a strange man, humorous but vicious, out of Villa, as he was in real life, but Conway's version had Wallace Beery playing Santa Claus." Although the film proved to be a reasonably popular attraction, it just barely broke even because of its bloated budget.

"I knew it never was going to work out," Hawks said of his stint at MGM. As should have been obvious from the start, the MGM way of making movies—of preparing stories and scenarios and casts before assigning directors, then shuffling them around and reshooting extensively, often using other directors, and all of this orchestrated from above by Mayer, Thalberg, and now Selznick—was utterly antithetical to Hawks's methods; Hawks later said, "I was glad to get out of that goddam place."

13

Screwball: *Twentieth Century*

After his exasperating year and a half at MGM, Hawks knew he needed a fresh start, and *Twentieth Century* marked the beginning of several things for Hawks, all of them very significant for his career. Since sound came in, he had directed six dramas—some heavier than others, all more brutal and harsh than the norm, with gangsters, prisoners, heavy drinkers, doomed soldiers, reckless racers, and desperate fishermen as their subjects. With the exception of a grafted-on Joan Crawford, women had not been central to these films, and while Ann Dvorak and Zita Johann had offered character-izations that were not without interest, it couldn't be said that Hawks showed any particular touch with actresses or female characters up to this time.

Nor had he done an outright dialogue comedy. All of Hawks's experi-ence had taught him the value of injecting humor where it might least be expected, but only in *Fig Leaves* in 1926 had he played a picture strictly for laughs. But with *Twentieth Century*, Hawks would help introduce what became known as a new genre to the screen—the screwball comedy, in which attractive players, one of them a major star, horsed around and bounced off one another in a manner normally expected only of comedi-ans or supporting types. Before this, as Hawks explained it, "they didn't have leading men and leading women make damn fools of themselves like they did in that picture." What's more, the film set a new standard in pacing comedy with its freewheeling approach and overlapping dialogue. The film version of *The Front Page* may have featured equally quick pronunciation of words, but Hawks always claimed that Milestone's direction created a "false" sense of speed through its cutting rather than the exchange of dia-logue. Many of the early 1930s Warner Bros. pictures also featured some pretty fast talking, but much of that derived from the individual, wise-guy styles of specific actors, notably James Cagney and Lee Tracy.

By leaving MGM for lowly Columbia, Hawks also reasserted the im-portance of his independence. Although it is not true, as he later claimed,

197

that he never signed long-term contracts with any studios, it is significant that at a time when most of his friends were forging important studio affiliations that guaranteed work and steady money, Hawks deliberately chose the nonaligned route so that he could keep his options open regarding material, actors, and control of his movements. After what had happened at MGM and, to a lesser extent, Warner Bros. and Fox, Hawks was determined to take charge of his career himself, to be beholden to the studio bosses as little as possible. After 1933, Hawks did not again make two films in a row for the same company until 1939–40, when he was able to call his own shots at Columbia on *Only Angels Have Wings* and *His Girl Friday*. Despite the fact that the mid-1930s did not result in Hawks's very best work, they were of vast importance in carving out his reputation, and bolstering his self-image, as an independent operator who would work on his own terms or not at all.

Hawks made running off to film *Twentieth Century* sound like the easiest thing in the world, and it was true that "everything that had to go right went right." The trick Hawks had up his sleeve after he lost *Viva Villa!* was the idea of making *Twentieth Century* practically overnight. Making himself look smarter than anyone else, as usual, Hawks loved telling the story of how he finagled five thousand dollars and ten weeks of vacation pay out of his pal Eddie Mannix when he left MGM, and at the end of that time invited Mannix to a preview. "He said, 'Of what?' and I said, 'A picture I've made since I left you.' And when he saw the picture, he said, 'Do you mean to say that you made that in the ten weeks while we were paying you $5,000 for a *vacation*?!' and I said, 'Yes.'" If true, this would have helped Hawks justify taking such a low salary for *Twentieth Century*, as he agreed to make it for just $25,000, or half of what he was making a few pictures back. It was one of the rare pictures on which the screenwriters made significantly more than the director; Hecht and MacArthur sold the play to Columbia for $25,000 and received another $14,525 for their adaptation.

As a friend of Hecht and MacArthur's, Hawks had attended a performance of *Twentieth Century* during its monthlong run at the El Capitan in Los Angeles in June and July 1933. By the time *Viva Villa!* was pulled out from under him, Harry Cohn had already unsuccessfully tried to recruit Rouben Mamoulian and, subsequently, William Wyler to direct a film version of the play. He then turned to the suddenly available Hawks, telling the director he had the job provided he could both make it cheaply and secure John Barrymore for the leading role of the overbearing theatrical producer. The Christmas holidays were approaching, but Hawks, intent upon showing up MGM and getting the film done in no time, made plans to leave for New York almost at once to work with Hecht and MacArthur.

Adapting the play wasn't just a simple matter of opening it up and inventing some new locations for the action (almost the entire play takes place during a sixteen-hour train trip). The work had its origins in a play called *The Napoleon of Broadway* written by a press agent named Charles Bruce Milholland and inspired by his former boss, the lordly theatrical producer Morris Gest. Milholland gave his manuscript to another Broadway titan, Jed Harris, who identified with the leading character but felt it wasn't a professional play. For a price, he convinced Milholland to let him give it to Hecht and MacArthur, from whom Harris wanted another play. Within three weeks, the speedy team delivered the first two acts to Harris, who could now see that the character of Oscar Jaffe was based on Gest, David Belasco, and, naturally enough, him.

Hecht and MacArthur had trouble getting around to the third act, however. After a long gestation period, interrupted by numerous screenwriting assignments, including *Scarface, Twentieth Century* opened on Broadway on December 29, 1932, to strong notices and a respectable run.

When Hawks decided to undertake the film, he went to Gregory Ratoff, who had played Oscar Jaffe in the Los Angeles run, for advice concerning potential changes and improvements. He came away convinced that the woman's part should be changed from an imperious grande dame to "Sadie Glutz" from Third Avenue. Hawks admitted that having no theatrical background—indeed, never even having been backstage—he was not particularly the most knowledgeable director for such a piece. He conceded, "If it hadn't been for Gregory Ratoff's help, I wouldn't have realized what things could be played around with or worked on."

Having received the playwrights' approval for the character change over the phone, Hawks boarded a train for New York, carrying with him a special parcel. In Mexico City that fall, Hecht had ordered six custom-made miniature wax tableaux by special artisans, but they were just now ready. Hawks had brought them over the border, and a couple of months later he finally presented the suitcase to Hecht in Nyack. "He opened it and there were six boxes of little wax statues that were the dirtiest things I'd ever seen in my life—a mother going down on her son, things like that," said Hawks. "They were really horrible but they were fabulously done by this erotic, crazy family down there who were great artists. Well, I was going to kill him. I got cold perspiration thinking about what could have happened if I'd got caught with those things. . . . Ben was always up to some crazy thing like that." Hecht had special shelves built in his library to show off his acquisitions, to the assorted delight and dismay of his visitors.

Hawks spent full days working with the writers, staying on top of them to ensure that the work got done and loving every minute of it. Often in the presence of the young theatrical producer Billy Rose, who was trying to initiate his own collaboration with Hecht and MacArthur, the three men batted around dialogue ideas and completely rewrote the woman's character, who became Lily Garland, née Mildred Plotka. At Hawks's insistence, they also significantly altered the structure. In the play, from the outset Oscar and Lily are seen going head-to-head in the train. For the film, Hawks requested a prologue that would reveal the essentials of the pair's relationship, showing their initial Svengali-Trilby phase as Oscar transforms her into a star, the nature of their love affair, and her eventual flight to Hollywood to escape Jaffe's ragings and possessive control. This prologue ended up lasting a half hour, boiling the substance of the original play to a mere hour on film, resulting in a thoroughly overhauled work that Hawks felt "had a whole lot more to it than the play."

The director kept pushing the writers beyond the point where they might have gone on their own. "I remember when we'd finished the script, they figured we were all done," said Hawks. "I said, 'Now we start on new, different ways of saying the same thing.' We had more fun for three days just twisting things around. I asked them, 'How do you say this— "Oh, you're just in love"?' Ben came up with 'You've broken out in monkey bites,'" (not realizing he had already used the line in A Girl in Every Port). The general pattern was for the men to sit around swapping lines, with Billy Rose, a former world champion in a shorthand competition, scribbling them down and a secretary typing them up at night. When they got a good idea locked in, Hecht would disappear to write it while Hawks and MacArthur played backgammon. "They taught me how to play. We would work for two hours and play backgammon for an hour. I started winning from them so they got together and decided that when I was their partner they'd lose so that I would always be on the losing end of it. They were so gleeful about this, but I saw what they were doing. If I threw a six and a three and I wanted a six and a four, I'd move it six and four. They never noticed. I won about $40,000 in IOUs from them and they never knew why the hell they were losing."

Before he left Nyack, Hawks helped his friends get their project with Billy Rose off the ground. Rose was determined to stand Broadway on its ear by producing a giant spectacle the likes of which had never been seen. Supposedly, it was Hawks who suggested that the most impressive backdrop for such a show would be a circus, while MacArthur offered that the world's most dramatic plot was *Romeo and Juliet*. Voilà, Rose's extravaganza would pit two rival circus families against one another, and *Jumbo*, which would finally open at the old Hippodrome in 1935, was born.

With a solid first draft in hand, Hawks returned home, where his critical challenge was convincing John Barrymore to play the part. The matinee idol of the 1920s and the most famous Hamlet of his generation, Barrymore had already begun his descent into broad self-caricature and erratic, alcoholic behavior. He wasn't a major box-office name but he was still a star, the key to Harry Cohn's desire to make the picture. Barrymore had had a tempestuous affair with Mary Astor shortly before she married Howard's brother Kenneth, but Hawks had never met the actor before heading up to his imposing mansion to tell him about the story and the role. As Hawks related it, when the actor asked why Hawks wanted him for the part, Hawks said, "It's the story of the biggest ham on earth and you're the biggest ham I know." Barrymore accepted at once and considered it "a role that comes once in a lifetime," deeming the film his favorite of the sixty-odd pictures in which he appeared.

Carole Lombard, who was born in Fort Wayne, Indiana, not far from Goshen, was Howard Hawks's second cousin. But even though she had moved to California at age six and worked for Allan Dwan in 1921, when he and Hawks were close, Hawks had never seen much of her, and he suspected, on the basis of her lackluster screen credits to date, that she was probably a bad actress. However, much as had happened with Ann Dvorak, Hawks saw Lombard "at a party with a couple of drinks in her and she was hilarious and uninhibited and just what the part needed." It is with Lombard that Hawks truly began "discovering" young actresses, shaping their screen personalities and fashioning what became known as "the Hawksian woman," an independent type with a mind of her own who would stand up to men and was not content "to sit around and wash dishes." Appropriately enough, Hawks's career as a Svengali commenced on a picture depicting the very same sort of relationship between a dominant man and a woman he remakes into a star. Just as significantly, it was the first time Hawks dared to pit a virtual beginner against an accomplished veteran in two equal leading roles; just as it would in later years, with Bogart and Bacall, and Wayne and Clift, Hawks's gamble paid off. It is a tribute to his directorial control and brilliance with actors that he could simultaneously handle the chore of keeping John Barrymore in line, which many directors were unable to do, and help Carole Lombard find the key to liberate her own personality on the screen, clinching her career from then on.

Still, there was a problem: the twenty-five-year-old former Mack
Sennett bathing beauty was petrified at the prospect of acting opposite the
screen's aging Lothario, not to mention carrying a picture with him. Fortunately, the problem was confronted head on and solved on the first day of
rehearsals. Hawks often asserted that his famous private bit of direction to
Lombard regarding how she should handle Barrymore took place on the
first day of shooting, but the celebrating "kicking" scene in the train was
not actually *filmed* until the third week of production, by which time
Lombard was very much in the groove of her performance. In rehearsal,
however, in a precise reflection of the predicament of her character,
Lombard was initially very stiff, "emoting all over the place. She was trying
very hard and it was just dreadful," explained Hawks. Barrymore was patient with her but at one point "began to hold his nose." Becoming concerned, Hawks asked the actress to take a walk with him. "I asked her how
much money she was getting for the picture. She told me and I said, 'What
would you say if I told you you'd earned your whole salary this morning
and didn't have to act anymore?' And she was stunned. So I said, 'Now forget about the scene. What would you do if someone said such and such to
you?' And she said, 'I'd kick him in the balls.' And I said, 'Well, he said
something like that to you—why don't you kick him?' She said, 'Are you
kidding?' And I said, 'No.'" Hawks's parting remark was, "Now we're going
back in and make this scene and you kick, and you do any damn thing that
comes into your mind that's natural, and quit acting. If you don't quit, I'm
going to fire you this afternoon." The direction worked, and Lombard's
natural spirited quality came through unchecked in her performance.
Hawks claimed, "She never began a picture after that without sending me
a telegram that said, 'I'm gonna start kicking him.'"

With Barrymore reporting two hours late on the first day, filming began
on February 22, 1934, with the scene of the telephone conversation between
Oscar Jaffe and the detective, played by Edgar Kennedy. Lombard began
work the next day with scenes in Lily Garland's dressing room, and sound
man Edward Bernds confirmed that the actress was entirely on top of her
role from the moment she started shooting. "She was great from the first
day," he recalled. Given a tight twenty-one-day schedule, the film was made
virtually in sequence, except for the theater scenes, which were bunched
together early in the shoot. Hawks had selected Joseph August, the cinematographer of his first two pictures, *The Road to Glory* and *Fig Leaves*, to man
the camera, and production rolled along just slightly behind until the third
week, when the interplay of the rapid-fire drawing-room scenes between

the two leads required so much rehearsal and refinement that filming fell five and a half days behind. But Hawks was trying something new, and everything depended upon the precise timing of the dialogue delivery, which made it "a completely high-pressure picture," in Hawks's view. "It isn't done with cutting or anything. It's done by deliberately writing dialogue like real conversation: *you're* liable to interrupt me and I'm liable to interrupt you— so you write in such a way that you can overlap the dialogue but not lose anything. It's just a trick. It's also a trick getting people to do it—it takes about two or three days to get them accustomed to it and then they're off. But you must allow for it in your dialogue with just the addition of a few little words in front. 'Well, I think—' is all you need, and then say what you have to say. You have to hear just the essential things. But if you don't hear those in a scene, you're lost. You have to tell the sound man what lines he must hear and he must let you know if he does. This also allows you to do throwaways—it keeps an actor from hitting a line too hard and it sounds much funnier." Hawks eventually found that his actors sometimes spat out their dialogue so fast that even he didn't understand it.

Although Hawks said he lost one day of shooting because Barrymore was drunk, the star was generally a model of dedication and cooperation, offering to work two days for free to make up for his delinquency, knowing his lines, and helping the director plan the onstage sequences. Barrymore devised his own Kentucky Colonel disguise for the scene in which he sneaks onto the *Twentieth Century* and improvised the very funny bit in which, once safely inside his compartment, he elongates his nose putty and concludes by picking his nose. After the rocky beginning, Barrymore became Lombard's biggest fan and supporter, giving her tips and rehearsing with her at length until Hawks was satisfied. After this high point, however, Barrymore's Hollywood career went into a steep decline. On his next picture, *Hat, Coat and Glove,* RKO was forced to suspend production when the actor couldn't remember his lines, and the deliberate self-caricature of *Twentieth Century* sadly degenerated into a general run of helpless self-parodies through the last seven years of his career. Hawks's own comportment was reserved, as usual. "The word that comes to mind is *austere,*" said sound man Edward Bernds, who later became a director himself. "He didn't go in for camaraderie with the crew. He didn't even seem to be directing, he never seemed to have conferences with the actors. Hawks seemed to take a well-played scene for granted. He took it in stride. He expected it. For Hawks, every scene had to be perfect, he wanted it to be perfect from beginning to end."

Filming wrapped up with scenes in Lily's apartment on Saturday, March 24, after twenty-seven days of shooting, six days over schedule. Two added scenes were shot in mid-April, and on May 3, *Twentieth Century* opened at Radio City Music Hall in New York. The critics were generally appreciative of the film's sophistication, expert playing, and direction. But *Variety*'s prediction that the film was "probably too smart for general consumption" was born out by business so lackluster that the film lasted only one week at Radio City. As Hawks noted, "The public wasn't ready for seeing two stars act like comedians the way those two did."

But resistance to the film then and now, regardless of its many sterling qualities, could also be due to several other factors that point to ways that Hawks's overt comedies differ from his other films, in which humor and drama are deftly combined in a manner that is so much like life. One can easily imagine audiences at Radio City in 1934 being put off by the patented Hecht-MacArthur sexual cynicism, in which all exchanges of desire and love between men and women are charades and power plays. Of course, set within the broader context of the theater, the leading characters are constantly "performing" in order to get what they want, and much of the comedy derives from this very role-playing. But the insincerity of the characters can simultaneously prove offputting, since the story's sympathy is clearly weighted entirely in favor of the brilliant thespians at the expense of the straight outsiders, who exist only to be buffaloed, bamboozled, and ridiculed, as is Lily's boringly normal boyfriend (a dull Ralph Forbes).

Hawks's direction in *Twentieth Century* was often praised in the same breath in which it was called "frantic," and the same could be said of his subsequent three outright comedies — *Bringing Up Baby, His Girl Friday,* and *Ball of Fire.* In the first three, particularly, Hawks pushed the pace to the breaking point, sometimes so far that it becomes more exhausting than funny. *Twentieth Century* and *His Girl Friday,* the two Hecht-MacArthur comedies, are also the only Hawks comedies not to feature shy, put-upon, often humiliated men; both of these have a powerful male figure who is officially the woman's boss, but to whom the woman manages to successfully stand up. Without Hecht and MacArthur, the women have their way entirely with the hapless men in Hawks's comedies.

Hawks preferred making comedies to dramas, but he also felt that it was "suicide' to announce to the audience that you are trying to be funny. Nor was Hawks interested in joke-derived humor, saying, "I can't remember ever using a funny line in a picture." For him, humor had to flow out of the characters and their attitude to what was going on around them.

But probably the point where Hawks's overt comedies and the rest of his work part ways most noticeably is in the style. Hawks's films, dramatic or comedic, are always very stylized, hermetic, and self-contained. In his best films, all seriocomic, the fantasy world that existed in the director's head was played out with a recognizable human and emotional balance that seems both natural and intensely poetic. But you don't feel the filmmaker's hand. The breathless comedies, even at their greatest, still fundamentally seem artificially engineered, utterly unnatural. Hawks was as clever, smart, and inventive as anyone else working in Hollywood during the 1930s and 1940s, but of all the most expert comedy directors of that period—Lubitsch, Wilder, Sturges, McCarey, La Cava—Hawks was the only one whose fundamental instincts and personality were not comic. At the same time, Hawks made some comedies that can be ranked with the best made by anyone, whereas it's impossible to imagine Lubitsch making *The Big Sleep*, Wilder directing *Red River*, Sturges tackling *Sergeant York*, McCarey or La Cava mastering the challenge of *Scarface* or *Air Force*. Without sending them up, of course.

14

Barbary Coast

After completing the added scenes for *Twentieth Century* in April 1934, Hawks went fourteen months without shooting any film, the longest such period since his unwanted unemployment in 1929 after being fired from Fox. This time it was different, however. His marriage was stagnant, but because of Athole's precarious mental condition, his concern for her, and his loyalty to the Shearer-Thalberg family, he felt constrained from doing anything about it. He was always open to little flings, but he knew that discovery of them could set Athole off into one of her deep depressions. Leading a bachelor's life was easier for him in New York, where his activities couldn't be monitored and keeping company with fellow carousers Hecht and MacArthur always guaranteed the presence of showgirls, aspiring actresses, and models. He spent whatever time he could there, and the five months—on and off—he was in New York, through the fall of 1934 and the following spring, represented the longest stretch of time he was to spend outside Los Angeles until after World War II.

This sabbatical was only possible, however, because of the collapse of a huge film project. After his quick, low-budget job for Columbia, Hawks started plotting his first true epic. Based on a 1926 historical novel by Blaise Cendrars, *Sutter's Gold* had been one of the projects undertaken by Sergei Eisenstein at Paramount during his ill-fated Hollywood sojourn of 1930. Although Westerns and pioneer stories had cooled off as a genre since *Cimarron* won the Oscar in 1931, Hawks became very keen on making this expansive tale about the Gold Rush. Looking for a way to do so, he found a receptive ear at Universal, one of only two studios where he had never worked in any capacity (the other was RKO), and he made a lucrative deal for what was certain to be a costly picture. Setting up offices in his own bungalow on the San Fernando Valley lot, he hired a new secretary, a beautiful, slim, divorced twenty-eight-year-old Mississippian named Meta Doherty Carpenter, who would work with him as secretary, and then script girl, with interruptions, for the next twenty-five years. She was put in charge of arranging his files and moving them from studio to studio, helping Athole at home, paying bills, and driving Peter and David back and forth to their grandparents' in Pasadena on weekends. To her distaste, she also became more involved with her boss's extracurricular activities than she cared to, handling Hawks's relations with any number of unsavory bookies, warding off the gambling-world types to whom Hawks owed money, and organizing the care and movements of Hawks's racehorses.

To work up a script on *Sutter's Gold*, Hawks called again upon Faulkner. Having earned himself some novel-writing time after his months of hard labor at MGM, Faulkner had begun writing one of his most ambitious and demanding works, *Absalom, Absalom!* but had become stuck and was willing to return to Hollywood for what Hawks swore would be a brief stay. Faulkner spent a month in Hollywood beginning in late June, turning out a full 108-page scene treatment of *Sutter's Gold* before returning to Oxford. This lengthy treatment was enormously detailed and so dramatically unwieldy as to be impossible to film. Faulkner continued to do some work on it after returning to Mississippi, but Hawks brought in John Barrymore's close friend, the former newspaperman Gene Fowler, to help chisel it into a script. However, when Universal, one of the cheapest studios in town, announced that they weren't prepared to spend more than $750,000 on the film, Hawks threw up his hands and walked away from it, knowing that such a logistically complex production would require a good deal more than that.

With nothing immediately in the offing, Hawks readily accepted an urgent plea from Hecht and MacArthur that he come East to help guide them in their latest project: producing and directing their own films at Astoria Studios in Queens. Determined to show up the philistines in Hollywood by making high-quality and commercial pictures on which the writers, of all people, were in control, Hecht and MacArthur cut a deal to produce four pictures for Paramount. At the time, Walter Wanger was in charge of the studio's Queens facilities, where many memorable early sound pictures—including the first Marx Brothers films and some Lubitsch classics—had been made but which were now less frequently used. Two men Hawks knew well, *Scarface* cameraman Lee Garmes and Arthur Rosson, had already signed up to help the writers with their dream undertaking, which was designed to demonstrate that good, professional-looking pictures could be made at much lower costs than the norm. To this end, Hecht and MacArthur took no fee for writing, producing, and directing in the expectation of receiving a healthy slice of profits, and stage actors were engaged for far less than Hollywood stars received. Their first production, *Crime Without Passion*, starring Claude Rains, was budgeted at only $150,000. Hawks had no artistic input on the film at all but was happy to help out his good friends and valued collaborators. "I came to New York and helped them get started. When they began to feel comfortable I got out of there and they finished it. I didn't direct the picture, I just told them what I would do." Their next collaboration would come sooner than they expected.

Hawks had known Samuel Goldwyn for many years but never worked for him, rightly suspecting that Goldwyn was one of those producers, like Selznick and Thalberg, who so thoroughly dominated their productions that the director was more like a go-between. However, when Goldwyn offered him sixty thousand dollars, more than he had ever received to direct a film and more than double his last salary, on *Twentieth Century*, Hawks could scarcely refuse.

Goldwyn had been trying to get a film called *Barbary Coast* off the ground for more than a year before Hawks became involved. In 1933, the producer had bought a book called *The Barbary Coast: An Informal History of the San Francisco Underworld*, published that year by Knopf and written by Herbert Asbury, the author of *The Gangs of New York*. Between June 1933 and October 1934, when Hawks signed on, Goldwyn spent nearly eighty thousand dollars having no fewer than eleven different synopses, outlines, treatments, original stories, and full scripts prepared by such estimable writers as Frances Marion, Marcus Goodrich, Joel Sayre, Kenyon Nicholson, Dwight Taylor, Nathanael West and Oliver H. P. Garrett. The assignment facing all of them, finding a strong approach to telling the story of San Francisco's wild birth pangs during the Gold Rush of 1849, became a much greater challenge when, after Goldwyn bought the book, Will Hays introduced much stricter censorship and morality guidelines, severely limiting the licentiousness that could be presented in what needed to be a bawdy tale. The producer sent an early draft to Gloria Swanson to gauge her interest and at one point announced that the project would star Gary Cooper and Anna Sten. Goldwyn could think of no director who would have been more at home during those days than "Wild Bill" Wellman, so he was enlisted. He couldn't figure out what to do with the project either, but he ended up earning $39,000 before he was replaced.

By the time Hawks came aboard in October 1934, Goldwyn had signed Miriam Hopkins and Joel McCrea to long-term contracts and had decided to star them together in the picture. Hawks's original notion was to pattern *Barbary Coast* after Sternberg's *Morocco*, one of his favorite films and one of Jules Furthman's best stories. That idea survives in the finished film mainly in the opening sequence, in which a mysterious blonde (Hopkins) arrives at night by boat in an exotic port and is treated solicitously by an older gentleman. Similarly, but only in general ways that resemble countless other stories as well, she takes up employment in a nightclub and must ultimately sacrifice the material wealth she enjoys as the mistress of an older man for the love of a handsome younger one. But with Furthman tied up at MGM on *Mutiny on the Bounty*, Hawks proceeded through the winter with writers Nat J. Ferber and Oliver H. P. Garrett, getting nowhere.

By March, Hawks suspected that Hecht and MacArthur could be approached about writing the script. Except for a successful New York run, *Crime Without Passion* had flopped, as had their second Astoria effort, *Once in a Blue Moon*. With their third, *The Scoundrel*, starring Noël Coward, finished but not yet open, the pair were ready to help themselves to forty thousand dollars of Sam Goldwyn's money, despite their lingering feeling of having been hoodwinked financially by the producer on *The Unholy Garden*. Even though Hawks's presence was the deciding factor in their agreeing to do it, they weren't above pulling a fast one on him, as Hawks realized when he had lunch with the writers' agent, Leland Hayward, at the "21" Club shortly thereafter. Hayward went on and on about how he had just sold the same story by the writers for the third time until Hawks asked if the story was about a man named Chamalis. It was indeed, and Hawks knew he'd been had, turning him sour on a story he hadn't been terribly fond of in the first place. "Every once in awhile they'd get into a story like this—a prostitute and a poet—and then they'd go kind of bad," he theorized. "The poet quoted poetry, and Miriam Hopkins was the evil woman from the Barbary Coast, and it all got out of hand. But Goldwyn liked it. I didn't, and I was stuck."

Nonetheless, comfortably away from the problems of home and with more young women available than he could possibly handle, Hawks stayed in New York for months, living in a suite at the Waldorf Towers while Meta Carpenter, whom he had brought along, stayed at the St. Moritz. Her living room became the place where weekdays, Hawks, Hecht, and MacArthur would work on the script, with MacArthur on the floor or the couch, Hecht up and down dictating, and Hawks, either reclining in a chair or walking around with his hands in his back pockets, interjecting and spinning off on the team's ideas. "Howard would nod, say a few things, but was best at pointing them in the right direction," Carpenter remembered. "He always had a good idea of where the story was headed." Weekends were often spent in

Nyack, where further script dictation would be intermingled with showfolk play, and Carpenter remembered one startling incident. The doorbell rang, and Hawks went to open the door. It turned out to be Tallulah Bankhead, and the moment she saw Hawks, she growled, "Damn you," and hit Hawks hard on the head. There were six raised eyebrows in the room, but nobody asked any questions about what might have happened between Hawks and the notoriously promiscuous actress.

By April they were well into the script. Hecht and MacArthur's Chamalis character was not entirely unlike Tony Camonte, a crude, unattractive thug whose law is the only law and whose illegal activities thrive in the anarchic atmosphere his rule-by-terror creates. In order to win the favors of the beautiful new arrival, whose fiancé he murdered in a gambling dispute, Chamalis gives her a lucrative job running the fixed roulette table, where returning prospectors are routinely cheated out of all their gold, then shot if they protest. Hecht and MacArthur can also easily be spotted in the character of the crusading newspaper publisher, Colonel Marcus Aurelius Cobb (political crusaders being otherwise entirely absent from Hawks's work), whose killing sparks the rise of the moralistic vigilantes and the downfall of Chamalis.

After *Scarface* and even *Viva Villa!*, Hawks had good reason to believe that joining forces once again with Hecht, on a subject with an outsized, violent man at the center of a turbulent, colorful world full of action, stood a strong chance of succeeding. In fact, it did extraordinarily well at the box office and was Hawks's biggest hit since *The Dawn Patrol*. But it was far from being this creative team's most copacetic collaboration. In mid-April Hawks wrote a rare letter, to Goldwyn literary assistant Merrit Hurlburd. He stressed that his idea all along was "that the Barbary Coast, being an unusual background, should have a story that could only happen here." It was also Hawks's idea that the strongest drama and suspense would derive from the two young lovers being in constant danger of death because of Chamalis's power. Again, this element only made it into the finished film in the final reel or so. Although he felt that they were writing under "a great deal of pressure and great haste," Hawks nevertheless claimed to be "really happy about it." He was ready to come home, however. "I'm so sick of New York and rotten weather, I'll do anything to hurry getting out of here."

Athole visited New York once during her husband's long stay, leaving the kids at home with their grandparents, and the separation actually did the marriage some short-term good. Despite Howard's general obliviousness to her needs and problems, Athole still loved him and desperately wanted to keep the family together. After the long absence, Hawks was happy just to get home.

Hawks and his writers ran through five complete drafts of the script in New York, and now Goldwyn was itching to get rolling. Allotted a $762,315 budget and a thirty-seven-day shooting schedule, Hawks had limited say in the casting. To join Hopkins and McCrea, Goldwyn borrowed Edward G. Robinson from Warner Bros. to play Chamalis—like his Mike Mascarenas in *Tiger Shark* for Hawks, another embittered man who loses a woman to a younger guy. Hawks had intended Adolph Menjou to play the newspaperman who solicits Hopkins on the boat, functionally the same role he had filled in *Morocco*, but Goldwyn imposed the pompous Frank Craven. David Niven got his screen start here in the tiny role of a Cockney sailor who crashes through a bordello window into the mud, but the highlight for Hawks was his discovery of Walter Brennan. Only forty but looking a good deal older, Brennan was an unknown playing bits and extra parts until a production man brought him to Hawks's attention. Hawks burst out laughing at the sight of the gangly actor in costume, whereupon Brennan asked him how he wanted him to do his test: "With or without?" "With or without what?" Hawks asked. "Teeth," Brennan replied. Hawks told him to keep his dentures off, and the part of the wharf rat Old Atrocity, scheduled as a three-day role, kept being expanded until Brennan worked for six weeks and made a name for himself. He won an Oscar on his next Hawks picture, *Come and Get It*, and the actor and director eventually did six films together.

Filming started on June 17 and was marked by a good deal of acrimoniousness, most of it triggered by Miriam Hopkins. From the outset, Robinson found Hopkins "puerile and silly," a snob of the first order who was always late, kept altering her dialogue, complained about everything, tried to upstage her fellow actors at all times, and wouldn't even feed her offscreen lines to her costar, a customary courtesy. No one, including Hawks, had a clue as to how to bridle the little prima donna, although Robinson was able to vent his anger at her in a scene that required him to slap her; he slapped her very hard indeed.

The set was also divided into deeply opposed political camps, with Robinson, Hecht, and MacArthur carrying the liberal banner and Hopkins, Hawks, McCrea, Brennan, and Harry Carey among the anti-Roosevelt conservatives. Although Hawks surely did not become involved, Robinson reported, "The arguments on the set were appalling; as a result, there was little socializing among us. There was a good deal of polite freezing and occasional bursts of rage." Hawks rewrote on the set more than usual, both to expand Brennan's part and in an attempt to improve Hopkins's dialogue. Hecht derisively described the action of the film as "Miriam Hopkins came to the Barbary Coast and wandered around like a confused Goldwyn Girl," and the two writers were upset enough at the "imbecility" of Hopkins's new dialogue to try to remove their names from the credits. All of this complaining, plus the continual problems of dealing with Goldwyn, made the film "a lot of trouble" to Hawks, who finished it in forty-four days, seven days over schedule and $10,118 over budget.

One amusing way to look at the film is to view Joel McCrea's highfalutin New York poet as a stand-in for Hecht and MacArthur, a young man who comes to California to stockpile loot and is ready to return East when he is waylaid by a beautiful woman and a childish big boss who plays by his own rules and can be seen as all the studio chiefs the writers ever worked for rolled into one. The film's one outstanding scene has Brian Donlevy's malevolent enforcer character, on his way to commit another killing one night, suddenly surrounded by a number of vigilantes. With a gun in his back, Donlevy is marched onward through the fog and muddy streets as the vigilantes conduct a mock trial that is preordained to end with Donlevy strung up by a rope. The scene has terrific quiet menace but, as Graham Greene astutely observed in his review of the film in the *Spectator*, it closely resembles a memorable passage in René Clair's 1930 film *Sous les Toits de Paris*, which was widely seen in the United States.

Although the film is nominally entertaining in a bland way, Hawks dismissed it as "a lousy picture, a contrived thing done more or less to order." The film's popularity can probably be explained by the large dose of conventional melodrama and the application of the Cecil B. De Mille approach of wallowing in sin and decadence for most of the story before allowing the forces of virtue and righteousness to triumph in the end. But the film is remarkable, and close to unique, in that there is virtually no trace of Hawks in the direction. Even in the handling of the dialogue or inanimate objects, areas where the director normally left his imprint regardless of a picture's overall quality, one would be hard-pressed to single out things that identify *Barbary Coast* as Hawks's work. The lack of a stronger underlying streak of sexual innuendo is also surprising, especially given Hawks's original intent to ape *Morocco*. Ray June's darkly atmospheric night photography is a plus, but the film also suffers from a dearth of any secondary female characters. The film overall stands as evidence that, at that time, a strong producer could effectively override the influence of a strong director. Certainly, the record shows that, with the possible exception of William Wyler years later, no director ever prevailed artistically over the dominance Samuel Goldwyn maintained over his own productions. As Hawks was soon to learn the hard way, a director ignored the will of Sam Goldwyn only at his own immense peril.

15

Flying High: *Ceiling Zero*

If *Barbary Coast* demonstrated how lugubriously the studio system could work, sacrificing all for the bottom line, *Ceiling Zero* showed how efficiently and beneficially it could function at its best. Hawks finished his work for Goldwyn in early August, signed to do *Ceiling Zero* a month later, was shooting by October 7, and was attending its sneak preview on December 19. In fact, in the seventeen-month period between July of 1935 and November of 1936, Hawks would shoot and open four pictures—*Barbary Coast, Ceiling Zero, The Road to Glory*, and *Come and Get It*. This was not unheard-of for directors who were part of the assembly lines at major studios and accustomed to knocking out three mediocre films for every decent one. But for a director who shuttled to different studios for each picture, whose films were major productions involving big stars, and who was intimately involved in the writing of his films, it stands as an exceedingly impressive achievement.

Of all the sound films Hawks made, *Ceiling Zero* was the least premeditated and consumed the least of his time. All the same, it could not be more Hawksian. The film sets the mold for any number of important themes, concerns, motifs, and stylistic traits Hawks would pursue and elaborate on in his best films over the next thirty years. It is here that his interest in the material (flying), his sympathy for the characters (adventurers), the pace (fast), and the cohesion of action based in a principal setting all come together for the first time. *Ceiling Zero*, a hit in its time, was seldom seen during the years when Hawks's critical standing was being built up by revisionist film historians, and it therefore has a reputation as a rather minor entry in the director's oeuvre. But the film played a major role in helping Hawks find his groove, determine what he could do best, and discover ways to treat male-female sparring that set him distinctively apart from other directors, in ways that still seem modern and audacious.

As it happened, Hawks saw the play *Ceiling Zero* on Broadway during its modest thirteen-week run at the Music Box in mid-1935. Hawks's inter-

214

est was piqued because the play starred his old *Scarface* friend Osgood Perkins (as Jake Lee, the role Pat O'Brien would play on-screen) and was written by Frank "Spig" Wead, a former lieutenant commander and veteran World War I flier from Annapolis who became a writer only after an accident landed him in a wheelchair for the rest of his life. (John Wayne played Wead in John Ford's 1957 biographical film *The Wings of Eagles*.) Although Hawks liked the play, which concerned daredevil airmail pilots in an age of dawning aviation conformity, he had nothing to do with setting it up as a motion picture, only coming onto it after several other directors proved unavailable.

A reader first brought the play to Hal Wallis's attention in late December 1934, and two more Warner Bros. readers, one of them the future illustrious screenwriter Dalton Trumbo, recommended it soon thereafter, with the proviso that the leading character of Dizzy Davis was "very censorable" and that "his conflicts with women would have to be toned down considerably." Wead sold the play to Warners in June for $21,000 and agreed to adapt it himself for an additional $6,750. High on the project, Wallis pegged it as the next costarring vehicle for the popular team of James Cagney and Pat O'Brien, who had already done three pictures together at the studio, and then set out to find a director. Wallis's wish list consisted of Tay Garnett, William Wellman, and Victor Fleming, but when none of them were available on short notice, Wallis very reluctantly agreed with Jack Warner and the picture's designated producer Harry Joe Brown that Hawks was the most suitable director for the job. Signing on the first week of September, Hawks said he liked Wead's script very much, then proceeded to start revamping it thoroughly with only a month to go before the fixed start date.

Wead's three-act play is set entirely in the operations office of Federal Air Lines at Hadley Field in Newark. The key men have been close buddies ever sine their military flying days, but their situations in life are now all quite different: Jake Lee has forgone flying for a responsible desk job supervising the airline's eastern division and has settled down into an agreeable marriage with Mary; Dizzy Davis, the wild man of the air, is a relentless skirt-chaser and an old combat ace who flaunts regulations and represents the old breed of free-spirited, maverick pilots and who, unbeknownst to Jake, was once involved with Mary; and Texas Clark, an outstanding pilot and a former roommate of Dizzy's, has had his old ways mightily curbed by his wife, Lou, who resents Dizzy's irresponsible influence. Then there's Mike Owens, formerly one of the boys but a victim of an accident that has left him brain-damaged; with the mentality of a child, he pathetically makes the rounds of the office, polishing the door handles, a stark reminder of the potential wages of their profession.

This, then, represents the classical Hawksian grouping of professional men involved in a dangerous job that holds out the prospect of tragedy on a daily basis. Their camaraderie and mutual respect are based on how well they do that job, and there is no room for those who can't cut it: in the opening scene a young, college-educated pilot is fired after he panics when flying through bad weather and parachutes to safety while letting his expensive plane crash. A pretty young girl (with a man's name—Tommy) is allowed into the group, protectively by Jake and Tex, wolfishly by Dizzy, only because she aspires to the same standards as the men do; when first seen, she has just completed her first solo flight, and her only stated goal is to fly as well as they do. Everyone else, regardless of their qualities, is an outsider, either a potential detriment to the continuity and excellence of the group (represented, in this case, particularly by intrusive government regulators and bothersome corporate minds) or simply irrelevant. The comradeship among these men is playful and kidding, even to the point of containing amusingly homoerotic overtones (taking cigarettes from each other's mouths, frequent touching, even, in the film, Cagney kissing O'Brien on the mouth); it is also rambunctiously competitive and expressive of the friendship. One might see it as adolescent; another, the ultimate way in which men can relate together while performing a job.

Hawks had demonstrated an affinity for these attitudes before in isolated ways, and in *Ceiling Zero* the intricacies of the relationships, and the means of expressing them poetically, are not worked out with the sophistication and depth that Hawks would later achieve. But in Wead's play, Hawks at last found the structure to ideally accommodate his concerns in the most concise, dramatic manner.

Once signed to direct the film, Hawks activated Wead's adaptation in numerous ways that both made it more exciting and better expressed some of his own concerns. Two female characters were cut out, one an air hostess named Jane, another an over-the-hill woman named Birdie who was Dizzy's common-law wife. In both the play and the film, the irrepressible Dizzy puts the moves on Tommy from the moment he sees her, but one early exchange between them went way beyond what Hays would allow:

DIZZY
Would you like to have me give you some instruction?

TOMMY (eagerly)
Will you teach me to fly upside down?

DIZZY
A couple of hops from me and you'll be on your back most of
the time.

Hawks indicated that Wead was a major womanizer during his ambulatory days but that, incapacitated by his accident, he could only write
about men like himself. In the play, Dizzy keeps coming on to Tommy time
after time, but Hawks felt that Cagney made such an excellent pass at June
Travis's Tommy the first time, only to be turned down, that any further
aggressive attempts would appear "ridiculous." The director therefore called
upon the entire crew to compare notes on what Dizzy should do next to
win Tommy over. A diminutive property man chimed in to say, "You know,
if I got turned down I'd say, 'OK, I got off on the wrong foot. I'm not going
to do it again, I promise. Just let's go on.' And then if I want to start something I say, 'Now, look, I promised to behave, but *you've* got to behave.' And
all of a sudden, the *girl* is making the passes." Hawks said, "So we did it that
way. But that was just a single phase of it. The other scenes were in the play
and they were good. We rewrote only the romance."

The romance was, indeed, vastly improved by moving out of the airport control office and into an Italian restaurant, where the interplay among
the principals in a couple of scenes is especially lively. One of the most
libidinous lines ever to get past the vigilant Hays Office is delivered when
Tommy, on her first night out with Dizzy, slips out on him to avoid an
awkward scene later. Now available for the rest of the night, Dizzy eyeballs
the fat Italian woman who helps run the establishment and makes a suggestive remark to her. At this, the ample proprietress falls into convulsive
laughter, upon which Dizzy remarks to Tex, "She thinks I'm kidding."

Consuming much of the play's second act, and omitted from the film,
is a very long talk in which Dizzy is ostensibly coming on to Tommy but
which has him spewing forth pages of dialogue extolling the virtues and
thrills of flying.

The third act was also improved for the film. In the play, Dizzy has
another long speech in which he explicitly states Wead's theme, that the
real days of airplane pioneering are over. The playwright also has Mary
forthrightly tell Dizzy that she's never gotten over him, whereupon she kisses
him, just in time for Jake to walk in. Jake then says that he wanted Dizzy to

come back to Newark just to confirm his suspicions about him and Mary. Hawks masterfully changed all this by deflecting the direct questions and building up implication and innuendo. In the play, Dizzy's suicidal run at the end, during which he tests out the new deicers designed to make winter air travel safer, is thus motivated out of guilt for having betrayed his closest friend. In the film, the act becomes more existential, Dizzy's way of realizing that time has passed him by; as an irresponsible pilot who, just to have a date with a girl, shirked a flying assignment that killed his replacement, Dizzy now admits that he's not a professional who is worthy of the group. In the manner he would always prefer, Hawks found a way to state through action and inference what Wead could only say in words. How Hawks transformed *Ceiling Zero* stands as an excellent example of how a strong director could make an independent piece of material his own in the classical Hollywood era. *Ceiling Zero* remains recognizably Frank Wead's work, but it also becomes thoroughly Hawks's as well because of the way in which the director kept pushing, twisting, and deepening it. Both Wead and Hawks benefited, in that the playwright's work was significantly improved and the filmmaker discovered how to say things important to him more effectively.

When Wead turned in his 142-page first-draft screenplay, it included an excruciating final sequence after Dizzy's death depicting an official ceremony at which the president of the Flying League of America awards a medal to Jake in Dizzy's honor and sanctimoniously praises the late flier for his pioneering with deicers. In fact, Warner Bros. was quite concerned about reactions from the airline industry. Five months before the film went into production, United Airlines expressed its displeasure with the play (which included explicitly disparaging remarks about the company) and the proposed film and suggested that the action of the piece be put back in time by ten years to reassure viewers that flying was not as precarious as it appeared in *Ceiling Zero*. The Aeronautical Chamber of Commerce of America wrote a letter to Will Hays, insisting, "The air lines do not employ pilots like 'Dizzy' in the play," and requesting that the film carry an introduction reassuring viewers that contemporary airlines "are operated in a business-like manner." This demand was agreed to, and Hawks personally played a big part in placating nervous aviation officials, even using by-then obsolete single-engine mail planes—a Northrop Gamma with an F-3 cyclone motor and F-50 cylinders—for the crash sequences.

Wead and Hawks continued to add more technical flying jargon to the script, but there was general agreement among Hawks, Harry Joe Brown, and Wallis that the love scenes were too repetitious and that the whole thing needed more humor, so Hawks brought in Morrie Ryskind for two weeks to work with Wead. The script was improved enormously in the process. Ryskind, the Pulitzer Prize–winning coauthor of *Of Thee I Sing* and a frequent writer for the Marx Brothers, was so ignorant of aviation that when his agent, Zeppo Marx, first told him about the assignment, he thought the title was *Sealing Zero*. His job was to "concentrate on injecting some humor into the human element of the story." But he was also asked to stretch the story out without making it seem padded, since Hawks planned to have the actors speak the dialogue at twice the normal speed. As Ryskind recalled it, Hawks said the average rate of dialogue delivery was 150 words per minute, which works out to about one page of script per minute. Therefore, no one was too alarmed when the final screenplay came out to 168 pages. There was some talk of Ryskind receiving cowriting credit, but Wead was furious at the prospect and Ryskind himself agreed that the playwright deserved solo recognition.

As for the cast, Cagney and O'Brien were a lock, but the other roles offered plum possibilities. For Texas, Hawks tested G. Albert Smith, who had played the part on Broadway, but finally borrowed Stuart Erwin from MGM; ironically, Erwin had replaced Lee Tracy in *Viva Villa!* but had not worked with Hawks, while Isabel Jewell, who was cast as Erwin's henpecking wife, was Tracy's girlfriend at the time. Hawks wanted Ann Dvorak to play Mary, but the role was too inconsequential for her, and it went to Martha Tibbetts. Most important, however, was the role of Tommy. Since the character is supposed to be nineteen and impressionable, it was a perfect part for a newcomer, and Wallis had one in mind: June Dorothea Grabiner, a lovely black-haired, green-eyed young woman Wallis and his wife had noticed at their hotel in Santa Barbara. Hawks agreed on her potential, and the role was hers.

With the Warners New York office very anxious for the picture, Wallis pressed for the film to start production quickly. But, in an unusual move, he granted Hawks four days of rehearsal. As one of the executive lieutenants noted, "Personally, I think with a man like Hawks, the more rehearsal time we can give him, the less time it will take when we start shooting. You know how *slow* Hawks works." The rehearsals no doubt helped, but they weren't enough to calm Wallis. Filming began on October 7, and within two days Wallis was fit to be tied. In his opinion, Hawks had only accomplished a half day's work in that time, and Pat O'Brien was "barking too much." Wallis was also dismayed that the massive shooting script hadn't been cut down further, although Harry Joe Brown rightly defended Hawks on this issue, pointing out that the dialogue was being played so fast that the running time would not be a problem. By the third day Wallis was even closer to a coronary, determining that what other directors accomplished in three hours Hawks took a full day to do. The very next day, Wallis received a stern missive from Joseph I. Breen of the Hays Office urging that the characterization of Dizzy as "an habitual seducer who cheerfully deserted his victims" be toned down as much as possible, that the idea that he intends to commit suicide on his final flight be eliminated, and that the film omit any suggestion that Mary used to be Dizzy's mistress—only the three most important plot points in the entire picture!

After a week of shooting, Wallis could no longer contain himself and fired off a memo that explains much about what drove him so mad about Hawks's methods, both on this picture and in the future:

> Hawks is getting next to nothing in his dailies. I just finished looking at Saturday's stuff, and there are a couple of close-ups of Buzz at his desk, and one little scene outside of about thirty seconds, and that's the day's work. I can't understand how it is possible to get so little work done. . . .
>
> I find that Hawks was on the inside, in the office, and shot the close-ups of the boy at the radio desk, and then went out—in order to stay in continuity he made a complete move to the outside of the office, shooting in, and this probably took four or five hours. There was no reason at all for doing this. He could have shot out of continuity and stayed on the interior and skipped it, and then picked up this outside sequence when he moved outside. . . . In any event, let's prevent him from doing it in the future.

Within several days, Hawks had gotten up to speed, and Wallis began to see that the results were good. It is possible that a few more days' rehearsal would have prevented the bumpy takeoff, but Hawks's methods of slowly working out the mechanics and timing of a scene, of honing character interplay, of rewriting on the set, of giving his leads a long leash to pursue flights of fancy of their own, of calling impromptu cast-and-crew conferences to see if anyone had any better ideas of how to play a scene, and of generally taking his time to ensure the best possible results ran completely contrary to the values of a man to whom counting the days and dollars was of primary importance.

Happy to be working on such congenial material and with such a spirited company of actors, Hawks established a loose, freewheeling atmosphere on the set, and except for the irksome specter of Wallis looming over it, he had a grand time making *Ceiling Zero*. Although most of the flying sequences used miniatures filmed in the studio or made do with phony cockpit mock-ups, the stunts of Dizzy buzzing the airfield upside down were done by the Hollywood ace stunt pilot Paul Mantz. At home one morning, Hawks asked his six-year-old son David, "How would you like to fly upside down?" and took him to the shoot for a memorable spin with Mantz. Amelia Earhart was briefly around as an unofficial consultant and took Meta Carpenter, who held script on the picture, on a ride over Los Angeles. Cagney was in a feisty mood and showed up on the set having grown a little mustache, probably to make himself look a bit older but possibly also to tweak the noses of the Warner Bros. executives, with whom he was feuding. This was to be Cagney's last picture for the studio before his walkout, which saw him make two pictures at Grand National before returning to Warners with a more favorable deal.

Cutting as it went, *Ceiling Zero* was finished in six weeks at a total cost of only $375,000. To show how the studio fixed things in its favor, however, 31 percent of this sum, or $116,250, represented studio overhead, charged alike to all films, while depreciation accounted for another 4 percent, meaning that the total direct cost was only $243,950, including $30,500 for Cagney and $16,000 for O'Brien. On December 19, just over two months from the time it started shooting, it had a successful sneak preview, then opened on January 16 in New York to strong reviews and good business.

With the exceptions of *Scarface* and, for many people, *Twentieth Century*, *Ceiling Zero* today plays as the most strictly entertaining film Hawks made up to that point in his career. Cagney's performance as Dizzy is dazzling, even audacious, brimming with bantam cock effrontery and a knowing, even lewd sexuality unmatched in any of his other films. He's given an entrance that would be hard to beat: after having been introduced over the radio with his irreverent patter, as well as with his friend Jake's buildup as "the best cock-eyed pilot on this airline or any other," Dizzy buzzes the field upside down, lands, and, upon jumping out of his cockpit, is affectionately tossed around like a human beanbag by all his cronies before landing in a heap on the tarmac at the feet of a disapproving federal inspector. The way O'Brien snaps out his dialogue, it's as if he stepped right out of *The Front Page*, even down to his character; his Jake Lee is Hildy Johnson as if he had quit working as a reporter and settled down with his wife and a city-desk editorial job. And June Travis (née Grabiner), as Tommy, could not be more appealing, making a striking entrance enthusiastically emerging from her plane after soloing, garbed—in what would become preferred Hawks fashion—in a pilot's uniform and an adapted Haile Selassie helmet. In very fast company, she holds her own with poise and humor, batting the come-ons back at Dizzy as quickly as he tosses them out. Along with Carole Lombard in *Twentieth Century*, she is the most self-sufficient, sexy, and forthright woman in Hawks's films to that time. It was to remain her career highlight, however, as she got stuck mainly with B pictures for the remainder of the 1930s, before concentrating on the stage.

In nearly a dozen ways Hawks's handling of the material in *Ceiling Zero* prefigures his more extensive treatment of recurring themes and situations in his later work. In more than a third of his subsequent films, Hawks would constrict the action to a limited physical space, a safe haven threatened by unpredictable elements trying to intrude from the outside. In *Ceiling Zero*, the impression of a rarefied, almost abstracted world in which philosophy is expressed through action is intensified by the flat, almost B-movie-fake sets; the impact of the characters' behavior, along with its thematic resonance, would be much different in a hyperrealistic setting. The machine-gun, overlapping dialogue direction, which Hawks initiated in *Twentieth Century*, is cranked up even more here, would reach its zenith in *His Girl Friday*, and would continue to be used judiciously throughout his career. The theme of competition between men, used initially in *A Girl in Every Port*, resurfaces here and would remain a thread through many later films. But the way he uses the "girl he used to go with" motif here, in the context of the friendship between Jake and Dizzy, echoes *The Dawn Patrol* and directly foreshadows the much more prominent use of the same situation in *Only Angels Have Wings*.

The vibrancy, casualness, and directness of the romance between Dizzy and Tommy provides a model for many that were to come in Hawks's films thereafter. Although the frank elements of the male-female relations in *Scarface, The Crowd Roars, Tiger Shark, Barbary Coast*, and even *Today We Live* give indications of Hawks's preference for keeping the sexual current close to the surface, it's as if *Ceiling Zero* helped teach him that he could push his characters to be considerably more suggestive and insolent, lessons that had their payoff specifically in the Bogart-Bacall films, but in others as well. As usual, there is the refusal to yield to the expected Hollywood sentimentality and mawkishness; Hawks liked his characters, men and women, to be available and ready to spark when the fuse was lit, and characters settled into marriage and domesticity continued to be pushed further into the margins, or eliminated altogether (witness how the portrait of Jake's marriage is painted with one quick, isolated scene of him and Mary sitting at home playing backgammon).

Hawks's preoccupation with crippling, disabling injury is placed front and center with the character of Mike, a pathetic walking reminder of what might befall any pilot who survives a crash. Hawks's fondness for the graceful but loaded physical gesture is present here in the exchanges of cigarettes and the small, unspoken things the characters do for one another, although such business would be elaborated far more extensively in later films, from *Only Angels Have Wings* and *To Have and Have Not* to *Rio Bravo* and *Hatari!* The specific incident of Texas's fatal landing in inclement weather is repeated in Joe's crash in *Only Angels Have Wings*, as is the stoic reaction to sudden death and deprivation. For Jake, the climax of *Ceiling Zero* surely must qualify as the most tragic day of his life, in that his two closest friends, Dizzy and Texas, are both killed in plane crashes. But after only the briefest of moments, Jake pulls himself together and buries his sorrow in his work rather than indulging it. Again, this instinctive stoicism, borne by many of the World War I generation though more evident in Hawks's work than in that of any other American director, was more eloquently and completely expressed later on but is squarely on display here, and not enshrouded in an alcoholic fog as it was in *The Dawn Patrol* and *Today We Live*.

Dizzy's plunge to earth after deliberately allowing his plane's wings to encrust with ice represents yet another explicitly suicidal ending in Hawks's work, a precedent set in *The Dawn Patrol*. But his next picture would mark the last of these, and Hawks later expressed his disapproval of suicide as the coward's way out of problems, and a simplistic and dramatically expedient way to conclude complicated, high-pressure scenarios. Beyond this, as he increasingly dealt with characters that he personally liked, he didn't want to knock them off. Keeping characters alive was also an astute commercial move. Hawks deliberately allowed Harry Morgan to live in *To Have and Have Not* though Hemingway had not, and what promises to be an unavoidably murderous finale in *Red River* is averted. And, wartime allegiances to the side, *Ceiling Zero* contains as specific an expression of Hawks's (and no doubt Wead's) political sentiments as can be found anywhere: with the threat of ever heavier government regulation cramping Jake's style in the way he runs the airline, Jake remarks that he just wants Washington "to leave us alone."

16

The Road to Glory

The Road to Glory represented a unique challenge in Hawks's career; tackling someone else's jigsaw puzzle and making it his own. The story is *The Dawn Patrol* set in the trenches instead of the air, an epic war film nearly as claustrophobic, intimate, and abstract as *Ceiling Zero*, a look at professionals doing their jobs within the much grander context of a cyclical view of warfare and history. It is also static and rather dull, recycling many of the ideas already stated in *The Dawn Patrol* and *Today We Live* but providing no new ones.

The jigsaw puzzle consisted of pieces of a French film with which Hawks and his collaborators attempted to interlock their own narrative. The new Hollywood company 20th Century–Fox was related in name only to the company for which Hawks had made all his silent films. Fox, which had fallen into bankruptcy, was merged in 1935 with Twentieth Century Pictures, which Joseph Schenck had created in 1933 with Darryl F. Zanuck after the latter left Warner Bros. With much fanfare, the new company set up shop at Movietone City, an expansive lot on Los Angeles's West Side between MGM and Westwood. Adjacent to the soundstages and executive offices was an enormous parcel of open space that for twenty-five years would serve as a superb back lot where scenes representing everything from World War I France to a Western street could be filmed. In the early 1960s, the increasingly valuable real estate was sold off and grew into Century City.

Zanuck was in charge of production for the new company, and one of his early moves was to purchase the American rights to a French film called *Les Croix de Bois* (*Wooden Crosses*), directed by Raymond Bernard and based on Roland Dorgeles's novel of the same name. The Pathé-Nathan production was a major attraction in Europe, as it featured a cast consisting largely of veterans intent upon revealing the war in all its unvarnished horror, and had its world premiere at the Geneva Disarmament Conference early in 1932.

An attempt by the French to make their own *All Quiet on the Western Front*, the film serves up its theme in the opening sequence, which hinges upon a dissolve from a division of soldiers standing at attention to an enormous field of crosses. Then, as everyone cheers the warriors enthusiastically mobilizing for the front, a victim is solemnly carried by. The picture, which is powerfully directed to bring its motivating messages home, stresses the endless periods of waiting the soldiers have to endure before becoming cannon fodder in a sustained battle that lasts for days. The story doesn't adhere very closely to specific individuals so much as it concentrates on the horrendous spectacle and sense of waste, useless carnage, and destruction. Like so many World War I stories, the film intended to describe a generation essentially wiped out by a pointless war, and it certainly succeeded in making its argument clearly.

Zanuck had no intention of releasing the French-language film in the United States but bought it instead for its spectacular and highly realistic battle footage, which would have been nearly impossible, and very expensive, to duplicate in Hollywood. Having worked well with him at Warner Bros., Zanuck then called in Hawks, who agreed that the French picture had "some fabulous film in it—marvelous scenes of great masses of people moving up to the front and through trenches—wonderful night stuff." Crafting characters and relationships that bore no relation to the French film, Hawks didn't strain himself thinking up a story. He merely took the cyclical premise of *The Dawn Patrol*, Irvin Cobb's anecdote of one officer replacing another in the job of sending out young soldiers to die, and brought front and center the love rivalry that he had pushed into the background in the earlier film, the one inspired by a World War I veteran and Princeton graduate. "He was completely shell-shocked and he'd been living on brandy and aspirin. He told us about a little girl who seemed to be patriotically influenced into living with him and taking care of him. I told Faulkner about this guy and we copied the idea," Hawks admitted. Hawks also cavalierly lifted from *Today We Live* the blindness motif and joint suicidal ending, where a sighted man and a blind one die together.

Hawks's enlistment for *The Road to Glory* kept the director working at an incredible pace, which, in addition to helping him cover his expenses and debts, kept him out of the house and at a distance from his problems with Athole. By late 1935, Athole was pregnant again, with the child expected the following May. Without a pause, Hawks went straight from Warner Bros. in late November to the Westwood lot, where he began sketching out a story for the war film with Joel Sayre, a young writer known for the college novel *Ricketay-Rax*. Just as they were starting, Hawks heard the horrible news from Mississippi: Faulkner's brother Dean had been killed while giving a flying lesson in the Waco aircraft Bill had sold him. Better than anyone, Hawks knew how this tragedy would affect his friend, having lived through the same thing five years before. Like Hawks, Faulkner had to identify the body, but he then went much further than that, working with the mortician all night in an attempt to make Dean's horribly disfigured face presentable for the sake of the widow.

On top of that, in early December Faulkner's financially strapped publishers were obliged to call in a loan they had made to him. The novelist was deeply into work on *Absalom, Absalom!* at that point, but his bank account was now depleted, forcing him to look again to Hollywood for some quick earnings. Although Zanuck was less than enthusiastic about hiring Faulkner, about whom the legends of epic drinking and preference for working "at home" were already growing, Hawks enjoyed sufficient sway to get his friend hired at a thousand dollars a week, on condition that he work with Sayre. This was fine with both Hawks and Faulkner, and the writer reported to the studio on December 16.

Although Faulkner would work closely with Hawks on this picture just as he had at MGM, this was not a "Howard Hawks production," as most of his previous pictures had been. Zanuck's designated associate producer on *The Road to Glory* was the elegant, well-educated Georgian Nunnally Johnson, a former journalist primarily known as a screenwriter. He and Faulkner hit it off immediately; they shared a pint at their first meeting, at which Faulkner poured out the story of his brother's death, then proceeded to get plastered together that night. Faulkner also got on well with the gregarious Sayre.

For the sake of his friend's continued employability more than that of the picture, Hawks admonished Faulkner not to go on one of his drunks until the script was finished. But still having nightmares about his brother's plane crash, bedeviled by the as-yet-unfinished *Absalom, Absalom!*, and frustrated by his domestic situation back in Oxford, Faulkner couldn't help himself. He was also stunned and unnerved by the woman he met in Hawks's outer office when he reported for work. Although Meta Carpenter had begun working as Hawks's secretary on *Sutter's Gold*, she had started after Faulkner had finished his own work on the project and so met him for the first time now. A lovely, intelligent honey blonde with a sweet Mississippi accent that made Faulkner feel right at home, she was impressed by the writer, who was cordial with her. Two days later, however, he turned up in the office drunk and badgering her to have dinner with him. Panicked, she retreated into Hawks's inner sanctum and begged her boss to inform his friend that she, as a well-raised southern girl, had no intention of going out with a married man.

Although Faulkner was back on good behavior while he and Carpenter worked together—she trying to decipher his tiny handwriting in order to type his script pages—he continued to invite her to dinner. Even after she finally accepted and began seeing him every night, his courtship remained slow and cautious. Well before they actually started a physical affair, Faulkner intuitively sensed that Carpenter, who had been raised just fifty-five miles from Oxford, offered the promise of an emotional outlet for him, a salvation from the oppressiveness of his life while in Hollywood, and later a way for him to express his pent-up passion after two years of not sleeping with his wife.

Hawks, who was always very correct with his attractive secretary, watched all this from a bemused distance, even though the affair involved two of the people most closely involved in his daily life. It certainly didn't hurt Faulkner's productivity, as he turned out as many as thirty-five script pages a day when five was considered the industry norm. Working right through to New Year's Eve, Faulkner and Sayre delivered a 170-page first-draft screenplay. Drawing on the Verdun veteran Hawks had met years before, the script opened with Captain Paul Laroche keeping company with the lovely nurse Monique and subsisting on a diet of aspirin and brandy due to the horrible pressure of his job: half of his company of the Thirty-ninth Infantry gets killed every time it goes to the front. Repeating the gambit from *The Dawn Patrol*, his new young lieutenant, Michel Denet, ridicules this record. Denet also begins an affair with Monique, which further places the men at odds. After numerous reckonings and battles, Laroche is blinded. Just as in *Today We Live* Robert Young's Claude considers himself useless to Joan Crawford's Diana once he's lost his sight and clears the path for Gary Cooper's Bogard, so does Laroche yield to Denet once he's blinded, by undertaking a suicidal mission with his father, in this case, rather than with his best friend.

The script went through four more drafts—all credited to Sayre and Nunnally Johnson, although the film itself would credit Sayre and Faulkner. Faulkner had left the picture "temporarily due to illness" on January 7 after having finished *Absalom, Absalom!* and going on the bender Hawks had warned against. Some of the significant plot points can rather easily be traced to Faulkner through his work on *Today We Live* and the unfilmed *War Birds,* as well as through aspects of his fiction. It is also conceivable that Carpenter's relationship with Faulkner may have influenced Denet's initial attempted seduction of Monique, which he undertakes while playing "Liebestraum" on the piano. Faulkner was entirely immune to the emotional power of music—"It's unnatural," he told screenwriter Harold Jack Bloom years later. "The only real music is birds singing."—but Carpenter was a trained classical musician whose passionate love for it was plain to her man. Captain Laroche's unusual attachment to his (unseen) sister harks back to *Scarface*, while it was Zanuck who suggested the rosary as a prop that passes among Laroche, Monique, and Denet. Nunnally Johnson claimed that the nearly entirely rewritten dialogue that appears in the script's fifth draft, delivered on January 27, just as the film was entering production, was all his, and it might well have been. All the same, Faulkner returned to the studio in late February and helped Hawks collate all the material from the various drafts into what he wanted for the film.

Not only was the material less than fresh, but the casting kept *The Road to Glory* from catching fire as well. Fredric March and Warner Baxter both belonged to Fox's stable of stars and were assigned to the picture by Zanuck. While competent and convincing as Denet and Laroche, respectively, they were also cold and uninvolving personalities unable, on their own, to bring the script to life. Then there was June Lang. Hawks's burgeoning reputation as a star maker took a hit this time. As Hawks said, "I was making tests one Sunday of about ten girls, and this girl appeared. . . . And she was so bad I said to the cameraman, 'My God, we've got to stay here a little while longer—this girl is so bad—it'll ruin her completely if we print this.' So I worked and worked and worked with her and turned out a scene, and Zanuck, Schenck and everybody went absolutely crazy about this girl. They took her on, and I was stuck with her."

Unfortunately, Lang's awkwardness is immediately apparent in the first scene with Baxter, where her high-school-drama-class stiffness helps get the picture off to a poor start. Her pencil-thin eyebrows and perfectly coiffed bangs do little to improve her credibility as a wartime nurse, but there is no denying her modelish beauty. In the end, Hawks felt that "she didn't annoy you" but "she was just a child and she thought like a child. It was terribly hard to do an adult picture with her." In story terms, he didn't believe that Monique was supposed to be in love with Captain Laroche, but "you really couldn't tell much from the picture because June Lang couldn't act, and it was pretty hard to get across an emotion of any kind." Hawks made the best of it, but admitted, "We'd have got more if we'd had a more experienced actress." One of the actresses he liked when he tested her that Sunday was twenty-year-old Clara Lou Sheridan, who had already done bits of no consequence in more than a dozen pictures. Her heavy Texas accent ruled her out as a French girl, but Hawks recommended her to Jack Warner, who signed her and changed her name to Ann Sheridan. She and Hawks had a fling some time thereafter, and more than a decade later he cast her in *I Was a Male War Bride*.

The filming was arduous. Even though the company was shooting only on the back lot, and not on some distant location, the long February and March nights were bitterly cold and difficult. Tempers grew short as the technical and logistical demands of the period war film made progress slow, and relations among the cast and crew became strained. Working with Hawks for the first time, the cinematographer Gregg Toland didn't achieve the sort of startling nighttime effects he created a few years later on *The Long Voyage Home*, but he expertly matched his style to the existing French battle footage and launched a strong friendship with Hawks in the process. Other compensations for the director included working with Lionel Barrymore, who gave a very good performance as Laroche's father, who slips into the company as the oldest private in the army and accompanies his son on the fateful final mission, and finally working with his friend the irrepressible Gregory Ratoff, to supply the nominal comic relief.

Hawks's characteristic understatement pays off in certain scenes, notably the creepy one, adapted virtually unchanged from the French film, in which the French soldiers hear Germans digging underneath their quarters with the intention of placing mines there and blowing them up. The quality of war as a never-ending night with no ultimate meaning is also strongly conveyed, although viewers who might see this as an antiwar tract along the lines of *All Quiet on the Western Front* are barking up the wrong tree, since none of the key creative personnel, including Zanuck, would have considered themselves pacifists. Hawks stated, "I've never made a picture to be anti anything or pro anything. I flew. I knew what the Air Force was up against. I used that theme from *Dawn Patrol* in another picture about war [*The Road to Glory*], and the theme is very simple. It's a man who's in command and sends people out to die and then he's killed himself and some other poor bastard has to send them out to die." Hawks also dispensed with the ghostly processional of war dead at the end, further emphasizing his cyclical, and defiantly nonpolitical, view of war. "I'll come back. I always come back. I'm eternal," Laroche tells his mistress at the outset, and he does, figuratively, as a different man, one who will be compelled to give the same speech and the same miserable orders, and probably to suffer the same fate.

Given the unrelievedly bleak mood of the film, *The Road to Glory* did fairly well at the box office, breaking a five-year-old house record in its opening at the Rivoli in New York and enjoying solid, if not spectacular, runs in major cities throughout the country. "Strictly a man's picture," *Variety* dubbed it, "but has done business on that score." But when Hawks returned to World War I one last time, five years later, he would take a very different, and more popular, tack.

17

Include Me Out: *Come and Get It*

With three pictures in release, a new baby on the way, and an income commensurate with that of any filmmaker in Hollywood, Howard Hawks should have had a great year in 1936. Instead, he spent it in the crucible both professionally and personally, enduring turmoil, frustration, and hurt brought on mostly by his own obstinacy, selfishness, and coldness. The year provided vivid examples of Hawks's will and stubbornness, his habit of just turning and walking away when things didn't go his way, no matter the consequences for others. A positive reading of his behavior would praise his resolve and sense of principle; a negative one would see simple childish petulance.

The difficulty of Hawks's home life led him to remove himself from it as much as possible through nonstop work and obsessive gambling. A new baby wasn't exactly what Hawks had had in mind when Athole got pregnant again; David was six now, Peter ten, and for some time Hawks had been unable to see how things between him and his wife would work out. Her breakdowns were just periodic but still always looming ahead. For her, even if her husband was scarcely around, having another baby made her happier than she had been in a long time and gave her the hope that this would help keep her faltering marriage together. If she was lucky, she didn't know about Hawks's ongoing affair with the statuesque showgirl and dancer Mary Lou Holtz.

Professionally, Hawks should have known what getting involved with Sam Goldwyn again would mean, but his need for money—and Goldwyn would provide a $3,500 weekly paycheck—outweighed his hesitations. Even if Goldwyn sometimes seemed, or played, the fool, no director ever put anything past him. Hawks thought he could this time, and he tried, but to no avail in the end.

Goldwyn's taste for big literary names and properties led him to inquire about Pulitzer Prize–winning novelist Edna Ferber's *Come and Get It* even before it was published in late 1934 and to eventually pay forty thousand dollars for the screen rights. Set in the author's native Wisconsin in the late 1800s and early 1900s, the sprawling novel centers on an unscrupulous lumber baron who rides roughshod over the land and his loved ones in pursuit of wealth and status. As far as Ferber was concerned, it was "a story of the rape of America," and the book's passionate ecological theme was the overriding impetus behind its writing.

Goldwyn put his forces to work on the project at once. Edward Chodorov was the first screenwriter assigned to the adaptation, but when Ferber was critical of the changes he made, particularly with the lead female character of Lotta, he was taken off the job. Ferber persistently badgered Goldwyn to hire Howard Estabrook to write the script, but as he was presently under contract to Fox and on loan to MGM, Goldwyn turned to Jane Murfin, who in November 1935 handed in a draft Ferber considered "excellent" through the first half but problematic thereafter.

The lead character was hard to cast. Barney Glasgow was written as a big, burly roughhouser who could take on any lumberjack on his crew, and the span of the story sees him age from thirtyish to his fifties. It remains difficult to think of any actor at any studio at the time who would have been ideal for it. Goldwyn tried to persuade his greatest rival, Louis B. Mayer, to loan him Spencer Tracy. But Mayer, who was then grooming Tracy for major stardom by giving him more sympathetic roles, rejected Goldwyn's overtures out of hand. Almost by default, the 1930s prototypical tycoon, Edward Arnold, got the part.

Choosing an actress to play the double role of Lotta was equally daunting. As written, Lotta was a pathetic, lame little barkeep who is loved, then dumped by the callous Barney Glasgow, who decides to marry up socially in order to guarantee his career and fortune. In distress, she marries Barney's best friend, the hulking Swede Swan Bostrom. They have a beautiful daughter, also named Lotta, upon whom the besotted Barney lavishes money and gifts in a foolish, pathetic attempt to make her love him and thus make up for his having deserted her mother. Instead, the young Lotta is attracted to Barney's son.

Just as she was beginning her role for Hawks as the mercenary saloon girl in *Barbary Coast*, Goldwyn announced that Miriam Hopkins would play Lotta in *Come and Get It*. Hawks, who made two other pictures in the meantime, eventually persuaded the producer that Hopkins wasn't the ideal choice. Abruptly, Goldwyn announced with considerable fanfare that Virginia Bruce had won the double role. Newcomer John Payne was also mentioned for the role of Barney Glasgow's good-looking son. Involved with *The Road to Glory*, Hawks bided his time.

While the director was still shooting in the trenches on the Fox back lot, he dispatched his ever reliable right-hand man Richard Rosson to begin filming second-unit footage in Idaho in mid-March. The crew's assignment was to capture dramatic footage of falling timber, camp work, logjams, huge trunks sliding down flumes, hundreds of cut trees freed from ice and snow by explosion and sent downriver, and other lumbermill activities that would make up an exciting montage at the beginning of the picture. The crew was rugged and expert, but there were significant problems nonetheless. A lot of the action proved very difficult to photograph, particularly the flumes, and when the company arrived in Lewiston, they found themselves in the midst of a particularly bitter labor dispute. Eventually, it took four months of intermittent shooting, in Wisconsin and Canada as well as in Idaho, to get everything they needed, but it was worth it, as Rosson topped even his work in *Tiger Shark*, delivering footage that most critics felt was the most exciting in the finished picture.

Hawks took on *Come and Get It* with considerable trepidation. Not only was he familiar firsthand with the sort of strangling effect Goldwyn had on directors, but he had serious reservations about the story and its commercial potential. He liked the first half, with its emphasis on the logging life, Barney Glasgow's ambition, and the great love he discards, but he thought the second half "pretty lousy." He considered the problems formidable enough to turn the assignment down, but he gave in when Goldwyn's wife, Frances, begged him to do it. There were plenty of reasons why Hawks was regarded as the ideal director for the film. Not only was it a rambunctious piece peopled by strong, lusty characters, but the story literally took place in the Hawks and Howard families' backyard. Edna Ferber had grown up about twenty-five miles north of Neenah, in Appleton, Wisconsin, where her father was rabbi to a small Jewish community. She had left that life behind to become a reporter and, by the 1920s, one of the most successful and prolific American novelists. Hawks sometimes claimed that Barney Glasgow was based on his own grandfather, a boast with a pinch of truth to it. The character was, in fact, a composite but was inspired mostly by the dominant Wisconsin lumberman and politician of the time, F. J. Sensenbrenner. A trait or two might have been taken from C. W. Howard, but the important thing was that Hawks knew this sort of man well; he had spent the first ten years of his life around such men, men like his neighbors Kimberly and Clark. When Ferber learned that Hawks was Charlie Howard's grandson, she concurred with the Goldwyns' decision to entrust her book to him.

Hawks had known Jules Furthman since the mid-1920s, when they were at Paramount together. Since then, the caustic writer's irreverent, cynical, slyly insinuating style had greatly enhanced the careers of his friends Josef von Sternberg and Victor Fleming. But because of his ongoing alliances with Ben Hecht and William Faulkner, Hawks had never had the occasion to work with Furthman. As he was intent, however, upon changing the first Lotta from a shrinking violet into "a big, luscious girl, full of bravado," a sexy saloon singer in the Dietrich manner, who better to call upon than the writer of *Morocco* himself?

The son of a prominent Chicago judge, Furthman had contributed to newspapers and magazines before turning to the screen in the mid-1910s. Forced to use the pseudonym Stephen Fox during the war years because of his Germanic name (while some people may have presumed that he was Jewish, he was not), he worked mostly at the Fox Studios through the mid-1920s, collaborating repeatedly with such directors as Maurice Tourneur, Henry King, John Ford, Clarence Brown, and Arthur Rosson and directing three films himself in 1920–21. He joined Paramount in 1925, just when Hawks was there, and soon rose to become one of Hollywood's top screenwriters. He came into his own in his work for Fleming and Sternberg, notably *Morocco* and *Shanghai Express,* which oozed with innuendo and understated, offbeat eroticism.

The problem with Furthman, however, was that he was one of the nastiest, most cantankerous characters to carve out a place for himself in Hollywood. As the years went on, fewer and fewer employers would tolerate him, despite his undeniable talent. Hawks said that he, Sternberg, and Fleming "were about the only people who could put up with the son of a bitch. . . . He was such a mean guy that we thought he was just great. He was bright, and he was short. He'd say, 'You stupid guy' to somebody who wasn't as smart as him. He needed help, but when he got help he was awful good."

Furthman's personal life was intensely private. When the wailing of his retarded son annoyed his neighbors, Furthman, along with his wife and son, moved to a remote corner of unfashionable Culver City, where in his specially designed greenhouse, he became an obsessive cultivator of orchids. Unlike most of Hawks's other illustrious writers, Furthman was the author of nothing outside of his screenplays, gave no interviews, left no papers, and thus remains one of the great enigmas of Hollywood. Pauline Kael once opined that Furthman wrote "about half of the most entertaining movies to come out of Hollywood." (Hecht, she said, "wrote most of the other half.") Hawks clearly demanded, and got, the best out of Furthman. But as the years and the films mount up, it becomes evident that Furthman's decisive influence over Hawks, both in the scripts he actually wrote and, indirectly, in further sharpening Hawks's own methods and concerns, cannot be overrated.

Hawks so charmed Edna Ferber when they met that she didn't mind when he mentioned how he wanted to alter a few things. He then hired Furthman, who, at Hawks's instruction, began changing things quite a bit. As everyone but Ferber and Goldwyn, who had "a great fetish for prominent writers," agreed, the story needed work. Just as he thought he could slip through David Selznick's net of total control on *Viva Villa!* because he'd be off on location, so Hawks was emboldened in his moves to change *Come and Get It* because of Goldwyn's prolonged absence from the studio. Hawks reported to the lot on April 1, when the producer was supposed to be in Europe. However, Goldwyn only got as far as New York, where gastrointestinal problems aborted the trip. Hawks went to New York briefly in late April to confer with Goldwyn at the Waldorf-Astoria, and shortly after the director returned to Los Angeles, Goldwyn was headed for the hospital to have several feet of rotting intestine removed.

It was during this time, with Rosson busy capturing spectacular logging footage and Furthman rewriting Murfin's script, that Hawks had to decide who would play Lotta. After ten years as a director, Hawks had launched Carole Lombard as a star, but he hadn't yet truly discovered an essentially unknown actress and put her definitively on the map. *Come and Get It* gave him the opportunity to do so if he found someone whom both he and Goldwyn believed could both pull off the double role and, in effect, carry the picture. Hawks ran endless reels of film — screen tests, upcoming pictures, private material — and was struck by one girl he saw in a student film, Antoinette Lees, who had the kind of fresh, spunky quality Hawks liked but was not quite ready for the lead. Nonetheless, Goldwyn put her under contract, changed her name to Andrea Leeds, and assigned her to play Barney Glasgow's daughter Evvie.

Then Hawks saw some rushes from a Bing Crosby musical currently in production called *Rhythm on the Range*, featuring a new Paramount contract player named Frances Farmer. Just twenty-two, Farmer had completed two pictures, but Paramount obviously hadn't figured out what to

do with her, not having offered her anything remotely challenging or interesting. An instinctive contrarian who had stirred up controversy as a University of Washington drama student when an essay she wrote won her a
trip to the Soviet Union, she was already becoming fed up with Hollywood
after less than a year there. But for Hawks, her high-strung temperament
merely added to the appeal of her extraordinary beauty; she was, he enthused, "the cleanest physical thing you've ever seen. She always looked
as though she were shining." Her natural blond looks and clear blue eyes
instantly reminded people of Lombard, and her sturdy build would be
another plus in the role of a Wisconsin North Woods girl.

Even more taken with her when she came in to read, ostensibly for a
small part, Hawks told Farmer at the end of their first meeting that she should
play the lead. The actress was all for that, and Hawks worked intensively
with her in preparation for a screen test. Against her director's wishes, however, she insisted on wearing heavy makeup for the test; deliberately giving
her free rein, Hawks stood by silently as she acted up a storm. When he
screened the result for her, she immediately recognized how bad she had
been, and from then on was Hawks's devoted pupil, following his advice
on all matters and trusting him implicitly. As research for a second test,
Hawks took her on a tour of Los Angeles dives looking for prostitutes or loose
women whose attitudes Farmer might adopt for her performance. Hawks
said that they finally found a waitress in a beer joint who would serve as a
fantastic model, and he asked the actress to come in every night for ten days
to watch her every move. On her own, Farmer apparently went even further to research the first Lotta, the saloon singer: "I went into the red-light
districts of Los Angeles, wearing a black wig to disguise myself, and studied
the girls who worked the streets. I learned their mannerisms. The way they
talked out of the sides of their mouths, with a cigarette dangling from a
corner. I acquired their speech inflections. I watched how they drank their
liquor and picked up their men. I mimicked their swagger, their cheapness.
And I completely immersed myself in the role, studying it from every angle."

For the second test, Farmer used no special makeup, only the black
wig, and "she was just fabulous," according to Hawks; "her whole attitude
changed, her whole method of talking." For Hawks, Farmer was the ideal
actress, a young woman with spirit and a natural rebelliousness who was
beautiful, innately talented, hardworking, and hung on every word he said.
Until the end of his life, he sang her praises, once saying that only Lombard
and Rosalind Russell could be mentioned in the same breath with her,

another time flatly stating, "I think that she had more talent than anyone I ever worked with."

Hawks casually mentioned that she went out with him on his boat a couple of times "wearing her sweatshirt and her dungarees and carrying a toothbrush in her pocket"—just the sort of comment he might hope would lead people to suspect he'd had an affair with her. It is possible, and most certainly Hawks would have liked to, but the evidence weighs against it: two years before, Farmer had married the young actor William Anderson, [who was just beginning his screen career under the name Leif Erickson,] and she was not known to have strayed outside her marriage until her later, disastrous affair with Clifford Odets; neither Hawks nor Farmer ever said as much themselves, and Meta Carpenter, who was with Hawks virtually every minute during the making of *Come and Get It*, believed nothing happened. On the other hand, Hawks was ultradiscreet, and as both he and Farmer were married, they conceivably could have made a point of keeping an affair absolutely secret from everybody.

Farmer was receiving a mere seventy-five dollars a week under her contract at Paramount, which asked for double that to loan her to Goldwyn; for her wonderful performance in *Come and Get It*, the actress received precisely $562.50, with Paramount pocketing the same amount. By contrast, Edward Arnold earned $52,500, and Hawks took home $73,150. But Farmer, well aware of the career-making opportunity at hand, threw herself into her role and, in working with Hawks, enjoyed the one genuinely rewarding professional experience of her aborted screen career. "Howard Hawks was one of the finest and most sensitive directors in the business," she said. "He gave every scene a minute examination, both psychological and visual, and under his direction I was secure and full of anticipation." Farmer wore her stiff, cumbersome costumes at home to become completely comfortable in them, and even though her voice was naturally low and resonant, just the way Hawks liked it, she worked with him to improve it further and pitch it slightly differently for each of her two characters.

With Goldwyn recovering from his operation in New York and no one at the studio able to restrain him, Hawks pushed Furthman further in his rewriting, especially of the early sections, to accommodate their new conception of the first Lotta and the outstanding actress Hawks had found to play her. On May 20, Athole gave birth to a baby girl named Barbara, but according to Meta Carpenter, Hawks disappeared that week, heading to Mexico on a solo trip. However, by May 30, his fortieth birthday, he was back in Hollywood to attend the premiere of *The Road to Glory* at Grauman's Chinese with Norma Shearer. Two weeks later, Hawks sued Universal for what he judged to be an unpaid $45,000 for his work two years before in preparing *Sutter's Gold,* which James Cruze had finally, and unmemorably, directed. Six weeks later, Universal and Hawks settled out of court for an undisclosed sum.

Rounding out the casting of *Come and Get It,* Hawks had no problems with Goldwyn contract player Joel McCrea for the role of Barney Glasgow's son, the young romantic lead, but amazed everyone by insisting on skinny Walter Brennan to play Barney's best friend, Swan Bostrom, "the strongest man in the North woods" and the man who ends up marrying Lotta. Also onboard was the lean, strikingly handsome tennis star Frank Shields, as the working-class kid Barney's daughter wants to marry.

Goldwyn wanted to get the picture rolling by the first week in June to ensure delivery to exhibitors before the end of the year, but Hawks's lingering dissatisfaction with the material, particularly the second section, caused him to delay until June 20. From the beginning, the atmosphere on the shoot was tense, "thick with strain, indecision, and malevolence," according to Meta Carpenter. This stemmed mainly from Hawks's unhappiness over the story line and his doubts about ever being able to shape it to his own liking. Despite the months of preparation, the director, Carpenter felt, "was putting scenes in front of the camera before he was completely satisfied that his players were ready." The ranks were not divided nearly to the extent they had been on *Barbary Coast* two years before, but feelings were mixed about Farmer; it took Edward Arnold practically no time to realize how good she was, but others considered her remote and self-absorbed. Hawks continued to work closely and patiently with her, and the unsettled feeling on the set was partially alleviated by Walter Brennan, who always lightened the mood, and cinematographer Gregg Toland, a sympathetic and generous collaborator for Hawks as well as the cast.

On July 4, with two weeks of filming completed, Goldwyn arrived from New York to continue his convalescence at his Beverly Hills home, although he was still too sick to go to the studio. This bought Hawks a bit of time, as did Goldwyn's preoccupation with how much film William Wyler was shooting on *Dodsworth,* the other Goldwyn production of the moment. Working on a customarily lavish Goldwyn schedule of fifty-four days and a $973,000 budget, Hawks wasn't particularly behind or over schedule, but he was fussing over Farmer's performance and adding plenty of business not laid out in the script; a barroom brawl climaxes memorably with participants dangerously flinging large metal serving trays around the room like Frisbees, something Hawks recalled seeing at a saloon in San Francisco. Hawks knew Goldwyn well enough to realize that his boss would be furious at any changes he made in the work of a big writer like Edna Ferber, so he tried to put off showing him anything, telling Frances Goldwyn that her husband should wait until he was entirely recovered before seeing the footage. Finally, however, Goldwyn would not be denied, and as Hawks had predicted, he blew his stack. "I found that Hawks had filmed a completely different story from what you had written," the producer wrote to Edna Ferber. "After I saw what he had filmed, I suffered a relapse for a full two weeks; it upset me so." Hawks asked Goldwyn to have associate producer Merritt Hulburd work with him to try to bring the story back around to what Goldwyn had in mind, and Hawks continued shooting, pressing further into the second part of the story, which he found particularly disconcerting.

According to Hawks, the end came after he delivered some newly written scenes in an attempt to placate his producer. Liking what he read, Goldwyn asked who the writer was, and when Hawks said he was, Goldwyn became apoplectic. "Writers should write and directors should direct!" he supposedly bellowed. Hawks later said that, deeply insulted by Goldwyn's obstinate silliness on this point, he quit; equally adamant about showing who was in charge, Goldwyn insisted that Hawks was fired. No one can say for sure, but Meta Carpenter recalled that after this fateful meeting, Hawks simply returned to the stage, picked up his things, and vanished without a word to his cast or crew.

This happened on Saturday, August 8, Hawks's forty-second day on the picture; according to the schedule, there were only twelve days of shooting remaining. For eight days, the production was shut down. For public consumption, Goldwyn and Hawks were described as having parted ways "amicably when impasse was reached over story angles and concluding episodes." Hawks even issued a statement "asserting that he believed Goldwyn should complete the picture in his own manner." But this was all a cover for violent feelings on both sides. As Meta Carpenter confirmed, "The rupture was far more bitter than that, and the amicability stressed in the news release was blatant fiction." According to Hawks, Irving Thalberg pleaded with him to patch things up with Goldwyn and finish the picture, but he refused to have anything more to do with the producer. For his part, Goldwyn brought Jane Murfin back to quickly rewrite the final scenes; then he had the brainstorm of getting William Wyler, who was just finishing *Dodsworth*, to take over *Come and Get It*. For any number of reasons, Wyler refused out of hand, which sent Goldwyn into such a fury that Wyler had to flee from the producer's house. But it shortly became clear that Wyler's contract obliged him to abide by Goldwyn's wishes or face suspension, in which case someone else would be brought in to finish *Dodsworth*. Facing the facts, Wyler reluctantly called Hawks to tell him what Goldwyn was forcing him to do, and, was surprised to learn that Hawks was still angling to get back on the project, although not to the point of becoming Goldwyn's obedient servant.

In the finished film, it is pretty easy to tell where Hawks left off and where Wyler began; the latter's scenes dominate the final half hour, and his more sincere, elegant, decorous style is apparent in the lavish garden party set piece and the assorted declarations of love that finally force Barney Glasgow to face his old age and allow his son and the young Lotta to go off together. Amidst the extreme conventionality of the film's final stretch is one crucial moment that foreshadows a famous Hawksian scene more than a decade hence: when Barney discovers his son kissing the woman he adores, he slaps him, whereupon Richard knocks his father down; at this, Lotta gets between them, much as Joanne Dru would intervene in the battle between John Wayne and Montgomery Clift in *Red River*. Ironically, the scene was staged by Wyler, although conceived by Furthman and Hawks.

A grouchy Wyler started filming his scenes on August 19, and if anyone was unhappier about the turn of events than Wyler, it was Frances Farmer. She legitimately felt abandoned, even betrayed, by the director who had left without explanation after winning her complete trust. "He brought her on and then left her high and dry," lamented Joel McCrea. "Well, Hawks didn't care about anybody except himself." Farmer hated Wyler's directorial technique of brusque, uncommunicative bullying and endlessly repeated takes, such a far cry from Hawks's quiet, attentive support. "Acting with Wyler is the nearest thing to slavery," she complained, although she still felt that her performance succeeded. "I was basically satisfied with my interpretation of the trollop, but the daughter role of a gentle, innocent girl was in no way challenging," she said, echoing Hawks's own reservations about the second half. For his part, Wyler, intensely aware of the actress's resentment of his presence, hated her right back: "The nicest thing I can say about Frances Farmer is that she is unbearable."

Wyler finally finished on September 19 after twenty-eight days of work, adding more than the ten minutes Hawks always alleged he had, but far less than what Goldwyn falsely claimed to Ferber: "I threw away most of what Hawks had photographed, put William Wyler on the picture and spent a good two months rephotographing it." Hawks shot for forty-two of the seventy days *Come and Get It* was in production. With the $172,848 spent on the additional work, the final budget came in at a hefty $1,111,200.

But the contentiousness was far from over. The bad blood between Goldwyn and Hawks was such that the producer initially removed his first director's name entirely from all advertising and publicity for the film, using only Wyler's. With the Screen Directors Guild still not recognized by the studios, there was no one in a position to officially object to this but Wyler himself, who wanted no credit at all and, for the rest of his life, did not consider it part of his true body of work. Rather than face the embarrassment of sending out a major film with no director listed at all, Goldwyn put both men's names on it, with Hawks's coming first. Even so, in interviews just before the film's release, Goldwyn went to great lengths to minimize Hawks's contributions. Still, the producer was confident that the picture would gross $2 million worldwide, thus ensuring him a profit.

After a heavily publicized world premiere in Frances Farmer's hometown of Seattle, *Come and Get It* opened commercially at the Rivoli Theater in Manhattan on November 11 and shortly thereafter in other key cities, to less than smashing results. *Variety* judged it "one of season's major disappointments. Campaign was big and good, notices were excellent, but it's apparent that Edward Arnold hasn't quite enough on the ball to pull 'em in alone. No femme names either, which is hurting." Ultimately, the film grossed $876,436 in the United States and half that overseas, leaving it well short of the break-even point. With *Dodsworth* an outright commercial flop, it was a poor year for Goldwyn.

The reviews of *Come and Get It* were, in fact, very good, always citing Rosson's spectacular logging footage at the beginning and commenting that the work of the two directors seemed to blend seamlessly. No doubt without his brother's knowledge, Bill Hawks cozied up to Goldwyn by wiring him as to how pleased he was with how the picture had turned out, and actress Louise Dresser cabled the producer to rave about Frances Farmer and insist that the newcomer was the perfect choice to play Stella Dallas in the new film Goldwyn was having trouble casting. Edna Ferber was two-faced, one day congratulating the producer for "the courage, sagacity and power of decision which you showed in throwing out the finished Hawks picture and undertaking the gigantic task of making what amounted to a new picture," on another refusing to do any publicity because she felt her motivating ecological theme had been completely ignored in the adaptation. The one real compensation for Goldwyn, such as it was, came at the

Academy Awards. The film editor Edward Curtiss, cutting his sixth and final feature for Hawks, was nominated, but Walter Brennan, validating Hawks's eccentric choice of him for the role of Swan Bostrom, won the first Oscar in the newly created supporting actor category.

Come and Get It, in the end, remains most compelling as the one film that reveals Frances Farmer as an alluring personality and might-have-been great star. Despite her literally breathtaking beauty, she was bland, and blandly used, in every other film she made, but she came entrancing to life for Hawks as the first Lotta. She also inspired Hawks in his most concerted effort yet to create a feminine screen persona from scratch, and the early Lotta certainly stands as the first fully realized prototype of the Hawksian woman. To achieve this Hawks required not only sufficient artistic inspiration and erotic stimulation from the actress with whom he was working but also total cooperation from her and, crucially, a guiding hand from screenwriter Jules Furthman. Despite his numerous successes, Hawks wouldn't find quite this synthesis again for nearly a decade.

18

Big Spender: RKO, *Gunga Din*,
and *Bringing Up Baby*

RKO had flirted with hiring Howard Hawks to direct a picture back in 1934, when *King Kong* creators Merian Cooper and Ernest Schoedsack were trying to launch a biographical film about the intriguing British World War I figure T. E. Lawrence, starring Ronald Colman, but this never materialized.

Sam Briskin, whom Hawks had known when he was general manager of Columbia Studios in the early 1930s, was now running the studio, although the most profitable pictures, notably the Astaire-Rogers musicals, came out of Pandro Berman's unit. Berman was loyal to one of the studio's most celebrated stars, Katharine Hepburn, although the actress's last several films had been bitter box-office disappointments.

Looking to add some high-powered directorial talent to the studio, Briskin contacted Hawks as soon as he heard about the blowup at Goldwyn. Although the contract was not finalized and signed until the following March, its basic terms were established at two meetings at the end of August and the beginning of September, at which Hawks's lawyer, Mendel Silberberg, extracted very lucrative terms for his client: over the course of two years, Hawks was to receive $130,000 per year, payable at $2,500 per week, for his exclusive services for directing up to three pictures per year. A complicated sliding scale was also negotiated by which Hawks would receive 10 percent of the gross of his pictures once receipts exceeded 1.75 times the negative cost, up to 25 percent once the gross exceeded three times the negative cost. Highly favorable option and credit clauses were included, as was the provision that the director was not to be assigned to an Astaire-Rogers picture.

At once, Hawks's agent, George Volck, sent Briskin a list of stories in which Hawks was interested. Foremost among them was a script by Zoë Akins and Hawks called *The Food of Love*, a frantic romantic comedy about a group of classical musicians on tour. It had some of the crazy, as well as

243

train-bound, qualities of *Twentieth Century*, just as it also dealt with slightly pretentious people in the arts. Among the fourteen other properties on the Hawks-Volck list were Sidney Howard's *Yellow Jack, Lulu Belle*, a Hecht-MacArthur story called *The Russian Ballet, Two Years Before the Mast*, and Rafael Sabatini's *The Tyrant*.

The studio countered with a project that had frustrated several screenwriters, including William Faulkner, over the years and had just been acquired that June when the producer Edward Small joined RKO. *Gunga Din*, Rudyard Kipling's 1892 poem, told of a British soldier's admiration for the loyalty and heroism of a native water carrier during a time of difficult campaigns against rebels in northern India. A year after the successes of *The Lives of a Bengal Lancer* and *Clive of India*, Small's Reliance Pictures had bought the rights to *Gunga Din*. Once Small became an RKO producer in June, the studio had Lester Cohen and John Colton, the author of *The Shanghai Gesture*, tackle the material, and King Vidor was mentioned as a possible director.

When *Gunga Din* was proposed to Hawks, he was immediately enthusiastic, and it's easy to see why: the devil-may-care, rambunctious, fun-under-pressure potential in it appealed immensely to his sophisticated teenage-boy mentality; the story was mainly about men on a mission; and it seemed like a surefire commercial bet. In a stroke of great fortune, Hecht and MacArthur were available immediately, and within two weeks Hawks was on the *Chief* heading for New York.

It is not known whether Hawks heard of Irving Thalberg's death before or after boarding the train on September 14, the same day Thalberg died, but he can hardly not have known that his brother-in-law had been bedridden since September 8 and in an oxygen tent for two days before his death. But Hawks went east anyway, escaping the afflictions of the Thalberg-Shearer clan, avoiding the gigantic funeral and relieved at the prospect of resuming his unfettered bachelor's life in Nyack and at his suite at the Waldorf-Astoria.

Working mostly at the hotel, Hawks, Hecht, and MacArthur had great fun throwing numerous diverse ingredients into the stew that became the *Gunga Din* script. In addition to the poem, the team turned to Kipling's 1888 story collection *Soldiers Three* for their three leading characters, an Irishman, a Scot, and a Cockney; threw in an almost unavoidable dash of *The Three Musketeers*, and lifted virtually intact the ending of *The Front Page*: in place of the editor Walter Burns seeing his star reporter and the latter's bride off on their honeymoon, then having him arrested for stealing the watch he gave him as a gift, the *Gunga Din* script had the Scotsman

1. Howard Hawks, age one.

2. and 3. Cephas and Chloe Hawks, Howard's great-grandparents.

4. The prenuptial party for Helen Howard in Neenah. Helen is the third woman from the left with the black choker, and Frank Hawks is at her side with his back to her. Helen's best friend Theda Clark is next to Frank with her eyes closed, and to her left is her future husband, Will Peters.

5. Corner of Jefferson and Sixth Streets, Goshen, Indiana, around 1900. Howard Hawks was born one block away.

6. Main Street, Goshen, Indiana, about the time Hawks was born. Dwight H. Hawks, druggist, is in the building furthest right.

8. Howard and Kenneth Hawks at table.

7. The Hawks-owned Goshen Milling Company.

9. The house Frank Hawks built in Neenah, 1904–06, 433 East Wisconsin Avenue.

10. Kenneth, William, Grace, and Howard Hawks, Pasadena, 1905.

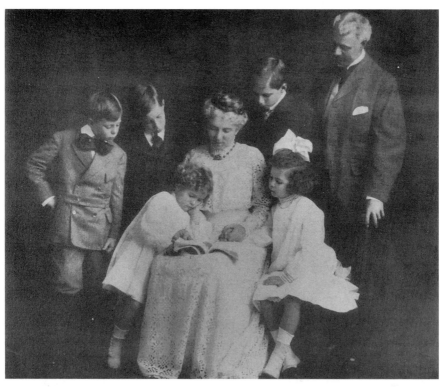

11. The entire Hawks family, June 1912. Left to right: William Ballinger, Kenneth Neil, Helen Bernice, Helen Howard, Howard Winchester, Grace Louise, Frank Winchester.

12. Howard and Kenneth in Army uniform, World War I.

13. Howard and Athole on their honeymoon, Hawaii, June 1928.

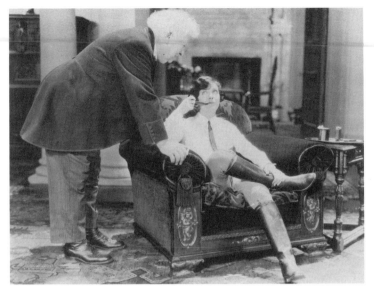

14. Hawks's work in the silent era prefigured some of the characteristic preoccupations of his later career. Here, May McAvoy wears men's clothes and smokes a pipe in Hawks's first film, *The Road to Glory*, 1926.

15. Sammy Cohen in drag in *The Cradle Snatchers*, 1927.

16. Nine men and one girl (Sue Carol), *The Air Circus*, 1928.

17. and 18. Two views of Victor Fleming, at left with a frisky Lupe Velez on the set of *Wolf Song*, 1928.

19. Directors William A. Seiter and Alan Crosland, Jack Warner, and Hawks on the links, early 1930s.

20. Hawks on location for
The Dawn Patrol, 1930.

21. Wife and mistress: Athole with
Ann Dvorak, early 1930s.

22. Hawks talks over a scene in *Scarface* with Paul Muni. Cinematographer Lee
Garmes is adjusting the camera above Muni, Vince Barnett is in the white hat with
the black band, staring at the camera, and Hughes production executive E. B. Derr is
seated to Hawks's left.

23. Athole and Howard.

24. David, Athole, and Howard.

25. David and Dad.

26. Suitably garbed on location for
Tiger Shark.

27. Jean Harlow.

28. With old flame Joan Crawford on *Today We Live*.

29. With Carole Lombard and John Barrymore on *Twentieth Century*.

30. Goldwyn studio portrait, mid-1930s.

31. Helen and Frank Hawks.

32. Directing James Cagney and June Travis in *Ceiling Zero*, as Pat O'Brien and Stuart Erwin are amused.

33. She was "the cleanest physical thing you've ever seen," Hawks said of Frances Farmer, here taking a break on *Come and Get It*.

34. Meta Carpenter, Hawks's longtime script girl and secretary, with the loggers on *Come and Get It*.

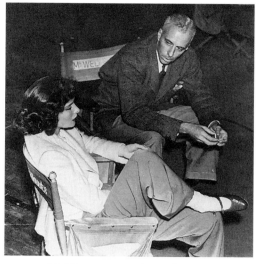

35. Trying to get through to Katharine Hepburn on *Bringing Up Baby*.

36. With Cary Grant and Rita Hayworth on *Only Angels Have Wings*.

37. Lionel Banks's set for *Only Angels Have Wings*.

38. "Admiral," David, Barbara, "Whiskers," and Peter Hawks at 1230 Benedict Canyon Drive, Beverly Hills, 1939.

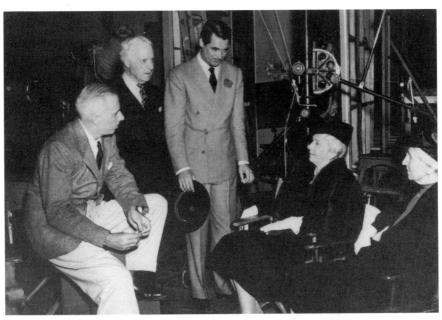

39. Howard, Frank Hawks, Cary Grant, Helen Hawks, and "Aunt" Katherine Ogden on the set of *His Girl Friday*.

40. and 41. Slim

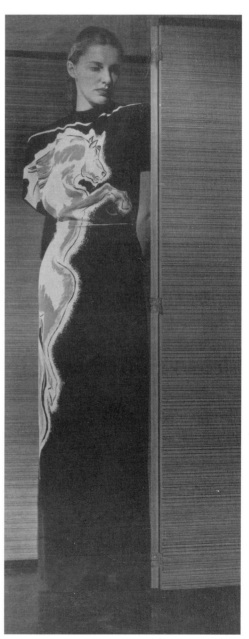

42. Howard and Slim cutting the wedding cake, four days after Pearl Harbor.

43. Traveling in style.

and his new wife depart after all the adventures were done, only to have the Irishman shrewdly arrange for his buddy's arrest for desertion.

At the end of October, by which time Hawks and his writers had the story line set and about thirty-five pages of script finished, Athole surprised her errant husband by doing something uncharacteristically bold and assertive: she went to New York to confront him about their marriage. Knowing that direct, emotional challenges to his behavior, authority, and independence were utterly abhorrent to Hawks, Athole couldn't really have expected much good to come from this approach, and it didn't. More adamant than ever that there was no hope of salvaging their marriage, Hawks sent her packing almost as soon as she arrived. Shattered by her husband's callous attitude toward her good intentions, Athole returned to Los Angeles and went into an unchecked tailspin, the worst emotional collapse of her life. After undergoing tests at UCLA Medical Center and being diagnosed as a schizophrenic, Athole entered Las Encinas sanitarium in Pasadena, an exclusive facility that treated mainly alcoholics. There, with the approval of her UCLA physicians, she underwent electric-shock therapy, which was designed to stabilize her condition for the moment. However, doctors were distinctly pessimistic about her long-term prospects, predicting an incurable pattern of breakdowns followed by seeming recoveries, leading to a major collapse resulting in total loss of identity.

Accepting, as did everyone else, the physicians' analysis, Hawks endorsed the prescribed treatment but kept his distance from Athole. Increasingly, the children, particularly little Barbara, were tended to by Hawks's parents. Norma, who might otherwise have been expected to look after her sister, was at that very moment suffering from a traumatic physical and emotional breakdown as a result of Irving Thalberg's death. After a long bout with pneumonia, the disease that had killed her husband, Norma was advised by doctors to give up her career for at least a year, and she repaired to Phoenix to convalesce through November and December. For good measure, Bill Hawks and Bessie Love, whose marriage had been deteriorating for some time, officially announced their separation at the end of September; by mid-December, the divorce became final, and Bessie, having been granted custody of four-year-old Patricia, moved to England. During this time, Hawks also received word of the death of Charles Furthman, Jules's brother and the screenwriter of *Underworld,* after a bout with pneumonia.

For Hawks, it was easiest, and most expedient, to stay well clear of all this unpleasantness, which he did until mid-December, returning just in time to spend Christmas with the family. As far as *Gunga Din* was concerned, Hawks was basically happy with what Hecht and MacArthur had done, although, as sometimes happened with them, they had either run out of steam or become distracted by other projects before satisfactorily finishing the third act. So at the beginning of 1937, Hawks called in Dudley Nichols. But the project became stalled over casting difficulties. Hawks wanted to use two MGM stars, Robert Montgomery and Spencer Tracy, to play the Scotsman Ballantine and the Irishman MacChesney, respectively, with British actors Robert Donat and Roger Livesey considered possibilities for the more secondary role of the Cockney Cutter. Sam Briskin upped the ante, asking Louis B. Mayer for the stellar trio of Clark Gable, Tracy, and Franchot Tone in return for the rights to the much-cherished *Rio Rita*, in which Mayer hoped to team Jeanette MacDonald and Nelson Eddy. But while Tracy and Tone might be available, even Hawks could do nothing to pry his friend Gable away from MGM on a loan.

When the to-and-fro over casting and budget considerations dragged into the spring, and as Edward Small, who hoped to produce *Gunga Din*, started to become frustrated over his position at RKO, Hawks began scouring about for another project to tackle in the meantime. Ironically, the property Briskin most urgently pushed upon him was another Edna Ferber story, an *Iron Horse*–like saga about the early days of railroading. *Lawrence of Arabia* was mentioned again, as was *Two Years Before the Mast*. Hawks held out for something in a different vein, however, and eventually found what he was looking for in a short story by Hagar Wilde that appeared in the April 10th issue of *Collier's* magazine.

A thinly plotted tale of a paleontologist, a rich society girl, and a pet leopard, the story was recommended by RKO's story department because the dialogue was "hilariously funny and the possibilities for further comedy complications are limitless," even if the frequent presence of the panther in scenes was viewed as a potential problem. Hawks liked it too, and the story was bought for an economical $1,004, although the wary Briskin, while agreeing to let Hawks proceed, expressed fears about the picture's ultimate cost, declaring, "I am not interested in making a big picture of this story."

A New York writer, Hagar Wilde had worked once before in Hollywood, for Howard Hughes on a four-week job. Briskin was warned that "the experience was so distasteful and unpleasant that she is rather soured on the movies," but she came out anyway and worked with Hawks for a few weeks fleshing out the characters and certain scenes. But Hawks soon recognized that he would need a professional screenwriter and turned again to Dudley Nichols, a former newspaperman, most of whose credits were heavy dramas for John Ford, most notably *The Informer*, for which he had recently won an Oscar. (Nichols was also a driving force behind the nascent Screen Writers Guild, of which he would be elected president in late 1937.) Hawks kept Wilde on to retain the original comic tone and keep the characters consistent with what she had originated, while Nichols developed the structure and incident. Curiously, *Bringing Up Baby* would remain the major aberration in Nichols's lengthy career, the only outright comedy among his fifty-odd lifetime screen credits. Hawks paid him his ultimate compliment, saying, "he was awful good."

As the script was labored over through the summer and grew to a mammoth 202 pages by the time shooting started, key casting was also finalized. Although Carole Lombard was briefly mentioned as a possibility for the dizzy heiress, there was never any real doubt that anyone other than Katharine Hepburn would play Susan. Because of her shaky box-office record, Hepburn had many detractors at the studio, and her cost was steep: her RKO contract, which still had three pictures to go, called for her to receive $72,500 (more if the picture went over schedule) plus 5 percent of the gross between $600,000 and $750,000, 7½ percent up to $1,000,000, and an incredible 11 percent of the gross from that point on. But Pan Berman was unswerving in his belief in her, and the role was tailored to her specifications.

The male lead posed more of a problem. The beleaguered, constantly frustrated scientist David Huxley didn't seem like a very dashing, attractive role on paper, and several prominent actors, including Ronald Colman, Robert Montgomery, Fredric March, and even Ray Milland, who had only just achieved top-billed status, turned it down. Cary Grant, who had just made his romantic-comedy leading-man breakthrough in Leo McCarey's *The Awful Truth* at Columbia, had a three-picture deal at RKO and was tempted by the prospect of working with Hawks and, once again, with Hepburn, but he felt he didn't know how to play an intellectual. But when Hawks suggested that he keep the bumbling, bespectacled, always-anxious screen character created by Harold Lloyd in mind, Grant got the only directing tip he needed and came aboard, for $75,000. For some of the key supporting roles, Charlie Ruggles came over on loan from Paramount, and the Irish actor Barry Fitzgerald was borrowed from the Mary Pickford Company. The dusky, twenty-one-year-old beauty Virginia Walker, who played David Huxley's snooty fiancée in a sexpot-behind-the-pince-nez fashion, was one of the first actresses Hawks put under personal contract, and he loaned her to RKO for the role. Romantically, however, it was Bill Hawks who took an interest in this Boston society girl, and she became his second wife when they eloped to Mexico the following June.

Before *Bringing Up Baby* got under way, however, Hawks became more deeply immersed in Hollywood politics than he ever would again. Never a joiner of organizations and much closer in mentality to a boss than to a labor activist, Hawks became involved in the nascent Screen Directors Guild almost entirely out of self-interest. The industry-controlled Academy of Motion Picture Arts and Sciences had always mediated in labor-management disputes, and the studios held virtually all the cards. However, when the U.S. Supreme Court affirmed the constitutionality of the Wagner Act in April 1937, it opened the door for Hollywood's struggling guilds to achieve some true influence. With the Screen Actors Guild and the Screen Writers Guild already signing contracts by late spring, the Screen Directors Guild, which had attracted only ninety members since its creation in February 1936, suddenly bulged to about 550 members with its decision to enlist assistant directors and unit production managers as Junior Guild members, making it a force to reckon with.

Hawks, a charter member of the guild, became chairman of the committee whose task it was to negotiate an SDG contract with the studios. The big bosses, represented by three friends of Hawks's, Darryl Zanuck, Eddie Mannix, and Jack Warner, already bruised by their losing battles with the other guilds, took the position that directors, by virtue of the fact that they "perform a service which is fundamentally creative," were part of the Hollywood elite, closer to them, the producers and executives, than they were to the rabble-rousing, socialist-minded leaders of SAG and the Screen Writers Guild. Even within the SDG, right-wing members such as Cecil B. De Mille objected to any alliance with SAG, due to its affiliation with the American Federation of Labor. Since the tycoons had welcomed directors as part of the exclusive Hollywood boys' club, they felt, couldn't everyone just be gentlemen about it and avoid all this unpleasant haggling and saber-rattling? The studio heads simply couldn't understand why the likes of Hawks, Eddie Sutherland, and John Ford, who composed the negotiating committee, would want lowly assistants and unit managers in their own guild, and at talks that began on August 4, they tried to persuade the directors to separate these underlings into a different organization in exchange for guild recognition.

At an SDG meeting on the evening of August 30, however, the SDG served notice that it had no intention of partitioning itself. The producers felt that they shouldn't negotiate with the directors just as the National Labor Relations Board had refused to negotiate with design engineers at the Chrysler automobile company on the basis that they were well-compensated creative artists. To the contrary, Hawks and guild attorney Barry Brannen pointed out at the meeting, directors had no contractual power to hire and fire and were therefore employees themselves, not management at all. "In practice," Brannen acknowledged, "a director may exert substantial influence in selection of cast or designation of members of the production unit, but this influence is exerted vicariously by means of recommendation and suggestion and not as a matter of right by any authority given him under his contract."

Balking at this ultimatum, the producers stiffened their position, insisting that it would deal with the SDG only if it represented actual motion picture directors. The committee expressed its astonishment that the producers would "attempt to change the internal organization of the other and opposite party" in labor negotiations, with Hawks protesting that this would amount to "nothing less than the dissolution of the guild!" On September 23 (the first day of shooting on *Bringing Up Baby*), spurred by the producers' refusal to negotiate, Hawks, Ford, and Sutherland issued a statement to the trade press blaming the producers for the stalemate and announcing that the SDG would be filing for certification with the NLRB. But from here on, Hawks played a significantly diminished role. In October, Frank Capra, Herbert Biberman, and Lewis Milestone took charge of the Inter-Talent Council, which coordinated dealings with the other guilds, and Capra assumed the chairmanship of the negotiating committee the following April, a month before he was elected SDG president. Still, a basic agreement and full guild recognition from the producers wasn't achieved until May 1939.

For Hawks, his own family history, fundamental instincts, and personal politics ran against the sort of FDR-style progressivism that the labor movement represented. (A cynical critic once suggested that if Hawks had ever made a film about American labor, it would have centered on the code of professionalism among strikebreakers hired by management—an unfair hypothesis but one perhaps not inaccurate in its assessment of Hawks's sympathies). Nor did Hawks ever lose much sleep worrying about the plight of the common man during the Depression. Hawks's lack of compassion and elite image of himself made him fundamentally ill-suited to active political engagement on behalf of any cause, and it was easy for him to see that Capra, King Vidor, Rouben Mamoulian, and others would be more effective than he in keeping up the fight for the SDG. Hawks's guild activity was always a matter of looking out for his own interests, which included increasing his salary, boosting his leverage with and independence from the studios, and gaining more artistic control.

Although the way the cast and story were coming together was creating considerable optimism about *Bringing Up Baby*, RKO still had cause for concern as the start date approached. The large salaries of Hawks, Grant, and Hepburn put the original budget at $767,676, and Briskin was advised more than a month before shooting that it was "suicidal" to make a Hepburn picture at that expense. "Hawks is determined in his own quiet, reserved, soft-spoken manner to have his way about the making of this picture," production executive Lou Lusty prophetically noted to the studio chief. "With the salary he's been getting he's almost indifferent to anything that might come to him on a percentage deal—that's why he doesn't give a damn about how much the picture will cost to make. . . . All the directors in Hollywood are developing producer-director complexes and Hawks is going to be particularly difficult."

Work on the film went slowly from the outset. The first problem was that Katharine Hepburn, who had never done "screwball" comedy, wasn't getting the hang of her part; Hawks had imagined that she'd have no problem because the role was such a close fit to her own background as a clever, imaginative, outspoken New England heiress, but she was trying too hard, desperately attempting to "act" funny, and constantly cracking up at her own antics and those of her costar. Although he was normally able to set uncertain actors straight with some simple, direct guidelines, Hawks couldn't figure out what to do with Hepburn. "I tried to explain to her that the great clowns, Keaton, Chaplin, Lloyd, simply weren't out there making funny faces, they were serious, sad, solemn, and the humor sprang from what happened to them. . . . Cary understood this at once. Katie didn't."

In a measure of desperation rare for the director, Hawks turned to Walter Catlett, a veteran comic long associated with the Ziegfeld Follies. After watching some rushes, Catlett agreed that Hepburn was overdoing it but initially refused to work with her, until Hawks got Hepburn to ask him herself. "Walter played a whole scene of hers out with Cary Grant, played it with every mannerism of hers, *very serious*, and she was entranced. She said, 'You have to create a part for him in the picture.' And I did." (Catlett was prominently featured as Constable Slocum.) "After that, she played perfectly—not trying to be funny, but being very, very natural and *herself.*" Hepburn also credited her costar with keeping her on the right track: "Cary Grant taught me that the more depressed I looked when I went into a prat-fall, the more the audience would laugh."

Hepburn and Grant, who with their respective mates at the time, Howard Hughes and Phyllis Brooks, socialized a great deal off the set, were utterly full of beans on the shoot, overflowing with energy and thrilled to be working together. "We wanted it to be as good as it could possibly be," Hepburn said. "Nothing was ever too much trouble. And we were both very early on the set. Howard Hawks was always late, so Cary and I worked out an awful lot of stuff together. We'd make up things to do on the screen—how to work out those laughs in *Bringing Up Baby.*"

Among the scenes Grant came up with was the priceless one in which, after Hepburn tears his formal suit in a swank supper club, he accidentally steps on her dress and rips off its rear, revealing her lingeried backside. To prevent everyone from glimpsing this, Grant first covers it with his top hat; then, once she has felt the breeze, they walk in step with him pressed as firmly up against her back as possible. Something similar had happened to the actor not long before at the Roxy Theatre in New York City, where he had been seated in the front row of the balcony with the head of the Metropolitan Museum and his wife. When Grant stood to allow the wife to cross in front of him to go to the bathroom, he found that he'd neglected to zip up his fly and began to do so, only to catch the woman's frock in it. The two then had to lockstep to the manager's office in order to find a pair of pliers to disconnect Grant's fly from the lady's garment. Hawks loved the story and fully caught its comically embarrassing spirit.

In a later scene, Hepburn accidentally broke the heel off her shoe. Immediately, Grant whispered to her the line "I was born on the side of a hill," whereupon she repeated the ad-lib as she continued to limp along. It was this sort of dazzling quickness Grant was to exhibit even more abundantly for Hawks two years later in *His Girl Friday.* Grant also provided his costar with some invaluable coaching for the final scene, in which she climbs toward him by ladder, then across his giant reconstruction on a brontosaurus, only to be saved by his outstretched hand when it collapses in a heap under her. "I told her when and how to let go," Grant remembered. "I told her to aim for my wrists, an old circus trick. You can't let go of that kind of grip, whereas if you go for the hands, you'll slip. She went right for my wrists, and I pulled her up. Kate was marvelously trusting if she thought you knew what you were doing." In general, Hepburn recalled, "Everyone contributed anything and everything they could think of to that script."

Working with the leopard, which was trained by a Madame Olga Celeste, provided an adventure all its own. Contrary to what RKO imagined, Hawks had the cat slinking through a great many scenes unleashed. Grant was terrified of it and played as few scenes with it as possible. (The avoidance of the actor's face in some close-ups, including those in which the beast rubs up against his legs, suggests the use of a double.) The star was not terribly amused when, as a practical joke, Hepburn dropped a fake leopard through the top of his dressing room. For her part, Hepburn suggested, "I didn't have brains enough to be scared, so I did a lot of scenes with the leopard just roaming around." Madame Celeste was always just outside camera range with a large whip, and Hepburn wore a heavy perfume that had the effect of turning the jungle dweller into a pussycat. But the actress had a very close call in one scene in which she wore a dress with a hem lined with little weights. When Hepburn swirled around and made the dress swing abruptly, it startled the leopard into making a lunge for her back, and only a swift crack over the head from Madame Celeste kept the cat from clawing Hepburn. From then on, the cat was not permitted to walk freely among the actors.

Hawks rarely complained about practical problems that held pictures up, but he had good cause here. "Now, if you don't think that was a hard one to make! Oh, that goddamned leopard—and then, the dog, running around with the bone. . . . Katie and Cary had a scene in which he said, 'What happened to the bone?' And she said, 'It's in the box,' or *something* like that. Well, they started to laugh—it was ten o'clock in the morning— and at four o'clock in the afternoon we were still trying to make this scene and I didn't think we were ever going to get it. I tried changing the line. It didn't do any good. . . . They were just putting dirty connotations on it and then they'd go off into peals of laughter."

But problems with the animals, as well as with actors just having too good a time, were scarcely the only reasons the shooting proceeded so slowly. As the studio had feared, Hawks himself set a very relaxed pace. Fritz Feld, who played a psychiatrist who advises Hepburn in the supper club, recalled nostalgically, "Often in the morning Howard Hawks would come in and say, 'It's a nice day today. Let's go to the races.' And we'd pack up and *go* to the races. Kate continued her custom of serving tea on the set. We all laughed and laughed, and were very happy." At the end of the scene Feld and Hepburn shared, Hawks sent in two cases of champagne. As Feld wistfully said, "Those were the good old days!"

The one story Hawks typically never failed to tell about *Bringing Up Baby* was an example of one-upsmanship over Hepburn. This is the version of it he related to Peter Bogdanovich: "I remember another time we were making a scene and Katie was talking so much she didn't hear me. We called, 'Quiet!' She didn't hear that. Called 'Quiet!' again, and she didn't hear it, so I just stopped everybody, and all of a sudden, in the middle of talking, she stopped and said, 'What's the matter?' I said, 'I just wondered how long you were gonna keep up this imitation of a parrot.' She said, 'I'd like to talk to you,' and she led me around to the back. She said, 'You mustn't say things like that to me. Somebody'll drop a lamp on you. These are my friends around here.' I looked up at the man on the lamps. When I was a prop man, this fellow had been an electrician—I'd known him for God knows how many years. I said, 'Pete, if you had your choice of dropping a lamp on Miss Hepburn or me, who would you drop it on?' He said, 'Get out of the way, will you, Mr. Hawks?' And Katie looked up at him and looked at me and said, 'I guess I was wrong.' And I said, 'Katie, *he* doesn't make it wrong, but you are. And I can tell you one thing, I'm gonna come up and kick you right in the behind if it happens again.' She said, 'You won't have to kick me.' And from that time on, she was just marvelous."

When RKO executives began seeing dailies of the film, their worries had to do with things like Grant's owlish glasses and Hepburn's out-of-control hair, which they believed reduced the stars' appeal. They had also expected a sweeter, more glamorous approach, as opposed to what they perceived as a hard, unromantic tone in Hawks's direction. But this hardly compared to their alarm when the schedule for RKO production number 999 began getting completely out of hand. There was nothing the studio's designated associate producer, Cliff Reid, could say to the far more powerful Hawks to get him to speed up, and the stress of his own impossible position made him physically ill.

By late October, the RKO executive suite was in a shambles. Sam Briskin, who had come to the studio nearly two years earlier from Columbia, was fed up with many things: the company's disorganization, partly caused by its being in receivership; the fact that his decisions were constantly being undermined by the conservative receivers; the fact that Pan Berman had first call on the studio's leading talent, and that he, Briskin, had only once had access to one of the company's top artists—Hepburn for *Baby*. In the first week of November, Briskin quit as vice president of production.

Two weeks later, Berman was officially put in charge of A pictures, while Leo Spitz took control of the B unit. Throughout all of this, *Bringing Up Baby* was conveniently ignored, and it didn't bother Hawks a bit that the administrative disarray resulted in there being no one on the lot who could intervene in the forceful way of a Hal Wallis or Sam Goldwyn. Originally, the film was scheduled for a fifty-one-day shoot, ending November 20. By that time, Hawks had barely shot half the movie. With scarcely a break for Christmas and New Year's, shooting finally finished on January 6, 1938, after ninety-one days, forty days over schedule; the duration was so unusual that *Variety* gave it special coverage. Fulfilling the studio's worst fears, the cost soared correspondingly, to $1,096,796.23, or about 40 percent above the already lavish original budget. Nearly a third of the overages were caused by an option and hefty penalty payments to the two stars that kicked in when filming ran past the limits earmarked in their contracts; Grant and Hepburn each ended up earning just over $120,000 for the picture, nearly $50,000 more than their original salaries.

The film's editor, George Hively, had been cutting the picture right along through production, so that RKO, desperate to see returns on their huge investment as quickly as possible, was able to make finished prints within a matter of days and hold two previews almost at once, on January 17 in Huntington Park and two nights later in Inglewood. Audience reactions could not have been better: An "excellent-plus" and an "A-plus" in two separate studio assessments. Despite the smash responses, Pan Berman felt the picture needed to be cut further and did so over Hawks's strenuous objections. A subsequent preview with the shorter, and final, version at the Chicago Theatre was equally successful, with the report of a "terrific" response from the sold-out house fueling great optimism in the front office that their *Baby* might just make some money after all.

As for the Hays Office, it found the dress-tearing incident "border-line business" that "may be deleted by a number of the political censors boards, both in this country and England"; indeed, the strict Ontario censors objected to Grant's slapping his hat against Hepburn's bottom and her retort, "Will you please stop doing that with your hat?" Hawks, Nichols, and Wilde had been clever enough to sneak their more subtle but quite outrageous sexual humor through under the censors' noses. Not only did the bone-in-a-box references get through undetected, but so did all the other "bone" jokes, including the one in the opening scene in which Grant's David Huxley, pondering the quite erect-looking dinosaur bone he holds in his hand, innocently remarks, "This must belong in the tail."

The early trade press served up excellent "money" reviews, and the reactions by mainstream critics were equally favorable. Everyone liked the picture enormously. "Audiences used to roar at this one," an RKO executive admitted, and Hawks often recalled that the laughter was so great that it prevented people from hearing many of the other funny lines. But despite it all, the picture didn't do nearly well enough at the box office to approach recouping RKO's investment.

The highly erratic commercial performance of *Bringing Up Baby* was deeply perplexing to the industry in 1938 and, in a sense, remains so today. With theater manager Cliff Work "guaranteeing a refund to any patron who does not enjoy this picture," *Baby* began its world-premiere engagement at the Golden Gate in San Francisco on Valentine's Day and, backed by great reviews, did bang-up business. As the film fanned out across the country, it did solidly in such markets as Los Angeles, Portland, Denver, Cincinnati, and Washington, D.C., but came up short of expectations in numerous other cities, especially in the Midwest. But the real shock of its disappointment hit with its opening on March 3 at New York's Radio City Music Hall. Grossing only $70,000 at the 5,980–seat house, where strong attractions generally pulled in $100,000 or more, *Bringing Up Baby* was precipitously yanked after only one week, suggesting, as *Variety* dryly noted, that "the Katharine Hepburn draw, as expressed in some quarters, isn't what it used to be." Subsequent runs in New York were equally weak. The film's box-office track record was utterly without comprehensible pattern and wasn't entirely bad by any means; its conspicuous flop in New York forged the impression of a failure where it mattered most, and the film needed to be a huge hit to compensate for the egregious budget overages.

In its initial run, *Bringing Up Baby* grossed just $715,000 in the United States. Overseas, it pulled in $394,000, bringing the total to $1,109,000. A 1940–41 reissue generated an additional $150,000. To trigger Hawks's percentage participation, the picture would had to have grossed $1,875,000, and it never came close. When all was said and done, RKO lost $365,000 on the film, fulfilling everyone's worst initial fears.

The common reasons advanced for the picture's relative initial unpopularity are that it was too sophisticated, that the characters were too intellectual, that there was no real romance in it, that the lighting was too dark for a comedy. Most famously, Katharine Hepburn was accused, in a list prepared by Harry Brandt, president of the Independent Theatre Owners of America, of being "box office poison," a distinction she shared with Joan Crawford, Greta Garbo, Marlene Dietrich, Kay Francis, and others.

But Hawks, who always insisted that there was something wrong with a film if it failed to win a large audience even if critics considered it great, had a more subtle reading of why the film fell short. He eventually concluded that *Bringing Up Baby* "had a great fault and I learned an awful lot from that. There were *no* normal people in it. Everyone you met was a screwball and since that time I have learned my lesson and I don't intend ever again to make everybody crazy."

It took a couple of decades, but *Bringing Up Baby* began building a reputation when it started being shown on television in the 1950s, and by the late 1960s, when film buffs started drawing attention to the sometimes underestimated talents of Cary Grant and Hawks, and to the wonders of 1930s romantic comedy, the film finally achieved its deserved position as one of Hollywood's most perfect and brilliant comedies. Perhaps nothing did so much to ratify the classic status of *Bringing Up Baby* as Peter Bogdanovich's 1972 hit comedy *What's Up, Doc?*, starring Ryan O'Neal and Barbra Streisand. After having paid homage to John Ford and Orson Welles with *The Last Picture Show* the year before, Bogdanovich, plausibly enough, told everyone how *Bringing Up Baby* had inspired him this time out, which was like an invitation to the press to compare the new film unfavorably to its model. Audiences didn't know or care, but suddenly *Bringing Up Baby* was being referred to as one of the greatest comedies ever made. It only took thirty-five years. But it did give the film a new lease on life, one that has continued ever since.

As a comedy, as well as a love story, the film represents a huge advance on Hawks's only previous farce, *Twentieth Century*. It is aggressive and dark but stops just short of spinning out of comic control toward the end and of pushing too far into the comedy of humiliation, that hallmark of his postwar comedies. His collaborators could not have been more felicitous, and it represented one instance in which all the fun the actors and filmmakers were having actually spilled into the picture for the audience's benefit.

There was, however, a price for the indulgence that helped create the greatness of *Bringing Up Baby*. And that price was *Gunga Din*.

With *Bringing Up Baby* finished and in release, Hawks had every intention of moving right back onto *Gunga Din*. Once Berman assumed full control of RKO's major projects, he, too, wanted to reactivate it, and in early 1938 he assigned the writer Anthony Veiller to cut down the Hecht-MacArthur-Hawks-Nichols script, which ran to 284 pages, enough for at least a four-hour movie. Berman and Hawks met numerous times during

February and March to discuss the picture, the result of which was a growing distrust on Berman's part that Hawks would ever toe the line when it
came to budget or scheduling matters; Hawks had plenty of excuses for
what had happened on *Bringing Up Baby*, but *Gunga Din* would be a far
grander production, one that promised, at about $1.5 million going in, to
have the biggest budget ever for an RKO film. Berman had no doubt that
Hawks could make a fine, rousing picture of *Gunga Din*, but nothing the
director said could make the producer forget that Hawks was, in his experience, "slow and difficult." Berman eventually made his decision: "I was
afraid he would go over budget so much that I would be in trouble. So I
didn't go with Howard. I went with George Stevens who, up to that time,
had made pictures quite reasonably for us." For his part, Hawks didn't
think much of Berman's overall track record as a producer, and he made
Berman's decision easier by telling him, "I don't think I want to trust myself
to your judgment."

The news wasn't broken to Hawks directly but, rather, to his brother
William, who was informed at a meeting with RKO brass on March 17,
1938, that not only was Howard off *Gunga Din* but the studio was termi-
nating his contract. Two days later, a distressed Howard wrote back protesting the studio's decision, stating that he would suffer "very substantial
damages" if he didn't make the film, and insisting that he was "ready, able,
willing and anxious to complete the direction of said photoplay *Gungha
Din* [sic], and to comply with all of . . . obligations under said contract."
On March 21, RKO sent Hawks a letter citing numerous contractual de-
faults and breaches on Hawks's part and informing him that their decision
to dump him was "neither arbitrary nor unreasonable," as he had claimed,
but "arrived at after mature deliberation. We believe, in good faith, that
sound business judgment makes this step necessary." Certainly the deciding factor in letting him go was that since the fall of 1936, RKO had paid
Hawks $242,500 (including a $40,000 payoff to get rid of him) for the privilege of losing more than $350,000 on *Bringing Up Baby*. The bottom line
on the studio's relationship with Hawks was not pretty.

Bringing Up Baby also proved to be the last straw in RKO's association with Katharine Hepburn. The studio had brought her to Hollywood
in 1932, given her starring roles from the outset, and tailored fourteen productions to her specifications. Now, even with her greatest ally, Pan Berman,
holding the reins of power, RKO could no longer justify pouring good
money after bad on this high-priced star. She had originally been announced
to play another dizzy heiress in *The Mad Miss Manton*, but Barbara

Stanwyck won that choice role when *Bringing Up Baby* went over schedule. Once the Hawks film was completed, RKO contemptuously offered Hepburn a part in a modestly budgeted programmer, *Mother Carey's Chickens*. When she refused it, the studio gave her the choice of taking the role or buying out her contract. Although most actors couldn't have afforded to do so, Hepburn's personal fortune afforded her the luxury of choosing the second option, which she did to the tune of $220,000. Her career upswing of *Holiday* and *The Philadelphia Story* lay just ahead.

George Stevens, ironically, ended up going forty days over schedule on *Gunga Din* (the same amount as Hawks had on *Bringing Up Baby*) and bloating the budget by some $400,000, to an enormous $1,909,669. Therefore, even though the film was a smash hit, it still didn't cover its costs in initial release. The Stevens film has been widely enjoyed and even loved over the years, but one suspects that Hawks, with his great feel for both adventure and comedy, would have made something more lasting and memorable out of it (though it remains doubtful whether Hawks would have eliminated or even softened what today seems an almost unbearable jingoism and white supremacy; this was a hallmark of the Hecht and MacArthur script, which Hawks had such a significant hand in shaping). *Gunga Din* remains one of the most prominent "might-have-beens" of Hawks's career, a picture that very well could have been one of his best, as well as one of his most successful. Hawks was acutely disappointed not to be able to make it. But there was consolation—both for him and for the public—in what he ended up doing instead.

19

Only Angels

In the wake of the RKO fiasco, Hawks had to dodge more trouble of his own making in the persons of underworld figure Ben Kaufman and bookie Donald Miller, whom he owed nine thousand dollars from a 1937 gambling debt. Hawks was now denying that he owed it, despite a promissory note payable the previous July 3, and went so far as to claim that since the debt stemmed from gambling, the transaction had been illegal and therefore could not be enforced: Charges were filed against Hawks in any event, but he managed to elude a summons served him on April 8 by having his household help lie that he was in New Orleans and wouldn't be back for a month. The case dragged on for another year until it was thrown out.

When he was supposedly in New Orleans, Hawks was, in fact, still in Los Angeles and once again submerging himself in Screen Directors Guild activities. At an April 12 meeting with Association of Motion Picture Producers President Joseph Schenck, Hawks and Capra reiterated the guild's basic platform and requested that the producers return to the bargaining table. On May 15, Hawks was elected second vice president of the guild, replacing Frank Tuttle, and was also returned to the twelve-man board of directors. At the same time, Capra was elected president of the 150-member organization, succeeding King Vidor, while Woody Van Dyke supplanted Lewis Milestone as first vice president.

When the SDG formally filed with the National Labor Relations Board on August 2, claiming that the major Hollywood studios were violating the Wagner Act and employing unfair labor practices in refusing to negotiate with the guild, the stage was set for the final phase of the directors' battle for full recognition by the producers. In mid-August, with Schenck and Zanuck finally back from an extended European trip, Capra called on Hawks and Van Dyke to rejoin him on the committee to negotiate with Zanuck, who spoke on behalf of the producers. After an initial meeting between the two sides on August 21, Zanuck announced that, with

Hollywood's international reputation at stake, "the civil war in the film industry must be ended." Responding to Zanuck's promising suggestions that an agreement was at hand, Capra, Hawks, and Van Dyke gave upbeat reports to membership at a meeting the following evening and proposed a postponement of the NLRB hearings.

The producers, however, quickly backtracked, reiterating their specious argument that directors were actually part of management and insisting on negotiating with full-fledged directors separately from assistant directors and unit managers. It took until February, and the threat of an implied directors' strike and boycott of the imminent Academy Awards, but the producers finally agreed to recognize the guild and enter into collective bargaining with directors. Ratification of the basic agreement, which finally did exclude unit managers but embraced certain creative rights for directors, such as two weeks' preparation time and "consultation" on casting, editing, and second-unit work, came on May 1, 1939.

For Hawks, this formative period marked the peak of his active involvement in guild affairs. From here on, he attended few meetings and was often in arrears with dues payments. The tedium of organizational politics, as well as the liberal labor-movement orientation of Hollywood unions in general, was not for him. Selfishly, he had got what he wanted out of the guild's formation—a bit more power over his own work, something he had been accruing on his own in any event.

On June 10, the Los Angeles area's latest racetrack, Hollywood Park, or "Warner Park," as it was dubbed within the industry, debuted in Inglewood. The grand opening, *Variety* observed, "was distinctly a Warner Bros. production, with the Warners doing everything but ride a horse." Responding to Hollywood's craze for the ponies, a passion they shared, the brothers Warner built the attractive and luxurious facility as a rival to Hal Roach's Santa Anita track east of the city. Its first season ran through July 23, and Hollywood Park instantly became a magnet for showbiz socialites, high rollers, and self-styled horse owners and experts, including Hawks.

In late June, Bill Hawks married Virginia Walker, whom Howard had prominently featured as Cary Grant's sniffy fiancée in *Bringing Up Baby*. For Howard Hawks, it was largely a recreational summer of going to the track, outings with Peter and David, making the rounds of nightspots with his eye constantly out for aspiring young starlets, and working out ideas for his upcoming film project. By summer's end, things would come together for him in very big ways on two major fronts.

On August 30, Hawks spent the evening gambling at the Clover Club, an exclusive enclave for the film-business elite on the Sunset Strip. Heading out of the private gambling salon, he noticed his acquaintance Albert (Cubby) Broccoli dancing with a very attractive young woman he'd never seen before. Afterward he took Cubby aside and, in his drawling, completely casual manner, asked, "Who's the girl you're with? I'd like to meet her." And so it was that Howard Hawks met Nancy Raye Gross, who, at a glance, was just Howard's cup of tea: a strikingly beautiful twenty-one-year-old, she had flashing eyes, a ready smile, and, at five feet, eight-and-a-half inches, a model's physique. She also possessed notable composure and a stylish, well-bred manner that was immediately apparent, as well as a sharp, no-nonsense wit that belied her age and proved instantly appealing to the sophisticated Hawks.

After a couple of dances, Hawks pulled out his usual line—"Do you want to be in movies?"—and was startled when his companion replied in the negative; it wasn't often that such a dazzling young woman making the rounds in Hollywood had no interest in becoming an actress. Regrouping quickly, however, Hawks, instead of asking her for a real date, invited her for a swim at his house the next day.

Aware of Hawks's industry reputation and struck by his imposing looks and sartorial elegance, young Miss Gross accepted. She was even more impressed when she arrived at 1230 Benedict Canyon; unlike most of the ostentatious and phony-looking Hollywood homes she had seen, this "was a beautiful, proper house . . . a lovely fieldstone building. The interior was English country house at its best, with tasteful chintz fabrics, real furniture, an excellent staff, and good food." After their swim, Hawks intently questioned his guest about her background, her interests, and why she had come to Los Angeles.

What he found out was that "Slim," as she was already known, had been born in Salinas, California—Steinbeck country—and had been raised, along with her beautiful blond sister, Theodora (Teddie), who was five years older, and her brother, Buddy, who was three years younger, in Pacific Grove, a small, sleepy beach resort town on the northern end of the Monterey Peninsula. Her father, Edward, was a prosperous businessman who owned much of what Steinbeck made famous in *Cannery Row*, and she grew up as a spirited, adventurous child. Although she was well brought up by her mother, née Raye Nell Boyer, and Raye's own mother, "Auntie Rydie," who also lived at the house, the family was not a happy one because of her father's severe, intolerant, unloving character. Although he himself was born Catholic, he had dropped the religion, and he hated Catholics, including the many Italians who worked for him, as well as Jews. Racially prejudiced and politically right-wing, the willful and hardworking Edward Gross was almost a caricature of a smug, close-minded Germanic tyrant in the style of the Kaiser—big-bellied, double-chinned, and, from a kid's point of view, no fun. He detested Christmas, never acknowledged birthdays, and would never allow his children to have friends over to play.

Family life was largely joyless and grim whenever Father was around, but the atmosphere turned truly tragic in the winter of 1928. In a dreadful accident, eight-year-old Buddy's long nightshirt was ignited by embers from the fireplace; the screaming child was chased around the living room by his mother and siblings, and much of his body was burned by the time Raye managed to wrap him in a carpet. Called home, Edward gave blood for a transfusion in an attempt to save his son's life, but to no avail.

Buddy's horrible death irrevocably tore the family apart. From that day on, Edward took Buddy's death out on his wife, blaming her for not saving him and even designing a family mausoleum with only four spaces, for him and his three children—Raye was to be excluded. Within a year, Teddie and Nancy were sent to convent school, where they became estranged from each other. Edward moved out of the house, leaving Raye alone there with her mother. Shortly after Teddie's graduation she, too, abruptly left the house and never spoke to her mother or sister again, turning instead to her father, who made her his business partner and heir apparent. Naturally, this brought Nancy closer to her mother, who in her divorce from Edward won a sufficient settlement to live comfortably in a Carmel hotel and allow Nancy to grow up with a measure of stylish luxuries, which included personal lessons in horseback riding, tennis, and swimming, as well as entrée into the area's monied social set.

At seventeen, Nancy met a wealthy, twenty-one-year-old socialite and brooding intellectual with whom she fell in love, and midway through her final year at her Dominican convent school she dropped out. The skinny teenager's excuse was ill health, and in search of a warm climate, her mother financed a winter-long stay in the restorative warmth of Death Valley. Staying at the comfortable but staid Furnace Creek Inn, which attracted some show-business clientele, the vivacious youngster attracted a good deal of attention. In time, she was taken under the wing of film stars Warner Baxter and William Powell. (Coincidentally, Baxter was about to start work for Hawks in *The Road to Glory*, while Powell, who had worked for the director in *Paid to Love*, would shortly become engaged to Hawks's momentary

flame Jean Harlow.) Powell, in particular, took a proprietary, fatherly interest in the budding beauty, and it was he who dubbed her "Slim Princess,"
of which the "Slim" part stuck. An initial visit to Los Angeles, during which
Bill Powell invited Slim and her mother to lunch, whetted the young
woman's appetite for a more glamorous, exciting life. Her circumstances
allowed her to travel to Los Angeles for a few days each month and to stay
at the elegant Beverly Wilshire Hotel; before long she became a regular
guest of William Randolph Hearst and Marion Davies at San Simeon, even
traveling with them privately to Mexico as well as their northern California
ranch, Wyntoon. In the process, she also became friends with numerous
film personalities, notably Cary Grant and David Niven.

By early 1938, her grandmother had died. Feeling the irrevocable pull
of Hollywood, its social scene and its eligible bachelors, Slim persuaded
her mother to move with her to Los Angeles. They moved into a house on
Sunset Boulevard near UCLA, and Slim was just getting the lay of the land
socially when, after attending a prizefight with Broccoli and *King Kong* star
Bruce Cabot, she met Howard Hawks. Even the most amateur psycholo-
gist wouldn't have a hard time figuring out what would have attracted Slim
to Hawks: she had always been in need of a strong, positive father figure,
and Hawks—gray-haired, commanding, gentlemanly in an Old World sort
of way, conservative, Germanic in his unbending reserve, and, at forty-two,
literally old enough to be her father—filled the bill in virtually every possible way. She was especially struck by Hawks's "candid" blue eyes (others
more often compared them to ice), which reminded her of her father's,
which were "the most piercing light blue eyes I've ever seen. It was as if a
pale fire burned in them."

At the same time, Nancy Gross clearly had her eye out for the big catch.
Trained in the social graces and like catnip to men, she never in her life
seriously entertained the notion of work, and each of her three marriages
represented a step up on the social and financial ladder. Superficially edu-
cated in literature, quite knowledgeable about classical music, already fashion conscious, and extremely at home at outdoorsy activities from riding to
fishing, she easily outclassed most of the women her age in Hollywood; and,
since she had no professional aspirations, she lacked the often off-putting
edge of aggressiveness and desperation of young hopefuls on the make.

None of this was lost on Hawks. In all these important respects, Slim
represented a welcome contrast to most of the women he knew. More than
that, she was a breath of extremely fresh air after the years with the unstable,
retiring, enervating Athole. Although he was never pushy, Hawks could

barely contain himself, and after their swim date, he invited Slim back another day for lunch. On this occasion, he trotted out his three kids and announced that he was married. Slim was shocked at this revelation, and when Hawks explained that his wife was mentally disturbed and currently incapacitated in a home, Slim momentarily considered bolting. But she was already hooked, enchanted perhaps not as much by the man she had known only for a few days but by what she called "the package," which included the "career, the house, the four cars, the yacht—this was the life for me." Over the years, some would privately call her a well-bred, high-class gold digger interested in social climbing above all, but Hawks didn't see it that way. For him, she would be the perfect trophy wife, the ultimate "girl" who would join him in the things he liked to do and always be beautiful and sporty and his. The things she couldn't already do, such as shoot and read scripts, he would teach her. And all his friends would be impressed and jealous.

For their third date, Slim had to get permission from her mother to stay out all night with Hawks in order to accompany him to the Bendix Air Races, a speed race from California to New York that started at 4 A.M. at the Burbank airport. As Slim remembered the exciting night, "I was sitting on top of a station wagon in order to have a better view of the departing planes. I said something that made Howard laugh. He was standing below me, holding on to the luggage rack. He looked up at me and said, 'You're the most remarkable thing I've ever seen. You're going to marry me.' 'Well, we'll see,' I said. 'But thanks anyway.'"

With that, Hawks and Slim began their romance in earnest, although it would be three years before his divorce from Athole would come through. At the time, it was a very difficult matter to divorce someone who had been judged mentally incompetent. However, even though she had been institutionalized, Athole had not been declared legally insane, which ultimately provided Hawks with just the loophole he needed to push the divorce through. During this time, although Slim continued to officially live with her mother, she and Hawks established a very open and public relationship, going everywhere together, entertaining, traveling to Mexico and Palm Springs, hiding nothing. Slim also quickly established a strong bond with the Hawks kids, especially the boys Peter, then fourteen, and David, soon to be nine, who adored her youthful energy and almost tomboy spirit of sport and fun.

From the point of view of Hawks's work, his career decidedly entered a new phase with the blossoming of his relationship with Slim. There is no question that the eight films he directed during the eight years he and Slim were involved—from *Only Angels Have Wings* through *Red River*—represent the greatest and most creatively vibrant period of his career. Not only that, but every one of the films, which also included *His Girl Friday, Sergeant York, Ball of Fire, Air Force, To Have and Have Not,* and *The Big Sleep,* was hugely popular at the box office, resulting in one of the most remarkably sustained runs of artistic and commercial success in Hollywood history.

Beyond this, however, the films were different in feel and treatment when it came to portraying relations between men and women, as well as in the fates accorded the leading characters. Gone now would be the reckless and sometimes suicidal heroes of *The Dawn Patrol, Scarface, The Crowd Roars, Today We Live, Ceiling Zero,* and *The Road to Glory,* as well as the powerful but pathetic older men unsuccessfully trying to make it work with younger women of *Tiger Shark, Barbary Coast,* and *Come and Get It.* Also absent during this period was the comedy of humiliation and emasculation that could be found both before (in *Bringing Up Baby*) and immediately after (in *I Was a Male War Bride*) his years with Slim. Hawks's sound films throughout the 1930s were, by Hollywood standards, notably short on conventional "happy" endings; when the young male and female leads actually got together at the end it was only after the deaths of other men who, while not evil, loved the women too hopelessly and were simply in the way. Even the ostensibly upbeat *Bringing Up Baby* concluded with the woman dangling in midair, precariously held by the man whose life's work she has just destroyed.

During the Slim period, the leading men and women were much more equally balanced, able to take the other's measure, decide what they wanted, and spend the greater part of the running time getting it. There was a sense, too, in most of these films that these men and women were made for each other, were meant to be together. For that reason, the viewer believed in and rooted for these couples more than for most others in the Hawks canon. Hawks made a point of never showing the domesticity and dullness of "real" marriage and family life, only satirically acknowledging the threat it represented in the guise of what might happen to Hildy Johnson if she were to marry Ralph Bellamy's sappy Bruce Baldwin in *His Girl Friday.* The sharp-witted, innuendo-laden, sexually electric pairings of equal partners, while present in pregnant form in some of Hawks's previous films and often mimicked thereafter, was the great hallmark of the Slim years, a fantasy of how things could be between a man and a woman that Slim inspired in Hawks and that he was miraculously able to realize on film with the considerable assistance of some of the greatest writing and acting talent of the day. When war and the West didn't take precedence, it was the intricate dynamics of sexual combustion between men and women that preoccupied the poetic engineer Howard Hawks during these years. For a while, Slim made it evident that Hawks actually had a beating heart somewhere behind his hard, impenetrable shell.

At the time he met Slim, Hawks was in the process of putting together the pieces of his next film. He had been through a rocky time professionally with *Come and Get It, Bringing Up Baby*, and *Gunga Din*, and he knew it was imperative to make a surefire commercial bet. But, as always, he was looking for maximum control and minimum interference, so he turned once again to Harry Cohn and Columbia, where he had virtual carte blanche as long as he could deliver a strong story for Cary Grant and one of his top female stars—in this case, Jean Arthur. Grant, who had rotating, nonexclusive deals at RKO and Columbia and was available for work at other studios as well, was desperately sought at that moment by Ernst Lubitsch to star opposite Garbo in *Ninotchka* at MGM. But the actor owed his next picture to Columbia and Cohn wouldn't let him off the hook, so he readily agreed to work again with Hawks, having enjoyed himself so much on *Bringing Up Baby*.

The story Hawks had in mind eventually became one of the screen's great fantasy adventures, but the irony is that in Hawks's mind, the film was virtually a documentary, in that "there wasn't one single scene in the whole picture that wasn't real." *Only Angels Have Wings* had its origins in the people and places Hawks encountered in Mexico while scouting locations for *Viva Villa!* Hawks often took credit for the film's story—in fact, his screen credit for it was dropped only at the very last minute—but the first document on record concerning the project is a seven-page synopsis called "Plane Number Four" by the screenwriter and former magazine feature writer Anne Wigton that was submitted to Columbia in January 1938. The synopsis bears a remarkable resemblance to the course of action in the finished film, establishing the setting as Baranca, "a little banana port on the coast of Equador" and describing the Dutchman's as "a combination general store, hotel, bank, restaurant and operations office of Baranca Airways." The main characters were mostly "crazy" fliers who daily flew hazardous missions in makeshift planes over the mountains and whose philosophy was "Live for today." Also of possible relevence was a 1937 RKO release, *Flight From Glory*, about down-and-out pilots flying rickety planes on dangerous routes over the Andes. For a sixty-seven-minute programmer with no particular

aspirations to complexity or depth of characterization, the film was unusually well received at the time and did not pass unnoticed by critics and
audiences. There is no way of knowing if Hawks, or any of his writers, ever
saw the film, but the setup and many of the plot points bear an uncanny
resemblance to the picture Hawks was soon to make.

In a rare instance of Hawks himself setting pen to paper, the director
produced a five-page document laying out his thoughts on the story. In fact,
in his brief treatment, called "Plane Four from Baranca," there is no story
at all, just a roughing out of a few characters and incidents based entirely
upon the people he had briefly met in Mexico. They were "outcasts," close
relatives of Cagney's irresponsible Dizzy Davis in *Ceiling Zero*. For Hawks,
"collectively and individually they were the finest pilots I've ever seen but
they had been grounded because of accidents, drinking, stunting, smuggling—each man's existence almost a story in itself."

The rawness of situations described by Hawks in some ways looks ahead
more to Henri-Georges Clouzot's 1953 French suspense classic *The Wages
of Fear* than it does to the film he shortly made: the men's "living accommodations were bad, they were lonely, women-starved," and they "flew
anywhere, carried prospectors to country almost impossible to reach in any
other way, dropped their passengers and picked them up three months later.
(A great scene took place after each of these trips on the pilot's return—
they all gathered over a map and each man made his own map to be used
in picking up the passengers in case of the death of the pilot who did the
outgoing trip.) They carried gold, silver, equipment, acid, dynamite,
T.N.T—anything that people would pay them to carry."

Hawks's treament dwelled upon such technical matters as the fliers'
jerry-built planes, poor navigational equipment, and short and swampy landing strips. Most important, the story would be "very real, as is always the
case with a group of men who may die tomorrow."

As for the characters, the central figure was to be the little band's leader,
Tex. "You could only guess at his history," Hawks wrote, "because he didn't
talk much even when drinking—and that was most of the time. Tex was
rather young and had been through a crash and resultant fire that had burned
one side of his face and left rather interesting scars. Because of this he hadn't
much expression, except in his eyes, but that was enough. He ran the outfit
the only way it could be run—by complete domination—what he said went
and everybody knew he'd do twice anything he asked to have done."

Equally important for Hawks, of course, was Tex's woman, and the
way he saw her fitting into the group and the men's activities qualifies her

as a real-life prototype for what became the fully realized Hawksian woman: "Just before I met him Tex had married Bonnie—they were a great pair. She was blonde, pretty, full of life and a great sense of humour. . . . Outwardly unlike Tex she was strangely like him otherwise. She loved flying as much as he did, not just the riding around but that strange love for the air that the men had. Bonnie had been married before to one of the other pilots. He had been killed and she had drifted and knocked around until meeting Tex. According to the various tales Bonnie knew immediately what she wanted and Tex did not—and so the war started."

One story Hawks particularly liked, although he had to know it would never get by the censors, had to do with the other pilots hanging a device used to record flight vibrations under Tex and Bonnie's honeymoon bed. Hawks testified that "on the night I met them Tex and Bonnie received a nicely framed record of their marriage night. Bonnie proudly hung it over the mantel in the living room."

For the subplots, there was "one story, particularly interesting, of a young fellow who had come down to fly with them. He had brought with him his wife, young and inexperienced as himself. He hadn't been able to fit in—lost his nerve and started to go to pieces. Tex had liked the wife and been contemptuous of the boy. Tex hadn't many morals or scruples and in a place where a good-looking white woman is practically never seen started after the wife. Bonnie complicated the whole situation, she did everything she could to get in Tex's way."

Hawks concluded his notations by stating, "This is the story I want to do, using the background of this group of men and their spirit—daily adventures—as a beginning. . . . Ending with Tex taking the boy's job on a dangerous flight resulting in the crash that scarred his face. The Boy and Girl sent back to the States and Tex and Bonnie carrying on together."

The screenplay to *Only Angels Have Wings* has always been viewed as the essence of Jules Furthman in its world-weary romanticism, cynical attitude toward sex, hard-shelled and stoic leading man, and footloose leading lady with a past. However, Furthman was but one of five writers (not including Hawks) who worked on the script between September 1938 and February 1939. Furthman created the characters, at Hawks's instructions, and pounded out the basic script, but Columbia acknowledged, in a certificate filed with the Academy upon the end of production, that the contribution of Eleanore Griffin and William Rankin "represented more than 10% of the value of the completed screenplay." Anne Wigton wrote and rewrote many of Cary Grant's scenes with both Jean Arthur and Rita

Hayworth, although Furthman was always on hand to fine-tune story points, punch up the bon mots, and apply the stainless-steel finish.

Unfortunately, the various script drafts by the different authors are not available to be examined, but such notes on them as exist indicate that co-writers Eleanore Griffin (who won an Oscar that year for her original story for MGM's *Boys Town*) and William Rankin initially centered the story around the inexperienced "Boy," observing his coming-of-age under severe performance and peer-group pressure. The "Girl" in this draft is written as a young society lady. Griffin and Rankin delivered two different treatments and one full script before bowing out.

Once Furthman took over, Cary Grant's tough Jeff Carter character, based on the Tex Hawks met, took center stage, and Bonnie was transformed into a vagabond showgirl in the mold of the lead women in Conrad's *Victory* and the Furthman-Sternberg *Morocco*. The "Boy" was cleverly re-molded into a Lord Jim of the air, an older man forever scarred by a failure of character which saw him survive when others perished. Hawks later claimed he was based on a man who, during the shooting of a Howard Hughes picture, parachuted out of a spinning plane before checking to see if his partner could also get out. The other man died, and Hawks said that the survivor "spent the rest of his life trying to prove that he was brave. He flew at every air circus in some little pusher plane that he'd built until he finally cracked up and killed himself. Barthelmess was playing that character." (Ironically, in the fascinating 1931 *The Sun Also Rises* knockoff *The Last Flight*, written by John Monk Saunders, Barthelmess had portrayed a pilot who had gone down with his plane in order to not leave his mechanic behind.) Furthman made the Lord Jim reference all but explicit in a great speech in which Sparks explains the code to the man's wife: "Captain deserting a ship . . . radio operator leaving his post. You are supposed to stay, and if you don't among your own kind you're a marked man. No matter where you go—your story travels ahead of you . . . and if they haven't heard it you think they have, so what they don't do to you, you do to yourself." The critic Robin Wood has also noted similarities between Thomas Mitchell's Kid and Singleton in Conrad's *The Nigger of the Narcissus*. The "Girl" took on the past of Hawks's real Bonnie of having been involved with one of the other pilots, who turns out to have been Jeff, raising the question of whether he will sleep with her again.

The art director, Lionel Banks, oversaw the construction of the sprawling Baranca set on the Columbia Ranch in North Hollywood, right next to the Shangri-La of Capra's 1937 *Lost Horizon*. The beautifully designed tropical village was covered by translucent tarpaulin stretched across beams that vaulted more than sixty feet above the ground, and the shooting area was controlled to the extent that a full array of lights was available to be mounted on the beams and scaffolding surrounding the set. However, to the consternation of the cinematographer, Joseph Walker, the space often resembled an exterior more than an interior because of the ease with which cold, rain, and changing sunlight seeped in through the tarp. The amiable and inventive Walker, Capra's regular cinematographer, had briefly worked with Hawks before, shooting makeup tests for *Twentieth Century*, and his shadowy, "sling-the-lamps-low" lighting style was enriched by striking the film's original release prints in a chocolate-toned sepia.

For the two most important roles other than Grant's and Arthur's, Hawks turned to one veteran and one newcomer. Since his great success in *The Dawn Patrol* in 1930, it had all been downhill for Richard Barthelmess in sound pictures. By 1938, at forty-three, he was virtually a forgotten figure. Hawks offered him the role of the disgraced flier Bat McPherson and shrewdly used the actor's physical flaws for his own devices. Not long before, the former silent star, whose original appeal was based to an extent on his boyish good looks, had undergone plastic surgery in Paris for bags under his eyes. Infection had set in, leaving him with deep crisscrossed marks, which only heavy makeup could conceal. To Barthelmess's distress, Hawks insisted that he appear without makeup because "those scars tell the story and are important to your character." Hawks also removed the thick wooden planks the smallish actor wanted to use to make him appear taller, which actually subtly accentuates the character's sense of inferiority in the many group shots with the film's generally rangy men.

At the same time, Hawks had his hands full with the twenty-year-old Columbia starlet Rita Hayworth. The former dancer had been around Hollywood for three years and had appeared in more than a dozen pictures without making anyone sit up and take notice. Conflicting stories abound concerning how she ended up in *Only Angels Have Wings*. Hawks sometimes claimed that he had noticed her in another picture and asked for her to come in. The most famous account, advanced from apocrypha into legend by the fan magazines of the era, had her campaigning for the role by showing up in a stunning new five-hundred-dollar dress at the Trocadero when she knew Hawks and Cohn would be dining there together. However, the truth was considerably more prosaic. George Chasin of the Small Agency, a young agent who would later represent Alfred Hitchcock, sat for several days outside Hawks's office until he was able to corner the director to talk up his client. Hawks told him that Linda Winters, a new twenty-year-old protégée of his brother Bill's—and later under her real name, Dorothy Comingore, the female lead in *Citizen Kane*—was set for the second lead, but Chasin managed to persuade Hawks to test Hayworth. On November 30 and December 2, Hawks shot tests with Winters, Hayworth, and the more established actress Rochelle Hudson in scenes with Barthelmess, Arthur, Sig Ruman, and other actors. Hayworth finally won Hawks over, with the director concluding that she had one of those "faces that the camera likes" and that her tremendous sexual allure was just the ticket for the part of the woman who had burned Grant's Jeff Carter so badly that he had turned against all women.

Victor Kilian, cast as Sparks, had served in the trenches for Hawks on *The Road to Glory*. But most of the other actors—Thomas Mitchell, fresh from *Stagecoach*, as Jeff's best friend, Kid; the genial Ruman as the Dutchman, the owner of the establishment; John Carroll, Allyn Joslyn, and Noah Beery Jr. as some of the other fliers—were appearing in their one and only Hawks film. Unlike John Ford and some others, Hawks was not interested in building a stock company and tended to reuse leading actors rather than supporting players, with the exception of Walter Brennan.

After seven more days of tests, production started in earnest on Monday, December 19, on the Columbia Ranch with the scene of Jean Arthur's Bonnie Lee arriving at the port of Barranca (now spelled with two *r*'s). Filming was scheduled to run forty-two days, until February 8, with release set for May. After six days of interior scenes on the Dutchman's set, which occupied stages 8 and 9 on the Columbia lot, it was back to the massive waterfront mock-up for five days of crowd scenes that carried the company through the New Year. Cinematographer Walker recalled that Hawks said next to nothing to him before filming began about what he expected from him. "He would leave the visual planning to me, then would come over to correct certain things and make suggestions. After the first day, he said, 'I like that mood, let's try to keep it.'" During the week of shooting with dozens of extras on the Barranca set, the crew had tremendous problems with wind and weather under the tarp, and Walker was very impressed with the way Hawks handled it all. "Nothing bothered him, he said very little, there was no small talk. He told me tersely what he wanted, and everything remained very calm. . . . At one point when we were waiting out a problem, we were walking along, he with those long strides of his, and I said, 'You just take these things so calmly. I think it's wonderful, but how do you do it?' Hawks said, 'I learned a long time ago when big trouble comes along and I let it get to me, I'd lose my breakfast. I never saw anything in this business that was worth losing your breakfast for.'"

One day Capra dropped by the set to visit Hawks and Walker and saw something that forever after defined Howard Hawks to him: "They were shooting a scene with some wind machines and a lot of heavy equipment and there was a lot of black smoke in the studio. I was friendly with Howard—as friendly as you could get—so I went over and I saw that everybody coming out was black and covered with smoke. But when Howard came out, he was absolutely untouched. His pants were pressed, his hair was in place and he didn't have a spot on him. I said, 'My God, even the smoke won't touch him.' That was Howard."

As much as he could, Hawks shot the picture in sequence in order to enhance the dynamics of group interaction. Cary Grant and the rest of the men were terrific and provided no problems, but, just as he had been unable to communicate effectively with Katharine Hepburn on *Bringing Up Baby*, he encountered heavy resistance to his methods from another pro, Jean Arthur. Questionable to begin with in the role of a showgirl knocking around Latin America, Frank Capra's greatest leading lady was simply too wholesome, irrepressibly upbeat, and unironical to fit comfortably into Hawks's world. She was not adept at improvising with the quicksilver Grant, and when Hawks would try to direct her to act in the sexy, subtly simmering way that he liked, she simply refused, saying, "I can't do that kind of stuff."

Hawks didn't hide his disappointment and resentment, and the feeling became mutual. At the end of the shoot, Hawks said that he told Arthur, "You are one of the few people I've worked with that I don't think I've helped at all. Someday you can go see what I wanted to do because I'm gonna do this character again." In a typically self-serving story, Hawks claimed that several years later he returned home to find Jean Arthur waiting in his driveway. She had just seen Lauren Bacall in *To Have and Have Not* and, according to Hawks, contritely confessed, "I wish I'd done what you'd asked me to do. If you ever make another picture with me, I'll promise to do any goddamn thing you want to do. If a kid can come in and do that kind of stuff, I certainly could do it." In later years, Hawks admitted that Arthur was "good" and attributed her inability to follow his direction to "a quirk." To see how Arthur is wanting in *Only Angels Have Wings*, and to realize how a certain sexual spark is missing as a result, one has only to imagine any number of other Hawks actresses from different eras in the role, not only

Bacall but Louise Brooks, Carole Lombard, Frances Farmer, Barbara Stanwyck, Ann Sheridan, or Angie Dickinson.

Hawks had just as much trouble with Rita Hayworth, but ironically, with an inexperienced actress he was able to get what he wanted; as Joseph Walker remembered, she "would do anything Hawks told her to do." Hawks personally didn't find her "terribly sexy," but did find that "she had a sex *quality* that came across . . . on the screen," so he emphasized that aspect of her personality at the expense of anything else. His choice certainly worked spectacularly well in terms of the film as well as her future, but at the time the hopeful actress felt that Hawks condescended to her and didn't take her seriously. "It was a difficult film for me," she later said. "I hadn't been in a big 'A' picture before and I was really frightened. Cary Grant was so lovely and kind to me. He said, 'Don't worry, it'll be okay.'" She added, "Mr. Hawks asked me to do certain things that I was very unhappy about, but between Cary and Hawks I did it. Cary is more genteel about things. Hawks is quiet. You can hardly hear him speak when he talks to you, but he's kind of hard." So bitter was she about Hawks's insensitivity to her that decades later, when the film historian John Kobal was preparing a biography of her and mentioned that he was going to talk to Hawks about her, "she froze, and suddenly, out of nowhere, she asked in a voice tingling with hostility, 'Why?'"

For his part, Hawks realized that she was shy and hadn't yet developed a performer's ego and that it would be a mistake to "ask for things that were beyond her." Instead, he posed her in the sexiest possible ways and tricked her to make her effective in scenes he realized she wasn't up to. He introduced her with dramatic brilliance, having all the men stop what they were doing and just stare as she comes down a flight of stairs. In her first solo scene with Grant, she was obliged to come into his office to begin a conversation that would summon up their past together. In the first rehearsal, having been given no instruction by her director, she entered very quickly and just looked blankly at Grant, prompting Hawks to laugh. He then suggested she try it slowly: come in, close the door, and lean back against it so that her form-fitting dress would do its work. "She did and she looked awful good doing it because she had that . . . dancer's quality . . . of assuming a position," Hawks said. He then had her say, "Like my hair this way?," telling the audience all it needed to know about their past; she and Grant kiss, after which she says, "I'm not so sure we should have done that." The finished scene carries a suggestive dose of the female insolence that Hawks would fully realize with Lauren Bacall in *To Have and Have Not* six years later.

Hayworth had a scene in which she was supposed to cry, but try as she might she couldn't make it convincing. Hawks solved the problem by moving the scene outside, turning the rain machines on, and letting the water drench her face. Most difficult of all for her was a long drunk scene in which she and Grant were supposed to discuss their past. When Hawks and Grant agreed that she wasn't "up to being a good drunk," the director told Grant to simply tell her, "You don't know what I'm talking about, do you?" and pour two pitchers of water and ice cubes on her head and then say a line while she reacted hysterically, upon which they could dissolve to a shot of him drying her hair and telling her to blow her nose. Later, while suggesting that Hayworth, "at her best, was slightly . . . unreal," Hawks admitted, "I'm not sure Rita *ever* really knew what it was all about."

Making changes constantly on the set with Furthman and the actors, Hawks worked at a deliberate pace, with the shooting schedule bulking up accordingly. By February 8, the day he was to have finished, the end was nowhere in sight. If Harry Cohn was concerned, he had nevertheless agreed to Hawks's nonnegotiable stipulation, and was forbidden from coming onto the set. First-unit filming didn't end until March 24, after seventy-three days, or thirty-one days over schedule. The film, however, was far from complete. Several other units were engaged to shoot portions of the picture, and a lot still had to be done. The ever-reliable Richard Rosson, with Russell Metty on second-unit camera, shot some night footage at Metropolitan Airport in Van Nuys. Later, Rosson flew to Las Vegas to photograph some snowy mountains, and most of the aerial footage was shot by Elmer Dyer; Hawks's good friend and Hollywood's top stunt pilot, Paul Mantz, flew the planes, working around Salt Lake City, and St. George, Utah; and Riverside, Bishop and Muroc Dry Lake in California, among other locations. Roy Davidson did all the miniatures, which included the freighter at sea as well as all the (obviously fake) plane takeoffs and landings.

Hawks returned to do retakes with Cary Grant and Victor Kilian as late as April 13. For unknown reasons, Charles Vidor (who, seven years later, would direct Rita Hayworth to her best performance in *Gilda*), and not Hawks, was called in to direct two days' worth of retakes and added scenes. Vidor made the interior scene of the mountaintop lookout with Barthelmess, Don Barry as the injured Tex, the doctor, the father, and the boy, as well as a process scene of Cary Grant and Rita Hayworth in the plane. Vidor also did a retake of a scene between the two in the Dutchman's, which was not identified in the production log; some of this material did not end up in the finished picture. Just before the release prints were struck, Hawks, making use of the precedent Frank Capra had set at the studio, managed to have his title-card credit changed from his usual "A Howard Hawks Production" to the possessive "Howard Hawks'" for the first time.

On May 10, a mere twelve days after the final scenes were shot, *Only Angels Have Wings* had its invitational premiere at the Pantages in Hollywood. Victor Fleming, just having returned to work on *Gone with the Wind* that day after a week's illness, turned out to see his friend's latest creation, as did many celebrities and most of the important cast members. Richard Barthelmess threw a party at Café LaMaze afterward, which Hawks attended. The official world premiere took place the following day at Radio City Music Hall in New York City. Except for some carping about the casting of Jean Arthur, the reviews on both coasts were flat-out raves. While calling the film a "standout," *Variety*'s Abel Green noted the similarity to *Flight from Glory* and reported that Barthelmess's entrance, marking his return to the screen after a three-year absence, was greeted with applause by the opening-day Radio City crowd. In Hollywood, and no doubt elsewhere, men were reported going nuts over Hayworth, issuing wolf whistles and shouting when she was on-screen. Never having had any luck creating a star at his studio, Harry Cohn took note, signed her to a new contract with a raise from $250 to $350 per week, and heeded Hawks's advice to wait until public reaction set in before rushing her into another picture. In short order, she landed on the cover of *Look* magazine and started receiving fan mail. Despite her miserable time on the set, the film marked Rita Hayworth's breakthrough.

Only Angels Have Wings was heavily promoted by Columbia, particularly in the national magazines, but with the opening of the New York World's Fair on May 3 essentially killing film business in the city that spring, the picture did just a "pretty good" $143,000 in its two-week Radio City run. Throughout most of the country, however, it proved a lively draw with notable staying power and ended up earning well over $1,000,000 in revenues, in the imprecise box-office accounting of the day, fulfilling Columbia's hopes for it as the company's third top grosser of the year, after Capra's *You Can't Take It with You* and *Mr. Smith Goes to Washington*. It was shortly announced that *Only Angels Have Wings* would be one of twelve titles to represent the United States at the first-ever Cannes Film Festival, set to open on the French Riviera on September 1, 1939. However, events in Europe that summer would delay the inauguration of the festival by seven years.

The distilled, microcosmic nutshell of a world Hawks created in *Only Angels Have Wings* has been called "a boy's own land," an "operetta seaport" that is "removed from reality, like the land of Tolkien's Hobbits." It has also been described as "a Racine tragedy," a "heady atmosphere of primal struggle" in which "Grant almost seems the high priest of some Sartrean temple," "a self-sufficient hermetic society with its own values" in which Hawks finds a setting "ideal for the expression of his metaphysic." It is, in fact, all these things, depending on how seriously one chooses to take the picture. The critic Dave Kehr has convincingly proposed the picture as representing "the equilibrium point" of Hawks's career. "The themes he was developing throughout the 30s here reach a perfect clarity and confidence of expression, without yet confronting the darker intimations that would haunt his films of the 40s and 50s." It is also true that *Only Angels Have Wings* finds Hawks simultaneously operating at maximum effectiveness as an entertainer and a commercial filmmaker on the one hand and a philosopher and intuitive artist-poet on the other. Even those who can't take the film seriously are forced to acknowledge its snappy, cynical, and suspenseful "White Cargo melodrama" qualities, as well as the dazzling allure of Cary Grant, who never looked better or so fully expressed his hard, dark side. The vast majority of more general viewers, including the critics and audiences of 1939, who enormously liked it but weren't about to start thinking of it as great art, could reasonably consider it a prime example of what Hollywood could do best, one of the most exhilarating films of what has often been called the best year in American film history.

Critics who began looking deeper into the director's work from the 1950s onward have found in *Only Angels Have Wings* one of the richest mines in all of Hawks. His ability to compress, to take a story that originally occurred over a period of many weeks and reduce the action down to little more than twenty-four hours; to boil down to essences; to convey meanings through gestures, physical objects, and composition; to obliquely state what in other hands would be blatantly put was never greater. His adolescent notions of stoicism and refusal to fear death were more clearly expressed here than in any of his other films: none of the later characters live so continuously in death's shadow, and nowhere is there a scene that so concisely states the stubborn denial of it as the famous "Who's Joe?" exchange. The manner in which Hawks delineated the importance of integration into the group achieved a standard here that Hawks often strove for in his later work and sporadically achieved but never surpassed. In terms of the purity with which it expresses its director's attitudes and personality, his quasi-existential, closet-romantic impulse to assert the importance of individual self-definition against the dark void of the outside world, *Only Angels Have Wings* can fully support the serious claims that have been made for it as "a completely achieved masterpiece." One can also use it to assess the limitations of his world and sensibility, and the film starkly puts to the test how deep and profound pulp material can ultimately be. The film greatly benefited from the renewed zest and romantic optimism Hawks was feeling at the time, as he was just in the initial throes of falling in love with Slim, the most important woman of his life.

The extent to which Howard Hawks lived in a fantasy world, however, can be seen in his imagining that *Only Angels Have Wings* was good because of some notion of documentary realism. In fact, the second-unit sequences of actual planes flying, the only recognizable exterior shots in the entire film, actually yank one out of the action, so disconnected are they from the artificial world of Barranca. The film contains a tremendous amount of truth and insight into people and behavior, but virtually no reality. Not since the greatest of the Sternberg-Dietrich collaborations—*Morocco, Shanghai Express, The Scarlet Empress, The Devil Is a Woman*—had so much distilled visual poetry, daring behavioral stylization, and eccentric, undiluted personal philosophy come through with such brazen but covert force in a first-class Hollywood entertainment.

20

His Girl Friday

None of his many interviewers ever thought to ask Howard Hawks about the identity of the young woman who read the part of Hildy Johnson at Hawks's request one night after a dinner party. Nor has anyone ever stepped forward to take credit for giving the performance that convinced the director that a sex change would lend a special angle to a remake of his favorite play. Nor, in fact, has anyone else ever mentioned having been present at this legendary evening at Hawks's home. So we have only Hawks's word that this event actually took place, with Hawks, the antithesis of the fast-talking, harddriving verbal type, playing the manipulative editor Walter Burns to the Hildy of some sweet young thing. But the story is good enough that one would like to print the legend, for it led to one of the greatest American screen comedies, an arguable improvement on its brilliant source material, a high point in Hawks's own career, and a culmination of the 1930s screwball genre from a man who was there at the start of it all some six years before.

In July 1938, Howard Hughes made the biggest headlines of his life when he completed his epochal round-the-world flight in the record time of just over ninety-one hours. Later that year, word began circulating that he was planning a return to the movies after his withdrawal in disgust, six years earlier, in the wake of *Scarface*. First, however, he sold the screen rights to *The Front Page* to producer Edward Small. With *Only Angels Have Wings* just barely into production, Hawks went to see Cohn to try to sell him on producing another version of *The Front Page* as Cary Grant's next starring vehicle for Columbia. Initially, Cohn imagined Grant in the reporter role, with the editor Walter Burns being played by the celebrated newspaper columnist and staccato-speaking radio commentator Walter Winchell, who had already appeared in a couple of pictures for Zanuck at Fox. When Hawks informed the studio boss that he wanted Grant to play Burns and a woman to appear as the reporter, Cohn, Hawks related, was initially aghast but quickly came around to his idea during the course of a single meeting. In early January 1939, Cohn bought the remake rights to *The Front Page* from Eddie Small.

With Hecht and MacArthur unavailable—Hecht was busy doing uncredited rewrites for Victor Fleming on *Gone with the Wind* and preparing his next film as a director, *Angels over Broadway*—the first screenwriter Hawks approached to ring the transformation was Gene Fowler. The man responsible for setting the playwrights back on track when they were having second-act problems during the writing of *The Front Page*, Fowler was a natural candidate for the job, but he resented, as Hecht did not, the changes Hawks wanted to make. Rebuffed, the director instead turned to another old Hecht crony, Charles Lederer, the prankish, wealthy nephew of Hearst's mistress, Marion Davies, who had begun his career polishing dialogue on *Scarface* and helping Bartlett Cormack with the adaptation of Lewis Milestone's 1931 film of *The Front Page*.

While remaining in Hollywood to direct *Only Angels Have Wings*, Hawks stayed in close contact with his writers as Hecht briefly accompanied Lederer to Palm Springs to help him revise the *Front Page* plotline. It was Lederer who took Hawks's basic notion the crucial extra step to make ace reporter Hildy Johnson the ex-wife of Walter Burns, who schemes to lure her back into his professional and personal life before she marries a straight-laced mama's boy the next day. Hawks credited Lederer's idea with making "all the scenes much better and the characters more definite. Now we knew what we were talking about—two people who had been married and in love and divorced. After that, it wasn't really a great effort to do the story. We were a little snagged up before that because the relationship was nebulous."

After Hecht helped him a bit more on structural revisions, Lederer remained in the desert to complete the first draft, which he presented to Hawks on May 22, just twelve days after the *Angels* gala premiere. Lederer did two more drafts by the beginning of July. But Hawks, feeling that the dialogue needed more punch, then decided to call in Morrie Ryskind, who had pitched in so helpfully on *Ceiling Zero*. Ryskind was a particularly apt choice, not only for his comic mind but because of his intimate familiarity with the material; his celebrated and frequent collaborator George S. Kaufman had directed the original Broadway production of *The Front Page*. Ryskind worked through the summer right up to the start of shooting at the end of September, by which time more than half of what Hawks considered the "finest modern dialogue that had been written" had been rewritten.

Changing Hildebrand into Hildegard enriched the dynamic of the story in obvious ways, enabling it to become "a very curious and complex romantic comedy in which love is expressed through work and work is expressed as love." Hildy becomes a markedly stronger character as a woman, doubly important to Walter and not only because of the romantic connection: Hawks made sure to include a scene not present in the play—Hildy's superb prison interview with murderer Earl Williams—that showed this celebrated pro *in action*, doing her job, proving how good she really is and thereby how worthy of Walter's high esteem. Her sex also changes the dynamic in the otherwise all-male courthouse pressroom and alters the focus of the scene in which Earl Williams's floozy Mollie Molloy tells off the "gentlemen of the press." It also, of course, required a total rethinking of the character to whom Hildy is engaged. In the play, Hildy's intended, Peggy Grant, was the one boringly "nice" individual in whom Hecht and MacArthur clearly had no interest. Bruce Baldwin, shrewdly written in the new *His Girl Friday* as being unqualified to enter Hildy's world of the newsroom and presented by Hawks as the only person who speaks slowly, is used as the butt of jokes to ridicule the safe, dull, conventional life Hildy is on the verge of embracing. He is also, however, given a vestige of decency and legitimacy that enhances his position as a mere foil and punching bag for Walter in his attempts to win back Hildy. He may be a chump, but as newly conceived for the film, he becomes, unlike Peggy Grant, not only an obligatory character but a memorable one.

Structurally, Hawks and his writers followed the pattern the director had first employed on his adaptation of *Twentieth Century*: adding an extensive "prologue" establishing the prior personal and working relationship of the central couple, then boiling down the play's three acts—in the case of *His Girl Friday*, into a tight seventy minutes—while largely retaining the constricted settings of the theater piece. The first twenty minutes of *His Girl Friday*, from Hildy's entrance through her long conference with Walter Burns and the luncheon they share with her fiancé, Bruce Baldwin, were entirely invented for the film. In creating this foregrounding material, Hawks moved the beginning of the action up to the daytime, which then eases into night as the story unfolds, the same progression used in *Bringing Up Baby*.

The original play boasts one of the most famous final lines in American theater history: after scheming to keep Hildy onboard long enough to help him with the Earl Williams case, Walter encourages him to leave to join his fiancée, giving him a watch as a parting gift; after Hildy has left, Walter reveals his essence by phoning the police and telling them to apprehend Hildy, since "the son-of-a-bitch stole my watch!" In the more relaxed pre-Code days of 1931, the original film of the play was able to get away with this line, which, eight years later, Hawks could not have done even if he'd wanted to. But by this time, Hawks felt the line had become so familiar that it was shopworn, and he wanted to find something better. This assignment fell to Morrie Ryskind, who came up with what he thought was a brilliant new ending, in which Walter and Hildy have a wedding in the newsroom and break into a huge fight as soon as they say "I do." Abner Biberman's Diamond Louie was to have had the last word: "I think it's gonna turn out all right this time." This was never shot, however, since Ryskind, a little proud of himself, laid it all out for a bunch of other Columbia scribes at a writers' hangout after work one evening. Just a few days later, one of the screenwriters who had been there told him that he had just seen Ryskind's ending being filmed on a nearby soundstage—for a different picture.

Ryskind was incensed but had no choice except to come up with yet another wrap-up. This time, he recalled, "I devised the one of a guarded marital reconciliation between Walter and Hildy. This was kept under wraps until Howard filmed it. Both Howard and I agreed that the romantic flavor of the new ending worked out better than our previous one, so in a way, I'm grateful to that writer at Columbia—who shall remain anonymous—for giving us the impetus to make a great film even better." The final ending cleverly sends Walter and Hildy out to take the train to Albany, Hildy and Bruce's original destination, in order to cover a labor strike, with Walter snidely remarking, 'I wonder if Bruce can put us up."

The Hays Office had no overriding problems with the screenplay it received before production but vehemently objected to repeated references to newspapermen as "the scum of creation" and "the scum of Western civilization," as well as to such untoward behavior as Hildy's bribe of the jailer, Louie's kidnapping of Mrs. Baldwin, and the idea of smuggling Earl Williams out of the court building. But censorship requirements impinged not at all upon anything significant in *His Girl Friday*.

While the procession of rewrites was under way, Hawks spent the summer realigning his family life. With Athole now under care in La Jolla, Hawks brought Slim more fully into his household, encouraging her to spend as much time as possible with his kids. They responded enthusiastically to this vital young woman, especially David, who found Slim an incredibly exciting partner in fun. Peter and David continued to live at the Benedict Canyon house, but Barbara, who was only three during the summer of 1939 and without a mother to care for her, was more often than not sent to stay with Hawks's parents in Pasadena. For a private getaway just for Slim and himself, Hawks proposed a car trip to Mexico, but the fun was diminished by Hawks's getting so lost that Slim feared that they'd never find their way back. There were the usual expeditions to June Lake near Yosemite, and Hawks was gratified by the way he could see a new family unit forming around him, with Slim as its spark plug.

Through August and September, as the storm clouds of war broke over Europe, Howard Hawks's main professional concern was finding the right actress to fulfil his idea of a man-woman *Front Page*. Although Cohn had announced Jean Arthur for the picture back in March, she and Hawks remained cool toward each other. So the offers went out to actresses at other studios: to Ginger Rogers, Claudette Colbert, Carole Lombard, and, most seriously, to Irene Dunne. Amazingly, all refused. Finally, with the start date looming less than two weeks away, Cohn arranged to borrow Rosalind Russell from MGM, where she had just finished work for George Cukor on the picture that would shortly establish her once and for all as an important star, *The Women*.

The announcement of Russell's casting proved particularly humiliating to the smart, good-humored actress, who had never met Hawks. Russell had read a *New York Times* story revealing how the director had approached every important actress in Hollywood "before Harry Cohn had stuck him with me." None too excited about the prospect of her first meeting with Hawks, Russell took a swim first and didn't bother to dry her hair, so that when she turned up at his office on the lot, he "did a triple take" before asking her in.

Taking the offensive with a director she was predisposed not to like, the plain-speaking actress bluntly confronted him with her knowledge that he hadn't really wanted her for the part. Hawks blandly told her that everything would be all right and quickly ended the meeting by instructing her to go to wardrobe and order a sharp-looking striped suit.

After four days of photographic, wardrobe, and makeup tests, production began on September 27 with the scene that would mark the beginning of the picture: Hildy Johnson arriving in the newsroom on her way to tell her ex that she's to be married the next day. The sequence includes one of the rare extended moving-camera shots in Hawks's work, albeit a highly effective one, in that it definitively establishes Hildy's relationship with, and dominance in, her workplace as she strides through a sea of well-wishing coworkers. The next day, Cary Grant reported to work for his initial scene with Roz Russell, one that involved, as did all their interchanges, a great deal of complex timed dialogue and business. Having enjoyed two very spirited collaborations with Hawks already, Grant was accustomed to, and in fact had earned, the loose reins the director gave him, but Russell was highly disconcerted because Hawks said nothing and just sat there watching her with eyes that she felt looked "like two blue cubes of ice." Unable to take it anymore, she went to her costar to express her dismay and ask if he thought Hawks approved of what she was doing. "Oh, sure, Roz," she said Grant told her. "If he didn't like it, he'd tell you."

This gave her enough confidence to confront Hawks directly and demand his thoughts. "Unwinding himself like a snake, he rose from his chair. 'You just keep pushin' him around the way you're doing,' he said. I could hardly hear him but I could see those cubes of eyes beginning to twinkle.

"He'd been watching Cary and me for two days, and I'd thrown a handbag at Cary, which was my idea, and missed hitting him, and Cary had said, 'You used to be better than that,' and Hawks left it all in. It's a good director who sees what an actor can do, studies his cast, learns about them personally, knows how to get the best out of them," she observed.

From then on, things went swimmingly between cast and director, with Hawks not only giving the actors freedom but encouraging them to come up with their own bits, lines, and flights of fancy. As precise and adamant about adhering to the script as Hawks could be on a "serious" film such as *Only Angels Have Wings,* he was loose and casual about such matters on his comedies, rightly feeling that the actors could bring inspiration and life to the material on the set that writers couldn't possibly think of in an office.

At the same time, Hawks the engineer was still very much present. Everyone always said that the original film of *The Front Page* featured some of the fastest dialogue ever delivered on-screen. Hawks devised a way to set a new speed record on *His Girl Friday* by having the actors overlap each other's dialogue. This technique had been tried before, of course, by him and others, but Hawks and his writers worked out a careful plan by which "we wrote the dialogue in a way that made the beginnings and ends of the sentences unnecessary; they were there for overlapping." He also cranked up the pace to where, by one count, the actors were speaking at up to 240 words per minute, compared to the average speaking rate of 100–150 (the drawling Hawks would have come in at something significantly slower than that). When some newsmen came to the set and remarked about the speed of the original, Hawks arranged to screen comparable sequences from both films at the same time to put the question to the test. The visitors were amazed at how slow the original seemed by comparison, leaving Hawks to surmise, "I guess we'd accomplished what we'd wanted, which was to make it fast."

The zany, unpredictable behavior on the set was great for the actors, but it "was hell for the cameraman," Joseph Walker recalled. "*His Girl Friday* was tough because you never knew where the actors were going to go." Comedies normally call for brighter, plainer lighting than dramas, and the look and mood was certainly a world apart from that on their last film together. Nonetheless, Walker had to pay special attention to his female star. "Rosalind Russell was very hard to photograph," he recalled, "because she had sagging jowls along her chin." His solution was to have the makeup man, Fred Phillips, "paint a sharp, very dark line along the edge of her jaw, blending it toward her neck. Then, hitting her with a high key light, that dark line became a strong shadow below her cheek, giving it a firm, youthful appearance."

At one point, Roz Russell became concerned that the unvarying torrent of dialogue would prove too much for audiences to take, but Hawks, with great insight, reassured her: "You're forgetting the scene you're gonna play with the criminal. It's gonna be so quiet, so silent. You'll just whisper to him, you'll whisper, 'Did you kill that guy?' and your whispering will change the rhythm. But when you're with Grant, we don't change it. You just rivet in on him all the time."

Given the green light, Russell quickly came up to Grant's speed and matched him, quip for ad-lib. She had a ball: "We went wild, overlapped our dialogue, waited for no man. And Hawks got a big kick out of it," she said. By now completely converted to Hawks's methods, she decided that "Hawks was a terrific director; he encouraged us and let us go. Once he told Cary, 'Next time give her a bigger shove onto the couch,' and Cary said, 'Well, I don't want to kill the woman,' and Hawks thought about that for a second. Then he said, 'Try killin' 'er.'"

On another occasion, Russell did something so unexpected that Grant broke character and, with a grimace directed at Hawks and the camera, said, "Is she going to do that?" Hawks left it in the picture, just as he did other jokes in which Grant refers to Archie Leach (his real name) and describes Ralph Bellamy's Bruce Baldwin character as looking like "that fellow in the pictures — you know, what's his name — Ralph Bellamy." Bellamy happened to be in watching dailies when Harry Cohn heard this for the first time. The studio chief erupted in a fury at the impertinence, but he eventually let

Hawks leave it in, retaining what has always been one of the picture's biggest laughs.

Despite her pleasure in the part, Russell began to feel that the combined efforts of Hecht, Lederer, Ryskind, and Hawks had pushed the piece somewhat in favor of the Walter Burns character, leaving him with most of the best lines. Taking matters into her own hands, she mentioned this to her brother-in-law Chet La Roche, the head of the advertising firm Young and Rubicam, who recommended one of his top copywriters to her. Out of her own pocket and unbeknownst to Hawks or the studio, the actress paid the writer, whom she would never identify, two hundred dollars a week to sharpen her lines, as well as, eventually, a few of Grant's. Because of the anything-goes, ad-libbing atmosphere on the set, Russell didn't have to clear her changes with Hawks, since she could just drop them spontaneously into her dialogue. All the same, Cary Grant began to suspect something was up; it got to the point where each morning he would greet his costar by inquiring, "What have you got today?"

The ghostwriter came up with the rude bit of nose-thumbing business for Russell in the restaurant scene in which Burns makes fun of his ex-wife's forthcoming train trip to Albany with her husband-to-be and prospective mother-in-law. That scene, which has no equivalent in *The Front Page*, proved to be one of the most complicated in the entire picture to shoot, as it involved three actors delivering very quick overlapping dialogue, perfect timing from the waiter and other bit players, and a great deal of precise innuendo and nuance in the line readings. (One will notice that food is served but virtually none is eaten during the scene; with the actors spitting the lines out so rapidly, there was no time for chewing.) With Hawks shooting in sequence and, as was always his custom, with just one camera, the scene came up a week and a half into production and took four days to finish rather than the allotted two.

The arrival of the great character actors playing the reporters in the press room meant more delays, as they all literally had to get up to speed with Hawks's requirements, and the intricate timing of these ensemble scenes meant continual adjustments and retakes. Hawks applied a lesson he learned from *Bringing Up Baby* to make his new film more palatable, in his view. He felt that audiences had had a problem with the earlier picture because he had made "all the characters crazy." This time, he was determined to play the supporting characters straight to offset the antic behavior of his leads. "Outside of one reporter and the funny man [Billy Gilbert] who came in with the pardon and the overdone mayor [Clarance Kolb], they were all pretty legitimate. I don't mean the reporters weren't funny, but they were legitimate. They had the cynical attitude of a bunch of criminal court reporters and were amusing mainly in the way they said things."

With Arthur Rosson helping out for three days of second-unit footage with the phone operators and shots of the jail courtyard, constructed at the Columbia Ranch, production was completed on November 21, seven days over the originally scheduled forty-two shooting days. Very uncharacteristically for the time, but consistent with his first speed comedy, *Twentieth Century*, Hawks used no music in the film except to build to the final fadeout.

Rushing the picture to completion just as he had done with *Only Angels Have Wings*, Cohn held a sneak preview for a regular audience in Pomona the first week of December. Any concerns he and the filmmakers might have had about the dialogue being too fast for viewers to grasp evaporated at that highly successful first showing. Screened for the press on January 3 as the first picture of 1940, *His Girl Friday* received across-the-board outstanding reviews, with virtually all critics approving the sex switch and therefore the legitimacy of remaking the beloved *Front Page*. Once again, a Hawks picture premiered at Radio City Music Hall, on January 11, where it grossed a good, if not sensational, $155,000 during its two-week engagement. As had *Only Angels Have Wings*, it performed better elsewhere, racking up terrific returns in Los Angeles, in the big eastern cities, and even in small Midwestern towns.

His Girl Friday has remained in high regard since then, a Hawks classic of its period whose reputation was further strengthened by the revaluation of the director's career from the 1950s on. Although theater critics and historians have been curiously silent on the subject, the handful of film academics — Gerald Mast and Robin Wood in particular — who have bothered to closely analyze the differences between *The Front Page* and *His Girl Friday* have come down decisively in favor of Hawks's film.

Because of the central role of a smart working woman torn between her professional talent and her domestic inclinations, the film has also served as a convenient focal point for discussions of Hawks's attitudes toward women. On the surface, of course, Hildy comes off as exceedingly modern, a sharp-dressed feminist before her time who can out-think, out-write, and out-talk any of her male colleagues, an unusual woman even in Hawks's world in that she long ago proved herself worthy of inclusion in the otherwise all-male group. Feminist critics, notably Molly Haskell, have praised Rosalind Russell's Hildy as one of the most positive and uncompromised female screen characters of the era. By contrast, one of the director's great champions, Robin Wood, attacked the final choice Hildy was offered between staying with Walter Burns or Bruce Baldwin as "much too narrow to be acceptable." Wood argued that "the only morally acceptable ending would be to have Hildy walk out on *both* men; or to present her capitulation to Walter as tragic." The point Wood misses, it would seem, is that throughout the film Hawks is making the case for Walter and Hildy being two of a kind and, therefore, belonging together. Sure, Walter takes advantage of her and manipulates her, as he does everyone. But he also brings Hildy fully alive, both personally and professionally. Hildy is at her most vital and creative with Walter, as he is with her; who else could Wood imagine being suitable for her? It almost seems as though Wood would rather she were alone than with a man who, for all his monstrousness, brings out the best in her.

As it happened, the film had a happy consequence for Rosalind Russell on a personal level. During the shoot, she became quite close to Cary Grant, adoring his humor and charm on and off the set. They went dancing together occasionally and Grant, who was seeing the actress Phyllis Brooks at the time, kept telling his costar about a good friend of his, the Danish-born agency executive Frederick Brisson. Finally he introduced them, and in 1941, Grant was the best man at the wedding of Brisson and Russell.

21

Slim, Hemingway, and An Outlaw

The comparison needn't be pushed too far, but there is a case to be made for considering Howard Hawks the cinema's closest equivalent to Ernest Hemingway. Born three years and about 120 miles apart, the two men shared an upper-middle-class, Midwestern, WASP background; an appetite for hunting, fishing, and other rugged pursuits; and an inclination to brag and take credit. Both men also made their decisive artistic marks with works haunted by the specter of World War I. Of course, the differences between them may have been even more significant: Hemingway had enormous problems with his father and mother that helped him develop a significant rebellious and ornery streak; he rejected the convention of an elite education for more plebian journalistic work, took part in the war, settled in Paris at a young age with the specific intention of becoming recognized as an important writer, and was politically engaged. Hawks, in contrast, accepted all the advantages of his pedigree, was friendly with his parents, never saw combat, felt aloof from social and political issues, and essentially bought, socialized, and married his way up the career ladder. Nevertheless, the two had in common a certain taste in material and a similar approach to character and story; a predisposition to strong, confident men (with discreetly revealed vulnerable streaks) engaged in dangerous work; a high regard for physical capability and mental professionalism; a preference for conveying meaning through their characters' actions, gestures, and looks; an exceeding intelligence and aversion to the pretentious; a sometimes adolescent view of human endeavor that could often be abruptly offset by stunning expressions of insight and maturity; an unusually developed sense of the moment, of the fleeting nature of relationships, love, and life; a cool, pared-down style ideal for describing the physical nature of things, as well as for eliminating from concern anything not immediately germane to what interested them in a scene; a wry humor; and a poet's way of refining and transforming the commonplace into the rarefied and deeply meaningful.

288

Most of Hemingway's work posed at least some censorship problems for Hollywood filmmakers, so, as of 1939, only one of his novels, A *Farewell to Arms*, had been made into a picture, an almost achingly beautiful, highly romanticized one directed by Frank Borzage for Paramount in 1932. The author had not cared for it, but he did approve of Gary Cooper as an ideal physical embodiment of his hero, Lieutenant Frederic Henry. Since that time, Hemingway's celebrity had continued to grow, but his literary reputation was stalled; after the publication of A *Farewell to Arms* in 1929, he had produced only two middling book-length works, *Green Hills of Africa* in 1935 and, two years later, *To Have and Have Not*. He had also spent a great deal of time covering the Spanish Civil War, raised money for the ill-fated Republican cause, and written a play about it, *The Fifth Column*.

In March 1939, in a frank attempt at a knockout punch to regain the heavyweight championship among American novelists, Hemingway embarked on a massive novel of romance, courage, and political commitment set during the Spanish Civil War. A month later, he was visited in Havana by a friend, the famous former football player Shipwreck Kelly, who told him that a friend of his, Howard Hawks, was interested in making a film of Hemingway's 1936 short story "The Short Happy Life of Francis Macomber." The writer became excited at the prospect, and the men began speaking in terms of a film shoot–cum–African safari that would occur as soon as Hemingway completed work on his book.

In October, while Hawks was in the midst of production on *His Girl Friday* and Hemingway was spending his first autumn hunting in Sun Valley, Idaho, plans were laid for Hawks, Slim, and Shipwreck to visit the novelist in December. But the novelist wouldn't be back in Key West until the middle of the month, so just after Thanksgiving, Hawks drove Slim cross-country for her first visit to New York City, which surpassed her wildest dreams. This most social of young women was in constant ecstasy as she met Hawks's friends from the Hecht-MacArthur circle at the most fashionable restaurants and boîtes in town. Things continued in high gear as they were joined by the spirited Shipwreck Kelly for the drive to the southern-most tip of Florida to meet the great writer.

Taking a breather from writing *For Whom the Bell Tolls*, Hemingway was rather depressed, as his soon-to-be ex-wife, Pauline Pfeiffer, had taken the kids away for the holidays, and the current woman in his life, the journalist Martha Gellhorn, who would later become his third wife, had gone to cover the war in Finland, leaving him quite alone at Christmas. He lit up, however, upon meeting Slim. As she put it, "There was an immediate and instant attraction between us, unstated but very, very strong." She was, she admitted, "starstruck," but she always insisted that there was no physical attraction on her part and that nothing ever happened between them. Like Martha Gellhorn, Slim was put off by the writer's sloppiness and poor hygiene. For his part, Hemingway, enormously attracted by her looks and wit, flirted with "Miss Slimsky" constantly but transformed his sexual feelings into a fatherly overprotectiveness. Slim remained in his life until his death, sparking jealousy in Hemingway's fourth wife, Mary; ironically, Slim's two husbands during this period, Hawks and Leland Hayward, were among the Hollywood figures with whom Hemingway had the closest dealings, which helped bring Slim back into his orbit time after time.

Hemingway found in Hawks a man after his own taste, a rugged, quiet-spoken gentleman who liked to hunt, fish, and drink. Home movies Hawks took of the visit show the group skeet shooting, carrying passels of freshly shot game birds, deep-sea fishing, and boating through swampwater, with Slim looking impossibly elegant at all times, Hawks creating a dapper and dashing impression, and a beaming, shirtless Hemingway puffing out his chest when caught by Hawks's lens. Behind all the socializing lay the subject of Hemingway writing for films; Hawks had already gotten William Faulkner to work for him, and while Hemingway had a much more commercially viable name than his southern rival, he also had considerably higher expenses and was always in need of more money. Still, Hemingway was nearly alone among major novelists in having refused the lure of big Hollywood paychecks. He had seen how F. Scott Fitzgerald had been humbled by studio bosses and rewrite men, and he was in a position just exalted enough to maintain a condescending attitude about the movie factories, willingly accepting their money for film rights but refusing to actually go there to work. Given that the studios intermittently tolerated even the needy Faulkner's wish to work at home in Mississippi, Hawks figured that the best approach would be to quietly present a carte blanche opportunity under which he and Hemingway would work however and wherever the writer wished.

It wasn't hard for Hemingway to see where Hawks was leading him and, unsurprisingly, he resisted. As for what came next, there is no account of it other than Hawks's own, one of his most outrageous examples of ballsy one-upsmanship. Hawks claimed that he told America's leading writer that he could make a film out of anything Hemingway wrote; "'I can make a movie out of the worst thing you ever wrote.' He said, 'What's the worst thing

I ever wrote?' I said, 'That piece of junk called *To Have and Have Not*. 'I needed the money,' he said. I said, 'Well, I knew that. At least I had to guess it.' He said, 'You can't make a picture out of that.' And I said, 'No, but the two leading characters were marvelous in their relationship with each other. What about if we told how they met?'" From that point on, Hawks maintained, the two men spoke in depth about the characters of Harry Morgan and Marie, what they were like and what happened to them. The extent to which Hemingway actually helped Hawks envision the sort of film *To Have and Have Not* eventually became is highly questionable, given that it has so little to do with the source novel, but whatever it was represented the only direct input Hawks ever got from the writer on one of his films.

As it happened, Howard Hughes had just paid Hemingway ten thousand dollars for the film rights to *To Have and Have Not* that July. Knowing this, and pretty sure at this point that he would soon be forming a new partnership with Hughes to make movies, Hawks may in fact have been shrewdly manipulating Hemingway for ideas on what he hoped would be his next picture. Also, if Hawks had the writer in his camp, Hughes would be hard-pressed to give *To Have and Have Not* to some other director. Even if he hadn't persuaded Hemingway to write for him, Hawks left Key West in excellent spirits, having befriended the world's most famous novelist, leaving the door open to further exchanges and potential collaborations.

If Hemingway needed money, so did Hawks. His gambling debts always had him living close to the financial edge. Sooner or later, his much-desired divorce would come through, but that would cost him plenty. And Slim's expensive tastes, added to his own profligacy, created cash outlays such as he'd never encountered before. Most of all, however, his ego and competitive side demanded that he make more. By almost any standard of the era, Howard Hawks made a great deal of money—$112,500 in the 1939 calendar year, during which he directed two pictures. But he knew that many other directors—men considerably less talented, in his view—were earning considerably more.

Willing to gamble on his ability to bring in a big box-office winner and anxious, as ever, to work independently, as far as possible away from the control of the moguls, Hawks renewed his association with the maverick Howard Hughes, who was now ready to get back into film production as an independent with a distribution deal at 20th Century–Fox. Early in 1940, Hughes signed two directors he had worked with previously, Hawks and Leo McCarey, to two-picture deals unlike anything the major studios were willing to acquiesce to at the time: standard salaries plus substantial cuts of the profits. Thus, they felt themselves to be partners with Hughes, not employees.

All through the preliminary stages of script work, casting, and pre-production, this arrangement worked just fine as far as Hawks was concerned. While McCarey and Hughes vainly tried to revive their coveted adaptation of the bizarre Hollywood novel *Queer People*, which the studio heads had lobbied to block some eight years before, Hawks and Hughes readily agreed to go ahead with a highly fanciful telling of the Billy the Kid story. Hawks said that in New Mexico, on his way back from Florida with Slim, he'd heard the legend that Billy had not really been killed by his friend Pat Garrett but that "when Billy fell in love, Pat Garrett blew the face off another man, said it was Billy the Kid, and Billy and the girl went off to Mexico and lived happily ever after." This sentimental fantasy has always been a fringe Billy the Kid legend, one that even Sam Peckinpah briefly indulged while making his film on the same subject thirty years later.

Starting with this premise, which again involved a sort of love story between two men that is disrupted by a woman who comes between them, Hawks took a very willing Slim back to New York in early February so he could work with Ben Hecht on a story treatment and the beginnings of a screenplay. At the same time, Hawks advised Hecht on the writer's next production venture, *Angels over Broadway*, which he hoped to start directing alongside Lee Garmes in the Bronx in March. Hawks's hand is evident in the cast Hecht assembled—leads Douglas Fairbanks Jr., Rita Hayworth, Thomas Mitchell, and John Qualen were all Hawks veterans—and when Hecht's hoped-for independent financing failed to materialize, Hawks provided the crucial link to Harry Cohn that enabled the film to proceed at Columbia, even if it meant relocating the shoot to Hollywood. Hecht's preoccupation with his own film prevented him from continuing with the Billy the Kid project, so Hawks returned to Hollywood and once again called upon Jules Furthman, who wrote an exceedingly ahistorical script about Billy the Kid, Pat Garrett, Doc Holliday, and a fictitious girl who ensnares Billy.

While the screenplay was being prepared, Hawks set in motion the purchase of the property where he would shortly build his dream house, where he and Slim would live. At first, Hawks couldn't understand why Slim didn't want to live in the lovely house he'd owned for so many years; after all, it was one of things that had impressed her so much when they first met. All the same, she couldn't help but think of it as Athole's home, and she eventually managed to persuade the man she was going to marry to find some new land and build a house just for them. In the event, it didn't take long to find just the right spot. Victor Fleming, just then in the flush of his career pinnacle of directing *Gone with the Wind* and *The Wizard of Oz* in the same year, lived in one of the loveliest spots in the Los Angeles area, in a gently sloped canyon along Moraga Drive off Sepulveda Boulevard in the foothills of the Santa Monica Mountains, near Bel Air and Westwood. Through a complicated process by which Fleming agreed to subdivide his property in concert with some surrounding land controlled by Security First National Bank of Los Angeles, Hawks was able to obtain an extraordinarily beautiful 105-acre plot just beyond Fleming's.

Located in a natural canyon above Hog Creek, with slopes rising to the east, west, and north and covered with shrubs and trees, the land was perfect for a gentleman such as Hawks who wanted to keep and breed horses, play host to guests in an impressive but relaxed manner, and create a superb outdoorsy environment for his young wife and growing kids. Once this was settled, Slim took it upon herself to supervise every element of the home's construction and decoration down to the tiniest detail. The look of what became the S-Bar-S Ranch at 1150 Moraga Drive was very closely based on Van Nest Polglase and Perry Ferguson's casual American ranch design for Katharine Hepburn's Connecticut home in *Bringing Up Baby*, but the actual architect was the celebrated Myron Hunt, one of Frank Hawks's closest friends in Pasadena and the designer of, among other things, the Rose Bowl. When it was finally finished, with a pool, vast lawns, stables, barns, horse paddocks, extensive wooden fencing around the corral, and a large garden planted entirely by Slim enhancing the comfortable but unostentatious wood-and-stone house, the estate was a masterpiece of understated taste and refinement, a rural paradise in an unspoiled urban setting, a man's castle with a very smart feminine touch. As David Hawks said, "Anybody would have loved to live in the stable."

On July 24, 1940, Athole—or, properly speaking, her sister, Norma on her behalf—filed for divorce. During this final period, Athole "was very in and out," as David put it. Misdiagnosed as schizophrenic and therefore incorrectly treated, Athole was in such a deteriorated mental state that she was easily "convinced by the doctors, her mother and sister to file for divorce, since they argued that she and my father didn't really belong together," observed Barbara. At the court proceedings, which Athole did not attend, Norma acknowledged that Athole was "mentally afflicted," but blamed this on Hawks's "cruel and inhuman treatment." The details and eventual settlement took nearly another year and a half to work out, but Hawks in the end agreed to pay a thousand dollars a month to support Athole (she also received additional money from Norma) while gaining full custody of the children, including Athole's son Peter, who turned sixteen in 1940; Hawks was also required to set up trust funds for the children. There is no question that breaking from her husband represented a terrible ordeal for Athole, but David said, "She coped. A lot of people would have committed suicide. She was very warm, very loving. When she was well, she was such a lovely person, really fun." Still, her troubles were real and unavoidable, and her son admitted, "I was shielded from it a lot. Maybe they just put her away at the first sign of any problems. We'd go visit her in these locations where she was put, but it was never explained to us. We just sort of gradually became aware of a mental illness problem."

That summer, Hawks worked to bring Slim and his children even closer together, and the best way he knew was through sports and shared outings. Hawks arranged for Peter, David, and Slim to learn skeet shooting under the instruction of Tommy Thompson at a range just south of the Santa Monica Airport, and he subsequently took them dove hunting in the Imperial Valley. Later, Hawks put in a shooting range at Hog Canyon that everyone agreed was one of the best in Los Angeles. They also went on a fishing trip to June Lake with Faulkner, whom David found to be "just a friendly, Southern good ol' boy who liked fishing." While Hawks was just a recreational Western rider, Slim was highly trained at dressage and jumping. However, her riding days came to an end late that summer when she fell and broke her leg, landing her in traction at the hospital for an extended period. After that, she refused to as much as mount a horse, even, she joked, one of her husband's Tennessee Walkers.

By August, Hawks had to turn serious attention to the Billy the Kid project, now known as *The Outlaw*. With Furthman's script coming along, Hawks concentrated on the casting, which promised to be fun since the two leads, Billy and the girl, Rio, would be played by unknowns. Working out of Hughes's offices at 7000 Romaine in Hollywood, Hawks looked at dozens of young hopefuls, including Gene Fowler's son Will and Wallace Reid Jr. for the Kid and, among the women, Beverly Holden, who had been up for Rita Hayworth's role in *Only Angels Have Wings*. Facing a final round of screen tests without being sold on anyone, Hughes found a prospect for the Kid in a dark-haired, physically compact twenty-three-year-old insurance clerk, Jack Beutel (soon changed to Buetel), while Hawks was taken with photographs of a nineteen-year-old aspiring model named Jane Russell that he'd received from an agent who had noticed them at a photographer's studio. Working in an improvised studio in the vast basement of the Romaine building with Lucien Ballard behind the camera, Hawks paired off his five male and five female finalists at random to enact "the beginning of the big rape scene, where Billy and Rio come eye-to-eye, she has a pitchfork laying in wait and he throws her in the hay. It was all close-ups," recalled Russell.

A few days later, Hawks called Buetel and Russell in to see him and separately showed them all the screen tests. For her part, Russell said, "I was astounded at how I looked. I had a very mediocre image of myself, so I was amazed and very pleased!" Without a word, Hawks escorted first Buetel, then Russell to his small office, sat down at his desk, and calmly said, "Well, you two kids have the parts." Russell never forgot how, when he announced this, Hawks "was so calm and quiet, but his eyes were twinkling, bright blue." But after she rolled back on her little cot and threw her hands over her head and Buetel similarly erupted, Hawks said, "Now that's what I want you to do, be totally spontaneous and natural." In fact, Russell had noticed Buetel from the first time she saw him at the tests and "had picked Jack out as the cutest boy there." On their way out of Hawks's office, they noticed a tall, thin man leaning against the hallway wall looking at them. It didn't take them long to figure out that this was Howard Hughes. It was clear, however, that "he didn't want to meet us, just to see us in the flesh," said Russell. "Howard Hawks and Howard Hughes had agreed on the tests, they had to agree on the discovery of Jack and myself." After a quick look, Hughes disappeared into Hawks's office. Russell wasn't actually to meet her longtime boss and benefactor until months later, after returning from location work in Arizona.

Hawks threw a party for his lucky couple at the Mocambo nightclub on the Strip, where they were thrilled to meet Gary Cooper, and the director gave the untrained new actress voice and posture lessons. "He wanted me to keep my voice low, and he said that girls should walk from the hips, not from the knees. He said I should take long strides" Russell remembered. Hawks took Russell to Nudie's, a famous cowboy outfitter, where he bought her some well-tailored Western clothes, and sent her to see Slim in the hospital, where she was still laid up in traction with her broken leg. Slim arranged an appointment with her favorite women's-wear buyer so Russell could be properly attired on location.

Even though MGM was proceeding with its own Billy the Kid picture, starring Robert Taylor, which looked as though it would beat theirs into theaters, Hughes and Hawks went ahead. Hawks cast two solid actors he'd worked with before and knew he could count on, Walter Huston and Thomas Mitchell, to play Doc Holliday and Pat Garrett, respectively. Much as had been done for *The Dawn Patrol*, an entire tent city was put up outside of Tuba City, Arizona, a small Indian town on the Navajo reservation about seventy-five miles north of Flagstaff. As locations went at that time, it was extremely remote, not easy to reach, and far from any luxurious amenities. With the still-mending Slim remaining behind, Hawks flew in with Lucien Ballard and was joined by Furthman, who continued to amend the screenplay as shooting began in the last week of November, as well as by Cubby Broccoli, whom Hawks made an assistant director. Not needed for the initial scenes, the voluptuous Jane Russell was immediately taken to be photographed in a series of revealing outfits that prominently featured what the publicity campaign later trumpeted were "two good reasons for seeing *The Outlaw*." After a few days of being pushed to pose in increasingly preposterous positions, Russell had had enough: "In tears, I went down to see Howard. He said, 'Look, Jane. You're a big girl. If you don't want to do something, the answer is "no." Cooperation is not always the best thing to do.' It's the best advice I ever got," Russell averred.

While this mythmaking was going on, Hawks directed the opening sequences: the introductions of Billy and Doc Holliday and the scene—the best in the entire picture—in which Thomas Mitchell's Pat Garrett tries to hit Billy in a saloon but gets knocked down by him instead. Just as he had on *Scarface*, Hawks insisted that Hughes come nowhere near the set while he was working, and he was reassured that his "partner" was hundreds of miles away in Los Angeles. This represented less protection than it seemed, however. As he began to see the rushes that were shipped back to him each day, Hughes started complaining by telegram and phone that Hawks wasn't taking advantage of the locale's scenic possibilities. He then took exception to Hawks's direction of Buetel. Russell felt that "Hughes identified with Billy the Kid and wanted him to be the antihero. Hawks wanted him to be smart-alecky. Hughes wouldn't hear of this. Hughes didn't want him cocky, but Hawks definitely did."

Suddenly, without warning, the boom was lowered: after just two weeks, Hawks was off the picture, Hughes would replace him as director, and the company would return at once to Los Angeles. This is one of several instances in Hawks's career where it remains debatable whether the director quit or was fired; either way, the decision was mutually agreeable. Hawks could already see that Hughes's personal interest in the story and his young stars was such that he'd be constantly interfering in a way that he never had on *Scarface*. Hawks's usual response to interviewers about his departure from the picture was, "We had different ideas about revealing women's bosoms, and things like that," so that when the chance to direct *Sergeant York* presented itself, he told Hughes, "You always wanted to direct, why the devil don't you direct this?"

Both Ballard and Russell remembered it rather differently, however. The cinematographer stated that Hughes strategically waited until a day when the crew was idle and Hawks and Ballard were off scouting a new location. At that moment, Hughes ordered the entire company home, save for the director and cameraman, who were left in the lurch. Ballard made no bones about it: "Howard and I were taken off the picture," he said. "We were told that we were to pack up and leave—very suddenly." Abruptly informed of the news by unit manager Cliff Broughton, Russell and Buetel were devastated that they were no longer to be guided through their film debuts by one of the top directors in Hollywood. When Hawks finally turned up, he told the kids that since "no one tells me how to shoot a picture," he had advised Hughes to take over in his place. He even invited them to fly back to Los Angeles with him, but Broughton warned them that Hughes would be furious if they accepted Hawks's hospitality, so they returned, as they had arrived, by bus. Later, when Russell finally met Hughes for the first time, she said that he told her, "Howard Hawks was spending too much money, so I'm going to shoot this in the studio." Ironically, a completely opposite story was reported in the press, with *Variety* stating that "Hawks pulled out when Hughes insisted on a budget of $1,500,000, which, Hawks contended, would have reduced the chances of realizing on a percentage basis."

To Russell's great disappointment, Hawks never directed her in any scenes. "I watched a little. I loved the way he directed Jack. I adored him, and got things from him I was able to use even though he was no longer there. He didn't take any shit off people. He knew what he wanted, and if he didn't get it, he removed himself." As he was saying good-bye, Hawks told both Russell and Buetel that he wanted to work with both of them again someday, and he meant it.

As for *The Outlaw*, the rest of the shoot was "painful," in Russell's view, in more ways than one. "Hughes wasn't really sure what he wanted and did it over and over and over. It was the most insane thing I've ever seen. Walter Huston had the right idea, because he just took it like a big joke," said

Russell. By contrast, Thomas Mitchell was none too pleased with Hughes's amateurism and made sarcastic and derogatory remarks about his new director's abilities throughout the shoot.

Encouraging the ever-present Furthman to outrageous extremes and oblivious to prevailing censorship norms, Hughes laboriously guided his ripe young stars through ridiculously stilted and contorted sexual situations, with Buetel striding around in tight leather outfits, Russell constantly posing for maximum mammary impact, and both of them enacting some kind of weird S&M ritual that would have been campy if it wasn't so dull. The extent to which Hughes tried to emphasize Russell's chest bordered on the demented, as he instructed his new cameraman, Gregg Toland, to devise shots that would allow viewers to peer all the way down her blouse. In one scene, he directed Russell to carry a tray so as to make it appear that her big breasts were, in fact, on it. When he looked at the scene later, he kicked himself for covering this action in a medium shot and spent ten thousand dollars to pay a specialist in optical printing to create a zoom in on the tray and its contents. It was a difficult effect to achieve but, as one Hughes aide vividly recalled, "When Hughes saw it, I never saw a kid so tickled in my life." The shot went into the picture. Hughes was so fixated that he privately ran shots of Russell's most overtly sexual posturings night after night in his screening room, and rumors have persisted over the years of special nude footage made for Hughes's delectation alone.

Unsurprisingly, the film was rejected outright by censor Joseph Breen, who was shaken to the core by its relentless obsession with Jane Russell's physique. He was extremely concerned that the film, if shown publicly, might spark a trend to "undrape women's breasts." The appeals, legal haggling, and recutting went on for nearly two years until, in a barrage of publicity orchestrated by the endlessly resourceful Russell Birdwell, *The Outlaw* finally premiered at the Geary Theater in San Francisco on February 5, 1943, accompanied by a special "stage epilogue" in which Russell and Buetel performed an embarrassing scene supposedly written for the film but never shot. By this time, Jane Russell had become an international sensation on the basis of her eye-popping cheesecake photographs. The film was briefly seized by the San Francisco police, then cleared, but after the landslide of attention and promise of great business, Hughes, preoccupied with his Spruce Goose airplane project, suddenly withdrew the film. More legal battles ensued until the picture was once again offered to the public, in altered form, in 1946, then again in 1950. The film generated millions of dollars in grosses over the years but, as Hughes confidant Noah Dietrich pointed out, the problem with *The Outlaw* was that it was a $450,000 picture that Hughes spent $3 million to produce. Despite all the publicity, free and otherwise, "he lost money on it," said Dietrich.

The film's overriding fetishism makes it clear that Hughes truly did have a very different picture in mind than anything Hawks would have made, and the result confirmed Hawks's belief that his intermittent friend had no talent as a director: "My idea of a good director is a man who chooses his own story and works on it, and casts his own picture and does everything about it, and he didn't do that, you know."

22

Sergeant York

It took Hawks no more than a week to land a new film, whereas it had taken its producer nearly twenty-two years to set it up. *Sergeant York* had been a passion of Jesse Lasky's ever since he watched from his Fifth Avenue office window on May 22, 1919, as the war hero Alvin York was showered with confetti by the population of New York City; Howard Hawks simply stepped into the breach when his departure from *The Outlaw* freed him to fill it. Not only was Hawks ready for this inspirational story of a Tennessee mountain man who overcame his religious objections to serve in the army and become famous by capturing 132 German soldiers; with war spreading in Europe, the public was also ready for it. As Helen Buchalter of the *Washington Daily News* noted the day after the film's dignitary-studded premiere in the nation's capital on August 1, 1941, *Sergeant York* hit the screen "at the precise moment when the American frame of mind is ripe to receive it." By becoming available at the critical moment, Hawks walked into the biggest hit of his career.

Lasky, of course, had given Hawks his first job in the industry, in the Famous Players–Lasky property department, during the twenty-year-old's summer vacation from Cornell, and had employed him again at Paramount as a story executive before Hawks became a director. Upon witnessing the extraordinary outpouring of emotion for York in 1919, Lasky had spent the next two days trying to convince York to star in a motion picture version of his life story.

Lasky was not the only showman who tried to make hay from York's sudden fame. Florenz Ziegfeld had wanted him to team up with Will Rogers in a folksy, inspirational sketch for his stage extravaganza, and Lee Shubert had offered to feature him in a revue. Despite his genuine need for money, York had categorically refused these and all other commercial proposals, stating, "Me, I don't allow Uncle Sam's uniform for sale."

Ten years later, after the arrival of sound films, Lasky once again approached York and was again turned down. Squeezed out of his job at Paramount in 1932, the once great executive soon became a pathetically marginal figure in the industry, losing his house and falling heavily into debt. In the winter of 1939–40, with the outbreak of war in Europe, it occured to Lasky that he might be able to prey upon York's patriotic sentiments as a way of finally bringing him around. The producer received no replies to his numerous letters and wires, so in February 1940, Lasky flew to Nashville and made the three-hour drive to Pall Mall, Tennessee, to court the man in person. The recalcitrant York, who had recently opened a modest Bible school, reacted coolly, but at least he didn't turn his guest down cold — partly because, for the first time, Lasky was not proposing that York play himself on-screen.

When Lasky returned two weeks later with a prepared contract, York wouldn't sign. Undaunted, Lasky continued to cajole the principled man, and when he came back a third time with a simpler contract, York, citing the need to combat Hitler as the reason, finally signed it, on March 21, 1940, in the old state house in Nashville in the presence of Governor Prentiss Cooper. York would receive fifty thousand dollars and a sliding percentage of the gross starting at 4 percent after the picture grossed three million dollars and growing to 8 percent after nine million dollars, with proceeds going to the York Bible School. Lasky announced that the picture, which would probably be filmed in Technicolor for RKO release, would downplay the war theme and instead be a "document for fundamental Americanism."

Still in financial straits, Lasky had to borrow in order to pay York the first half of his advance, as well as to wrap up control of three essential York-related properties: *Sergeant York And His People,* by Sam K. Cowan, *Sergeant York: Last of The Long Hunters,* by Tom Skeykill, and *Sergeant York: His Own Life Story and War Diary,* edited by Skeykill.

RKO quickly cooled on what executives envisioned would be an expensive production, so Lasky started his hunt for studio backing at the top. MGM's Louis B. Mayer was enthusiastic but, as he had done with David O. Selznick on *Gone with the Wind,* demanded a heavy price for his participation. Not wishing to lose control and a sizable share of any profits, Lasky weighed his other options, immediately ruling out Paramount, which had dumped him, as well as Universal, 20th Century–Fox, and Columbia, where various personality conflicts existed between him and top executives. With few possibilities left, he went to Warner Bros., where the ultrapatriotic Harry Warner prevailed upon his brother Jack to make the deal. The studio paid

Lasky $40,000 for the written material, gave York his second $25,000, and agreed to an $88,500 producer's salary as well as to paying Lasky 20 percent of the rentals after $1.6 million domestic and $150,000 foreign. After $2.5 million in rentals was reached, Lasky's share would increase to 25 percent.

Delighted that his perseverance had paid off so handsomely, Lasky returned once more to Tennessee, this time in the company of the writers Harry Chandlee and Julien Josephson. A veteran screenwriter, Chandlee was chosen partly because he had spent part of his youth near the Tennessee-Virginia border and had written a 1915 picture, A *Magdalene of the Hills*, that evinced knowledge of mountain folk. For ten days, the Hollywood men interviewed locals, scoured back issues of newspapers, and talked with former Governor Roberts of Tennessee, who had performed the Yorks' wedding ceremony. After exercising "considerable persuasion," Lasky convinced York to give them a thorough look at the love letters York had written to his sweetheart, Gracie, while overseas. York himself entertained them by staging a down-home turkey shoot before their departure in late April.

Prodded by Warners' and Lasky's desire to begin production before year's end, Chandlee and Abem Finkel, who replaced Josephson, handed in a 105-page, scene-by-scene treatment in mid-July. Studio enthusiasm for *York* was high; Robert Buckner, an intelligent writer and valued story editor, advised production chief Hal Wallis that the film could emerge as a *Mr. Deeds Goes to War*. Implicit in this view of the project was the expectation that Gary Cooper would play the lead. Cooper was the only actor Lasky could envision in the role, but landing him posed a major problem. Cooper was under contract to Sam Goldwyn, Lasky's former brother-in-law, and the two men had been on bad terms for twenty-five years, since Lasky had pushed Goldwyn, then Samuel Goldfish, his treasurer and film salesman, out of his company. Furthermore, Goldwyn had just loaned Cooper to Warner Bros. for *Meet John Doe*, and Jack Warner was certain he wouldn't be able to get him a second time, as he was then ranked as the number-five box-office name in America, after Gable, Garbo, Deanna Durbin, and Errol Flynn. Goldwyn, however, coveted Warners' biggest star, Bette Davis, for his upcoming adaptation of *The Little Foxes*. Warner made it a policy never to loan Davis out, but he made his one and only exception in this case, and the two players were exchanged in a direct swap.

Unexpectedly, Cooper himself was against it. Approaching his fortieth birthday, he was wary of playing a famous and younger man (York was thirty-one at the time of his exploits) and was frankly scared of the demands the role would make on him. "In screen biographies," the actor opined, "dealin' with remote historical characters, some romantic leeway is okay. But York's alive and I don't think I can do justice to him. He's too big for me . . . he covers too much territory." Throwing a monkey wrench into their plans, he gave Warner Bros. and Lasky a flat "no" when first approached. Lasky kept working on him, however, and in August brought York to Hollywood for a brief visit to meet the actor, during which they spoke of virtually nothing but hunting. To generate publicity, Lasky variously announced that Cooper was the only movie star York liked or even knew about and that one of the conditions of his deal was that Cooper play him (the two looked not at all alike, and York sported a trim little moustache). Cooper began to weaken, later saying, "What got me to change my mind was York, who wanted me to do the picture. Even then I wasn't convinced. When we met I realized we had a few things in common. We were both raised in the mountains—Tennessee for him, Montana for me—and we learned to ride and shoot as a natural part of growin' up."

Warner Bros. announced Cooper for the lead in September. But still without a director or final script, the studio privately hedged its bets, considering both James Stewart and Henry Fonda, although neither was under contract to the studio; as late as November 15, Ronald Reagan did a screen test for the role.

A great deal of similar skirmishing went on concerning the appropriate director. In August, Lasky approached Goldwyn's top director, William Wyler, but he was in New York preparing for *The Little Foxes* and, while claiming interest, begged off until he could see a finished screenplay. Wallis's first choice was Victor Fleming, but he was already preparing *Dr. Jekyll and Mr. Hyde* at MGM. Henry Hathaway was tied up at Paramount, Henry Koster had obligations at Universal, and after giving consideration to Norman Taurog and Henry King, Jack Warner personally wooed King Vidor in November, to no avail.

The hoped-for December 2 start date had come and gone when Lasky learned that Hawks was out of a job and available. Wallis, who had happily avoided working with Hawks in the five years since *Ceiling Zero*, reluctantly agreed to allow Lasky to offer the script to the director, principally because he knew that Hawks's participation would virtually guarantee the willing cooperation of Gary Cooper, who was still hemming and hawing despite his commitment to the project. The initial problem, however, was that Hawks found the Chandlee-Finkel script "bad." In his self-serving account of his initial meeting with Lasky, Hawks claimed to have told the producer,

"Look, close your door, and tell the secretary no calls, and tell me why the hell you bought this story." Lasky proceeded to relate the drama he wished to film, something Hawks found at total variance with the screenplay he had read. "Jesse," Hawks said, "I'll make the picture if it's O.K. with you that I just do the story you told me." Startled, Lasky immediately agreed.

The way Hawks always told it, he also promised to deliver Gary Cooper, even though, by this point, the star would have had serious problems backing out of his agreement. The story is worth relating, however, in that it illustrates both Hawks's egocentrism and his obsession with getting the upper hand over studio executives in general, and Hal Wallis in particular. Hawks said, "I called Cooper, and I said, 'I just talked to Lasky. Didn't he give you your first job?' Coop said yes. 'Well,' I said, 'he's broke, he's got the shakes, he needs a shave, and he's got a story that I don't think would hurt you to do, or me.' He said, 'I'll come over and talk to you.' And he came over, and he said, 'Where's that new gun of yours?' He didn't want to talk about anything. Finally I said, 'Look, Coop, we have to talk about this.' He said, 'What the hell is there to talk about? You know we're gonna do it.' So I said, 'Well, come with me, and if I say "Isn't that right, Mr. Cooper," you say, "Yup." So we went over and saw Hal Wallis, and I said, 'We'll do the picture for you if you stay out of our way and don't interfere at all. Isn't that right, Mr. Cooper?' 'Yup.' 'We're gonna change the plot, the story around. Isn't that right, Mr. Cooper?' 'Yup.' 'I'm gonna use Johnny Huston as a writer.' Well, they had to say yes, and we started to work on it."

Hawks's deal, dated December 16, paid him $85,000 for twelve weeks' work; with overages, he ended up receiving nearly $110,000 for directing *Sergeant York*. The picture was also to be billed as "A Howard Hawks Production," even though Lasky and Wallis would be the producers of record, and Hawks demanded extra time to prepare a new script. To this end, he recruited thirty-four-year-old John Huston, who was then a fast-rising fair-haired boy among Warner Bros. screenwriters. Hawks had had a passing acquaintance with him since directing his father, Walter, on *The Criminal Code* and was pleased when Wallis teamed him with Howard Koch, the writer of the legendary Orson Welles radio broadcast *The War Of The Worlds* who had made a strong impression with his scripts for *The Sea Hawk* and *The Letter* in his first year in Hollywood. Working practically round-the-clock, including weekends, through Christmas and the New Year, the two writers delivered eighty-three pages of the rewrite by the end of the first week of January 1941, less than a month before the new start date of February 3.

Embittered over having been taken off the picture, writer Abem Finkel got hold of the new draft and fired off a nine-page memo to Wallis in which he attacked what was being done to his and Chandlee's work: "I have, of course, long since despaired of protecting the script from the blundering stupidities of Messrs. Cooper, Hawks, Huston and Koch." Finkel complained that the simple Tennessee mountain folk were being changed into "background color . . . for laughs," that York was being shown drinking when he had actually quit in 1914, that it was now made to appear as if Gracie "came on" to York, and that Pastor Pile was being turned into a "hell and brimstone shoutin' preacher" when, in fact, he had written to President Wilson defending York's conscientious-objector status. "It is my considered opinion," he wrote, "that you must be on your guard against any 'bright idea' on the part of Messrs. Hawks, Huston or Koch if you would avoid a helluva mess."

Hawks never actually met York, but he sent him dozens of questions and received the answers on Dictaphone recordings. Overall he remained concerned about making such an extraordinary story—the only ostensibly biographical one he would ever attempt—believable to audiences. Alvin Cullom York was one of eleven children in a family of farmers in the Cumberland Mountains of Tennessee. A blacksmith, hell-raiser, and acknowledged great shot, York was hired as a young man by Rosier Pile, the pastor of the Church of Christ and Christian Union and, after he "got religion," became an active church leader. At age twenty-eight, he fell in love with a fifteen-year-old neighbor, Gracie Williams, but her parents vigorously disapproved of the match. Two years later, York, along with every other available young man, was drafted into the army. Though he objected on the basis of his religious convictions, he finally had little choice but to report to Camp Gordon in Georgia. During basic training, Captain C. E. B. Danforth, impressed with York's sincerity, allowed him to go home for two weeks to decide whether or not he could fight, and York actually did spend a day and a night on a mountain wrestling with his dilemma. Returning to Georgia, York was assigned to Company G of the Second Battalion, 328th Infantry, a part of the 82nd Division, which was dubbed the "All-American Division" due to its thorough mixture of men from all parts of the country. The company became part of the first American army offensive, the St. Michel drive. With York now a corporal, it moved to the Argonne Forest, where it was under fire for a record twenty-six days.

The incident that made York famous took place near Chatel-Chehery on October 8, 1918. York's battalion, on its way toward a railroad behind

German lines, suddenly found itself in the midst of machine-gun cross fire in a shallow valley. Sergeant Bernard Early and sixteen men managed to capture one group of German gunners, but an intense barrage from guns on an adjacent ridge killed six soldiers and seriously wounded three more, including Early. The others scrambled for cover, but York, finding himself exposed, used his sharpshooting talents to kill some twenty-five German gunners. A German major, evidently fearing that his entire force would be destroyed, whistled his surrender, whereupon York and seven other soldiers guided their prisoners through two German lines, collecting additional prisoners as they went. When it was all over, 132 German prisoners, including several officers, had been captured, and the action succeeded in the objective of taking the railroad.

After being decorated by France and Italy, York received the U.S. Congressional Medal of Honor and was received as a conquering hero. When he returned to Tennessee, however, he found that his fame made no difference to Gracie's parents, but he married the girl anyway. The only fees he accepted came from appearances on the lecture circuit, and he poured all the money into aiding an impoverished local school.

A nation's need for heroes and the government's propaganda machine may have been responsible for exaggerating York's role somewhat and creating the impression that he had done it all singlehandedly; the man's awareness of this, as well as his innate modesty, was undoubtedly responsible for his shunning the spotlight at the time. Nevertheless, there were those who persisted in questioning, and even denying, York's heroism. In his memo to Wallis, Abem Finkel cautioned Warner Bros. against using Corporal William S. Cutting as a possible technical director on the film. "Cutting is the guy who claims York hogged all the credit unjustifiably. . . . He also insists that it was he, not York, that brought the prisoners back and that York pulled a fast one on him by bringing in these prisoners while Cutting was asleep in a shell hole." York, Finkel pointed out, always admitted that he hadn't done it alone.

As it happened, Cutting had already written to Lasky claiming that he and five other men had played a major part in the exploit and that York's role had always been vastly overemphasized. Warners paid Cutting off with $250, but this started a ball rolling that threatened not to stop. The studio discovered that to tell the tale properly, some thirty-five to forty individuals would have to be paid to sign releases agreeing to their depiction in the film. The size of these payments proved to be highly inconsistent. Some men were satisfied with as little as five dollars, but Captain C. E. B. Danforth, for one, demanded and received fifteen hundred dollars. The inequity of the sums eventually made its way into the press, as did further attacks on York's character. For example, an unsigned letter printed in the *Boston Globe* at the time of the picture's release, written by a man who claimed to have been in York's unit, maintained that York was "yellow. . . . We recall one morning as we were to go 'over the top,' York went stark mad with fear. He jumped up on top of the parapet and started to holler, 'I want to go home. For God's sake why isn't this war over.' Sgt. Early said, 'If you don't shut up, I'll blow your brains out.'"

Whatever the truth, Hawks was mainly interested in making it all palatable dramatically. He began by coming up with the idea of the Tennessee turkey shoot and reapplying the motif in the battlefield when York picks off the German gunners. Searching for turkeys, York would gobble, a bird would stick its head up, and York would shoot it. "So in the war," Hawks said, "he was looking down a line of German trenches—the Germans were all hidden—and we had him gobble, and they'd stick their heads out, and he'd shoot one of them. Well, the audience was amused by that and didn't take it too seriously. So he got eighty prisoners that way and marched along and when he came to a bunch of Americans he wanted to get rid of them, but they didn't want to take them, so he had to keep on going. That way we really had fun with it and the illogical quality was overlooked." Hawks also claimed that he and Cooper came up with the idea of York's licking his finger and wetting the rifle sight before taking aim, which became another well-remembered bit of business from the film.

Huston operated under the conviction that the film's version of York's heroics was very close to the truth. He was also taken with the notion of York as a reformed drunk who rationalized killing by convincing himself that his actions saved lives on balance. "I spoke with York on numerous occasions and he told me—and this is the fascinating part—that he was convinced that if he did it, he would save hundreds of human lives. He said, 'If I destroy this machine gun, I'll save thousands of people.' He thoroughly believed it when we spoke about it.

"York was a very amusing fellow, and I tried to put this across in the film," Huston testified. "I tried to show his comic side. And dramatically, he was a terrific character. I don't believe that the film delivers a terribly profound and relevant message. . . . We weren't trying to make *All Quiet on the Western Front*. That was a film which set out to show the First World War in all its horror, all the better to shock the viewer so that he won't repeat it. . . . We chose to tell the story of a man, a particular case. It's completely infantile and absurd to want to try to find an overall moral in it. I believe that Hawks, who is a great director, is a reactionary man, at least in his life. But you don't feel this in the films he makes, nor when you work with him."

Certainly, levity ended up being more important to the finished film than any commentary about the futility of war, a distinct contrast to Hawks's previous World War I films, *The Dawn Patrol, Today We Live,* and *The Road to Glory.* With the need to take up arms again becoming increasingly apparent, the mood had changed since Hawks made those pictures, and the patriotic impulse that had originally engaged Lasky and the brothers Warner easily prevailed over Hawks's own pessimism and the liberal-left politics of both Huston and Koch.

With one exception, the casting fell nicely into place. Walter Brennan, also on loan from Goldwyn, was a natural choice for Pastor Pile, although shortly after shooting began, Wallis demanded that the actor's makeup be changed because his huge, bushy black eyebrows made him look "very much like Groucho Marx." Brennan had been with the 101st Field Artillery in World War I and had seen action near the site of York's exploit.

Margaret Wycherly, whom Hawks found "a superb actress," played the important part of York's mother but ultimately found herself with hardly any lines to say. "As we were rehearsing," Hawks remembered, "I told her to cut out a line. 'Oh, that's one of my best,' she said. Well, we played the scene and I told her to cut out a couple *more* lines and pretty soon she said, 'I'm not going to have *any*thing to say.' I said, 'That's a good idea—let's just play it without your saying anything.' And it made a much better scene. As he went away, his sister says, 'Why is he going, Mom?' and the mother says, 'I don't rightly know.' They *didn't* know, and *he* didn't know. They were going off to war, and I thought it was best not to take sides in the argument." The fifteen-year-old actor Dick Moore, who played York's younger brother George, remembered things rather differently. "Margaret Wycherly was a pain in the ass," he said. "She had a superior New York theater attitude. She was kind of a joke on the set. She was very grand."

The only role that posed any casting problems was that of York's sweetheart, Gracie Williams. When Hawks and Howard Hughes parted ways on *The Outlaw,* Hawks had relinquished any financial participation in the picture, with the proviso that he could borrow Jane Russell anytime he wanted. Having liked Russell a great deal but not gotten to work with her, Hawks tested her for Gracie the first week of January, and both he and Lasky were happy with the result. Wallis, who was leaving for Washington, D.C., to attend FDR's third inauguration, wasn't convinced. "I agree with you that Jane Russell is very attractive, but I hardly think she is the type for *Sergeant York*. She doesn't look like the simple, backwoods country girl to me." Familiar with Hawks's taste for provocative, knowingly sexy young women, Wallis was troubled by the director's inclinations in casting this part and warned him that "any attempt to try to make her a sultry, sexy, wild creature that might be played by Paulette Goddard will, I am sure, meet with violent objections from the Yorks." Wallis added that Jack Warner had voiced similar concerns. Wallis then argued in favor of another young actress Hawks tested, Suzanne Carnahan, but finally Hawks tried out an attractive, coquettish sixteen-year-old, Joan Leslie, and cast her just before shooting began. June Lockhart, a year younger than Leslie (and twenty-five years younger than Cooper), won the role of York's sister.

With an initial budget of $1 million and a shooting schedule of forty-eight days, *Sergeant York* began production on February 3. That morning, Cooper received telegrams from York, General John J. Pershing, and Secretary of State Cordell Hull, who had been the congressman from York's district in Tennessee and was being portrayed in the picture by Charles Trowbridge; Lasky informed Wallis that these wires "pepped Gary up enormously." At the end of the day, unit manager Eric Stacey, the studio's watchdog on the production, related to management that the star had been a half hour late in showing up in the morning, "which is nothing unusual for Cooper, I can assure you." He also reminded Wallis of Hawks's leisurely work habits, which had always annoyed the production chief. "Mr. Hawks has been in the habit of providing tea and cake for his staff every day. This was done today, and much appreciated, and I can honestly say that no time was lost by so doing."

Hawks would later claim, "We had no trouble at all—we just *sailed* through the picture." From his point of view this was undoubtedly true, but the studio, at the time, saw things differently. Hawks spent the first five days filming on the Blind Tiger Café set and at the end of the first six-day work week was already four days behind schedule. As usual, Hawks was taking his time, letting the actors get a feel for their roles and ease into the picture.

Dick Moore, who played York's younger brother, had appeared in more than one hundred pictures since he was eleven years old, but he still felt insecure as an actor. In the café scene, in which he comes to take a drunken Alvin home to their mother, Moore felt stiff and uptight standing there patiently with his rifle. "Hawks sense of how to get the best out of me, and to make me comfortable, was uncanny," Moore said. "At one point in the scene, I smiled, accidentally. He said, 'Very good, we'll try another one.' But he took me aside and said, 'Everything you're doing is good, but at no time in this entire picture does George have to smile. Don't think you have to. Only when you feel like it.' So I totally relaxed. How he sensed that I'll never know." With *Sergeant York*, Moore's whole attitude about acting changed. "The thing I admired about Hawks was the sense of freedom he instilled in me. . . . He was a very subtle director, he would just give suggestions. He was courtly, gracious, and treated his actors with respect, even diffidence." Gary Cooper took the teenager under his wing, teaching him how to throw a knife and talking Moore's mother into buying him his first rifle. "I became an outdoors person because of my experiences on that picture," Moore said.

The following Monday, Lasky went to see Warner and Wallis to request a ten-week shooting schedule. While filming was getting under way, the art director, John Hughes, was supervising construction of the 123 sets required for the picture, including an enormous farmland and mountain set on a revolving merry-go-round base (to allow for different perspectives), with a two-hundred-foot stream and 121 trees. Because of the high ratio of settings to the number of sound stages available, throughout the shoot the art department was forced to wait for the company to finish with one set before demolishing it and quickly building the next; both the rewriting and the scene construction on *Sergeant York* barely kept up with the pace of shooting during the initial weeks. This merely contributed to an enormous squeeze at the studio as a whole; by March, production at Warner Bros. reached an all-time high, with 5,030 people on the payroll working on eight pictures on twenty-two stages.

During the second week of shooting, Hawks received a memo from Wallis gently insisting that he speed up his work pace, the sort of missive that had become irritatingly familiar to him during *Ceiling Zero*. With the picture a week behind schedule after only two weeks of filming, a meeting was held to weigh solutions. The main problem was that the script was composed of many short scenes requiring a great deal of set-up time, but for economy's sake it was decided to eliminate two major sequences from the end of the picture—a big wedding scene and the spectacle of York's reception in New York City.

Hawks's rapport with his cast and crew was excellent, and the director was very happy with the way things were proceeding, except for the front-office pressure. He objected to the fact that the picture was still officially listed as being six days behind schedule when, in fact, the studio had agreed to Lasky's request for an extended schedule. Furthermore, certain factors were out of his control. Joan Leslie, for instance, was forbidden to work past 6 P.M. because of her age. On more than one occasion, work at the Warners' ranch had been scheduled, but heavy rains had forced last-minute rescheduling onto interior sets that were not entirely ready. Uncooperative dogs and mules held up filming of certain scenes: while Hawks was getting what he needed for most shoots with an average of between one and three takes, what should have been a simple dialogue exchange between Cooper and Erville Alderson became a twelve-take farce when a mule, which was supposed to stand still, kept moving around. Finally, the scene had to be restaged so that the animal's newly bound front feet couldn't be seen by the camera.

At the same time, it didn't escape the attention of Stacey, the unit manager and Wallis that Hawks was up to his old trick of writing new dialogue on the spur of the moment. As Stacey told his boss in explanation of a very late start one day, "I noticed both the actors had yellow pages and the dialogue had been rewritten."

As usual, Warner and Wallis were not welcome on the set, but Hawks was not about to banish his old mentor Jesse Lasky from the stage. All the same, the director wasn't afraid to let his producer know when his presence was unhelpful. When Hawks was trying to figure out how to stage a scene of York plowing the field, Lasky was standing right behind him with a guest. Dick Moore recalled that Lasky whispered something to his companion, whereupon Hawks announced to the room, "They called for quiet on the stage." Lasky promptly turned and left the set with his guest.

The fourth week of shooting started out to be notably difficult. Hawks came down with a very bad cold and requested that the scheduled exterior location work be postponed so he could stay indoors. This put his less-than-ideal relationship with the art director, Hughes, on the spot; feeling that the indoor-for-outdoor sets on which Cooper was to be seen plowing looked phony, Hawks demanded that they be changed and announced that he wanted to play the scene at night, with the "character silhouetted in a night sky and with no trees." He also had words with Wallis's spy Stacey, who instantly reported to his boss that "Mr. Hawks made a very sarcastic crack — something about shooting a schedule and not making any picture."

Hawks suffered through the week. He had Lasky, Huston, and Koch come on the set one day to rewrite the scene in which the mountain men

register for the draft. The following day, he patiently waited as bit player
Frank Orth kept blowing his few lines, requiring sixteen takes of one shot
and thirteen of another. The last day of the week, however, proved the most
productive of the entire shoot to date; having averaged fewer than two pages
of script per day up to that point, Hawks sped right through four and a half
pages of dialogue in Pastor Pile's store, ending the week with a burst of
enthusiasm.

The following week, Hawks was feeling better, but the cinematographer, Sol Polito, fell ill and was replaced, mainly for the big meeting-hall
sequence in which York "gets religion," by Arthur Edeson, who had shot
Ceiling Zero for Hawks and would soon handle the camera on the outdoor
war scenes. That week, after constant pressure from Lasky, Warners finally
upped the production from a forty-eight to a seventy-two-day shoot, or more
than double the average for an A picture at the studio. "Physical construction" problems were officially blamed for the previous delays, but this didn't
stop Wallis from continuing to complain to Hawks, not only about what he
considered the director's slack working methods but also about the pacing
of the scenes, which he felt was on the dull, slow side.

At the same time, Wallis and Warner secretly began planning to as-
sign a second-unit director to simultaneously shoot all the war footage, feeling that it would take Hawks forever to get around to it and another eternity
to finish it. Hawks knew, of course, that some second-unit material would
be used, but he was upset when the studio suddenly announced that stunt,
action, and B-movie director B. Reeves Eason, nicknamed "Breezy" for his
quick—some would say slipshod—shooting style, had been personally chosen by Lasky to direct the second unit. Hawks told his old boss, "I think we
are making a great mistake to put a man on the second-unit work who is
not a dramatic director," but he had little choice but to acquiesce.

At about the same time, in early March, an importrant budget meeting among the principals was called by the studio. Tired of being blamed
for all the overages, Hawks told Warner and Wallis that he had sometimes
been made to wait on the set for Lasky to deliver new pages of the script to
him; he also insisted that the screenplay contained more material than could
ever be used in the finished film. Lasky maintained that everything included
was necessary. On March 10–11, Hawks astonished the studio by knocking
out an uncustomary forty-four setups in making the turkey-shoot sequence;
at the end of the second day, he had a tête-à-tête with Wallis in the director's
station wagon and received permission to keep Huston and Koch on to
rewrite the final portion of the script, which still bothered him.

Work proceeded efficiently through the rest of March, and when the scenarists finally finished their rewrites, Lasky felt compelled to send a note to Wallis: "I do not want to let the occasion pass without expressing to you my feelings about these two splendid boys. In spite of pressure, they maintained an enthusiasm for the work that I am sure will be reflected on the screen." Wallis kept any comments about Hawks to himself from this point on, and as of April, only the weather could be blamed for the mounting delays. Breezy Eason no sooner arrived on location in the Santa Susanna Mountains, where two miles of trenches had been dug, than he was greeted with more than a week of torrential rain. Several of Hawks's scenes, including the fox hunt, had already been switched from exteriors to interiors because of both his illness and inclement weather, resulting in a more studio-enclosed picture than he originally intended, but Eason had no alternative but to wait it out. Showing Breezy up, Hawks even completed the long sequence in the G Company barracks in two, rather than the allotted three, days, although he was then tripped up when Cooper couldn't shoot for several days because of health problems.

With a June release planned, Wallis personally took charge of the fine cutting of the first seven to eight thousand feet of the picture, up through the training-camp sequences. Hawks finally moved out of the studio onto San Fernando Valley locations at the Warner Ranch and Sherwood Forest, where the first thing he did was to have a shooting range set up so he and Cooper could indulge in target practice every day at lunch. Hawks put himself back on schedule with the grand accomplishment of finishing the firing-range scene, a seven-page sequence featuring Cooper and seventy-eight extras, in one day, which prompted the skeptical Stacey to tell Wallis, "Hawks is very consistent in making good speed on long sequences . . . after he has gotten the whole thing worked out." In fact, Wallis's concern was shifting to Eason; he complained, "I can't seem to make much out of Eason's dailies," and, deciding that Eason's scenes lacked scope, he attempted to solve the problem by sending him 250 more extras.

Although stars of his magnitude normally were not required to take orders from second-unit directors, Cooper worked for about three days with Eason, mainly in long shots during battle while surrounded by dozens of extras at a time when Hawks was doing scenes set in the German headquarters. On April 26 and 28 the two units merged, with Hawks taking over and restaging aspects of the battle. With this done but the picture not yet entirely finished, Hawks announced that he was leaving on May 1 to attend the Kentucky Derby. Given no notice at all, Warner called in the contract director Vincent Sherman to cover the final sequences. On April 30, Hawks rehearsed them in Sherman's presence, with particular attention to the scene in which York is decorated, and Sherman executed them according to Hawks's plan the following day. Sherman recalled that Hawks instructed him, "'Feature the people who are doing the decorating. We've seen enough of Coop.' Seeing the picture later, he was right. He had an uncanny sense of story, of what was important in a scene." Eason shot two more days of the trenches and the German machine-gun nests, and filming of *Sergeant York* finally wrapped on Saturday, May 3, after seventy days of actual shooting, two days under the final allotted schedule. Weather had limited Eason to twenty days of filming on a thirty-three-day schedule. The studio also announced that Cooper had appeared before the cameras for fifty-four straight days, excepting Sundays and sick days, a record for any star. The final budget, including a 39 percent studio overhead, came to $1.6 million.

With Hawks out of town and the premiere less than two months away, Wallis continued to supervise the cutting and scoring of the picture with the film's editor, William Holmes, and composer, Max Steiner, just as the publicity department geared up for a media onslaught of mammoth proportions. The first public preview, in a 150-minute cut without any war montages, was held on June 16, and York was duly wired that it had been a great success. After one more preview, the final print, running 134 minutes, was sped to New York in time for the July 1 world premiere. The day before, York was met at Penn Station by Cooper and numerous dignitaries, and a marching band accompanied them in a parade up Fifth Avenue to 82nd Division headquarters, where a motorcade awaited to transport them to a reception at City Hall with Mayor La Guardia. Making no secret of its enthusiasm for the picture's combat-ready attitude, the government sent a special train from the nation's capital carrying Mrs. Roosevelt, General Pershing, Wendell Wilkie, and several senators and congressmen. York and Cooper attended the invitational debut along with members of the 82nd "All-American" Division and Generals Pershing, Hugh Drum, and Lewis B. Hershey. York made a dozen patriotic speeches, which were picked up by the national wire services, and Broadway was blacked out for thirty seconds at midnight on June 30–July 1 to dramatize the illumination of the *Sergeant York* sign at the Astor Theater, where the film opened with a top ticket price of $2.20 on a two show per-day road-show basis, with more shows added due to the demand. Dr. Norman Vincent Peale enthusiastically endorsed the picture, and Generalissimo Chiang Kai-shek requested and received a print to show to his troops in China. To top off the dream come true of any publicity department, FDR himself saw the film, said he was "thrilled" by it, and invited York to the White House.

The critical reaction to *Sergeant York* was so unanimous that it is difficult to find a single negative or even lukewarm review from the time of its release. Sensitive to the film's manipulative, propagandistic nature or not, all the critics commented upon its remarkable timeliness and generally greeted it as a new American classic, the most important film to have come out since *Gone with the Wind* nearly two years before. Everyone rhapsodized about Cooper, and Lasky's name was often mentioned in the context of a magnificent comeback and career capper.

Despite his prominent billing, however, only seldom was Hawks given much credit for the picture's success, other than to say that he did a fine or highly professional job. By contrast, when Frank Capra had taken *Mr. Smith Goes to Washington* to the capital for its premiere in 1939, the director was the center of attention. *Sergeant York*'s director, however, was nowhere to be found at its opening. On the eve of the greatest critical and popular success of his career, Hawks was back home in Beverly Hills, sporting with Slim, housebreaking the two eighty-five-pound English mastiff pups he had just bought, and preparing to start *Ball of Fire* in a month's time.

Warner Bros. played off *Sergeant York* very slowly, milking its extraordinary timeliness for all it was worth. After playing in exclusive runs at inflated prices in major cities past Labor Day, the picture gradually spread into other markets until it entrenched itself as the number-one film in the country throughout the fall, breaking box-office records in many markets. The film was a phenomenon of staggering proportions, and its reputation was enhanced even further by the role it played in helping to quell the braying of some virulently right-wing politicians in Washington. Incensed by what they viewed as Hollywood's role as self-appointed cheerleader for joining the war, isolationists and America Firsters in the Senate launched some loudly publicized hearings before an interstate commerce subcommittee on September 9. The subject was the allegedly insidious content of Hollywood movies, particularly the "warmongering" dramas that dared to suggest that the Nazis represented a threat, that Americans ought to extend a helping hand to Britain and perhaps prepare the join in the battle themselves. As always, attacking the film industry made for headlines, but when *Sergeant York* began building in popularity, editorial writers all over the nation began using the film as a club to demolish the Capitol Hill reactionaries, stating that the filmed biography of a religious pacifist's conversion to a war's righteousness represented "the full and complete answer" to the senators' rants. By late October, the hearings fizzled out.

Thrilled with the gold mine Jesse Lasky had brought them, Warner Bros. executives were nonetheless upset at the hefty percentages they were contractually forced to pay the producer; once the picture passed $1.6 million in rentals (the amount returned to the distributor from the total box-office gross), Lasky got twenty cents of every dollar. The studio tried different strategies to hold on to more money, such as offering to buy back points, delaying payments inordinately, and pleading that since the foreign market had become so limited due to the war, Lasky ought to understand and give up his share of overseas revenue. Lasky's contract had no loopholes, however, and the sixty-one-year-old producer crowned his career by making $2 million on the film, which ultimately returned $6 million in rentals from the domestic release alone, making it the third biggest box-office attraction in film history, after *Gone with the Wind*, which then stood at $18 million, and *Snow White and the Seven Dwarfs*, which had earned $7.15 million to that point (in 1941, a film was generally considered a hit if it returned $1 million to the studio). Cooper, who also had *Meet John Doe* and *The Westerner* out that year, was declared the number-one box-office draw in America, while *Variety* ranked Hawks as the industry's number-three "money director" on the basis of this one film, following Arthur Lubin, who directed three popular Abbott and Costello comedies that year, and the late Victor Schertzinger, who was also responsible for three successful releases before his sudden death. After the United States entered the war, the picture experienced another surge of publicity as countless news stories told of men, including two ministers, withdrawing previously stated objections to combat duty and enlisting after being inspired by the picture.

Not surprisingly, *Sergeant York* was nominated for a dozen Academy Awards. Although *Citizen Kane* was a prime contender in most categories, John Ford's *How Green Was My Valley* won the top Oscars, for best picture and director. The only *York* wins went to the editor, William Holmes, and to Cooper, who had won the New York Film Critics award for best actor and accepted his first Oscar from James Stewart, who was already in the Army Air Corps, having been the first major film star to enter the military. Cooper closed out his brief Oscar speech by saying, "It was Sergeant Alvin York who won this award. Because to the best of my ability, I tried to be Sergeant York." Hawks received his only Oscar nomination for the film. Years later, when they were old in Palm Springs, John Ford, who won four

Academy Awards for direction over the years, would rib Hawks about how he, Ford, had beaten him out of the Oscar undeservingly.

Hawks finally received a honorary career Oscar in 1975, but before that he always claimed it didn't bother him that he hadn't won. "I don't think much of some of the pictures that have won, so I don't think it would mean much to me. . . . It hasn't anything to do with the fact that I didn't ever get one myself. . . . And I listened to too many speeches of acceptance that would have made a good comedy." Lasky was undoubtedly more disappointed than Hawks at not going home with a statuette, but he was full of plans and projects and surrounded by people who suddenly wanted to work with him again. The producer announced that his next project would be a history of the Boy Scouts, and adding that he and Hawks would work together again on another biographical venture, *The Adventures of Mark Twain*. Neither film happened as planned, and although he produced several more pictures through the 1940s, he was in debt again in the years before his death in 1958.

That *Sergeant York* is not now ranked among Hawks's most enduring or admired films is a result of several factors, including its very success at the time of its release, its historical timeliness and consequent datedness, and its folksiness, visual phoniness, and propagandistic nature. None of the copious post-1950s critical analyses of Hawks's career devotes much attention to the film; with its rigidly set story, preordained ideological and political intent, origins as a producer's project, heavy studio feel, and focus on the inner journey of an individual rather than the actions of a group, *Sergeant York* has generally been dismissed by students of Hawks as atypical of his work in general, a more conventional Hollywood product than was his norm. Citing how unusual it was for a Hawks film to deal explicitly with major moral, religious, and patriotic issues, Robin Wood argued that "it is precisely these factors that work consistently against the film's artistic success. One feels Hawks continually hampered by having to 'stick to the facts'; an intuitive artist, he is ill-equipped to handle big issues on any but a superficial level."

Looked at today, the skill that went into the film still appears impressive and Cooper remains remarkable, but the film does suffer in comparison to Hawks's best work in that it seems not only conventional but unsurprising. Much of the humor is genuinely earned, and Hawks's one audacious invention, the turkey gobbling, clinches the picture with comedy at its dramatic high point; on one hand, the device is inspired, while on the other, it undercuts any serious consideration of York's pacificistic inclinations or qualms about killing. More than on any of his other films, Hawks had considerable real-life material and predetermined attitudes he was forced to accomodate on *Sergeant York,* and so had less room in which to maneuver to his own liking. But while the film was not viewed as a personal triumph for Hawks, it greatly enhanced his standing in the industry and took him less than half a year to complete, start to finish.

23

Catching Fire

At just about the same time Hawks met Slim, he began a relationship with another individual, with whom he would form the most important professional association of his life. Influential but not yet a dominant force in motion pictures by 1940, Charles K. Feldman always bore the trappings of success. One of the most intelligent and cultivated agents in Hollywood, he was handsome, persuasive, married to a celebrated beauty, host of some of the town's most elegant parties, and holder of a client list that included some of the most sophisticated and distinguished artists in films.

Female stars loved Feldman. His dalliances with some of them continually threatened to dash his marriage, and even those with whom he never got involved adored him for his constant attention, lavish gifts, and solicitous, soothing style. At the same time, he was equally at home with his many tough-guy clients and the studio moguls; among the latter, he was particularly close to Darryl Zanuck, Jack Warner, and David O. Selznick.

The one tycoon with whom he was decidedly not on friendly terms was Louis B. Mayer, for Feldman had stolen away the girl Mayer coveted for himself. This may have made Feldman persona non grata at MGM, but it actually enhanced Feldman's reputation among many in the Hollywood crowd, who enjoyed imagining Mayer's insulted rage at being humiliated by a mere flesh peddler.

In 1928, Feldman had opened a law office, concentrating on show-business clients, especially agents. However, when he realized how much more money agents were making than he was, he decided to shift into that field himself, and in 1932 he opened a talent agency with Ad Schulberg, the vivacious, popular, left-wing-activist wife of about-to-be-deposed Paramount production head B. P. Schulberg, who had left her for actress Sylvia Sidney. Ironically, Schulberg was just beginning an affair with, of all people, Louis B. Mayer, the first serious extramarital involvement of the studio chief's life. The Schulberg-Feldman Agency, which initially specialized in writers but shortly added several big-name stars to its roster, was inaugurated with a lavish party on July 18, 1932, at their Taft Building offices; the pair were later joined in their partnership, first by Noll Gurney, then by the agent Sam Jaffe.

In 1933, at a party in Beverly Hills, Feldman, then just twenty-nine, met Jean Howard. In retrospect, Howard claimed that it was love at first sight for both of them. Feldman had no trouble sweeping Jean Howard off her feet; however, the entanglements of their lives made their involvement considerably more complicated than that. Feldman was still in a passionate relationship with the stunning Mexican actress Raquel Torres, and his attentions to Jean Howard were something less than consistent and faithful. Howard was under contract as an actress at MGM, where she had worked, ever so briefly, under Hawks's direction in *The Prizefighter and the Lady* the year before. Louis B. Mayer had taken an intense personal interest in her welfare; although she always claimed that there was never anything physical between them, there is no doubt that Hollywood's most powerful boss was infatuated with her, arranging for her to spend evenings on the town with him, hiring a private detective to follow both Feldman and Howard, and, according to Howard, offering her $5 million to marry him. Howard eventually decided enough was enough and told a devastated Mayer that she was returning to Feldman. Soon after, Feldman and Howard were married.

Even if Feldman himself was not welcome in Mayer's office in the aftermath of this wild interlude, Ad Schulberg certainly was, and it was she who handled the agency's MGM contract players, including Norma Shearer. After another year, however, Schulberg left to form her own agency, upon which Feldman formed an alliance with a former law associate of his, Ralph Blum. Mayer was finally forced to do business with Feldman personally in 1936, when his biggest star, Greta Garbo, insisted that Mayer hire Feldman's client Charles Boyer to appear opposite her in *Conquest*.

Charlie Feldman and Jean Howard were an enormously popular Hollywood couple, but they were not without their problems. Charlie's philandering led to several temporary separations, and while he was not a compulsive womanizer, he was in the business of cultivating beautiful young actresses who not only saw him as a way up the Hollywood ladder but were genuinely attracted to him. For a man like him, sporadic dalliances were all but inevitable, which forced Jean Howard to decide whether or not she was capable of looking the other way.

In 1935, when Feldman-Blum moved offices, Feldman got to know William Hawks, whose Hawks-Volck agency maintained offices in the same building in Beverly Hills. Feldman's initial encounters with Bill's brother Howard were casual, but by 1939 a real friendship was developing, with the men often meeting for lunch at the Brown Derby down the block or at Victor Hugo to discuss deals, stars and starlets, and horses, as Feldman and Hawks had a major gambling fixation in common. In addition, neither was a fan of the long-term studio contract, Hawks because he hated being tied down to one studio, Feldman because he believed there was more money to be made in making deals on a picture-by-picture basis. Both men felt a strong impulse to produce films independently, and although it would take awhile, their strongest bond was based on blazing this trail together, to their mutual profit.

Feldman quickly caught on to Hawks's propensity for self-aggrandizement, but he enjoyed it and over the years got a big kick out of listening to Hawks tell others tall tales he knew to be whoppers, just to watch their reactions and to see how far Hawks would go with them. Jean Howard said that Feldman would often come home smiling and shaking his head saying, "He really is the biggest liar that ever happened." Jean asked if Hawks believed what he was saying, and her husband would insist, "He believes every word he's saying." For her part, Jean found Hawks "a very attractive man . . . very polite but a cold kind of fellow. He wouldn't be somebody that I would wave to across the street and say, 'Hi, Howard.'"

But while Hawks and Feldman were becoming increasingly close, their wives had little time for each other. Jean Howard felt that Slim was a social climber and sensed almost at once that Slim wasn't very happy with her man, even more so when Slim realized that Hawks was much less interested in hosting or even attending glittering Hollywood parties than she was. Jean resented the way Slim seemed to copy both her style of entertaining and her taste in home decoration, and before long she found excuses to avoid any invitation to accompany her husband to the Hawks home. One time she resorted to getting high on some marijuana Errol Flynn had given her to get through an evening with the Hawkses. One way of reading this is that Jean saw an uncomfortable amount of herself in Slim. Jean had few equals within the inner circle of Beverly Hills society, and the frostiness between her and Slim happened to be the result of two very like-minded women trying to occupy the same turf.

In 1940, Bill Hawks decided to quit the agency business to become a producer. That May, he announced the formation of United Producers

Corporation, a group composed of Hawks, his longtime client Ronald Colman, and four others, all represented by Feldman: Charles Boyer, Irene Dunne, Lewis Milestone, and Anatole Litvak. The company intended to produce ten pictures for RKO over a period of three years, five of which would star Ronald Colman. The first of these, the inconsequential comedy *My Life with Caroline,* starring Colman under Milestone's direction, was released a year later. With his brother no longer representing him, Howard Hawks was free to join Feldman, and the first deal the agent made for the director was the lucrative one for *Sergeant York.* Better yet was the fee Feldman would extract from Sam Goldwyn for Hawks's next film.

It was immediately prior to this that Hawks made his first and only trip to the Kentucky Derby, near the end of the *Sergeant York* shoot. Slim said that chez Hawks, listening to the running of the Derby on the radio "was treated like an on-the-spot broadcast of the Resurrection." Hawks's eyes would actually well up, she reported, at the playing of "My Old Kentucky Home," such were his sentimental fantasies of being a great horse breeder from bluegrass country.

Hawks's excuse for leaving the shoot of *Sergeant York* a day before finishing it was that he had a horse running in the Derby. Of course, he had no such thing. Scheduled to depart by train, he and Slim instead flew as far as Kansas City, where Hawks insisted that they deplane and drive the rest of the way so that Slim could get a feel for the South, even though Slim could see that the real reason was that Hawks was airsick. They rented a car and, as so often happened, Hawks got lost, taking them on an inadvertent detour all the way to Cleveland before arriving in Louisville. Once they arrived, they found, also with great difficulty, the less-than-imposing home of Hawks's acquaintance "General" Miles, a hee-hawing, rotund, older southern gent who was hosting a number of guests for the weekend. Hawks's behavior there, as witnessed by Slim, seems unique in his entire life: "Howard was a fellow whose most relaxed and carefree moments were fraught with a kind of Brooks Brothers button-down dignity. On meeting him, you had the curious feeling that both of you were under water. But with the General, he emerged. Now he too was full of hearty laughter and rib-punching joviality. Howard was suddenly a stranger to me. It was the most complete metamorphosis I have ever seen in a human being."

The day of revelry continued through a drunken picnic and finally to the main event at Churchill Downs, by which time Slim was so fed up that she remained furious for the rest of the trip. The whole experience was, in fact, so disagreeable that she made a point of never returning to Kentucky again. Hawks, however, became "horsier than ever," to the point that he soon bought several racehorses, which, Slim said, "struck me as an excuse to justify his excessive gambling habit . . . which was so out of control he would bet on his own horse."

While Hawks was away, Feldman was busy lining up his new client's next job and was in touch with Hawks about it nearly every day as Hawks and Slim pushed south to Nashville, Florida, and the Keys and then on to New Orleans, where they selected a vast number of Louisiana antiques for their future home. On June 4, the day after he and Slim arrived home, Hawks had a meeting with Sam Goldwyn about his next picture. The result was a clever, congenial entertainment as sweet and relaxed as most of his comedies were brash and frantic, one that also contained the oddest professional group ever portrayed in a Hawks film.

Even before *Meet John Doe* and *Sergeant York* came out in 1941, Sam Goldwyn was chagrined at how all of Gary Cooper's biggest hits were the ones he made on loan to other studios rather than the five he had thus far made in-house. Determined to develop better material for his most valuable star, Goldwyn arranged to borrow one of the hottest writing teams in town, Charles Brackett and Billy Wilder, from Paramount. Unhappy over the way his work was being treated at Paramount, Wilder was chomping at the bit to launch his directing career but agreed one last time to work strictly as a writer, persuaded by the staggering amount Goldwyn was willing to pay: $7,500 for the story, another $79,800 for the script. In addition, Wilder insisted on being allowed to observe every day of the shooting from beginning to end in preparation for graduating to the director's chair himself, which he did the following year.

After rejecting everything remotely appropriate for Cooper in Goldwyn's development files, Wilder pulled out a fourteen-page story he had once put together with Thomas Monroe. "From A to Z" concerned a British linguistics professors named Professor Thrush who, at the age of ten, had written "a much spoken of thesis on 'The Faults in Shakespeare's English Grammar.'" Thrush found Babe singing in a 42nd Street burlesque house, and the ensuing conflict between the rarefied academic environment and Babe's bruising underworld acquaintances ended in "the triumph of science and knowledge over brute force, of intellect over integrity, of Einstein over Capone."

Through the late winter and early spring of 1941, while Cooper was in the middle of *Sergeant York*, Brackett and Wilder tore into the script, tailoring it for the star by changing the leading character to a shy American and fleshing out the wonderful roles of the seven older professors with whom the younger man would work in preparing a new encyclopedia. They even identified specific actors, including Walter Brennan, in the script.

When it came to selecting a director, Goldwyn had to admit that none of his contract directors had managed to show Cooper off to maximum advantage. Since the whole project was being built around the actor, the producer reluctantly agreed that anyone Coop wanted was all right with him, even the dreaded Howard Hawks, who hadn't set foot in his studio since the nasty split on *Come and Get It* five years before. In his favor, Hawks had subsequently proved himself as an ace comedy director with *Bringing Up Baby* and particularly *His Girl Friday*, so Goldwyn went along despite his private feeling that Hawks had "no character." So if Hawks was responsible for nudging Cooper over the edge into committing to do *Sergeant York*, the actor might be said to have returned the favor on what became *Ball of Fire*. Not that Hawks needed much convincing. He found the screenplay outstanding, later commenting that "Brackett and Wilder were *superb* writers and they could make almost anything good." Of course, Hawks had to find a way to somehow claim the material as his own, insisting that when the writers were stuck, he clarified everything for them by pointing out that their story was really *Snow White and the Seven Dwarfs*, with Babe, now Sugarpuss, as Snow White and her gangster boyfriend as the evil queen. Wilder, however, pooh-poohed Hawks's credit grab.

Charles Feldman waited until the perfect moment—June 17, the day after the first preview of *Sergeant York*—to nail down Hawks's $100,000 directing fee, "at which figure, Goldwyn promptly proceeded to faint"; this was the most Hawks had ever received for a single picture. Warner Bros. was simultaneously trying to arrange for Hawks to direct Orson Welles in its adaptation of the George S. Kaufman–Moss Hart Broadway comedy smash *The Man Who Came to Dinner*, but Hawks was spoken for.

Once he was on *Ball of Fire*, Hawks's first challenge was to cast the female lead, a problem exacerbated, as it had been on *His Girl Friday*, by several surprising rejections, but once again the final choice proved felicitous. Having just won an Oscar for her dramatic performance in *Kitty Foyle*, Ginger Rogers, Goldwyn's first choice, spurned the role of Sugarpuss O'Shea as too frivolous now that she had established herself as a serious actress. Carole Lombard disliked both the character and the story, and Harry Cohn refused Goldwyn's request for Jean Arthur, whom Hawks did not want anyway, although the actress went public with her anger over being denied her chance at the part. In late June, Hawks filmed tests with twenty-three-year-old Betty Field, who had just scored in Lewis Milestone's film *Of Mice and Men,* as well as with longtime second banana Lucille Ball. Cooper finally suggested his *Meet John Doe* costar, Barbara Stanwyck, whom everyone agreed would be ideal.

Production began on Monday, August 6, 1941, with a forty-eight-day shooting schedule. By Hawks's standards—and to Goldwyn's delight—filming zipped along relatively efficiently. Hawks began each day by watching the previous day's dailies and was usually on the set by 9:20 A.M.; after a month, the company was only four and a half days behind schedule, with the slight delays due to rewriting and an eye inflammation that briefly put Cooper out of action. The septet of Oscar Homolka, Henry Travers, S. Z. "Cuddles" Sakall, Tully Marshall, Leonid Kinsky, Richard Haydn, and Aubrey Mather were cast as the graying professors, and Hawks personally decided which of them should play which roles. Kinsky, who had known Hawks since appearing in a small part in *The Road to Glory,* said that the character actors "had a certain amount of freedom, we were able to suggest some things." At the same time, the director persisted in his shameless way of appropriating other people's ideas as his own. "He never gave credit for anything," Kinsky observed. "He rented people, the finest and the best, and then called what they did his own. . . . [Once] I told him, 'We're old-fashioned professors, and we'd sing the old university hymn "Gaudeamus igitur" after a few drinks. If we didn't, there'd be something wrong with us.' On the set, after a few rehearsals, Howard stopped and said, 'I have an idea: these men studied in Vienna. I think they'd sing "Gaudeamus igitur." No old-fashioned professors' group would spend an evening without singing that.'"

Other than what he borrowed from his collaborators, Kinsky found that Hawks had very few suggestions to offer in rehearsals, although "you felt that he was the boss of the whole thing. He had the same talent, but in a different way, that Wyler had. He would just have you do it, then do it again, without explaining why. Gary Cooper was the easiest person in the world to work with. It was like working with a beautiful horse. So honest, so truthful." On *Sergeant York,* Cooper had been concerned about capturing the simple, religious nature of a real-life figure, while on *Ball of Fire,* he complained to Hawks that some of his dialogue was too complicated and difficult to deliver. Nevertheless, their collaboration was once again the definition of congeniality.

Kinsky found Barbara Stanwyck "professional but cold" and recalled that she never became a part of the collegial camaraderie that developed among the men in the cast. But Stanwyck's professionalism suited Hawks just fine, as he enjoyed working with her enormously and always ranked her among the best actresses with whom he ever worked. The feeling was not entirely reciprocated, however. Stanwyck confided that while she thought Hawks did a competent job, she felt the picture lacked a certain spark of inspiration, and she secretly regretted that Billy Wilder, present at all times on the set, hadn't directed it instead.

Fresh off *Citizen Kane*, Gregg Toland had deeply explored the possibilities of deep-focus cinematography since working for Hawks on *The Road to Glory* and *Come And Get It*. Hawks, whose films were conventionally well-photographed without being innovative visually, found the technique suitable "when you didn't give a damn what the people looked like, as with the old professors. The harsher the lighting, the better they looked." The director thought deep focus "was only good with a group like that, because they worked as one person—I always thought of them as one actor. 'The professor' meant all of them—I seldom singled one out. . . . Anyway, it was kind of a stylized thing, and you had to adapt your style to it. I never tried for depth of focus on a picture where it would intrude." Hawks was impressed with Toland's solution to one photographic dilemma. Cooper was to enter a dark room where Stanwyck was in bed. Hawks wanted only her eyes to show but didn't know how to avoid revealing her face as well. Toland's answer: Have Stanwyck do the scene in blackface.

To shoot the location footage, Arthur Rosson took a second-unit crew to New York City and worked all over town, including at Yankee Stadium during the World Series. After the film had been shooting for two months, it was nine and a half days behind its original forty-eight-day schedule. Due to the rewrites, however, shortly before the end Goldwyn officially extended the schedule to fifty-eight days. But with shooting rolling into mid-October, the real pressure to finish was coming not from Goldwyn but from Cooper, Stanwyck, and Hawks. They were all invited by Ernest Hemingway to join him in Sun Valley for a hunting vacation, and this just couldn't wait. Hawks responded, as he sometimes managed to do, by knocking off a hefty six and a half pages of script in one day, then pushing ahead without delay to the final major sequence, Sugarpuss's performance of "Drum Boogie." (Benny Goodman singer Martha Tilton dubbed Stanwyck's vocals, and bandleader Gene Krupa improvised the variation, "Match Boogie," played with a pair of matches on a matchbox, which Hawks liked and threw into the film.) The picture wrapped on October 16, officially one day ahead of schedule, with a final budget of $1,152,538, including 15 percent for overhead and contingencies. Cooper outearned even Hawks, taking home $150,000, while Stanwyck received $68,333, markedly less than the writers.

Once again, Hawks, with more interesting places to go and people to see, left final editing and postproduction work to studio hands. Rushing the picture to completion so as to ride on the coattails of *Sergeant York*'s immense success, Goldwyn scheduled the first sneak preview for the first week of November but suffered an unusual embarrassment in the process. By gentleman's agreement, the Hollywood trade press did not review new films at sneak previews as long as the screenings were held sufficiently outside of Los Angeles. The suburb of Glendale, however, was considered fair game, so when *Variety* got wind that *Ball of Fire* would be snuck at that town's Alexandria Theater, the critic Bill Brogdon was dispatched to the event. But once Goldwyn discovered that Brogdon was present, he refused to proceed with the showing. According to the *New York Post*, "a riot broke out," with people demanding that Brogdon be thrown out on the street. Goldwyn ended up taking the print and his guests to a theater in Pasadena.

Goldwyn was then distributing his pictures through RKO, and the company made it their first release of 1942. The film enjoyed an excellent three-week run at Radio City Music Hall beginning January 15 and did exceedingly good business everywhere, generating $2,200,000 in rentals to rank as the year's twenty-fifth biggest box-office attraction.

Ball of Fire doesn't rate with Hawks's best comedies of the period, *Bringing Up Baby* and *His Girl Friday*, although it remains utterly charming for the brash cleverness of the dialogue, the heartwarming geniality of the professors, and the expert comic playing of Cooper and Stanwyck. At 111 minutes, it runs too long, and Hawks was not able to pace it at the same speed as his previous comedies, albeit for good reason. The film "was about pedantic people," Hawks pointed out. "When you've got professors saying lines, they can't speak 'em like crime reporters." He added, "It didn't have the same reality as the other comedies, and we couldn't make it go with the same speed."

As Robin Wood observed, the film charts a favorite Hawks theme of conflicting characters' "mutual improvement through interaction," but the dynamic of the plot is directly opposed to those of his comedies of "irresponsibility." Unlike *Bringing Up Baby*, where Cary Grant's academic life is thoroughly disrupted by Katharine Hepburn, or *His Girl Friday*, where Grant's unethical high-handedness rides roughshod over any notion of propriety, the world of civilized values is respected and reaffirmed here. The tough-guy gangster stuff feels off-putting as well as annoyingly artificial in this context, underlining the fairy-tale conceit of the entire story, and Hawks sides with respectability and rectitude in *Ball of Fire* for the only time in any of his comedies. This said, he also recognizes the need of his leading man to be loosened up by a spirited woman of the world, a theme that never varied in his work or personal life.

As soon as filming concluded, the Hollywood contingent left for Idaho, where Hemingway and his three sons had arrived in September for antelope hunting. As he had in the two previous autumns, Hemingway, who had married the writer Martha Gellhorn the previous fall, was staying gratis at the plush, twelve-unit Sun Valley Lodge, a year-round resort that desperately needed the kind of publicity Hemingway's presence could bring it. Gary and Rocky Cooper had visited the season before, and this year Hemingway, now at the peak of his success and fame, broadened the invitation to include Hawks and Slim, whom he hadn't seen since their Key West visit nearly two years before, as well as Barbara Stanwyck and her husband, Robert Taylor. Because Hemingway's two younger sons, Patrick, thirteen, and Gregory, almost ten, were so close in age to David, Hawks's twelve-year-old son also got to go, skipping school for a couple of the best-spent weeks of his childhood. Also on hand was Hemingway's buddy Robert Capa, the great Hungarian war photographer, who became friendly with Hawks and Slim and took pictures of the group hunting and partying that beautifully document the time. Coincidentally staying at Sun Valley, although not explicitly as part of Hemingway's group, were Leland Hayward—perhaps the only Hollywood agent with more class and sophistication than Charles Feldman—with his actress wife, Margaret Sullavan, and the producer William Goetz and his wife, Edie, Louis B. Mayer's daughter.

Following Hemingway's lead in mostly glorious Indian summer weather, the group hunted partridge and pheasant, swam, played roulette, and drank at night. Hemingway wasn't particularly taken with Robert Taylor, but he enjoyed the spunky Stanwyck and liked Cooper as much as ever; the year before, Coop had shown Hemingway up with his expert riflry, so the writer was pleased when Sergeant York asked for pointers to improve his skill with a shotgun.

As for Hawks, when the director talked in general terms about his notions for making a film about trotting horses, Hemingway urged him to hire his old friend Evan Shipman, a poet and horse expert, as technical adviser. He also challenged Hawks to slug him in the belly as hard as he could causing Hawks to break his hand. Hemingway later wrote that he found Hawks "a very intelligent and sensitive man with a lovely girl," and there was no doubt that it was this "girl" who most occupied his thoughts. The strong, disturbing, unmistakable connection between Hemingway and Slim instantly reasserted itself here, although, at least on Slim's part, there was no way they were going to start something physical. But Hemingway persisted in sticking close to Slim while hunting and hovering solicitously after hours.

In her memoirs, Slim recounted two notably revealing stories about Hemingway's feelings for her. The writer told her that his two young sons "asked him what falling in love is. 'Well,' Ernest said, 'do you remember when you first met Slim?' Gregory piped up, 'Boy, I sure do.' And then Ernest said, 'Well, what did it feel like?' 'Like being kicked in the stomach by a horse,' Gregory said. Papa laughed. 'That's just what falling in love is like.'"

On another occasion that fall, Slim remembered, she had just taken a shower and went to dry her hair in front of the fireplace, where she found Hemingway and Capa. Hemingway asked if he could brush her hair and, receiving permission, brushed it for a very long time. "When he was finished, he dropped the brush on the floor in front of me and said, 'You don't know what that was like. It was very, very difficult. Both for Capa and me. You're a very provocative woman. I can't be around you too much.'" Slim made light of this, diffusing the tension and allowing the good times to continue.

The underlying reason for the trip was to work out a strategy for Hawks to get the directing job on *For Whom the Bell Tolls*. In the year since its publication, the novel had become the biggest best-seller since *Gone with the Wind*, putting Hemingway back on top of the heap among American writers. Paramount's record purchase price of $115,000 for the motion picture rights was rising to $150,000 because of the book's enormous sales, but nothing concerning the film's production had been locked down. The studio hadn't begun to figure out how to handle the book's touchy political and sexual elements, nor had a director been definitely selected. As a favor to Cooper, who would play the lead, Cecil B. De Mille had read the novel in galleys to help press Paramount into buying it but passed on tackling the film himself. Sam Wood, a former assistant of De Mille's, was announced by Paramount for the job in June 1941. But since Cooper had contractual director approval and hadn't officially been signed himself, the door seemed just sufficiently ajar for Hawks to slip in if everyone played their cards right.

Hawks went along with all this out of a desire to work with Hemingway and Cooper, as well as to take the helm of what could easily have been the most prestigious and commercially successful film of his career to date. By the second week of November, Paramount had secretly agreed to give the picture to Hawks. At the crucial moment, however, Hawks's uncertainty about the project asserted itself and he responded that he "might be interested if Cooper is definitely the lead and Hemingway writes the script." Since he knew perfectly well that Hemingway would never actually sit down to write the screenplay, Hawks had to realize that this requirement would dash his chances to direct the picture.

The irony in all this, and the reason for his ambivalence, was that Hawks privately loathed *For Whom the Bell Tolls.* Up to then, he had loved nearly everything Hemingway had written, and they shared a great deal in the way of aesthetic tastes and codes of behavior. But Hawks found the new novel pretentious, overblown, and too overtly—even distastefully—political. Hawks knew that because of the novel's fame and prestige and the author's undoubted surveillance of the project, he wouldn't be able to change it very much, unlike the drastic overhaul he would give *To Have and Have Not.* More than most filmmakers of the time, Hawks steered clear of august literary properties that could not be tampered with; when he had dared fiddle with *Come and Get It,* he was booted off the picture, and he was able to turn *The Front Page* inside out only with the express blessing of the coauthor, a good friend. Whatever lie Hawks told Hemingway concerning his feelings for *For Whom the Bell Tolls* is lost to time, but it was not a film Hawks was particularly eager to make or was crestfallen over not having done, at least until he saw how much money it earned.

The film Sam Wood directed, starring Gary Cooper and Ingrid Bergman, was a success beyond anything anyone dared imagine upon its release in 1943 but so turgidly directed that one can't help but fantasize about what a Hawks version could have been like. It remains, in theory anyway, one of the great might have beens of his career, concerned as it was with a small group dedicated to a dangerous mission, the stoic denial and dedication of a capable American hero, and the enticing beginnings of a great romance with great star power. On the other hand, the novel was very much about political commitment and self-sacrifice, the profound impulse toward democracy and humanism versus fascism and destructiveness. Wood was oblivious, even hostile to these elements, but there is little reason to believe that Hawks would have been more responsive to them. Hawks probably could have figured out a way to make a version of *For Whom the Bell Tolls* that would have been terrific on his own terms. But given the novel's stature, this would never have been countenanced at the time, so it's a moot point, and Hawks was wise to recognize it. He was better off—artistically, if not financially—with *To Have and Have Not.*

24

Air Force

Air Force is going to be the real stuff. —Howard Hawks

Many weddings have been victimized by rain, storms, and all manner of bad weather. Some have been marred by unruly guests, embarrassing faux pas, and even no-show participants. But few had what Hawks's and Slim's had: Pearl Harbor.

It seemed to have taken forever but, finally, more than three years after Hawks and Slim met, the final details of his divorce settlement with Athole were resolved and they were at last free to marry. Now that their future together was in no doubt, Slim threw herself into planning the Hog Canyon home, and Hawks put the Benedict Canyon house up for sale and rented a temporary residence for himself, Slim, and the kids in Bel Air, adjacent to the Bel-Air Country Club golf course.

By the beginning of December, everything seemed in order: the wedding date was set for December 11, Hawks had made what he thought were marvelous plans for the honeymoon, his current film was the biggest hit in the country, *Ball of Fire* was opening in a month, and Slim, after much debate, had decided not to invite her father to walk her down the aisle. Then, on Sunday, December 7, they awoke to the news that Pearl Harbor had been bombed by the Japanese. The United States was going to war. Slim, however, was not to be denied, and four days later, the wedding went ahead exactly as planned.

Howard Hawks and Nancy Gross were married in a small, formal ceremony at Hawks's parents' Pasadena home. Dr. Roderick Dhu Morrison of Altadena officiated, Bill Hawks was the best man, Slim's schoolgirl friend Dixie Cavalier-Carlisle was her bridesmaid, and Gary Cooper gave her away. The fashion-conscious *Los Angeles Times* reported, "The bride wore a wedding gown that had been in her family for four generations. It is an old-fashioned, ivory satin dress with a slight train and a deep, lace collar. She wore an old lace and tulle veil. She had carnations in her hair and her bouquet was all carnations." Slim admitted that at the last minute, as she

331

was standing at the top of the stairs, she developed cold feet and told Cooper she didn't want to go through with it. Coop told her it was too late to back out, and down they went.

Hawks had arranged for them to travel by train to New Orleans, then on to Miami, where they were to share a house with the newlyweds Shipwreck Kelly and the 1930s' most famous debutante, Brenda Frazier. However, because army troop trains were already receiving priority on the tracks, the honeymooners' train was endlessly delayed. Once in Miami, Hawks spent most of his time golfing or fishing with Shipwreck, abandoning Slim with Frazier, a spoiled rich girl whom she found utterly vapid and uninteresting. Hawks's plans to continue on to the Bahamas and Cuba had to be scuttled because of the war, but by this time Slim was too disillusioned about the honeymoon trip to care and just wanted to return to Los Angeles as quickly as possible.

By the time they got back, Hawks found that quite a few of his friends had already enlisted for military duty. Jimmy Stewart, Darryl Zanuck, and John Ford were already commissioned officers, while Frank Capra, William Wyler, and John Huston would be entering the U.S. Army Signal Corps as soon as they disposed of their obligations on current pictures. Forty-five years old and a veteran of World War I, Hawks did not have to consider actual duty in the armed services. But rather than sign on to make government documentaries, as had Capra, Wyler, Huston, and any number of other filmmakers, Hawks opted to stay stateside, where he spent the next year and a half working exclusively on major studio projects heralding the war effort.

Although there was no doubting his patriotism and dedication to the cause once the United States declared war, nor the slightest suggestion that he was an America First proponent or isolationist, there is reason to believe that Hawks was a latecomer in supporting U.S. involvement in the war. His close friend Christian Nyby, a film editor in the 1940s, said that, ironically, the director of *Sergeant York* felt throughout 1941 that the United States was being railroaded into the war and afterward was "teed off" because of his suspicions that FDR had known about the Japanese plans for Pearl Harbor two days before the attack occurred. According to Nyby, Hawks never softened in his view of Roosevelt as "a pompous ass." With a beautiful young wife, a gorgeous new home, and an earning power matched by only a handful of other Americans at the time, Hawks made his choice: he stayed home and signed a contract that would guarantee him a minimum of $100,000 per year, with the opportunity to make much more.

In the wake of *Sergeant York*'s breakaway success, Hawks was inundated with offers. Jean Gabin, the recently arrived French star, asked for Hawks to guide him through his first Hollywood picture, John O'Hara's adaptation of Willard Robertson's 1940 melodramatic best-seller *Moontide*, and Zanuck and producer Mark Hellinger, hoping that Hawks could help mold Gabin into another Gable or Tracy, pursued the director at length before giving up and settling for Archie Mayo. Zanuck also tried to persuade Hawks to direct *Ten Gentlemen from West Point*, about the early history of the academy, which Henry Hathaway eventually took on. There was talk of a Gary Cooper–Barbara Stanwyck Western called *Cheyenne* that William Hawks would produce at RKO, and that studio also approached Hawks about reuniting with Cary Grant and Rosalind Russell on a war-oriented project called *Bundles for Freedom*.

After preparing *The Outlaw* and then doing *Sergeant York* and *Ball of Fire* back-to-back, Hawks was physically spent, almost ill, and told Feldman that he needed to rest and recuperate before launching into another picture. He refused another future box-office giant starring Gary Cooper, Sam Goldwyn's inspirational biography of Lou Gehrig, *The Pride of the Yankees*, which Sam Wood also ended up directing. Hawks was tempted, but Feldman reported to his staff that the way he was feeling, Hawks "didn't care whether he did the picture or not, if he was going to be rushed into it." Warner Bros. paged Hawks to take the reins on the Edna Ferber Western *Saratoga Trunk*, but Hawks didn't want to work with Errol Flynn and told Hal Wallis he'd consider it if Cooper would star (which he did, opposite Ingrid Bergman, under the ubiquitous Sam Wood). Warners also proposed to Hawks *The Hard Way*, which Vincent Sherman ended up directing memorably, as well as Jesse Lasky's Mark Twain biography, which Irving Rapper eventually took on.

One Warner Bros. picture Hawks definitely was not involved with was *Casablanca*, his own claims to the contrary. One of Hawks's tallest tales was about how, one day, he and Michael Curtiz were supposedly commiserating about the lousy projects Warner Bros. wanted them to do, Curtiz complaining about how he didn't know anything about Tennessee hill people and Hawks moaning about a silly story about a bunch of people who meet at Rick's nightclub. Between them, he said, they agreed to swap pictures, and the rest was history. However, *Sergeant York* began shooting in December 1940, eighteen months before *Casablanca*, so the timing is considerably off. Warner Bros. did send an early draft, called *Everybody Goes to Rick's*, to Hawks while he was working on *Sergeant York*, as it did to Curtiz. But

Slim, whom Hawks had trained to read and analyze scripts for him, told Hawks it was terrible—granted, this was a long way from what the final screenplay would be like by the time shooting was completed. Curtiz agreed to direct the film in March 1941. When he saw the finished film, Hawks said he liked it, but claimed it had "an awful musical comedy quality" and admitted, "I never had any faith in my doing anything like that."

When Hawks and Slim were married, Slim was referred to in the press as a "film writer," a typically Hawksian exaggeration that nonetheless had an explanation, even if no one was asking. In the first of what were to be many schemes by Hawks and Feldman to buy literary properties and then sell them to the studios, Hawks brought to his agent's attention "Phantom Filly," a story by George Agnew Chamberlain published in the *Saturday Evening Post,* which was bought in the names of Nancy Gross and the CKF [Feldman] Corporation for $7,500, written into a script by Feldman client Winston Miller and unloaded to Fox for $60,000, resulting in a huge profit for Slim and Feldman. Henry Hathaway directed the picture in 1944.

In late November, two weeks before Hawks's wedding, Feldman was trying to put over another idea, that of selling Hawks and Gary Cooper as a package. Even though Feldman didn't represent the actor, who was still under contract to Goldwyn, the prodigiously creative agent argued, "I am thoroughly convinced, because of Hawks' relationship with Cooper, that Gary will definitely do almost anything that Howard wants to do." Of course, any studio in town would have been interested in these two men under any terms that were remotely realistic, but Feldman was zeroing in on the un- likely target of Universal, which did best with such lowbrow fare as Abbott and Costello comedies and Deanna Durbin musicals, since he believed he was most likely to win the greatest profit participation and artistic con- trol from the studio most eager to land such prestigious talent.

Feldman's brief to Universal on behalf of his client emphasized his recent successes and his friendship with Hemingway, "who is now working on a new book and to whom Hawks has given ideas." Feldman further argued that Hawks deserved to get considerably more than Universal's highest-paid director, Gregory La Cava, whose deal called for $125,000 and a percentage, saying that La Cava, "in my opinion, isn't one tenth of the director that Hawks is." As it eventually transpired, Universal would end up with Hawks but not Cooper, the one they actually coveted.

At the same time, Feldman had Hawks close to a lucrative one- picture-per-year deal at Fox, but the studio backed down, just as it did with a similarly expensive deal for Capra. The week before his wedding, Hawks had a dinner with Cary Grant at which they agreed to make two pictures together over the next three years.

After all these overtures, proposals, and negotiations, Hawks ended up signing two different contracts in early 1942, each of a long-term nature the likes of which he had avoided in recent years. The first, which he signed in February, was with Warner Bros., where he agreed to make one picture per year over the next five years for $100,000 per picture. For each production, Hawks was obliged to sixteen weeks of work, beyond which he would earn $6,250 per week. Warners was not yet amenable to paying their talent percentages, but Hawks did receive wide latitude in his choice of stories, and knew that he and Feldman would be able to sell just about any property they wanted to Jack Warner for a big profit.

Two months later, Hawks signed a long-brewing deal at Universal to produce and direct three pictures over three years. Again, he would receive $100,000 for sixteen weeks of work, but he was also cut in for 50 percent of the net profits. Here, the budgets would be lower—no more than $650,000, not including the salaries of the producer-director and the stars—but Hawks could get his "A Howard Hawks Production" credit in letters 75 percent the size of the title, whereas Warners would only allow it to be 40 percent. Hawks optimistically believed that with everything neatly set up and the top stars in Hollywood dying to work with him, he could make two pictures per year and earn more than $200,000 per year and still have twenty weeks left over. All those zeroes looked nice on paper, even if it was sheerest fantasy that he could ever be that prolific.

Before Pearl Harbor, Hollywood had produced a number of contemporary combat films. A *Yank in the R.A.F.*, starring Tyrone Power, was the fourth most popular film of 1941; *Dive Bomber, I Wanted Wings,* and *Flight Command* had stressed the importance of military preparedness. But once the war started, the film industry immediately joined hands with the government to produce ultrapatriotic, even blatantly propagandistic entertainments designed to bolster the war effort. Warner Bros.' first wartime drama to hit the screen was Raoul Walsh's *Desperate Journey*, starring Errol Flynn and Ronald Reagan as pilots trying to make their way out of Germany. But the studio's first major push was on behalf of what became *Air Force.*

Hawks always said that Major General Henry (Hap) Arnold, head of the Army Air Corps, asked him to make this film, which was intended to promote the Air Force's role in turning the war around from its disastrous start. Hawks had known Arnold through flying circles for some years, but the contact that launched *Air Force* began at a higher level, between Arnold and Jack Warner. Warner, who from this time on liked to be referred to as Colonel Warner, was, with Zanuck, the most gung ho of all the studio heads, which is reflected in the extraordinary wartime output of his studio. Once Arnold arranged for the cooperation of the War Department, Warner brought Hawks and the screenwriter Dudley Nichols onboard to prepare the script.

Hawks said it was Arnold who proposed the basic story "about the flight of B-17s that had left Hamilton Field up in Northern California and gotten past the point of no return when they heard over the radio that the Japanese had hit Pearl Harbor. They got in there that night, in all the smoke and everything, and were afraid of being hit again, so they were sent down to Manila." The idea was to concentrate on the crew of one plane, and the Air Force appointed Captain Samuel Triffy as technical adviser to Hawks and Nichols. Resurrecting a method used on *Scarface*, Hawks and Nichols tacked red, yellow, and blue cards to a large cork board to lay out story strands and characters. They initially miscalculated, however, since the first draft of Nichols's script begins with fifty-five pages of character development before the plane even takes off. This was quickly remedied, and the film benefited enormously from having the group of men thrust almost immediately into action.

Leaving Nichols to continue writing, the producer, Hal Wallis, to concentrate on the logistics of organizing the shoot, and Slim to check into Good Samaritan Hospital in Los Angeles for the first of many "rests," Hawks took a trip to Washington, D.C., in mid-May to consult with Hap Arnold and the War Department Motion Picture Board of Review. On the train he got to know another general and an older sergeant, the latter of whom supplied the basis for the service veteran played in the film by Harry Carey. The excited, proud little boy in Hawks came bursting out when he was embraced by all the military top brass. He boasted that he found that the Air Force's gunnery manual was a useless document that couldn't teach a soldier how to hit anything. Arnold supposedly challenged Hawks to rewrite it, which Hawks claimed he did. Arnold's parting directive to the director was, "Tell the story of how the Japs laced hell out of us. Then tell how we struck back at them with our own medicine. Tell the whole story — its bitterness and sadness and bravery. Tell the story of the greatest fighters the world has ever known." Hawks then joined Captain Triffy in Tampa, Florida, where the exteriors would be shot; not only would Drew Field serve as a plausible stand-in for Hickham Field in Hawaii, but the ongoing fear of a

Japanese invasion on the West Coast completely ruled out filming with any Japanese-marked planes in California.

To get a head start on a picture Jack Warner was adamant to have in theaters by December 7, the first anniversary of Pearl Harbor, the miniature unit began shooting under the director Roy Davidson on May 18 in the ocean off Santa Barbara. They spent fifty-nine days creating scenes duplicating combat in Makasar Strait, the Coral Sea, Haruna, and the Celebes Sea.

On June 15, Hal Wallis was shocked when Dudley Nichols submitted a 207–page screenplay, nearly double the normal length for a feature film. Not only that, but the script was still incomplete. Hawks and Nichols had long since decided to make the plane, the *Mary Ann*, rather than any actor, the star of the picture. Helping set a predictable pattern for future combat films, the bomber crew was composed of a societal cross-section, mostly played by relative unknowns—John Ridgely's stoical captain, Gig Young's upper-class WASP, George Tobias's comic Jew (similar to his character in *Sergeant York*). The only major name in the cast was John Garfield, whom, Hawks said, had always loved *Scarface* and was simply interested in working with him.

Many logistical problems had yet to be solved, and both Boeing and the Air Force were having trouble securing a Flying Fortress that could be spared for a significant period. Warners finally rented a mock-up interior from Paramount, and Hawks began filming in it on June 18 with his ten actors. With the script in such a tentative state, it was impossible to set a precise budget and shooting schedule, but a hefty $2 million and seventy-two days were allocated going in. Because of the long schedule, Hawks's salary was bumped up to $150,000. Hawks's favorite assistant director, Jack Sullivan, was at his side again, as was the cinematographer James Wong Howe, with whom he hadn't worked since *Viva Villa!* in Mexico. Originally, the film was to have been shot by Sol Polito, who had done *Sergeant York*, but Howe ended up with the job, assisted in the special effects and rear-projection work by the veteran Hans Koenekamp. The entire first month was devoted to interior bomber scenes with the core crew, and Hawks moved along at the reasonable pace of one and a half to two pages of script a day (although at this rate, Nichols's full screenplay would have taken more than two hundred days to film). Hawks covered many of his set-ups in a single take, but a handful of difficult group shots required as many as twenty-two takes.

After completing three days of hospital interiors, the company departed Los Angeles by train on July 21 for the 58½-hour journey to Tampa. Hawks found things far from well when he arrived. Setting up headquarters at the Tampa Terrace Hotel, Hawks learned that while the War Department was trying to cooperate the best it could, because of the demands of the war it had come up woefully short on equipment, including lights; that requisitioned electrical supplies and gasoline were going to be difficult to come by; and that many adjustments were going to have to be made in the script as a result. Furthermore, it was the hottest summer in Tampa in thirty-four years; the entire company was ordered to take daily salt pills and drink lime and quinine water. Although Hawks later claimed that he shot all the action himself without the aid of a second unit, the facts were otherwise. None other than Breezy Eason headed up the second unit, which worked out of nearby Mather Field while Hawks remained at Drew. Eason concentrated mainly on aerial shots coordinated by the great flier Paul Mantz, who had flown stunts on *Ceiling Zero,* and photographed principally by Elmer Dyer, who had worked on all of Hawks's other aviation films, with assistance from Charles Marshall and Rex Wimpy. In Florida, Eason shot for nineteen days, covering just about all the aerial footage for the picture, including the Zero attacks, while back in Los Angeles he directed an additional twelve days of Japanese ship movements, battle material, and explosions.

From the start, problem begat problem. The enormous lamps Howe set up to facilitate night shooting attracted swarms of insects, so that Howe was forced to erect an extra bank of lights one hundred yards away and turn it on first, which distracted the bugs long enough to allow for about one minute of shooting. Asian extras were at such a premium in Florida that in most cases local Cubans were recruited to play Japanese and Hawaiians; for certain close-ups, a few Chinese were found, and Howe, Chinese himself, submitted them to what he called the "cruel system" of lighting, or head-on illumination without any relieving or softening spotlights, resulting in a harsh, high-contrast look of evil. Engine noise drowned out much of the dialogue, planes developed problems or were called away for essential government use, rain caused delays, the crew constantly complained about being forced to live in barracks and to eat military rations, and virtually all the main actors came down with severe colds or the flu as a result of the extended waits during night shooting. To top it off, Jack Warner was becoming irate, not only at how little footage was coming back from Florida but at how the scenes he saw in dailies were not necessarily those in the script. Hawks was up to his old tricks again, and in early August both Warner and Wallis ordered the director to speed things up and not change dialogue or rearrange scenes on location.

Hawks's wired reply to Warner, which calmed the anxiety in Burbank for a week or two, gives some indication of the difficulties he was going through. It read, in part (with punctuation added): "First, as to field across from Drew, recent rains made ground too soft to hold airplanes, trucks and equipment. . . . Your information about yesterday was not correct. We planned four nights' work in succession & used yesterday to rehearse action. We took lamps from the studio for this purpose. We got only long shots because an actor suffered from heat prostration and will be confined to bed for several days." Hawks went on to list myriad other technical hurdles, concluding, "It is not my intention to make excuses, but we believe we have been under difficulties which we have now overcome & with any luck should accomplish the work we set out to do in the estimated time. One thing I assure you, Jack. Not one of us wants to stay down here any longer than is necessary to get a good picture."

It was true that Hawks was modifying Nichols's dialogue constantly on location, partly with an eye to paring it down to the minimum and partly to make it more realistic. Hawks had the technical adviser, Triffy, by his side at all times, and Triffy was impressed with the way Hawks was on top of every detail and made every scene come alive, turning it into "more truth than fiction." In his determination to make the picture as authentic and powerful a portrait of aerial warfare as possible, Hawks was as demanding with his stunt fliers and crew as he was with his actors, to the point where Triffy, who flew both American and Japanese-marked planes for the filming, came to see Hawks and his allies as "ruthless! Absolutely ruthless! If they could have damaged [an] airplane in flight so I would have had an accident, they would have done it. Really! I couldn't trust them. I mean it." When he saw the finished film, Triffy was satisfied with its military authenticity, except for the instance in which John Garfield picks up a large machine gun and brings down an attacking Japanese fighter plane.

A strange publicity item released by Warners at this time stated, "So pretentious are plans for the Hal B. Wallis production of *Air Force* at Warner Bros. that budget and time restrictions have been completely scrapped; director Howard Hawks' only obligation to the company is to 'bring in the greatest air picture ever filmed.'" In reality, the reverse was true, and Hawks responded to the pressure by shifting into unheard-of seven-day work weeks and obeying Warner's command to save film by making only one take of all shots. On August 22, Wallis ordered Hawks to return to Los Angeles on

August 26, but Hawks flatly refused, insisting that he absolutely needed three days beyond that to shoot B-17s returning to the airfield at dusk. Later, even Wallis admitted that what Hawks and Howe captured on film for this sequence was worth the extra time. As Howe was setting up his lights for the sequence in the late afternoon, he discovered that his generator was on the blink. He explained the problem to Hawks, who was less than helpful. As Howe told it, "He said, 'Don't tell me that. That's not my problem, that's your problem.'" Howe made do by using signal flares with the reflectors from the lights, which achieved superb results: "They flickered and it was wonderful, because the airport was—the landing field was supposed to be on fire—in flames." The flames and drifting smoke being cut by the planes and their landing lights and propellers created a brilliant effect and Hawks congratulated his cinematographer on his ingenuity.

Finally, on August 30, after thirty-one days, the company decamped for the long trip back to California. The train pulled into Union Station at 8:15 P.M. on September 2, and the following morning Hawks was in Hal Wallis's office being told in no uncertain terms to shoot only precisely what was needed, to stop rewriting every scene, and to speed things up. Hawks naturally responded by proceeding with rewrites of several significant sequences. Hawks decided that he wanted to end the film on a "clever" note, with the exhausted men thankfully "getting into bed, feeling the mattress, etc.;" after their tremendous effort, it was doubtless what he felt like doing after having had only two days off during the entire Florida shoot. Jack Warner instantly vetoed this, insisting that the film needed an "up ending" of the men being congratulated and recognized for their heroics. This argument dragged on for weeks. Hawks realized that further work was needed on a couple of scenes, particularly the one in which Captain Quincannon (John Ridgely) dies, which the director found grossly sentimental in Nichols's script.

As it happened, the financially desperate William Faulkner had arrived at Union Station on July 24, a matter of hours before Hawks left from there for Tampa, to work under contract at Warners for a paltry $300 per week, concentrating on a screenplay about Charles De Gaulle and the Free French movement that was never made. During his first week back in September, Hawks called on his old friend and, in two days, Faulkner wrote a vastly improved version of Quincannon's death, in which the crew gathers around his bed and helps the expiring man run through the cockpit checklist, as they have done so many times, and imagine that he is taking off once more. It was an impressive conceptual piece of writing, as well as a quintessential example of Hawksian professionalism and stoicism. The other scene was of a more comic bent, with George Tobias, as the Brooklyn boy making fun of California, delivering the one recognizably Faulknerian line: "The sun shines and nothing ever happens, and before you know it you're sixty years old."

On September 11, the production was officially declared three weeks behind schedule, and more than half of the scenes remained to be shot. By September 17, the seventy-two-day schedule had been exceeded. Through the remainder of the month Hawks pushed along at the deliberate pace of about a page and a half per day. On October 2, a further second unit, headed by the film editor George Amy, was created to knock off some exteriors and process shots; on the same day, Warner unilaterally announced that the picture would wrap on October 17, regardless of what had or had not been shot. Hawks responded the next day, a Saturday, by covering more dialogue — three pages' worth — than he had in a single stretch in weeks, but on Sunday he decided upon a different strategy to combat Warner's increasing harassment.

The Warners press release stated that because Howard Hawks had come down with a bad streptococci infection, Vincent Sherman was taking over as director of *Air Force*. Officially, then, Hawks was just out sick; in fact, he was feigning illness in protest of what he considered the executives' ill-considered, high-handed manner. Hawks was betting that upon seeing Sherman's dailies, Warner, if not Wallis, would readily recognize the superiority of Hawks's work and ask him back. As Sherman recalled, "I thought [the rough cut] was very good, but the last thing Wallis said to me was, 'I don't want the script changed, not a word.' On the set the next morning we were rehearsing, and someone said, 'You can't say this because Howard changed something earlier.' I called Hal Wallis and said I had to change something. He said, 'Okay, but don't change anything else.'"

Sherman was directing scenes of the crew in the bomber, and he found that "the actors were working in the Hawks style, underplaying. Wallis came on the set and said, 'Can't you get some life out of them? Bump 'em up, bump 'em up, they're flat.' But that was Hawks's style. I think what Hawks was going for was to let the audience supply the emotion. He didn't portray hysteria. But I boosted them up a bit, even though I thought it was wrong. On the second day, Jack Warner said my first day's dailies were 'great, they're great. Keep it up. I want you to finish the picture.' Later that day I asked Hal Wallis what was going on, and he said, 'Never mind. It's none of your business. And whatever you do, don't talk to Hawks.' I didn't know exactly what the problem was, but I presumed that Wallis was displeased that Hawks was changing the script."

On Saturday, October 10, as Sherman was shooting an exterior of the bomber in a clearing, Hawks suddenly showed up on the set at 3:30 P.M. "I could hear things going on," remembered Sherman, "and later I got a call telling me I wouldn't be working tomorrow." It turned out that assistant director Jack Sullivan, a Hawks loyalist, had been calling Hawks every night to tell him what was going on. That Sunday, Sherman met privately with Hawks, who told him he didn't hold him responsible for what had happened. "He said, 'I just want to tell you about the kind of man you've been working for,' and he went on a tirade about Wallis. It turned out Howard was not ill at all. I learned about the major rift between Wallis and Hawks, and Howard was very bitter about Hal Wallis. They were two very strong personalities. Wallis had a big problem about Howard's habit of rewriting scripts. He felt a loss of authority with Hawks."

Hawks told Sherman he intended to reshoot some of what the substitute had done, "just because I want to show Wallis who's doing this film." Years later, Hawks claimed that Warner didn't like anything Sherman shot and was begging Hawks all the while to return to the studio; he also claimed he didn't use any of Sherman's "lousy" footage in the final film. To the contrary: the day after Hawks returned, Sherman was put in charge of an additional unit that shot simultaneously with Hawks's for five more days to hasten the picture's completion. Hawks did do a handful of retakes, but he also had to shoot the hospital scenes, some tail and bubble gunner stuff, and numerous process shots. After a fourteen-hour final day, *Air Force* finally wrapped on October 26. The picture had shot for 105 days, thirty-three days over its original schedule. Hawks had managed to shoot 164 pages of Nichols's 207-page original, with the remaining scenes merely eliminated.

Because of the delays, it was obvious by now that the film was not going to make its hoped-for December 7 opening date. But Jack Warner was still anxious to mark the anniversary, so the studio boss traveled to Washington to present the hastily cut picture to Secretary of War Henry L. Stimson, Hap Arnold, and numerous other military brass. As expected, the response was positive, but the Office of War Information expressed serious concern about what the other Allies would make of a line in the epilogue stating that Americans would have to win this war alone. Shortly thereafter, the Hays Office objected to John Garfield's line "Damn 'em! Damn 'em!," uttered when he sees what the Japanese have done to Pearl Harbor, but Warner Bros. won its appeal based upon the precedent set by Clark Gable's "Frankly, my dear, I don't give a damn," in *Gone with the Wind*. The long cut originally featured one additional battle, but walkouts toward the end at public previews prompted its quick elimination. Hawks wanted to shorten the picture further, particularly the final battle scene, but a satisfied Warner declared on January 18 that no more changes would be made and quickly began showing the film to government dignitaries, aviation executives, and the press.

Air Force had its world premiere on February 3, 1943, at the Hollywood Theater in New York City, replacing *Casablanca* after its three-month run. The reviews were excellent, praising the film for its apparent authenticity, dramatic excitement, and morale-building qualities and comparing it favorably to the English war-effort hit of the moment, Noël Coward and David Lean's *In Which We Serve*. Hawks personally received more credit than he had on *Sergeant York* because of his prior mainstream reputation as a director of aviation pictures. The director was further praised for avoiding the usual "Hollywood hokum" and for centering on a group of men rather than the heroics of a single star. Even the critic for the *Daily Worker* admired the film's portrayal of "the new relationships among men being developed by a people's war." The only recurring criticisms were directed at the obvious overlength and at the film's flagrantly false suggestion that the local Hawaiians of Japanese descent helped sabotage Pearl Harbor.

Although not in a class with *Sergeant York*, *Air Force* still proved to be a powerful commercial draw, ranking as Warner Bros.' fourth biggest earner of 1942 with $2.7 million in rentals. There are numerous worthwhile angles from which to consider the film. Perhaps the most wonderful thing about it is the way it embodies, in an inspiring and uncloying way, the ideals of democracy. Because of the expert handling of the interlocking story strands and emotional and dramatic impact, the idea of diverse individuals coming together for the common good is indelibly expressed; as Robin Wood put it, "it is the triumph of individualism placed at the service of something beyond itself." At the same time, Hawks's preferred method of abstracting his protagonists from a context of real life and society comes heavily into play. Military hierarchies, tradition, and family and emotional ties are secondary to the functioning of the group. Of all the Hawksian groups over the years, the one in *Air Force* is unique in that there is no one whose natural talents make him a distinct leader. John Garfield's rear gunner Winocki, like Richard Barthelmess's discredited flier in *Only Angels Have Wings*, may have caused another man's death some years before, something for which the captain, at least, holds him responsible. In all of Hawks's previous war films, as well as in others featuring civilians, the director chose to have at least one character commit suicide as a way to assert himself, resolve a dead-end situation, or admit his unsuitability for the group good. But from this point on, it is as if Hawks changed his mind about suicide both as a dramatic device and as a human act. In *Air Force* he instead has Winocki transform his negative emotions into a positive force for himself and those around him.

The film takes the form of a perilous journey, almost like a classic Western in which the protagonists must improvise under the constant threat of ambush. More often noted by critics is the picture's function as a microcosm — not as a simplistic one representing different ethnic aspects of America but virtually as an organic microcosm of democracy, with the men representing the parts that make up the plane, which in turn is part of a specific fleet, which itself is just a portion of the total war effort. Hawks's movie is equal parts physics, action, and emotion, all balanced by the master engineer to run beautifully together, even if on the spare parts of propaganda, nationalism, and expediency.

25

The Bel-Air Front

Slim had promised her husband that when he returned from the demanding shoot in Tampa, he could look forward to moving into his new home. But much to her annoyance, the war had created a few inconveniences. Priority given to war-related goods meant endless delays in the shipment of their Louisiana furniture, so the house was barely furnished; there was not yet any gas; and even Hawks's money and connections couldn't immediately secure them the 125 feet of scarce electrical wire they needed to illuminate the house. In time, however, it all arrived, and the Hawkses—five of them, at first—finally moved into what Lauren Bacall later called the most beautiful house she had ever seen.

Slim had done her job to a fare-thee-well. The Hog Canyon home was decorated in discreetly fabulous taste; it was luxurious but comfortable American design at its best. Anything anyone could want—pool, stables and corral, huge wooded grounds—were at hand; it was in the city, close to both work and the sea, yet it had a completely rural flavor. Despite her own aversion to bluegrass country, Slim even accommodated her husband's wish for the white rail fences he had admired so much in Kentucky.

Although the Hawks children all officially moved into the house in Hog Canyon, they were in various states of flux at this point in their lives. Having graduated from Beverly Hills High School, Peter had enrolled at the Arizona State University but in 1942 was drafted and entered the Army Air Corps, based at Hamilton Field in Northern California. David entered eighth grade at Emerson Junior High in West Los Angeles. But separated from all of his friends, he began falling in with a quasi-delinquent crowd, which later led his father to send him to the Black Fox Military Institute, a boarding school in Hollywood.

Barbara, at just six years old, was another, more delicate matter. After the divorce, Athole had taken Barbara with her to Santa Barbara, where they stayed in great luxury for a few months at the exclusive San Ysidro Ranch,

345

which was owned by Ronald Colman, followed by a spell at the lodge in Sun Valley. When the burden of taking care of an active child proved too taxing for the unstable Athole, Barbara moved in with her father, first on Bellagio Road and then, briefly, at Hog Canyon. The highlight of this short spell was her friendship with their neighbor Victor Fleming's two daughters, Victoria and Sally. "I'd always spend Saturday night with the Fleming girls," Barbara remembered, "and Sunday breakfast was always a huge buffet."

Hawks, however, was hardly a candidate to be a fully responsible, attentive father who could be expected to look after the daily needs of a little girl, and Slim didn't see why she should be called upon to single-handedly raise a daughter not her own. So Barbara was sent to live with Grandpa and Grandma Hawks in Pasadena. Seventy that year and having had five children of her own, Helen Hawks was far from thrilled about the prospect of raising another one, but was able to face the challenge with the help of her closest friend, Katherine Ogden, who had lived with Helen and Frank since shortly after seeing her young soldier husband drown on their honeymoon around the time of World War I. Katherine, who had never remarried or had children, was delighted to have Barbara in the house, and even if the little girl was terrified of her "aunt" much of the time, she still received much doting attention from her. She was enrolled in a girls' school, Westridge, three blocks away, pursued her passion for horses, and saw her father infrequently, mostly on holidays. "My grandparents' house had a telephone room," Barbara recalled, "and my grandmother always thought she was being so smart, going in there, and five minutes later a phone call would come from Dad after he hadn't called for a month."

As soon as Hawks checked off of the Warner Bros. lot at the end of October after thirty-four weeks of work on *Air Force* (more than twice the amount he was expected to work on any picture under his deal), he told Charles Feldman he had no intention of going back to fulfill the rest of his contract. He was livid at the way Hal Wallis had treated him throughout the shooting, capped by his treachery involving Vincent Sherman. He categorically refused to work with Wallis again, which would make his life at the studio quite difficult. After a month's cooling-off period, Feldman agent Ned Marin arranged an evening's get-together with Hawks and Jack Warner, but Hawks was still too hot about it all to agree to come back just yet; even if he did, he told Warner, he would only deal with the front office, never with Wallis.

While Hawks busied himself up to a point with his first production for Universal, most of his time was occupied plotting new projects and business schemes. He talked to Feldman every day and saw him almost as often. The idea of a Hawks–Gary Cooper team package was revived. Feldman didn't represent the actor, and even persistent encouragement from Hawks couldn't persuade Cooper to change agencies. But the real stumbling block to the team deal, as before, was the resistance of most of the studios to giving away a large percentage of their profits.

The closest they came to a deal was at RKO, which was willing to completely finance any Hawks-Cooper ventures to the tune of $1.5 million pay them $350,000 per picture, and cut them in for 50 percent of the profits, an amount Feldman hoped to increase. To Hawks's disappointment, Cooper went ahead with his own individual deals elsewhere, even though a project turned up that seemed ideal. In the wake of *Sergeant York*, everyone in Hollywood was looking for a similar true-life inspirational story, and they thought they saw one in Eddie Rickenbacker, the World War I flying ace. Tough and very savvy, unlike York, Rickenbacker played it cool while half of the top producers and agents in Hollywood courted him, including Selznick, Jack Warner, Feldman, and brass from MGM, Fox, Paramount, and United Artists. Feldman's pitch, of course, was that only the director and star of *Sergeant York* could do justice to Rickenbacker's story. Feldman was in the midst of negotiating potentially unprecedented percentage deals for Hawks and Cooper at Universal and Fox on the Rickenbacker project, urging Hawks to go to New York to convince Rickenbacker, when he abruptly accepted another offer. Hawks and Feldman had no choice but to turn their attention elsewhere; in this instance, in the direction of a beautiful young woman who had turned both their heads.

Ella Raines was a saucy twenty-one-year-old fledgling model when David O. Selznick made a screen test with her and a young Broadway actor, Gregory Peck, in New York in 1942. Charles Feldman happened to be sitting in with Selznick when he ran the test, and much to the producer's consternation, the agent decided to sign the young lady immediately. Inviting her to California, Feldman had a green Dodge and an apartment on Durant Drive in Beverly Hills waiting for her, took her to the Brown Derby, and began plotting her motion picture career.

One of Feldman's key clients was the French émigré actor Charles Boyer. In another of his money-making schemes, Feldman discussed with both Boyer and Hawks the idea of forming a company that would discover, acquire, and train new talent, then turn around and lease the performers to the studios at great profit. In addition to the financial side, this prospect appealed to Hawks enormously because he always preferred working with young performers he could shape and mold as he saw fit, who wouldn't resist his methods or feel like they knew it all already. As soon as he saw Raines, he knew she was someone he definitely wouldn't mind spending long hours with in training. Trim and coltish, she had the clear-eyed, direct look he so liked, a wholesome countenance with just a hint of sophistication and earthiness.

Introduced by Feldman, whom Raines liked at once, Hawks took her to the Brown Derby, and after droning on about business and her career, turned the conversation with the subtlest of come-ons. "Do you ride?" the director inquired. Raines took him up on his invitation, and, she said, "I spent the next two weeks out at his ranch." She knew that he was married, of course, but thought better than to ask any questions. She put it simply: "I never saw Slim." Hawks even showed off his latest conquest to some of his movie-star friends, including Clark Gable and Spencer Tracy. Raines, of course, could barely contain herself over all this attention and said of Hawks, "I loved him and adored him. I didn't think he was a cold person at all. He was very charming, very thoughtful, very kind."

Already the gears were turning for Raines to do another, more elaborate screen test, which Hawks would direct, and for Raines to become the first and exclusive property of the new Boyer-Hawks outfit, called B-H Productions. This professional association gave Hawks a good excuse, once Slim returned from another of her "rests," for having Raines come around the house on Sundays, when he would go over scenes with her in preparation for the test.

The fling with Ella Raines may or may not have been Hawks's first since marrying Slim, but it was the first significant one, and it was at this time, scarcely a year into their marriage, that Slim began to figure out that her husband was no different from most of the other famous and powerful men in Hollywood. Hawks often would not show up for dinner when his wife was expecting him, pleading late work or an important meeting. He would quietly slip in at four in the morning, and she would lie in bed, wide awake, pretending to be asleep; she even had to confront the old telltale sign of lipstick on his collars. Slim started hearing the rumors, eventually even learning the names of some of his dates, but, remarkably for such a spirited young woman, she never confronted him about his philandering, accepting it as a fact of life for a successful, famous man in Hollywood.

Virtually anyone who could fool around did, and Hawks, even more so now that he was keeping company with Feldman, had constant opportunities. The number of major directors who did *not* stray outside their marriages could literally be counted on the fingers of one hand, and in Hawks's macho crowd it was considered de rigueur. Before, he had always competed with Vic Fleming and come in second, but now he could imagine that he was taking up the slack, since Fleming had changed his womanizing ways after his marriage. But Fleming was the real thing, a man innumerable women lost their hearts and heads over. In his own diffident way, Hawks managed to fill up his scorecard but left no one swooning in his wake; Harlow aside, women rated Hawks "a gentleman" in the sack as in the rest of his life, not someone who went wild once the doors were closed. In Slim's opinion, Hawks didn't have the sexual compulsion to be a Don Juan but pursued constant conquests to fulfill his own fantasy of himself as a great lover. Even though Slim represented his ideal woman, the sexual dynamic between them was never vital or overwhelming. As she lamented, "Even at the height of our courtship he was a tentative partner. Sex was simply a physical need that had no relation to the person he was with."

All the same, Ella Raines was happy with him for a while, especially since he was following through on his intention to put her in a picture. After *Air Force*, Hawks planned a similar, if much more modest, war film as his first production for Universal. *Corvettes in Action*, as it was initially called, would glorify the role of the fast little ships that escorted large freighters and other vessels in convoys across the North Atlantic and that were particularly effective in battling submarines. The oceangoing equivalents of small fighter planes, they were "known for courage." One of the film's characters declares, "They ain't pretty ships, maybe, but brother, they got a lot of guts." After *Air Force*, the Royal Canadian Navy was more than willing to participate. Planned for a medium budget, without top stars, it was a film Hawks decided only to produce, not direct. Instead, he gave that job to his old associate Richard Rosson, who hadn't done a picture in six years. Lieutenant John Rhodes Sturdy of the Canadian Navy, a Feldman client who lived in Montreal, wrote the script, although the prolific screenwriter Edward Chodorov did an uncredited major rewrite. Since Hawks would not be directing it, the film was placed outside his overall Universal deal. Feldman negotiated for his client to receive $35,000 plus 30 percent of the net profits.

But just as interesting for Hawks as his renumeration was the chance to try out his new leading lady. Unlike *Air Force*, *Corvettes* was not an all-male action picture, and there was a nice, relatively undemanding part of a young woman whose brother is killed at sea and who must then stand by as her other brother and new boyfriend head off on a perilous new voyage.

For both Hawks and Feldman, there was no doubt whom they intended to put in the role. In early January 1943, B-H Productions signed Ella Raines for twenty weeks at three hundred dollars a week, with an option for six and a half years. A couple of weeks later, Hawks, seeing no reason to share the actress with anyone else, deviously tried to push Boyer out of the picture, even though the deal had been finalized. Feldman was furious at Hawks for this, calling his behavior "terrible and wrong and unfair" and threatening to take on the responsibility for Raines's contract himself if Hawks didn't patch things up with Boyer, which he was convinced to do.

On February 2, Hawks directed Raines's test, a scene with Randolph Scott, already cast in *Corvettes*. Hawks lavished every attention on the newcomer, posing her effectively for the camera and coaching her in delivery. As a favor to Boyer, Hawks also directed the Frenchman and Raines in a scene, and Boyer came away even more ecstatic than the others, which was saying a lot. The Feldman office decided that the "girl definitely has terrific ability and with careful handling should be star material." Boyer indicated that he would seriously consider her for a picture he was planning, and Hawks had cleverly planned the test so that, if successful, it could be inserted intact into *Corvettes in Action*, which it was.

The picture, eventually called *Corvette K-225* started shooting at Universal on February 4, and Hawks was there hovering over Ella Raines. "The first morning he was there with me in hairdressing," Raines remembered. "He didn't like what they were doing, so he took a hairbrush and brushed my hair and said, 'I want her to look natural.' He helped me through all my scenes." Hawks also consulted closely with the cinematographer, Tony Gaudio, about the lighting for Raines. Knowing very well that physical action, not directing actors, was Dick Rosson's strong suit, Hawks was on the set to supervise all the shooting done on the sound stage. This was a mixed blessing as far as Universal was concerned, since Hawks's overconcern with rewrites and last-minute suggestions slowed the shooting down enormously and inflated the budget accordingly in a film whose appeal would depend much more on Rosson's footage of real ships at sea.

Originally scheduled for six weeks of shooting in California before Rosson's action unit would assemble in Canada, the picture dragged on for thirteen weeks and two days, finally wrapping on May 7. Rosson left Los Angeles four days later for Nova Scotia, where he shot a convoy coming into harbor, and then traveled across the Atlantic to the British Isles, during which time he and cinematographers Harry Perry and Bert A. Eason captured exciting footage of corvettes and other ships in action. The crew also shot at shipyards in Montreal and, briefly, back at Universal before calling it quits in early July.

To Universal's dismay, what had been intended as a modest war film with a $736,670 price tag (including 20 percent overhead) had spiraled 40 percent over budget to $1,031,630, more than many a major film with big stars. When it opened in September, it was received for what it was, a pretty routine entry with some unusually authentic oceangoing footage. Nor did its box-office returns justify the additional expense, for by the time it played itself out, *Corvette K-225* had generated a thoroughly unremarkable $1,067,540 in rentals in the U.S. and Canada. Foreign business made possible by the end of the war enabled the picture to edge into profit by 1946, giving Hawks the most insignificant of returns on his percentage. As for Ella Raines, her role seemed utterly incidental to the main action and hardly worthy of Hawks's unstinting attention.

Shortly after *Corvette* was finished, Boyer and Hawks assigned rights to the actress to Universal, where she quickly won the leading role in Robert Siodmak's *Phantom Lady*. Being peddled around by her sponsors made Raines feel "like a piece of horseflesh," but it didn't mean that she was out of the lives of the men who had brought her to Hollywood. Hawks's interest may have waned after a few months, but Feldman started an affair with her and grew so deeply involved that Raines became the straw that broke the back of his marriage. Like Slim, Jean Howard knew her husband strayed, but she tried to ignore it and believed that her position in his life was never truly threatened. This time was different, however. Though by her own account she "had never been a wife to go in dresser drawers," Howard was dismayed to come across a tie clip on Feldman's dresser inscribed "'For Keeps, E.R.' And I thought, 'Who in the hell is "E.R.?"' Well, it turned out to be Ella Raines."

During this entire period, scarcely a week went by that Charles Feldman wasn't approached by one studio or another for Hawks to direct a major film. This would have required prying him out of his Warner Bros. contract, but Hawks seemed determined enough to do it under the right circumstances. RKO wanted him for a big adaptation of Pearl Buck's *China Sky*, about a doctor fighting alongside the Chinese during the war, which finally went to Ray Enright. Hawks was enthusiastic about MacKinlay Kantor's story *Happy Land*, about a smalltown Iowa druggist coming to terms with the death of his son in the war and wanted to make it "on an unpretentious basis" for Universal, but Hawks's only choice for the lead, the inevitable Gary Cooper, decided it wasn't right for him, so Hawks backed off as well. Hawks was also attracted by Joseph Shearing's novel *Moss Rose*, a murder melodrama set in period England, and maintained an interest in the project for several years, bringing Jules Furthman in to rewrite the script, planning to film it in Britain, and even fixing a budget ($734,975) and a ten-week shooting schedule. Other projects took precedence, however, and Gregory Ratoff ended up directing it for Fox in 1947.

By the early 1940s, the Feldman-Blum Agency had become so successful that Charlie Feldman began pursuing the next stage of his career, his true goal — producing. Antitrust laws prohibited big talent agencies such as MCA from producing films themselves, but Feldman got around this by agreeing not to take commissions from his own artists should they work in one of his productions. His first picture was the bruising melodrama *Pittsburgh*, a vehicle for two of his top stars, John Wayne and Marlene Dietrich, who, as unlikely a prospect as it may have seemed, began an affair during the shoot. Feldman was so well liked by studio heads that he was constantly being invited to take important executive jobs, but he declined them all, preferring the freedom of remaining an independent producer. His agency was doing far too well for him to give it up to devote himself entirely to producing, but, virtually alone among agents of the time, he possessed the creativity, will, and energy to do both.

In mid-1942, in a combined surge of imagination and patriotic enthusiasm, Feldman conceived a project which, had it come to pass, would have been by far the most ambitious and all-encompassing Hollywood feature to emerge from World War II. Designed as a United Nations–themed propaganda film for the Allied cause, it dealt with virtually every front on which the war was being fought, from China and the Soviet Union to North Africa and the French underground. It would have run eighteen reels and cost $4 million. Had Feldman had his way, it also would have broken down the usual narrow-minded ways the studios, agencies, and labor unions did business, as he wanted the film to be a cooperative venture where altruistic ideals, not profit, would have been the motivating force. The film got to the very brink of production, but even though it was never made, it is worth examining at length since it was the most gargantuan and, in many ways, most atypical project Howard Hawks ever attempted. It also could easily have landed Hawks, Feldman, William Faulkner, and others in hot water several years later with the House Un-American Activities Committee.

Charlie Feldman had his brainstorm in the spring of 1942 during an evening at Jack Warner's house. Among the films the mogul screened that night was a Paramount short that contained excerpts of a speech by Vice

President Henry Wallace stressing the importance of the "common man" in the worldwide "people's war" against fascism. Stirred by this notion, Feldman shortly conceived of an episodic film that would spotlight that fight as it was being carried on in several different parts of the world. To begin putting the pieces together, he enlisted the enthusiastic help of his client Edward Chodorov, and by summer's end they had assembled an extraordinary team of writers, including Clifford Odets, Lillian Hellman, Dalton Trumbo, Ben Hecht, Pearl Buck, Edna Ferber, Maxwell Anderson, Leon Feuchtwanger, Franz Werfel, Sidney Buchman, George S. Kaufman and Moss Hart, and, for the music, Jerome Kern.

While Chodorov concentrated on coordinating the writers' work, Feldman spent weeks twisting arms in a vain attempt to convince film industry leaders to get behind his desire to make *Common Man* on a non-commercial charity basis. In his view, the war effort justified, even demanded, this one major exception to business as usual in Hollywood, and he tried to shame key organizations, notably the Motion Picture Producers and Distributors of America and the Screen Actors Guild, into supporting him. The idea was that no one would be paid, no star would work more than twelve days, and all profits would go to a charitable war fund. Numerous Feldman clients and friends, including Marlene Dietrich, Irene Dunne, Randolph Scott, Merle Oberon, Jean Arthur, and Margaret Sullavan, volunteered to participate, and directors Alexander Korda and Lewis Milestone both expressed an interest. But the MPPDA showed not the slightest inclination to help Feldman; Chodorov noted "We have met unbelievable opposition from high places in getting this project rolling, not the least of which has been the recently passed ruling by the Actors' Guild Board prohibiting its members from participating in 'charity' pictures."

Though the industry at large would not support a film to benefit the war effort, several studios were interested. Because of the superior profit percentage he could obtain there, Feldman was initially inclined to place the picture at Universal, but the price tag was out of its league. MGM and Fox entered the hunt, but by the beginning of 1943 the patriotic fervor of Jack Warner carried the day, with Louella Parsons trumpeting that "Jack is so sold on the idea the big budget didn't phase him." Under the terms of the deal, 50 percent of the net profits would go to United Nations Group charities and Warner Bros. would get the other half, with 2½ percent of the world gross going to the Motion Picture Relief Fund.

After spending time negotiating with the War Production Board in Washington, D.C., and enlisting the *Time* magazine foreign correspondent

Stephen Laird and the radio writer Norman Corwin to help further with the script, Feldman officially announced the project at the beginning of 1943, with Dietrich, Charles Boyer, Claudette Colbert, Leslie Howard, and Ingrid Bergman as only the first of the many stars who would appear. He could easily have decided to use as many directors as there would be episodes, but it was thought better to employ one director to oversee, shape, and give a consistent tone to the work of the many writers. When it was clear that *For Whom the Bell Tolls* wasn't going to fall his client's way, Feldman immediately took the new project to Hawks.

Quite prepared to make this his major contribution to the war effort, stimulated by the prospect of working with so many outstanding writers, challenged by the staggering logistics, and sharing Feldman's belief in the film's commercial potential, Hawks agreed to sign on, as long as Warner, and not Hal Wallis, would oversee the production for the studio. Nervous that the film would miss its historical moment, Feldman got the gears moving as fast as he could, prodding Hawks to settle on several particular stories and whip them into shape. The director immediately called on Faulkner to write two of the episodes and made overtures to Hemingway, Sinclair Lewis, and others for contributions. Joris Ivens, a celebrated Dutch documentary filmmaker, was later engaged as technical adviser for his intimate experience of the war and conditions in other countries.

As work pressed ahead at a rapid pace through the spring, the filmmakers found a way to frame the diverse episodes. "Abraham Lincoln Comes Home," a cantata with music by Earl Robinson and libretto by Millard Lampell, portrayed the funeral procession of the assassinated president in a way that inspirationally conveyed the never-ending struggle for freedom; this would be wrapped around and threaded through the entire picture to lend it thematic continuity and growing resonance. Spinning off from this would be the numerous contemporary war stories: "The Diary of a Red Army Woman," the story of a heroic Russian peasant girl who flies in bombing missions and loses her young husband in the war, written by Violet Atkins and William A. Bacher, from a story suggestion by Isabel Donald; "Ma-Ma Mosquito," from a 1940 story by Dean S. Jennings about a tough old Chinese grandmother recognized by Chiang Kai-Shek for leading resistance against Japanese occupation; "American Sequence," with a story by Hawks and dialogue by Faulkner; the "English Episode," about a young British pilot, by John Rhodes Sturdy, the scenarist of *Corvette K-225*; "French Sequence" by Faulkner, in which a Frenchwoman, raped and prostituted by the Nazis, resists to help the Allies; "Greek Sequence," by Hawks and

Faulkner, based on the story "The Weapon," by Georges Carousso, about how the Athenians resisted the Axis by mocking them; and a Norwegian story for Ingrid Bergman, which was never written. While retaining the basics of the original sources, Faulkner made at least three passes at the entire screenplay himself and, more than anyone, can be considered the main author of the overall work.

The picture, now titled *Battle Cry*, was to open with a prologue defining a "battle cry" as something that "rises out of man's spirit when those things are threatened which he has lived by and held above price," something worth fighting for so that he and his family will "be not cast into slavery, which to a man who has once known freedom is worse than death." A train whistle resembling the words "Free——dom! Free——dom!" turns into Paul Robeson's voice chanting the same thing. Little black children scream, "Again, Uncle Paul! Go like a train again!" and he does. An old southern Negro explains to the kids that Lincoln's body wasn't actually on the Freedom Train "because Lincoln was freedom, and freedom wasn't dead. So Abraham Lincoln wasn't on that train." At the end of the prologue, Robeson's face is superimposed over a head-on shot of the locomotive as he sings the "Freed——dom!" cantata.

The action opens in early 1942 at the Springfield, Illinois, railway station. Young Fonda, who bears a certain resemblance to Abe Lincoln, is waiting to be transported off to a war he doesn't understand. Grandpa explains that the nation has now got the same fight on its hands that Abe had — the fight for freedom and against slavery. The story then flashes back some seventy-seven years to when Grandpa, as a little boy, was standing at the same station watching Lincoln's funeral train arrive.

Flashing forward, Fonda is now stuck in the African desert with a group of Americans, an English officer, and two prisoners, German and Italian officers. Among the Americans are a nineteen-year-old southerner named Akers; a paralyzed, stoical Negro soldier who goes by the name "Private America," and a by-the-book army regular named Sergeant Reagan. The various episodes occur as stories told by these characters, and throughout the philosophical discussions generated by the men in the desert concerning their reasons for fighting and the importance of freedom, the image of the Freedom Train reappears.

After the telling of several stories, the mixed group votes on whether to stay put or forge ahead into the desert, and much is made of the democratic voting process. At this point the crippled Negro speaks out, saying that Abraham Lincoln gave him the vote and much more, but he questions, in the manner of Sergeant York, whether killing is right under any circumstances, given the decrees of the Bible.

The Freedom Train speeds by once again, with reenactments of Lincoln's life and the shooting at Ford's Theatre; then the funeral train turns into a roaring express, with the cheering faces of American troops beaming from the windows.

The desert group votes to stay at their compound, upon which a Corporal Loughton tells the tragic "French Sequence."

The climax begins at the desert outpost just before sunrise. A Nazi tank approaches, whereupon the sneaky German officer trains a commandeered machine gun on his captors, only to be shot by the Italian officer, who is shown throughout to be highly civilized, with his forced obedience to the German merely representing a temporary lapse. The tank and garrison continue to fire on each other, the noise finally blending into the sound of the Freedom Train, which is superimposed over fighting tanks and finally overcomes them as Robeson sings his cry for freedom. The trainful of G.I.s finally passes by, and the final image contains a slogan written on the last car: BERLIN TOKYO OR BUST.

On July 28, second-unit director Roy Davidson, who had done the miniature work on *Air Force*, shot 130 seconds of footage of burning wheat fields for the Russian and Chinese episodes in the San Fernando Valley. Four actors and thirty-six extras took part. This, alas, was all that was ever shot on *Battle Cry*. On August 4, word came down from the Warners front office to halt all work on the picture and to cease making any further charges against it, due to what was viewed as an alarmingly escalating budget, which had already climbed to $232,348 before filming even began. Stunned at the cancellation on the brink of production after so much work had been poured into it, Hawks and Feldman could only console themselves with the money they earned for not having made a picture. Having spent very little to buy them, the pair sold four of the diverse stories to Warner Bros. for $79,500, and Hawks personally collected the full $100,000 due him as salary for the second film under his five-picture deal. For his trouble, Faulkner received $17,340.

In so many ways, *Battle Cry* was antithetical to what Hawks generally preferred in a screen story: it was explicitly political, very liberal in slant, episodic, riddled with flashbacks, attentive to diverse cultures, and encompassing many different times and places. Reading the script, it is difficult to imagine Howard Hawks truly getting behind any of these conceits and sympathies. Yet one can only deeply regret that the picture was never made.

Although its tone and stance come across clearly in the script, how successful it could have been as a unified, not to mention personal, film is not clear at all. It would have been fascinating to see if Hawks could have pulled together such an ambitious, over-reaching project, one so unlike anything else he ever attempted. It would have been one of a kind for Hollywood as well, but the system was not as conducive as it would become to this kind of mad, obsessive venture that threatened to spiral out of control as easily as it could clean up at the box office. And who would not have been curious to see a cast that was to have included, in addition to the stars previously mentioned, Gary Cooper (as Fonda), Bette Davis (as Ma-Ma Mosquito), Humphrey Bogart, Ida Lupino, Lauren Bacall, John Garfield, Ann Sheridan, and George Raft?

But it was not to be, so Hawks and a particularly disappointed Feldman had to assess their fall-back position. They didn't know it for sure yet, but as it turned out they were sitting prettier than ever.

26

Not in the Script: *To Have and Have Not* and *The Big Sleep*

Slim was his ideal woman. The things Slim missed, he put into Bacall. —Christian Nyby

Howard Hawks tried many times to arrange a meeting between Ernest Hemingway and William Faulkner. The two great, proud authors always resisted the idea, however, so the closest Hawks, or anyone, ever came to getting them together was on the credits of *To Have and Have Not*. Hawks often claimed that when Hemingway turned down his offer to work on the adaptation and doubted that the director would ever be able to make a film from that novel, he taunted the author by saying, "I'll get Faulkner to do it; he can write better than you can anyway." This may well have been typical after-the-fact bravado on Hawks's part, but there is no doubt that he took some perverse pleasure in having his genuinely good friend Faulkner rewrite his more arm's-length pal Hem to his own specifications. However, it was a long time coming to that, and Faulkner was far from Hawks's mind when he initially got around to figuring out how he would crack the nut of *To Have and Have Not*.

After having first visited Hemingway in Key West in 1939, Hawks had been forced to bide his time in tackling the picture because of his split with Howard Hughes. Originally, Hawks intended to do it as his second picture for Hughes, after *The Outlaw*. Hughes knew that Hemingway was in urgent need of cash in May 1939, when the author was still trying to finish writing *For Whom the Bell Tolls*, and induced him to sell it outright for a paltry ten thousand dollars. Four years later, Hughes would part with the book only for an enormous profit, especially if Hawks was the buyer, and the tycoon ended up forcing Hawks and Feldman to cough up $92,500 for the rights. This was one literary deal on which the two partners weren't about to make a profit of their own; knowing full well what they had paid Hughes, Jack Warner reimbursed them for exactly the same amount.

For Hawks personally, this was unfortunate, because his reckless gambling losses, along with the expenses involved in the upkeep of Slim and Hog Canyon, had once again placed him in big hole. In June 1943, the IRS filed a levy with Warner Bros. against Hawks in order to collect $81,476 in unpaid back taxes. An arrangement was quickly made under which the studio initially withheld two thousand dollars per week from his five thousand-dollar salary; it was later altered to a 50 percent deduction of whatever his weekly paycheck might be (the amount varied between three and five thousand dollars, depending upon the advances he received at the start of a specific production). By September, Hawks urgently needed thirty thousand dollars in cash to pay off more gambling debts, and Warners obliged with an advance of 30 percent of his total salary for *To Have and Have Not*. Hawks thought nothing of withdrawing all the money from the household bank account to bet on races, leaving Slim holding the bag when trade and service people turned up demanding payment. As she put it, "His gambling was a compulsion that turned the entire household upside down.'

When *Battle Cry* fell apart, Hawks was ready to move along quickly to his next picture under his Warner Bros. contract, and they agreed on two films the director would do back-to-back. After the Hemingway story, Hawks would direct the film version of *Dark Eyes,* a 1943 Broadway farce about some Russian refugee actresses who, during a long weekend on a Long Island estate, convince a well-heeled capitalist to finance their play. Having paid far too much money for it, Warners was anxious to place it in reliable hands so that it would have a good chance to become a major film attraction.

To Have and Have Not suddenly became a "go" project when Humphrey Bogart agreed to star in it. After appearing in thirty-five films at Warner Bros. in seven years, Bogart had emerged overnight as a romantic, if still tough, leading man in *Casablanca,* and the studio was now anxious for him to follow up in the same vein. Barring any direct contribution from Hemingway himself—now a moot point in the wake of the huge success of *For Whom the Bell Tolls*—Hawks had always intended to use Jules Furthman on the adaptation, so shortly after *Battle Cry* came to its abrupt end, Furthman was put to work on the script, at $2,500 per week.

The way in which *To Have and Have Not* moved from page to screen has been analyzed by numerous scholars and from various points of view, with special attention to how the finished film does, and does not, reflect the contributions of Hemingway, Faulkner, and Hawks and, secondarily, Furthman and the whole *Casablanca* ethos. The various drafts of the screenplay have been combed over by several academics, notably by the Hemingway expert Frank M. Laurence, the Hawks specialist Gerald Mast, and the Faulkner scholar Bruce F. Kawin, who edited and wrote an introduction to the screenplay for publication. All of these writers offer valuable insights into the evolving, quicksilver nature of this most unexpected and near-miraculous adaptation, as do numerous other Hawks critics and commentators on the Bogart-Bacall phenomenon.

From almost every possible angle, however, this is the decisive film of Howard Hawks's career, the one in which nearly all of his vital interests intersect in some way. Hawks aficionados can argue about the relative differences in greatness between *To Have and Have Not* and, say, *Bringing Up Baby, His Girl Friday, Only Angels Have Wings,* and *Rio Bravo.* But if one isn't turned on by *To Have and Have Not,* if it doesn't make a viewer "see the light," as it were, then it is doubtful if any of his films will.

Hawks scholars can also use the making of the film, as well as the result, as a perfect example of the auteur theory in action. The director on this picture was surrounded by several highly powerful personalities and artistic voices: perhaps the two greatest novelists of the first half of the twentieth century, another very individualistic writer, a major star with his own indelible image, and a studio with, arguably, the strongest "personality" in the film industry. And yet, through the strength of his own will, Howard Hawks was able to bend all these exceptional forces to effect a maximum expression of his own worldview. No matter the degrees to which one can detect elements of Hemingway, Faulkner, *Casablanca,* or, for that matter, Conrad, Sternberg, and the demands of Hollywood escapism, the film *To Have and Have Not* is, beyond doubt, exactly the work its director intended it to be, and would have been nothing like this in the hands of anyone else.

Strictly from his own perspective, Hawks accomplished many things with *To Have and Have Not*: he finally worked from a story by his favorite modern author and stood it on its head, collaborated with his two preferred screenwriters, added some of the screen's most famous dialogue to the Hollywood anthology, elaborated the persona of one of the cinema's greatest stars, achieved his long-cherished dream of creating a new star from whole cloth, unintentionally launched a celebrated and enduring love affair, made a screen personality out of a popular song composer, named his leading man and lady after himself and his wife, had at least two affairs on the side (and did not have another he desired), made a great deal of money, and created a work that has stood the test of time as one of the great, audacious romantic-comic melodramas.

Even more than with most Hawks shoots, the filming was leisurely and very often rare, uproarious fun. But it was also highly charged, with erotic currents coursing in sometimes conflicting directions on and off the set, secrets dearly kept when the truth was clear to all, games being played between the filmmakers and the studio brass, a director alternately thrilled-with and infuriated at his young discovery, and writing that was barely staying one step ahead of the staging of scenes. If there are a half dozen film shoots in Hollywood history one might like to have witnessed—*Intolerance, Queen Kelly, Gone with the Wind, Citizen Kane,* and *Rebel Without a Cause* might rank among them—*To Have and Have Not* would certainly be one.

Hawks said that the one thing he liked about the novel *To Have and Have Not* was that "the two leading characters were marvelous in their relationship with each other," and he claimed that he and Hemingway spent several days knocking around ideas about how Harry Morgan and his wife, Marie, had met, which is what Hawks wanted to make the film about. Even if Hawks and Hemingway did have these discussions, very little of what the author suggested can possibly have ended up in the script, so far removed from Hemingway are the picture's characters and viewpoints. As James Agee commented at the time, "It has so little to do with Ernest Hemingway's novel that I see no point in discussing its faithfulness!"

In fact, the first four of the book's twenty-six chapters supply the film with some basic characters and what was intended, until the last minute, to be its setting: Harry Morgan, a struggling charter-fishing-boat operator during the Depression; his refusal to transport to Florida some Cuban revolutionaries, who then get gunned down; his rummy friend Eddy (later abetted by another mate, Albert); his pathetic day with the chiseling American client Mr. Johnson, who not only loses two big fish but Morgan's costly rod and reel, then skips town without paying him; Morgan's being forced, for financial reasons, to carry human cargo he could do without, and the Pearl of San Francisco Café, a waterfront hangout in Havana. Beyond this, however, the novel charts choppy waters the film never contemplated: Harry's loss of an arm and his boat, a wife and kids back in Key West, and a bifurcated focus between the desperate Morgan and a bunch of alcoholic society layabouts centered around a self-important writer, Richard Gordon, whom Hemingway cruelly based in part on John Dos Passos. The story is one of inexorable decline and destruction, climaxing thematically with Morgan's defeatist rumination, "No matter how, a man alone ain't got no fucking bloody chance."

Furthman's first screenplay draft, which he finished in early October and which ran an exhorbitant 207 pages, does reorient the story toward how Morgan meets a provocative young lady, but it also includes a heavy dose of *Only Angels Have Wings* and a precursor of *Rio Bravo* in the balance. Set in Cuba under Machado, most likely in early 1933, it begins with the Mr. Johnson fishing episode, includes the Rummy's line, "Was you ever bit by a dead bee?," and prominently features a couple, Decimo and Benicia, who own the Pearl of San Francisco and very closely resemble the Mexican owners of the hotel and bar in *Rio Bravo*, except that here Morgan was once involved with Benicia. Corinne (later Marie), bluntly described as a "wench," picks up Johnson in the bar and steals his wallet, occasioning the first encounter between Morgan and Corinne, who already call each other Steve and Slim. Three Cuban student revolutionaries offer Morgan five thousand dollars to run them to Cienfuegos in order to rob a bank, but he refuses, stating his political sympathies: "It's nothing to do with me one way or the other." Soon thereafter, one of the students mistakes Mr. Johnson for Morgan and guns him down, which brings in the Cuban police investigator Caesar, a "slick," sophisticated pal of Morgan's (later transformed into the film's obese Captain Renard). Morgan is forced to kill one of the revolutionaries after they kidnap the Rummy; then, in an episode similar to the smuggling of Chinese to Key West in the book, Morgan and a Negro mate carry a shipment of what they're told is liquor but is actually dope across the straits, where they are attacked and injured by Coast Guard guns. Unlike Morgan in the book, however, the film's leading man does not undergo an amputation.

A bit more than halfway through, two sophisticated New Yorkers arrive at the bar, Sam Essex and his "sleek, beautiful" twenty-five-year-old wife, Sylvia. Fulfilling the identical role that Rita Hayworth's Judith did in *Only Angels Have Wings*, Sylvia is the woman who jilted Morgan and then ran off with his best friend, who has since died and been replaced by Essex. Morgan and Sylvia engage in some ferocious verbal sparring, making clear that the spark is still there, prompting Corinne to get drunk. Corinne has a real liquor problem and has good reason to feel inferior to the much cooler and wiser Sylvia. Essex intends to hire Morgan to take him fishing, but the revolutionaries kidnap the Rummy again and Morgan is finally obliged to take them, with Essex and the Rummy in tow, to Cienfuegos, where the Cubans pull off the bank job. With some overlapping of incidents from the novel, the aftermath is messy, as Morgan again abjures any political kinship with the insurrectionists, the Rummy is killed, and Morgan, with Essex's help, manages to turn the tables on the rebel criminals.

Back at the hotel, Sylvia is waiting for Morgan in his room and, in a warped and cynical reworking of the *Casablanca* climax, proposes a sneaky scheme in which Morgan will come along with her and Essex back to New York, her husband will set Morgan up in a job, and then Sylvia will leave Essex. But Morgan now likes Essex, and Sylvia correctly guesses that Morgan is taken with Corinne, so she hands him her pearl necklace to give to Corinne with a parting line from *Othello:* "The robbed who smiles steals something from the thief."

As Bruce Kawin has pointed out, aside from specific plot and character points, the overriding difference between Hemingway's and the Hawks-Furthman version is that the Harry Morgan of the novel is progressively beaten down by events until he is destroyed, whereas the film's Morgan, specifically written with Bogart in mind, manages to prevail and come out on top after his assorted setbacks (the only irreversible tragedy, the Rummy's killing, is eliminated in later drafts). Hawks always detested stories about "losers," which is probably the main reason he disliked Hemingway's novel in the first place, so it was elemental for him to turn Harry Morgan into a winner. It is also clear that Hawks and Furthman originally intended to create two women characters of equal weight who kept outdoing each other in insolence and toughness; at this stage, Hawks didn't know who might be capable of filling the roles and therefore wasn't certain which to emphasize, but he had his hopes.

"Slim" would never have come to life on the screen as she did without Slim. In the February 1943, issue of *Harper's Bazaar*, Slim Hawks noticed a full-page color photograph of a striking, frank-looking young woman posed in front of a door marked "American Red Cross Blood Donor Service," a woman she felt had "a bit of the panther about her." Knowing her Svengali husband was looking for another girl to mold and develop into an actress, and quite certain that he would respond favorably to this kid who looked so very like herself, she wasn't surprised when, upon seeing the model, he called Charlie Feldman at once to have him contact her and arrange to bring her to California for a test.

The legend has come down through the years that Hawks asked his secretary to find out about her and that, instead, she mistakenly sent her a ticket, landing eighteen-year-old Betty Jean Perske on the unsuspecting director's doorstep. (the Bacall name, which came from her mother's side of the family, had just one "l" until Hawks added a second one to make the pronunciation clear; he also came up with her new first name.) However, Bacall makes it clear that her Uncle Jack was fielding several offers in response to the photograph and accepted Feldman and Hawks's invitation west only after due deliberation and first meeting with David O. Selznick's New York representative and turning down an offer from Columbia. Uncle Jack was familiar with Hawks's very successful recent films and recommended accepting his offer of the trip plus fifty dollars a week until the test was made.

Bacall arrived at Los Angeles' Union Station on April 6 and was taken directly to meet Feldman at his office (some biographies of Bogart and Bacall have her going straight to Warner Bros. for tests, which is patently absurd). Put up at the modest Claremont Hotel, in Westwood, she dined with Feldman that night and quickly developed a terrific crush on him, but felt safe because he was married. The next day, she met Hawks for the first time, at lunch with Feldman at the Brown Derby in Beverly Hills, a block from the agent's office. Although Bacall was shaking with nerves, Hawks was impressed as she related the routine details of her life to him. He also flatly rejected Feldman's suggestions about fixing her teeth, emphasizing again that he preferred a natural look. For her part, Bacall found Hawks imposing and terrifying, "an odd person," undemonstrative, "inscrutable," and "very sure of himself."

With Hawks preoccupied with *Corvette K-225* and *Battle Cry*, his new discovery's test kept being put off, first for a week, then for another. Entertained and catered to attentively by Feldman and his wife, Jean, Bacall met with Hawks occasionally, was mesmerized by his boasts about what he done for other actresses, and was absorbed by his many stories about his various cinematic triumphs. She had no reason not to believe them all, but even at this stage she noticed that "he always came out on top, he always won." She was stunned when Hawks made a casual anti-Semitic comment; it suddenly occurred to her that Hawks didn't know she was Jewish, and now, terrified of losing her chance, she determined to keep it a secret. One day sometime later when Hawks took her to lunch, she was caught up short once again when he abruptly said, "Do you notice how noisy it is in here suddenly? That's because Leo Forbstein just walked in—Jews always make more noise." Again, she said nothing but was so upset that she confided it to Feldman, who just laughed it off and said, "That's the way Howard is. Just don't pay any attention to it." Confronted years later with Bacall's charge of anti-Semitism, several of Hawks's Jewish friends swore that Hawks always knew Bacall was Jewish and calculatedly dropped these comments just to see how she would react.

At the end of April, Bacall went for the first time to Warner Bros., where Hawks told the makeup artist in no uncertain terms that he did not want his protégée's eyebrows plucked, hairline shaved, or teeth straightened. He also ran her through a scene from *Claudia* with Charles Drake, one of his actors from *Air Force*. The next day Hawks shot a full-blown test and decided at once to sign Bacall to a seven-year contract, which he shared equally with Slim, beginning at one hundred dollars a week and escalating by the end to $1,250. With this, the young actress took a small apartment in Beverly Hills within walking distance of Feldman's office, brought her mother out from New York, and embarked upon Hawks's patented training program for lowering and strengthening her voice. As she remembered him explaining his approach, he said, "When a woman gets excited or emotional she tends to raise her voice. Now, there is nothing more unattractive than screeching. I want you to train your voice in such a way that even if you have a scene like that your voice will remain low." Bacall's method was to project passages from *The Robe* into the empty canyons off of Mulholland Drive in as low and loud a voice as possible. Bacall's speaking voice tended to be low anyway, but this training, along with her ceaseless smoking, accentuated it and helped keep it that way.

By summer, Hawks was considering his discovery for the part of the pregnant Russian pilot in "The Diary of a Red Army Woman" episode of *Battle Cry*. All through these months of waiting, Bacall took singing lessons, socialized frequently with the Feldmans, soaked up Hawks's wisdom about acting and filmmaking, came to like Slim enormously, and, in September, turned nineteen. That season, the Hawkses threw one of their few enormous Hollywood parties, with innumerable celebrities in attendance but, as Bacall noted to her consternation, virtually no Jews, an almost impossible anomaly in Hollywood. "Slim told me that her husband didn't want any Jews in his house," Bacall revealed. "The only Jew he let in was Feldman." When *To Have and Have Not* was set as Hawks's next picture, he was tempted to use Bacall in one of the roles, but he still wasn't sure about which woman's role to favor, nor if Bacall would be up to carrying the picture paired one-on-one with Bogart. Wanting to see how they looked together, Hawks took Bacall to the set of *Passage to Marseille* to meet Bogart, but it was a brief, unremarkable encounter. Bacall had never found Bogart attractive or particularly interesting on-screen, and the same held true in person; her dream was to costar in a movie with Cary Grant.

Furthman completed his second script draft by the end of December, reduced in length by nearly sixty pages. Here, Slim seems like more of a straight-out prostitute than ever, and the degree of insolence between her and Morgan is cranked up high from the outset, with Morgan objecting when she calls him Steve, her responding by changing it to Stephen, and him one-upping her by calling her Skinny instead of Slim. Eddie's part is enlarged, Colonel Caesar is replaced by Captain Renard, Sylvia is transformed into Helen, who now has no husband, and the piano player Cricket is introduced. The sense of Morgan's and Slim's financial desperation is increased, and the ending is changed, with Morgan taking the decision to leave Helen and return to Slim into his own hands, rather than letting Helen sacrifice herself.

Toward the end of the year, Hawks told Warner Bros. he wanted to go to Cuba to consult with Hemingway, not so much about the script, which could only have roiled the writer, but to engage his help in smoothing over any problems with local politicians. There was already some concern that a major Hollywood film depicting crime, revolutionary students, and general licentiousness in Cuba would not foster goodwill between these allies during wartime, and Hemingway made an initial gesture to mend matters by talking to State Department representatives in Havana and by offering to intercede with top Cuban officials, including Batista himself. Hawks also insisted that he wanted to scout locations for a second unit, but Warners flatly ruled out any foreign shooting.

In any event, Hawks did not make the trip, and while Slim oversaw a full array of Christmas festivities at Hog Canyon, he concentrated on preparing Bacall for her test to see if she was capable of standing up to Bogart. For the test, Hawks had ready what later became known as the "whistle" scene, ultimately the most famous in the picture. Beginning with Morgan, played by John Ridgely in the test, and Marie about to call it a night, it has her coming into his room and offering him a bottle, then making the first move and kissing him, him asking why she did that, her answering "I've been wondering whether I'd like it," kissing him again, and then uttering the famous parting lines: "What's more, you don't have to do anything. Not a thing. Oh, maybe just whistle. You know how to whistle, don't you, Steve? You just put your lips together and blow." (Her equally famous "It's even better when you help" was added to the scene only during the actual shooting.)

Hawks always claimed in interviews that this "was a scene I wrote as a test for her. I had no idea it was going to be in the picture, but it worked out so well that I wanted to use it." Slim had a different view, remembering that her husband used not only her name, look, and clothes for the character but her manner of speaking and expressions. She said that Furthman insisted that she deserved script cocredit for *To Have and Have Not* "because so much of the material is yours. The character certainly is," and Slim implied that many of the most memorable lines came right out of her mouth. Hawks or, more likely, Furthman may also have had a long memory, since the "whistle" scene dialogue is very similar to that in the intertitles for a sequence in Rudolph Valentino's last film, the 1926 *The Son Of The Sheik*, which concludes with the line, "When I want her, I whistle."

Unless Bacall completely crashed in the test, Hawks was pretty sure going in that he wanted to use her in the film; the main question was whether he would have to split the female interest between two roles or place all his chips on her. Warner Bros., however, which preferred developing its own stars to indulging the whims of prima donna directors, was opposed to Hawks's discovery on principle, and Jack Warner's lieutenant, Steve Trilling, told his boss that he would "try, as much as possible, to talk him out of Betty Becall [sic]." All the studio could realistically do, however, was ask Hawks to test some of its own actresses along with his discovery, so on December 31, Hawks made short tests of the aspiring actresses Dolores Moran, Carol Matthews, and Georgette McKee, along with Bacall.

After rehearsing all through New Year's, however, Hawks gave over all day on January 3 to Bacall. She and Ridgely rehearsed all morning with the cinematographer, Sid Hickox, and a full crew working as if on an actual shoot, and after lunch Hawks spent six hours slowly taking them through the entire scene for the cameras. Hawks was patient and, in his understated way, endlessly encouraging to the novice, making her feel, as she said, "secure." By the end of the day, Bacall felt she had done well; for Hawks's part, he was positive now that he'd found a sensation, and it was only a matter of showing it to Feldman, Warner, and Bogart before he could tell his terribly anxious young hopeful that she had the role.

The rest of the casting quickly fell into place. When the Sylvia/Helen role was meant to be as, or more, important, than Marie, there was some talk of casting Ann Sheridan, whom Hawks had recommended to Warner after testing her for *The Road to Glory* years before. But the diminishing size of the part, as well as Sheridan's suspension from Warners at that moment, tabled this idea. No longer in need of a big name, Hawks became interested, in more ways than one, in Dolores Moran, and decided that her fleshier, more voluptuous looks would contrast effectively with the willowy

Bacall. Walter Brennan was the only possible choice for Eddie the rummy and he was borrowed, not without the usual difficulty, from Goldwyn. Dan Seymour, a rotund former nightclub performer who had just played the doorman at Sydney Greenstreet's Blue Parrott club in *Casablanca*, was originally tested to play one of the Cuban revolutionaries, which he found absurd. Not long after, he said, "I got a script and I read it, and it's nothing like the scene I did. On the front it said, 'Dan Seymour, Capt. Renard.' I read it and found out it was the Vichy policeman." Hawks personally out-fitted him in a beret, requested that he be padded to bulk him up even beyond his 305 pounds, and asked that he use only the slightest of French accents. Marcel Dalio, the superb French actor who had also appeared in *Casablanca*, was an easy choice to play Gerard, or "Frenchy."

As for Hoagy Carmichael, the enormously successful and personable songwriter had written tunes for numerous films and had performed a bit in one but had never harbored any ambitions as an actor. Virtual neigh-bors, Slim and Carmichael's wife, Ruth, became very friendly, and the Carmichaels were shortly frequent guests at Hog Canyon. "I was rather fascinated with Hawks because I knew he had what you call class and under-standing and intelligence," Carmichael said. "I was delighted we could be friends. Before I knew it, when I was in New York, I got a wire from him asking me if I'd like to be in the picture." When Carmichael got back to California, Hawks shrewdly made him feel comfortable by testing him playing "How Little We Know" on the piano, accompanied by Bacall. Carmichael was right at home sitting at the keyboards, and no one could have seemed more natural portraying a sympathetic saloon pianist than the genuine article himself. Among his crew members, most important to him was his favorite assistant director, Jack Sullivan, who set the quiet, some-what formal tone on the set as much as Hawks himself did. Dan Seymour described him as "a deadly Irishman and, just like Hawks, he never showed any emotion. He was not someone you could be intimate with." The pic-ture also marked Hawks's first collaboration with the film editor Christian Nyby, who became a good friend and longtime associate of Hawks. A protegé of Harry Warner's, Nyby was always on the outs with Jack, who fired the young cutter, only to find himself overruled. Reserved and physically not dissimilar to Hawks, Nyby, at his director's request, was on the set for most of the shooting. "Howard never gave me cutting instructions," Nyby said. "He felt it was up to me to do my job."

Hawks kept Furthman working on the script through January and into February but, feeling he could use a couple of extra minds bearing down on the material, called in two mystery-writer friends, Cleve F. Adams and Whitman Chambers, to provide additional help. Working separately, they came up with very little and, in Adams's case, less than that, as he proceeded to replace Furthman's great, tough dialogue with a weak watered-down alternative. For his part, Furthman got through most of one more revision by mid-January and delivered his final solo draft in mid-February. Still set in Cuba, this version beefed up Marie's role even further, modeling her more explicitly on the characters he had written for Dietrich in *Morocco* and *Shanghai Express*, and even stealing a couple of his own lines from the latter. When Shanghai Lily is asked why she is going to Shanghai, she flippantly replies, "To buy a hat," the same reason Marie was now given for coming to Cuba. He also attempted to recycle that film's most famous line, "It took more than one man to change my name to Shanghai Lily," but *Shanghai Express* had been made before the Code, and this did not slip past the watchful eye of Joseph Breen. Another lift, this time from *Morocco*, was Marie's sarcastic remark when she sees Morgan carrying a woman who has fainted: "You trying to guess her weight?"

Now that he felt Bacall had what it took to put his idea of the character over, Hawks urged Furthman to push Marie's hard-edged dialogue and one-upsmanship lines as far as he could. Explaining his intentions to Bogart, Hawks said, "You are about the most insolent man on the screen and I'm going to make the girl a little more insolent than you are." When Bogart told him there was "fat chance of that," Hawks replied, "I've got a better than fat chance. . . . In every scene you play with her, she's going to walk out and leave you with egg on your face."

Among Furthman's other changes for this draft, the "whistle" scene is worked in, although in a different way. Also in desperation, Morgan agrees to transport some Japanese for a sinister Mr. Kato, whom he subsequently kills. On a second illicit voyage with the Cuban bank robbers, one of them kills Eddie, but Morgan manages to shoot them before they do the same to him, whereupon he returns the stolen loot to the authorities. At the end, Helen still believes Morgan is going to return to New York with her until Morgan changes his mind just before getting on the seaplane with her.

With shooting due to begin in two weeks, Warner Bros. was obliged to send the script to moral watchdog Joseph Breen; the studio was not pleased by his response. In a six-page, single-spaced rebuke of Furthman's screenplay, Breen wrote, "The general unacceptability of this story is emphasized by its overall *low tone* and by the suggestion that your sympathetic lead, Morgan, is a murderer, who is permitted to go off unpunished." Objecting strenuously to the "scummy" feel and "a kind of flavor of 'pimpery' to the entire proceedings," he insisted that all the characters be "*softened*," that all the women characters be changed "to get away from any possible suggestion that they are prostitutes," that the studio "remove from the script the business of the men sleeping in the women's rooms," and that Morgan's killings of Kato and the Cubans be clearly made acts of self-defense. Breen then enumerated three dozen instances in which the script willfully violated the Production Code, making it impossible to approve unless many changes were made.

But another problem suddenly sprang up that, for a moment, at least, seriously threatened the picture's proceeding. The Office of the Coordinator of Inter-American Affairs decided that the nature of the story ran directly counter to the interests of the United States' Good Neighbor Policy with Central and South America and intimated that the film would therefore not be granted an export license, thereby placing all overseas markets off-limits. Jack Warner wanted to cancel the production, but Hawks obtained permission from Inter-American Affairs to set the action in Martinique, a French-controlled territory that lay outside its domain. Hawks called on his most resourceful script doctor, William Faulkner, to perform some emergency surgery.

Faulkner solved numerous problems on the script. Having recently written an unproduced epic screenplay for the studio on Charles de Gaulle and the Free French, the writer was au courant with issues regarding the anti-Vichy movement and saw at once how the the conflicts in *To Have and Have Not* could be updated and altered to reflect war intrigue in the Western hemisphere. The film would now begin politically, with some local blacks appreciating the large "V" torn into a Pétain poster. The Cuban revolutionaries cum criminal terrorists would become members of the Gaullist underground, the local authorities became personified by Captain Renard, both smuggling missions were eliminated, Helen and her husband were "Casablancanized" into resistance fighters in need of Morgan's help, Marie became his sole romantic interest, and Eddie was not only beefed up as a character but spared from dying as well. Faulkner solved the problem of sleeping arrangements by simply having everyone stay in the same hotel, and he facilitated the Morgan-Marie encounters by placing their rooms directly opposite each other. He also cut down the quantity of Marie's drinking and, by jettisoning the smuggling, effectively did away with what appeared to be Morgan's murderous side. To suit Hawks's taste for compressed storytelling, Faulkner also boiled the time frame down to a very eventful three days, a far cry from the three seasons of the novel.

Faulkner had about a week to make these major conceptual adjustments; the rest would have to be done as shooting progressed. Between January 19 and February 16, the ever-reliable Roy Davidson shot twelve days of second-unit footage of fishing, boat maneuvers, rum running, and robbery coverage, off Balboa and Laguna Beach; after a break, he subsequently shot five more days of related material. Principal photography began on Tuesday, February 29, with scenes involving Morgan, the American fisherman Johnson, and sixty-five extras in the San Francisco Café. The very next day brought the first exchange between Bogart and Bacall, in which Morgan meets her with Gerard in the hallway and tosses her a box of matches so she can light her cigarette. Bacall was beside herself with nerves, trembling so much that she couldn't even catch the matchbox or light her cigarette without her hand shaking. However, Bogart was a prince, making light of it and joking around with her until she relaxed. The next day was devoted to the two stars' first scene alone, with Morgan roughly threatening to take Johnson's wallet away from Marie, then quarreling with her about what she's done and how they will dispose of the money. At this early stage, Hawks took things slowly to make sure the two actors got off on the right foot, and he made things easier for the still nervous Bacall by breaking the dialogue down into very short shots. In the beginning, he uncharacteristically did as many as fifteen takes of each setup, introducing a fair amount of new dialogue into the scenes on the set, shaping the scenes, and his new star's performance, until he was fully satisfied. Eventually, as Bacall's confidence grew, along with Hawks's faith in her, he was able to reduce the number of takes.

The modus operandi had Faulkner working just one to three days ahead of the shooting. Generally, the reclusive writer preferred to work in Hawks's bungalow, which was directly across from Hal Wallis's. Occasionally, when a scene hadn't quite gelled, the director asked him to the set, where they would confer sotto voce or repair to Hawks's portable office whenever Hawks needed a line, and where Faulkner could quietly observe the efficient work of the script girl, Meta Carpenter, with whom he had resumed his passionate love affair from the 1930s after the failure of her marriage to the pianist Wolfgang Rebner. Dan Seymour recalled that Faulkner would sometimes sit in a chair next to Hawks, who would ask, "'How did that sound, Bill?' Faulkner would nod, go off for a shot of Scotch and come back with a new line that was always better." Faulkner also made a point of visiting the set whenever Hoagy Carmichael was due to perform.

In her autobiography, Bacall cogently described what she considered Hawks's "brilliantly creative work method." Each morning, "We would sit around with only the work light on and read through the scene, and he'd throw in lines that he or Slim or someone had come up with the night before. We'd try things, or he'd say, 'Why don't you try that?,' or someone would suggest something and he'd say fine. He always had Furthman around because he always said, 'If there are five ways to play a scene, Furthman will always come up with a sixth.'" Several published accounts have stated that Furthman left the picture after Faulkner was engaged, but in fact he was always on call to help punch up dialogue or find a new angle on a scene; for example, he completely rewrote the bullet-removal scene in the cellar, including its withering repartee between Marie and Helen, just before it was shot in mid-April. Only after the actors had digested all the changes and worked out their movements did Hawks bring in the cinematographer, Sid Hickox, to set the lighting and camera angles. Dan Seymor said that Meta Carpenter had the hardest job because she was always "furiously writing down everything while Hawks would suggest ways of doing it. . . . Lots of times, only a half hour before shooting a scene would we decide how it would be done." Bacall considered it "the perfect way for movie actors to work," but only a director with Hawks's confidence and power at the studio could get away with such a relaxed approach in the film-factory climate of the era.

Meta Carpenter, a vastly experienced pro by this time, considered this approach "a dangerous way to make a motion picture" and credited the fact that it worked this time to Faulkner's industriousness, craftiness, and superb sense of story structure. While the writer slaved away to add heart to Furthman's clever, playful, often intoxicatingly sexy surfaces, the company of filmmakers and actors had an exhilarating time, charged with professional as well as personal tensions. Artistically, the film was a high-wire act in which one of the nation's great writers created a taut line on which a great director and a core group of uniquely inspired actors danced some breathtaking variations, always landing on their toes. Emotionally, the arrows of desire, suspicion, jealousy, and resentment were pointing in potentially deadly cross patterns.

Unlike his relationships with Gary Cooper, Cary Grant, and, later, John Wayne, Hawks was not a close friend of Bogart's. They scarcely knew each other before starting work together, they were at opposing ends politically, and Bogart didn't hunt, ride motorcycles, or indulge in Hawks's other would-be manly pursuits. As if to show that he could boss around even the toughest actor in Hollywood, Hawks self-servingly told a story about how he noticed that Bogart returned from lunch on the first day having had several drinks. He immediately upbraided the actor, saying, "Either I get a new leading man or you get a new director. I don't want anybody who's gonna drink during the day. I don't think anybody's that good. I have to get the best out of 'em, and if I don't get it, I don't want to make the picture." Thus chastened, according to Hawks, Bogart said he wouldn't drink, paving the way for a strong working relationship in which Hawks actively sought the star's suggestions, as he always did with anyone he felt was "any good."

Bogart's domestic situation was founded upon drinking and fighting. Not a philanderer in the Cooper-Fleming-Hecht-Hawks mold, Bogart had twice been married to and divorced from actresses before wedding Mayo Methot, another actress, who then let herself go physically, could land only minor film roles, and could keep up with her hard-drinking husband shot for shot. By this time, six years into their marriage, a customary evening chez Bogart consisted of Methot's becoming so loaded that she hurled both insults and objects such as ashtrays at her husband, often driving him out of the house. Once she actually stabbed him, and another time she attempted suicide by cutting her wrists. They were known around town as the Battling Bogarts, but despite the chaos and unhappiness, Bogart felt a strong responsibility toward his wife and had not really come close to leaving her, much as he might have thought about it. According to the biographer Joe Hyams, Hawks once asked Bogart if he could get an erection without first having a fight with Mayo. At first taken aback by Hawks's bluntness, he then replied, "You know, I guess you're right. I probably couldn't."

Nearly all the scenes shot during the first two weeks involved both Bogart and Bacall, and no one in their vicinity was oblivious to the heat lightning that blazed between them almost from the outset. Meta Carpenter, who was there every second, said, "That Humphrey Bogart and Betty Bacall were in love was evident after the first days of shooting." The publicist Mickey Seltzer observed, "The electricity between them was not to be believed. It was so tangible you could feel it in the air. I knew something was going to come of it." There were telltale signs, such as the flowers that appeared daily in Bacall's dressing room, the way each of them would hang around the set to watch the other work, the daily lunches. For her part, Bacall testified, "I don't know how it happened — it was almost imperceptible." She said that around the third week of shooting, Bogart, who was done for the day, came into her dressing room to say good night, impulsively kissed her, and asked her for her phone number, which she gave him and which he called later that night. (From the start, they carried over their screen names, Steve and Slim, into their private life.) Bacall is also sure that the sharp-eyed Hawks picked up on their involvement "fairly early on" and decided to use it to the film's advantage, even if he was boiling about it inside.

And boiling he was. As Bacall became increasingly more attentive to Bogart than to her mentor, a disturbing combination of resentment, jealousy, insulted ego, and wounded pride grew in Hawks, fostered by the knowledge that there was nothing he could do about it. Bacall knew that Hawks "had quite a crush on me, but of course he was tangling with the wrong people because there was no way he was going to get anywhere, with Bogie and me involved. He wanted to be my Svengali. He told Bogie to get a room at the Ambassador, he threatened to send me to Monogram. He was really burned up. Bogie always said he'd never send me to Monogram, he'd never do the things he threatened to do. He finally forgave me, but he couldn't handle it."

Part of Hawks's fantasy about discovering a nobody and molding her into the ultimate movie star was that she would naturally fall in love with him, but in Bacall's case he was thwarted on every front. After all, his wife had spotted her first and had become fast friends with the youngster, perhaps partly a preemptive move at first but obviously a genuine one as well, given that the two women remained very close until Slim's death nearly fifty years later. Slim turned up on the set of *To Have and Have Not* with unaccustomed frequency; Dan Seymour said, to coin a phrase, "Slim watched Hawks like a hawk." And, unbeknownst to him, Bacall simply didn't find him appealing "that way." Bacall admitted, "He was an attractive man because he was so talented and smart and successful, and some women would naturally be attracted to that, although I wasn't. He was remote." It was against Hawks's nature to make the first move with a woman, but so infatuated was he with Bacall that early on he persuaded an intermediary to urge her to come see him. One thing Bacall didn't include in her autobiography was her belief that one of the reasons Hawks always kept Furthman around was that the writer acted as a pimp for his boss. "Furthman suggested to me that I give Howard a call," Bacall said. "He said Howard would like it. But I said no way."

In fact, through her entire life, Bacall "was always terrified" of Howard Hawks: "I always was nervous around him. He was always very intimidating." Although there was no way Hawks could remain oblivious to what was going on between Bacall and Bogart, Bacall, not sure what he knew, desperately tried to keep the relationship a secret, just as Bogart needed to keep his wife in the dark about things if he had any hope of getting her to agree to a divorce. Bitterly aware that his protégée was slipping away from him just as he was brilliantly fashioning her image for worldwide adoration, Hawks nonetheless kept his anger on a low boil through most of the shooting, professionally capitalizing on the sparks flying between his costars on the set and, by extension, on-screen. Shortly before the wrap Hawks ordered Bacall to his house one night and, in Slim's presence, dressed her down for her irresponsible and ungrateful behavior, threatened to sell her contract to Monogram, the lowest of the lowly Poverty Row companies, and predicted that Bogart would forget about her as soon as shooting was completed. "He had this very tight-lipped way of talking when he was mad," Bacall vividly remembered. "He didn't raise his voice, but he could be rough."

In interviews decades later, Hawks painted over all the melodrama and never let on to his own hurt feelings; he even pretended that he had helped engineer the romance and urged it along for the sake of the picture: "Without Bogie's help I couldn't have done what I did with Bacall. Not many actors would sit around and wait while a girl steals a scene. But he fell in love with the girl and the girl with him, and that made it easy." One of Hawks's more astounding claims, given Bacall's perceptions of his anti-Semitism, was his later insistence that he warned Bogart to curb his own slurs against Jews if he wanted to have a chance with Bacall; according to this story, Bogart had no idea Bacall was Jewish at the onset of their romance and only learned when Hawks told him. Ironically, Bacall was doing everything she could to prevent Hawks from finding out, lest he lose interest in her professionally. Knowing details of Bogart's life with Mayo Methot, Hawks also boasted that he instructed Bacall never, but never, to fight with Bogart if she wanted to keep him.

If things didn't go Hawks's way with Bacall, nor was his life with Slim altogether to his liking at this point. Bacall felt that Hawks was not so much in love with Slim as he was "very proud of her. He loved the way she looked, she was so beautiful and classy." But Bacall "never felt a sense of fun or sex between them," and she learned that Slim knew all about her husband's affair with Dolores Moran, whom Slim derisively referred to as "Dollarass Moron." It is possible that Hawks launched into this casual relationship partly out of spite when he realized he would be getting nowhere with Bacall. During the shoot, he also had a fling with a tall, brown-haired extra named Dorothy Davenport, whom Dan Seymour remembered as "a Slim type."

Despite the deceit and ill-feeling revolving around Hawks, the contagious thrill sparked by Bogart and Bacall's romance defined the prevailing mood of the shoot. Despite the pressures they were under, the two stars joked around constantly at work and met surreptitiously at the end of the day and sometimes at night. William Faulkner, who would receive his first screen credit in eight years on *To Have and Have Not*, achieved new regard in Hollywood thanks to the picture, and he and Meta Carpenter found a measure of the happiness they had once shared, until he abruptly announced to her that his wife and daughter would be coming out for the summer. Walter Brennan was a joy as always, Dan Seymour and Marcel Dalio were delighted to be playing prominent parts in a major picture, and Hoagy Carmichael could hardly believe that he was actually acting in a picture; as Bacall said, the songwriter "looked up to Howard so much, and Howard made an image for him that he'd never had before."

For her part, Bacall couldn't get over the irony of being a virginal, nineteen-year-old "nice Jewish girl" cast as a sexually knowing woman of the world and thrown in among these tough, seasoned men. Like the persona that was being created for her, The Look, as it came to be known around the world, began as a false pose as well. Because she was so nervous at first, Bacall held her head down to minimize her shaking, then would look up with her eyes without lifting her chin. When enhanced by Hickox's lighting, this proved so provocatively sexy that Hawks would just instruct Bacall to give Bogart The Look and she would know what to do.

It took Bogart to wake Bacall up to the fact that much of what Hawks had been regaling her with for months was purest fiction. "Very early on, Bogie said, 'You don't believe the stories Howard tells, do you?' I said, 'Of course I do. Why not?' Bogie told me that he made things up as he went along. Bogie never believed any of the stories Howard told." After this, Bacall was able to deduce that Hawks "had quite an active fantasy life. In his stories, he always won, he always came out on top. He got his release through his work and his inventions. His inventions in his work, I think, meant everything to him, and I guess he more or less succeeded in making them his life.

"He was a great director, as long as I did the work," Bacall reflected. "I thought he was the best real movie director I ever worked with. I think he was really way ahead of anyone else in terms of dealing with men and women. He had great wit in dealing with them. The films don't date at all, they're completely modern. He believed that women should behave like men. He gave you a great sense of security that made you feel like you'd come out on top. And it was fun." Pranks were the order of the day. Hoagy

Carmichael played the whole picture with a toothpick in his mouth, which added a memorable aspect to his character. "It was a gimmick, like George Raft and his nickel," he observed. "I thought of it and Howard didn't say he liked it, but didn't say he didn't."

As per Hawks's policy, Jack Warner was not welcome on the set. Despite this, he called down one day to announce that he was bringing over the gossip columnist Louella Parsons. As Dan Seymour remembered it, the assistant director, Jack Sullivan, "told Hawks, who went out the door, got into his car and left the lot. Then Sullivan sent all of us home. By the time Jack Warner walked on the stage with Louella, Howard Hawks, Bogie and Bacall were gone. Jack Sullivan said, 'We're through for the day.' Michael Curtiz heard about this and tried to get away with it, but he couldn't. Warner and the others were afraid of Howard Hawks because he was so cool."

Bacall remained surprised that Hawks actually wanted her to sing in the picture. Her vocal training was coming along, but no one knew if she would sound good enough for her singing voice to be used, so Hawks kept his options open. To find a singer whose voice would match up plausibly with Bacall's husky tones was not easy, and quite a few were tried, including the deep-voiced black singer Lillian Randolph, Dolores Hope, and the teenaged Andy Williams. Williams finally prevailed, and it was his voice that emanated from the playback machine on May 1 when Hawks at last came to filming "How Little We Know." As was customary, Bacall sang along while Carmichael tinkered away on the silent keyboard, and as she did, Hawks liked what he heard and told her to keep going. When she was done, he decided to record her again singing the song, so, despite the legend that has come down over the years that Andy Williams's voice was dubbed over Bacall's (a legend so generally accepted that it became a correct answer on *Jeopardy*), the truth is that Bacall sang her own numbers in *To Have and Have Not*.

As he preferred to do, Hawks shot as much in sequence as possible; with Faulkner rewriting as they went, it would have been difficult to do otherwise. Warner Bros. scheduled the production for forty-eight days, but with the playful approach brought to this picture, as well as the care Hawks lavished upon his new star, shooting was already six days behind schedule after just fifteen days of work. Hawks filmed the key pair of scenes in Marie's and Morgan's rooms, ending with the "whistle" line, over three days, March 27–29, at the beginning of the fifth week, a week or two after Bogart and Bacall had started their relationship for real. On some of the key shots featuring Bacall, Hawks made between nine and thirteen takes, an unusual number for him, but worthwhile to ensure that he got exactly what he wanted from her. Quite apart from his romantic interest in her, Bogart got a charge out of acting opposite Bacall: "She gives you back what you send. It's like a fast game of tennis. If you put over a good ball and somebody muffs it, you can't have a good game. But if somebody drives it back hard, you drive back hard, and pretty soon you have a good game."

Shooting continued through April on the scenes set in the cellar and the San Francisco Café, with the two big musical numbers, "Hong Kong Blues" and "How Little We Know," staged near the end. Filming finally ended on May 10 after sixty-two days, fourteen days behind schedule. The original budget of $1,056,182 was exceeded by some 50 percent, as the picture, including overhead, cost $1,557,655. Hawks received his $100,000 according to his Warner Bros. contract, $30,000 of which had been advanced to him up front to cover some pressing gambling debts. The egregious discrepancy between the two writers' salaries bluntly points up the penuriousness of William Faulkner's contract with Warners: Jules Furthman earned $47,750 for his work, while Faulkner received a mere $5,000, or less than Whitman Chambers and Cleve Adams got for their momentary and insignificant contributions to the script. Warner Bros. issued Hawks and Feldman a flat $125 per week to cover their payments to Bacall.

All along the way, Hawks cagily held Bacall back from the press, carefully plotting to build public interest in a slow crescendo that would reach its peak with the film's release. Two fabulously successful sneak previews convinced Warners that they had something special. The studio's publicity chief, Charles Einfeld, went bonkers when he saw the film with an audience, reporting to his staff, "Nothing like Bacall has been seen on the screen since Garbo and Dietrich. This is one of the biggest and hottest attractions we have ever had. If this sounds like I'm overboard, well I am." For months, newspapers and magazines stirred up interest in "The Girl with 'The Look,'" while, in Hollywood, Bacall endured a summer during which she could find only furtive moments with Bogart, who was with his wife on his yacht off Newport. Hawks was convinced that he had been right all along in seeing that Bogart would never leave his wife for Bacall. Furthermore, he was so pleased with Bacall's work in the film that he decided he could forgive her dalliance and agree to Jack Warner's request for an immediate follow-up for Bogart and Bacall, certain that she would rebound to his sage influence.

Ever since giving the go-ahead on *To Have and Have Not*, the studio had been expecting Hawks to follow it with *Dark Eyes*, the stage piece that had three wonderful lead roles for women. Initially, Hawks and the intended producer, Robert Buckner, had been intrigued by the Warners' intentions of casting Garbo, Dietrich, and Fanny Brice, but this fanciful idea had fallen by the wayside, and now the studio wanted to proceed with some combination of Alexis Smith, Faye Emerson, Ann Sheridan, and Jane Wyman, all-American girls totally unsuited to play sophisticated Continental "artistes." Hawks momentarily turned his attention to two other projects, *Pillow to Post*, a wartime housing-shortage comedy, and *Chicken Every Sunday*, an adaptation of a play about a family boardinghouse in Tucson, circa 1900.

None of these projects were suitable for Bogart and Bacall, however, so, in his limousine riding back from the first *To Have and Have Not* preview, Jack Warner asked Hawks if he had anything in mind. In fact, Hawks had already kicked ideas around with Faulkner and had come up with the possibility of Raymond Chandler's detective thriller *The Big Sleep*. As it happened, Warner Bros. had considered buying the book when it was published in 1939, but its sordid plot points involving pornography, nymphomania, homosexuality, police corruption, and unpunished murder seemed to pose too daunting a censorship challenge. Hawks glibly assured the studio chief that, as before, he could iron out any difficulties. Claiming that he already had the first half entirely blocked out, Hawks insisted that he could have a completed screenplay passable by censor chief Joseph Breen, who had succeeded Will Hays, ready within three or four weeks, and the entire picture finished before the end of the year.

Knowing Hawks, Warner can only have laughed to himself at this rash prediction, but he didn't hesitate to give the go-ahead, feeling that the Hawks-Chandler-Bogart-Bacall combination was as close to a sure thing as he could get. Chandler at that moment was just entering his greatest vogue in Hollywood; *Double Indemnity*, which he cowrote with the film's director, Billy Wilder, had scored a big hit that spring, and *Murder, My Sweet*, the second adaptation of *Farewell, My Lovely*, was already under way at RKO. With Chandler under exclusive contract as a screenwriter at Paramount, there was no possibility of hiring him for the adaptation. So Hawks engaged Faulkner, increasingly unhappy with his Warner Bros. enslavement, whom he knew would at least be able to break down the novel in a constructive way. But to speed things along, and for help on dialogue, Hawks wanted another writer. Hawks read little but mystery novels, and one that had recently impressed him was *No Good from a Corpse*, written by a first-time novelist named Leigh Brackett with a tough, hard-boiled prose style. Hawks called the writer in and was, as Brackett recalled, "somewhat shaken when he discovered that it was Miss and not Mister Brackett, but he rallied bravely and signed me on anyway, for which I have always been extremely grateful."

Just twenty-eight years old, short, and taken to dressing in the simple, somewhat outdoorsy manner Hawks admired, Brackett had spent much of her childhood in Pasadena, not far from the Hawks home. Hawks was also won over by Brackett's taste in literature, as her heroes were very close to his own—Hemingway, Kipling, and Steinbeck, in addition to Chandler and Hammett. Having been previously employed in Hollywood only by Republic Pictures on a cheap horror film, she was understandably stunned and a bit bewildered to be summoned by the likes of Hawks to work with the great Faulkner on a story by her god Chandler. "What have I got to offer? as it were," she quipped. Hawks was willing to risk $125 per week on her, which was more than all right with Brackett: "I'd have done it for nothing."

Hawks's directive to his writers was, "Don't monkey with the book—just make a script out of it. The writing is too good." This was willfully perverse and, if true, self-deceiving, since never in his career was he content to simply transcribe an existing text on-screen. Unlike John Huston, who always insisted on fidelity to the original text, for Hawks irreverence was more like it, adherence to some preexisting literary standard quite irrelevent to what interested him. Hawks was invariably driven—by his creative urges, his need to put his own stamp on someone else's creation, his ego, and his entire artistic process—to free himself from the constraints of literature, to spin a tale his own way, to make something organic gel from the combination of talents assembled on a particular picture. To be sure, *The Big Sleep* ended up resembling its source much more than did *To Have and Have Not*, but Hawks's original instructions to hew closely to the novel stand as ironic, in that it was he, more than his writers, who strayed significantly from it.

Hawks rated Chandler, along with Hammett and Hemingway, among his favorite authors. He once remarked, "Chandler's dialogue is in some ways just as good as Hecht's and MacArthur's, though it was more limited. He really wrote only about Marlowe, but it was awfully good." Hawks also felt that Chandler, who was in his early fifties by the time his novels starting becoming popular, had an advantage in having written most of his important work before he began being taken seriously, so "he didn't get a chance to be self-conscious about it."

Due to the august literary names involved, the adaptation of *The Big Sleep* has been far more intensely scrutinized than that of any other Hawks film except *To Have and Have Not*; scholars specializing in Chandler, Faulkner, and Hawks have all taken close looks at it. Especially helpful is the work of Roger Shatzkin; the very title of his essay "Who Cares Who Killed Owen Taylor?" frankly addresses the issue no one can avoid when discussing *The Big Sleep*: that the plot is so complicated that even the original author couldn't say who murdered one of the characters, but that it didn't matter because everything else about it is so dazzlingly good. If there was a pivotal film in Hawks's career, after which his storytelling technique became more discursive, more leisurely, and less tightly plotted, it is this one. As Hawks later stated: "I'm learning more about characters and how to let them handle the plot, rather than let the plot move them." It could easily be argued that after *The Big Sleep*, Hawks's films begin to suffer from loose, casual plotting and that their quality depends to a great extent simply upon how successful he is at getting away with it, or, on his terms, how good his scenes are. As Meta Carpenter so astutely noted, it was a risky way to make a movie, the equivalent of walking a tightrope without the net normally provided by a tightly knit, well-constructed story. It is perhaps not coincidental that the most convoluted, heavily plotted story Hawks ever took on was the one that triggered this significant change in artistic attitude.

Hawks-Feldman, of which Hawks was now president, bought *The Big Sleep* for twenty thousand dollars, with an agreement that Warner Bros. would in turn pay him $55,000 for the literary rights as well as a completed screenplay—Hawks could keep the difference if there was any. With his impeccable story sense, Faulkner was entrusted to devise the structure, but the approach to the actual writing proved rather unusual. Brackett described her initial meeting with her partner on the lot: "Faulkner came out of his office with the book *The Big Sleep* . . . and said: 'I have worked out what we're going to do. We will do alternate sections. I will do these chapters and you will do those chapters.' And that was the way it was done. . . . I never saw what he did and he never saw what I did. We just turned our stuff in to Hawks." Brackett acknowledged, "It's a confusing book if you sit down and tear it apart. When you read it from page to page it moves so beautifully that you don't care, but if you start tearing it apart to see what makes it tick it comes unglued." In fact, it is possible, with some difficulty, to fit all the pieces of the novel together, and Faulkner and Brackett actually went to considerable lengths to clarify some of the details left a bit vague by Chandler.

Aside from conforming the action of *The Big Sleep* to the requirements of the Production Code, the main challenge the filmmakers faced was to transform a detective story heavily anchored in the first person into a suitably amorous and balanced vehicle for Bogart and Bacall. No matter what happened before, the ultimate goal was to arrive at an ending very much like that of *To Have and Have Not*, in which the audience is buoyed by the feeling that Bogie and "Baby" will stay together. This was by no means an easy matter, requiring more than a year of work.

Although no Raymond Chandler novel was designed to be easily squeezed into a nutshell, the original work, a clever amalgam of four of his stories, concerns gumshoe Philip Marlowe being hired by the wealthy, aged General Sternwood to investigate his wild daughter Carmen's gambling debts. In fact, Marlowe shortly learns, Carmen is a subject in some lewd photographs taken by drug dealer–pornographer–extortionist Arthur Geiger, who is murdered in Carmen's presence. Marlowe saves Carmen and sees two men leaving Geiger's place, the infamous chauffeur Owen Taylor and Joe Brody, who now intends to blackmail her with the photos himself. In short order, Geiger's male lover Carol Lundgren murders Brody, thinking he was the one who killed Geiger, when, in fact, the killer was Taylor, who by now has turned up drowned in his boss's car in the Pacific Ocean.

The classic story that Hawks always told, with slight variations, was that Bogart asked him who was supposed to have killed Owen Taylor (Leigh Brackett claimed that it was she whom Bogart initially asked). Hawks admitted that he had no idea, and when Faulkner and Brackett confessed that they couldn't figure it out either, the director wired Chandler, who responded, "I don't know." (Jack Warner supposedly later complained about the needless expense of seventy cents for this "silly" telegram.) Despite that, in their first-draft screenplay, Faulkner and Brackett explicitly answered the question by fleshing out a scene of Chandler's in which the detective discusses the case to date with the district attorney. In it, Marlowe surmises: "So Taylor killed Geiger because he was in love with the Sternwood girl. And Brody followed Taylor, sapped him and took the photographs and pushed Taylor into the ocean. And the punk [Lundgren] killed Brody because the punk thought he should have inherited Geiger's business and Brody was throwing him out."

Hawks filmed this scene, and it was included in the original cut of the picture that was shown only to G.I.s overseas in 1945. A year later, when the film finally went into general release, the scene was eliminated from the picture, thus leading to the mystery that would forever after surround Owen Taylor's fate, and to the overriding reputation of *The Big Sleep* as an indecipherable picture.

With Marlowe having identified the killers of both Gerger and Taylor, it would seem that Marlowe's job for General Sternwood is finished. However, Marlowe learns that the old man is also searching for the missing husband of his other daughter, Vivian, a man named Rusty Regan. After striking some sparks with Vivian, Marlowe finds the nude and nubile Carmen throwing herself at him in his apartment, but he tosses her out. Some time later, Carmen tries to shoot Marlowe but finds that he's replaced the live ammo with blanks. The secret behind the whole story is that Carmen has killed Regan for rejecting her sexually and wanted to exact the same revenge upon Marlowe. Vivian was, in fact, an accomplice after the fact, having helped dispose of her husband's body. To disguise Regan's death, the gambling operator Eddie Mars had hidden his wife, Mona, away and put the word out that Regan had run off with her. It all ends with Carmen about to be institutionalized and Marlowe heading off to deal with Mars.

Complicated, yes. Impossible to figure out, no. In the 1970s, Hawks admitted, "I can't follow the story. I saw some of it on television the other night, and I'd listen to some of the things he'd talk about and it had me thoroughly confused because I hadn't seen it in twenty years." But by cutting the one scene that best explained the knotty plot points, Hawks proved good to his word that "you don't really have to have any explanation for things"; that is what he felt he had learned by the time he was done.

At the outset, when Faulkner and Brackett began writing, upon Hawks's instructions "we both tried to stick as close to Chandler as we could," said Brackett. The writers pursued the joint goals of laying out the story as lucidly as possible and anticipating the primary objections of the Breen Office. In the first draft, which was written with incredible speed, between August 29 and September 14, Geiger was reduced to a straight blackmailer rather than a pornographer and extortionist; Lundgren became Geiger's business associate, not his lover; Carmen, of course, was dressed on her surprise visit to Marlowe's, and her psychotic fury over her sexual rejection was changed to jealousy of Regan's and Marlowe's attentions to Vivian. The screenwriters' new ending had Carmen, to regain the favor of her father, pretending to commit suicide by shooting herself with the gun that was, at last use, filled with blanks. Little did she know, however, that the butler had replaced them with real bullets.

The revised, "temporary" screenplay was finished barely two weeks later, on September 30, and was the one Hawks used as the basis for his scenes when he started filming on October 10; it had taken just six weeks to produce a shooting script, and if he could somehow hold to the forty-two-day schedule, Hawks would wrap on November 28 and fulfill his prophecy of delivering the picture by Christmas. In the climax of this new version, Carmen confesses her crimes to Marlowe at Geiger's house, whereupon she walks out the front door and is gunned down by Mars's goons. Hawks was never happy with this conclusion, but private talks between Hawks and Chandler gave birth to another ending that the author liked a great deal but evidently couldn't pass muster with the Production Code. This one similarly had Marlowe and Carmen in Geiger's house, with Marlowe, but not Carmen, realizing that the first person to walk out the door would be gunned down. Disliking the role of "playing God" with Carmen's life, he decides to flip a coin to decide if he should tell her. He does not, but is about to stop her when she pulls a gun, ready to shoot him. As she opens the door, machine-gun fire tears her to pieces. Chandler lamented that it couldn't be used, commenting, "All I know is it would have been a hair-raising thing if well done."

Hawks had so much confidence in his material, his stars, and his own ability to solve problems along the way that he wasn't the least concerned about proceeding without an ending or a finished script; after all, Faulkner had done splendidly on *To Have and Have Not* working barely one step ahead of the filming. Bogart, he felt, looked like his old self again after a summer on his yacht, and as far as he knew, Bogie and Bacall had not even seen each other in at least three months. Over the course of the summer, Bacall had come back into Hawks's good graces, taken more singing lessons, spent many evenings at Hog Canyon, and cooperated with the press buildup for *To Have and Have Not*. Though forced to abandon the idea of a liaison with his protégée, Hawks had seen enough over the years to convince him that the Bogart-Bacall affair was over, allowing him to resume his position as her Svengali. In fact, there was good reason for him to believe this, and Bacall began to fear it herself. At the time *The Big Sleep* started production in early October, Bacall had barely spoken to Bogart in weeks; under incredible strain, he told her that since his wife had stopped drinking, he'd promised to give his marriage one more try. So while Bogie and Bacall resumed their jokey, sparring ways during working hours, the underlying mood between them was much more brittle and uncertain than it had been when they had begun their first picture together less than eight months before.

Then there was the matter of casting the secondary roles, particularly the women. Hawks decided that one of the ways his Philip Marlowe would differ from Chandler's was that, partly as a fulfillment of his usual fantasy and partly as a result of Bogart's screen persona, he would be more sexually aware and available, as best seen in the bookshop scene, in which there is little doubt what happens after the lovely clerk closes the shop on a rainy afternoon to share a bottle of booze with Marlowe. Another Hawks invention was the sexy female cabdriver, played by Joy Barlowe, who gives

Marlowe her card and offers to help him again any time he needs another "tail job," adding, "Night's better. I work days."

For the bookseller, Hawks was delighted with a nineteen-year-old Texas newcomer, Dorothy Malone. Hawks said that the scene was never intended to be taken as far as it went, but they were able to do so simply because "the girl was so damn good-looking. It taught me a great lesson, that if you make a good scene, if we could do something that was fun, the audience goes right along with you." Like Bacall, Malone was so nervous doing her first important scene that her hands shook while she attempted to get the drink, prompting Hawks to have the bottom of the glass filled with lead so she could handle it.

For the treacherous, nymphomniacal Carmen, the most important female role other than Bacall's Vivian, Hawks tested several unknown actresses. For a while, the leading contender was Sonia Darrin, but then Hawks was struck by a glamour photo of a former model and up-and-coming actress named Martha MacVicar. Initially signed by Selznick, she had begun her career inauspiciously at seventeen at Universal in monster movies. When Hawks took an interest in her, Warner Bros. signed her up and changed her name to Martha Vickers. Hawks worked with her closely to push her sexual suggestiveness to the breaking point, and they were so successful that Raymond Chandler felt that "she shattered Miss Bacall completely." At some point along the way, Hawks started an affair with her, which lasted for some time. However, she later incurred the scornful wrath Hawks reserved especially for those who didn't listen to him: after playing ingenues in a couple of unmemorable pictures, she came to him to complain when Warner Bros. let her go. Hawks recalled saying, "'Why don't you just keep on playing that character we did?' She said, 'Well, that girl was a nymphomaniac!' I said, 'Well, that isn't a bad character.' Oh, she was so *good*. Silly dame." Censorship standards may have decreed the severe toning down of how the Carmen part was written, but the way Vickers played her, like a lewd, lascivious child ever on the lookout for mischief to stir up, encouraged thoughts of boundless depravity and fully warranted Marlowe's great lines about her, such as "You ought to wean her, she's old enough." As consolation, Carmen runner-up Sonia Darrin was given the smaller part of Agnes, Geiger's secretary. A sarcastic young woman herself, Darrin was on the set when it was asked who killed Owen Taylor, and she burst out, "It must have been Hawks."

For the secondary male roles, Hawks considered H. B. Warner for General Sternwood; Paul Stewart, John Ireland, and George Macready for Eddie Mars; Dan Duryea for Brody; Ireland and Freddy Steele for Canino, and Walter Sande (Johnson the fisherman in *To Have and Have Not*) and Lee Tracy for Bernie Ohls. Tantalizing as some of these choices would have been, Hawks decided to cast somewhat against type, with his earnest *Air Force* pilot John Ridgely as the sinister Eddie Mars, the Western hero Bob Steele as the thug Canino, the veteran stage actor Louis Jean Heydt as Brody, and Regis Toomey as the D.A., Bernie Ohls.

Because of his continuing gambling debts and the heavy bite the IRS was taking out of his Warner Bros. salary, Hawks was determined to make sure his profit participation paid off this time on what he was positive would be another big hit. Going over budget would hike the breakeven point along with it, so Hawks decided to cut production costs wherever he could, beginning with the art direction. Some of the sets, notably those for the Sternwood mansion, were all anyone could ask for. But he doubled up some other sets, dropped locations when studio substitutes would do, and skimped to such an extent that in some instances, *The Big Sleep* looked perilously close to a B movie, with its anonymous backgrounds and dark shadows hiding the lack of production values.

Shooting in virtually precise sequence, Hawks began production on October 10, 1944. Some of the high-spirited atmosphere from the early stages of the *To Have and Have Not* shoot returned, superficially covering the tremendous tensions that simmered just below the surface. Driven to distraction by Bogart's decision to stay with his wife, Bacall saw her severe case of nerves reappear, with her shaking evident whenever she had to light a cigarette or pour a drink. She relied heavily on Hawks to get her through, reinforcing his belief that he had regained the upper hand with her. But Bogart was still very much in love with Bacall and determined to be with her; the incredible emotional strain of his last days with the desperate, belligerent Mayo drove him to nights of little sleep and very heavy drinking.

Nonetheless, the picture provided a means for the two lovers to once again spend their working days together, and the electricity between them, spurred by the hothouse atmosphere and the provocative, insolent characters they were playing, became palpable once again. The early weeks included the shooting of not only the sexually charged scenes between Bogart and Bacall but those featuring Martha Vickers, Dorothy Malone, Sonia Darrin, and Joy Barlowe—in line with Hawks's vision of an ideal world, every woman in *The Big Sleep* makes a pass at Bogart. As Cecelia Ager later observed in her astute review of the film in *PM*, "Except perhaps for the showgirls in a Metro musical, there has never been assembled for one movie a greater and more delightfully varied number of female knockouts. But whereas Metro showgirls at least look content, every woman in *The Big Sleep* is feverishly hungry for love . . . and though every one of them would prefer Humphrey Bogart, they settle instantly for anybody."

Barred, as usual, from the set, a frustrated Jack Warner sent down this immortal memo: "Word has reached me that you are having fun on the set. This must stop." The writers, actors, and director took their time in order to extract the maximum character and suggestiveness from every situation. Bogart wanted his Marlowe to be the hardest man imaginable but found that some of his dialogue was a bit gentle. Assuming that the woman writer on the team was responsible for this, he had a word with Brackett about it, only to learn that Faulkner had written the exchanges he considered too soft. From then on, Bogart went straight to Brackett, whom he nicknamed Butch, whenever he wanted any of his dialogue toughened up, and the two launched a mutual-admiration society; Brackett said, "As far as I was concerned, he was the greatest actor that ever happened." Brackett particularly admired the way he could take his final pages for a scene five minutes before the cameras rolled, "put on his horn-rims, go off in a corner, look at it, and . . . he'd have it right down, every bit of timing, and he'd go through about fourteen takes waiting for the other people to catch up with him." Despite Bogart's personal turmoil, Hawks had the greatest of respect for Bogart and proved it by daring to put him in every scene. Hawks astutely observed that "there are only a few actors in the world you can have in every scene and not get tired of them. But I don't think you get tired of Bogart."

During the third week of filming, Bogart left his wife and moved into the Beverly Hills Hotel, where Bacall was able to sneak in to see him. Hawks once again felt betrayed and forced Slim to call her emotionally distracted friend to straighten her out and to advise her not to alienate her director any further.

A week later, Bogart devastated Bacall by telling her—just before she was due to go on the stage to perform a scene—that he was going back to his wife, who was entering a hospital to dry out. Not long after that, barely out of the hospital, Mayo hit the bottle again, sending Bogie on a bender that, very uncharacteristically, left him incapable of reporting for work; Bogart was normally an utterly dependable professional, but these days and nights were the most difficult of his life. To cover up for him, Hawks told Jack Warner that Bogart was exhausted since he had been working for thirty-six straight days. However, since Marlowe appeared in literally every scene, and virtually every shot, of the picture, Hawks was hard-pressed to shoot around his star; that day, the Friday after Thanksgiving, Hawks managed by arranging to record Bacall singing, appropriately enough, "Her Tears Flowed Like Wine."

Hawks had just about had it with the emotional turmoil swirling around his two stars. Just as he had during *To Have and Have Not*, Hawks demanded that Bacall come to his house, and she knew what that meant: a major dressing-down. As she recalled, Hawks said, "Look, I'm not going to go on with this. I can't have anyone under contract who won't listen to me. Bogart likes his life—he likes the drinking and he likes his wife—you're throwing away a whole career because of something that's just not going to happen. . . . So you'd better make up your mind—this is your last chance." A contrite Bacall obediently came to dinners at Hog Canyon, where one night her hosts set her up with Clark Gable, with whom, unbeknownst to Hawks, Slim had had a serious but unconsummated flirtation during the summer. Though flattered, Bacall wasn't the least bit distracted from Bogart by Gable. Shortly thereafter, Hawks had it out with Bogart as well, stopping work one afternoon to "straighten him out relative the 'Bacall' situation, which is affecting their performances in the picture." Through the holiday season of 1944, the Bogarts' marriage was sputtering through its last gasps, with Bogart making divorce preparations, then relenting over Christmas, going into one of his worst tailspins.

According to the original schedule, the picture was supposed to have wrappped by November 28; by that date, Hawks had made his way through not even half of the 195 scenes of *The Big Sleep*. The film was seventeen days behind, and to some extent this was due to Bogart's emotional stress. However, physical problems had taken their toll as well: Hawks, Bacall, and John Ridgely all fell ill, while Bob Steele and Tom Rafferty, cast as Carol Lundgren, both injured their ankles. For two days after Christmas, no work could be done as Bogart had called in sick, but the unit manager, Eric Stacey, reported to studio brass that on December 26 Bogart did not turn up because he was "very drunk" at home, adding, "I really do not feel that Bogart's condition can be straightened out over night since he has been drinking for approximately three weeks and it is not only the liquor, but also the mental turmoil regarding his domestic life that is entering into this situation."

The other reason for the slack pace was the continual rewriting of the screenplay. Through the first half of the shooting, Hawks was continually pushing Faulkner to further condense the vast amount of material in the script. Hawks also did his own share of rewriting, notably in two scenes. The first was the expository scene between Bogart and Bacall in Marlowe's office which—in contrast to his earlier attempts to stay under budget and on schedule—Hawks rewrote on the set all morning, rehearsed for more than two hours after lunch, then shot, finally rolling the cameras for the first time at 4:30 P.M. The second was a scene in Eddie Mars's office, which Hawks similarly rewrote nearly all day while the cast and crew waited, finally making the first take at 4:40 P.M.

As *The Big Sleep* moved into its much more complicated—and, as far as the script was concerned, much less well worked out—second half, Faulkner began to ease himself off the picture and out of Hollywood. He was desperately anxious to return home to Mississippi—it was a toss-up as to who was drinking more during this time, Faulkner or Bogart. He told Meta Carpenter, "I have to get back to my own writing. . . . I'll never get it done in this town. Sometimes I think if I do one more treatment or screenplay, I'll lose whatever power I have as a writer." Certain that Hawks could carry on without him, Faulkner requested a six-month unpaid leave from the studio, beginning December 13, but as a favor to his friend he wrote twelve pages of revisions on the train, after he had gone off salary.

Hawks again called on Jules Furthman; up until then, his only contribution to the film was having supplied the orchids for the opening scene in General Sternwood's greenhouse. Unlike *To Have and Have Not*, in which Furthman's influence was more decisive than that of either Faulkner or Hemingway, *The Big Sleep* employed the writer's talents mostly on a straight craftsmanship level, sharpening dialogue and condensing and reshaping scenes for the final portion of the script. Furthman also had to find a new ending. From the outset, Faulkner and Brackett, aware of the enormous potential for censorship problems, had bent over backward in an effort to anticipate them. As a result, there were surprisingly few objections from the Breen Office once the initial script was submitted to it in early October. The office's concerns mainly surrounded Carmen's character: she was to indulge in no thumb-sucking or "any other activities . . . which might give a questionable flavor to her character," and it must be clear that she is not "being blackmailed by means of some nude or lewd photographs." The censor's overriding worry, however, was the ending, for it was completely inadmissable that "Marlowe deliberately sends Carmen out to her death." Hawks didn't like the Faulkner-Brackett wrap-up either, nor did it serve the desired purpose of bringing Marlowe and Vivian together at the end.

During the two weeks before Christmas, using the revisions Faulkner wrote on the train and those Furthman was now producing, Hawks made drastic cuts and changes in the screenplay. Despite a lavish bedroom set built for a scene in which Marlowe was to pay a second visit to General Sternwood, Hawks replaced the sequence with a simple phone call, eliminating fifteen pages of script and four or five days of shooting. Over a lunch meeting with Jack Warner's deputy, Steve Trilling, the director ennumerated the cuts he wanted to make that would save a week's work, just as he was shooting up to four or five pages of script per day, unusually high for him. A couple of days were devoted to script conferences and discussion of revisions, but they resulted in net time gained due to the number of pages dropped from the schedule. Bogart's "illness" immediately after Christmas gave Hawks and Furthman precious additional time to work on the script. Specifically, Furthman rewrote the scene in Marlowe's office in which Vivian offers him five hundred dollars to close the case, the scene in which the D.A. tells Marlowe to lay off, the car sequence between Marlowe and Vivian in which she says that she killed Regan, and the entire ending, copies of which Hawks was able to give to the actors only on January 5, the day they started shooting it.

In later years, Hawks claimed, "The end of the story was done by the censors." They said, 'Howard, you can't get away with this.' And I said, 'O.K., you write a scene for me.' And they did, and it was a lot more violent, it was everything I wanted. I made it and was very happy about it. I said, 'I'll hire you fellows as writers.'" Hawks grossly exaggerated the artistic abilities of the censors, as well as the sort of work they would actually undertake. There is no written record of the Breen Office suggesting any ending at all, so it was undoubtedly conveyed in a personal meeting between Hawks and the office's representatives that they would accept an ending in which Marlowe forces Eddie Mars out the door of the house into machine-gun fire from his own men, which would suggest that it was he, and not Carmen, who killed Regan and would also make Marlowe the agent for Mars's proper fate. From Hawks's point of view, this solution did wrap everything up neatly, and allowed him and Furthman the considerable latitude of including Vivian in the climax and allowing her and Marlowe to be together at the end.

With scenes being condensed and jettisoned almost daily, Hawks was able to rush the film to completion by January 12, finishing with a second reshoot of Marlowe and Vivian's first scene together, in her sitting room. The picture took seventy-six days to shoot, thirty-four more than the number originally allocated. But as Eric Stacey noted in his final report to the front office, because of innumerable economies impemented by Hawks, the picture was only fifteen thousand dollars over budget and would probably end up no more than fifty thousand dollars over once normal music and post-production costs were added.

Hawks had come a long way from his original admonition to the writers: "Don't monkey with the book." From the strenuous attempt at clarity undertaken by Faulkner and Brackett, Hawks and Furthman led *The Big Sleep* to a place where the leading characters were surrounded by a darkness in which the threats could be identified or explained only with great difficulty, and yet they prevailed anyway. On January 21, after a week in Palm Springs, Hawks returned to Warner Bros. to do two retakes of Vivian in her sitting room. For the moment, *The Big Sleep* was finished; final editing and scoring were done, and some prints were made. But more than a year would pass before the film would take the final form in which it is known today.

After a huge press buildup centered around "Baby" Bacall, which included a record sixty-two interviews in New York on a seven-day promotional trip, *To Have and Have Not* opened in October 1944. Reactions to her and Bogart were great, and it was generally conceded that the advance ballyhoo surrounding a hot new personality was, for once, fully warranted. But while critics grudgingly admitted to finding the film passably entertaining, the overall attitude of reviewers was mildly condescending and dismissive; they minded less that the picture strayed so much from its source than that it seemed like a reheated *Casablanca*. Looked at strictly from that angle, it is easy to see how they felt: *Casablanca* is lush and romantic where *To Have and Have Not* is hard-edged and cynical; Bogart is beautifully dressed and always in command in the first film, while in the second he is a bit grubby and backed into uncomfortable corners by circumstances; the supporting cast of *Casablanca* is beyond compare, full of distinctive and colorful character actors, while the lineup in *To Have and Have Not* grows threadbare after you get past the leads; and the former is loaded with highly charged melodramatic scenes involving truly evil Nazis, next to which the villains in the latter seem somewhat minor league.

But *To Have and Have Not* arguably represented the high-water mark of Hawks's career to date, the most fully realized version of his intuitive view of how a man should behave in the world and how a man and a woman in love should interact. Understated, stylized, and poetic, the film exists on two levels of fantasy: first, as the Furthmanesque exotic outpost of *Morocco*, *Shanghai Express*, and *Only Angels Have Wings*, where characters intensely play out their fates in a contained setting during a compressed period of time, and second, as the most refined projection of Howard Hawks's sexual imagination, in which a very knowing, yet actually not widely experienced young woman meets an older man, knows at once what she wants, and proceeds to tempt, tease, and taunt him into an instinctive, erotically charged rapport. One may well ask what happens to Steve and Slim after they sail out the door at the film's end; indeed, their long-term prospects would seem not much better than those of the couples in *Only Angels Have Wings, His Girl Friday,* and *Ball of Fire.* In fact, if one chooses to take Hawks's view of the film literally as a speculation on how the man and wife of *To Have and Have Not* met, then the novel can serve as evidence of their sorry fate. But Hawks was profoundly uninterested in what came after, in the realities of married life and the complexities of mature emotions, and he displayed this indifference in his work by avoiding the depiction of married or settled couples to an extent unmatched by any other major Hollywood director. Until the end of his career, Hawks was almost singularly obsessed with how a new couple sparked until they clicked; after that, he didn't care. *To Have and Have Not* is Hawks's ultimate expression of How It Should Be between a man and a woman; everything prior to it was in preparation for it, and everything after it was in some way an attempt to recapture the ideal he had once achieved. Hawks went on to make quite a few more exceptional films, but just as Slim forever remained the dominant woman in his life, "Slim" remained the ultimate Hawksian woman.

These notions, however, were the furthest things from critics' minds at the time. Regardless of what they thought, audiences ate up *To Have and Have Not.* Opening in an exclusive run at the Hollywood Theater in Manhattan on October 11, 1944, the film grossed a sensational $46,200 in its first week, the second-highest weekly total in the history of the house, and played sixteen weeks, the second-longest run ever at the site, during which it pulled in a terrific $393,000. Warner Bros. held the film back from any further engagements until mid-January 1945, when it began opening in other major cities, including Los Angeles, and racking up huge numbers almost everywhere. It set a new one-week record gross of $430,000 for the New York City RKO circuit and posted records or near records in many other situations. It generated some $4 million in domestic rentals in 1945.

Given the box-office bonanza blossoming from the first Bogart-Bacall pairing, one might have thought that Jack Warner would have rushed to satisfy the public's desire for a rematch and brought *The Big Sleep* out later in 1945, shortly after *To Have and Have Not* had closed. The first preview of the mystery thriller was held on February 22, less than a month after the final shots were made, and despite a favorable reaction, it was apparent that Bogart and Bacall lacked the impact as a couple they had had in their first outing, because they had less to do together. Hawks at once saw the problem, but for the moment he did nothing. A month later, Bogart and Bacall, confident that his divorce would at last come through, announced their engagement, and on May 21 they were married.

Wanting to cash in on Bacall's name, Warner assigned her to a new film, *Confidential Agent,* in which she was hopelessly miscast as an upper-class British girl opposite Charles Boyer and was insensitively directed by Herman Shumlin. But Warner insisted upon rushing *Confidential Agent* into release due to its wartime theme and because he thought Bacall was "about hundred times better in *Confidential* than she is in *Big Sleep,* and we want to keep this woman on top." But when the Shumlin picture opened disastrously in October, leaving reviewers utterly baffled as to what had become of the sultry temptress who had seduced them in *To Have and Have Not,* Warner recognized his error and resolved to do something to salvage *The Big Sleep*.

In its original version, *The Big Sleep* had its world premiere in Luzon, the Philippines, in August 1945 and by October was being shown to American servicemen on dozens of bases overseas. But Hawks knew that further strengthening of the Bogart-Bacall relationship was needed, and he backed Charles Feldman's approach to Jack Warner with the idea of giving Bacall "at least three or four additional scenes with Bogart of the insolent and provocative nature that she had in *To Have and Have Not*." Feldman warned that after *Confidential Agent,* "if the girl receives the same type of general reviews and criticisms on *The Big Sleep,* you might lose one of your most important assets." Warner agreed at once, almost as if the retakes had been his own idea, and Philip Epstein, the coauthor of *Casablanca,* was brought in to write the needed scenes.

Epstein wrote twelve pages of new material, almost entirely with an eye to upping the sexual stakes between Marlowe and Vivian. Given that this sort of thing was Furthman's specialty, that he had been the last writer on the film before, and that he had played a decisive role in shaping Bacall's screen image in the first place, it is not clear why he was not brought back to write these scenes. The best guess is that Jack Warner had more than a bit to do with the decision. Epstein's major contributions were two double entendre–loaded scenes between Marlowe and Vivian. In the first, Marlowe and Vivian talk about love, with Vivian saying, "Carmen's easy — men know that—You have to work harder and longer on me," to which Marlowe responds, "If an extra half-hour makes you feel more respectable. . . . " "Good night, Mr. Marlowe," Vivian says. The other was the famous horse racing–as–sex café scene, which could not possibly be spiked with more innuendo. Marlowe admits to Vivian, "You've got a touch of class, but I don't know how far you can go," to which Vivian replies, "That depends on who's in the saddle." This prompts Marlowe to speculate as to whether Vivian is a front-runner or likes to "come from behind."

Other additions written by Epstein were the scene in the parking lot of Marlowe telling off Eddie Mars; Marlowe's short speech about the chauffeur, Carmen, Geiger, and the compromising photographs; a revision of a scene of Marlowe entering the Sternwood mansion in which some of the butler's lines were given to Vivian, further beefing up her part; and redrafts of the scene in the hideout with Marlowe, Vivian, and Mona Mars (played by the harsh Pat Clark initially, but recast with the more conventional Peggy Knudsen for the reshoot); the one between Carmen and Marlowe in his apartment; and, crucially, Marlowe's face-off with the D.A. This last scene, in which Bernie Ohls tells Marlowe to lay off the Sternwood case, was a streamlined substitute for the original one, in which, among other things, the killer of the chauffeur Owen Taylor was identified and the entire plot to that point was summarized. Jack Warner personally ordered the replacement shot to speed the story along, and Hawks complied, but of all the new scenes added in 1946, this one does not seem like an improvement, as the new version not only removed considerable information but erased much of the ambiguity and suggestion about why Marlowe wanted to continue his investigation, just as it further flattened out Ohls's character.

In the year since the film had wrapped, relations between Bogart and Bacall and Hawks had become strained. Hawks had long since sold his interest in Bacall to Warner Bros., and when it became clear that the couple intended to stay together and get married and that Hawks had been dead wrong about Bogart's intentions, he washed his hands of them. Even Bacall's close friendship with Slim had suffered. So when the group reassembled for six days of reshoots on January 21, 1946, the attitude was strictly business. Nonetheless, with the help of the great dialogue and bold confrontations Epstein had created, they were easily able to reenter the provocative, sizzling groove they had been working in, on and off, for two years. On January 28, *The Big Sleep* finished shooting for good, and on February 8, the new and final version was previewed for the first time. The feeling that the extra work had been worth it was shared by everyone, prompting Warner to wire his East Coast executives with the news: "in my opinion we have [a] one hundred percent better picture."

Whether or not Warner was right can now be judged by contemporary audiences, since the 1945 version, hitherto seen only in exceedingly rare 16mm prints, was restored by Bob Gitt of the UCLA Film & Television Archives and presented to the public in 35mm for the first time in Los Angeles in July 1996. It is impossible to claim that the original cut is better, since the added material produces such intense sparks and provokes such thoroughgoing pleasure. All the same, the earlier version possesses a richness of narrative satisfaction, a thrill of dramatic discovery, that was sacrificed in the reshooting and cutting. The two cuts are very different in effect, with the original 116-minute film having been trimmed of twenty minutes to make way for eighteen minutes of new footage, creating a final running time of 114 minutes. A comparison of the two versions reveals *The Big Sleep* as the indisputable turning point in its director's career. The first cut represents the culmination of Hawks's dedication to narrative, to classical storytelling principles, to the kind of logic that depends upon the intricate interweaving of dramatic threads. The revised, less linear cut sees him abandoning these long-held virtues for the sake of "scenes," scenes of often electrifying individual effect, but scenes that were weighted heavily in favor of character over plot and dramatic complexity. When Hawks saw that he could get away with this, it emboldened him to proceed further down this path through the remainder of his career, with results that were variable in terms of the intent and quality of his work.

The Big Sleep finally opened in New York City on August 23, where it broke the opening week record at the Strand Theater with a tremendous gross of $84,000; public interest was so great that the house ran almost around the clock, closing its doors only between 3 A.M. and 9 A.M. The six-week run there generated a total gross of $378,000, making for one of the theater's best engagements ever. Spurred by reviews affirming that the old Bogie-Bacall magic was back, the film soon spread across the country, and through September and October it remained steady as the number-two film in the nation, just behind Hitchcock's *Notorious*. By the end of the year, it had done more than $3 million in box-office rentals, making it Warner Bros.' third-biggest film of 1946.

The qualities of *The Big Sleep* are self-evident. It is, as Hawks intended it to be, massively entertaining on a moment-to-moment basis, with Bogart etching the definitive Philip Marlowe, every woman in the film fairly oozing sexuality, a mood of sinister uncertainty draping the action, and a mystery being unraveled whose dubious clarity is at least matched by its scandalous fascination. The sense of intangible threats lurking in the darkness of the world at large, the Conradian danger present in so many Hawks films, is especially helpful to this deeply mysterious puzzle in which everyone is suspicious and most are guilty of something. It is not the personal film that *To Have and Have Not* was, but it does reflect the steel-eyed, unsentimental, sly, sexually excitable, and ruthless sides of its director, all of which serve this material extremely well. As Cecelia Ager wrote in *PM* in the most perceptive contemporaneous review, the film "evokes the fond indulgence that a blue-eyed, rosy-cheeked, good little boy meets when earnestly relating the very naughtiest daydream the dear little fellow is able to think up." She also put the dazzling skill evident in individual sequences in perspective by comparing it to "cutting and polishing rhinestones to simulate diamonds, instead of just cutting and polishing diamonds. They are marvelous fakes."

With *The Big Sleep*, Hawks had now scored seven major hits in a row, a record all but unmatched in Hollywood. His commercial success had earned him a virtually free hand at Warner Bros., where his position was condusive to his doing just about any project he wanted. And yet he chafed at being under contract, at not truly controlling his own destiny. He still looked back at the unfettered manner in which he and Hughes had made *Scarface* as an ideal he had been unable to recapture since. More than anything, Hawks wanted his independence, to not have to deal with Jack Warner or Sam Goldwyn or Louis B. Mayer, to own and profit by his own work. Due to his tremendous success as a director, Hawks was able to get what he wanted. But knowing how to handle it when he got it was another matter altogether.

27

The Urge to Independence:
Red River

As the war years began drawing to a close, Howard Hawks, who was approaching his fiftieth birthday, acquired some curious new pastimes. Long
gone were his days of flying, sailing, and tennis, and even his taste for hunting began to subside as he got older. But his passion for all manner of engines and vehicles, preferably fast and unusual ones, persisted. During the
making of *To Have and Have Not*, he distracted himself by building an
automobile from the ground up on the Warner lot, joined occasionally by
David, who as a teenager was beginning to share his father's interest in hot
cars. But the most unusual, and almost comical, manifestation of this mania
was the middle-aged men's motorcycle gang that gathered every Sunday
morning at Hog Canyon. Sporting the curiously proper and British name
of the Moraga Spit and Polish Club, this informal group "didn't care too
damn much about the usual social life that centered around how big you
were," according to Hawks, but nonetheless consisted largely of prominent
Hollywood names: Hawks, Vic Fleming, Clark Gable, Ward Bond, Keenan
Wynn, Andy Devine, Van Johnson, William Wellman, and, as the only
woman with a chopper, Wellman's wife, Dotty, who, according to Slim,
had the biggest bike of all and was the best rider. Other regulars included
the stuntman Cary Loften, the test pilot and certified wild man Vance
Breeze, the aviation innovator Bill Lear, later of Learjet fame, and Al
Menasco, whose Menasco Aircraft Company made airplane engines in
Burbank.

Sometimes numbering as many as twenty cyclists, the gang would
gather at Hawks's house at 10:30 A.M. in full leather gear and special jack-
ets. The men then spent at least an hour polishing their machines to show-
room conditions while discussing their machines' performance and fine
points, whereupon they would peel off for a couple of hours of noisy cruis-
ing through the hills off and around Mulholland Drive or into the San
Fernando Valley. Afterward, they either returned to Hog Canyon, where

Slim dutifully served up a big lunch she'd spent the morning preparing, or adjourned to Andy Devine's ranch, where the jovial Western character actor "had this long 'Liar's Bench' made for our house. All the riders would sit and drink beer and tell lies about what they'd been doing on their motorcycles." The only biker who tried to outdo the others in terms of speed and fancy maneuvers was Fleming. Otherwise, the main competition, such as it was, stemmed from having the spiffiest, most polished machine. Most of the bikes at that time were Harleys, although Hawks and Gable each had a four-cylinder Ariel Square Four. In addition to his own Harley, Hawks along the way acquired a Triumph, a Zundapp, and, just to one-up the others, a rare German BMW, which he bought from a policeman.

It hardly escapes notice that several members of the group, notably Bond, Wynn, and Fleming, were extremely right-wing, and vague stories have circulated over the years about how Hollywood's first motorcycle gang was actually a bunch of celebrity thugs prone to roaring through the streets of Hollywood on the lookout for liberals and lefties. While Bond and a couple of his cronies apparently indulged this fantasy from time to time, it wasn't on Sunday mornings with the rest of the bunch, who were in it for the social and mildly macho gratification. Any political views voiced were no doubt conservative, but the Moraga Spit and Polish Club was as innocuous, and somewhat silly, as its name.

Hawks's chronic preoccupation with vehicles, which Slim tolerated with no enthusiasm, assumed its most peculiar manifestation when he bought, at untold expense, an elaborate land yacht that he imagined would take Slim and him off on fabulous journeys to unknown destinations. The two-toned green contraption consisted of a special cab attached to an enormously long trailer that resembled the inside of a yacht. After Slim stocked it with the requisite utensils, Hawks decided to take the unwieldy thing on its inaugural voyage. By the time they reached the end of Moraga Drive, Slim felt so ill that she insisted that they return home at once, so Hawks made an ungainly U-turn and, while attempting to park, did not clear the eave of the stable, which sliced like a can opener through the top of the trailer. Neither Hawks nor his wife ever took it out for a second spin.

Shortly after the war ended, a new sport was taken up by the Hollywood elite: croquet. Commonly thought of in America as a children's pastime, the game, when pursued seriously, is as vicious as polo and second only to cricket in the length of time required to play. In addition, the necessity of a large, perfectly flat, immaculately manicured, expertly measured grass playing field, as well as costly English equipment, restricts access to the privileged few, annointing it with further snob appeal in the film capital. The sport had long been popular in society and show-business circles in the East, with the critic Alexander Woollcott as its "high priest" and other enthusiasts including Averell Harriman, Richard Rodgers, Vincent Astor, Moss Hart, Herbert Bayard Swope, and George S. Kaufman. It was Hart who was most responsible for bringing croquet west by introducing it to Darryl Zanuck. Soon Hawks became one of its prime adherents as well, followed by such others as his brother Bill, Tyrone Power, Cesar Romero, Samuel Goldwyn, Gregory Ratoff, Otto Preminger, André Hakim, Joseph Cotten, Douglas Fairbanks Jr., and Louis Jourdan, who was the best player. William Powell, Slim's friend from the mid-1930s, was the official cheerleader of the Palm Springs club.

Because of the vast acreage of Hog Canyon, Hawks's compound was easily able to accommodate an impeccable regulation croquet lawn. Matches could easily last all day and sometimes continued well into the evening. While Hawks, Zanuck, and the other diehards feverishly pursued their new game, nonparticipants, including Slim, Robert Capa, Lew Wasserman, and Constance Bennett, would play ruthless poker inside.

Naturally, the East Coast veterans looked down on the Hollywood neophytes, and Zanuck took Moss Hart's joking put-downs as a slap in the face that demanded satisfaction. Thus was born the East-West croquet championship, which pitted Hart, Tyrone Power, and the agent Fefe Ferry for the East against Zanuck and Hawks for the West. The three matches were played on July 6–7, 1946, before some three hundred spectators seated in a gallery set up at Hawks's home. Special floodlights were installed to allow play to continue after dark, and the playoff was considered such an event that *Life* magazine covered it with a two-page spread highlighted by photographs taken by Jean Howard. Zanuck and Hawks won the first game, but, as Hart observed, "they became drunk with success and lost control very early" in the night game, then lost again the next day, giving the tiny winner's cup, presented by Slim, to the East. Among those in the crowd on the first day was Howard Hughes, who the next afternoon would nearly die when he crashed his experimental XF-11 plane into two homes in Beverly Hills.

As Hart noted, croquet, when properly played, "is a fascinating adult game, requiring skill, stamina and iron nerves," and Hawks possessed those qualities in spades. Unlike the emotional and ill-mannered Zanuck, Hawks approached the contests with the calm precision of the engineer that he was, which took nothing away from the fearsome power with which he knocked opponents' balls away. The fad for croquet continued into the next decade, but it reached its peak at Hawks's home that weekend. Hawks received official recognition for his standing in the sport when he was inducted into the Newport, Rhode Island, Croquet Hall of Fame.

Later in July, the summer's other major social event at Hog Canyon took place: the wedding of director Jean Negulesco to Dusty Anderson. A wild-spirited Romanian whose prankishness and competitiveness made him good company for Zanuck, Negulesco was a quickly rising director at Warner Bros. and met Hawks socially through Feldman. He had Hawks's number, knowing full well that the director was "a preposterous, imaginative, and inspired liar," but thought it better just to grin and bear it than to challenge him. But he also admired Hawks tremendously, calling him the "Great White Father" and coming to him whenever he had a story problem. Negulesco was also crazy about Slim—"I considered her to be perfection," he admitted—and actually asked her to get to know Dusty Anderson and give him her opinion before he proposed marriage. Slim not only approved but threw the wedding, which took place in an idyllic spot at Hog Canyon on a little rise surrounded by trees, blooming flowers, and buzzing hummingbirds. Hawks stood in as best man, although he slipped away from the wedding celebration as quickly as possible to get a croquet game going.

It was during the war years that the first noticeable cracks began to appear in the monolithic studio system. Provoked by Jack Warner's wresting away of the best picture Oscar for *Casablanca* at the Academy Awards ceremony in 1944, the film's producer, Hal Wallis, left Warner Bros. later that year to form his own production company, releasing through Paramount. After long flirting with a partnership with Hawks, Gary Cooper created his own company, International Pictures, and personally produced *Along Came Jones*; it wouldn't be long before numerous other top stars, including Bogart, would follow suit. Mervyn LeRoy became the first director with his own autonomous deal at Warners, something Michael Curtiz would later emulate. Directors whose careers had been interrupted by military service came back in a new, more serious mood, determined to make films that said something, that had social and thematic weight. To this end, Frank Capra, William Wyler, and George Stevens, along with the producer Sam Briskin, formed their own company, the short-lived Liberty Pictures, and John Ford formed Argosy Pictures with Merian C. Cooper. Other prominent directors who hadn't gone to war also broke their studio chains: despite grave warnings from Hawks, Preston Sturges made the ill-advised decision to leave Paramount after a string of hits and become partners with Howard Hughes, and even Victor Fleming, by then in his early sixties, left MGM after fifteen years to join the independent producer Walter Wanger in making the giant-budgeted *Joan of Arc* with Ingrid Bergman, with whom Fleming became involved in a desperately intense May-December love affair.

For years, Charles Feldman had shrewdly made his clients far more money than they would have seen otherwise by generally steering them clear of long-term studio contracts in favor of picture-by-picture deals. By the late 1930s, he began having some luck in pioneering the packaging of clients and material, thus giving talent a bit of leverage in a system in which the studios held all the cards, and in the early 1940s he had muscled his first producer's credits on *The Spoilers* and *Pittsburgh*. In February 1943, during the effort to get *Battle Cry* off the ground, Feldman and Hawks had formed H-F Productions. At first it was a simple partnership whose function was to acquire literary properties that Hawks wanted to make into films, with the idea of selling them to the studios for far more than it had paid. Toward the end of 1944, while in the middle of production on *The Big Sleep*, H-F bought three very interesting books, all of which were turned into excellent scripts that Hawks was very serious about directing.

In October 1944, Samuel Fuller was a G.I. who, having made the D-Day crossing four months before, was pushing through France toward Germany. The publication of his mystery novel *The Dark Page* during some of the toughest days of the war was later immortalized by Fuller himself in *The Big Red One*, when the Fuller character has trouble convincing his fellow dogfaces that he is the author of the book they're reading on the front lines. But the true story went further than that. Hawks and Feldman bought the screen rights to the novel for fifteen thousand dollars, an unimaginable windfall for a soldier about to enter the final winter of the war. When he finally managed access to a typewriter in Germany in December, Fuller made only one request of Hawks: that the premiere be held for the entire First Division. The novel combined elements of *The Front Page* and *Double Indemnity*, telling of a newspaper editor who commits murder and pushes his favorite reporter to try to solve the case.

Hawks saw *The Dark Page* as "a very unusual relationship between two men . . . a form of love story between two men, where the love of the editor for the reporter and the editor's pride in the work of the reporter allows him to egg the reporter on to uncovering the crime committed by the editor." Hawks hired Jules Furthman for $25,000 to write the adaptation after the writer finished his work on *The Big Sleep*, and when Hawks later left Warner Bros. and formed his first production company, Monterey

Productions, along with Feldman and Slim, he essentially sold the novel and script to himself for a five-thousand-dollar profit. Monterey hired Fuller, now returned to Hollywood, to write a new script, for which he received an additional five thousand dollars.

After considering Edward G. Robinson, Bogart, and Cary Grant, and failing to interest Gary Cooper in the material, Hawks briefly entertained doing it with unknowns, but when Feldman convinced him it was the sort of story that demanded stars in the leading roles, Hawks decided to sell. Edward Small's syndicate, Motion Picture Investors Corporation, which not so coincidentally arranged the financing for Hawks's *Red River*, bought *The Dark Page* from Hawks for $100,000, and Small ultimately produced a disappointing version of it, Phil Karlson's *Scandal Sheet*, starring Broderick Crawford and John Derek, in 1952. When Fuller found out about the sale he exploded, and he threatened legal action over the fact that Hawks had made more than fifty thousand dollars' profit horse-trading his work. He also accused Feldman, who was his agent as well, of sharing in the profit, a charge Feldman denied by claiming that his only payment had been 10 percent of the original fifteen-thousand-dollar sale. Fuller, who became a director himself in 1949, finally calmed down and, in later years, was sorry only that Hawks didn't make the film himself as originally planned.

Within two weeks of acquiring *The Dark Page*, in October 1944, H-F bought two other novels, *The Black Door* and *Dreadful Hollow*. Written by mystery specialist Cleve Adams, whom Hawks had hired briefly on *The Big Sleep*, *The Black Door*, for which H-F paid four thousand dollars, had the potential to rival that film in its portrayal of rampant corruption and pervasive evil. As adapted by Leigh Brackett, it was a lewd, licentious tale that would have offered Bogart an opportunity to take the sexual insolence of his Philip Marlowe to an even greater extreme. The story, later variously known as *The Turning Door* and *Stiletto*, sees former narcotics agent James J. Flagg pulled into a convoluted drugs-and-gambling scheme on the pretense of being hired by a senator to keep track of his wildcat daughter. Brackett wrote it in breezy, highly entertaining style, and her dialogue, particularly in the provocative sex scenes, is notably sophisticated. While derivative of both Chandler and Hammett and no less confusing than *The Big Sleep*, it would seem to have had all the makings of a winning commercial picture if done by a combination such as Hawks and Bogart. As had been the case with *The Dark Page*, the pair's mutual disaffection, and the director's departure from Warner Bros., left it by the wayside.

Dreadful Hollow was something altogether different and would have marked a radical departure for Hawks had he ever made it. H-F purchased Irina Karlova's gothic horror novel for $2,500 two years after its publication, and Hawks never considered anyone other than William Faulkner to adapt it. Because the only known copy of the script reposed in Hawks's possession, this major screenplay remained utterly unknown to Faulkner scholars for decades, as it was not even mentioned in Joseph Blotner's exhaustive 1974 two-volume biography. Even now, it is not entirely clear when Faulkner actually wrote the script, since he did not date it, but the best guess would be around 1947. Although quite different in surface intent from "A Ghost Story," *Dreadful Hollow* bears an equally fascinating kinship to Faulkner's work as a novelist, recalling his frequent theme of grievously inbred, twisted families, with the difference that these characters have roots in Transylvania rather than the American South.

Jillian Dare, a pretty nineteen-year-old, takes a job as a paid companion to the Countess Ana Czerner, at an English house called the Grange, which is also occupied by a threatening woman named Sari. Strange events, including a rabbit found with its throat torn out and its blood removed (this after Sari has been glimpsed in the kitchen with a bowl of blood), and a large, batlike shape that flies at Jillian and spits out a curse in a foreign tongue, make her fear she's going mad. Sari confines her to her room, which leads Dr. Clyde, whose father knew Czerner's secret, to appeal to the police.

Later Jillian is discovered being readied to give blood to the Czerner clan. The countess, in the form of a bat, swoops down at the intruders, but the crazed Sari catches her and axes her to death, chopping off her head, then follows her to the grave.

Faulkner's approach to the potentially ridiculous events is consistently intelligent, as he maneuvers around clichés and wins confrontations with far-fetched plot developments, investing the script with sufficient suspension of disbelief to make it work. Even more than the effectively drawn atmosphere, the dialogue is outstanding, full of funny local dialect, which is written like his southern speech even though the setting is Britain. Violent and a bit perverse for its time, and featuring a leading role that gave Hawks a perfect excuse to discover a new actress, the script excited Hawks, who tried for years to interest studios in backing it. Warner never thought much of it and, a few years later, when he was under contract at Fox, Hawks tried unsuccessfully to push the project on Zanuck, who felt that it followed "familiar patterns like *Dragonwyck* and *Hound of the Baskervilles*." Decades later, after the deaths of both Faulkner and Hawks, producers occasionally inquired about the script, but the rights quagmire, along with its relatively "straight" treatment of vampires by contemporary standards, have left it still unproduced.

One more project that came Hawks's way was *Moss Rose*, Joseph Shearing's novel about a chorus girl who worms her way into high society in late Victorian England, with near-calamitous results. Again, Hawks hired Furthman to write the script, and when he was anxious to leave Warner Bros. in late 1944, he sidetracked discussions of other projects by insisting that he was planning on leaving imminently to make both *Dreadful Hollow* and *Moss Rose* for Fox in Britain, the latter most probably with Ginger Rogers in the lead. After Hawks dropped it, Furthman's *Moss Rose* script remained at Fox, where Tom Read and Niven Busch rewrote it and Hawks's old friend Gregory Ratoff directed it to moderate effect in 1947.

Underlying everything during this period, from his numerous purchases of material to his procrastination over directing any more pictures for Warner Bros., was Hawks's growing desire to break free and make films independently. Jack Warner realized he'd have to make some kind of settlement with Hawks, and in May 1945, four months after *The Big Sleep* wrapped and just before Bogart and Bacall were married, Hawks sold his half-interest in the actress to Warners along with his share of the profits in the films he made at the studio, and packed up and moved into the H-F office at Famous Artists on Wilshire Boulevard; in August, his remaining obligations to the company were officially canceled. Hawks always claimed that he received a flat $1 million in the exchange. Mysteriously, however, nowhere in the bulging archives of both Warner Bros. and Feldman is there any record of such a transaction. Of all of Hawks's expansive claims, this is among the more plausible; at the same time, it could have been his way of demonstrating that he came up a winner despite losing Bacall.

In mid-May, Hawks and Slim went to Palm Springs for a week, and it was very likely there that the utterly unexpected happened: Slim became pregnant. For at least a couple of years, Slim had known that her marriage wasn't working, yet a woman as shrewd, status conscious, and well supported as she wasn't about to leave her comfortable situation without a well-conceived game plan. In 1944, Hawks had been so solicitous after her mother's death, tending to all the arrangements and taking her to Palm Springs to recover, that Slim was willing to overlook Hawks's subsequent indiscretions and aloofness for some time thereafter. In the interim, Slim, through her friendship with *Harper's Bazaar* editor Carmel Snow, began appearing frequently on fashion magazine covers (Hog Canyon also received increasing photographic attention), and Slim was on the point of having to decide whether or not to accept Snow's offer to become the West Coast editor of *Harper's Bazaar* when she learned she was expecting. Overcome with both nausea and insomnia, she remained mostly bedridden throughout her pregnancy, wondering, as she remembered, "how I was going to raise a child in a loveless home, for the prospect of fatherhood had not changed Howard in the least." Far more interested in his pictures, his horses and gambling, his cars and motorcycles, and any girl he might manage to attract than in anything to do with Slim or their baby, Hawks become so irresponsible and inattentive during Slim's pregnancy that his own mother told him to shape up. But nothing could induce him to truly change his ways.

Predictably, then, when Kitty Stephen Hawks was born on February 11, 1946, at 9:49 P.M., her father was not around. He eventually turned up, but he didn't even drive his wife and daughter home from the hospital, arranging for an ambulance to do so instead. If Hawks was to have another child at all in his fiftieth year, he definitely wanted a son—as might be gleaned from his daughter's middle name, an inside joke on *To Have and Have Not*. As for her first name, the incredulous have always wondered if Howard Hawks could actually have named his child after the birthplace of aviation. Of course he could, and he did. But that was the first and just about the last thing he did for her, as Hawks couldn't be bothered to pay any attention to her.

Not that he was terribly involved in the lives of any of his kids. Peter, who turned twenty-one in 1945, had developed a passion for airplanes that far exceeded that of his stepfather, especially after his wartime stint with the Army Air Corps. Shifted out of El Rodeo School in the Beverly Hills school district and away from all his buddies by the moves to Bellagio Road and then Moraga Drive, David spent the eighth grade at Emerson Junior High in West Los Angeles, where he began getting into trouble. With this, Hawks enrolled him in the Black Fox Military Institute, where the student body featured quite a few spoiled and unruly rich Hollywood boys; future director George Englund was the cadet major at the time. Even though Black Fox was only a half-hour drive from Hog Canyon, at Melrose and Wilcox in Hollywood, David was forced to board there for two years. After that, David said, "I had a plan of how to get out of going to Black Fox for another year, by telling my father it was full of delinquents." Without taking the time to investigate David's claim, Hawks freed his son to go to the public University High School (Uni) nearby in West L.A., but there David fell in with the hot-rod crowd; by giving him a 1938 Ford coupe for his six-teenth birthday in October 1945, Hawks could not have better played into his son's hands. "It wasn't a bad group of people I was hanging out with," David recalled, "it's just that we went out racing on Friday nights, and it was illegal." Giving birth to L.A.'s post-war drag-racing scene, David and his pals would roar down Pico Boulevard well into the night until some of them got arrested and the rest took off for home. "It was far from being a gang kind of thing, but the police cracked down on it. I remember my dad saying one night after I came home late that if I ever got picked up, he wasn't going to come down and get me out, to wait to call him in the morning. It was the same way with everything else. I didn't smoke or drink, and he didn't tell me that I couldn't. He just lent me his pipe and watched me turn green. . . . He never said I couldn't do anything, he just wanted me to know that I would have to take responsibility for whatever I did."

Barely lasting the year at Uni, David was then sent to board at Webb School in Claremont, about two hours to the east. Despite the fact that he should properly have been entering his senior year, he was forced to join the junior class and therefore graduated a year late. One point in Webb's favor was that students weren't allowed to have cars, but one celebrity sprig well known to the Hawks family, Irving Thalberg Jr., was expelled during David's time there for keeping a car hidden in a nearby orange grove. Whereas he had gotten Cs at Uni, David made better grades at Webb since "there was not much else to do." Thanks to his improved academic record and the fact that the school's founder was a Princeton man, David was accepted at the New Jersey Ivy League university for the fall term of 1948.

Although David always remained very fond of his father, he did have one complaint: "He was never very open with praise. Once I came upon a letter describing how he came for the only time to a high school football game. In it, he praised how well I'd done in the game and it did me good to read him praising me. He never said anything to me at the time. I think it was very hard for him to open up." The letter in question is one Hawks wrote in November 1947 to Shipwreck Kelly, who had tossed the football around with David some ten years before. In it, he wrote that David, who was by then six feet, two inches tall and weighed 160 pounds, "caught everything that came his way and ended up by making two touchdowns and setting up a third, and to my great delight not missing a ball that he could get any-where near."

For her part, Barbara, who turned nine in 1945, was quietly being raised by her grandparents and going to school in Pasadena. She generally saw her father on holidays and on arranged vacations during the summer. Very occasionally, the kids saw their mother, who during this time lived mostly in an apartment not far from Hog Canyon, on Hilgard in Westwood near UCLA. Athole was allowed to drive and so was able to get around, although she had very few friends and nothing in particular to do. Every so often, her attacks would recur, sending her back into the hospital at UCLA.

Hawks's growing children were not in a position to complain about their father's extreme distance from them, but Slim, once she was back on her feet after her daughter's birth, resolved to take her life into her own hands. Without telling him, she decided "very early that Kitty was not to be Howard's baby. I would have the sole responsibility for her forever, and so she was mine." In early April, needing to get away from the oppressive atmosphere at home, Slim left her baby of less than two months with a nanny to go to New York, where she built up her ego with a two-week round of partying with friends and some new gentlemen admirers. Wanting more, she hopped down to Nassau, which proved less exciting, so she called Hemingway in Cuba and procured an invitation to join him and his wife of six weeks, Mary Welsh, at Finca Vigia, his compound southeast of Havana.

Still aroused by Slim's presence, Hemingway greeted her at the airport with the provocative comment, "Miss Slimsky, why don't we ever find each other *between* marriages?" Most evenings were spent with the crowd that gathered around Hemingway at the great El Floridita bar in Havana, and Slim endured an uncomfortable four-day fishing trip with the newly-weds. Despite Mary's resentment, Slim was enormously refreshed and buoyed by Hemingway's constant attention and praise. Things also took an interesting turn when some unexpected show-business personalities turned up and more or less imposed themselves on Hemingway: David O. Selznick and Jennifer Jones, the agent and producer Leland Hayward and his wife, Margaret Sullavan, and CBS's founder and owner William Paley. They tried to induce Slim to join them on their continuing cruise of the Caribbean, but she begged off, realizing she couldn't ignore her obligations in Los Angeles forever.

Once back home in May, Slim reluctantly joined her husband for a short stay in Palm Springs without Kitty, to little effect on her marriage. She then, at last, eagerly embraced her role as mother, but with the knowledge after her trip that there was a different life out there for her; she didn't know how or when she would find it, but she was now on the lookout for her chance. Hawks became suspicious that his wife might be having an affair with the photographer and compulsive ladies' man Robert Capa, who took advantage of Hawks's standing invitation to visit his house by spending an inordinate amount of time hanging around the pool and drinking his booze. But Capa was mostly unhappily killing time between rare opportunities to see his true secret lover, Ingrid Bergman.

In the end, it was Hawks himself who created the circumstances that fostered Slim's break from him. On Bastille Day, July 14, the Hawkses went to a Sunday night dinner party at David Selznick's. As he sometimes did, Hawks bowed out early but insisted that Slim stay on. Slim enormously impressed Leland Hayward, who was there without his wife, and he insisted upon taking her home. Hayward, an endlessly dynamic, appealing man of forty-four, had blue eyes much warmer than Hawks's and a salt-and-pepper crewcut and was known as much for the quality of his female conquests— Garbo, Hepburn, Sullavan—as for their quantity. Dropping Slim off at home, he asked her point-blank why she didn't ditch Hawks, since there was so obviously nothing between them anymore, and tempted her with the thought that there was a lot out there waiting for her if she would only leave her husband. Contriving a way to see more of her, Hayward hired Slim as costume consultant for the national tour of *State of the Union*, one of his first outings as a producer. For the first and last time in her life, Slim took a job, and it enabled their romance to begin without raising anyone's suspicions. Slim's involvement with Leland Hayward also inadvertently led her to help her husband make his second big discovery of the 1940s, this time of an actor who would become one of the idols and legends of his era.

Not having finished *Viva Villa!* or *The Outlaw*, Hawks was ready to tackle a Western, this best-defined of film genres that had proven so successful for almost every important director of his generation. The pulp writer Borden Chase was an acquaitance of Hawks's through horse circles and in January 1946, Hawks bought Chase's story about the nation's first major cattle drive. Hawks paid fifty thousand dollars for all rights and hired Chase for $1,250 a week to write the screenplay. Early on, however, Hawks could see that he would have trouble with the belligerently right-wing Chase, who refused to collaborate with Hawks or anyone else and became incensed at the mere suggestion of any changes. With its grand theme of how the creation of a cattle empire helped build a nation, its epic movement, its contrast of an old authoritarian ethic with a newer and more democratic one, and its elemental conflict between an older man seeking revenge upon the foster son who took away his herd, Chase's dramatic architecture was sound and full of tremendous potential. His straightforward, sometimes colorful dialogue was quite suitable for films, though as a prose stylist he was crude, bombastic, repetitive, and utterly lacking in nuance.

As published in the *Saturday Evening Post* in installments from December 1946 to January 1947, *The Chisholm Trail* told of Thomas Dunson, a "bull of a man . . . with eyes that looked out at you like the rounded gray ends of bullets in a pistol cylinder." Splitting off from a wagon train with one bull and a wagon, he meets a boy, Matthew Garth, whom he takes under his protection. Plotting the beginnings of a giant herd of cattle, he kills a Mexican who disputes his right to the land he is now claiming as his own.

Jumping twenty years ahead, Matthew is on his way back from fighting for the South in the Civil War when he stops at the River Palace and is attracted to saloon singer Tess Millay, the companion of a blustering gambler named the Donegal. Back in Texas and ready to move his thousands of cattle to market in the North now that Matthew has returned, Dunson takes on Cherry Valance, a "charming and impudent" hired gun, to join his thirty other men in the drive. Cherry has also known Tess, giving him and Matthew a sort of *A Girl in Every Port* relationship. Demanding total obedience from his men, Dunson insists upon driving the herd the long way through to Missouri, despite the many reports of trouble with outlaw gangs there and Cherry's insistence that there is now a railway line closer by at Abilene, Kansas.

After a nocturnal stampede and the arrival of a nearly dead rider warning of a border gang, several men rebel against Dunson and Matthew, who kill five of them. Cherry Valance rounds up the remaining three, who are shot by Dunson. Despite an easier crossing to the west, Dunson insists upon making a dangerous crossing of the Red River, which now marks the border between Texas and Oklahoma. The loss of three more men sparks a full-scale mutiny, which Matthew joins by stating that he will drive the cattle to Abilene himself. At this betrayal, the old man vows to kill Matthew, but as he goes for his gun, Cherry Valance shoots Dunson in the shoulder. Turned out by the man he raised as his son, Dunson swears to come back for him and hang him.

As Matthew and the men drive through the Nations, they run across a wagon train headed by the Donegal. With him are a dozen sporting women, including Tess Millay. After a long evening campfire, Matthew deliberately stampedes the cattle under threat of an Indian attack, which arrives the next morning. Tess flirts heavily with Matthew and Cherry Valance, which enrages the Donegal, who draws on Cherry, with fatal consequences for himself. Tess, hardly crushed by the loss, continues to provoke Matthew, announcing that she will now change course and accompany him to Abilene even though he doesn't want her to. All the while, Dunson and ten hired guns are rapidly advancing on Matthew and the herd.

After a nighttime lightning storm, during which many steers are shot to prevent them from crushing a broken wagon in which a woman is having a baby, Cherry decides to quit the herd and stay with Tess's wagon train, which trails about a mile behind Matthew. Cherry virtually proposes to Tess, but when she says she wants a man with real money, he slinks off to plot his takeover of the herd. He then tries to ambush Matthew during another river crossing but botches the attempt. Dunson arrives in Tess's camp and, after a long talk, offers her half his empire, once he claims what's his, if she will bear him a son. When Cherry turns up, the two men shoot it out; Cherry hits Dunson in the shoulder again and would have killed him if Tess hadn't brushed his elbow as he fired. This gives Dunson his chance, and he kills Cherry.

Having reached Abilene and the railroad, Matthew collects more than eighty thousand dollars for the cattle and puts it away for Dunson to collect, as promised. But as the men celebrate, Tess comes into town to inform Matthew that Dunson has shot Cherry, that she's agreed to go off with Dunson, but that she'll throw it all away if he'll leave with her now. Of course, he can't cheat destiny that way, so at high noon the next day, the two men face off in town. They draw, and the younger one is faster, but Matthew finds himself unable to shoot the man who taught him everything he knows. Dunson, ailing from the wound Cherry gave him, fires away but can't hit his target as he loses strength with every squeeze of the trigger, and finally crumbles to the dust. An epilogue has Matthew and Tess returning to Texas with Dunson in the back of their wagon. After they cross the Red River, the old man gets out to stand on Texas soil one more time before he dies.

When Hawks read Chase's screenplay and the parallel short novel in late March, he brought in a bright, Yale-educated twenty-nine-year-old named Charles Schnee, who had recently dropped law in favor of screenwriting. His only credit to date was on John Berry's *From This Day Forward*, for which he wrote additional dialogue, but he would shortly break through with his scripts for *They Live by Night*, *The Furies*, and *The Bad and the Beautiful*. Working under Hawks's guidance in Palm Springs while Slim was off on her East Coast spree, Schnee made numerous changes in Chase's narrative. The first was to give Dunson a woman he leaves behind at the beginning of the story. When she turns out to have been killed in an Indian attack on her wagon train (information imparted in the typically Hawksian manner of a found bracelet Dunson had given to her), it enriches the story's meaning and Dunson's character in multiple ways: when he quits the wagon train, Dunson is thus parting company not only with the other men's laws but with the "civilizing" influence of women, thereby freeing him to establish his own rules. It also makes him at once embittered and more ruthlessly determined than before; as Hawks said, leaving the woman he really loved "would make him all the more anxious to go through with his plans. Because a man who has made a great mistake to get somewhere is not going to stop at small things." Matthew, with his cow, serves to replace her as the sole object of Dunson's love, an affection for "love stories between two men" being something Hawks and Chase had in common.

In the interests of streamlining, Schnee eliminated Matthew's trip back from the war, thereby delaying Tess's entrance until far into the story, which many have viewed as a flaw. He tightened the time jump between the two sections from twenty to fourteen years. He took out Cherry's injuring Dunson in the shoulder during the mutiny, removed the Donegal, made Tess into a professional card sharp (foreshadowing *Rio Bravo* and *El Dorado*) to get away from the suggestion that she was a prostitute, excised the hard-to-film nocturnal storm scene as well as Cherry's death, and added the Indian attack, in which Tess is shot with an arrow.

The climax, however, remained up in the air. To Chase's disgust, Hawks, who increasingly refrained from killing off remotely sympathetic characters, would not allow Dunson to die in the end. As the Schnee-revised shooting script had it as the film went into production, Dunson stalks Matthew to the Abilene Hotel, which has an enormous wheel of fortune on the front of it. When Dunson yells at Matthew to draw, the young man points out, "You're always saying what's to be done." Finally, Dunson draws and fires but repeatedly hits the wheel of fortune, spinning it round and round. Then Cherry Valance steps out of the crowd and challenges Dunson, but Matthew is quicker on the draw and shatters Cherry's gun hand. At this, Dunson, an interesting antecedent to John Chance in *Rio Bravo*, screams, "I've told you! And told you and told you! I need no help from you or anyone!" He twice slaps Matthew full across the face with the back of his hand, pushing his head back against the wheel of fortune so that it stops, and finally takes Matthew's gun from him and smashes it. At last, Matthew hits Dunson, but Dunson beats him to a pulp. Once Matthew is knocked out, it's discovered that Cherry's bullet hit Matthew in the shoulder so that he couldn't use his left, to which Dunson says, "Of course. I could see. Do you think I'd've fought him fists if he hadn't? He'd've killed me. Don't forget! I taught him how to fight!" The film then ends with the three principals crossing a river in a wagon and Dunson, upon touching, smelling, and tasting it, asking if this isn't the Red River and then getting out on the other side.

To play the three main characters, Hawks originally wanted Gary Cooper as Dunson, Cary Grant as Cherry Valance, and the good-looking nonactor Casey Tibbs, then the reigning national champion rodeo rider, as Matthew. Cooper was initially cool to his intended part, feeling Dunson was too mean and unsympathetic for an audience to tolerate. Hawks was sure he could bring him around, so he was quite surprised when Cooper declined the role in favor of Cecil B. De Mille's pre–Revolutionary War "Western" *Unconquered*.

But Charles Feldman had the right actor waiting in the wings: his longtime client John Wayne. Duke, who was about to turn thirty-nine, had won World War II on-screen in a series of action pictures and had just produced his first film, *Angel and the Badman,* at Republic. But he was still hovering vaguely in the B-plus picture category and not working for top directors except occasionally for John Ford, whose cavalry trilogy was yet to come. Delighted at the prospect of working with Hawks, whom he knew a bit through Feldman and Ford, Wayne was not so much concerned about Dunson's brutal personality as about playing an older man. Hawks supposedly said, "Duke, you're going to be one pretty soon, why don't you get some practice?" and Wayne was won over. Not hurting matters either was his compensation, which was set at $50,000, $10,000 more for every week over twelve weeks of shooting and 10 percent of the profits, with a profit of $75,000 guaranteed.

Despite their best-laid plans, Hawks and Cary Grant hadn't found a way to work together again since their sparkling back-to-back-to-back trio in 1938–40. As originally written, Cherry Valance would have been an amusingly different sort of character for Grant to play, but he didn't feel it was a big or important enough part and understandably begged off. Not needing a star for the film's third role, Hawks remembered John Ireland from his screen test for *The Big Sleep* and signed him to play Cherry for the bargain rate of five hundred dollars a week.

To play the many cowboys, Hawks rounded up a colorful combination of reliable old friends, such as Walter Brennan, Harry Carey Sr., Paul Fix, and Noah Beery Jr.; newcomers; and the almost inevitable loan from the Ford stock company, Hank Worden. (Brennan made five thousand dollars per week, an incredible amount for a character actor.) But the plum role, of course, was Matthew. Directing a real-life cowboy like Casey Tibbs would have represented an interesting challenge, but Hawks became doubtful that the untested young man could stand up next to Wayne; when Tibbs broke his arm in a fall, his screen career was over before it started. Hawks then decided he wanted to cast Jack Buetel, whom he had directed ever so briefly on *The Outlaw*, but Howard Hughes seemed intent upon thwarting Buetel's career, refusing to loan him out to anyone. Buetel, of course, was beside himself, but there was nothing he could do, and he made only a few B Westerns in the 1950s before vanishing from films.

So Hawks had to look elsewhere. Biographies of Montgomery Clift state that Hawks had been impressed with the rising Broadway star in the Tennessee Williams–Donald Windham play *You Touched Me!* The director, however, never spoke about it, and there is no indication that he even visited New York anytime during its run. Ironically, Leland Hayward was Clift's agent, and it was Hayward who played the aggressive matchmaker between Hawks and the actor. By this time, the beautiful, hypersensitive Clift had been around Hollywood a bit. He'd even signed a six-month contract at MGM but wisely refused Louis B. Mayer's tearful entreaty to extend it to seven years. Snobbishly disdainful of the place he called "Vomit, California," the twenty-six-year-old Clift wanted to become a movie star, but on his own terms.

It wasn't until late summer, with filming looming just ahead in September, that Hayward gave Clift the *Red River* script. Although costarring in a Western opposite John Wayne was about the last thing Clift ever expected to do, he was intrigued and could easily sense both the role's star-making potential and the picture's commercial possibilities. With his trusted New York theater friends hopelessly divided over whether or not he should do it, Clift returned to Los Angeles to meet Hawks, knowing the part was his if he wanted it but still utterly ambivalent about it.

With Hayward anxious to clinch the deal, Slim proposed that her new lover bring Clift to Hog Canyon for a luncheon with her husband. Tickled to be seeing Hayward on her home turf, she took Clift for an after-lunch walk around the grounds, during which she claimed to have convinced Clift to take the role by insisting that he would learn a great deal from both Hawks and Wayne. When they got back to the house, Clift told the two men, "I've decided to do it. She talked me into it." As if sleeping with Hawks's wife was not enough, Hayward also extracted a king's ransom for Clift's services: $50,000, which, when extra-week overages and a bonus were added on at the end, eventually came to $75,000, putting Clift in the same ballpark as Wayne on his first trip to the plate. It was a startling fee for an unknown newcomer, and not at all easy for Hawks and Feldman to swallow; Feldman was sure he could maneuver Hayward down to $30,000 or $40,000, and he and Hawks had originally hoped to sign Clift to a long-term deal themselves. But Hayward and Clift would have none of it and got things entirely their own way.

Still, Hawks took charge of his "discovery" in his usual manner and immediately challenged Clift to learn how to ride. "Now look, this is a Western," he said. "If you can't sit on a horse, you may as well go right home." Total preparation and deep immersion in a part were Clift's stock-in-trade, so he left for location in Arizona almost at once and spent three weeks with a top cowboy, learning to ride, rope, and shoot. Clift was a superb pupil, and by the time filming started he fit in effortlessly with the more experienced cowboy actors. There would be other questions about Clift, specifically in the mind of John Wayne, but those could only be answered once shooting began.

Hawks was on the make as usual in regard to casting the women's roles. Late in 1945, he met a striking actress in her early twenties named Jan Zweigart, who took the professional name of Jana Garth. Very much in the Hawks-preferred tall, blond, slim, high-cheekboned mold, she had made a stunning impression in a production of *Saint Joan* in her native San Francisco, where she was discovered by the film director George Cukor. She was madly pursued by agents, producers, directors, and men in general, but she decided to sign with Hawks because of his track record of catapulting actresses straight to stardom without years of building up through small parts.

In the view of her close friend, the future director Curtis Harrington, "She was a natural aristocrat. She was arrogant, very high-strung and neurotic. She was beautiful and she knew it. But she was real, very honest and direct." Sexually, Harrington said, "she was a very free spirit" and had flings with a number of prominent Hollywood men but not, it seems, with Hawks. Nonetheless, her mentor put her through the usual "yelling in the hills" training and by summer decided to cast her as Fen, the young woman

Dunson leaves behind. This wasn't good enough for Garth, who had read the script and expected to be given the female lead of Tess Millay. Impulsive and headstrong, she refused to play the smaller part and just turned her back on Hawks, his film, and her contract. Success in Hollywood continued to elude her, and eventually she moved to Italy, where she became romantically involved with the prominent author Curzio Malaparte. But things continued to spiral downward for her, until she killed herself. Malaparte proceeded to give appallingly egotistical interviews to the press about "the girl who committed suicide over me."

When Garth shocked him by refusing to play Fen, Hawks, on a moment's notice, cast the up-and-coming 20th Century–Fox starlet Coleen Gray, whom Zanuck agreed to loan out. For the much more crucial part of Tess, Hawks had long since settled on another of his recent discoveries, Margaret Sheridan. This wholesome but sultry looking "lush Irish beauty," as Hawks enthused, was a Los Angeles native, five-foot-six with dark brown hair and blue-green eyes. When Hawks noticed her photograph in *Vogue* in early June 1945, he instantly put out the search for her. But when he finally got her number and called her at her freshman dorm at the University of Southern California, she hung up on him because she thought it was a prank call. At that time, Sheridan's gorgeous face graced a beer ad posted on dozens of billboards all over Los Angeles, including one next to the USC campus, and guys on campus had taken to calling her and claiming to be Darryl Zanuck or Jack Warner. As soon as Hawks could clear up the matter of his own identity, he signed Sheridan to a personal contract, and she quit school and embarked upon the Hawks program of heavy training, which included dance, singing, and gymnastics and drama and voice coaching.

Extremely attracted to her physically and prone to giving her gifts from Saks, Hawks was more convinced of her screen potential than with most of his protégées and began having glamour and cheesecake photographs taken that made her look like a prettier, more refined Jane Russell. By the time *Red River* was taking shape, there was no question in his mind that Sheridan would play the main female role, and she started learning card tricks and fancy dealing techniques Hawks wanted to incorporate into some scenes. But in the spring of 1946, Sheridan suddenly fell hard for former Navy pilot William F. Pattison. They quickly married, on May 15, 1946, but in August, when Hawks could finally confirm that production would begin monmentarily, Sheridan was forced to admit to her mentor that she was already nearly three months pregnant and couldn't possibly do the picture. Although he wasn't pleased, Hawks was outwardly gracious, reassuring her that there would be other opportunities down the line.

In a bind, Hawks gave the part to another actress he had just put under contract, Joanne Dru. Dru had the makings of a good comedy and musical performer, in Hawks's opinion, but he always regretted having to cast her in *Red River*, for which he thought she was ill-suited. "She did a very good job for the fact that she'd had no experience or anything," Hawks allowed, but he felt that Sheridan "would have been six times as good." Sheridan retreated from the film world for several years to raise her daughter, while Hawks, true to his word, continued to propose her for numerous parts until, finally, she made her debut in *The Thing*. But she had missed her chance. "When she came back she wasn't the same girl," Hawks said. "If she'd only done *Red River*, she'd have been a big star."

The financing for *Red River* was set up by Feldman, with Hawks's full complicity and knowledge. After considering the names Sunset, Wilshire, and Ambassador Productions, they settled on the more evocatively western monicker of Monterey Productions for their company, which was incorporated at the end of 1945 with Hawks, Slim, and Feldman as the principal shareholders. In exchange for their ownership positions, the principals all loaned Monterey amounts totalling nearly $80,000 for initial operating expenses, specifically the purchase of Chase's story. Feldman, who would serve as executive producer, and Hawks initially set the budget at an unrealistic $1,258,000 for a seventy-two-day shoot, but by May this was increased to $1,750,000. Hawks would receive a relatively standard $125,000 to produce and direct, but he and his wife also stood to rake in 57 percent of the profits based on their majority ownership of Monterey. Feldman, who would receive 24 percent, began shopping the project around to several prospective partners, including Universal Pictures, Sam Goldwyn, David O. Selznick, Joseph Schenck at Fox, and even Joseph P. Kennedy, who hadn't been actively involved in the film business in more than a decade.

Instead, Feldman worked out a scheme by which the film would be funded by a combination of private financing and bank loans. A crafty former actor and agent, Edward Small had for twenty years been a successful but artistically undistinguished independent producer working mainly with United Artists. Knowing Feldman and Hawks well, he rounded up a group of eight other wealthy show-business figures, mostly lawyers and distribution executives, to form a syndicate blandly known as the Motion Picture Investors Corporation. To cover the rest of the film's budget MPI agreed to advance $675,000, with an additional $900,000 supplied by a loan from Security-First National Bank in Beverly Hills. Shortly thereafter, the picture landed at United Artists under a multipicture deal Eddie Small made for his productions. UA would receive its distributor's share first, followed by MPI and the bank; only after they were paid off would Monterey receive its monies.

At first, Hawks figured on shooting the picture on its natural settings in Texas. Governor Coke R. Stevenson assured the company of the state's complete cooperation in everything from water, power, and transportation, "lenient application of State Humane Laws in 'stunt' scenes," "cooperation of the Labor Commissioner's Office in avoiding interference by unions," and advantageous prices on cattle. But Hawks needed a location where the diverse terrains for the separate sections of the story would be easily available, to prevent time-consuming moves of the base camp and cattle. Potential locations were scouted in Oklahoma, New Mexico, and Mexico before an ideal spot turned up in Arizona. Businessman C. H. Symington of Detroit, whose brother had gone to Yale with Kenneth Hawks, owned a large spread in the remote southern part of the state, twenty-five miles from the Mexican border. The town closest to the property was Elgin, population seven, which was on a large plain with an elevation of five thousand feet. Nearby were the Whetstone Mountains and Apache Peak, and the area's scenery was so diverse that the company never had to range farther than fifteen miles from camp.

At once, the ranch was transformed as if it were an army encampment. The Anderson Boarding and Supply Company put up seventy-five portable tents equipped with electricity and running water for the cast and crew to stay in. No one could complain about the accommodations at Camp Anderson, or the food, which was uncommonly outstanding for a location shoot. The only set needed in Arizona was for the picture's climax at Abilene, which consisted largely of false fronts, but construction work started on four stages at the Goldwyn Studios in Hollywood on sets for the interior and night scenes that would be shot there subsequently. The costumer Joe De Young quit before production began, but not before making dozens of sketches of the proper outfits for the various characters, with special attention to distinctive hats, since Hawks believed that this was the easiest way for audiences to recognize otherwise undifferentiated characters, such as the cowboys. Characters in *Red River* wear a stovepipe and derby in addition to the regular cowboy hats, and when he arrived in Arizona, Hawks was so pleased with Clift's dedication to learning cowboy ways that, as a vote of confidence, he gave his young star an old hat Gary Cooper had given him, and its weather-beaten look was perfect for the picture.

Hawks also gave all the principals in the film "Red River D" belt buckles based on the design Wayne's Tom Dunson draws in the ground. Hawks went to a silversmith in Nogales to have these gifts made, and each of the beautiful buckles, on which gold inlays marked the banks of the river, was initialed for its intended recipient, with the men, including Wayne, Clift, Walter Brennan, Russ Harlan, David Hawks, and a few others, getting full-sized buckles and the women, Joanne Dru, Slim, and Barbara Hawks among them, receiving smaller versions. Wayne wore his in many subsequent pictures, and at one point, he and Hawks exchanged buckles in a gesture of friendship. Hawks lost his—the one initialed J.W.—but David Hawks was extremely impressed years later when he noticed that the enormous sculpture of the Duke in front of the airport in California's Orange County that bears his name correctly has the initials H.W.H. engraved on the buckle's facsimile.

The company originally intended to start shooting by August 26, but there were too many loose ends for Hawks to get away that soon. Clift, Joanne Dru, and Coleen Gray were cast only at the last minute, the logistics were demanding, and the script needed more work, which would persist right through shooting. Even the title continued to be a topic of much back-and-forth. Chase's original *Break Of Dawn* had been abandoned in favor of the more historical *The Chisholm Trail*, which is the title the *Saturday Evening Post* wanted to use for its serialization. It was Hawks who came up with *Red River*, which everyone else objected to for many reasons: it had only incidental relevance to the story, it didn't begin to suggest the epic scope the film would have, and it smacked of such previous Republic B Western titles as *Red River Valley* and *Red River Renegades*. Feldman hated it so much that he tried to buy the title of Antoine de Saint-Exupéry's aviation novel *Wind, Sand, and Stars* and, when that proved impossible, implored his staff to come up with a close approximation. At one point, *Stampede* was announced as the new title, but Monogram already owned it. Hawks, who naturally wanted the serialization to serve as advance promotion for the picture, was upset when the *Post* refused to substitute his title for Chase's.

There were also uncertainties about key production personnel. Hawks desperately wanted Gregg Toland, who had done such dramatic work with western landscapes and parched faces on Ford's *The Grapes of Wrath*, to be his cinematographer. Toland had just finished Wyler's *The Best Years of Our Lives* and was technically available, but Sam Goldwyn, to whom he was under contract, knew very well Hawks's tendency to go way over schedule and, needing Toland to be free for *The Bishop's Wife*, declined to loan him out. Instead, Hawks picked Russell Harlan, who had been shooting for ten years but was just beginning to move up from B Westerns to more prestigious projects. This began a close association that continued through seven films and seventeen years. A rugged, no-nonsense former stuntman with a rarified artistic side, Harlan could easily have played one of the parts in the film.

Hawks debated at length whether or not to shoot in color, as Selznick had done with his giant Western *Duel in the Sun*, but he felt that color film at that time still looked "garish" and was not as conducive to evoking a period look as black-and-white. To compose the score, Aaron Copland's name was advanced; he had just won a Pulitzer Prize for *Appalachian Spring*, but Hawks, who liked the music in his films to be minimal and self-effacing, went instead with his good friend Dimitri Tiomkin, who had first worked for him on *Only Angels Have Wings*. Tiomkin created an outstanding soundtrack for him this time and would go on to score four more pictures for him.

Just before leaving Los Angeles, Hawks also had to spend a great deal of time on the screenplay to placate Joseph Breen, who found it "wholly unacceptable" for approval under the Production Code for numerous reasons: the various killings by Dunson and Matthew seemed like outright, unpunished murders; Dunson was unduly brutal in general; the women were all clearly prostitutes; Matthew and Tess Millay clearly had "an illicit sex affair," and animals seemed to be in store for abusive treatment. On August 23, Hawks had a long meeting with Breen, at which he assured the industry's morality watchdog that all of those problems would be reversed, to the point of consulting the American Humane Society regarding the animals.

Breen, however, still had dozens of specific objections to the script, which in its first draft was, for a Western, unusually loaded with sexual references. In particular, Walter Brennan's character of Groot, the cook, was constantly making off-color comments, such as "It'll make a better man out of me in less time it takes a rooster to make a chicken grin," and "Women don't seem like much till you ain't been getting none," all of which had to go. Groot was also used as an exasperated witness to Dunson and Fen's leave-taking, making faces as Dunson tells his woman he loves her and will send for her, then fingering his long black whip as they embraced and kissed; Breen didn't care for this at all. Cherry Valance and Matthew also got off quite a few suggestive remarks, and in general, the original script was spilling over with what, for the time, were very frank and natural remarks from men without women—dreams, fantasies, braggadocio expressed in terms unlike anything ever heard in a Hollywood Western. Hawks was forced to eliminate the Donegal's women because they were all, bluntly, whores, as well as to cut anything that suggested that Matthew and Tess slept together, especially the night before Dunson was to arrive in Abilene, when Tess tried using sex to convince Matthew not to face the older man; in the finished film, the only tip-off as to the extent of their relations is the reappearance of Fen's bracelet on Tess's arm. Breen was also upset that Tess agrees to bear Dunson a son with no mention of marriage, and any number of references to Matthew's many past affairs had to go. In short, the *Red River* script, originally so sexed up, was almost entirely sanitized by Joe Breen.

Hawks finally got away at the end of August and stayed briefly in Tucson before moving on to Nogales and finally Camp Anderson at Elgin. Filming started September 3, on a seventy-six-day schedule, with scenes between Dunson and Groot and then the introduction of Clift's Matthew. John Ford had sent along a fare-thee-well note to Hawks saying, "take care of my boy Duke and get a great picture." With Wayne, Hawks's main challenge was helping him find a comfortable approach to playing a man who was, presumably, fourteen years older than he was. At first, Hawks felt that Wayne was overdoing it, and as he had done before, notably with Walter Catlett and Katharine Hepburn on *Bringing Up Baby*, he asked Walter Brennan to give the Duke some pointers. But Wayne rightly rejected Brennan's suggestions to shuffle and slump more when he walked, feeling it would detract from Dunson's stature. In fact, Wayne had never looked bigger on-screen than he did in *Red River*, and he subtly conveyed middle age through the exertion necessary for his physical scenes and his fatigue at the end of the day.

As for Brennan, Hawks remembered his initial meeting with Brennan at the start of *Barbary Coast* and asked the actor to work "without"—teeth, that is. Brennan initially balked but Hawks goaded him into it, resulting in the funniest running gag in the picture, in which his Indian pal Chief Yowlachie wins his dentures in a poker game and gives them back to Brennan only at chow time. But Hawks could not talk Wayne into performing a scene in which Dunson gets his finger caught between a saddle horn and a rope and some of the boys cut it off. Wayne didn't think it was funny, and it is hard to imagine Dunson submitting to this, but the Duke admitted he was wrong when he saw how well the gag worked for Kirk Douglas in *The Big Sky* a few years later.

In a very short time, Clift had acquired the look, the saddle skills, and the diffident attitude of a fine cowboy; Hawks himself taught him the distinctive little hop he made into the saddle's stirrup and suggested the business of putting a strand of wheat in his mouth, rolling cigarettes and lighting them for his costar, and rubbing the side of his nose while in thought. But while the skeptical Wayne soon came to see he was working with a good actor, he simply couldn't believe that compact, refined-looking, five-foot-ten kid could stand up to him or look believable in a fight with him. "He's a little queer, don't you think?" Wayne had asked his secretary after his first, off-putting meeting with Clift in Hollywood.

Hawks's initial direction to Clift was to not compete with the big man on his own level. "No, don't try to get hard, because you'll just be nothing compared to Wayne," the director instructed, suggesting instead that Clift underplay his scenes with a pensive cool that Hawks was betting would contrast well with Wayne's ferociousness and overpowering physicality. Clift's stage-trained approach, in which he studied his lines for hours, was "baloney" to Hawks, and he decided to cure him of it at once by performing an improvisation with Wayne on a subject of Clift's choosing. For Hawks, it was a character's attitude that mattered more than the specific lines, and that the actor be alive to the possibilities of a scene and the other actors; The last thing he wanted was an actor who was locked down, in another world. The improvisation opened Clift's eyes; as Slim had predicted, he would learn a lot working with Hawks and the Duke.

While *Red River* was getting under way, members of Hawks's family were making some important changes in their lives. With her husband safely away, Slim was able to see a lot more of Leland Hayward, and by mid-September he had already asked her to marry him, despite the fact that they were both still married to others. Discharged from the Army Air Corps, Peter headed back to Arizona State, while David was entering junior year at Uni and sharing the Moraga Drive house with Slim. Almost as soon as his father left, David starting going a bit wild, and after a face-off, Slim was forced to call Hawks to tell him that she could no longer deal with his unmanageable teenage son and that Hawks ought to give him a job on the picture to keep him out of trouble. (No mention was made that this would make it far easier to conduct her affair with Hayward.) So Slim put David on the train and sent him out to his father, who had the prop master, Bob Landis, put him to work.

But David's best memory was not of the shoot but of a bear-hunting trip he took with Wayne and Clift. "We had an old Army sergeant as a guide. It was near the Mexican border. We were looking for smaller Mexican brown bears and we rode and rode through the mountains. We never saw any bear but we did get lost. The guide admitted that he didn't know the way back. So John Wayne took charge, and he really and truly led us back. One horse fell, lost its footing and broke its leg, and we had to shoot it." Writing to a friend about this incident, Clift joked, "You see what happens when you turn a bunch of fascists loose in the hills?" David worked all the way through the production, including on the Hollywood stages, before going back to school.

Less fortunate was Peter, who visited the location and was driving back to Tempe on September 23 with a girlfriend and another couple from school when he had a terrible automobile accident, breaking his knee, fracturing his pelvis, and suffering severe lacerations. David went up to see him in traction in Tucson, and shortly Slim flew in to visit him while on a mission of her own: to have it out with her husband, face facts that Hawks had never acknowledged, and agree on a separation. Leland Hayward's name was never mentioned, but the news of the Hawks's split made both Louella Parsons's and Hedda Hopper's columns, with the former reporting that a divorce would be pursued as soon as *Red River* was finished, the latter giving the reason as "Slim's reluctance to play mother to children almost as old as herself."

To remove herself from the firing line, Slim shortly made another of her escapes, this time back to Idaho to see Hemingway during hunting season. Slim, Mary, Hemingway, and the writer's two sons spent several days shooting partridge. But on October 31, when Slim was unloading her Browning 16-gauge automatic shotgun, one shell accidentally discharged, singeing hair off the back of Hemingway's neck. After a long pause, Slim threw her gun down and became hysterical, yelling, "I almost killed my friend."

Hemingway and Mary were getting along particularly well that fall, and with Slim now in love with Hayward, the edge was off their flirtation, even if the mutual attraction was still there. As Hemingway confided in a letter, Mary asked him, "'Papa I don't have to worry about Slim do I?' I told her no, honestly. And there it was."

In Arizona, the shooting of *Red River* progressed slowly. Even with the reliably experienced second-unit director Arthur Rosson handling most of the heavy logistics with the cattle, it seemingly took forever to get some scenes done. As Hawks remarked, "Go out and try to tell fifteen hundred cows what to do!" Rain Valley Ranch, where about half the film was being shot, lived up to its name with downpours that delayed work. Symington instantly regretted having rented his property for the movie, complaining after only two weeks that they "are just about ruining my ranch." Borden Chase, who came to location to keep working on the script, boozed it up constantly and was contrary with Hawks about everything from dramatic emphasis and the weapons the characters carried to the type of cattle Hawks used. Historically, all the cattle should have been longhorns, but since there were simply very few of them to be had, Hawks had no choice but to put the longhorns close to the camera (another time-consuming procedure) and leave the Herefords in the backgrounds. Chase continued to gripe about Hawks and his changes for the rest of his life, while Hawks countered "Chase wasn't content with writing a story; he wanted to tell you how to do it." Finally, he said, "I thought he was a goddam idiot."

Even though many people remembered *Red River* as a friendly shoot, the company was divided into opposing camps and stray offshoots. Wayne's misgivings about Clift were mild compared to the scorn of some members of his hard-drinking, ultramacho entourage, including the makeup man Web Overlander, who sneered, "Clift couldn't take a piss by himself. Hawks must be an idiot if he thinks that s.o.b. can act." Later, Wayne told a journalist, "Clift is an arrogant little bastard." Naturally, the sensitive Clift noticed the gulf between the Wayne clique and himself. At first, he tried to be one of the guys, accompanying Wayne and David Hawks on the bear hunt and sometimes sitting in with his costar and director at their frequent nocturnal poker games, but Clift later noted, "They tried to draw me into their circle but I couldn't go along with them. The machismo thing repelled me because it seemed so forced and unnecessary." Clift, whose moods always fluctuated dramatically, spent a good deal of time alone and even left the location entirely when he had enough time off. He shared a tent with Walter Brennan and Noah Beery Jr., and after the initially amusing Brennan started recycling his anecdotes for the third and fourth times, the two younger men "turned to each other in self-defense" and developed a strong friendship.

Hawks may have been turned off by Clift's intense, ultraserious personality, but unlike Wayne and the rest, he was very excited by what he was doing in front of the camera. "He *worked*—he really worked hard," Hawks said admiringly. Clift also continued to learn. The young actor thought that his biggest scene in the picture would be the pivotal one in which he takes over the cattle drive from his mentor. "Don't be too sure about that," Hawks warned Clift, whereupon he went to Wayne and told him that Clift was looking forward to walking away with the scene. When the cameras rolled, Wayne, on Hawks's advice, looked away from Clift, glancing at him only briefly, while quietly but fiercely delivering his devastating lines, concluding with, "Every time you turn around, expect to see me, 'cause one time you'll turn around and I'll be there. I'll kill you, Matt." There was nothing Clift could say, and Hawks, after letting him stand there for a moment, told him off-camera to just walk away. Afterward, Clift admitted to his director, "My big scene didn't amount to much, did it?" and Hawks told him, "Anytime you think you're going to make Wayne look bad, you've got another think coming."

But the big test would be the climactic fight scene. As in Chase's original, Dunson is injured by Cherry, although not so seriously that he can't shoot accurately. Building up to it stunningly by having Dunson relentlessly ride, then walk through a sea of cattle, Hawks had Dunson try to provoke Matthew into drawing by shooting all around him, even nicking him, then becoming disgusted and beating him silly one-handed while Matthew passively takes it all. Only then, when Dunson thinks it's all over, does Matthew respond with one big surprise slug, landing Dunson in the dust. Hawks spent four days choreographing and photographing the battle down to the most minute gesture, having Clift kick Wayne and then ram him with his whole body, thereby working around the size imbalance as much as possible. Crucially, he also kept the fight short. More than thirty years later, Hawks admitted that "My arm's still sore from trying to show Montgomery Clift how to throw a punch."

The bigger problem was the resolution Hawks devised for the fight. Hawks could not bring himself to kill off either of the leading characters, by now having turned against "killing people off for no reason at all"; in a departure from his serious films of the 1930s, he wanted his audiences to leave happy. So to let Dunson live, he reworked the scene to have Tess Millay step in with a gun and tell the two brawlers that they're being foolish, that they know they love each other and should stop acting like boys and make up. Chase was just the first of many to criticize this turn of events, calling it "garbage," and Clift disliked it because "it makes the showdown between me and John Wayne a farce." Hawks defended the logic of the scene but also acknowledged that it was "rather corny," that he never really cared for it. He thought that Joanne Dru's performance was partly to blame, but he still felt that the basic emotions and actions of the scene were valid.

"If we overdid it a little bit or went too far, well . . . I didn't know any other way to end it." The only person to recognize that Hawks had stolen this ending from another picture was Borden Chase: it was the conclusion to *The Outlaw* that Hawks and Furthman had devised six years before. When Howard Hughes found out a few months later, it was one of the few times Hawks couldn't just take the high road about one of his deceptions.

As usual, Hawks beefed up Walter Brennan's part, almost a nonentity in Chase's original story, as filming progressed, particularly using it as a way to give many scenes a humorous, upbeat tag, which effectively preempted any sour aftertaste Dunson's remorseless behavior might have created for some viewers. Aside from the ending, the most significant story change Hawks made on location was the radical hatchet job he did on Cherry Valance's character. This was due almost entirely to Hawks' displeasure with John Ireland. In stark contrast to Monty Clift, Ireland didn't take his big break seriously, didn't work hard, didn't become a cowboy. Instead, he was usually drunk or stoned, and unreliable in his scenes. He also started an affair with Joanne Dru, whom he later married. (It has often been claimed that Hawks became incensed because the director himself was involved with Dru, but it was her husband, Dick Haymes, who would have had cause to be jealous.) Everything about Ireland's approach to his work rubbed Hawks the wrong way, and he reacted by whittling his part down as much as he could, giving his lines to others, and depriving him of his pivotal role in the story's climax.

Nonetheless, Ireland did get to share one of the film's most memorable scenes, the one in which Cherry and Matthew compare guns and have a tin-can-shooting competition. As soon as Cherry signs on for the drive, he and Matthew head off together for their mutual sizing up. "That's a good-looking gun you were about to use back there. Can I see it?" Cherry remarks, to Matthew's amusement. "Maybe you'd like to see mine," he adds, as they swap weapons. "Nice. Awful nice," Cherry enthuses, before they match each other shot for shot hitting the can. The scene, not in the script, was an inspiration Hawks had on location and has often been cited as a prime and quite funny example of the homosexual subtext in much of Hawks's work. Real Hollywood insiders have long chuckled at an even more private meaning to the "mine is bigger than yours" motif of the scene, since John Ireland was well known to pack one of the biggest pistols in town, right up there with Milton Berle and Dan Dailey.

Red River marked a poignant transition in the lore of the cinematic Old West as the only film in which Harry Carey and his son, Harry Carey

Jr., appeared together, even if they didn't work in the same scenes; it was the father's second-to-last picture, and the son's third. Carey Sr. and Hawks had maintained a mutual admiration society ever since *Air Force*, the actor feeling that he gave the best performance of his life in that film and his director expressing his regard by giving him a Tennessee Walker, even though Carey already had fourteen horses. All the same, while Carey's wife, Olive, adored Hawks and was very friendly with Slim, Carey himself found Hawks too distant and reserved for his taste and did not enjoy his experience on *Red River*. Already quite ill, Carey played the cattle buyer at the end of the picture, and Hawks became unusually severe with him when the actor couldn't give him a certain look he wanted. "There was no problem with the dialogue," his son said, "but he didn't do it the way Howard wanted and Howard wasn't nice about it."

Harry Jr., then twenty-five and fresh from Raoul Walsh's *Pursued*, wasn't part of the original cast of *Red River* but was hired after Hawks fired an actor who called in sick when he was actually drinking in Tucson. Since the character doesn't make the long trek to Abilene, he decided not to bother recasting it until returning to Hollywood, at which point John Wayne suggested Carey. Hawks, the actor remembered, wrote most of the character's dialogue on the set and suggested giving him a slight stutter. This gave Walter Brennan the opening he needed, and the great character actor continually pestered the kid about how he wasn't stuttering right and demonstrated by "doing this stuttering thing like it was an affliction," to the vast amusement of the director. Hawks also found a typically indirect way of bolstering young Carey's confidence. "When we started shooting it, Howard said, 'Cut' during the first take. I thought, 'Oh, God, that's it,' and Howard said, 'Duke, you got out of character there, you were smiling,' and Duke said, 'Well, I guess I did it because he was doing such a good job,' and that made me feel great." At another point, Hawks asked Carey if he knew any cowboy songs and had him sing his choice, "Ridin' Old Paint," to the accompaniment of actor Glenn Strange's guitar, as the scene began; a year later, Burl Ives sang the same tune at Harry Carey Sr.'s funeral.

In mid-November, the company decamped for Los Angeles, where filming resumed at the Samuel Goldwyn Studios. One of the stages contained an enormous, 110 x 120–foot simulated desert that was used for all the nighttime camp scenes, the Indian raid, and various close-ups. *Red River* remains lodged in the memory as an expansive, outdoor film, but if watched closely, it reveals itself to be shot significantly inside. The opening scene, for instance, is striking for its wagon-filled landscapes and the sight of

Dunson and Fen cutting well-defined figures against the sky. Jarringly, however, most of their dialogue exchanges were done later in the studio against a rear-projection screen and intercut with the location footage to less than graceful effect. The entire film is marked by this technique, something numerous other pictures, such as *The Treasure of the Sierra Madre*, were also guilty of during this transitional period from traditional studio work to vastly increased location shooting.

After the adventure, uncertainties, camaraderie, competition, grudges, and overall excitement of the Arizona expedition, the Hollywood shoot was altogether more routine. John Ireland continued in his provocative behavior, launching an affair with Shelley Winters—visible in just one shot in the finished picture as a dance-hall girl—that was at least partly carried on, according to more than one cast member, in a covered wagon on the soundstage. One day when Ireland was needed for a scene, Hawks sent Harry Carey Jr. and stuntman Cliff Lyons to find him, which they did, in the selfsame wagon, snoozing away. Lyons awakened him by giving him a powerful kick in his side. Later, Hawks said that Ireland apologized for his lack of professionalism during the shoot and, promising to change his ways, begged for another chance on another picture. But Hawks had had more than enough.

With the main company ensconced at the studio, Arthur Rosson remained in Arizona to stage the stampede. Using several cameramen and thirty-five wranglers, it took thirteen days to shoot the monumental sequence and its related footage, which may have involved more large animals than any sequence ever filmed to that time. Seven men were hurt, thirteen horses and mules were crippled, one steer died, and sixty-nine steers were injured or crippled in the course of the filming. Rosson headed back to Hollywood in late November, and Hawks finished with the actors just before Christmas, one month over schedule.

All along, Hawks and Feldman were facing a financial whirlpool, as the logistical considerations, the constant rewriting, and the director's usual slow pace sent the budget way beyond initial projections. In late August, Monterey took an additional $200,000 loan from Security-First Bank, so that when shooting began the budget had already inched above Feldman's $1.75 million ceiling; anything beyond that would result in the Monterey partners losing percentage points in the picture. By the time the company returned to Hollywood from Arizona in early November, Feldman and Hawks were trying to figure out if there was any way of retaining a participation position in the film, but they soon saw that they had overspent their way out of their anticipated windfall. After borrowing another $111,000 from the bank, Monterey was forced to go to Eddie Small and his MPI partners, who were in a position to extract stiff terms for the money the filmmakers needed. MPI invested a further $639,000, bringing its total exposure to $1,314,000, or a bit more than half of the film's final $2,836,661 budget. In exchange, Small's group essentially got virtually all of Monterey's share of the profits.

Hawks would end up with his $125,000 producer-director's salary and nothing more for many years, meaning he would make less than he had under contract at Warner Bros. when he directed *Air Force* several years earlier. Worse, in December, Monterey was required by the IRS to attach $34,051 of monies payable to Mr. and Mrs. Howard Hawks. He was hoisted with his own petard, his entire reason for leaving Warners shot down by his own fiscal irresponsibility. Naturally, Hawks would point the finger elsewhere: sneaky moneymen, incompetent budget-makers, the elements. But this time, he truly had no one else to blame but himself. He and Feldman were the producers and had arranged the financing, and both of them knew that Hawks hadn't finished a picture on schedule in years. They in no way planned for this, and Hawks paid dearly for it, not even so much financially—he could always earn plenty of money as a director for hire—as in independence, in the control he had sought over his career. Like virtually all the other big directors who thought they could control their own destinies after the war, Hawks's dream of life without meddlesome moguls and irritating executives collapsed, even though he made a tremendously successful picture. His failure to monitor his own spending forced him directly back into the clutches of the studios from which he had spent years working to free himself.

28

Slim Walks, Money Talks

Ironically, Mrs. Howard Hawks received more publicity when her marriage was essentially over than she had at any time during it. After Hawks returned from Arizona, he was seldom at home, but when he was, the big chill was on. Knowing full well what was going on but, like Slim, not about to bring it up, Hawks stonewalled his wife, froze her out of his life. Even after he finished shooting *Red River*, he seldom saw Slim, and even when he was around the house, he could spend days and not say a word to her. It was bizarre behavior that no one, not even Slim, could ever fathom; they had agreed during Slim's quick trip to Arizona in September that there was little left between them, and yet they were caught in a no-man's-land where the next step had not been decided. Despite his general absence from Hog Canyon, Hawks's simple presence in town prevented Slim and Leland Hayward from seeing each other every day as they were now accustomed to doing, and Slim was too nervous to accept Hayward's suggestions that his lover join him in La Jolla or Palm Springs.

What brought Slim and, by extension, Hawks into the limelight during this trying period was Slim's unexpected coronation in 1946 as the Best Dressed Woman in the World. There was never any question that Slim Hawks sported one of the classiest and most original wardrobes in the United States. Shunning the pretentions of haute couture, she selected clothes that bespoke health, physical activity, the outdoors, comfort, a vaguely masculine refinement, and smart good sense. Expensive clothes and jewels also looked great on her, of course, and at five feet, eight and a half inches and 125 pounds, she appeared at home in virtually anything from work clothes to the most elegant gown. But winning the title voted by 150 designers and fashion editors of the New York Dress Institute was a shock. The favorites were always women like the Duchess of Windsor, a four-time winner, or the Duchess of Kent, and the bias was otherwise entirely in favor of vastly wealthy East Coast socialites; for a member of the movie colony and native

Californian to be recognized was simply unheard-of. Also unusual was the fact that most of the voters had never met Slim, knowing her only from her photographs in *Harper's Bazaar*, where editor Carmel Snow had promoted her for several years and advanced her as the first "California Girl." But Slim's fresh look and "specifically American type of chic" won the voters over, with a *Vogue* editor defining the winner's appeal as "the sexiness of the sultry sports girl — the ability to wear a skirt and a shirt and a pair of thong sandals and still outdo the girl in the black slip."

A major spread in *Life* magazine featured Slim in five poses and another photograph of her with Hawks (sporting his silly mustache). The write-up claimed that she spent ten thousand dollars a year on clothes, not including jewelry, furs, and her maid's salary, and that her glass-doored wardrobe contained nine fur coats, twenty-four suits, forty-seven dresses, thirty-five evening gowns, and so on, right down to 120 pairs of shoes. Also in her collection was a solid gold barrette she had copied from a ten-cent-store model and which clamped her hair back in a simple way that became popular after she wore it in a magazine photograph.

Honestly surprised and amused by her honor, Slim joked of the voters, "If they ever saw me running around in my blue jeans and wild shorts they might change their minds," then revealed that she changed clothes twice a day "in jig time," mostly wore shorts or slacks, did not own a Paris gown, hated white fox and see-through Lucite bags, and lived by the following fashion rules: "Never dress for other women, dress for men, don't follow fads and always be mysterious." Even though she had never really worked, Slim said that she was considering taking a regular job, either for her close friend David O. Selznick or as the West Coast editor of *Harper's Bazaar*. Such was Slim's standing in the fashion field that she became the first "consumer" to receive the Neiman-Marcus award, normally reserved for designers of great talent and influence.

While Slim was receiving all this public notice for her terrific taste, as well as ardent personal attention from Leland Hayward, Hawks tried to overcome the humiliation of his cuckolding through the usual course of younger women. One of his discoveries in early 1947 was a strikingly beautiful dark-haired model named Katherine Cassidy, née Icede. More voluptuous than the usual Hawks protegée, Cassidy, already earning top modeling fees at twenty, was noted for designing many of her own clothes. Very taken with her, at least physically, Hawks put Cassidy through his usual dramatic and vocal hoops, although her Hollywood career never progressed beyond a major photo spread Hawks arranged in *Life* magazine.

As far as *Red River* was concerned, Hawks was sure he had something special: his gamble with Wayne and Clift had certainly paid off, the size of the picture was suitably impressive, and everyone in his circle smelled a box-office winner. But the film posed by far the biggest editing challenge of any of his films to date, as the episodic narrative, the absence of some seemingly inevitable confrontations—between Matthew and Cherry or with the much-discussed border gangs or with Indians—and the sheer quantity and diversity of the filmed material made the picture far tougher to shape and mold than the much more tightly controlled, dialogue-dominated films he normally made. Chris Nyby was under contract to Warner Bros., but Hawks managed to borrow him as soon as the cutter finished *Pursued* for Raoul Walsh, and Nyby spent several months, both during shooting and after, splicing and pruning the picture into shape. In late February, Hawks showed the rough cut to a small group of trusted friends, including Zanuck and Gregory Ratoff, with the latter telling the director that the people who saw it thought it was "out of this world."

Still, during the spring of 1947, Hawks had to face the hard fact that no matter how well *Red River* did, he was highly unlikely to make any more money from it, at least not anytime soon, and he had better take another job fast. Not only did a divorce from Slim promise to drain his resources, but the government was taking a great deal of money to pay off back taxes, and he was even way behind in alimony payments to Athole. His gambling debts continued to mount as well. Hawks left behind no accounts, but his losses easily totaled in the tens of thousands during this period, and he persisted in eluding bookies when he owed them money. Instead of coming to the house, however, certain bookies now knew to approach Famous Artists, where Feldman was also a heavy player, and demand payment on Hawks's behalf. The agency always obliged, with reimbursement handled internally later on.

As always, Hawks appeared and pretended to have far more money than he actually did, but much as he hated to face it, he was forced to instruct his agent to find him the highest-paying job possible. Feldman confided to his associates at Famous Artists that "he is desperately in need of funds" and began sizing up possible deals. Most of the studios, of course, were anxious to hire a director with such a track record, one who could automatically bring with him a big star, and hefty percentage deals for top directors were now a reality. Jack Warner, for starters, was willing to take Hawks back with the same sort of autonomous production deal that he'd given Michael Curtiz; Hawks was very interested, but Harry Warner stalled the deal. Columbia seemed on the verge of offering him a minimum of $150,000 plus 50 percent, and Hawks, who owned 50 percent of *Twentieth Century* with the studio, said he would be willing to remake that film for them. As before, Harry Cohn remained willing to do "anything that Howard wants." Zanuck wasn't offering a profit participation but had a staight $200,000 standing offer for Hawks's services that would include a substantial advance, but when Hawks tried to press *Dreadful Hollow* on him, Zanuck could muster no enthusiasm. There was even talk of Hawks making an independent deal at the longtime B-movie studio Republic, which had just initiated a new premier class of production with bigger budgets to attract major directors. Ben Hecht had been the first with *Specter of the Rose*, Feldman would produce Orson Welles's *Macbeth* there that summer, and Hawks's friends Allan Dwan, Lewis Milestone, and John Ford were among the others who would shortly be lured to Republic by the promise of wide artistic latitude. Hawks immediately considered trying to revive *The Dark Page* with Bogart and Cary Grant starring, but when it became apparent that it might take a year or more for them to be available at the same time, Hawks proposed doing it without big stars, which interested Republic boss Herbert Yates much less.

The best bet for Hawks was to set up a deal for a property he already owned, and by far the most interesting one was *The Sun Also Rises*. Hemingway's first great novel, about the so-called Lost Generation after World War I, had long tempted filmmakers and actors anxious to capture the glamorous ennui of Jake Barnes, Lady Brett, and the others as they made their way from the bars and bistros of Paris to the running of the bulls and the corrida at Pamplona. But since the novel's publication in 1926, no one had been able to lick the script, at least in part because the censorship problems bound to accrue from such matters as Jake's impotence, Lady Brett's adultery and promiscuity, and the drunken, lascivious behavior of the other characters. As part of their divorce settlement, Hemingway had given his first wife, Hadley, the screen rights, and she sold them to RKO in 1932 for $14,500. This was far less the novel's potential worth, which Hemingway remained bitter about for years. The following year, the rights were sold for $25,000 to Fox, which came the closest to making it, with Clive Brook as Jake and Constance Bennett as Lady Brett, but the project was flatly rejected by the Hays Office. Ann Harding, a patrician star of the early 1930s, bought it in 1935 and for ten years harbored the dream of producing it as a vehicle for herself. Rowland Brown, acting on behalf of Feldman and Hawks to keep the price reasonable, purchased the rights from her in 1945, and a year later the agent-director team assumed full legal possession.

Preoccupied with *Red River*, Hawks did nothing with the Hemingway project at first, but when Samuel Fuller visited Hawks's office one day to discuss a possible writing job, he noticed several books on the shelf above Hawks's desk. "I own all these," Hawks offhandedly said. Taking a closer look at some of the familiar titles, including *The Sun Also Rises*, the young screenwriter replied, "Well, I own them too," whereupon Hawks said, quietly but with emphasis, "No, Sam, you don't understand. I *own* them." When Fuller enthused about the Hemingway, Hawks asked if he would be interested in writing the script, but was stunned when Fuller, carried away with excitement, suggested his idea for a great opening scene: in a tent near the front during World War I, an injured Jake Barnes is on the operating table; the nurse is Brett, and the light from the lantern shines upon her as we hear Jake's balls drop, one, then the next, into a bucket. Thus, in one vivid scene would the audience be clued in to the nature of Jake's malady and Brett's knowledge of it. (Though Hemingway never explicitly detailed the injury in the novel, he elsewhere indicated that Jake lost not his balls but his penis, leaving him with the ability to still feel sexual desire but unable to do anything about it. Fuller misunderstood this, while Hawks's insight into this crucial component of the story remains unclear.) Needless to say, Fuller did no work on this script.

All of the companies approached about Hawks's services were very keen on the prospect of his making *The Sun Also Rises*, but without a script or even a clear idea on Hawks's part of how to get around the problems that had stumped everyone else for so long, the project obviously couldn't move ahead anytime soon and would not solve Hawks's immediate need for cash. The project was put on hold, to surface as an ever-intriguing possibility at several points over the next few years.

Suddenly, Hawks got a call from the last man in Hollywood, except for Louis B. Mayer, he ever expected to work for again—Sam Goldwyn. After having reduced his productivity during the war and finally won his long-cherished Oscar for *The Best Years of Our Lives* as well as the Irving Thalberg Award from the Academy, Goldwyn was resuming a schedule of two films per year. Several of his big stars had either played out their contracts or slipped away during the war, but in 1943 he signed the multitalented comic entertainer Danny Kaye and launched him on an enormously successful screen career in a string of Technicolor comedies and musicals. The fourth of these, *The Secret Life of Walter Mitty*, was due out in July, and Goldwyn had the brainstorm that Kaye's vehicle for 1948 should be a remake of *Ball of Fire*, then only five years old. At the enormous price of $100,000, Goldwyn hired Harry Tugend to adapt Wilder and Brackett's script.

In various interviews, Hawks claimed that Goldwyn came to him practically begging for an idea for Kaye and that he, Hawks, hatched the *Ball of Fire* idea, but Tugend was hired in January and finished his first draft in March before Hawks was even approached by Goldwyn. All through the winter, Goldwyn had intended to have William K. Seiter direct, and it was only in March, after Seiter proved unavailable, that Goldwyn spoke to Hawks in Palm Springs. For reasons that were never spelled out but undoubtedly had to do with the success of the original picture, Goldwyn decided that Hawks, who obviously didn't respect him and always caused him trouble, was the only man for this job. Hawks didn't want to take it, but Goldwyn finally made him in an offer that, in Hawks's current desperate straits, he simply couldn't refuse — $250,000. In one interview, Hawks stated that he earned $25,000 per week, but had this been the case he would have made, with overages, $350,000 for the job; Goldwyn had wisely hired him at a flat rate.

Hawks dealt with Goldwyn without even informing Feldman, and the agreement was reached by the beginning of April, just as Monterey was closing up its offices on the Goldwyn lot. It was a deal that, as even Hawks later admitted, Goldwyn came to regret, due to its pointless extravagance — he was paying his director nearly four thousand dollars more than he was paying Danny Kaye, and for as anonymous and indifferent a piece of work as any journeyman would have done for one-third the price.

After his deep and passionate involvement in every phase of his last several pictures, Hawks couldn't have cared less about this one, and the result was what he unequivocally called an "altogether horrible experience." At first, he said, Goldwyn wanted to set the story in 1922 with a New Orleans musical backdrop. This seemed both preposterous and musically limiting, so the slant was changed, with the professors no longer researching slang but modern jazz. The constant evolution of the script is testified to by the revolving door for writers that kept spinning right through production, with little input from Hawks. After Tugend completed a second draft, Phil Rapp did a rewrite, whereupon the excellent writer Daniel Fuchs spent nearly as much time on revisions as Tugend had on his adaptation. Other writers were called in for spot work: former Kaye screenwriters Melville Shavelson, Robert

Pirosh, Ken Englund, and Everett Freeman all worked on punching up his dialogue; Roland Kibbee was paged just to write the Buck and Bubbles material. An extraordinary collection of jazz greats was assembled for the picture—in additon to clarinetist Benny Goodman, who would play one of the professors, Goldwyn brought aboard Tommy Dorsey, Louis Armstrong, Lionel Hampton, Charlie Barnet, and Mel Powell—but the army of writers was unable to give them anything interesting to do or say. Entitled *That's Life* during production, *A Song Is Born*, as the picture was renamed, ended up as an unusual instance of a picture with no screenplay credit, other than the citation for Wilder and Monroe's original story. Whether this was the result of a Goldwyn decree or because no one wanted it is unknown.

In what was otherwise a desultory shoot and film, the musicians represented the one saving grace. Hawks, whose own musical talent was limited to playing two songs on the banjo, liked jazz and popular music and got a kick out of the jam sessions on the set. On numerous occasions, according to Virginia Mayo, Hawks "would stop the action and just listen to them play, which wasn't very professional. Mr. Goldwyn wouldn't like him wasting time like that." Hawks sometimes invited the musicians up to his house, where his daughter Barbara remembers some incredible evenings when Goodman, Powell, and a couple of the others would play and cut homemade 78 recordings into the small hours. All the same, Goldwyn's squareness asserted itself in the narrow latitude he allowed Hawks and the musicians, jamming the latter's contributions into narrowly defined corners, mostly early in the picture, and instructing his director not to let the white and black musicians get too close together; even Hawks, not exactly known for his broadmindedness about race relations, balked at this and claimed to have become good friends with Louis Armstrong.

Hawks knew from the outset that he was stuck, and it only got worse. As Virginia Mayo observed, "This wasn't his own film, it was Mr. Goldwyn's film. Mr. Goldwyn was the boss." Danny Kaye, known for his wild exuberance and inventive antics, seemed straitjacketed by the part of the bashful academic. What's more, he was temporarily separated from his wife, Sylvia Fine, which not only meant that she wasn't there to write any specialty numbers or comedy for him but that he was, according to Hawks, "a basket case, stopping work to see a psychiatrist twice a day." In fact, Kaye had one shrink appointment per day, at noon, but the result was the same, with his director finding him "about as funny as a crutch."

Even worse, after having promised Hawks that he wouldn't have to use her, Goldwyn imposed Virginia Mayo, Kaye's costar in all his previous films, as the female lead. Hawks gave Mayo a miniversion of his routine for beginning actresses, sending her to an empty soundstage and making her scream to lower her voice. "That didn't work for me," Mayo said. "I just got hoarse. I just had to try the role the way I ordinarily would." But Hawks lavished most of his attention on the actress's looks. "He liked every woman to sort of resemble his wife," Mayo declared. "I had to wear clothes that were patterned after his wife Slim. And even my hairdo was patterned after Mrs. Hawks' hairdo." Receiving little concrete direction from Hawks, Mayo watched *Ball of Fire* numerous times and privately rehearsed her scenes in imitation of Stanwyck. Nor could Mayo sing her own number, which was dubbed by Jeri Sullivan. Hawks considered Mayo, in a word, "pathetic."

Once again, Hawks rounded up a genial bunch of character actors to play the professors but was saddled with Steve Cochran, whom he had tested for *The Big Sleep* and didn't like, as the heavy (one arguable improvement the film made on *Ball of Fire* is that there's less of the cornball gangster stuff). Aside from the musicians, the one compensation for Hawks was working again with Gregg Toland. Unlike *Red River*, however, for which Hawks had badly wanted his favorite cinematographer, *A Song Is Born* was utterly devoid of challenge or interest pictorially, and looked it. That it was Hawks's first film in color mattered to him not at all; Toland gave the film the bright, lavish look Goldwyn expected for his Danny Kaye comedies, but from a compositional point of view, he and Hawks approached their assignment so perfunctorily that they often just repeated setups from *Ball of Fire*. Hawks was so uninterested that he didn't even attend dailies and, late in life, claimed never to have seen the finished film.

On all fronts, Hawks was enduring one of his most dispiriting seasons. During the spring, prior to the shoot, he spent as much time in Palm Springs as *Red River* would allow but happened to be home during the period Slim was overwrought with worry about Leland Hayward. As he had once four years before, Hayward began hemorrhaging beyond doctors' ability to stop it. Slim called in her own doctor, who performed an operation and concluded the bleeding was due to tension. Even through this, Slim's attachment to Hayward was never discussed with Hawks, who, Slim said, "behaved like the gentleman he had been brought up to be. He knew I was suffering and he went out of his way to be sympathetic and supportive." When Slim was telephoned with the reasonably optimistic results of the operation, she was in her room and, she thought, alone. Then, as she recalled it in her memoir, the following scene played itself out:

Unknown to me, Howard had entered the room during this call. When I looked up, he was standing at the foot of my bed, watching my face.

"Is he going to be all right?" he asked, as though we were talking about an old friend of ours.

"Yes, I think so."

"Good," he said softly. "I know how much you care for him. I'm glad he's going to be all right."

With that, Howard was gone. And I sat there for a long time, in total disbelief that my marriage had just ended with the most impeccable ease and grace.

On June 5, as Hawks was testing potential professors for *A Song Is Born*, Slim moved out of Hog Canyon and took a house with sixteen-month-old Kitty a few minutes away in Brentwood. The details of the settlement would be worked out later, and it would take nearly a year for Hayward to obtain a divorce from his wife, Margaret Sullavan. But now, after several years of a household bursting with teenage kids, rich bikers, croquet players, illustrious guests, animals, and, above all, Slim's sunny exuberance and spirited sense of fun, Hog Canyon was quiet. Sure, Hawks could bring his girls there openly now, and David would be around through the summer, tinkering with cars and bringing dates by before leaving for Princeton in the fall. But without Slim, the parties were over. Hawks had built the house for her, and she had decorated it, furnished it, maintained it, bestowed it with her impeccable taste. With Hawks as its sole master now, the atmosphere became muted, the help idle, the rooms empty.

A Song Is Born began shooting on June 16 on an allotted seventy-six-day schedule that was then augmented to an incredibly cushy eighty-one days; it almost seemed padded to take Danny Kaye's shrink appointments into account. Filming was briefly interrupted in early August when Hawks became ill, but even with the leisurely timetable and the director not wanting to spend a minute longer on it than necessary, production fell gradually behind. Shooting finally ground to a halt on September 26 after eighty-seven days, eight days behind schedule. The budget was a lofty $2,851,983—incredibly, virtually the same as that of *Red River*; there can be no question which made better use of its money.

United Artists had originally hoped that *Red River* would be ready for release that summer, but with Dimitri Tiomkin's score just completed and Hawks's attention diverted elsewhere, it wasn't even ready for its first sneak preview until July 8. Another preview was held two weeks later, and while reaction was good, everyone agreed that the film was far too long. Tiomkin exclaimed, "If I never see another cow in my life, it will be too soon." Feldman gave Hawks a number of notes, some of which were heeded, while others were not: the picture was at least twenty minutes too long, with "too many cattle scenes," and cuts should largely come in the first half; there were too many "yahoos" at the start of the drive, and at least a half dozen individual scenes were too long and could be cut by as much as half. Hawks was so enamored of the film that Chris Nyby had to be brutal at times and force him to shorten it, and Feldman still wanted to change the title to something indicative of the size and importance of the story. All the same, the film was in excellent shape compared to the financial and legal quagmire surrounding it on all sides.

United Artists, which had been started as an idealistic dream by Charles Chaplin, D. W. Griffith, Douglas Fairbanks, and Mary Pickford in 1919, through which the filmmakers would control their own destinies, was in its most perilous straits ever in the late 1940s. Always the subject of fractious disagreements between surviving founders Chaplin and Pickford, the company was considered such a poor risk at that time that its banks either suspended loans to it or demanded 100 percent guarantees on them. Making matters worse, some of its key producers, disenchanted with the corporate disarray, decided to withhold their product, thereby diminishing cash flow and creating a further reduced sense of confidence that UA could properly release a big picture. United Artists was finally able to force delivery of the films, but because they were all flops, the company became even more anxious to get *Red River* into release; at least this one, executives felt, looked like a surefire winner.

The mess at UA, along with the additional cutting Nyby was doing and Hawks's daily chores on *A Song Is Born*, enabled Hawks to put off any decisive action regarding *Red River* until the fall. The moment he finished shooting the Goldwyn picture, Hawks left for New York, *Red River* in hand, and proceeded to set up screenings for friends, including Monty Clift, who saw it there for the first time and was one of the few who was less than pleased. The actor found his own performance "mediocre" but told a friend, "I watched myself in *Red River* and I knew I was going to be famous, so I decided I would get drunk anonymously one last time." Among those whom Hawks pointedly did not invite to the showings, which he impudently held at the United Artists projection room, were UA's executive staff, with the exception of the company's new president, Gradwell Sears. This created great ill will internally and marked an admission, as far as the lawyers were concerned, that Hawks had at last finished the film. While Hawks was still in town, attorneys representing UA contacted him at the Warwick Hotel to demand delivery of the picture, along with 236 positive prints that had been contractually due on August 1. Unless he delivered within thirty days, Hawks was told, he would be considered in breach.

As usual, Hawks ignored such threats; having failed to sell the picture to a different distributor, he at least wanted plenty of assurances that it would be handled in the major way it deserved. Through it all, Hawks hadn't a leg to stand on legally, as UA's contract was airtight and clearly entitled the company to the film's negative—once it was finished. But Hawks returned to Los Angeles and continued to play games, pretending the film wasn't really finished and otherwise stalling for time. He spent Thanksgiving in Palm Springs with Eddie Small and his wife, and at the end of the month received word that UA was demanding arbitration, in view of its own good faith and belief in the indisputability of its claim to the film. Outrageously, Monterey responded that the film was still not finished, that considerable work remained to be done, and that it desired a change of venue from New York to Los Angeles because the company was in debt and had no funds. Nonetheless, a hearing was shortly set for the American Arbitration Association on March 3, when three men—arbitrators selected by Monterey, UA, and an impartial third party—would settle the fate of *Red River*.

In the meantime, members of the MPI group were becoming extremely restless. In February, with the arbitration still a month away, MPI vice president Maurice Cohen served notice on Monterey that Hawks's failure to complete the film on schedule "has caused us great and irreparable damage for which we will be forced to hold you responsible." In essence, MPI, as the primary financing party, threatened to take *Red River* away from Hawks and deliver it to UA themselves. In response, Monterey charged that the film was made under MPI supervision and pointed out that MPI itself was now in breach for failing to meet the deadline for payment of John Wayne's guaranteed $75,000 profit share.

Literally the next day, on February 17, Howard Hughes notified MPI that any release of *Red River* would constitute an infringement of his rights, since the ending, in his view, plagiarized the climax of *The Outlaw*. Stating that Hawks had worked on the story of *The Outlaw* and was paid for it, Hughes concluded, "It would seem to an impartial observer that the similarity complained of must have been the result of taking from a common source," or stealing. Hughes threatened immediate legal action.

At this, MPI officers suddenly became less eager to take over the picture, bewildered at what they might be expected to do with a picture with no ending. Monterey attempted to further stall by insisting that the combination of Hughes's complaint and MPI's move to take over the picture made it impossible for the company to send anyone to represent it at the arbitration hearing in New York. The arbitrators would have none of this, however, and proceeded to unanimously find in favor of United Artists. Monterey was thus forced to deliver the negative to the Pathé Lab in New York, but MPI warned that no prints should be struck until the ongoing dispute with Hughes was resolved.

Given Hawks's lifelong casual attitude about "borrowing" dialogue and bits of business that had worked before, there was no question that Hughes had good reason for being miffed. Specifically, Hawks had lifted a memorable detail from the final showdown in The Outlaw in which Doc Holliday tries to force Billy the Kid to draw by firing at him, nicking his earlobes in the process, and there was no way Hughes was going to let him keep that. But the main reason Hughes moved against Red River was to settle a longstanding grudge: Hawks had done this to him before, when he helped himself to the ending of Hell's Angels for The Dawn Patrol. Hawks fought him by having his secretary, Helen Ayres, compile a list of other Westerns with similar sequences—she came up with about a dozen, including the recent Randolph Scott feature Gunfighters—and, in a heated phone conversation, Hawks defied Hughes to prove that this sort of scene was not one common to Westerns. Still, Hughes was determined to extract his pound of flesh and compel Hawks to make the changes he demanded or face the prospect of a protracted lawsuit, which would hold up the release of Red River for as long as The Outlaw had been delayed.

Hughes had another motivation as well. Having just taken control of RKO studios, Hughes was looking for a way to pry three of his productions— The Outlaw and the as-yet unreleased Vendetta and Mad Wednesday—away from United Artists so he could reassume control of them. All through the weeks that he was pressing for changes in the ending of Red River, Hughes was dickering over these pictures with UA president Grad Sears, whose persuasiveness and willingness to accomodate the tycoon broke down Hughes's stubborness and, more than anything, paved the way for Red River to come out both on schedule and in a form very close to what Hawks intended.

The precise manner in which the final release version of Red River was agreed upon is open to some question, since Hawks was vague about details and the stories Christian Nyby told about it are rife with contradictions. In his book *Howard Hawks, Storyteller*, the film scholar Gerald Mast quotes Nyby at length about how Hughes notified Monterey of his objections to the showdown sequence only a week before the film's scheduled openings in the Southwest in August 1948. (It had already been reviewed by the trade press in July.) According to this account, Hughes came to the cutting room and made Nyby cut the scene in sixteen different ways, but never to his satisfaction. Fed up, Nyby offered Hughes the chance to cut the sequence himself. After some further slight adjustments, in the end Hughes was mollified by cutting fifteen seconds from the picture.

At the very least, Nyby compressed the time frame in which all this occurred, as Hughes filed his copyright suit in Federal court on August 13, and *Red River* didn't open in Western territories until September 1. At the same time, Hughes misrepresented the similarities between the pictures, particularly in the matter of the earlobes: Dunson nicked Matthew on the cheek, not the ears; if the lobes had been hit, the result would presumably have been visible in subsequent shots, which were not reshot or replaced.

More perplexing is the question of why two distinct versions of *Red River* were made — one in which a written chronicle entitled *Early Tales of Texas* serves to connect the chapters in this highly episodic film, another in which voice-over narration by Walter Brennan's character, Nadine Groot, bridges the gaps in time and place. Two Hawks specialists, Gerald Mast and John Belton, have analyzed the differences between the versions in great detail, with Mast, along with Leonard Maltin, preferring the diary version and Belton coming down in favor of the narration, as does Peter Bogdanovich. As this split opinion indicates, there are things to be said for and against each version. The diary version runs seven and a half minutes longer; in addition to cutting the shots of the pages, other cuts for the latter version included a lengthy description by Cherry Valance of a beautiful woman who told him about the railroad to Abilene and a scene showing Matthew's nervousness at night as Dunson is catching up to him. There are also differences in the musical score, with the diary version containing more vocalizing than the voice-over edition. Most important, however, the showdown between Dunson and Matthew is significantly cut in the latter version. As Gerald Mast observed, all of Dunson's initial dialogue — ordering Matt to draw, warning, "Then I'll make you draw," and so on — is missing in the voice-over version, leaving him to just fire away. Also removed are the progressively tight shots of Matthew's unblinking eyes as Dunson shoots at him — only the last one remains.

There is no question that the diary version constitutes the picture in its earlier form, although, as *The Big Sleep* demonstrates, that doesn't necessarily mean that it is definitive. Hawks told Bogdanovich, "The one with the book was the first cutting and it wasn't any good." He explained, "It was meant to be with narration, which shortened it and brought it closer to you because we had a very distinctive voice doing it." Hawks even claimed that he never saw the diary verison until it was on television.

Although Hawks seldom employed voice-over narration in his pictures, he had just done so to good effect in *The Big Sleep* and would use it again in *The Big Sky* and *Land of the Pharaohs*. That Hawks would passively permit a film so important to him to be printed up and distributed in a form that he expressly disapproved of testifies to several things: his habit of not following a picture all the way through postproduction, the general confusion that surrounded *Red River* in the final months before it came out, and the extent to which Hawks had, by that time, virtually washed his hands of it, since there was no financial incentive in his further involvement. Still, Hawks's negative opinion of the diary version can perhaps be looked at partly as Monday morning quarterbacking, since, in most ways other than the pure enjoyment of Walter Brennan's vocal commentary, the voice-over version represents a reduction of the first and longer cut, especially where the climax is concerned. In the absence of any documented reasons why two versions were created, it seems likely that the voice-over edition was made with an eye to foreign markets, where several minutes' worth of English-language text on the screen would have been highly annoying. The voice-over version was also more suitable for television, although the diary version, to Hawks's annoyance, frequently turned up on the tube with its hard-to-read written text. Ironically, the *Red River* released on video with the promotional line, "Restored Director's Cut," is the diary version, the one Hawks himself pointedly disapproved.

In any event, all this was done without any overseeing or even input from Hawks, who had trusted Nyby to shape the mass of diverse footage in the first place and had now left the final crucial decisions in his hands. Hawks left Los Angeles in mid-August and sailed from New York on the *Queen Elizabeth* on August 21, on his way to shoot *I Was a Male War Bride* in Germany.

Like a plane taking off under seemingly impossible conditions, *Red River* finally made its way into theaters at the beginning of September 1948, exactly two years after it had gone before the cameras. But even as it played strongly in the Southwest and the plains states, squabbling continued in

the executive suites where its destiny was being controlled. Hawks's unwillingness to turn his picture over to UA had largely been predicated on his
lack of confidence in the distributor's ability to market it and secure the
best theaters. In July, he was placated by an unusual agreement under which
Goldwyn's sales organization, headed by the shrewd James A. Mulvey, would
handle *Red River* on a freelance basis in exchange for 3 percent of the gross.
In mid-September, the verbal deal was called off, partly because Mulvey's
slow playoff pattern annoyed the MPI partners, but mostly because the
Goldwyn sales arm was increasingly busy with *A Song Is Born*, which was
competing with *Red River* for the same theaters in some cities, creating a
conflict of interest. At this point, with Hawks's endorsement, Grad Sears
took personal control of the selling of *Red River*, which opened in New York
and other major eastern cities on September 29, to huge business. By mid-
October, when it finally debuted in Los Angeles, it was the number-three
box-office film nationally, after *Johnny Belinda* and *Sorry, Wrong Number*,
and two weeks later it moved up to number one.

All this did Hawks little good financially, since he had long since spent

Releasing through Hughes-controlled RKO, Goldwyn launched *A
Song Is Born* in New York and Chicago on October 19, to some unusually
nasty reviews. But even though the musical didn't ring up the colossal numbers of Danny Kaye's earlier crowd pleasers, the film did very strong business, playing for more than two months in some of its first-run engagements.
Strikingly, in the first week of November, *A Song Is Born* was the number-
one box-office film in the nation, and *Red River* was number two. In those
days no mention was made of the fact that the same man directed both films,
nor was Hawks around to promote the fact himself, but the double-barreled
success did testify to Hawks's remarkable and unbroken commercial winning streak that now stretched back across nine films and ten years. The
two films remained in the top dozen box-office attractions through Christmas, and *Variety* announced that *Red River*, with domestic rentals of
$4,150,000, was the number-three film of the year, just slightly behind the
Bob Hope–Bing Crosby smash *Road to Rio* and MGM's lavish musical
Easter Parade. Hawks was declared the number-six "money director" of the
year. The film was Hawks's most popular since *Sergeant York*.

All this did Hawks little good financially, since he had long since spent
himself out of a meaningful share of the profits. Because he had worked on
a deferral, Hawks didn't receive any of his $125,000 salary until the picture
officially went into profit after the 1952 reissue, and even then his share
was only $56,405, the rest going to Athole, Slim, and Feldman; subtract
taxes, and Hawks cleared less than $30,000 for all his work, which makes it

more apparent why he felt forced to accept A Song Is Born and his subsequent contract at Fox. For its part, A Song Is Born ultimately took in $2.4 million at the box office, very good but not good enough compared to the unnecessary amount Goldwyn spent on it.

But the book was far from closed on Red River and Monterey's problems. From the time the company departed Arizona to years after the film had come and gone from theaters, the filmmakers were beseiged with lawsuits from creditors whom Hawks, in line with his usual treatment of everyone from bookies to the corner grocer, had left in the lurch. Among the twenty-eight claimants were an assistant director, Southern Pacific rail, thirty-one actors, and the rancher who had rented them the steers. The most egregious grievance was that of John Wayne, whom one would have thought no one in Hollywood would want to alienate. Despite UA's agreement to compensate the star first, full payment of his guaranteed profit was not forthcoming until 1952, although Famous Artists placated him with loans in the interim. As of 1952, creditors were still owed approximately $175,000 by Monterey.

Most incredible of all was the company's failure to reimburse Pathé Laboratories for its processing and printing of the film. In order to not hold up the film's release any further, the lab generously turned out the full order of more than four hundred prints in 1948 without immediate compensation. Unfortunately, no one—not Monterey, MPI, or UA—took responsibility for the bill (it was actually MPI's obligation), and it got to the point where, at 10 A.M. on July 20, 1951, the lab held an auction to get what it could for the film's negative and soundtrack. The catch was that the buyer would not own the rights to the picture, but the true owner, for lack of the elements, would be effectively prevented from making 16mm or TV prints. Even though Pathé was owed less than five thousand dollars, up to the day of the auction, the interested parties were all acting like cagey poker players, bluffing one another by not stepping up and paying off the small debt. In fact, the ploy worked for MPI, which managed to buy the thirteen cans of negative and sound at auction for fifteen hundred dollars. But Pathé then immediately announced plans for another auction, on August 21, at which an enormous amount of other Red River material would be sold to the highest bidder. Hawks's business associate Ed Lasker won with a bid of $2,777, the price of the lien plus costs. Hawks had Lasker buy the material because, since it was not copyrighted, he and Feldman were afraid that another buyer would use it in another film or television show. In any event, it remains astonishing that the makers of so great and valuable a film could treat their creation, and those who helped them achieve it, in such a cavalier fashion, with so little regard for its condition and eventual fate.

In 1953, in the wake of the reissue, some profits began trickling in, with 69 percent going to MPI, 25 percent to Monterey, and 6 percent to John Wayne. The following year, Monterey actually received $15,602 in profit participation, of which 18½ percent went to Hawks and 10 percent was given to Slim. Despite periodic offers for the television rights, Monterey finally sold *Red River* outright to UA in 1957 for $225,000. MPI had been dissolved the year before after making its partners a great deal of money, while Monterey, whose shareholders did considerably less well, followed suit two years later, but not before having to pay off the $18,000 still due some creditors. Thus ended, with a whimper, Hawks's long-abandoned dream of being a true independent producer in total control of his own destiny.

Critically, *Red River* was as well received as any straightforward Western was permitted to be in the 1940s or 1950s. During those two decades, when Westerns were at their greatest and most abundant and therefore taken entirely too much for granted, the only Westerns nominated for the best-picture Oscar were *The Ox-Bow Incident, High Noon,* and *Shane,* the first two among the most socially conscious Westerns ever made. Essentially, if your aspirations did not include political and symbolic commentary beyond the normal scope of the genre, you could forget serious consideration from the critics and tastemakers. The same went for John Wayne, who got very good reviews for *Red River—Variety* spoke for many when it said that he "has his best assignment to date and he makes the most of it"—but the lion's share of the attention went to Montgomery Clift, who became the raging heartthrob of millions of teenage girls.

Still, time and perspectives change and, as good and unusual as Clift was in the film, the film historian Jeanine Basinger more recently made the incisive point that "a nonmovie lover is the person who walks out of *Red River* talking about Montgomery Clift." Hawks always liked to say how John Ford, who allegedly helped edit certain sequences in *Red River,* told him upon seeing Wayne's performance as Dunson, "I never knew the sonofabitch could act." Wayne backed the story up, stating that, "Jack never respected me as an actor until I made *Red River*," and it was immediately thereafter that Ford starred Wayne in a series of roles that were much more complex and demanding than any he had offered him previously. In any event, nothing Wayne had done before quite prepared the viewer for the sheer force and turbulence of his performance as Dunson; there is no question that it was his breakthrough role.

Like the similar independent ventures of Capra, Wyler, Stevens, Sturges, Hitchcock, Lang, and others, Hawks's didn't last long—just one film. Because of the tremendous autonomy Hawks had commandeered at the studios prior to this, he didn't have appreciably more artistic freedom on *Red River* than he'd had on any of his earlier pictures, nor did he have the slightest inclination to use his freedom to make "art" films, such as Ford's *The Fugitive,* or message pictures even in the mainstream vein of Capra's *It's a Wonderful Life.* The secret to Hawks's enduring success was that there was no difference between the manner of films he wanted to make and what the studios craved; he just wanted to make them on his own terms, without the interference of meddlesome producers and executives, and at maximum profit to himself. Being left to his own devices, and exposing himself financially to his investors when he hadn't nearly the expertise or self-discipline to beat them at their own game, proved fatal to his dreams of continued independence. But he made a classic film in the process, and *Red River* introduced him to the only place other than the modern world he was ever to find accommodating to his imagination: the American West.

29

Skirting Trouble:
I Was a Male War Bride

Although time would prove her wrong, Slim felt that Hawks was being very civilized about the divorce. And the feeling was mutual, for, although she could have tried to clean her husband out, she didn't feel motivated to do so. In their property settlement, Slim agreed that she could be supported "in her customary manner" by just five thousand dollars in alimony from Hawks per year, to terminate in the event of her remarriage, and six thousand dollars in annual child support for Kitty. She would also keep her two cars, the money in her personal checking account, her interest in Monterey and some other business ventures, selected furniture, silverware and bric-a-brac from the house, and her clothing and jewelry. The jewelry, much of it bought by Hawks or, at least, with his money, consisted of more than fifty items and was worth in the tens of thousands of dollars. With Slim poised to marry Leland Hayward as soon as both divorces came through, perhaps it seemed pointless for her to press for too large a settlement, although something could have gone wrong with Hayward. As far as Hawks was concerned, once Slim moved out, he washed his hands of her and Kitty; his view on his little daughter was that since she would never remember him anyway, she could be raised by Leland Hayward as his own.

At that time, however, obtaining a divorce was a protracted matter. Hawks and Slim can truly be said to have broken up at summer's end, 1946; she moved out in the spring of 1947, and the property settlement was agreed upon at the end of the year. Slim and Kitty left Los Angeles and moved in with Hayward in New York City the following spring, but her divorce was not definitively granted until June 6, 1949; four days later, she and Hayward married at Bill and Babe Paley's estate in Manhasset, Long Island, with David Hawks up from Princeton to give the bride away.

The groundwork for another 1949 wedding was also being laid during this time, as Peter Hawks left Arizona State for the San Francisco Bay area, where he had spent the war years, took a job as a purser with Southwest Airlines, and soon became serious with a young woman named Shirley Godfrey. Barbara, now on the verge of puberty, was still living in Pasadena with her elderly grandparents and "Aunt" Katherine, who were beginning to slow down, and attending Westridge.

With essentially no family responsibilities, other than the financial, Hawks had fewer ties than he'd had in twenty years. Through the winter, spring, and summer of 1948, he golfed frequently, was constantly at the track, did a little horse trading, and continued gambling heavily, resulting, as usual, in heavy losses. This year, he had a partner in bad luck, as Feldman rolled up losses well into five figures. Hawks was habitually on the phone to one of his bookies the first thing every morning and would often place large bets based on hearsay and hot tips. When short for cash, he would insist that one of the junior agents at Famous Artists cover the bets, the sum to be deducted from his earnings later. While persisting in this recklessness, he blithely continued to stiff legitimate businesses to which he owed money, even down to the little Bel-Air market at the foot of Moraga Drive, which regularly settled for ten or twenty cents on the dollar from Hawks after waiting many months for payment.

Hawks's active involvement in Directors Guild affairs had been minimal since the late 1930s, but under the new president, George Stevens, Hawks was corralled into joining the public relations committee, along with Leo McCarey, George Sidney, Norman McLeod, and Norman Taurog. The group drew up a publicity agenda by which directors would be guaranteed credit in all advertising controlled by a film's producer, embracing newspaper, magazine, and radio ads. This was something Hawks could wholeheartedly get behind, although the guild faced a longer and tougher fight in pushing through their long-sought demand that a director be able to present his cut of a film before studio executives could take scissors to it.

As far as broader politics were concerned, the ill winds of blacklisting, security clearance, and red-baiting were already swirling in Hollywood, but while most of those in Hawks's circle—Wayne, Cooper, Furthman, Fleming, Nyby, Carmichael, Brennan—were ultraconservative, Hawks personally had little more patience for the rhetoric and bullying of the right than he did for the left. As his son David said, "Dad didn't like people who were in politics." Because he basically agreed with them, Hawks could humor and not argue with his right-wing friends, but there was no way he was going to join them; When stuntman Cliff Lyons approached Hawks about joining the virulently anticommunist Motion Picture Alliance for the

Preservation of American Ideals, Hawks pretended he didn't even know what Lyons was talking about, even though two close friends, Gary Cooper and Clark Gable, had been among the organization's earliest members. Years later, Chris Nyby vaguely alluded to how Hawks worked "behind the scenes" for the conservative cause during the blacklist days, but when pressed, he could point to nothing of substance to back his claim. Persistent questioning of many members of both the left and right in Hollywood yielded no one who had the slightest feeling that Hawks became politically involved in any direct way during the polarized Cold War years. Hawks had his sympathies, no doubt, but true to Harry Morgan, he believed in minding his own business.

And business was good, better for Hawks than for many in the film industry. For all the directors who had thrived in the studio system from the early 1930s through the end of World War II, the immediate postwar period represented a turning point critical to defining the direction of the remainder of their careers. A number of the more hard-nosed old "pros," including Michael Curtiz, Raoul Walsh, William Wellman, Henry Hathaway, Henry King, Clarence Brown, Mervyn LeRoy, and even John Ford, continued much as they had before, making one or more films of variable quality a year and hanging on more or less as long as the aging moguls for whom they worked. A fortunate few, notably Cecil B. DeMille, Alfred Hitchcock, William Wyler, Billy Wilder, and George Stevens, were able to transform enormous box-office success and (except for Hitchcock) some well-timed Oscars into an extraordinary degree of producer-director autonomy. A much larger group of other directors of comparable prewar reputation—Frank Capra, Frank Borzage, Leo McCarey, Fritz Lang, Rouben Mamoulian, William Dieterle, Edmund Goulding, Mitchell Leisen, Busby Berkeley—were able to continue their careers for a while but had clearly lost sync with public tastes and, arguably, even their own talent. As Hawks said privately about these men, "They've lost the wrinkle in their belly." In other words, they got fat, something Hawks would never allow to happen to him.

For his part, Hawks represented an almost singular case. In theory, he should have been among the dominant producer-directors, but despite the prominence of Hawks's name on some of the biggest commercial attractions of the period leading to this decisive time, a combination of factors conspired to keep him out of this select group. Unlike DeMille and Hitchcock, he was not associated with a specific type of picture, nor did he have a strong public image; unlike Stevens, Wyler, and sometimes Wilder, he rejected high-brow and "significant" think-piece material, thereby disqualifying himself from serious consideration by the East Coast tastemakers and literary-oriented critics. Partly for this reason, he was never recognized at the Oscars, and he never made that single, career-defining blockbuster that would forever separate him from the crowd. For critics and anyone in the public who thought about it, Hawks was still more a solid all-rounder than a distinguished, selective artist, closer to Milestone and Wellman than to Ford, Stevens, or such attention-getting newcomers as Huston, Mankiewicz, and Kazan.

In fact, from the coming of sound onward, the director whose career Hawks's arguably most resembled was that of King Vidor. Vidor made twenty-eight sound films while Hawks made thirty-two, and Vidor's long affiliation with MGM is roughly comparable to Hawks's tenure at Warner Bros.; each functioned well and with considerable latitude at his respective home studio, doing much of his best work there, but each maintained a sufficient arm's length so as never to become swallowed up by the studio's style and mentality. Bracingly steely and smart, Hawks and Vidor each pushed for independence whenever they could, although the impulses behind Vidor's *Hallelujah!* or *Our Daily Bread* were strictly ideological and intellectual in nature, contrasted to Hawks's more mercantile motives. Both made epic Westerns as their first films after World War II, moved at will from genre to genre and studio to studio, strayed at their peril into 1950s historical epics, and never quite got their due from the industry.

Although several of Hawks's post-1948 films were very successful with the public, they are, with but one exception (*Rio Bravo*), much less popular now, decades later, than any number of his earlier pictures. The reasons why are complex and should emerge in time. On the one hand, the later films remain as adventurous in spirit and modern in temperament as the earlier ones; a couple of them are also markedly better than their reputations would indicate. At the same time, however, Hawks's almost infallible judgment, his uncanny knack of being right in the long run even when he looked wrong in the short term, and his virtually unerring talent for casting began to cough and then sputter; in the nearly twenty-five years after casting Montgomery Clift in *Red River*, Hawks launched just one actor or actress of significance—James Caan—after having discovered or introduced so many in the prior fifteen years. His slow decline was also marked by a couple of uncharacteristic lapses in judgment, as well as by an aesthetic retrenchment that resulted in one of the great conservative works of art, two or three others that come awfully close, and one spectacular and fascinating folly. The paradox of Hawks's postwar career, and the challenge of grasping it fully, lies in the pull between the unceasing modernity and unsentimentality of his point of view, his accelerating withdrawal from the prevailing currents of contemporary taste and thought, and his relaxed and generous, rather than inward and contemplative, brand of serenity.

Through the spring and early summer of 1948, Howard Hawks was the subject of much jockeying for favor among studio executives, including Jack Warner, Dore Schary, the new vice president in charge of production at MGM, and Harry Cohn. Despite the ongoing problems with Monterey, however, Hawks was undeterred about working independently if someone would put up the money. If he or she were successful enough, any artist in Hollywood in the late 1940s had the motivation to form a corporation, since the federal income tax on people making more than $100,000 per year now stood at a staggering 68 percent; those few earning $500,000 or more were taxed at a rate of 88.6 percent. More irritated than ever that he had failed to sign Monty Clift to a personal contract, Hawks now talked to the hot young actor about forming a corporation together. But Clift was in the catbird seat at Paramount, with his pick of scripts and directors, and the combination of his painful indecisiveness and his unwillingness to place himself at anyone else's command would have mitigated against the success of the venture. Hawks also revived the idea of an ongoing partnership with Cary Grant, allied with independent producer Eddie Small.

However, in recent years, Hawks had socially and personally drawn closest among all the moguls to his croquet partner, Darryl F. Zanuck, so it was not surprising that, given roughly equal terms and opportunities at several studios, he would choose to work for 20th Century–Fox. Hawks felt more at home temperamentally with Zanuck, a fellow Midwesterner and the only non-Jew among the studio chiefs, than he did with the other big bosses. But probably more important was that Hawks believed that Zanuck wouldn't hover over him and interfere in silly ways, and that Zanuck understood story better than any executive since Thalberg. Although he put business first and was incredibly tough-minded, Zanuck was also the most politically rational of the studio heads at that time; although he made the obligatory public statements against communist influence in the industry, Zanuck, believing that his colleagues were overreacting, was the only industry leader who refused to sign the famous Waldorf agreement in November 1947, in which executives effectively initiated the blacklist by stating that they would not hire the Hollywood Ten or any Communist.

Hawks's Fox deal evolved over several months through the first half of 1948, as Zanuck talked over ideas with the director while Feldman and studio lawyers haggled over terms. Zanuck most wanted Hawks to take on *Twelve O'Clock High*, a major production about American fliers based in Britain, but Hawks was dead set against doing another film about the war. In May, Zanuck brought him another idea. For several months, the studio had been struggling with what seemed like a funny idea based on an autobiographical account by one Henri Rochard, a Belgian officer accidently hit by a car and tended to by an American nurse named Catherine, to whom he later became engaged. When he and Catherine planned their trip to the United States upon his discharge, Rochard was informed that he could likely only "be admitted into the United States under the provision of Public Law 271, which regulates the entry of War Brides."

When Zanuck first showed him the material, Hawks was far from overwhelmed but felt there might be some potential in the *Bringing Up Baby* element of a smart woman almost completely dominating a man who becomes progressively more humiliated by circumstances. To try to reproduce the formula, he again recruited *Baby* creator Hagar Wilde to work, as she had before, with a more experienced writer, in this case perennial wise guy and *His Girl Friday* scenarist Charles Lederer. Working from the screenwriter Leonard Spigelgass's first draft, the pair took two months to hammer out a revision under Hawks's watchful eye while the complicated details of the production were worked out.

After considering all his other options, Hawks signed a Fox contract in June that, most important to him, gave him adequate leeway to leave to make a film elsewhere. The deal called for him to direct four pictures during a six-year period at $8,250 per week, but periods between pictures could be extended if he were making an outside picture and certain conditions were met. As it panned out, Hawks made $165,000 on his first Fox film in thirteen years, more than he did on *Red River* but a far cry from his haul on *A Song Is Born*. There was never a question of anyone other than Cary Grant playing Rochard, but the first notion for his bride was to cast Ava Gardner, who had just broken through as a star. However, Hawks wasn't sure Gardner had what it took to play opposite Grant and shortly decided to use someone he had wanted to work with since testing her for *The Road to Glory* a dozen years before. In the interim, Ann Sheridan, with her winning personality and comic flair, had become a star in spite of the fact that she was seen in very few first-rate films. Always a good sport and a quick reactor in the manner of Rosalind Russell, Sheridan seemed like just the ticket opposite a Cary Grant unleashed by Hawks.

For the second female part, that of Sheridan's pert, efficient roommate, Hawks could cast whomever he wanted, so he cast his current girlfriend. Just eighteen when Hawks met her, Marion Marshall had started modeling three years before, to make money after her father died. Before long, she was noticed by a 20th Century–Fox casting director, who signed her for the studio. She debuted in a small role in Anatole Litvak's *The Snake Pit* and quickly made a strong impression on men around Hollywood. The producer A. C. Lyles, for one, remembered her as "one of the funniest women in town, with a wonderful laugh," and her fresh beauty attracted attention everywhere. She went out with Hawks for the first time on February 26 and continued to play bits in other Fox pictures while Hawks plotted a bigger future for her.

I Was a Male War Bride was just part of a major trend toward overseas filming that snowballed in the late 1940s. There were many reasons for it. To some extent, it was because the wealthy elite who produced, directed, and starred in movies had essentially been stuck in Hollywood for many years because of the war and relished the chance to work and play in the rebounding glamour capitals of Europe. After hitting an all-time peak in attendance in 1946, the industry was perceived to be in a crisis, hit by shrinking audiences, political problems, and the Supreme Court decision forcing the studios to relinquish their theaters. Industry leaders were suffering a crisis of confidence, with the careers of such titans as Louis B. Mayer, David O. Selznick, and Sam Goldwyn drifting or in flux, and foreign films were enjoying unprecedented success with American audiences: in 1948, for the first time, a foreign-made film, Laurence Olivier's *Hamlet,* won the Oscar for best picture; *The Red Shoes* was an unexpected sensation; and Roberto Rossellini snatched Ingrid Bergman away from Hollywood and began starring her in his minimally scripted, commercially marginal Italian productions.

There was also a compelling financial reason to shoot films on foreign locations. After the war, many countries, in order to keep much-needed cash inside their borders, imposed laws that forbade American companies from removing monies from those nations. It was estimated that by 1949 American film companies had approximately $40 million impounded in Great Britain alone. These frozen assets could be spent only internally, meaning that the only way film companies could use the money their films made in certain countries was to produce films there, which poured further funds into the local economies. Spurred by this, as well as by his own taste for the European high life, Darryl Zanuck announced in the summer of 1948 that 20th Century–Fox would spend $24 million, half of it frozen funds, on twelve European-produced motion pictures during the coming year. Not surprisingly, quite a few of these, including two of the first, *Princes of Foxes* and *War Bride*, importantly involved clients and associates of Charles Feldman, who would also spend much of the next two decades in Europe.

Germany, however, was not on the usual list of glamour European locations at the time. Pockmarked by widespread destruction and with foreign troops still stationed everywhere, it was hardly conducive to serving as a backdrop for anything other than what it was, a devastated nation not yet back on its feet, though a couple of films had already used it as such. It seemed inconceivable that anyone could make a film in Germany at that time and not take into account the repercussions of the war, but leave it to Howard Hawks to figure out a way to tell a story almost completely set in postwar Germany that was utterly devoid of politics, any mention of the war, or, for that matter, many Germans.

The schedule called for the company to spend several weeks in Germany, beginning in late September, then move to London to complete filming in studios there before Christmas. Even before anyone left the States, however, there were ominous signals concerning the British phase of the shoot. With the unions suddenly in the ascendant under Prime Minister Atlee's leftist Labor government, the film industry in the U.K. was becoming much more prickly about foreigners barging in and allegedly taking jobs from qualified English workers. The Brits immediately ruled out the possibility of Hawks importing the cinematographer he wanted, Russell Harlan, for the English portion of the shoot. Then, in mid-August, the powerful Association of Cine-Technicians, representing film crew members, decided to harden its stance against all outsiders. Since there were competent English directors currently without work, Howard Hawks should not be allowed into the country to direct the film, the association contended. Fox, of course, found the union's position absurd; fortunately, so did most of the rest of the British film industry, and the ACT reversed its decision a week later.

Leaving Los Angeles with both his status in Britain and the final cutting of *Red River* still unresolved, Hawks alit briefly in New York before sailing on the *Queen Elizabeth* on Saturday, August 21. At fifty-two, he was traveling to Europe for the first time; prior to this, his only trips out of the country had been to Hawaii, Mexico, and Cuba. His traveling companion was the effervescent, worldly Charles Lederer, and the two would spend the voyage working on the script and hanging out at the first-class bar. Following on the next sailing would be Cary Grant, who would stop in England to introduce his girlfriend, Betsy Drake, to his mother, and Ann Sheridan and Marion Marshall.

The German shoot was based in Heidelberg, and despite the status of the picture, as well as Hawks's and Zanuck's military connections, conditions were far inferior to what Hollywood artists were accustomed to on foreign locations. The hotel was mediocre and the food so poor and unvarying that Grant and Drake would fly to Strasbourg or Switzerland whenever possible for gastronomic relief. The players were paid in U.S. Army script, which they could then convert into marks. But the cast and crew were initially startled by the flourishing black market and the chaotic political conditions, from which they were only partially protected by their prestigious status. Although one of Zanuck's staff producers, Sol Siegel, had been on the picture longer than the director and received producer credit, Hawks still ran his own show. Lederer kept hammering away at the screenplay, and shooting began on September 28, as the bite of fall was first being felt. Virtually every scene scheduled for Germany was an exterior, and many of the locations were rural, which placed the filmmakers very much at the mercy of the elements. Unfortunately, while the weather in the film looks uniformly splendid, clear, and bright, this was hardly representative of what the company faced most of the time. Many days were spent sitting around waiting, and Hawks remembered one occasion when they were in a valley and the sides of it became entirely black with clouds.

Coincidentally, on the same day Hawks began filming, one of his favorite collaborators and best friends, his neighbor Gregg Toland, died at his home of a coronary thrombosis, at only forty-four years of age. Just before he died, Toland had perfected something he had been tinkering with for a decade, an "ultimate focus" lens that would stop down to f/.64 and was designed to achieve many times the usual clarity and depth of focus. Although Hawks's straightforward visual aesthetic never pushed Toland to the heights of greatness the cinematographer achieved with other directors, the two loved working together and Hawks wished he could have teamed up with him more often. So much did Hawks admire his friend that he named his last child after him.

The story of *War Bride* was one of humiliation and frustration, both bureaucratic and sexual, as one barrier after another prevents Captain Rochard from consummating his marriage to Lieutenant Gates; it takes the entire length of the film for him to get into a position to do so, and then only after he's been forced to pose as his wife's bride. It was a situation that, in real life, could only be taken as grim, if not tragic, so the film stands as a definitive example of Hawks's talent for turning any piece of material into comedy if at all possible. As he said, "Whenever I hear a story my first thought is how to make it into a comedy, and I think of how to make it into a drama only as a last resort."

As in *Bringing Up Baby* and *His Girl Friday*, his inspiration was Chaplin, whose genius made great comedy out of everyday adversity, setbacks, and inequities, and he hoped to take it much further in *I Was a Male War Bride*. In this line, he wanted Cary Grant to play it straight, especially in the climactic section in which the actor must wear a clunky-looking woman's uniform and a horsehair wig. (Grant only appears in drag for ten minutes of screen time, although people remember it as the dominant piece of business in the picture.) In one of his more amazing stories, which unfortunately can't be verified but which one would like to have seen to believe, Hawks said that after Grant had behaved very effeminately in rehearsal, he decided to show his actor how straight he wanted him to play it: "Without saying anything, I got into a WAC's costume with my legs sticking out and put on a red wig, you know, and went over to this general's party—he didn't know who I was. I pulled out a cigar and asked him for a light and he had the strangest expression you've ever seen. He didn't know what was happening. Grant started to laugh and said, 'You're right.' So we did that same thing—being *completely* straightforward—not a bit feminine at all."

Similarly, there was a scene in which a military clerk asks Grant's character if he is pregnant or has ever had any female trouble. When Grant instinctively answered in an embarrassed manner, Hawks had the actor reverse it by responding to the questions very earnestly—"Nothing but, Sergeant"—and letting the sergeant be the uncomfortable one, which made the scene much funnier. As Hawks pointed out many times, his comedies were not filled with one-liners and jokes but were made amusing purely through the attitude of the teller to the story. "The only difference between comedy and tragedy is the point of view," he said, and Hawks's point of view toward men being dominated by women was to crank up their discomfort as much as he could.

As adept as any director Grant ever had at encouraging the actor's imagination and setting him loose, Hawks filmed scenes repeatedly to milk as much humor from them as Grant was able to give. As he had done on many previous pictures together, Hawks urged his actors to ad-lib, and Lederer was on hand throughout the German portion of the shoot to help them polish their impromptu dialogue and business. Ann Sheridan, who loved making the film despite all the problems, described the prevailing work method this way: "Howard Hawks would sit on the set and he'd say, 'Well, I'm not quite satisfied with this scene. What would you say in a situation like this?' So we'd sit and think, and it was inevitably Cary [who] would tell you what to say. Howard is a very clever man. He picked brains. And he had a very clever brain to pick [in] Cary Grant, believe me."

Although his days as an acrobat and vaudevillian were now far behind him, Grant still liked to do his own stunts, and the silent film–like gag of his being lifted up on a railroad crossing gate was one he, Hawks, and Lederer devised on the spot. Many of the early sequences have Sheridan driving a military motorcycle with Grant in the sidecar, and normally, doubles would probably have been used for everything other than close-ups. But Grant saw no reason not to do the scenes himself, and with a little prodding from Hawks, the always cooperative Sheridan agreed to drive the motorcycle herself, even in a downpour. Nonetheless, she was always scared doing it, and she broke down and cried when she accidentally ran over a goose and killed it. However, this was the only blemish, at least until they got to England, on what Sheridan otherwise always considered the happiest experience she ever had shooting a picture.

Waiting out inclement weather at every turn, the company shot briefly in the fifteenth-century village Zuzenhausen, marked by narrow cobblestone streets and stone houses, before pushing on to the port of Bremerhaven. The only labor problem in Germany was triggered by Hawks's decision to use American officers' wives as extras and to compensate them at the low rate being paid to the Germans. Surprisingly, it was the Germans who complained about this, pointing out that using real Americans cheated the Germans out of much-needed work. The Germans insisted that everyone should receive normal Hollywood scale for extras, and Hawks, not wishing to rock the boat and not needing a great many extras anyway, complied.

After several weeks, Cary Grant began feeling nauseated and short of energy, but he continued working. In early December, after nine weeks of slow progress, the company finished on the German locations and, within seventy-two hours of its arrival in England, was filming again on the biggest stage at Shepperton Studios, where the interior sets representing U.S. Army Command Headquarters had been built. Although ensconsed in luxury at the Dorchester, Hawks was instantly hit with unwelcome frustrations. When cinematographer Russ Harlan, who had shot in Germany, was not allowed in because of union restrictions, Hawks settled for a Canadian, Osmond H. Borradaile, who had started his career with Jesse Lasky in Hollywood in 1915 and whom Hawks had known at Paramount in the 1920s. Still, he was an odd choice to light all the black-and-white interiors, since he had mainly distinguished himself with his spectacular location cinematography. For a director whose comedies generally have an unusually dark, high-contrast look, *I Was a Male War Bride*, particularly in the studio interiors, has an especially glum, under–art directed look. This can be rationalized as being a visual correlative to the oppressive bureaucratic conditions and the ravaged postwar German landscape, but it still makes the film rather less welcoming initially and less pleasing to savor in retrospect.

Hawks was always accustomed to working at his own leisurely pace, into lunch hours and past dinner if necessary, in order to get scenes working right. He rarely kept his eye on the clock, and he believed in anyone on the set being able to pitch in if it could help the quality of the film. In the union-dominated Britain of the new Atlee Labor government, however, the working hours were rigidly set and adhered to, and God forbid if an actor or an assistant director should pick up a prop and move it a few inches. Hawks complained to an English journalist at the time, "Sometimes I go home at nights feeling I haven't earned my salary. . . . In Hollywood we knock off for lunch because we're feeling hungry, but here I may have to break off in the middle of a take, because everybody has to go off to lunch on the dot." In exasperation, Hawks one day offered the crew triple pay for a half hour's incursion into their lunch break, but the union wouldn't permit it. The strict regulations shortened the workday and decreased efficiency, and left Hawks feeling that the union's uncooperative attitude was reason enough not to shoot again in Britain; at that time, he was planning to make *The Sun Also Rises* with locations on the Continent and studio work likely for the U.K. Now, he was completely turned off the plan and would look elsewhere.

Then there were the health problems. The first to succumb was Randy Stuart, who played the small role of the smart-talking WAC named Mae; she contracted jaundice. Hawks himself came down with the hives or something like it, "an itch that started on the top of my head and went right through my balls and everything down to my feet." Navy personnel who had contracted something similar during the war had relieved the condition with seawater, so Hawks soaked endlessly in a bathtub filled with salt-water and finally got better. Then, shortly after arriving in England, Ann Sheridan came down with pleurisy, which turned into pneumonia. There was little Hawks could film without her, so shooting was suspended for two weeks beginning in late December while she recovered. Marion Marshall said that as elemental as conditions had been in Germany, things were much worse in England, and she blamed the many illnesses of the cast and crew on the lack of decent food. "Pickings were slim; at least it was difficult to obtain food we were used to—like eggs, for instance." Although he never mentioned it, Marshall said that Hawks lost twenty-five pounds while in England. For her part, Marshall was the only principal in *War Bride* who managed to survive the shoot without getting sick.

During the layoff, Hawks received shocking news: Victor Fleming was dead. Hawks's best friend had spent the previous year directing his biggest picture since *Gone with the Wind*, a $4.6 million production of *Joan of Arc* starring Ingrid Bergman. Fleming had had a passionate affair with the actress during the shooting of *Dr. Jekyll and Mr. Hyde* in 1941 and had resumed it when they began working together again. Not only did he agonize over his relationship with Bergman, who was married and also conducting simultaneous love affairs with the photographer Robert Capa and musician Larry Adler, but *Joan of Arc* proved to be an artistic, logistical, and financial nightmare that strained Fleming's abilities to the breaking point. Uncertain that he had found the right approach to the always daunting story and tortured by what he felt was a doomed love for his intoxicating star, he worked incessantly, ate little, and drank far too much.

After *Dr. Jekyll*, it had been Fleming who had left Bergman, but this time it was the other way around. In the summer, with filming and the affair over, he had flown off to the Canadian Rockies to get away and try to pull himself together, and by year's end, *Joan* was doing strong business in the big cities, although it never really had a chance of making back its cost. He made his final public appearance at the *Joan* premiere at the Beverly Theater in Beverly Hills on December 22.

At New Year's, Fleming, his wife Lou and their daughters Victoria and Sally stayed at the Beaver Creek Guest Ranch, owned by the Hollywood producer Louis Lighton. Located about twenty miles east of the small town of Cottonwood, Arizona, the ranch was very remote and off the beaten path. On the afternoon of January 6, 1949, Fleming complained of chest pains and returned to his cottage. When the pains got worse, however, he sum-

moned the operator of the lodge, Charles Stimpson, and they started for
the tiny Marcus Lawrence Hospital in Cottonwood. They never made it,
though, as Fleming died en route.

It was pointless for Hawks to even think of trying to get back for the
funeral, but Leland Hayward and Slim flew in from New York, and Slim
stayed with Lou, Victoria, and Sally for a week afterward. More than two
hundred people turned out on January 10 for the services at St. Alban's
Episcopal Church in West Los Angeles, which included a short eulogy
written by John Lee Mahin. The pallbearers were Mahin, Clark Gable, Hal
Rosson, and Lee Bowman. Hawks was listed among the twenty-six honor-
ary pallbearers, who also included the likes of Leland Hayward, Jules
Furthman, Lew Wasserman, Ward Bond, Spencer Tracy, Jack Conway,
Laurence Stallings, Douglas Shearer, Henry Hathaway, King Vidor, Walter
Wanger, and Eddie Mannix. Also in attendance were Louis B. Mayer, Sam
Goldwyn, James Stewart, Andy Devine, Brian Aherne, John Wayne, Van
Johnson, Hoagy Carmichael, and Mike Romanoff.

Most people blamed the stress of *Joan* for Fleming's death. What
became apparent from the obituaries is that Fleming, in a gesture of vanity
familiar to many movie stars, had gone to great lengths to conceal his age,
which was listed in various publications as anywhere from fifty-nine to sixty-
four. He was actually just short of sixty-six.

But there was more to come. Back in England, almost as soon as Ann
Sheridan had recovered enough to begin working on *War Bride* again, even
if only for six hours a day, Cary Grant suddenly became gravely ill. At the
end of January, they were filming the breakthrough love scene in which
Sheridan finds Grant inside a large haystack after he'd inadvertently crashed
into it riding in the sidecar of the runaway motorcycle. Henri and Catherine
then admit how they feel about each other and utter lines which borrow
liberally from *To Have and Have Not*, when Catherine says, "Well, that was
a little better," and Henri replies, "Certainly, you see. It could have been
even better if I'd had some cooperation."

Shot through with penicillin and feeling barely ambulatory, Sheridan
was just making it through when Grant complained that he didn't like the
scene. Hawks found this odd since he and Grant had just rewritten it themselves; Sheridan, seeing that Grant looked bad, felt his forehead, which was
extremely hot. Sensing that something was amiss, Hawks called it a day and
sent Grant back to the hotel; at two in the morning, the actor was on his
way to the hospital with a life-threatening case of hepatitis. This was com-

plicated by jaundice, and although initial press announcements stated that production would resume within ten days, it shortly became clear that Grant wouldn't be returning to work anytime soon.

Although they only had about three weeks of filming left, Hawks and Fox decided to close down the production in England and return to California, where they would await their star's recovery; the $200,000 that the studio had already paid the British labor unions would have to be recouped on its next production. Thorough photographs were taken of all the sets so they could be reproduced on Fox's stages in Los Angeles, and some of the cast, including Marion Marshall, left as early as February 10. Hawks concluded his business and was glad to leave England behind when the *Queen Mary* sailed from Southampton on February 19. Arriving in New York six days later, Hawks stayed there only briefly, not bothering to visit David at nearby Princeton, before heading for home and warmth. Despite his upbringing in the frigid north, Hawks had entirely lost his taste for Eastern winters.

Feeling better, Ann Sheridan visited Paris and Rome before returning to California, while Cary Grant remained bedridden for weeks. Fleeing the hospital at the earliest opportunity, he sent Betsy Drake home and spent the rest of his time convalescing at Pamela Churchill's Mayfair flat. It was the worst illness Grant had ever suffered through, and he later confessed that he nearly died from the hepatitis. Having lost what has been variously reported as anywhere from twenty and forty pounds, Grant knew he needn't rush home, since time was required to build up his strength and weight, and took a slow boat, the *Volendam*, which sailed to Los Angeles via the Panama Canal. He regained his health as the weeks passed and finally arrived home on April 7. At the end of April, after a three-month break, he made some tests to ensure that he'd gained enough weight to match what had been shot before and shortly picked up where he left off, now with Norbert Brodine as cinematographer. As Hawks puts it, "Cary ran into a haystack on a motorcycle and came out weighing twenty pounds less." Scenes of the couple trying to make their way onto a Navy boat back to the States were shot at the San Pedro docks, and production finally wrapped on May 27, 1949, exactly eight months after it started. The budget was in the neighborhood of $2 million, although it is difficult to state precisely because of the $200,000 left behind in Britain and the layoff, which saw the cast kept on at full salary but at Lloyds of London's expense.

During the hiatus, it had fallen to a young second assistant at Fox named Paul Helmick to try to make sense out of the footage shot thus far and help determine exactly what was still needed. Hawks didn't forget the outstanding job he did at this, and an association began that would last the rest of Hawks's life. Subsequently, the film editor, James B. Clark, had one of the most difficult jobs on the picture, linking up all the disparate pieces shot in three different countries at different times.

An even greater problem, however, were all the changes demanded by the Breen Office. Because of the ongoing rewriting and the company being far away in Germany, Lederer's script was not even received by the MPAA until the end of October, a month after shooting had begun. To the filmmakers' dismay, Breen found the entire project unacceptable "because of the great amount of sex-suggestive lines and situations. This is particularly true of the element of sex frustration on the part of the leads after they have been married." Since several weeks of film was in the can by the time the MPAA expressed its objections, there wasn't much Hawks could do but hope for the best when he finally presented it with the finished picture. An example of a line that Hawks was later ordered to cut was Catherine's early warning to Henri, "If you lay a finger on me this trip, you're going back to France minus a couple of parts you probably value." There were also references to the French as "frogs," innuendoes about the sexual urges of dogs and bulls, and a shirtless backrub that all eventually had to go. However, it was the entire premise of the story's second half that turned Breen red. In his notes, the chief censor stated that "playing around with the deferment of the marital act could not be approved." He also pointed out that "comedy derived from the fact that a married couple are unable to consumate their marriage would be unacceptable."

Hawks and his editor did have to cut a great many of the more overt sexual innuendoes from the final print, but, his confidence bolstered by his past ability to slip some surprising things past the censor, the director took a big chance in the second half that Breen and his cronies would approve on the screen what they had objected to on paper. While they forced him to cut a joke in which a bystander was startled to see two women—actually Catherine and Henri in drag—eagerly kissing, Breen and company were won over by Hawks's treatment of his risqué subject and approved the picture more or less as filmed.

Fox rushed the picture through final postproduction to have it ready for release by August, and most critics were similarly disarmed by Hawks's sly treatment of what seemed like a potentially silly story. Even Cary Grant was delightfully surprised by the result. Grant attended the premiere in New York the final week of August despite his apprehension that a good film could never have resulted from such a problem-plagued shoot. The next day he told the *New York Times*, "I just saw the picture and the audience laughed themselves sick. I've been in many comedies but I've never heard an audience react like this one. I honestly feel it's the best comedy I've ever done."

Some viewers find *I Was a Male War Bride* virtually unbearable for the excruciating humiliation and sexual torture Cary Grant's character is forced to endure; young men, in particular, often find nothing funny in it. *War Bride* is very much a middle-aged man's film, the work of a man in his early fifties who, however much he had always enjoyed putting his male comic figures through the wringer, was now disposed to take a more dispassionate view of the urgency of sexual consummation. The most prolonged and overt of the numerous examples of cross-dressing and sex-role flip-flopping in Hawks's films, it also runs bracingly counter to the perception of Hawks as a conservative upholder of the status quo, for very few non-noir films of the late 1940s ridicule bureaucracy, the establishment, and conventional mores as disrespectfully as does *I Was a Male War Bride*.

The film certainly did the trick with audiences. After first opening in Los Angeles in mid-August to excellent returns, the picture grossed a sensational $376,000 in its four-week run at New York's Roxy Theater and rang up comparable returns nearly everywhere else. It was the number-one film in the nation for two weeks running in late September, was the third biggest money picture for October, and ended up as the number-three attraction for the entire year with $4.1 million in rentals, tied with *The Snake Pit* behind *Jolson Sings Again* and Fox's *Pinky*. This made *War Bride* Hawks's third most popular film ever, after *Sergeant York* and *Red River*. The budget overages meant that Fox's profit was not as great as Zanuck would have liked, but the mogul was still more than happy with the first fruits of his new collaboration with Hawks.

As soon as Hawks returned to the United States, he began trying to find a picture he could slip in between Fox assignments. *The Sun Also Rises*, which Burgess Meredith, Paulette Goddard, and Franchot Tone desperately tried to buy from Hawks that year for themselves to star in, remained the project Hawks most frequently mentioned, and he maintained that he intended to do it independently, with Montgomery Clift and Margaret Sheridan starring, then sell it to a distributor. Feldman even took the step of registering the title with the MPAA. All the same, little work was being devoted to solving the script problems, and it remains a mystery why Hawks didn't hire one of his usual crack writers, such as Lederer, Hecht, or Furthman, to get the upper hand on the celebrated story that attracted him, and many others, so much.

At the same time, Hawks wanted to pursue his idea of an ongoing partnership with Cary Grant. The project Hawks most fancied was a comic version of *Don Quixote* starring Grant in the title role and the Mexican comedian Cantinflas as Sancho Panza. Hawks always pointed to the example of Chaplin when people objected to his intention to turn this tragedy into a comedy, even speculating, "I think that Don Quixote's the basis really for the Chaplin character." There is no evidence that Hawks ever even engaged a writer to begin an adaptation, but certainly *Don Quixote* would have provided a supreme opportunity for Hawks to cross the lines between tragic adventure and comic misadventure as often as he pleased. It also represented the only time Hawks thought about tackling such a revered literary classic, which may be one reason he never pursued it more seriously. Nonetheless, it was an idea that never went away, for as late as the early 1970s, Hawks was still talking about doing it, "Before Cary gets too old or I get too old."

Meanwhile, Hawks and Zanuck jousted and parried as to what film the director might next do at Fox. Zanuck tried to sell Hawks on *Fourteen Hours*, a drama about a man threatening to jump off a building which Hawks said he'd be willing to do only if he could turn it into a Cary Grant comedy. Zanuck also pushed a Philip and Julius Epstein script called "Mable and Me" and proposed "Angel Face," a curious Charles Schnee political melodrama that featured such in-joke character names as Eva Lang, Governor Fuller, candidate Joe Huston, Molly Keyes, George Kirkwood, and a drunk named Mickey Nolan and that bore no relation to the 1953 Otto Preminger film. But while his clout was at its peak in the wake of *War Bride*, Hawks was still unable to push through either of the projects that seemed most immediately feasible. *Dreadful Hollow* remained unexceptional to Zanuck, but the alternative at least seemed to have possibilities.

Once again delving into the *Saturday Evening Post* for material, Hawks became interested in "Morning Star" through, of all people, Leland Hayward, who had bought the rights when Robert Spencer Carr's science-fiction love story was first published in 1947. The story centers upon a strong, brilliant scientist, Brian Dale (to have been played by Gary Cooper), who is working at the atomic bomb lab at Los Alamos, New Mexico, testing a new rocket designed to make the first flight to Venus. Among the other resident geniuses is Eva Morgenstern (Morning Star), an alleged Russian refugee who seems both overpoweringly bright and oddly disturbing to Brian (Margaret Sheridan, again, was intended for this part). After a meteor shower, Brian induces Eva to acknowledge her true identity: she is an emissary from Venus. What's more, her kind has been here before, but they were taken by earthlings to be angels or saints. It is clear that Brian and Eva were meant for each other in a cosmic sense, that it is through this couple's love that alien worlds can come together. Eva eventually returns to her mother planet on her own, whereupon Brian quickly volunteers for the first flight to Venus, from which he returns in triumph.

There are obvious Ayn Rand elements here, as well as an expression of the popular sci-fi theory that Venus is populated by beautiful women. The material had the potential to be dangerously corny, but it was written with great conviction and warm appeal. It would certainly have provided Hawks with the challenge of creating his most sincere love story, and would appear to have contained great commercial potential. But while admitting that the story was "unique," Zanuck put Hawks off by insisting that the treatment was not sufficiently developed and that the production would probably be exceedingly expensive. As late as 1952, Ray Stark at Famous Artists, working on behalf of Hawks, tried to interest Dore Schary, Jack Warner, and Stanley Kramer in backing the picture, but to no avail.

What was slowly becoming clear was that Zanuck was happy to have Hawks aboard his ship but had no intention of letting him steer the course; Hawks would make films Zanuck wanted him to make, never the other way around; nor would Zanuck play the sucker as Jack Warner so often had and pay advanced prices for material Hawks had bought for far less. Partly because Zanuck and Hawks were friendly and similar in some basic ways, Zanuck had Hawks's number and wouldn't let him get away with the sorts of things Hawks would pull repeatedly on Warner and even Goldwyn. From Hawks's point of view, his deal at Fox was a one-way street in terms of doing projects he really cared about. In this sense, he really had been better off at Warner Bros., and as soon as he realized this, his eye, quite understandably, began to wander.

Peter Hawks, now twenty-five, married Shirley Godfrey in the summer of 1949, but his stepfather did not bother making the trip north to San Mateo for the wedding. Although Hawks avoided formal occasions whenever he plausibly could, one reason he may have steered clear of this one is that he knew Athole would be there, and the two were on the outs to such an extent that she sued him later that summer. In her complaint, filed on August 31, Athole stated that Hawks owed her four thousand dollars in alimony, as well as the stipulated 10 percent of his net income, or an additional $39,112 for the relevant period of November 1, 1943 through August 17, 1949. Hawks had been through this once before, in 1943, and this time he resisted by employing every legal stalling tactic he and his lawyers could think of, even though it meant halting work on the home Hawks was building in Palm Springs, which Athole attached to the suit. He paid her a small amount in 1952, but it wasn't until 1955 that the matter was finally settled by a judgment that forced Hawks to pay Athole $55,382, including accumulated interest.

As the decade drew to a close, with his next-door neighbors Vic Fleming and Gregg Toland dead and no one else living at Hog Canyon, Hawks revved up his outside social life, dining out and partying often at La Rue's, Romanoff's, Chasen's, Ciro's, and the Mocambo, often in the company of Feldman, Gregory Ratoff, Cyril Gardner, George Raft, Clark Gable, and Otto Preminger. The social season reached its peak with an enormous party at Feldman's on December 17, which Hawks attended with Marion Marshall and which boasted such other guests as Gable, the Goldwyns, Jane Wyman, Kirk Douglas, Gertrude Lawrence, the Arthur Kennedys, the Charles Boyers, the Tyrone Powers, the William Holdens, the David Nivens, Anatole Litvak, Clifton Webb, Spyros Skouras, Arlene Dahl, Irving Rapper, and a young politician from Massachusetts making the rounds of Hollywood, John F. Kennedy.

Hawks's romance with Marion Marshall had proceeded in fits and starts. In May, word slipped out that they were on verge of getting married, which prompted a denial from Marshall that they were even engaged. On New Year's Eve, the couple went public with the announcement that they would be marrying soon, probably on February 26, the second anniversary of their first date. Plans went ahead accordingly but, suddenly, on February 24, amidst rumors of serious problems, the wedding was abruptly called off. Jane Greer, a good friend of Marshall's, suggested that the young actress was disappointed that Hawks wasn't proposing her for any big film parts, and Marshall, who fancied herself a new Carole Lombard, was particularly irked that Hawks didn't more aggressively pursue remaking *Twentieth Century* at Columbia, with her in the female lead. When the wedding was canceled, Hawks disappeared to Arizona, while Marshall commented, "There is nothing to say, it's just over. We came to the decision some time ago. We just decided not to say anything about it." Ironically, Marshall promptly signed a contract with Hawks's old nemesis Hal Wallis, who cast her in films opposite Dean Martin and Jerry Lewis; in 1952 she married the director Stanley Donen. Through the 1960s, Marshall was married to the actor Robert Wagner. She eventually became a prominent Beverly Hills dress designer with her own shop.

30

An Old Boss, A New Mate

Although no one, with the probable exception of Feldman, knew the full extent of Hawks's financial problems, Hawks was treading on thin ice by the time 1950 arrived. Unable to induce Zanuck to back "Morning Star" or "Dreadful Hollow," Hawks told Feldman to set up another deal for him at a different studio so he could receive a new infusion of cash and have a card to play against Zanuck. Hawks put his middle name on the shingle of his new production company, formed to supplant the moribund Monterey, and Winchester Pictures struck a three-picture deal with RKO, agreed upon in the final week of February, when Hawks was to have married Marion Marshall, and finally signed in May.

Hawks had not worked at RKO since having been dismissed from *Gunga Din* more than a decade before, and many things had changed at the studio, none of it for the better. After producing the postwar flops *Mad Wednesday* and *Vendetta*, Howard Hughes had announced that he was once again abandoning the motion picture business. The industry was therefore stunned when, in May 1948, he bought a controlling 24 percent in RKO from Floyd B. Odlum's Atlas Corporation. Realizing everyone's fears, Hughes soon began running the studio into the ground.

Under his erratic, reckless stewardship, Hughes eviscerated a strong company that, in the immediate postwar period, had ranked number-three in box-office earnings after MGM and 20th Century–Fox. He drove away his successful head of production, Dore Schary, who was quickly hired by MGM; fired seven hundred employees, or 33 percent of those on the regular payroll, within four months of his takeover; instantly kowtowed to Justice Department pressure to separate RKO's theater chain from studio operations, thus breaking ranks with the four other majors and leading the way for the splintering of the true studio system; placed himself in the forefront of the anticommunist witch-hunt that saw many of the studio's top talents placed under clouds of suspicion or driven from the studio; and reduced budgets and the number of pictures to a fraction of their former levels. Almost overnight, RKO became a virtual B-movie studio, for which Hughes's patented lurid campaigns failed to compensate. Hughes didn't want serious and talented filmmakers on the lot, and they didn't want to work for him. After a period of peak profitability, RKO lost increasing amounts of money in each of the first three years it was controlled by Hughes, with film-generated revenues plummeting an astounding 77 percent during that period.

It was when matters got that bad that Hughes—who didn't even maintain an office on the lot, preferring to remain squirreled away at the Goldwyn Studios—was convinced that he had to make a few A-type pictures in order to bolster the studio's image in town and to generate some major profits. When Hawks signed on, he joined Walt Disney, Sam Goldwyn, and the producer Edmund Grainger among the group that Hughes expected to generate big grosses for RKO. Even though he still resented Hawks for *Red River*, Hughes implicitly believed in him as an almost infallibly commercial director. As for Hawks, he knew that Hughes would be far too busy to meddle in his productions and felt that he had a special understanding of the tycoon since, unlike most other filmmakers, he had always landed on his feet after his dealings with Hughes. Under the new agreement, Hawks would produce and direct two pictures and produce, but not direct, a third, all within a twenty-seven-month period ending in August 1952. Hawks would receive $175,000 apiece for the first two and $125,000, less the director's salary, for the third. Winchester was to retain ownership of the films, although specified penalties would reduce Hawks's ownership and/or salary if the budgets exceeded $1.5 million on the first two, $1.25 million on the second.

Anxious to make another Western and on the lookout, after *Red River*, for another story about a Great First Time, Hawks settled quickly on A. B. Guthrie Jr.'s novel *The Big Sky*, about an early expedition of explorers and trappers who travel up the Missouri River from St. Louis to Montana in the 1830s and the subsequent lives of two of them. Ironically, the book had been passed on by RKO at the time of its publication in 1947, when a reader's report dismissed it as "lacking any sort of plot which might be suitable for picture purposes." Presumably, the report objected to its long, sprawling, and diffuse narrative, as well as to the fact that the two halves of the story occur seven years apart. It appears likely that the book came to Hawks's attention through Gary Cooper, who had bought the rights to Guthrie's new novel, *The Way West*, which went on to win the Pulitzer Prize. Winchester was able to obtain the earlier book for only thirty thousand dollars, where-upon Hawks hired *Air Force* and *Bringing Up Baby* writer Dudley Nichols, who had also written numerous John Ford films, including *Stagecoach*.

Deeply convincing as a detailed portrait of how things were in the unexplored West, Guthrie's novel was praised for its historical authenticity and clearly bespoke its author's intense feeling for the land. It is also, to be sure, a rambling narrative, which begins with the journey up two thousand miles of river by a curious band of loners, adventurers, and misfits, most of them Creole French. The book relishes its characters' antisocial attitudes, dwells at length on the hunting, and is quite rough and frank at times, dis-cussing how such men dealt with the clap and interacted with different tribes of Indians. The main characters are Boone Caudill, a Kentucky boy in his late teens who runs away from home and meets the slightly older Jim Deakins. Together, they join the largely French crew of the *Mantan*, a keelboat heading upriver with a runaway Blackfoot princess, Teal Eye, who is to be returned to her people in exchange for favorable trading rights.

Guthrie's manner of storytelling is episodic and discursive, and little conflict is generated among the leading characters or members of the crew. But Hawks, deciding that he would devote his entire film to the boat jour-ney, had strong ideas how to change that. Guthrie does very little with the relationship between Boone and Jim, but Hawks saw that latent in that friendship lay an excellent potential "love story between two men." In the novel, the Indian girl Teal Eye, found in St. Louis after having been kid-napped by a rival tribe, is only ten or twelve years old during the keelboat trip, or decidedly too young to figure in a romantic triangle with the two white men. By advancing her age by about eight years, Hawks created the compelling, if predictable, added dynamic to the plot. One of the central characters in the book is the group's wise and extremely colorful hunter, Dick Summers, an old coot who "speaks Injun," knows the territory like the back of his hand, and possesses a sixth sense about the ways of nature and all its creatures. Hawks decided to basically transpose Summers's per-sonality onto one of the book's much-discussed but little-seen characters, Boone's long-lost mountain-man uncle, Zeb, who turns up in the novel only in one episode, when the river travelers find the rather disagreeable old man working as a hunter for a company fort.

The first half of the novel charts the voyage of the *Mandan* into unex-plored territory and ends shockingly with the Blackfeet's massacre of the entire crew; only the hunters Caudill, Deakins, and Summers manage to escape with their lives. The second half picks up the trio seven years later

and evolves into a movingly tragic tale of men who belong nowhere, neither with the Indians, whose ways they have largely adapted, nor with "civilized" white society. Hawks streamlined it into the story of a successful
journey, one in which the men's hard work pays off and the various conflicts, both within the group and between the group and the two forces
opposing it, the Indians and the big trapping company, can be resolved.
He also took certain key characters from the novel's abandoned second half,
including the Blackfoot simpleton Poordevil and the menacing trapper
Streak, and worked them into the story of the river journey. Hawks essentially dismantled Guthrie's novel and rebuilt it according to his own interests, which lay much more in the area of the interaction among men rather
than in the bigger picture of history and the implications of the white man's
incursion into the wilderness of North America.

Hawks's new secretary, Lorrie Sherwood, worked with Hawks and
Nichols at their initial story meetings and, subsequently, taking the writer's
dictation; she said that Hawks laid down to Nichols how he wanted the
characters changed and the story to unfold. Nothing, she said, went into
the script that Hawks had not either thought of or personally approved.
"Everything Mr. Hawks did was his," Sherwood averred. It could accurately
be said that Hawks did the "adaptation" of *The Big Sky*, while Nichols wrote
the screenplay, which, it should be noted, contained virtually no dialogue
taken from the novel. He did so quickly, turning out a 220-page first draft
in two months.

Lorrie Sherwood would remain an important member of Hawks's team
for the next several years. A thirty-year-old Oklahoman of Irish-Indian descent who had once been married to a professional football player, Sherwood
was cute, gregarious, and fun-loving, as outgoing as her boss was reserved.
Having previously worked in publicity and casting for Sam Goldwyn, she
had just finished a job for Fred Zinnemann when she met Chris Nyby, who
sent her to see Hawks. When she drove up to Hog Canyon on a weekend to
meet him, she was greeted by the sight of four men playing croquet, one of
them—Darryl F. Zanuck—wearing a French bikini. Like all of Hawks's
other female secretaries and assistants, Sherwood maintained that Hawks
was always gentlemanly and respectful and never crossed the line between
the professional and the personal. At first, the chatty Sherwood was a bit
unnerved by Hawks's long silences, but she soon learned that with him
"there was a time to talk and a time to shut up."

In *The Big Sky*, much would depend on the quality of the personalities playing the main roles. Hawks's first choices for the two male leads were

Gary Cooper and Arthur Kennedy, even if Cooper was a good thirty years too old for either of the parts as written. Hawks then began juggling such intriguing combinations as Robert Mitchum and Marlon Brando, Mitchum and newcomer Charlton Heston, Cooper and Montgomery Clift, then Brando and Clift, Brando and Sydney Chaplin. However, when Brando, who had just worked for Feldman on A Streetcar Named Desire, demanded $125,000, it was too much for Hawks, who in a pique announced that he didn't need big stars and would shoot the picture with unknowns.

Desperate for a major title from Hawks, RKO had insisted on a start date of no later than September 1, 1950, for the director's first production. In an attempt to rush it, in early August Hawks organized a location-scouting trip to Jackson Hole, Wyoming, and Eugene, Oregon, manned by prospective second-unit director Arthur Rosson and four others, who spent ten days checking out potential river-area shooting sites. Hawks joined them for four days and approved Jackson Hole as a suitable base of operations. But it was apparent to everyone that there was no way to get such an ambitious picture before the cameras in time to beat the winter. With Hawks securing a promise from Hughes to keep Mitchum's schedule free for the following summer, both sides agreed to postpone The Big Sky one year.

For his second RKO picture to direct, Hawks had the astonishing idea of doing a sex-reversal version of Cinderella, entirely in drag, with Cary Grant as the mother, James Stewart and Danny Kaye as the daughters, and Ginger Rogers as Prince Charming. Hawks claimed that all the actors were enthusiastic to do it, although there is no evidence that a script was ever even attempted. It remained, however, a cherished project that Hawks and Grant discussed frequently over the next couple of years. Hastily, another picture had to be readied for an almost immediate shoot. The material was far from anything in which Hawks had shown an interest in the past, except for "Morning Star"; it also provided him with the means of making by far his most politically charged film.

"I thought it would be fun to take a stab at science fiction," Hawks said. He originally found the 1938 story "Who Goes There?" by John W. Campbell Jr. (originally signed with the pseudonym Don A. Stuart) in a magazine he idly picked up at the army PX in Heidelberg during one of the innumerable delays on I Was a Male War Bride. "I was sitting there with nothing to do and no place to go and got to wondering: 'What are people from another planet like?' I don't see why they should be so entirely different."

Hawks paid nine hundred dollars for the story, only to junk most of it for his screen treatment. Campbell's fifty-seven-page tale involved a group of thirty-seven American soldiers and scientists in Antarctica who discover an alien being that has been frozen in ice for twenty million years. The long first section is devoted to a debriefing on how the beast was detected and dislodged, followed by a debate over whether or not to thaw it out. The device on which the remainder of the story turns is that the alien, once revived, is able to transform itself into various guises, including those of its victims, thereby making it exceedingly difficult to combat.

Needing a script quickly, Hawks called upon two of the fastest and cleverest minds he knew, Charles Lederer and Ben Hecht. Although Lederer had become one of Hawks's closest friends, Hecht had passed out of Hawks's orbit in the decade since *His Girl Friday* and had recently alienated many people both inside and outside the industry with his extreme Zionism, particularly his fund-raising and propaganda writing on behalf of the militant—many said terrorist—Irgun Zvai Leumi. While continuing his screenwriting career, Hecht threw himself into raising money and arms for the Irgun, which was dedicated to forcibly removing the British from Palestine. Hecht had drawn harsh criticism from both American Jews and the British for publishing a letter in fifteen major American newspapers in which he concluded with the following message to Jewish freedom fighters: "Every time you blow up a British arsenal, or wreck a British jail, or send a British railroad train sky high, or rob a British bank, or let go with your bombs and guns at the British betrayers and invaders of your homeland, the Jews of America make a little holiday in their hearts." As a result, Hecht's name was banned from British screens for two and a half years.

Even though Hawks privately scorned Hecht's extracinematic activities—he even privately implied that denying the writer screen credit on this picture constituted his own form of punishment for Hecht's political shenanigans—he knew the subject would never come up between them and was therefore irrelevant to the matter at hand: developing a strongly dramatic approach to a story dominated by windy scientific speeches and debates. At first, Hecht wasn't in the least enamored of the project. But the offer of a thousand dollars a day got him to the table; his interest increased when they decided to tell the story through the eyes of a newspaper reporter; and he soon realized that this modern-day horror story could serve as an effective allegorical vehicle with which to poke fun at growing Cold War paranoia about communism. It is very probable that Hawks remained entirely oblivious to this second level of meaning in the story, but then the mischievous Hecht often had his own private motives for what he wrote. For his part, however, Hawks managed to keep Hecht's involvement with the project such a secret in Hollywood that, decades later, Chris Nyby professed never to have known that the legendary writer had worked on his first picture.

To speed the work along, Hawks convened the writers daily at Hog Canyon. He later would greatly exaggerate by claiming that they finished the script in seven or eight days, but it actually took the better part of six weeks. Together, Lederer and Hecht earned sixty thousand dollars for their work, or far more than anyone else on the picture but Hawks himself. Joining the three creators most days at the house was Hawks's new partner, Edward Lasker. A wealthy young man from Chicago, Lasker worked on Los Angeles accounts for his father's advertising agency, Lord & Thomas, before succumbing to the glamour of Hollywood social life. In 1947, he married Jane Greer, which earned him the enduring enmity of Howard Hughes, and he gradually entered Hawks's circle through their mutual interest in horses and the track. Lasker was often invited for croquet at Hog Canyon, and he and his wife socialized with Hawks and Marion Marshall before that romance broke up. Their main differences were religion and politics for, like Feldman, Lasker was Jewish and a Democrat. But these things didn't matter, simply because they never came up. Tall, imperious, taciturn, and always impeccably dressed, Lasker and Hawks were, in many ways, cut from the same cloth; by the early 1950s, Lasker maintained, "I was Howard's best friend."

With Feldman increasingly involved with the day-to-day demands of film production in addition to his enormous list of clients, Hawks was in need of some help on the business side of his life. In Lasker's view, "I don't think he had any business sense. I never knew for sure, but I always sensed he was broke." Chris Nyby suggested that there was an ulterior motive for Hawks's friendship with Lasker: "Ed Lasker was rich, and he would help Howard guarantee loans when he needed the money, so Howard brought him into pictures." When Hawks formed Winchester, he invited Lasker to become his partner, to be credited as associate producer on each picture. For Lasker, a man with no motion picture experience whatsoever, this was beyond his wildest dreams.

Hawks's one previous foray into producing another director's work, *Corvette K-225*, had not proved memorable on any level, but his financial crunch had motivated him to include just such a provision in his RKO contract; it would be an easy way to pick up an extra $125,000 or so. Studio executives, however, were taken aback when Hawks, instead of selecting a known quantity to direct, drafted one of his own cronies who had never exposed a frame of film before. Hawks had considered handing the job to Charles Lederer; he had directed one previous film, and he obviously knew the material. But after the rescue job Nyby performed on *Red River*, Hawks had expressed his gratitude by assuring his cutter a shot at directing, and Hawks decided to throw the new project his way. In all candor, Nyby later speculated on the main reason he got the job: "Hawks knew he probably couldn't have controlled Lederer as much as he did me." Hawks selected the story and prepared the script; hired some of his most trusted collaborators, notably the cinematographer Russell Harlan and the composer Dimitri Tiomkin, to ensure a professional result; planned to oversee it to make sure all went smoothly; and set a moderate budget of $860,240, which, with 25 percent studio overhead, came to $1,075,300. Hawks's generosity to Nyby did not extend to the protegé's salary; of the $50,000 the RKO contract specified for a directing fee, Hawks parceled out just $5,460 to Nyby, keeping the remaining $44,040 for himself.

The part of the job Hawks enjoyed most, and that he largely reserved for himself, was the casting. At long last, he would be able to launch his discovery Margaret Sheridan in a starring role. There were no female characters in Campbell's original story, but Hawks created the role of Nikki especially for her. The story's nominal hero, Captain Patrick Hendry, would be played by Kenneth Tobey, who had played a sailor skeptical of Cary Grant's womanhood in *I Was a Male War Bride*. Again, Hawks surprisingly came through on his promise to make him a lead in a later picture. From *War Bride*, Hawks also brought back William Self, while for another role he found a muscular, good-looking young Texan, Dewey Martin, whom he signed to a two-year contract.

But Nyby was responsible for finding the two actors who would become the most familiar faces to emerge from the production that was now called *The Thing*, albeit for their subsequent work on television. Nyby's next-door neighbor was George Fenneman, who, after his making his screen debut in *The Thing*, became famous as Groucho Marx's announcer on *You Bet Your Life*. And when Nyby met James Arness, an aspiring actor, at John Ford's Memorial Day party, he was convinced that the towering young man would be perfect for the role of Streak in *The Big Sky*, which was then still on the boards. Hawks agreed and cast him, but when the Western was post-poned, he gave Arness the thankless title role in *The Thing*. Arness, of course, recovered to make a career out of *Gunsmoke*.

Of the countless changes Hawks, Lederer, and Hecht made from story to script, among the most important were moving the setting to the North Pole in order to introduce the element of American surveillance of the Soviet nuclear threat; creating a female lead who fully participates in speculating about alien invasion and in devising a way to kill the Thing; and making a film in which, for arguably the first time in a Hollywood production, sci-ence-fiction and horror were equally mixed, as well as one in which the struggle was just as much between the scientists and the military as between men and an alien. One element Hawks took credit for introducing was the critique of scientists and, by extension, intellectuals, in that the biologist played by Robert Cornthwaite is the main culprit for the Thing's escape. However, this view was present, if in more implicit form, in the original story. On the downside, the screenplay vastly reduced and simplified the powers of the monster, eliminating its ability to mutate, a decision no doubt inspired by the virtual impossibility of creating convincing special effects.

Howard Hughes was dubious about the entire project from the out-set; after all, he had signed Hawks to bring some class to RKO, not creaky monster movies. Even his cast and crew were a bit skeptical. The script boy Richard Keinen said, "We all thought this was the dumbest thing we'd ever heard of. We thought, 'What is Howard Hawks doing making this stupid horror film?'"

Hawks sent Hughes a string of notes and memos assuring him that the picture would be extremely scary in a modern way and that the Thing would be unique, nothing like the usual Frankenstein creature. The beast in the original story was, indeed, out of the ordinary, with three red eyes and blue wormlike hair. The producer made the makeup artist Lee Greenway, who was also a well-regarded painter and sculptor, go through eighteen versions of makeup designs for the Thing. None of them satisfied Hawks, who finally got fed up and dismissively told Greenway, "Make him look like Frankenstein." A more playful contribution came from the prop depart-ment, which made the little "thinglets" growing in the laboratory out of condoms. No one noticed, however. In any event, the beast wouldn't even be clearly shown in the final film, the better to emphasize the threat of the unknown. Although grateful to be working at all, James Arness was so embar-rassed by his appearance that he usually lunched alone during shooting and otherwise kept his distance from the others in the cast, except for Dewey

Martin; in subsequent years, he similarly refused all invitations to participate in reunions or sci-fi celebrations centering on *The Thing*.

Hawks claimed to have invited the heads of three major electronics companies to his home for dinner on the pretext of asking them to suggest the best way of killing the Thing. Less receptive were the army and air force, both of which refused to cooperate since the story was predicated on a belief in flying saucers, a phenomenon that the military was then strenuously trying to downplay. Official sanction, however, was hardly crucial to the production.

Hawks sent Nyby and a few crew members to Alaska to scout potential locations, but any suitable spots were simply too inaccessible to accommodate a cast and crew of one hundred. Instead, the major exteriors would be filmed at Cut Bank, Montana, a town of twenty-eight hundred people fifty miles south of the Canadian border and forty miles east of Glacier National Park. Cut Bank was chosen, largely on the advice of Hughes himself, because it was, statistically, nearly the snowiest place in the United States and it had a huge military airfield, recently abandoned, that had been used for reconnaissance flights by B-29s toward the Soviet Union.

In the second half of October 1950 the most memorable showdown in the history of the Screen Directors Guild took place between factions of the right and the left. Cecil B. DeMille and his fellow archconsevatives unsuccessfully tried to oust guild president Joseph L. Mankiewicz over the issue of a loyalty oath. Tensions ran high, with John Ford publicly rebuking De Mille after the latter cast aspersions on such eminent directors as Billy Wilder, William Wyler, and Fred Zinnemann because of their foreign accents. No longer an SDG officer, Hawks was nowhere to be found during this crucial episode in the guild's history. As Ed Lasker remarked, "He would never get involved in something like that."

Shooting on *The Thing* started on October 25, but more in theory than in reality. With the actors remaining on call in Los Angeles, Hawks, Nyby, and the crew flew up to Montana in two TWA Consellations provided by Hughes. The art department had done its job, building a small compound on which the eaves of the roof were only two feet above the ground, so that even the slightest amount of snow would make it look as though it was buried nearly up to the top. But the problem was that there was no snow at all. Due to stay in Cut Bank for just a few days, the company waited. And waited. And it never snowed.

After a while, the men began to go stir crazy. One day, the script boy Richard Keinen and some other crew members were forlornly hanging around the airport site, about ten miles outside town. A couple of little boys turned up to play and asked the men what they were doing there. When told that they were waiting for snow in order to shoot a movie, one boy said, "It doesn't snow here." Keinen assured them that it snowed more here than just about anywhere else, but the boy corrected him: "It snows a lot in town, but it doesn't snow here at the airport. That's why they built it here, because the wind keeps the snow away and the runways clear."

Not quite willing to decamp based on the word of a little kid, Hawks decided to stick it out, certain the snow was bound to arrive as winter neared. A lot of poker was played and liquor drunk to sooth the frayed nerves. Lasker, who was new to it all, learned one lesson about working with Hawks the hard way. "After one week, I went to Howard and said, 'Howard, we've been up here for a week and we're already six days behind schedule.' Howard just froze and said, 'Don't ever talk to me about that.'" In desperation, the crew created artificial snow and the cast was flown up in the hopes of doing some general shots, but Lasker said that the company "finally got perhaps only one shot up there." The seven weeks on location were a total waste, to no avail on-screen.

Abruptly, an act of God brought everyone back to Hollywood. On December 15, Hawks's father, Frank Winchester Hawks, died quietly at the family home on Bellefontaine Street in Pasadena, at the age of eighty-six. When his son got the news in Cut Bank, he said not a word to anyone and spent the evening bowling with companions as if nothing had happened. The next day, however, he announced that the location jaunt was over and that everyone was to return home. Upon arriving, Hawks went directly to the house, where Barbara, who was just starting high school, was still living. She was there along with Hawks's mother and Aunt Katherine. Private services were held at the home. Helen Hawks went into a decline upon her husband's death, from which she never recovered, and she died on August 27, 1952, at eighty-one. Aunt Katherine moved to Santa Barbara and lived into her nineties in a residential hotel.

Improvising their way through the scenes they intended to shoot in Montana, the company relocated to the eighty-nine-acre RKO ranch in the San Fernando Valley, which was made to look like a frigid wasteland by treating the ground with salt, tempered Masonite, and photographic solution, which froze everything. The salt caused problems when the solution melted, however, running off into adjacent orchards and contaminating the water used to irrigate them; RKO was forced to pay damages. The most famous exterior scene, that of the crew forming a ring around the submerged flying saucer, was filmed while cast members baked in their heavy garments in one-hundred-degree-plus weather. Dewey Martin testified, "It was terrible. We had to wear those huge parkas, the fur-lined jobs. They were using plastic and cornflakes for the snow, and they had these big wind machines blowing it in our faces. And it would get down in the neckline, and down into our heavy underwear. I'm telling you it was rough." Sharp-eyed viewers have noted that a crease is visible in the enormous cyclorama, revealing that the skyline in the scene is actually a backdrop, while Nyby admitted that in one of his aerial shots for the same scene, taken in Montana, there are briefly visible a horse, trailer, and some men sweeping the ice, although no one ever complained about it. The company generated no goodwill when it filmed the blowing up of the flying saucer; the explosion was much bigger than anyone anticipated, and Nyby was only slightly exaggerating when he said, "We broke all the windows in Van Nuys and North Hollywood."

Initial interiors were shot at the RKO Studios, but Hawks soon came up with the idea that the Thing should turn off the heat in the compound as part of its battle against the earthlings. "Wouldn't it be nice if you could see the breath vapors?" Hawks mused, which meant that somebody had to figure out very quickly how to accomplish this. After some half-baked experiments with putting ice, hot soup, or coffee in actors' mouths, it was decided that the entire set would be rebuilt at an icehouse on Seventh Street on the east side of downtown Los Angeles. The temperature remained at a constant twenty-five degrees, and script boy Richard Keinen recalled it as being "so cold that you could only stay in there for twenty-five minutes at a time. The only nice thing I ever saw Howard Hawks do by way of showing camaraderie with common workers was to send out for this whole bunch of hand-warmers." Lorrie Sherwood said, "The only time I saw Mr. Hawks somewhat disheveled and not well dressed was in the icehouse. Usually he was all Abercrombie & Fitch, but in there, he had to wear the blankets and earmuffs and hand-warmers and everything else, just like the rest of us."

As a publicity gimmick, Hawks insisted upon a closed set throughout the shoot and even prohibited the RKO publicity department from releasing any photographs or information about the picture. James Arness, who was replaced by a stuntman for many of the more violent scenes that required the Thing to catch on fire or jump out a window, was not even allowed to venture off the soundstage once he was in makeup. In the end, though, it wasn't one of the more physical scenes that proved the most difficult to shoot, but one in which George Fenneman was required to spout a page of scientific gobbledygook; as Ken Tobey remembered it, "George didn't even know what he was talking about, and it took him thirty takes to get through the speech." Keinen said that Fenneman was so terrified that he called a halt to his acting career then and there.

The perennial question surrounding *The Thing* has always been, Who actually directed it, Christian Nyby or Howard Hawks? The sum of participants' responses make the answer quite clear. Putting it most bluntly, Ed Lasker said, "Chris Nyby didn't direct a thing. One day Howard was late and Chris said, 'Why don't we get started? I know what the shot should be.' And I said, 'No, Chris, I think we'll wait until Howard gets here.'" Ken Tobey testified, "Chris Nyby directed one scene. Howard Hawks was there, but he let Chris direct one scene. We all rushed into a room, eight or ten of us, and we practically knocked each other over. No one knew what to do." Dewey Martin, Robert Cornthwaite, and Richard Keinen all agreed that Hawks was the director, and Bill Self said, "Chris Nyby was a very nice, decent fellow, but he wasn't Howard Hawks."

Hawks was always a diplomat and a gentleman on the subject; for once, he didn't attempt to take credit, even though it was due him. Having prepared the production so carefully and attended rehearsals, Hawks explained that on "the very first day of working, Chris came in and said, 'Look, I'm in trouble. It's a lot different making scenes than taking the stuff you give me and putting it together. I need help.' So I used to be there. I'd come in and watch him rehearse a scene in the morning and I'd say, 'I think I'd tackle it this way.' People say Nyby didn't have anything to do with it. Well, he did have something to do with it. But he needed some help."

It was really Nyby who, for the rest of his life, would walk the tightrope of not taking too much credit away from Hawks but at the same time trying to hang onto his one claim to fame. Nyby explained, "Each morning Hawks would come in and sit down with the actors around a table and go over the script. Then we'd rewrite the scene. Everybody had a hand in it. I had never directed actors before, so Hawks had more of a hand in talking to the cast. He was the—well, you might call him the chairman of the board." Richard Keinen said, "People have no idea how strangely that picture was made. We'd come in in the morning, and no one knew what we'd be doing that day. We sat around in a big circle and Hawks would read off the lines but with no characters assigned to them. He'd talk it out and get suggestions and write it out while everyone waited around. We'd finally shoot the scene at four or five in the afternoon. It was weird for the actors, because they never knew when they would be gotten by the Thing, so they never knew when they came to work if it would be their last day. But we had a lot of fun on the picture."

At one point in early January, while Hawks directed what was officially called second-unit footage of the Thing burning up, Nyby and thirteen others were sent back to Cut Bank to try to supplement the paltry footage obtained earlier, but ferocious weather turned this into another useless trip. The one crew member to speak up on Nyby's behalf was the soundman Clem Portman, who pointed out, "Chris was in charge of postproduction. I don't remember Howard being in the dubbing room at all. I assumed Howard had stepped aside and let Chris handle things." Of course, this was nothing unusual for Hawks, who typically wasn't around for postproduction on any of his films.

Nyby suffered when the film was released to critical and commercial acclaim because everyone, particularly members of the industry, believed that Hawks was responsible for it. "Unfortunately, it was too big a success for my own good," Nyby lamented. "Nobody believed a first-time director could have such a big hit. They gave all the credit to Howard." Hawks even gave trade interviews in which he bolstered his protegé's contributions to the film, but it didn't help Nyby get any further first-class assignments. He was offered a couple of B horror movies at Universal and Columbia. "But," Nyby explained, "after doing a successful picture, being relegated to cheap schlock would be admitting that Howard Hawks directed *The Thing*. So I refused their offers." Nyby later went into television before directing a handful of feature films, none of them at all notable. Robert Cornthwaite subsequently worked with Nyby several times in television and was struck by one characteristic: "Chris was so much a disciple of Hawks that he was the only director I knew who didn't say 'Action' but instead only said 'Camera' when a scene was to start, in imitation of the unique way Hawks did it."

Years later, Nyby put it this way: "When you are being taught to paint by Rembrandt, you don't take the brush out of his hand. You listen and watch him paint. The same when you're working with a great director like Howard Hawks."

Making just his sixth picture, Robert Cornthwaite, whose own mother, he was amused to say, used to babysit for the young Howard Hughes in Beaumont, Texas, adored working with Hawks. "If there was ever a dictator on the set, it was Howard Hawks. He was an autocrat. But he was very considerate in explaining things, he would take an actor aside. He was a good writer, particularly good at trimming a line down to where it was witty.

He always went for humor. I felt inspired by his approach to things, because he encouraged the actor to contribute. He told me, 'I'd like you to take that last scene and write it yourself.' I tried it myself and he said, 'That's the way we'll shoot it.' There was a real sense of participation."

Even in this open, collaborative atmosphere, however, Hawks kept his distance from the others. Keinen testified that, "He was standoffish, but a very clever man. He was a sphinx-like character. I had gone to high school with his son David and I mentioned this to him as a way of possibly breaking the ice, so to speak. But he just stared at me. It didn't mean a thing to him." At one point, one of the actors made the mistake of calling Hawks by his first name. "He was just frozen out," Cornthwaite recalled. "Hawks just walked away. It simply wasn't done."

Richard Keinen attested that *The Thing* "was Hawks' baby right from the beginning. Hawks did everything. He dreamed up the idea, he had the script put together and he rewrote everything on the set. Nobody else had any input at all." The surest sign that Hawks, and no one else, was in charge was the way the schedule and budget soared. Completely contrary to Hawks's later claim that "it was shot very rapidly," what was originally intended to be a nine-week shoot finally finished on March 3, 1951, after nineteen weeks. However, due to the cheap cast, sets, and, especially for a science-fiction film, minimal special effects, the overall cost only increased by 25 percent, to $1,257,327, including overhead.

Bill Self was told at the time that Hawks didn't take directing credit on *The Thing* because it was planned as a low-budget film, one in which RKO didn't have much confidence. But, as critics have been saying ever since it was released, *The Thing* is a Howard Hawks film in everything but name. The opening scene of various members of the team bantering is so distilled as to be a virtual parody of Hawksian overlapping dialogue. Even more than *Only Angels Have Wings*, the picture presents a pristine example of a group operating resourcefully in a hermetically sealed environment in which everything in the outside world represents a grave threat.

This fear of the unknown exists in many Hawks films, but the sociopolitical climate of the early 1950s gives *The Thing* its extra resonance, as does its position at the forefront of countless other paranoid expressions— conscious or not—about the specter of communism. *The Thing* was not only the first modern "creature" film, but, more important, it was the first to link inhuman, devouring, alien beings with the Red Menace. Unlike the slightly more ambiguous *Invasion of the Body Snatchers*, there could be no doubt about the evil equation in *The Thing*: its characters, mostly military men, were explicitly placed on the front line in the Cold War against the Soviet Union, and Hawks's (and Nyby's) sympathies clearly lay with these intuitive can-do men and against the emotionless eggheads, even if both camps were bunglers. Ben Hecht's elitist, irreverent attitudes may have provided the springboard for the film's nose-tweaking posture (Hecht had no use for either Marxists or the McCarthyite Right), but Hawks, Lederer, and Nyby, all conservative men, took the allegorical anticommunist warning much further through their concluding admonition: "Watch the Skies."

It was not in Hawks's nature to do so, so it is therefore ironic that *The Thing*, for which he didn't even take authorial credit, marked one of the rare instances in which he functioned as a trendsetter rather than a refiner: for years to come, the screen was filled with aliens and monsters that somehow carried with them the baggage of the communist, thermonuclear, antidemocratic, brainwashed, "foreign" threat. *The Thing* can be said to have directly spawned this entire subgenre, just as it stands as the unavoidable granddaddy of the more recent wave of *Alien*-style mutant beast shockers.

For both reasons, *The Thing* was one of Hawks's most influential creations, still cited as a key film in the lives of such prominent directors as Ridley Scott, John Frankenheimer, Tobe Hooper, and John Carpenter, who went so far as to remake *The Thing*, with gory and horrific explicitness, in 1982. Carpenter recalled seeing the original at the age of six and said, *"The Thing* was the first movie that made me jump out of my seat—literally." The picture provoked a more divided reaction among science-fiction writers, but it is admired by some prominent authors in the field, including Arthur C. Clarke and Michael Crichton, who went so far as to say, "I am convinced that *The Thing* is the best SF film ever made." As for the original's author, John W. Campbell Jr. rather regretted the enormous extent to which the filmmakers changed his story, particularly the elimination of the shapeshifting element, but had to admit they did something right since it was so successful.

At least one woman fainted from fright at the film's sneak preview in Pasadena, but the only significant change made after this first public showing was the elimination of the love scenes between Tobey and Sheridan, which were felt to slow down the action. No doubt because it was so prominently touted as a "Howard Hawks Production," in the manner of most of his other films, *The Thing* received the sort of serious attention from the press that was customarily denied to examples of culturally despised genres. Most critics found it scary, entertaining, not unintelligent, and well made, almost as if Hawks had directed it himself.

Even with Hawks's name looming above the title, theater owners were skeptical that a black-and-white science-fiction film with a no-star cast could do strong business in class first-run situations. RKO, concerned that the public might associate the picture with Phil Harris's hit 1950 comic novelty song of the same name, lengthened the title to *The Thing from Another World*. But all fears quickly proved groundless, as an effective campaign and intense local ballyhoo in particular cities kept the film between second and fourth place at the box-office nationally for five weeks running between mid-April and mid-May. It was the number-two film for the entire month of May, behind *The Great Caruso*, and enjoyed particularly outstanding runs at such prestigious theaters as the Criterion in New York and the Pantages in Los Angeles. In London, it shocked the trade by breaking the twenty-one-year-old box-office mark in its first week at the London Pavilion. Its eventual earnings were less than sensational but, with rentals of $1.95 million, it ranked as RKO's sixth-biggest earner of 1951 and forty-seventh overall, moderately ahead of the other alien-invader classic of the year, *The Day the Earth Stood Still*, which arrived in September.

In late 1950, Hawks was squiring around a young Powers Agency model and hopeful actress, Elizabeth Threatt, with whom he often went dancing, and was also dating Jane Wyman, Ronald Reagan's ex. But at a New Year's Eve party, Hawks met a young woman seemingly made to order for him: very attractive and stylish, slim, vivacious, and forthright, twenty-two-year-old, Donna Hartford, who went by the name of Dee, was a model with ambitions to make it big in pictures, the sort of striking, perfectly groomed woman who turned heads wherever she went.

Dee and her younger sister Eden were originally the Higgins sisters from Salt Lake City, but they left a difficult home life for New York, where they launched careers as teenage models and girls-about-town and adopted their new surname. Ironically, they wound up in Hollywood thanks to Howard Hughes. Walter Kane, a Hughes aide whose most important duty was recruiting new girls for his boss, brought a photograph of a model with a knockout figure to Hughes's attention. Hughes predictably responded by having Kane track her down and sign her up, but more than a year later, when she appeared in an RKO comedy ironically called *A Girl in Every Port*, Hughes realized he had the wrong girl. It had been Eden that Hughes was interested in.

Dee soon realized that RKO had signed her up by mistake, but by then it was too late. Fate played its hand heavily in 1950–51 in determining the lives of the Hartford sisters, for when Eden came to the set to visit, she met the film's star, Groucho Marx. Although she was twenty-four to his sixty, they began dating; and though Groucho, like many in town, suspected that the Hartford sisters might be gold diggers, Eden eventually landed her man.

Thirty-two years separated Hawks and Dee, and there was little question about what appealed to one about the other. The relationship heated up so quickly that by June Hawks had to deny widespread rumors that they were engaged. With his own financial condition quite the opposite of Groucho's, Hawks similarly felt there was no reason to rush into a third marriage. In late 1950, Hawks was still in trouble with the IRS, and RKO and Winchester were instructed to advance him no further money until $19,353 in back taxes were paid up. So urgently did Hawks then need cash that for a while in early 1951, unable to wait for a lump-sum payment, he asked the studio to put him on a straight salary basis so he would get weekly paychecks. Hawks's financial strain even induced him to embarrass himself by asking his respected friend and colleague John Ford for five thousand dollars while driving him somewhere. Ford just listened as Hawks explained his predicament, and the older man procrastinated about giving an answer until they arrived at his destination. Ford then said, "Howard, I appreciate your plight. But I've just managed to save one million dollars, and if I gave you that money, I wouldn't be able to put away the million," whereupon he got out and walked away.

Also to get more money rolling in, Hawks set in motion the third and final project under his RKO contract. One of the big best-sellers of 1950 was William E. Barrett's timely and inspirational novel, *The Left Hand of God*, about an American flier trying to escape the embattled China of 1947 disguised as a priest. The trappings of the story—the resourceful pilot hero, a gorgeous young nurse, the endangered outpost of humanity trying to stave off violent and unpredictable forces—had obvious outward appeal to Hawks, who certainly would have played up the adventure and romance angles.

Hawks managed to spring Faulkner from his lingering commitment to Warner Bros. to adapt the book, and even though the writer had, in December, reached the pinnacle of his career by receiving the Nobel Prize in Literature, Faulkner didn't want to let his old friend down and accepted the assignment. Flying out to Los Angeles at the beginning of February, Faulkner installed himself at the comfortable Beverly-Carlton Hotel in Beverly Hills, instantly resumed his affair with Meta Carpenter, and agreed to a deal with Hawks whereby he would receive two thousand dollars a week and a substantial bonus if he finished the job within four weeks. Very occasionally, he would meet Hawks at his offices at RKO, then venture across to Lucey's for a few drinks. More often, he would meet Lorrie Sherwood for double bourbons at Musso & Frank's or at Hawks's house, where he would dictate to her "so slowly," as she recalled. Faulkner turned in his 198-page first draft with one day to spare and about a week later returned to Mississippi, from where he did periodic revisions for additional pay. But the results, while craftsmanlike, were disappointing—rather dull and sincere, with an abundance of narration—and the project was put on the back burner.

With *The Thing* finally finished and released in the spring, Hawks turned his full attention back to *The Big Sky*. As before, the main frustration lay in the casting. Despite his promise from the previous summer, Hughes now adamantly refused to make Robert Mitchum available. Hawks, Lasker, and Nyby all assumed it was because Hughes still harbored a grudge over the *Outlaw–Red River* issue, but adding fuel to the fire may have been Hughes's double frustration over Lasker's marriage to Jane Greer and Hawks's relationship with Dee Hartford; taking professional revenge on men over women he wanted was standard practice for Hughes.

John Wayne, Hawks's other leading candidate, was booked solid and simply couldn't fit in what promised to be a shoot no shorter than that for *Red River*. So for the role of riverboat explorer Jim Deakins, Hawks settled on Kirk Douglas, one of the top new postwar stars. Douglas was scarcely his first choice, but Hawks figured his intense physicality and confidence would serve the film well; ironically, his $125,000 price was exactly what Marlon Brando had asked for the year before, only to have been rejected out of hand by Hawks as too high.

Where the producer-director now intended to save money was with the role of Boone Caudill, the leading character in the book, a "White Savage" ultimately at home neither in white society nor among the Indians. The choice came down to two young actors from *The Thing* whom he had under personal contract, Ken Tobey and Dewey Martin. After watching them closely on *The Thing*, Hawks decided to give the plum part to Martin, a perfect fit for the role physically but still callow and inexperienced as an actor. Hawks did save money, however, paying him just $6,325. For the key female role of Teal Eye, the Blackfoot princess who comes between the two men, Hawks cast his fashion-model discovery Elizabeth Threatt, who was said to be of Cherokee and English descent and had used the middle name Coyotte, adapted from her actual middle name Coyote, during her New York modeling career, although she dropped it when she came to Hollywood.

With *The Big Sky*, Hawks believed that he could follow up on the achievement and reputation of *Red River*, not only with another story of early

Western trailblazing but as a deeper exploration of his perennial interest in "a love story between two men" in which serious emotional sacrifice is required to maintain the friendship—one that has been placed in jeopardy, as usual, by a woman. The working out of the conflict between sustaining the male relationship and allowing one of them to go off with the woman they have both loved is accomplished here with a maturity and complexity new to Hawks.

Even if the picture is not fully realized, the two men are forced to confront the dilemma head-on, transcend it, and embrace it to the benefit of all three people involved. As Arthur Hunnicutt's Uncle Zeb deftly summarizes the situation that pertains to so many Hawks films, "Ain't it funny. Two men is friends, then a girl comes along, and then pretty soon they ain't friends no more. And now with one of 'em walking out on what the other one woulda give his right arm fer, I kept wonderin' what they'd do to settle it." Fortunately, in *The Big Sky* there is no forced confrontation or melodramatic showdown; each man simply acts wisely and maturely, accepting nature's course.

Emboldened by the success of his fast-and-loose attitude to narrative in *Red River*, Hawks took an even more casual approach with the structure here, figuring that if the individual scenes were strong enough, the film would be too. The confidence behind such an attitude is evident in the film. By the start of shooting, Dudley Nichols had gotten the script down to 187 pages, and with Hawks operating autonomously at his own production company, no one at the studio was in a position to question it.

Hawks still, however, had to answer to the Breen Office, which saw much to object to in Nichols's script. The censors were concerned about such matters as the potential for great brutality in the fight scenes, the vulgarity of many of the French expressions, the prominent role of Boone's dead brother's scalp as a prop, Uncle Zeb's many lewd expressions, and the characters' heavy drinking. Although the censors objected to it, Hawks got away with the line "She's wild and pretty like a virgin woman"—surprising, given all the fuss over the word *virgin* in *The Moon Is Blue* two years later.

But the central problem, because it was so crucial to the resolution of the story, was Boone's sleeping with Teal Eye, only to awake the next morning to discover that he has "married" her, an event signaled in the original screenplay by having Teal Eye finish putting on her clothes and fastening her belt. It took a long meeting between Hawks and Lasker and the MPAA to work out an acceptable alternative: when she symbolically cuts the thong holding back the flap to her wigwam with Boone's knife, she initiates an unknowing Boone into marriage, Blackfoot style, and he has nothing to say about it.

On the first of June, Hawks chartered a DC-3 from Paul Mantz to take the second-unit director, Arthur Rosson; the cinematographer, Russ Harlan; the unit manager, Art Siteman; and a few others up to Jackson Hole for another location hunt. Virtually all the exteriors would be shot in and around Grand Teton National Park, with the Snake River filling in for the Missouri, and Hawks later proudly claimed that *The Big Sky* was the first major outdoor picture without a single process shot. The budget, including 25 percent overhead, was set at $1,712,174; the first unit would shoot for forty-seven days (revised upward to fifty-seven days by the start of production), with twenty-eight days allotted to the second unit. Despite its growing popularity, especially in big period films, color cinematography still did not appeal to Hawks. "Dirt looks more like dirt in black-and-white," he reasoned. "If you photograph a picture like mine in color you expect someone to suddenly come forth and sing 'By the Waters of the Minnetonka.'" After final preparations were made in Hollywood, Hawks, along with his son David and most of the top crew members, left for Wyoming the second week of July and stayed at the luxurious Teton Lodge in Moran while a new Camp Anderson was put up.

Art Rosson, who had now been doing this sort of thing for Hawks for twenty years, began shooting his second-unit coverage of river men working the keelboat in the second half of July. Hawks and the rest of the company arrived by the end of the month, and the director nearly had a calamitous mishap before he ever got to work. On the day that he was supposed to have his mandatory physical, Hawks decided he'd rather go fishing and invited Lorrie Sherwood out on a small boat. When a dam on the Snake River was opened, the torrent of rushing water swept them swiftly downstream until Hawks managed to grab onto an overhanging tree. It was only when Russ Harlan and some of his camera crew happened to notice them that Hawks and Sherwood were rescued.

Nor did principal photography begin auspiciously on August 3, as inclement weather nearly kept Hawks was from shooting his first scene. He couldn't start up again until August 8, but even then filming proceeded at a slow pace because of the combination of highly changeable weather conditions and Hawks's usual relaxed pace, which included extended visits from Dee, Jane Greer, and Famous Artists agent Ray Stark, who brought up his son Peter as well as Douglas's six-year-old son Michael. Hawks's fifteen-year-old daughter Barbara spent the summer on location, was given a bit part as an Indian girl, and developed a major crush on Kirk Douglas. "He said, 'When you're eighteen, call me,'" she remembered. Hawks, dapper in his custom-made cowboy gear, rewrote constantly on his omnipresent yellow legal pad, handing his revisions daily to Lorrie Sherwood, who typed them up while working from the back of a truck. Coordinating the crew, the movements of the boat, and the ever-changing locations was an enormous, time-consuming task, but Hawks's decision to hire mostly real river men to crew the *Mantan* paid off both in efficiency and authenticity.

Plenty of journalists rolled through, especially since two major locations could be visited on one trip to Wyoming that summer—George Stevens was filming *Shane* just forty miles away on the other side of the mountains. For his part, Kirk Douglas was soon shacked up with his costar Betty Threatt, and they carried on a hot affair that continued on past the shoot. Before long, Douglas was encouraging her to behave like a star and demand to be treated as one (although she was getting all of $5,000 for her work). As Lasker recalled, "In one scene she had to dive into the water, and, with Douglas's backing, she told Howard that she wanted the set clear. Howard said, 'We'll clear the set when you're a star.'" It never happened. After testing for but losing the role of the prostitute in *From Here to Eternity* to Donna Reed, Threatt disappeared from the film scene.

Although no open animosity developed, Hawks and Douglas never hit it off in a big way, and the director realized early on that while Douglas was in his element playing heels and heavies, he wasn't terribly convincing portraying friendship or warmth. Hawks's films depended greatly on casting, and he quickly knew that this time he had gotten it wrong and should have held off making *The Big Sky* until he could get the proper actors. At the same time, the strong-willed Douglas, who would shortly start producing his own pictures, didn't particularly cotton to Hawks's leisurely working habits. "Nowadays, with the tremendous emphasis on costs, you couldn't do that," Douglas observed, "nor is it my concept of how a movie should be made."

Still, Hawks got Douglas to perform a scene that John Wayne had refused to do in *Red River*. It was one of Hawks's favorite stories, about how he tried to convince Wayne that his character should mangle his finger between a rope and saddle horn and need to have it amputated by Walter Brennan. "Wayne said, 'You think that's *funny*?' 'Oh,' I said, 'if you're not good enough then we won't do it. I'll do it sometime with somebody who's a better actor.' So I did it with Kirk Douglas, who is not as good an actor, but Kirk did it, and it was very funny. Duke saw it, and he told me, 'If you tell me a funeral is funny, I'll do a funeral.'"

What Hawks's method sacrificed was money and hard-driving narrative momentum. What it generated was a tremendous feeling for territory
being penetrated by white men for the first time, for the humor and tragedy emanating from the diverse cultures present in the West in 1832, a sense
of life being lived in a curious and adventurous way. The one actor in the
cast who hit exactly what Hawks was looking for was Arthur Hunnicutt, who
was only forty but, like his counterpart in old-coot roles, Walter Brennan,
looked much older. The Arkansas native was seasoned and seemed part of
the landscape in a way that the other actors did not.

As shooting pushed on through the second half of August, the company was plagued by intermittent rain and, more frequently, bad light, which
kept the average number of pages shot down to under one per day. When
a surprise early storm of rain, sleet, and snow hit on September 11, Hawks
decided to pack it in and return to Hollywood the next day. At that point,
the production was fourteen days behind schedule. Anyone else would have
been exasperated by the problems, but Hawks was still thrilled with the
landscapes they were able to capture and particularly by Russ Harlan's beautiful black-and-white photography. Shooting the St. Louis street scenes on
the Fox backlot but the remainder of interiors at RKO Pathé, Hawks continued at his sluggish pace while two second units continued on location.
Art Rosson shot a great deal of needed river footage, while Chris Nyby had
his usual bad luck attempting to shoot in Montana. He was supposed to
film a buffalo hunt on the Crow Reservation, but the animals were spooked
and run ragged due to the annual thinning of the herds that had just taken
place. It then snowed heavily, forcing him to give up.

The scene Kirk Douglas had to perform on his last day required him
to swim in water on a soundstage. As he was coming down with a bad cold,
he told Hawks he didn't want to do it that day, especially with all the wind
machines blowing. According to Ed Lasker, "Howard said, 'You can stay in
bed all day tomorrow once the picture's finished.' So Kirk did it, and ended
up in the hospital with pneumonia. He was sore that neither Howard nor I
ever came to see him in the hospital." What Lasker didn't add was that
Douglas was staying in a room that Lasker had donated to the hospital.
Douglas recalled, "I heard Eddie was telling people: 'Isn't it funny that Kirk's
in the room I donated?'" The actor was sick for weeks and weak for months
thereafter.

When production closed on November 12, Hawks was thirty-five days
behind schedule, having shot for an incredible ninety-two days. The budget wound up at $2,546,336, including overhead, not quite as much as *Red*

River but very high for a film without a heavyweight cast and far more than RKO was spending on any other picture at the time.

As before, Hawks gave Nyby free rein in the cutting, telling him basically what he wanted but leaving the detail work to his trusted editor. For one scene that Hawks hadn't covered properly in which a bulldozer in high gear had pulled a raft downriver too fast, Hawks had said, "Don't worry about Chris, he'll figure out a way to cut it together." With all of Hawks's and the cast's additions, the script as shot came to 216 pages, enough for a three-and-a-half-hour feature. With tremendous difficulty, Nyby cut the film down to somewhere around two and a half hours and, after a series of public previews, pruned it further to 138 minutes. All through the trimming, Hawks kept redoing the voice-over narration, with input from Dudley Nichols, until finally he told RKO production executive Ned Depinet he could remove nothing more. (At one point, Nyby reversed gears to add some footage: For a private screening of one version at Ed Lasker's house, Nyby cut some hardcore stag film footage into a wrestling scene between Dewey Martin and Elizabeth Threatt.) Further sneaks were successful, but the widespread view among audiences, studio executives and the trade reviewers was that it was still too long. Hawks told Depinet that "it gets down to a decision either we want a shorter picture that definitely is not as good or let it stand." Hughes balked endlessly at approving Hawks's cut, and no one, including Hawks, could even get him on the phone for his comments. Lasker said that, on their own, he and Nyby managed to take out nearly another twenty minutes, but that Hawks put it all back.

Finally, on August 6, 1951, at a time when *High Noon* was the most popular film in the country, RKO held the world premiere of *The Big Sky* at the Woods Theater in Chicago, with Douglas, Martin, and Hawks flying in for the hoopla. (Jane Russell was in town at the same time to promote the opening of *Son of Paleface* at the renovated Oriental a half block away.) Hawks later accurately stated that initial business was outstanding (it did $35,000 opening week), but fancifully claimed that RKO immediately shortened the picture in order to cram in more shows per day, only to see the grosses plummet. In fact, the original long version was used, not only through the quickly tapering four weeks of the Chicago run, but upon the film's major openings at the end of August in New York and Los Angeles. Benefiting from mostly outstanding reviews, the film performed strongly at the Criterion in Times Square (although not nearly as well as *The Thing* had at the same theater) but was unaccountably soft on the West Coast, an accurate forecast of the mixed public turnout that followed throughout the country. For one week in September, it was the number-two film in the nation, and it ranked fifth at the box-office for the entire month. But it generally struggled, and the ultimate domestic take of $1.65 million didn't come close to matching the large production nut. It was also the lowest return for any Hawks film in well over a decade, the first one significantly under $2 million since the 1930s. Hawks's extraordinary winning streak, of eleven hit films (including *The Thing*) in thirteen years, was officially over.

Among the most interesting of the numerous rave reviews *The Big Sky* received was that from Hollis Alpert in the highbrow *Saturday Review*. He began by complaining that Howard Hawks was nowhere to be found in *Who's Who*, a shocking omission, and noted, "He is one of the select Hollywood few, a man who may choose, not only his own pictures but his studio connections as well." It was an astute insight for the time, one that not only foreshadowed by many years the eventual serious attention Hawks received, but points up how Hawks, despite his incredible track record and the prominence of his name above the titles of all his films since the 1930s, had not managed to make himself a national brand name. His career remained incoherent, his touch invisible, to most critics and viewers.

After years of inaccessibility, the 138-minute version of *The Big Sky* recently resurfaced on cable television, albeit in a highly variable print in which certain sections, particularly the reinstated scenes, look like bad 16mm dupes. The two versions are not radically different, and in a way, the long-lost material is more of the same—if you like the picture at 122 minutes, then there's more to like. If you don't care for the ambling pace and anecdotal structuring, then the picture is apt to seem even more leisurely. Hawks maintained, "They took out most of the story of the Indian girl and Dewey Martin. The scenes that made the relationships good were gone so all of a sudden you were hit with this strange relationship and you didn't know where it came from."

Hawks was only partially right. The sixteen minutes of cuts came from four significant scenes, or portions of scenes, having been chopped wholesale from the picture. The first major elision was of a scene between Jim and Boone; after they meet, fight, and agree to travel together, the two young men bed down together by a campfire and have a long talk during which Jim makes a major breakthrough by getting the dead-serious Boone to laugh. The scene has an important function in cementing their friendship, but most interesting is that it is written virtually like a romantic seduction, with one man trying to break down the resistance of the other and achieve an intimacy. The longest deleted sequence was a skirmish with Indians, which ends when the not-all-there Indian, Poordevil, kills another Indian with a bow and arrow and then scalps him. The entire sequence is very gracefully filmed, although it is arguably of minimal importance from a dramatic point-of-view. The third excision, much later on, was of a bullet being removed from Jim's leg; in the short version, there is an awkward cut from the preparation for the procedure to Boone handing his friend the bullet; the actual extraction was deleted. The final cut took out the second half of a key scene, in which Boone, having now unwittingly "married" Teal Eye, gives his rifle to her father, the Blackfoot chief; missing is a chat between Jim and Zeb in which the latter talks about a man he knew who married an Indian squaw then left her, only to come back to find that she had killed herself. This speech obviously lends more weight to what Teal Eye has done and raises the stakes over Boone's eventual decision whether or not to stay with his bride.

Hawks was too hard on himself when he judged *The Big Sky* a failure. Accepting all the blame, he said, "It should have been a really good picture. It's my fault." The film has a great deal to recommend it if one gets in sync with the pace, which corresponds to the slow mode of transportation depicted and the far-from-straightforward progress of wilderness exploration; this is a journey marked by bends in the river rather than the flat plains of *Red River*. It is true that the drama is seldom urgently compelling, that it lacks the stark conflict and magnetic characters of *Red River*. It is also the case that Hawks, despite his best attempt to present not only an Indian character but the colorfully assorted French-speaking pioneers of the period, didn't find a way to bring Teal Eye to meaningful life. Granted that Hawks was never adept at portraying cultures other than those with which he felt a personal affinity, but he still managed a reasonably evenhanded portrait of the Indians here, showing some to be good and some bad, but respecting them on their own terms. All the same, the film is genial in the manner of several of the more relaxed Hawks films to come, deeply appealing for the innumerable times the characters help and support one another in unspoken ways, and quite successful in giving the viewer a feeling for the discovery of the land, of pushing known boundaries, physical and emotional. The film also rewards multiple viewings, offering up further riches upon deeper investigation. Truly, the problem lay in the casting; if he had made the same film with, say, Brando and Mitchum in the leads, it could have made all the difference.

31

The Fox at Fox: *Monkey Business* and *Gentlemen Prefer Blondes*

By the early 1950s, the real world began to encroach upon Howard Hawks's paradise at Hog Canyon. An immaculately manicured preserve throughout the previous decade, 105-acre estate was surrounded by hills in a way that seemed to ensure against the city crowding in on its owner. However, the Los Angeles postwar boom knew few limits, and the property on the hills above Hawks's home to the north and west were bought in April 1950, by one Elwain Steinkamp, who planned to divide it up into thirty-six lots for houses. In due course, excavation, clearing, and grading were done. Hawks foresaw, to his annoyance, that he would soon have dozens of neighbors looking down on his private domain.

But annoyance became fury during the first three months of 1952. A phenomenal deluge pounded Los Angeles, playing the usual havoc on the streets and mountain passes of a city seriously unprepared for anything more than light rainfall. Down and down it came, until one day Hawks found—literally—tons of mud, rock, and debris covering his property. Steinkamp, his associates, and his contractors had stripped the land of vegetation and moved the earth above around with no regard to the consequences of a rainstorm. The result was a lavalike flow that rolled over the lawn, trees, shrubbery, and fences and despoiled, to varying degrees, Hawks's house, stables, barns, and horse paddocks. In some spots, the mess was several feet deep. Rivulets formed in the surrounding hills, channeling even more water straight into Hog Canyon; erosion was severe on Hawks's property immediately beneath the development, and a great deal of topsoil was washed away. One of the unfortunate consequences was the ruination of much of Hawks's career memorabilia, including the scripts from all of his films, which he had carelessly left out in the barn.

Naturally, Hawks filed a lawsuit against Steinkamp and his numerous partners, charging that his work had been pursued "in a careless, negligent and improper manner" and that nothing had been done to compact

494

and stabilize the earth or to install any drainage controls. The suit asked double Hawks's estimated $185,000 in damages. The defendants tried such tactics as claiming that the avalanche was an act of God and an unavoidable accident and even that Hawks should have known better than to build a house at the bottom of a canyon where one day such a thing was bound to happen, but the court found that there was no question that the defendants had been negligent. It took until 1957 for the final judgment to be rendered, at which point Steinkamp was ordered to pay Hawks $64,596 in damages, plus court costs. By this time, Hawks didn't even own Hog Canyon anymore.

By the spring of 1952, RKO already looked like a slowly sinking ship, and Hawks was searching for a good way to jump off. Like just about everyone else, the director couldn't pin Hughes down to a meeting or even get him on the phone, even though he was anxiously awaiting his approval of his cut of *The Big Sky*. Dore Schary, now at MGM, wanted Hawks to direct a Cary Grant film, but Hughes couldn't be reached in time to obtain the clearance. Hughes did want Hawks to go ahead with *The Left Hand of God*, but only if he could do it for $1.5 million with Kirk Douglas in the lead. By this time, Hawks had cooled off entirely on the project and adamantly refused to consider using Douglas. With Hughes determined to hold Hawks to his contract, numerous counterproposals were made, but time went by, Hughes sold *The Left Hand of God* to Fox, and, in the fall of 1952, Hughes relinquished control of the studio, if only temporarily. But it was the opening Hawks needed to escape any further commitments to RKO.

Hawks's RKO contract did provide for him to continue meeting his preexisting obligations to 20th Century–Fox. Zanuck was anxious to get him back in the fold, Hawks needed to keep earning money, Cary Grant was under contract to the studio, and Zanuck and producer Sol Siegel had a comedy for which they felt the Hawks-Grant combination would be ideal. *The Fountain of Youth*, or *Darling, I Am Growing Younger*, as it was soon called, was originated by Harry Segall and handed off to I. A. L. Diamond, a young writer shortly to become renowned as Billy Wilder's partner. Both Zanuck and Siegel were pleased with Diamond's elaboration on the original, but when, in early October, Hawks signaled his availability, Diamond was off and Hecht and Lederer were on. As soon as *The Big Sky* wrapped in mid-November, Hawks and Zanuck spent a weekend in Palm Springs sorting through the story in detail, at which point the writers shifted into high gear, delivering their rewrite on December 10. Siegel read it overnight and raved to Zanuck that "they have rescrambled all the elements of our script and have done an amazingly good job considering the short period of time they were on it. My feeling is that if Cary likes their version there is nothing to worry about. This can still be the funniest picture of the year."

The story turned on the discovery of a youth serum that makes adults behave like spirited college kids or, with an extra dose, schoolchildren. It was an age-old theme, and, like *The Thing*, it gave Hawks the chance to needle scientists, which he did right from the beginning by having a monkey be the one who "discovers" the youth potion. It was a premise pregnant with both farcical and serious potential, and while the film was intended primarily as a broad comedy, Hawks was not oblivious to its serious aspects, nor was Zanuck.

Following his usual instinct, Hawks wanted to cast a very young actress opposite Grant and show that Grant's character, Professor Barnaby Fulton, a close relative to the paleontologist in *Bringing Up Baby*, had "turned into sort of a fogey; then he was rejuvenated and remained younger for the rest of his life. That was the point." No theme could have been closer to Hawks's heart at that very moment, as, at fifty-five, he was in the flush of a major romance with a woman in her midtwenties. He was very partial to the script's summation line, "You're only old when you forget you're young," and until the end of his life, Hawks rarely spent time with people anywhere near his own age, preferring to socialize with men and women decades younger than himself. Hawks kept suggesting well-known young actresses, particularly Ava Gardner, for the film, but even then Grant had begun resisting costarring opposite such young women (not always successfully), and Fox finally decided to give the part to Ginger Rogers, a choice that didn't thrill the director. At forty-one, she was the oldest leading lady ever to appear in a Howard Hawks film; remarkably, she and Grant played the only leading couple in any Hawks sound film already married when the story begins. Furthermore, Hawks had originally envisioned that only Grant's character would regress into childish behavior by using the drug. But Rogers insisted upon doing the "getting young thing" as well, and Hawks was forced to acquiesce, though he realized that the antics performed by Grant would seem tiresome when Rogers repeated them.

In all events, Rogers's casting helped prevent Hawks's personal conception of the piece from coalescing, something he unkindly took out on her during filming. From the start, he kept the relationship formal and remote by addressing her only by her real name, Virginia. Rogers was a first-rate caricaturist, and one day she sketched a fine portrait of Hawks, accentuating his stern visage and turned-down mouth. As Robert Cornthwaite, who had a small part in the picture, remembered it, "Hawks kept walking up and down ignoring it, while Ginger was glancing up expectantly hoping for a compliment. He never said anything and, finally, she rubbed it out. I don't know if it was a coincidence or not, but in the next scene he humiliated her, . . . saying, 'No, no, no, Virginia, not that way,' over and over, but not telling her what to do, until she was devastated."

Hecht having moved on to other projects, Lederer continued to revise the script to Hawks's and Zanuck's specifications. Hawks, for example, came up with the running gag involving the water cooler as the source of the youth formula and instructed that while everything the characters did "under the influence" should be funny, it should also have serious consequences later on. For his part, Zanuck insisted that the film "should leave the audience with this thought: 'Be satisfied; let well enough alone; let nature take its course; youth is not all it's cracked up to be. The green pastures which we see in the distance aren't always so green when seen close up.'"

Although Hawks and Lederer loaded the script with nearly as much sexual innuendo as they had the much-laundered *War Bride* screenplay, no one expected the Breen Office to unilaterally object to the entire premise of *Darling, I Am Growing Younger*. But it did, stating that this comedy about a youth-restoring formula "amounts to a story of the invention of an aphrodisiac, which mainly exploits the . . . 'sex-sational' aspects of this drug." In the submitted shooting script, the main reaction Ginger Rogers's Edwina has to the drug, called Cupidone, is to get her husband on a second honeymoon and into bed, while Charles Coburn's Mr. Oxly is motivated to use the formula as a sex stimulant in his relationship with his voluptuous young secretary, Miss Laurel, played by Marilyn Monroe. All of this was utterly unacceptable to the MPAA, which forced the drug to be renamed B-4 and changed Oxly's interest in the elixir to a commercial, rather than personal, one. The censors also objected to "the light attitude towards marriage," hardly a surprising element in a Hawks film, and innumerable suggestive lines and bits of business. Among the problems: Oxly's continual leering at his secretary; Edwina's far-too-explicitly revived interest in sex on the honeymoon; and a climax in which a nude Barnaby pulls Edwina into the shower with him. Also requested for elimination were lines and words, such as "Tonight, we're staying home for intellectual reasons" and even "old poop." Most of the revisions were made and, as a result, the tone of the film overall was shifted from one of adolescent horniness to juvenile silliness.

With Chris Nyby just then in the throes of trying to pare *The Big Sky* down to a reasonable length, Hawks began shooting *Darling, I Am Growing Younger* on March 5, 1952. The director had Grant wear much thicker glasses than he had in *Bringing Up Baby* and noticeably slowed down the actor's dialogue delivery in order to emphasize the character's advancing age. He once again forced Grant to act opposite a scene-stealing animal, although the actor didn't mind the chimp nearly as much as he had the leopard. As always, Hawks structured his comic gags organically from the material and for his performers and had the rejuvenated Grant behave in ways that struck him as specifically appropriate to and funny for the former acrobat and music-hall performer; when Barnaby first takes B-4, he exults by executing a one-armed cartwheel. Robert Cornthwaite said, "Cary Grant contributed a lot to his part. He had a remarkable memory of the games he had played as a kid, which he used for his character, and he brought a wonderful childlike quality to it."

The veteran character actor Charles Coburn was a delight, and he proved adept at stealing scenes even from the seasoned Cary Grant. In one early scene, Coburn managed to make his costar all but disappear by enshrouding him in cigar smoke. Later, as Grant recalled, "he had to chase and squirt Marilyn Monroe with a siphon of soda, a moment he approached with glee. Any seeming reluctance, he later explained, was only his indecision about *where* on Marilyn's . . . um . . . *ample* proportions to *squirt* the soda. Miss Monroe seemed to present so many inviting parts. Everyone on the set awaited the moment with goggling eyes. You could hear a pin drop. Eventually Charles gave it a healthy squirt, and missing Miss Monroe, he hit me full in the puss, thereby completely obliterating me from the scene again." (In the film, Grant is nowhere seen being squirted by Coburn.) Hawks liked Coburn enormously and was willing to coddle the seventy-four-year-old actor in an indulgent way. To conserve his energy for the actual shooting, Coburn often napped in a chair he kept near the set. As Cornthwaite recalled, "He snored very loudly, and he often did so right through a take. It would often disrupt takes, but Mr. Hawks would just do it over again. He wouldn't allow them to wake him up or interrupt him. He was very considerate of him."

As for Monroe's limited but prominent appearance in the picture, it was the last of the initial, pneumatic sex-kitten phase of her career—her next picture, *Niagara*, gave her a full-blown lead and true stardom. Forced to wear a dress she detested, she was out of sorts during the shoot, and even though she was only in a few scenes, the company was forced to work around her. The reason, everyone learned later, was trouble with her appendix, which was removed as soon as she completed her role. Neither Hawks nor Grant responded to her allure in the least. Hawks, in Cornthwaite's view, was disdainful of Monroe as a talent and a person and was using her services only because, as Hawks put it to Cary Grant and John Wayne, "I think the overdeveloped quality in that little girl is going to be kind of funny." Grant remarked, "I had no idea she would become a big star. If she had something different from any other actress, it wasn't apparent at the time. She seemed very shy and quiet. There was something sad about her." Cornthwaite shared a scene with her and flatly said, "Marilyn was terrified. She had just a few words, and she rehearsed them again and again. . . . She was very determined to do the things she was scared of." Hawks believed that Monroe had a horrible inferiority complex, and he invariably noted inaccurately that "nobody dated her, nobody took her out, nobody paid any attention to her." In fact, it was during the shooting of this picture that she began dating Joe DiMaggio; she often had to be torn from long phone calls with him to go to work. They were a serious item by the time of *Gentlemen Prefer Blondes*, and they married in 1954, so it is hard to imagine what Hawks was thinking. Putting it charitably, one could say that Hawks and Monroe developed no special rapport with each other on their first collaboration; more bluntly, Hawks considered Monroe "so goddamn dumb" that she was wary and afraid of him from then on. Still, Hawks admitted that she did a fine job in the film and that "the camera liked her."

Monkey Business, as the picture was retitled toward the end of production, fairly flew through shooting, especially by Hawks's standards, wrapping after eight weeks on April 30. Scarcely three weeks later, on May 22, Hawks was back behind the cameras, directing perhaps the most desultory twenty-seven minutes of footage he ever exposed. Hollywood had never been especially partial to omnibus films, but the recent success of three British pictures based on stories by W. Somerset Maugham—*Quartette, Trio*, and *Encore*—inspired the studio to allow producer André Hakim to give the format a try with *O. Henry's Full House*, from tales by one of America's most famous authors and with segments directed by top in-house talents. The episodes had begun shooting the previous November, and all but the final one were in the can—Henry Koster's *The Cop and the Anthem*, Henry Hathaway's *The Clarion Call*, Jean Negulesco's *The Last Leaf*, and Henry King's *The Gift of the Magi*.

Saying he did the job simply as a favor to Zanuck but talked into it by a $28,000 paycheck for one week's work, Hawks didn't care at all for the story, an eight-page ironic comedy about two small-time con men in rural Alabama who kidnap a ten-year-old boy with the intention of collecting two thousand dollars for his safe return. The child turns out to be a terror, however, and they end up accepting his father's demand of $250 in cash to take the kid off their hands. Nunnally Johnson had done a straightforward adaptation, but when Hawks inherited the oddball cast of radio humorist Fred Allen and professional cynic Oscar Levant to play the kidnappers, he called in Hecht and Lederer to do a quick rewrite. This, along with the performers' ad-libs, threw the tone off more than it altered the course of the story itself; Hecht and Lederer concentrated on the cynical kibitzing between the two men, which was elaborated upon by the comic performers themselves, but in the end it really didn't matter. *The Ransom of Red Chief* was a lost cause, a silly little story that holds the unfortunate, if not unique, distinction of being a comedy without a single laugh in it. Hawks managed a couple of scenes of boldly protracted slow-burn comedy, but the only truly Hawksian touch, and only noticeable by a sharp eye at that, is the outrageous attention seeking of a sexy Tobacco Road floozie (Gloria Gordon) in the background on a porch as the men visit town. If this represented Hawks's idea of the sort of backwoods nymph he imagined for *Sergeant York*, one can only be relieved that Hal Wallis put his foot down in that instance. Also rather startling is Hawks's view of children as expressed by this episode and the films he made on either side of it. Granted, the boy in *Ransom* was portrayed by Lee Aaker very much as written in O. Henry's story, but the depiction of children here, in *Monkey Business*, and in *Gentlemen Prefer Blondes* makes kids, collectively, out to be nothing short of little terrorists, and there are very few other children in Hawks's films to balance this perspective out.

It was one of those pictures that was a lot more fun to make than to watch. Lorrie Sherwood said that, because of Fred Allen and Oscar Levant, "I never had so much fun in all my life, and Mr. Hawks had a wonderful time." Hawks liked both men enormously and socialized frequently with Levant in years to come. Levant also developed a big crush on Dee. In one important scene, the kidnappers were supposed to be asleep on the ground in their nightgowns when a large bear prowls through the camp. At the last minute Hawks decided to use stuffed dummies for the scene, and the entire crew was then stunned when the bear, named George, went directly over and clamped his jaws around the head of the dummy that was supposed to be Fred Allen.

Dampening the high spirits were the reactions of studio executives, who, Hawks admitted, were "horrified" when they saw that he had turned the story into something of a slapstick burlesque. Critics and audiences weren't much better disposed to Hawks's episode. Having made the film in imitation of some English art-house hits, Fox decided to launch it on September 19 at the tiny Beverly Canon Cinema in Beverly Hills, just around the corner from Feldman's Famous Artists offices. To everyone's amazement, it broke the house record with a $9,200 opening-week gross and went on to a fourteen-week run. Clearly, then, the film had an appeal to the same upscale audience that patronized foreign films. However, it was obvious to everyone that *Ransom*, which was placed next-to-last in the sequence of stories, was a misfire. By the time the film debuted in New York City, on October 16, Fox had removed Hawks's episode entirely, telling the press that it was felt that the overall feature, which ran 117 minutes with *Ransom* included, "would be a better picture without it." With the *Full House* title no longer truly applicable, wisecracks ensued about how Fox ought to change it to O. *Henry's Four of a Kind*. It enjoyed extended runs at the Trans-Lux in New York, the Surf Theater in Chicago, and at similar big-city art houses around the nation. The highest it ever ranked at the national box office was number eleven one week in early November, but this was achieved in limited release. In this light, its eventual earnings of $1 million were hardly disgraceful.

While *The Big Sky* was still playing at the Criterion, *Monkey Business* opened at the Roxy in New York on September 5 for a strong three-week run. Reviews and audience response were mixed, however, bearing out Hawks's contention that miscalculations in casting and structuring hurt the film. As it fanned out around the country, the picture failed to live up to the studio's hopes that it would be the comedy sensation of the year, on a par with *I Was a Male War Bride*. It peaked at number seven in popularity nationally in mid-October, ranked number eleven for the month, and finished the year in a disappointing forty-seventh place at the box office, with just $2 million in rentals.

Ironically, *Monkey Business*, an overtly commercial comedy of no particular distinction, shortly became the unlikely rallying point for a handful of French critics advocating recognition for Hawks as a serious artist, as Hawks would discover to his surprise when he got to Europe. Some of the most sophisticated students of Hawks's work have made cogent cases for the preeminence of the film among the director's comedies. Robin Wood described it convincingly as his most "organic" comedy, matched it intriguingly with *Scarface* as a portrait of the reversion to primitivism, and admired the way the subsidiary characters—elderly Oxly, the naked baby boy, Edwina's disapproving mother, the immature Miss Laurel—fill in the various stages of life not embraced by the age-reversing trips. Gerald Mast praised its immaculate structure; convincingly presented the film as, in many ways, the mirror image, or extension, of *Bringing Up Baby*; and pointed up the Shakespearean parallels in both pictures. Both critics applauded the manner in which *Monkey Business* interlaced its thematic concerns with humor, as well as the way excess pushed an ostensible comedy to the brink of tragedy.

Still, the best Hawks films are those in which one feels that the process of making the film helped it find its natural and proper form, and this is nowhere evident in *Monkey Business*. Aside from some of the unusually muted moments devoted to discussion of the Barnaby-Edwina marriage, most of the action seems mechanical and laborious, almost as if done by rote according to a preexisting plan. In fact, the film remains most resonant for its depiction of a long-term marriage—unique in the director's work—and its utterly fantastic means of reviving a dwindling relationship, something Hawks could never do in life. The sweet renewal of Barnaby and Edwina's marriage by the end of the film was, as far as Hawks was concerned, purest fantasy.

Through the summer of 1952, Hawks considered many changes he might want to make in his life. The mess and construction going on around Hog Canyon made him think for the first time about selling it; many of his friends were heading off to Europe to make films and even to live, and there were stories, especially *The Sun Also Rises*, that he wanted to make there; if he did this, he would want to unload his horses and reduce his entanglements at home. Making the whole plan more enticing were the hefty tax benefits he would accrue if he were to work overseas for eighteen months to two years. And perhaps he would marry Dee after all; if Hawks made the right deal with a studio, they could live lavishly overseas while he prepared some pictures, and Feldman told him that there were plenty of European producers ready to drop bags of money at the feet of a director of Hawks's stature. His parents were now dead and his boys were basically on their own. Barbara, now sixteen, would soon be sent to board at a girls' school. She had been refused by the exclusive Marlborough School, as were all girls from show-business families, including the Disney daughters, and enrolled instead at Westlake School near UCLA, where her cousin, Katherine Thalberg, was entering her senior year. It wasn't a boarding school per se, but two "old maid" teachers lived there, and they watched over Barbara and the few other girls who needed a place to stay. Basically, there was little standing in the way of Hawks turning over a new page and possibly making a lot of money in the process.

However, he still owed Fox one more picture and was open to trying something new there too. *A Song Is Born* to the side, one of the few genres Hawks had never tried was the musical comedy. In 1947, Hawks had spoken to Feldman about trying to do a movie musical, so when, surprisingly, Zanuck and Siegel proposed one to him, he was game. *Gentlemen Prefer Blondes* was a title that had already resonated throughout show business for more than twenty-five years. Anita Loos's 1925 book was one of the sensational and defining works of its era, a frank and ultimately rather downbeat look at a socially ambitious girl's life in the Roaring Twenties. Loos and her husband, John Emerson, turned it into an equally successful play in 1926. In 1949, a Broadway musical version, with a book by Loos and Joseph Fields and songs by Jules Styne and Leo Robin, became the rage, and Carol Channing became a star playing Lorelei Lee and singing "Diamonds Are a Girl's Best Friend."

Two years later, the show was still packing them in in New York, and with movie musicals at one of their all-time peaks of popularity, the film studios were outdoing themselves to win the rights. In November 1951, 20th Century–Fox won out, paying $150,000, with Zanuck intending it as a vehicle for his biggest musical star of the 1940s, Betty Grable. By the time Hawks and Lederer were assigned to the project the following June, shortly after *Monkey Business* wrapped, Zanuck and his staff had seriously rethought their intentions for it. Grable's star was on the wane, her salary was up to $150,000 per picture, and Zanuck, although he had no personal sense of Marilyn Monroe's potential, was allowing himself to be persuaded that perhaps this phony blonde was for real and ought to star as the musical stage's ultimate blond gold digger. His greatest incentive was her price, which had reached its contractual ceiling of fifteen hundred dollars a week, with five years to go. Monroe was so incensed by this that she left the William Morris Agency in favor of Charles Feldman, but even he, who was so close to Zanuck, couldn't twist the tycoon's arm on this point. Monroe ended up earning only eighteen thousand dollars on *Gentlemen Prefer Blondes*.

But if Zanuck was to cast Monroe, he wanted insurance in the way of a major costar in the role of Dorothy; at Hawks's suggestion, he got it in the form of Jane Russell. Howard Hughes, to whom Russell was still under contract, only rarely loaned out his most famous female star, but Hughes owned a minority share of Fox and could sense that the musical would be a winning vehicle that would only raise her stock in Hollywood. Furthermore, Hawks had waived his financial interest in Russell on the understanding that he would be able to borrow her anytime he wished. The time had come to cash in this chip, but it still came at a steep price: Hughes demanded, and got, two hundred thousand dollars for Russell's services and forced Fox to also engage her entire RKO entourage, including the cameraman Harry J. Wild and the makeup, hair, and wardrobe personnel. When Russell and her team arrived on the Fox lot, it was like Cleopatra arriving in Rome, and the good-natured actress played it to the hilt just for the fun of it.

Hawks and Russell, who had remained friendly over the years, were delighted to be working together at long last. Part of the understanding was that Dorothy's role, more of a supporting part originally, would be built up to equal status with Lorelei's in order to justify the top billing Russell, by Hughes's decree, would receive. After it was decided that the 1920s setting should be updated and that only the two lead characters, theme, and locales would be retained, Lederer, assisted by Lorrie Sherwood, sweated through the summer to drastically overhaul the material. Pointing out that the film had virtually nothing to do with the book and little to do with the play, the writer observed, "I had to make it up from scratch because there wasn't any story. . . . What amazed me was that the musical had no book to speak of, and you realize that it was actually a success as a revue rather than a musical story of a book." At the same time, it had to be decided which songs from the show would be kept and how many new tunes might be needed. Ultimately, three of Styne and Robin's Broadway originals were used: "I'm Just a Little Girl from Little Rock" (transformed into the duet "We're Just Two Little Girls from Little Rock"), "Bye Bye Baby," and the immortal "Diamonds Are a Girl's Best Friend." Hawks's friend Hoagy Carmichael and Harold Adamson collaborated on two fresh compositions, "Ain't There Anyone Here for Love?" and "When Love Goes Wrong, Nothing Goes Right." In the end, songs and dances filled roughly 40 percent of the finished film.

Although he had no gift for it himself, Hawks loved music, and in his nonmusical pictures, he often created scenes of group singing, which served to bring his diverse characters together in a communal activity. Hawks insisted, however, upon *not* directing the musical numbers in *Gentlemen Prefer Blondes*. He had no background in musical theater, of course, and no feel for choreography, and he probably realized that an expert in the field could do a much better job. The expert Fox chose was the ace choreographer Jack Cole, who had put Rita Hayworth through her paces in *Cover Girl, Tonight and Every Night*, and *Gilda*. Intense, wiry, neurotic, demanding, and personally shy, he was a highly gifted man who frankly described his role with female stars as a combination brother and mother, which is what he became for Monroe on six pictures through the end of the decade.

To give everyone an idea of what he had in mind for the numbers, Cole staged a test run of "Diamonds Are a Girl's Best Friend" with Monroe lying on a black-and-pink Empire-style bed "wearing nothing but diamonds with a little horse's tail coming out of her ass with a little diamond horsefly on the tail," as Cole remembered it. With Monroe seeming to be nude in her diamond-studded tights, the number was a knockout, but everyone agreed it was far too sexy for the finished film. Still skeptical of Monroe's talent, Zanuck refused to believe that it was actually her voice on the playback and insisted that she come sing for him in his office to convince him, which she did. Monroe sang all her own numbers in the picture, with the exception of the brief "No, definitely no . . ." introduction to "Diamonds Are a Girl's Best Friend," which was dubbed by the band vocalist Gloria Wood.

Given the problems he had recently gone through on *Monkey Business*, Lederer knew that the Breen Office would be vigilant in the case of this new film. While the MPAA was able to accept the basic premise of *Gentlemen Prefer Blondes*, it took immediate exception to the "Two Little Girls from Little Rock" number, which it found "a glorification of immorality." This was eventually ironed out with some changes in the lyrics, but Breen vetoed such suggestive phrases as "bosom companions" and "for two reasons," as well as part of what became the most-quoted line in the film: "Those girls couldn't drown. Something about them tells me they couldn't sink"; the latter was resolved by eliminating the second sentence from the line. However, the MPAA went on breast alert, insisting on seeing costume stills for all the outfits the stars would be wearing in the picture, just to make sure that they did not "attract focal attention" to their breasts or leave them not "fully covered."

Zanuck, active as always on story points, insisted that the film maintain its credibility by emphasizing the love story between Dorothy and the detective Malone, as well as Dorothy's genuine affection for Lorelei. Zanuck also invented the entire dockside opening sequence in which the Olympic athletes become mesmerized by the sight of the two women approaching the boat, ending with the "couldn't drown" line. In the studio head's view, "This is not a satire. It is a solid and honest comedy in the same terms as *I Was a Male War Bride*, for instance. In *War Bride*, the audience knew that our people had a very real problem and they never lost sight of that no matter how ludicrous the comedy seemed at times." Hawks couldn't have disagreed more, as he was about to turn what had been a satire into a burlesque.

As the original early November start date was pushed back once, and then again, the press began to predict a giant feud between the two stars or, as columnist Earl Wilson inevitably dubbed it, "The Battle of the Bulges." In fact, Russell, a down-home gal with no pretenses or complexes despite her status, welcomed Monroe at once and gained her confidence professionally and personally. She stuck with her endlessly through rehearsals and privately confided to her about life as the wife of a professional athlete, as Russell's husband, Bob Waterfield, was the Los Angeles Rams' quarterback, while Monroe was trying to cope with Joe DiMaggio's habits and circle of friends. The tight relationship carried over to their performances; as Norman Mailer much later observed, "Never have two women gotten along together so well in a musical."

Russell was also of invaluable help to Hawks on the picture, literally his lifesaver. Unable to communicate with Monroe, and with her increasingly resistant to anything the director said, Hawks acknowledged, "It wasn't easy, that film, but it wasn't difficult because I had Jane there. . . . I'd hear them talking, Marilyn would whisper, 'What did he tell me?' Jane wouldn't say, 'He's told you six times already,' she'd just tell her again." When not taking her cues from Russell, Monroe relied on her drama coach, Natasha Lytess, who Hawks silently abided for a while. Before long, however, he had to put his foot down. In one scene involving Monroe, Hawks was satisfied with the first take. But instead of looking at her director, Monroe checked with Lytess, who thought they should do it again. Hawks grudgingly obliged, but after nine or ten more takes, none of them as good as the first, Hawks had had enough and told his star, "When I say 'cut,' I want you to look at me, not at Natasha." Lytess also sat in for the musical numbers, irritating Jack Cole as well. The producer, Sol Siegel, tried to position himself as a diplomat between the warring parties, but things only got worse. At one point, when Zanuck asked him how filming could be sped up, Hawks replied that he had "three wonderful ideas: replace Marilyn, rewrite the script to make it shorter, and get a new director." Hawks had Lytess kicked off the set, but Monroe responded by staying in her dressing room and turning up later and later for work. Lytess was back within a week, although she was required to sit further away from the camera. On nearly all of her scenes, Monroe asked Hawks if she could do it "just one more time." Hawks would say, "Okay, but you were good," and then turn around and quietly mutter, "There's no film in the camera, is there?" before letting her continue. Jane

Russell said, "I liked Marilyn Monroe very much, but she wasn't playing it straight with Hawks and that annoyed the hell out of him." Hawks was simply the first of several distinguished directors driven to distraction by Monroe's lateness, insecurity, and reliance upon drama coaches.

Other than that, Hawks had some fun with *Gentlemen Prefer Blondes*. Shooting finally started on November 17, and Hawks was amused at what he had gotten himself into. For starters, his taste for subdued colors was useless in the face of the garish, eye-popping Technicolor that this brassy, $2 million musical called for. "You got color that really came out and hit you," Hawks said. "There was no sense in trying to dodge it." He had no trouble accepting this because, for him, "the girls were unreal; the story was unreal; the sets, the whole premise of the thing was unreal. We were working with complete fantasy." For him, Monroe and Russell were walking caricatures of sex, and he confessed, "I never thought of either of them as having any sex," adding that their obvious, showy "kind of sex isn't my line at all." Monroe, in particular, he found not only colossally dumb but profoundly vulgar. Appreciative, however, of the effect she had on others, he played with it and helped make her into a great star in the process. Zanuck was won over by Monroe in the first week's dailies, and studio-wide enthusiasm made it a bit easier to tolerate her contrary behavior and the maddening delays. So high was Hawks on the picture that he confidently predicted to a reporter who visited him on the enormous luxury liner set on stage three of the Western Avenue lot that it would bring in $10 million.

For once, Hawks was not making changes on the set. Lederer was not even around, because, according to Jane Russell, "Everything was so well prepared." Russell said Hawks was "a perfect gentleman, just like always," who basically "let me do my own thing." Unlike many people, Russell "found him a very warm man," partly because he was quite like her own father, who was also outwardly stern and reserved. "In both cases, I learned to read them, to know when they liked or disliked something." Because of their close friendship, Zanuck was the only studio boss Hawks ever allowed on one of his sets, but Zanuck knew where the line was drawn. Lorrie Sherwood recalled, "When it was time to shoot, he'd say, 'Well, see you later, Howard.'" Sherwood agreed that Hawks had everything "exceptionally well planned" on this picture. "But he just didn't like to be rushed." Hawks got a huge kick out of Russell's hand-picked cinematographer, Harry Wild, whose regular explosions of rage became a pressure-releasing running gag for the director. "Harry Wild would jump up and down on his felt hat, he'd get so mad," the assistant director, Paul Helmick, remembered.

"Howard got more laughs out of him than anyone." Fortunately, Hawks liked his work as well, as did Monroe, who was pleased that Wild didn't favor Russell.

Still, most of the women's attention went into their preparation for the musical numbers, which didn't involve Hawks. "Howard Hawks had nothing to do with the musical numbers," Jane Russell said. "He was not even there." Gwen Verdon, who was Jack Cole's assistant on the picture, said, "I never saw Howard Hawks except for the scene of the boat leaving the dock. I was with Jack all the time, . . . and we never had a meeting with Howard Hawks." Cole drove Russell and Monroe, who had no dance technique or professional training, devilishly hard, and they were willing accomplices. Often, when Russell would knock off after hours of grueling rehearsal, Monroe would want to stay another couple of hours to work with Cole and Verdon. "Marilyn, strangely enough, could do almost anything you would ask her to do if you could show it to her," Verdon said. Unlike Hawks, Cole was able to say, "I never had any trouble with her. Once she came late, and I said, 'Marilyn, don't ever come late for me.'" She never did again. Cole worked out imaginative moves for his stars that made them look like much better dancers than they really were. However, as Verdon pointed out, "the ladies basically walked everyplace or they were carried everyplace, so they didn't really have to do dance steps."

Two production numbers in particular stood out: "Diamonds Are a Girl's Best Friend," toned down from Cole's sexy original rendition, with a glamorously decked out Monroe surrounded by a host of tuxedoed admirers, and the outrageous Carmichael-Adamson special "Ain't There Anyone Here for Love?," in which Russell's inquiries fall on the deaf ears of a bunch of bodybuilders narcissistically consumed by their exercises. The number ends with Russell being knocked into a swimming pool by one of the athletes, which was, in fact, an accident that Fox decided to go with. The gay aspect of this knockout number is so overwhelming that one can't even properly refer to it as subtext, which may be the reason it has often been cut for television airings. But it is impossible to include the song in the list of Hawks scenes bearing homoerotic innuendo for the simple reason that he didn't have a hand in its creation, aside from having suggested that Carmichael compose additional songs for the film.

The question naturally comes up as to who directed, from a camera point-of-view, the musical numbers if Hawks did not. According to Gwen Verdon, "Jack decided where the camera would be in consultation with the director of photography." However, what concerned Cole much more than the camera angles was how the different shots would cut together, so "if he had the slightest doubt about anything fitting together, he'd go to the editor [Hugh S. Fowler] to ask if it would work. Hawks just stood by and let Jack do what he wanted to do."

Charles Coburn, who had enjoyed himself on *Monkey Business*, was having the time of his life at seventy-five playing opposite the two bombshells. "Work? This is work?" he queried a visitor. "This is sheer, unadulterated joy." Coburn indeed seemed to be having a high old time as the mining king all too ready to bestow his rocks upon Lorelei. But the film has a serious problem with the male characters in general. With the bland Elliott Reid playing the detective to whom Dorothy takes a liking and the cringing Tommy Noonan appearing as Lorelei's rich lover boy (with spectacles, as always, signifying eggheaded ineffectuality for Hawks), the range of manhood on display is simply too limited and unimposing, either elderly or wimpy. All of Hawks's recent films—*A Song Is Born, I Was a Male War Bride, Monkey Business,* and even *The Big Sky*—had dealt to some extent with the frustration and emasculation of the male lead, but here they are like toy popguns opposite the double-barreled dames.

Principal photography wrapped on January 22, 1953, with Hawks dispatching his portion of the film in an efficient nine weeks despite Monroe's recalcitrance. Only a month away from a wedding and his departure from California for what he intended to be a long sojourn abroad, Hawks left the editing and other postproduction details on *Gentlemen Prefer Blondes* to others, under Zanuck's supervision. Many people misremember the film as having been shot in CinemaScope. In fact, *Gentlemen Prefer Blondes* was one of the last major Fox pictures shot "flat," before the widescreen technique was introduced; *The Robe,* the first CinemaScope film, started shooting February 24, just a month after Hawks's musical was completed.

Naturally, the studio publicity machine geared up to full steam in the months before the film's release. Monroe and Russell were on the cover of *Life* magazine in May, and on June 26 they knelt down together, necklines plunging, over the cement in the forecourt of Grauman's Chinese Theatre in Hollywood to imprint themselves for posterity at the spot where the film would soon open. After an invitational preview the night before, *Gentlemen Prefer Blondes* had its world premiere at the Roxy Theater in New York City on July 15, 1953, and grossed a stupendous $128,500 in its opening week at the 5,886–seat house, which was just 314 seats smaller than Radio City Music Hall. In its six-week exclusive run, the picture pulled in a sensational $625,000 at this Manhattan showcase alone. The film was number one in the nation by the first week of August, dropped to second place for a week, then held the number-one slot for another two weeks. By the end of the year, the picture had generated $5.1 million in rentals for Fox, good for ninth position on the year. It was the biggest box-office hit Hawks had ever had, with the exception of *Sergeant York*, which still stood at $6 million. Still, *Gentlemen* was far exceeded by Fox's nonmusical CinemaScope follow-up later in the year, Jean Negulesco's *How to Marry a Millionaire*, starring Monroe, Betty Grable, and Lauren Bacall, which pulled down $7.5 million in rentals.

Some of the East Coast reviews of *Blondes* were a bit sniffy about the vulgarization of the material and its having "gone Hollywood," but even the starchiest observers had to admit that the gals had something going for them and that Monroe might actually have some talent. It has always been challenging for critics to fit the film into the context of Hawks's career, other than as an example of his extraordinary versatility and his abilities as an entertainer. One could begin a theory about Lorelei and Dorothy as female versions of the two sailors in *A Girl in Every Port*, but it can't be extended very far. Ultimately, the film can be enjoyed for its very "unreality" and, of course, for its two lead performances, the musical numbers, and its sheer mythic and camp value. But, unlike the way he attacked, reshaped, and transformed material not his own on so many occasions in the past, Hawks seems rather along for the ride on *Gentlemen Prefer Blondes*, passively accepting the story and character values created by others. The same could be said about *Monkey Business* and *The Ransom of Red Chief*, making his early 1950s Fox period one of the least interesting of his career from the point of view of Hawks's aspirations and accomplishments.

32

In the Land of the Pharaohs

Like Lorelei Lee, Dee Hartford got her man. Having set her sights on one of Hollywood's most successful, if not richest, producer-directors, she landed her catch. That she was beautiful and well groomed went without saying, and while she may not have had Slim's refinement and infallible sense of style, her personality was even more gregarious. She revitalized and provoked Hawks; she called him on his fabrications and pushed him where others were afraid to. More than anyone he had ever been with, Dee challenged him emotionally and psychologically; she didn't take everything he said and did unquestioningly, didn't tolerate his silences, didn't let him off the hook. This kept him on his toes more than he was accustomed to, and he liked it.

Hawks's friends smiled to each other about the intended marriage; the grey fox wanted to show everyone that he could still score, that his elegant, gentlemanly, soft-spoken ways hadn't lost their effect. Family members were privately disappointed, even disapproving, feeling that Hawks was just trying to show off but had actually succumbed to the young woman's calculated wiles. Dee may or may not be a gold digger, they thought, but there was something a little less classy about her than her predecessors. She wasn't Slim, and she wasn't a Shearer. As one friend said, "It was a marriage of ego and convenience."

The ceremony took place at six in the evening on Friday, February 20, 1953. Fifty-six guests gathered at Hog Canyon to watch Howard Hawks get hitched for the third time. Dee was twenty-four, Hawks fifty-six. Time would tell if such a marriage could last. Bishop B. J. Summerhays of the Brentwood Church of Jesus Christ of Latter-Day Saints performed the ceremony, Dee's sister Eden was the maid of honor, and William Hawks acted as his brother's best man for the second time in less than twelve years. Hawks wore a black suit adorned with a white carnation, while Dee looked strikingly modern in a small round hat with veil, a tight-fitting white dress fea-

511

turing narrow straps that exposed most of her shoulders, and long gloves up to her elbows. The evening soiree was as much a bon voyage party as a wedding celebration, for the couple was booked to fly to New York the following morning, then sail on the *Queen Mary* for Europe on Wednesday, February 25.

The Hawkses enjoyed a glamorous, if chilly, honeymoon crossing, and the newlyweds' photo aboard ship appeared in newspapers around the world. Upon arriving in Paris, they took a sumptuous apartment at 3 Square Trocadero with a full view of the Eiffel Tower across the Seine. Hawks stressed to Feldman and everyone else that, after making four major features in quick succession, he was determined to relax with his bride and take a vacation. In early April, they went to Italy, where Hawks hobnobbed with executives of Ferrari and other sportscar manufacturers and tried out the latest models on their private tracks. A few months later, he bought a Ferrari and, subsequently, an Alfa Romeo. By the time they arrived in Rome in midmonth, Hawks said he wanted to do a picture about cars, and in August he expressed an interest in Hans Ruesch's new novel, *The Racers*, which Julian Blaustein produced the following year, with Hawks's friend Henry Hathaway directing.

Even while he was on his extended honeymoon, work and potential projects were never far from Hawks's mind. Back in Paris, Hawks announced that his next picture would be the long-aborning *The Sun Also Rises*, with Gene Tierney as the besotted, adulterous Lady Brett Ashley, Montgomery Clift as the American newspaperman Jake Barnes, and Dewey Martin as the Spanish matador. The prospect of Clift, at the height of his talent and beauty in the wake of *A Place in the Sun* and *From Here to Eternity*, as Barnes under Hawks remains one of the most tantalizing missed opportunities of both men's careers, but Hawks still hadn't cracked the censorable, unfilmable aspects of Hemingway's story.

Feldman set Hawks up with numerous top European producers, including Robert Haggiag and Angelo Rizzoli and the executives of Lux Films in Rome but warned him about the many hustlers and shysters who would surely try to sweet-talk him into shady business schemes, saying, "You will find that you will be giving all of your time listening to many and various promotions and then end up disregarding ninety-eight percent of them."

Hawks spent the spring and summer in the cafés, at late dinners, at the popular Fouquet's on the Champs-Elysées, and at Alexandre's, a favorite late-night spot among the international film crowd, including Vittorio De Sica and Hawks's friends Anatole Litvak and Lewis Milestone. As he strolled along the quais, he was almost certainly unaware that one of the little magazines lining the book stalls, *Cahiers du Cinéma*, was at that very moment proclaiming him a genius. But, in fact, the concept of Howard Hawks as Great Artist was officially hatched with Jacques Rivette's polemical piece "Genie de Howard Hawks" in the May 1953 issue. The article opened with an incredible statement: "The evidence on the screen is the proof of Hawks's genius; you only have to watch *Monkey Business* to know that it is a brilliant film. Some people refuse to admit this, however." Rivette went on to compare Hawks favorably to Molière, Corneille, and Murnau. Rivette's impassioned view was shared by other young cinemaniacs at the magazine, notably François Truffaut and Jean-Luc Godard, who published rapturous reviews of *Gentlemen Prefer Blondes* after its Paris opening. Truffaut's piece, published in *Arts* magazine, was entitled "The Professional Secret: Howard Hawks, Intellectual."

Possibly through André Hakim, the Egyptian-born producer of *O. Henry's Full House*, who was proposing another teaming, Hawks met some wealthy and well-connected Egyptians late in the summer. Most conspicuously of all, he met the deposed King Farouk of Egypt, a regular at Fouquet's, who proposed that Hawks make a film about his life. Hawks humored him and strung him along, going so far as to announce at one point that he would actually make such a film. Hawks also met other Egyptians interested in backing him to make a picture in their country, and these contacts started Hawks thinking about Egyptian subject matter; they also made it possible for Hawks to help arrange for his old friend Gregory Ratoff to make *Abdulla the Great*, a dismal, forgotten film pertinent only in that it briefly introduced Hawks to his next leading lady, Joan Collins, who was considered for a role, and possessed plot elements strikingly similar to those of *Land of the Pharaohs*.

Late that summer, Hawks bumped into Jack Warner in the lobby of the Georges V Hotel, and again on the Riviera. In the course of just a couple of meetings, the two men sketched out the sort of deal no studio head would have dreamed of offering a director just a few years before, quite like the one George Stevens had just made to produce and direct *Giant*: complete financing from Warner Bros., $100,000 plus 50 percent of the profits for Hawks, and a $35,000 advance for an optional second picture. On such an arrangement, the studio normally insisted on a provision stipulating that for every $10,000 the film went over budget, the producer would lose one percent of his profit share. Hawks's attorney Gregson Bautzer was able to whittle his client's loss down to half that and also excised a clause that would have permitted the studio to take over the production if it exceeded its budget by 10 percent. Hawks also obtained possessive billing above the title, à la Alfred Hitchcock, $1,000 in weekly living expenses, a car, and a secretary.

Warner and Hawks didn't agree upon a project immediately. Feldman had been telling his old client for months that, with the industry currently in such disarray, a man with such a distinguished and successful record as Hawks was in a position to make a killing. Big films on the wide screen seemed to be the ticket, a suspicion confirmed on September 16 when the first CinemaScope production, 20th Century–Fox's *The Robe*, debuted. In its opening week at the Roxy in New York, it grossed $264,500, far more money than any film had ever made at any theater in a single week in the history of the medium. Suddenly, of course, everyone rushed to imitate it, and Feldman just happened to own a script that Hawks and Warner could move on immediately. "Song of Ruth" was a Biblical screenplay by Maxwell Anderson and Noel Langley, and Hawks was tempted to do it on the basis of *The Robe*'s success. Feldman also had a "Solomon" project in the works with, of all people, John Wayne interested in the part of the wise Hebraic leader. Warner was lukewarm on both proposals but was interested in another epic idea Hawks had mentioned, one about an Egyptian pharaoh and his obsessive construction of the first pyramid. Such a film wouldn't be "Biblical" per se, but Fox was already going ahead with its CinemaScope production *The Egyptian*, so perhaps the lack of a Judeo-Christian religious theme didn't matter.

Hawks's idea at that point amounted to no more than a vague notion, but it was enough for Warner to immediately advance him money. According to Noël Howard, Hawks's new right-hand man in France, the director got the final go-ahead from Warner while staying at the luxurious Eden Roc in the South of France. "Where is Egypt?" Hawks asked Howard, looking out over the Mediterranean. When Howard pointed to the horizon, Hawks stared out across the dark blue sea for the longest time, then drawled, "Nooooël, I'm going to build a pyramid."

Hawks went right to work in September, setting up a new production firm, the Continental Company, and looking for a writer. He first approached Anthony Veiller, who had recently worked for John Huston on *The African Queen* and *Moulin Rouge*, and then tried to recruit Ben Hecht, a rather unlikely choice for a story about the glory days of Egypt. Feldman kept pushing "Song of Ruth," telling Warner, "Hawks feels it can outgross any De Mille film and can be made in Egypt immediately while he is preparing the pyramid story." Backing off "Ruth" entirely, Warner instructed Hawks to get on with building his pyramid.

To this end, Hawks made it his first order of business to hire the great Hungarian-French art director Alexandre Trauner, who had designed *Le Jour Se Leve, Children of Paradise,* and Orson Welles's *Othello*. The impish, cherublike Trauner was Hawks's precise physical opposite, and the two were to make an amusing-looking pair throughout production as they traipsed around the desert, with Hawks calling his new friend Troy instead of his usual nickname, Trau. Hawks hired Noël Howard as his second-unit director. An American expatriate and bon vivant, Howard was an aspiring director who had worked for Victor Fleming on *Joan of Arc* and got the best tables in restaurants by deliberately slurring his name when phoning for reservations: "A table for two for this evening for Monsieur Noël C-h-oward, s'il vous plaît."

While Howard and Trauner launched into research as to how the pyramids might have been constructed, Hawks flew from Paris to Rome on October 17 to join Jerry Blattner, assigned by Warner to look after the studio's interests in the production. The next day, they flew to Egypt, where they met with Wing Commander Waguih Abaza of the Ministry of National Guidance. Advised that the short-lived Naguib government was determined to abolish graft, Warner had warned them against making any payoffs. After another meeting, with Abaza and heads of various other administrative departments, Blattner told Warner, "It is obvious that they are bending over backwards to have a big production made in their country." On the downside were the tiny Egyptian studios, with their limited equipment and power, and the fact that the authorities were very clear about not wanting anyone "directly concerned on the side of Israel" to be brought in to work on the production. Hawks was inspired by seeing the actual pyramids and settings for his epic, telling Warner, "The more I go into the story and conditions of making it the more sure I am we've got a big one, real big." Privately, Blattner, whom Hawks liked—surprising, given his customary disdain for middle-level functionaries and yes-men—cabled Warner, saying that while Hawks was "enthusiastic," he suspected the director was "lacking experience how organize energetic company away from America," and he recommended appointing a strong producer. Knowing Hawks's position as actual producer could not be encroached upon, Warner determined to select a reliable unit manager and assemble as much of the company as he could himself. "This has to be this way," Warner advised Blattner, "otherwise Hawks not only slow but may never finish picture."

After being accompanied on an exploratory trip to Upper Egypt by Dr. Mohamed Anwar Shoukri, a historian assigned to the picture, Hawks brought Noël Howard to Egypt, where for a few days they scouted around, admired the gold relics at the Cairo Museum, and were outfitted by tailors for the most fashionable desert wear. But what most excited Hawks was the unexpected opportunity to take the inaugural flight of BOAC's jet service between Cairo and Paris. Howard said that Hawks, who had never flown in a jet, was so delighted he jumped for joy like a little boy, exclaimed, "Gee whiz! A jet!" and actually slapped him on the back.

Soon thereafter, Hawks and Dee took a villa near Cannes, where he began assembling a team of collaborators. Art Siteman, last with Hawks on *The Big Sky*, became associate producer; Paul Helmick, assistant director on *Gentlemen Prefer Blondes*, would work again in that capacity, and Hawks had no problem with Warner assigning Chuck Hansen, who had been unit production manager on *The Big Sleep*, as unit manager. In his biography of Robert Capa, Richard Whelan claims that Hawks made an offer to the celebrated still photographer to codirect the picture, but this is a highly unlikely prospect for which there isn't a shred of evidence in any of Hawks's or Warner Bros.' documents relating to the film.

By mid-November, Hawks still had not signed his contract. Blattner signaled his concern to Warner, fearing that Hawks might be thinking of taking the deal elsewhere. While he shared Blattner's anxieties, Warner was nevertheless proceeding with the financing. Based on Hawks's reports of how cheaply everything could be done in Egypt, Warner initially fixed the budget at an absurdly low $1.36 million, not including a fee for a leading actor, and allocated the use of blocked funds in several European nations, South Africa, and possibly other countries as well, payable in Egyptian pounds through a special account. Warners actually became the first American company to receive a financial concession from Egypt under which the government would not insist upon payment in U.S. dollars but would accept the importation of unlimited amounts of foreign currencies. Blattner predicted "a considerable book profit on such transfers." Warner Bros. had so many frozen lire in Italy that Warner decided to make two films in Rome at the same time, *Helen of Troy*, directed by Robert Wise, and the interiors on *Land of the Pharaohs*.

Now installed with Dee at the luxurious Plaza Athenée Hotel in Paris at Warner Bros.' expense, Hawks was finally forced to confront the fact that he still had no story, much less a script. Unable to engage Veiller or Hecht, Hawks pursued the august historical poet and novelist Robert Graves, but this went nowhere, so Hawks turned to his old friend Faulkner. Despite the thirty thousand dollars that had come with winning the Nobel Prize, the writer was still far from flush, admitting a need to do "hack work of some sort," so the fifteen thousand dollars plus living expenses to work for Hawks again were enticing. He by no means felt like taking off and spending months in Europe and Africa, but, he took the job because "Hawks asked me."

Faulkner had always worked with other writers on any of his scripts for Hawks that got produced, and the director knew that the plot needed any help it could get. Hawks made a last-ditch effort to get Hecht, but when that proved impossible, he hired someone he had never worked with but who came highly recommended: Harry Kurnitz, a sophisticated screenwriter, playwright, and novelist who, plagued by political suspicion and memories of a painful divorce, was living in Europe at the time. Rangy, bespectacled, very funny, and a close friend of Hawks's future brother-in-law Groucho Marx, he had a reputation for great facility and productivity, which, in the end, proved to be lifesaving qualities.

Hawks always claimed that he and Kurnitz were waiting at Orly Airport on December 1 to greet Faulkner, but Noël Howard insisted that he alone was there to receive the news that due to bad weather, the writer's TWA flight had been diverted to Zurich, where the passengers were put on a train for Paris. When Howard nervously went the next morning to tell his boss that Faulkner was missing, Hawks had gone to play golf. Moments later, a couple of gendarmes delivered Faulkner to Hawks's room, inebriated and bleeding from a head wound. After Faulkner slept for a while, Howard took him briefly to Harry's Bar, then directly to his rooms at the Hotel Crillon because he didn't want Hawks to see Faulkner in his ghastly condition. It seemed that Faulkner had drunk his way across the Atlantic, thought he was in Paris when the plane landed in Zurich, and resisted getting on the train. Upon arriving in Paris, he headed straight for the all-night Bar Vert, where he was assaulted by some ruffians. Picked up by the police, he managed to get out the words, "Hawks — Plaza," whereupon he was escorted to the hotel.

One of Hawks's Egyptian acquaintances, a man named Raoul, had a villa in the Italian summer resort town of Stresa, on Lake Maggiore, that he was happy to let Hawks use; with the town virtually shut down as winter closed in, there would be no distractions from the job of coming up with a script for Land of the Pharaohs. In a spasm of last-minute panic, Hawks decided to hire yet another writer, Harold Jack Bloom, a twenty-nine-year-old New Yorker who had just earned his first screen credit, as cowriter of

The Naked Spur, for which he would soon receive an Academy Award nomination. His agent, Alain Bernheim of Famous Artists, mentioned Hawks's plight to him at Alexandre's one night, and the next day, while Bernheim set up a meeting, Bloom hit the library to research pyramids. That night, Bloom met Hawks at the Ritz Hotel, and, he recounted, "I told him my premise, which became the premise of the movie, about the Greek who is able to figure out a way to build a pyramid so it couldn't be broken into. . . . He looked at me sideways, but said, 'I like that.' Then he asked, 'Are you prepared to go to Italy?' I said, 'Of course.'"

Shortly thereafter, Hawks, Dee, and Faulkner began driving south, through the Alps, into Switzerland, and on to the Lake District. Bloom took a train from Paris with Raoul, whose wife met them in Milan and drove them to Stresa. "When I got there," Bloom recalled, "who should open the door but Faulkner. 'Hello, you must be Bloom,' he said. He always called me Bloom, and Kurnitz Kurnitz. I had no idea when I met Hawks that Faulkner was going to be on the picture. By the time I got to Italy I had it all figured out how to do the whole picture. But Faulkner had talked to Hawks about doing it all as a pirate movie, with the treasure and the evil girl who tries to take it away from the pharaoh. It was a joke, because he didn't see movies and didn't like them. He thought they were for children."

Kurnitz arrived in short order, and, surrounded by glorious pine forests where the writers could seek inspiration, the group began getting down to work. Faulkner simplistically felt the film was *"Red River* all over again," and both Kurnitz and Bloom quickly began to see that their celebrated colleague's heart wasn't in it. Hawks, whom Bloom sensed "was intimidated by the literary stature of Faulkner," remained the picture of generosity and indulgence to his old friend, even offering him a profit share of the film. Feeling excluded from the older men's club of two, Bloom and Kurnitz formed a fast friendship of their own. Faulkner, Bloom said, "frustrated me. He didn't like films and he wouldn't read new books. I asked him what books he'd read recently and he said, 'I don't read new books. I only reread the classics.'" By contrast, "Harry Kurnitz was maybe the funniest man I've ever met in my life. To me he was salvation. If it wasn't for Harry, I think I would have been out of there in a week or two."

As Hawks, Faulkner, Kurnitz, and Bloom toiled on the script, they realized that none of them knew a great deal about antiquity or had a distinct point of view on it. Hawks himself was especially interested in only two elements of the story: the idea of a megalomaniacal leader who spent his life on a mammoth building project, and the physical mechanics involved in sealing off the tomb chamber so that no one could ever break into it. The germ of the former idea actually lay in an earlier project of Hawks's about the building of a Chinese airfield during World War II, which for political reasons was never produced. In Trauner's view, "Hawks thought of the pharaoh like a tycoon in Hollywood." For Bloom, the director's identification with the lead was total: "He was like a pharaoh himself, a Hollywood pharaoh." At the very least, the pharaoh represented Hawks's fanciful notion of himself, entranced with wealth and power, bewitched by a sexy young wife, and invaluably aided by his (perhaps not coincidentally Jewish) designer-architect. Given his lack of fleshed-out ideas for the story and his urgent need for them, this influence should not be underestimated.

To make any serious headway on the script, Hawks and the writers had to be clear on how they were going to show the pyramid was built, since this was the point of the story, and their savior here was Trauner. Although the pyramids have been the focus of endless fascination and study over the centuries, no one has entirely figured out how they were constructed, how the five-thousand-pound stones were transported and then lifted into place on what were, for centuries, the tallest structures in the world. Having "called all the Egyptologues around," Trauner consulted Jean Philippe Lauer, considered the world's leading Egyptologist, who laid out all the leading theories about pyramid construction, then proposed his own notion, which involved a series of ever-narrowing ramps running alongside the pyramid, upon which man-drawn sleds carried the stones. Trauner was convinced that this approach "was correct in an archeological sense." Trauner also had long sessions with Hawks during which he sketched out his plans for the pyramid at various stages of construction; although he said Hawks, the former engineering major, never drew anything himself, some photographs do reveal the director hovering over architectural plans, pencil in hand.

As for the crucial matter of the ending, in which the dead pharaoh's burial chamber is forever sealed with his entourage of loyal servants as well as his treacherous wife inside, Lauer presented an assortment of ideas, given the fact that each actual pyramid was sealed with a different system. Later, in Egypt, Lauer showed Trauner and Howard one small and quite recent tomb that had been sealed in a clever way: at the appointed time, sand-filled pottery encasements were smashed, allowing sand to spill out and the stones above to lower, enclosing the sarcophagus. Presented with this technique, Hawks expanded it to apply to the entire interior of his pyramid, turning it into an ingenious hydraulic device that would lower the giant stones into a closed position, from which they could never be lifted. Trauner found that

Hawks became uncommonly involved in these matters, noting, "Once a propman, always a propman."

Hawks had a particular disdain for the Cecil B. De Mille school of filmmaking and was never partial to spectacle per se. All the same, according to Bloom, "He wanted to do a Cecil B. De Mille epic all of a sudden. . . . and he wasn't really suited to that. It became a drawing room story." Scholars have often chuckled at the director's explanation for the artistic failure of *Land of the Pharaohs*—"I don't know how a pharaoh talks"—but this problem really does lie at the heart of the picture's difficulties. Hawks's art was based on dialogue, gesture, and behavioral exchanges, and his not knowing how a given character would react in a specific context deprived the film of the kind of spontaneity and nuance that can be found in his best work. When Hawks posed the question to his collaborators, Faulkner supposedly suggested that perhaps he should speak like a Kentucky colonel, while Kurnitz proposed that King Lear might serve as a better model. Hawks told them to go ahead and do whatever they liked, because he would rewrite it anyway. Hawks, of course, tended toward modern colloquialisms, and successive script drafts reveal a clear progression from somewhat arch, occasionally pompous writing to material that was sparer, swifter, and sometimes jarringly contemporary. Bloom tried to push a sociological view of the pyramid project on Hawks, with little success. "My premise was that the building of the pyramids had created a middle class. The Pharaoh needed managers, the people who designed and engineered the pyramids. Egypt went broke, and then the people who built them could go anywhere. The wealth of Egypt disappeared with them."

Bloom and Kurnitz worked out a suspense element to the climactic sequence of the sealing of the pyramid, with Dewey Martin and a young girl successfully escaping and Joan Collins trapped behind. Dramatic as it might have been, Hawks did not use it, probably, Bloom noted, because it would have been difficult to stage.

Bloom noted that Hawks and Dee didn't give the impression of a normal husband-and-wife relationship: "He acted like he was her husband and she acted like she was his daughter, even his granddaughter." It didn't take long for Dee to become restless and bored in Stresa; there was absolutely nothing to do, and all the restaurants were closed. According to Bloom's Israeli girlfriend, who got to know Dee fairly well, Dee had another reason to be frustrated: there was no way she could see her French boyfriend, whom she had met in Paris. A ski resort setting, however, would attract less notice, so Dee persuaded her husband to move on to St. Moritz for the holidays, which they did on December 19. They were soon joined at the new, ultra-luxurious Suvretta House by Noël Howard, as well as Charles Feldman and Jean Howard, who were long since divorced but still close friends. Even King Farouk turned up. Although he was a beginning skier, Hawks lived up to his reputation as a sportsman, joining Dee for regular outings on the slopes, while the writers managed to get considerable work done in the mornings. Things slowed down quite a bit however, after the substantial imbibing done at lunch. Faulkner habitually fortified himself with two martinis and a half bottle of Chassagne Montrachet '49 at midday and became pleasantly distracted when Jean Stein, the nineteen-year-old daughter of MCA founder Jules Stein, attached herself to him at Feldman's Christmas Eve party and wouldn't let go. Warmed by her attention, Faulkner was nonetheless depressed by the collection of wealthy international frolickers and flew off the day after Christmas to Stockholm, passing through London before returning to St. Moritz on January 6. Jean Stein was still there, waiting for him.

On January 5, the group had a big party to celebrate Harry Kurnitz's forty-fifth birthday, and the following day, when Faulkner got back, Hawks mailed a fourteen-page outline of the story to Jack Warner in Hollywood. "I really believe it is the best thing I've ever worked on," Hawks enthused to Warner. He summarized the story as that of "a Pharaoh who accumulated the greatest treasure in the world, takes twenty years to build a tomb where he can be buried with it. He makes the mistake of falling for a beautiful young bitch." Hawks also cited the historical fact that pharaohs, even when they became old, were periodically required to run about a mile in public to prove they were in good physical condition and proposed a sequence, never shot, in which "the Queen gives him a hard night the night before the test and the poor bastard barely makes it."

As had happened previously with Hawks scripts on which Faulkner worked, each of the writers tackled different sequences separately. Bloom recalled, "I had difficulty with it because I would write twelve pages a day but then I wanted to edit it, but Howard wanted everything, the unedited pages. Faulkner was not writing anything at all, it was all verbal. Harry wrote twenty pages a day, out of which Hawks would find one or two pages."

Curiously, Hawks never considered a major star for the leading role. After toying with the idea of Sydney Chaplin as Pharaoh, Hawks settled on the English actor Jack Hawkins, who had been appearing in films for more than twenty years and was well-respected but not a box-office name. Hawks made the point to Warner that "almost every one of our actors should be

fairly good figures because the costumes make a fat man look pretty bad."
As far as the females in the cast were concerned, he said, "The evil young
queen should be the most beautiful, sexy girl we can find. I hope to find a
new one and ran across one whom we will test. She is Swiss, speaks
English, French, Italian and German. Saw a little test that is awful good
but will reserve an opinion until we make our own." That girl turned out to
be seventeen-year-old Ursula Andress. Thanks to the test Hawks saw, however, Paramount quickly signed her up, making her unavailable to Warners.

Ten days later, as promised, Hawks sent the ninety-one-page rough
draft to Burbank, confessing, "Am very pleased with it as it represents only
five actual weeks work," and terming it "the most adaptable yarn for Cinema-
Scope that has yet been found." Hawks bluntly stated that Pharaoh's obsession is an effort to provide meaning for his life, while the evil young queen
is trying "to make their work meaningless." Nellifer, the Cypriot princess
who becomes the pharaoh's bride, was clearly being written on the highly
insolent model of Slim in *To Have and Have Not,* and the big initial sex
scene in this draft was arresting. After Nellifer has been put in the dungeon
for disrespect, the pharaoh goes to visit her there. With Nellifer bound by
chains, they launch into passionate sex, and the next scene sees her happily installed in the pharaoh's apartment. In the final film, the equivalent
sequence takes place in the pharaoh's quarters without any bondage accou-
trements, his passion provoked when she bites him.

Hawks warned Warner that because both MGM and Fox were having some trouble with pictures they were making in Egypt, some "trained
help" there would be valuable. Approving the outline, the first draft, and
Hawkins's casting, Warner upped the budget to $1.75 million, although he
was privately advised by Blattner that $2 million would be a more realistic
figure, given the various unpredictable elements involved.

In St. Moritz, Hawks welcomed many of his key crew members, including Russ Harlan, Chuck Hansen, Paul Helmick, and about a dozen
others, for an initial production meeting. When the special-effects man
announced that he was about to begin construction of thirty chariots for
the pharaoh and his officers, Noël Howard, who was in charge of research
and historical accuracy, was obliged to inform the group that, as the wheel
didn't exist in Egypt at that time, neither did chariots. Nor, according to
the hieroglyphics of the period, did horses or camels. The film's animal
wrangler was devastated by this news, and at the end of the meeting Hawks
took Howard aside and said, "I'll make a deal with you. . . . I give up the
horses but, for God's sake, Noël, let me have camels."

At the end of the stay in Switzerland, Hawks let Harold Jack Bloom go, with both realizing that the collaboration had not been a terribly fruitful one, as their sensibilities were too different. Faulkner, too, bothered Bloom for many reasons. Not only was the great writer not interested in contemporary fiction, but, Bloom said, "I couldn't make Faulkner laugh. Only he could make himself laugh. He also said things about blacks that were, to say the least, not very nice, although publicly he cultivated a paternalistic stance toward them." Bloom never sensed anti-Semitism in Hawks, but he speculated, "He could have been anti-Semitic in the specific sense that he resented his bosses, who were all Jewish. On the other hand, he adored Ben Hecht."

From St. Moritz, Hawks moved on to Rome, where he took rooms at the Ambassador Hotel and worked further with his remaining screenwriters, who were staying on the Via Veneto and socializing with Bogart and Bacall, themselves in Rome on John Huston's *Beat the Devil*; for his part, Hawks kept his distance. On January 25, Hawks dispatched another revision of the script to Warner, one in which the story was more fleshed out and the dialogue more colloquial, and on February 10, he and his closest associates made the flight from Rome to Cairo.

Hawks and the other company VIPs lodged at the luxurious, touristic Mena House at Giza, some forty-five minutes from downtown Cairo. Built in the nineteenth century, set amid beautiful gardens at the desert's edge, and rather resembling an Arabian Beverly Hills Hotel, the Mena House was literally across the street and two hundred yards away from the three great pyramids, Cheops, Chephren, and Mykerinos. (The Mena House appears as itself in MGM's *Valley of the Kings*, a suspense film about Egyptian grave robbers, circa 1900, that wrapped in January, just before Hawks and company checked in.) There was also a huge pool, a first-class bar, and room service, major considerations for this group, which alternated between intense activity, both on the script and logistical matters, and indolent leisure. Despite his protestations that he had never played, Noël Howard was dragooned by Hawks into a round on the hotel's nine-hole golf course. Howard duffed his way through a few holes until finally calling it quits when one of his drives sliced violently to the side into the desert and scored a direct hit on the behind of a mangy camel, which galloped off in panic, dropping its female passenger to the ground. Fortunately for Hawks, Kurnitz, a fine golfer, was available as a replacement partner.

Hawks and Howard scouted locations around Giza and met intermittently with authorities, while Kurnitz did the lion's share of the writing. In the wee hours of February 15, Hawks and Kurnitz waited together at the Cairo airport for Faulkner to arrive. Alarmingly, he had drunk a bottle and a half of brandy on the flight from Paris and had to be taken directly to the Anglo-American Hospital. He was slow to recover, and after moving to the Mena House, he came down with a bad cold. Unexcited by Egypt and with other things on his mind, Faulkner worked mechanically, feeding some mediocre material to Kurnitz, who reworked it. Kurnitz later claimed that only one line of Faulkner's wound up unaltered in the finished film: the pharaoh asks the architect Vashtar, "So . . . how is the job getting along?" Realizing how unhappy and unproductive his friend was, Hawks had him polish a few sequences, which earned him an additional five thousand dollars, then let him go on March 29 after a stay of five weeks, and just before the beginning of principal photography.

One of the most taxing scenes, involving the extraction of granite blocks from a quarry, was scheduled to be staged first, on April Fool's Day; it was part of Hawks's strategy to send back some amazing shots right off the bat to keep Warner Bros. off his back. Working at Aswan, they took over an actual ancient quarry and filled it with extras for a setup of truly awesome dimensions. Repeating an effect Hawks had made with cattle in *Red River*, a panoramic shot showing three thousand extras in the enormous quarry was designed to be even more impressive by splicing together two such camera moves, the cut hidden by placing a giant plastic boulder in front of the camera mid-pan. It took a day to pull off and lasts for only a few seconds on-screen, but it was worth it.

To get all the extras to work in unison, the assistants had to come up with little singsong phonetic phrases that the men could chant. After running through a few, such as "Lift that barge!" and "Get a little drunk!," the three thousand sweating, nearly naked men were taught one more slogan, which shortly came roaring repeatedly out of the quarry: "Fuck Warner Bros.!" When Hawks heard this, he nearly laughed, and his driver said that in the car on the way back to the hotel that day, Hawks smiled all the way and kept quietly repeating, "Fuck Warner Bros., Fuck Warner Bros."

A bit later, Hawks wrote to Feldman, "A funny thing happened. Tenny Wright, who is an old friend of mine, came in the other day and had just finished telling me he had to get back to Rome on Monday because *Helen of Troy* had their big day's work then. They were using 800 people. My assistant came up about our next day's call and said 'Mr. Hawks about tomorrow . . . I've ordered 2,200 people but I think we're a little short. What about making it 2,600?' Tenny sat there with his mouth open and two days later saw us use over 6,000." Determined to break the all-time record for number of extras, Hawks pressed his lieutenants and the Egyptians and one day used twelve thousand extras, visible for just a few seconds in the finished film. Near Cairo, Trauner and Howard had located the foundation of an actual unfinished pyramid, then excavated and dressed it for use in further scenes of unprecedented spectacle. Habitually dressed in khaki safari shirt and pants and a wide-brimmed hat, Hawks quietly commandeered his troops like a veteran general; Noël Howard noted, "He had the look, the immobility and the muteness of an Egyptian statue." Hawks got some very impressive footage of men pulling the massive blocks around the construction site; it had taken some three million stones weighing five thousand pounds apiece—and thirty years—to build the actual Khufu pyramid.

Uncertainties surrounding the casting dragged on even after the start date; ten days later, Jack Hawkins still had not been signed. Hawks sent Warner an urgent cable: "Hawkins agent Al Park causing great deal trouble. As each situation cleared Parker makes new and difficult demands." If Hawkins's arrival was delayed any longer than April 14, the film would have to shut down. Tackling the problem personally, Warner cabled J. Arthur Rank, to whom Hawkins was under contract, and the British film tycoon arranged matters just in time for filming to proceed uninterrupted.

Despite the cooperation of the local government and the supply of upward of ten thousand Egyptian army regulars to appear as slaves, there were countless problem of heat, language barriers, censored international communications, equipment failure, the arrival of Ramadan, and even a headline-causing incident in which Egypt accused Warner Bros. of smuggling because Trauner had bought a mummified bird and his assistant was caught with it at customs. At one point, a fight broke out among some extras, resulting in the death of one man; at another, some army extras mutinied and charged the film crew, resulting in Hawks and Russ Harlan actually having to fend them off by throwing rocks at them; later, the threat of hostilities with Israel caused the disappearance of virtually all the extras overnight. Although the Egyptians had been granted no say on the content and story line of the picture, they proved highly sensitive in the matter of portraying themselves as historical slaves. Furthermore, word arrived from Hollywood that the Breen Office had found many scenes in the screenplay highly "sex suggestive" and in need of revision.

The final 138-page script felt significantly overwritten, which forced Hawks to continually streamline it as shooting progressed. The story he finally settled upon was set in the twelfth year of the reign of Cheops II. To fulfill his obsession of building an eternal monument and resting place for himself, the pharaoh is obliged to engage the services of the architect Vashtar, a member of the defeated tribe of the Kushites. Both were good characters, and the best dramatic potential in the script as written resided in the parallel stories of these two men, master and talented slave, who were working on the same task, one by choice, the other by command. This potential was only partially achieved, and the script and film were both pulled down from its initially intelligent level by the emphasis in the second half on the beautiful and duplicitous Princess Nellifer of Cyprus, who objects to her people being enlisted as slaves for the pharaoh's massive project, becomes his second wife, carries on with his captain in charge of guarding the treasure, and ultimately brings ruin upon everyone, which allows Vashtar to lead his people to freedom.

Throughout the shoot, Warner Bros. was convinced that it had an all-time winner on its hands. Studio representative Mort Blumenstock cabled Warner in April, reporting, "This footage . . . makes anything De Mille has done about Egypt look like child at play." Equally excited was Feldman, who told Hawks that he wouldn't be surprised if the film grossed $20–30 million. The agent added, "Jack Warner is really overboard about the rushes to date. Confidentially, he feels that [it] is the greatest stuff he has seen in his life."

None of the Egyptian footage involved the pivotal character of Nellifer, but as location work progressed into mid-May and a transfer to the studios in Rome grew close, apprehension mounted over her casting. Early on, Hawks had actually spoken of using Dee in the part, but her pregnancy removed the embarrassing possibility of a showdown with Warners on this question. Hawks then became quite intrigued by an English model, Ivy Nicholson. A supermodel before her time, this exceptional beauty was famous all over Europe and very much in the favored Hawksian mold—very tall and lean, with straight hair that framed her face in a way that made many think of Cleopatra. In April she flew to Cairo to shoot a test, the key scene in which Princess Nellifer seduces the pharaoh. Unfortunately, she made the fatal mistake of biting Hawkins's hand to the bone in the scene, infuriating the actor, who had agreed to do the test with her as a favor to Hawks. Suffering from a 102-degree fever and barely able to continue working, Hawks wired Warner: "After working with Nicholson decided too great risk personally to put in such important part. . . . Believe good chance of getting Gina Lollobrigida if can get your decision immediately." Or, as Trauner less diplomatically put it, Nicholson "was very beautiful, but a little cuckoo."

It didn't take Hawks long to figure out that he wouldn't be able to effectively mold the Italian actress, but then he recalled a sexy young English actress he'd met in Paris the year before when Gregory Ratoff was casting his King Farouk picture. Joan Collins, like Jack Hawkins, was under contract to Rank, but after some initial hassles, a deal was worked out for the sultry twenty-year-old to play Nellifer at fifty-six hundred English pounds for eight weeks, with an option to use her in two additional films over the next three years. The dark-haired Collins, who had already appeared in nine British films, usually as a bad girl, didn't even do a test for Hawks, and her sexuality was unusually overt for Hawks's taste. Hawks took a greater personal interest in the young starlet Luisella (Luisa) Boni, whom he cast as Nellifer's slave girl Kyra and whom he considered putting under personal contract; in the end, her poor command of English scotched the idea. For the first queen, Hawks used the beautiful Algerian-born actress Kerima, who had caused a bit of a stir with her debut in Carol Reed's *An Outcast of the Islands* three years before.

On May 25, as Hawks and his crew were packing up for their departure for Rome the next day, word arrived of the accidental death in Indochina of the photographer Robert Capa, killed when he stepped on an Vietminh antipersonnel mine while covering troop movements. Hawks had always been taken with this devil-may-care adventurer, who easily could have been a character in one of the director's films and very nearly did become one twenty years later. Capa had even been due to visit the Egyptian location to cover it for *Life*, before deciding, as usual, to go where the action was, whereupon his Magnum partner Ernst Haas came instead. Both Noël Howard and Trauner took their friend's death particularly hard.

Safely installed back in Rome after the unpredictable months in Egypt, Hawks was finally able to bring Jack Warner up-to-date on the vicissitudes of the shoot to date. Never much of a letter writer, on June 13 Hawks felt compelled to take pen in hand:

> I know a couple of letters to you have been stopped because I added some things about Egypt. It happened to us all and is just another odd thing about that country. . . . It is the greatest place as far as photography, light and scenic values in the world but all hell to make a picture in. The last month was the worse. What they call Ramadan was on. This means that they don't eat or drink from sunrise to sunset and it slows them down to a walk. It naturally slowed us too or we would have been finished a week or ten days

before we did. The bad break was that it took us into a spell of hot weather and dust storms. [One] day it was so hot two camels died of heat right in a scene and 66 men collapsed and were carried in during one hour. . . . Two days later a dust storm—you may have seen a little of it in the rushes. It was a funny feeling one minute looking at 3,000 men lined up for a shot and two minutes later you could only see about 50. . . .

We've got a great crew Jack, I don't know of any bunch that has taken such a beating and gone on with such spirit and cooperation. Your telegrams about the rushes helped. I posted them and the boys would say, "Well, if we're getting that kind of result we'd better keep going." Outside of the weather we had the people to deal with. They are different than any nation I have seen so far. They are tricky, lie like hell, make promises they don't intend to keep, have no idea of time.

They are like children in some ways, and like master minds in others. . . . Dozens of fights each day, right while a scene was being made. . . . One village we were working in, an argument occurred about a dog. A man threw a rock at another man's dog. The families of the respective men joined in. That evening the man who threw the rock had his throught [sic] cut and just before we arrived for work the next morning the owner of the dog was shot and killed. . . .

Our sets are ready and look very good. Have shortened a lot of scenes in the script and eliminated some others and believe there is no reason why they can't be as good as the outdoor stuff. . . . Even with the outdated studios and equipment it seems like heaven compared to Egypt. . . .

Jack I don't understand this argument about publicity. I do know that if we could get together and talk it would be settled in no time. . . . I don't agree with you that I have nothing to do with publicity or thinking of ways to help sell the picture. . . .

For ten years have been doing exactly what I am now and it's worked very well. . . . You remember the campaign on Bacall for *To Have and Have Not*. That was started by Conlon [Hawks's personal publicity man Scoop] and me with the help of some friends on the various magazines. . . . It was not done by the studio publicity department and am very sure of this statement. Conlon and I continued to work together on *Red River* and *The Thing*. . . .

I'm sure you will remember that both of those pictures were successful and in my opinion had excellent handling.

Conlon and I put in weeks of work before this picture ever started not on things usually handled by the publicity department but on trying to reach out for a few more avenues. We wrote letters to editors and others. I think you'll see the results in a little while and will be pleased and I assure you they won't conflict in any way with the studio publicity. I think this all started because of the stills. . . . It was impossible to process the stills in Egypt. [They] would have been subject to censor, so we decided to bring the film with us and develop it here which we did. It will be finished in a few days and sent immediately. . . .

Best regards, Howard.

Within a couple of weeks, both Hawks and Warner might have wished that publicity squabbles were all they had to worry about. Sets were built at two small studios, the Centro Sperimentale and the Scalera Studios; the latter, the oldest in Rome, were so primitive that they didn't even have permanent toilet facilities. Because of equipment problems, the continual rewriting of scenes, and the ambitious and time-consuming lighting designs of the cinematographer Lee Garmes, shooting proceeded at a painfully slow pace. Garmes, who had worked so creatively with Hawks on *Scarface*, was brought in to shoot the Rome interiors, as Russ Harlan was exhausted and extremely depressed over the incredible poverty of Egypt and the conditions under which children grew up there. Nonetheless, Harlan stayed on to shoot second-unit footage and to knock off a promotional short for Egyptian tourism that Warner Bros. had promised to make in exchange for location privileges. In Italy, Harlan shot some additional sequences, notably exteriors, such as the pharaoh's test of strength when he wrestles the bull.

Joan Collins immediately jumped into a rollicking affair with her on-screen lover, Sydney Chaplin, and the two annoyed Hawks to no end by staying up most of the night partying on the Via Veneto. After a couple of weeks of gorging herself on pasta and wine, Collins had put on eight pounds, and Hawks told her bluntly that "Princess Nellifer should not look as though she is four months pregnant." Both she and Chaplin had trouble keeping their rolls of fat from overflowing the outfits and skin-clenching jewelry that had looked just right during costume fittings. Censorship required that Collins not expose her navel, so a fake red ruby was found to fill it. Sensitive about her protruding stomach, she sucked it in for the first take, but this sent the ruby shooting out onto the floor, to general hilarity. An unamused Hawks said, "For God's sake, get some airplane glue. Get anything to keep the damned thing in place." As she and Chaplin continued their carefree romance, their giddy mood spilled over onto the set. In the key scene in which Chaplin's character declares his love for the princess, the actor began cracking up as he delivered his solemnly passionate lines. Soon Collins couldn't keep a straight face either, and after a few takes like this most of the crew members lost it as well. Hawks could barely contain himself but, of course, as Collins admitted, "The angrier Howard Hawks became the more we laughed." Finally, Hawks bawled them out in front of everyone, called shooting off for the day, and sternly warned Chaplin and Collins to shape up fast if they wanted to have careers after this picture. Realizing that she was stupidly risking a big break with one of the world's leading directors, Collins resolved to go on the wagon and turn in early from then on, although it wasn't easy since Chaplin continued to carouse the nights away.

Hawks's mood wasn't improved by his growing suspicion that the script might have intractable problems after all. In Egypt, Hawks and his team could easily deceive themselves into thinking they had a great picture on the basis of the extraordinary spectacle they were capturing on-screen. Once in the studio in Rome, they couldn't avoid confronting the hackneyed dialogue and story line, as well as their lack of a solution for these problems. Jack Hawkins, who had taken his role in large measure because of Faulkner's involvement, frankly felt that "some of the lines we were expected to speak were unspeakable." Hawks reassured him in one instance by saying, "I'll find you another. I have more used lines at my fingertips than anyone you know." Hawkins ended up thinking that *Land of the Pharaohs* was "a perfectly ridiculous film." Even Joan Collins realized that it was "a hokey script with some impossible dialogue." Much of the problem lay less with the pharaoh's dialogue than with Hawks's total conception of the Nellifer character, on which his formula for creating sexy young things went too far; she is a sexual vulture, a treasure-hungry villainess without a shred of refinement or sensibility. While the pharaoh was plausible enough, Hawks and his writers were entirely unable to bring any fresh conception to the female lead; coincidentally or not, Nellifer greatly resembled the evil character played by Bella Darvi in *The Egyptian*. Although Collins's lusty playing gives the film its greatest entertainment value, the conventional thinking behind the nature of the role makes the film resemble other epics of ancient times much more than it otherwise would.

Similarly, *Land of the Pharaohs* presents the usually egalitarian Hawksian group at its most imbalanced. Uniquely among the director's films, this one features a dictatorial leader whose will is obeyed either by loyal subjects or slaves; the only way this task can be achieved is by threat or force, and the value of unique individual contributions is denied. The one exception lies in the strong relationship between the pharaoh and his loyal top adviser, Hamar, very appealingly played by Alexis Minotis; while Hamar is obliged to do his leader's bidding, their brotherly camaraderie resembles that found in many other Hawks films. Otherwise, on this one occasion, Hawks tried an approach far afield from his usual formula, but it didn't work, which helps explain his retrenchment and recycling of stories during the final decade of his career.

It was Noël Howard's impression that Hawks was utterly obsessed with wealth and gold, and that he became ill at ease when the names of extremely rich men, such as J. Paul Getty and Howard Hughes, were even mentioned. One day Howard's feelings were confirmed when he went to look for his boss and finally found Hawks alone down in the treasure chamber set, silently admiring the phony gold and jewels, his head moving from side to side as if it were a camera panning the room. Howard didn't interrupt him, but when Sydney Chaplin abruptly entered the scene, Howard said, "Hawks spun around. His mouth open, he threw him such an outraged look that Syd stopped dead in his tracks. Hawks quickly regained his habitual poise. With a grand gesture, sweeping the decor, he said with deep conviction, 'Sydney, look at all this . . . isn't it . . . *beautiful?*'

"Sydney gave the wondrous sight a quick glance. 'Not bad,' he said, walking back up the steps. 'You should see my old man's cellars!'"

By mid-July, Jerry Blattner was able to assess what the final production costs would be. In his estimate, the film could be expected to wrap on about August 19 at a cost of $2.75 million. Stunned, Warner fired off a blistering telegram to Hawks:

> In my wildest imagination never would believe could go this figure. When we originally met in Paris you estimated you could make this picture for one million dollars plus some top star salaries of obtainable. You finalized this, setting budget $1,360,000. Then after you had scouted locations and fully estimated all the costs of the performers salaries and costs we revised this budget by amendatory agreement under date January 25 at $1,750,000 which was ample to cover all requirements. Now it is estimated you are going over one million

dollars over that figure and I want to go on record with you. Howard I cannot permit this as it is not good business and will expose me to criticism from our entire organization.

Warner went on to deny Hawks permission to import bulls and bullfighters from Portugal for a new sequence he wanted to shoot, claiming the Society for the Prevention of Cruelty to Animals wouldn't permit it anyway, and signed off by saying, "All my conversations with you in Europe were to avoid exactly what is happening. . . . I only went into deal on your firm promise that . . . you would keep within the budget."

The very next day, Hawks responded by stating that he could shoot the bullfight sequence (which had replaced the endurance run as the test of the pharaoh's strength) in one day and pointed out that the problems on his picture were in many cases identical to those being suffered on *Helen of Troy*, which Robert Wise had just finished directing for Warners in Rome. "Everything possible is being done to better these conditions or overcome them including working till seven or eight each night. . . . I can understand your anxiety and appreciate it but please also understand that after eight long months seven days a week working under every conceivable adverse condition I want to finish as soon as possible without jeopardizing what we already have."

After raving about the footage coming back from Egypt, Warner was a bit let down by what he saw from Rome, and he voiced concern that Hawks wasn't using the CinemaScope format well in his interiors, as the director was showing a tendency to stay too far away from his actors. Having used CinemaScope as the raison d'être for making an epic, Hawks in the end found it clumsy and "good only for showing great masses of movement." At face value, Hawks's visual style always seemed relatively plain and straight-forward, but his reactions to CinemaScope, however old school, reveal an exceptional sophistication and awareness regarding the implications of the visual component of cinema. "We have spent a lifetime learning how to compel the public to concentrate on one single thing," he explained. "Now we have something that works in exactly the opposite way, and I don't like it very much." He also pointed out that because of the difficulty of cutting in the same way as before, "you lose speed as a means of exciting or aug-menting a scene's dramatic tension." Hawks never used the wide-screen format again, even on an outdoor film such as *Hatari!*, which might have seemed to demand it.

Hawks also had big problems with the editing. On the advice of Lewis Milestone, Hawks originally hired a Russian-English cutter named Vladimir Sagovsky. Probably referring to the difficulties of editing CinemaScope, Hawks told him before leaving for Egypt, "I want this picture cut differently than any other picture ever made." Unfortunately, Sagovsky took him literally, cutting in close-ups where there should have been long shots, and vice versa. Seeing his material assembled this way upon his return from Cairo, Hawks threw up his hands and insisted to Jack Warner that he needed a new editor. To the director's delight, Warner sent over Rudi Fehr, an erudite, German-born film lover who had been a top editor and the head of the studio's editorial department for many years; if anyone could help set the picture straight, Fehr could. Seeing that Hawks had Sagovsky "shaking in his boots," Fehr asked to keep his predecessor on for a while so he could save face. After looking at the assemblage, Fehr told Hawks that "the story doesn't begin until page fifty-four." Reel by reel, Fehr undid Sagovsky's damage and attempted to give the footage shape and flow, with Hawks giving notes after each screening. It went slowly, for as Fehr told Warner, "One thing I have learned about Mr. Hawks is that you have to bring your suggestions up again and again, he might not buy them the first time, but the second or third time he lends an ear." Fehr's great chance to shine lay in the climactic sequence of the tomb being sealed off, and he made the best of it, creating the most effective montage sequence in any Hawks film with his expert assembly of boldly composed shots of massive stones falling into place and forever confining the treacherous Queen Nellifer, as well as the pharaoh's loyal entourage, in the gold-filled tomb. Still, Fehr felt he never succeeded in the alchemy that was being asked of him. "I tried restructuring it, but it didn't work and Howard knew it. I felt the picture could have had a better screenplay. They never solved their problems."

Although he continued to simmer over the budget, Warner finally permitted Hawks to quickly film the bull sequence when the director assured him no animals would be killed. For the scene, the company traveled south to a spot along the coast just north of Naples, where there was an existing ranch with a bullring. On the way, however, the stuntman who had crashed Hawks's Alfa Romeo once before in Egypt had another wreck in the same car, which he was driving down for the director's use. Because of the plethora of foreign actors being used, Fehr estimated that 75 percent of the picture was dubbed, and Warner cabled to tell Hawks that he would be in Rome around the middle of August and to insist that Hawks return to

Burbank for the remainder of postproduction. One particular bone of contention was Dewey Martin, whose Brooklyn accent was painfully obvious in the midst of the mostly British leads, but Warner learned that Martin's contract with MGM wouldn't permit his being dubbed. Later, after Fehr returned to Hollywood, he was asked to shoot some miniatures of stones falling to incorporate into the climax, effects that look particularly unconvincing in the finished film. Noël Howard also shot some miniatures representing the pyramid's interior.

Finally, on August 9, after more than four months of grueling work, *Land of the Pharaohs* completed production. An exhausted troupe celebrated at a giant wrap party in Borghese Park, and several friends later recalled having been surprised that Hawks did not seem at all impressed by a young French starlet to whom he was introduced there, Brigitte Bardot, fresh off a bit in *Helen of Troy*.

Rome was just entering the fabled period when it became known as "Hollywood on the Tiber," and after a brief vacation in Portofino the Hawkses, who were expecting a child in the fall, were able to partake of the thriving night life. They moved into a beautiful apartment across from a park, at 77 Via Bruxelles in the fashionable Parioli district particularly favored by show-business figures. One night at the Hostorio del'Orso, Hawks, Dee, Fehr, and the composer Dimitri Tiomkin were already seated when King Farouk, preceded by his bodyguards, walked in with an enormous Italian girlfriend. After they greeted each other, Hawks asked the king to join their party. Farouk proceeded to consume an enormous quantity of expensive caviar, much to the chagrin of Tiomkin, who had invited the Hawkses and Fehr to dinner. Tiomkin's discomfort amused Hawks to no end, as it did when Tiomkin, thinking he could curry favor with the king, mentioned that he knew his mother. Only later did Tiomkin learn that Farouk and the queen mother were not even on speaking terms. For a long time, the king tried to wheedle a screening of *Land of the Pharaohs* out of Hawks and Tiomkin, but to no avail, since showing it to the deposed monarch might seriously upset the present government. Over the summer, Hawks's teenage daughter Barbara came to visit, hit the town with Noël Howard with her father's consent, and was taken dancing by Fehr.

Tiomkin had come to Rome to score *Land of the Pharaohs* only under heavy pressure from Hawks, since he was desperately afraid of flying. He adored the director, however, and the prospect of creating what was to become the most expensive musical score ever done for a motion picture up to that time was too much to resist. Tiomkin composed a striking, sometimes brutal score with an emphasis on brass and choral chanting; strings were used to underline the appearances of Nellifer.

During his August visit to Rome, Warner was mollified by Hawks and pleased with what he was able to see of the picture itself. *Land of the Pharaohs* was the subject of a seven-page spread in the September 20 issue of *Life* magazine; five days later, Hawks saw the complete first cut of the picture, which ran two hours and twenty minutes. Confiding to Feldman that "the picture seems better than I thought," Hawks continued to encourage Warner about its progress and sent him a story, written in his own hand, which he said he would like to film next, about a man in Newgate prison awaiting death, who marries a girl so that she can inherit a fortune and is subsequently pardoned and shares in her wealth.

Warner let this one pass without recorded comment, but on a personal level, the two men continued to get along amicably. Warner had his camera department procure a 16mm Cine-Kodak "Royal" movie camera with a 25mm lens, which Tiomkin brought over for Dee's use, while Hawks personally picked out a new Bentley, which he arranged for Warner to receive.

A few weeks later, Hawks wired Warner that the film was all cut and ran two hours and fifteen minutes. He added, "Dee also has been busy lately in production boy, weight eight pounds running time 24 hours!" Gregg, named after Hawks's friend Gregg Toland, was born on October 22 by Cesarean section at Rome's International Salvador Mundi Hospital. Hawks, at fifty-eight, was delighted to have another son.

Hawks delivered *Land of the Pharaohs* to Jack Warner in early November, eleven months from the time writing on it had begun. On November 16, his boss responded:

> On Friday I cabled you that the first running of *The Land of the Pharaohs* was enthusiastically received by everyone. . . .
>
> In going over the future as far as you are concerned . . . this is the way we see it. . . . Unless we get an important subject, we would not want to make a deal at this time. We believe that stories such as "Dreadful Hollow" . . . would be a waste of time. The picture would end up as the bottom half of a double bill, and all the effort put into the making of it would be wasted. . . .
>
> I am not going to tell you that [*Pharaohs*] hasn't a chance of recouping its cost and making an important profit but when you spend $2,800,000 for a picture plus the cost of prints, advertising,

distribution, foreign dubbing and all that goes with it, you really have to gross a tremendous sum before making any money. In our opinion, the motion picture industry is in too precarious a position for us to take this chance now. However . . . if you come across a subject which can be made in . . . England as an Eady Plan quota picture . . . we would be interested.

Because of the many years we have known each other, I do not want to make any statement which will put you in the position of keeping you from doing something else where you can get an attractive deal. However, we are interested in making a deal provided we can set the budget and not exceed it within reason. . . .

Can assure you that our Company will not a leave a stone unturned on *Pharaohs*. I hope that it will come off as you put in a lot of hard work to make it all possible. You deserve high praise for having accomplished an important task.

To recover from the laborious year, Hawks played a lot of golf, made little excursions out of Rome, and then took his family on a long trip through Europe. Leaving Rome for Switzerland in early November, they picked up a new Mercedes and drove through Germany, the Netherlands, Belgium, France (with a stop in Paris), then went on to Klosters, near St. Moritz, where Hawks and his wife skied nearly every day and had so much fun that they stayed on through February. During that time, the next step in the creation of Hawks's vaunted critical reputation was made; in the February 1955 *Cahiers du Cinéma*, the great film theoretician André Bazin published an article entitled "Comment peut-on être Hitchcocko-Hawksien?," which addressed the question of how such commercial directors as Hitchcock and Hawks could be discussed as serious artists, an issue that would be taken up in the United States some ten to fifteen years hence.

On May 6, Warner cabled that the first sneak preview of *Land of the Pharaohs*, the night before at the Encino Theater in the San Fernando Valley, had been "excellent." The film was judged a bit too long, however, and Hawks, acting with the advice of his brother Bill, quickly approved a list of twenty-two cuts, all minor and designed merely to speed up the action. Both Warner and Feldman felt that the next preview, at the Huntington Park Theater on May 26, was "wonderful," and Feldman told Hawks to expect about $4–5 million as his cut of the profits on the picture. Equally confident, Warner began showing the film to the press; considering the eventual reception of the film, many of the initial reviews were surprisingly good. Billy Wilkerson, the publisher of the *Hollywood Reporter*, went so far as to send the following telegram to Warner: "Up to last night I felt the greatest spectacle of all time was Griffith's *Intolerance* but your *Land of the Pharaohs* makes it look like a two-reeler."

Still, despite all of Warner's sustained enthusiasm through the shoot and the expectations that *Land of the Pharaohs* would emerge as one of the blockbusters of all time, the company finally realized that this was not a film that was going to play for months and win Academy Awards. Going the opposite route, Warner Bros. developed a sensationalistic campaign keyed around such tag lines as "The Barbaric Love That Left the Great Pyramid as Its Landmark!" and "Her Treachery Stained Every Stone of the Pyramid." The epic did strong business in its initial West Coast openings on June 24, playing, of course, the Egyptian Theater in Los Angeles, but dropped off rather sharply in subsequent weeks. When it spread out to major cities around the country over the next couple of weeks, the same pattern was repeated—solid openings, but no legs. Feeling guilty over having let Hawks down, Faulkner agreed to appear at a Warners cocktail party for the premiere in Memphis and submitted to interviews to help promote the picture. One of the other writers, Harold Jack Bloom, was appalled by the final result and felt that Hawks had blown a real opportunity to make something unusual.

Reposing at the Villa Capri in Cannes, Hawks was buoyed by the initial returns, but it was shortly clear that his original hopes were to be excruciatingly underrealized. Perhaps it was the fact that the story was pagan, rather than Biblical; maybe it needed a real star or two; possibly Warner was right in suspecting that the public was surfeited on ancient exotica for the moment, and no doubt Hawks was onto something when he observed, "I should have had somebody in there that you were rooting for. Everybody was a son of a bitch." In any event, the public proved royally indifferent to *Land of the Pharaohs*. When it finally opened in New York City on July 26, it was at the Mayfair Theater, not one of the more high-end houses in town; in five weeks there, it grossed a lackluster $89,500. The highest it ever rose in the national box-office rankings was number four, during the week including July 4. An accounting five years later showed that the budget had run to $3.15 million. With prints, advertising, distribution expenses, and the rest, the film had ultimately cost Warner Bros. $5,716,120. U.S. and Canadian rentals amounted to $2,001,481, and the total worldwide was $4,181,909; this left Warners $1,534,211 in the hole for its trouble. All Hawks ever received for the picture was $100,000 plus expenses, or less than he had been earning a decade earlier when he was chafing under the frustrations of a Warner Bros. studio contract.

There was an ultimate irony. After taking a look at it, the new Nasser regime in Egypt promptly banned *Land of the Pharaohs* because, in its opinion, the characterization of the bearded Vashtar and his oppressed tribe made it appear that a Jew had designed the pyramid. Then, in 1959, the film ended up being reissued on the bottom half of a double bill with *Helen of Troy*.

33

Sojourn in Europe

The conventional wisdom concerning Howard Hawks's mid-1950s layoff from filmmaking—at three months short of four years, the longest hiatus between shoots in his entire career—is that he was licking his wounds after the crushing disappointment of *Land of the Pharaohs*, that he took time off in Europe to reassess what went wrong and didn't return until he had a very clear idea of how he wanted to proceed. This impression was fostered by Hawks himself, who claimed that he soured on the film business during that period and said, "I thought I would quit, and I did for a while."

While there is no doubt that Hawks needed to regain his enthusiasm and get a better fix on the stories he wanted to tell, the fact is that Hawks aggressively, even desperately tried to get films made all through this period. Even while he continued to live lavishly at the most fashionable addresses, Hawks suffered financial setbacks that made his situation even more urgent. But a combination of insufficiently prepared scripts, a balky star, a major standoff with a studio, a broken leg, and missed deals translated into a protracted dry spell that coincided with the deterioration of his third marriage.

Despite the tremendous rigors of the shoot, all through the postproduction and prerelease period of *Land of the Pharaohs*, Hawks was consumed with ideas and possibilities for new projects to begin as soon as possible. Once again, his thoughts returned to *The Sun Also Rises*. Refusing offers for the rights from Robert Hakim and Orson Welles, Hawks told Feldman that he now wanted Marlon Brando to play Jake Barnes and that he believed filming would have to span a year; he would send a unit to Spain in the summer of 1955 to shoot the running of the bulls, then return the following year with his actors, since it would likely be impossible to safely cover both at the same time. Feldman kept telling his friend that making an "important deal" would be no problem, but Hawks failed to make any progress on a script, and the following year, he sold it to 20th Century–Fox.

"I thought it was hard to do," Hawks confessed. "Zanuck paid through the nose for it, then six months later he called me up and said, 'Howard, how were you gonna make that?' I said, 'Darryl, I'll be glad to tell you for $100,000.'" Under heavy censorship constraints, Zanuck went ahead anyway, with Henry King directing a turgid 1957 adaptation distinguished only by a couple of the performances.

The producer Sam Spiegel, fresh from winning an Oscar for *On the Waterfront*, began pursuing Hawks to direct a film from a novel he owned called *The Bridge on the River Kwai*. Hawks discussed story ideas for this prisoner-of-war thriller with the writer Carl Foreman, whom he liked despite having despised *High Noon*, and proposed numerous changes and new characters from Pierre Boulle's novel. "I wanted Noël Coward to play a fairy that thought of marvelous ways of killing the enemy," he said. Years later, he maintained, "I couldn't stand Sam Spiegel so I left it." But in early 1955, he revealed his true reservations to Feldman: "I don't believe I'll do it. First, I think it's a good story, probably get great reviews as a picture but I don't think it will make money. It's a war story, no dames, expensive and too damn much work for no gain." Instead, in the same letter to his agent, he proposed another idea: "What would you think of doing *The Last Days of Pompeii*. It's a good yarn, very well known, and could have an amazing ending with the volcano and fire."

Hawks and his family spent an extended Christmas holiday in the Alps, mainly at Klosters but occasionally venturing to St. Moritz, where more of the international crowd gathered. "Dee and the baby are fine and if I could find a story everything would be perfect," Hawks confided in a rare note to Feldman. "It's about time," he admitted, "to think of something else." New financial pressures also weighed on him, as in February, Hawks was commanded by the court in California to once and for all pay Athole $52,382 in back alimony, which he finally did in May. Installed back in Paris at the Royal Monceau Hotel the following month, he was joined by Feldman, who spent nearly two months there largely occupied with attempts to set something up for Hawks. In response to Warner's letter about the optional second picture, for which Hawks had already been advanced $35,000, Hawks proposed two ideas to start as early as the summer. The first was a romantic drama, *The Daughter of Bugle Ann*, which he felt he could shoot in Ireland on a relatively low budget with Richard Burton and a yet-to-be-discovered actress. The other was an American female pioneer story, *Rugged Land of Gold*, which was meant to star Audrey Hepburn, one of the rare established actresses with whom Hawks was ever keen to work. The feeling was evidently mutual, but Hepburn's heavy schedule and the lack of a script conspired to thwart it. There was also talk of Hawks collaborating with Irwin Shaw, a prominent American in Paris, on a story for Cubby Broccoli, who had just launched his producing career in London. Most intriguing in terms of its atypicality was a project called "I'm Going to Have a Baby." Derived from Martha Martin's "I Will Live and Have My Baby," which was published in the *Ladies Home Journal*, the story dealt with a young woman who becomes stranded in the wilderness shortly before she is to give birth. In its theme and potential for transcendent meaning, it somewhat recalled Hawks's lost first film, *The Road to Glory*, and was unusual for him in that it focused exclusively on one person cut off from group interaction. None of these ideas made it to the script stage.

Consuming the lion's share of Hawks's and Feldman's attention was a story much more obviously in the director's line. All Hawks had was the basic idea, a loose account of one season in the lives of hunters who capture animals in Africa for zoos. Without being developed in the least, it contained all the basic Hawksian elements: a risky, adventurous profession being carried out in a remote location, endless opportunities for group interplay and interdependence, the possibility of introducing one or more women into a basically male environment, and a commercially appealing subject with plenty of room for major stars. Other pluses for Hawks included the opportunities for a prolonged stay overseas and an exciting shoot, although a studio head might look at the same circumstances rather more skeptically.

To play the leading role of the chief hunter, Hawks thought of no one but Gary Cooper. The two men hadn't worked together since *Ball of Fire* in 1941, and their relationship cooled somewhat after the actor unwisely turned down *Red River*. Nonetheless, Cooper always maintained that there was no one he loved working with more than Hawks, provided the project was right. Back on top again after his Oscar for *High Noon*, Cooper was currently greatly in demand among top directors, having just signed to do *The Friendly Persuasion* for Wyler and *Love in the Afternoon* for Wilder. During a stay in Paris in April, Cooper met numerous times with Hawks and Feldman. Despite a certain hesitancy about the story, the actor trusted Hawks enough to agree to appear in *Africa* — pending his approval of the script. This was enough for Hawks to announce the news to the press in May, a month before *Land of the Pharaohs* was due to open. With that, he repaired for the summer to Cannes, where he, Dee, and Gregg took an apartment at the Villa Capri while Harry Kurnitz tried to develop a first draft of the script.

Over the next year, a desultory and degenerating scenario unfolded, typical of the film business, perhaps, but unusual among Hawks, Cooper, and Warner, three men who had known each other for so long. In September, Cooper made it clear that, despite his handshake with Hawks, he was in no way committed to *Africa* until he saw a finished script. Hawks prodded Kurnitz to at least get through a first draft, whereupon he immediately commenced a second, with many changes planned to beef up Cooper's part and increase the quotient of comedy. In early October, Cooper flatly told Feldman that he wasn't interested in the project, which prompted a quick withdrawal by Warner, who was in no mood to embark upon another African adventure with Howard Hawks. Still, Feldman and Hawks persisted, submitting a second draft to Cooper while privately approaching John Wayne and William Holden to gauge their interest. Having already spent some forty thousand dollars on the script and research, Hawks threatened to sue Warner Bros. for breach of contract. Through the winter, Feldman badgered Cooper persistently while awaiting a new draft from Hawks, which was not forthcoming, until Cooper finally and definitely told him, "You know I am crazy about Howard. You know I want to do a picture with him, but I don't want to do this story." At this, Hawks decided he had no choice but to sue Warners for reneging on its deal, which sent Jack Warner into a fury since it was his contention that his agreement to produce *Africa* was entirely dependent upon Cooper's involvement.

Meanwhile, numerous other possibilities were coming Hawks's way. Out of the blue, Dino De Laurentiis, one of Italy's hottest young producers, who at that moment was making *War and Peace* with King Vidor, approached Hawks with another Tolstoy adaptation, *Resurrection*. Hawks got into advanced talks with British investors to shoot a picture in England and made a serious attempt to acquire the rights to two properties previously filmed by Warner Bros., *The Mask of Dimitrios* and Somerset Maugham's "The Letter," in which he wanted to star Ingrid Bergman and Richard Widmark. When Bergman turned out to be booked for more than a year, he considered using Jennifer Jones.

Late in 1955, after the French release of *Land of the Pharaohs*, Hawks sat for the first of what were to be several long interviews with the French film magazine *Cahiers du Cinéma*, which had "discovered" him two years before. Hawks was interviewed by three fanatical admirers: Jacques Becker, the distinguished director of the classic *Casque d'Or*, and two film critics in their twenties who had just begun directing shorts, Jacques Rivette, the author of the enshrinement of *Monkey Business*, and François Truffaut. The discussion mainly centered on *Land of the Pharaohs*, but then turned off into more theoretical areas, in which Hawks greatly impressed the eager French cinephiles with his thoughtfulness and well-articulated opinions.

Periodically through 1955 and 1956, Dee would return to Los Angeles with Gregg and stay with her sister and Groucho Marx, who were now married. As Groucho described the situation in a letter to Arthur Sheekman,

> When I casually invited Eden's sister to spend a week or two, I had no idea it would lengthen into six. And the way she eats, one would think that the baby is still inside of her instead of fouling up my house with baby toilet seats, wet bed sheets and flying rattles. Her nurse is very eager to appear on my show as a contestant, and nails me every time I come out of my bedroom. My bedroom exits are becoming more infrequent all the time. Beginning Monday, I am holing up in my boudoir until the taxi (with Mrs. Hawks) leaves for International Airport.
>
> As a matter of fact, Dee is a charming girl—both pretty and bright—and if she were here alone, without the nurse, the baby and Eden, I'd have a hell of a time."

One reason Groucho didn't mention for Dee's prolonged stay was that she had an unspecified operation, from which she recuperated partly in Palm Springs. Not long after her return to Europe in November, the family was off again to Klosters, this time to the Haus Am-Taoback, for another winter of skiing and socializing. This season, however, proved to be much less enjoyable than the last. Slim sent Hawks a late Christmas present by way of a lawsuit. Having gotten wind that Hawks was putting Hog Canyon on the market, Slim saw this as her chance to collect the $40,000 that her ex-husband owed her, as well as the $11,300 he had neglected to pay for Kitty's child support. The following spring, Hawks, with his brother Bill handling the transaction, sold his beautiful home for an underpriced $58,000 to the Tower Oil executive Howard Keck, and later that summer he was able to have Slim's suit dismissed on the promise that he would meet all his existing obligations under their original property settlement. He then chose to ignore the matter entirely, forcing Slim to take legal action repeatedly in years to come in an attempt to get her ex-husband to live up to his legal responsibilities. Hawks's behavior in relation to Slim and Kitty is hard to fathom, although it certainly stemmed from some combination of arrogant stubbornness, a conviction that he needn't pay since Leland Hayward and Slim had far more money than he did, a lack of liquid cash, and a lingering resentment of Slim for having left him. Relations between the two were strained when they existed at all, and Hawks undoubtedly knew that Slim bad-mouthed him to her show-business and society friends. Slim remained very close with such former mutual friends as Bacall, Bogart, and Hemingway, whereas Hawks did not. When Slim had an affair in the mid-1950s with the writer Peter Viertel, she described Hawks to him as "a great pillar of nothing."

Setting Hawks further back in early 1956 was an accident on the slopes at Klosters. When Hawks took up skiing, Chris Nyby warned him to start on short skis and gradually work up to long ones. The proudly self-confident Hawks would have none of this and gamely used full-length skis from the outset. He got by with this for a couple of seasons. Lorrie Sherwood, who by now had become both secretary and girlfriend to John Huston and was working for him in Europe, by chance met Hawks skiing at Klosters that winter and said, "He was doing all right. He wasn't what I'd call a good skier; he was a good learner." His mishap had nothing to do with fast, reckless skiing down treacherous, steep runs. Rather, Hawks tripped up in slow, sloppy conditions near the bottom of the mountain, where people often don't pay close attention to what they're doing. Hawks broke his leg and was laid up at the Haus Am-Taoback for weeks, well into April. Feldman wagged his finger at him in a letter, saying, "Always told you to lay off those goddamn skis [sic]. It is for the 'young uns,' believe me, Howard." A month short of his sixtieth birthday, Hawks was forced to concur, and he willingly gave up his short-lived skiing career.

On his feet again, Hawks returned to the Hotel Raphael in Paris and, in May, filed suit against Warner Bros. for breach of contract, fraud, and deceit over the *Africa* project. Hawks claimed he was out of pocket $43,742 in payments for the screenplay and further demanded $136,000 for his fee and $1 million in "lost profits." The real bone of contention was the issue of Gary Cooper's script approval: Hawks maintained that the studio had deliberately withheld the information that Cooper had such rights "in order to induce and secure the plaintiff's agreement to the terms" of the contract. The suit was to sit in limbo for some time to come.

Through the spring and early summer, Hawks lived a gentleman's life of leisure. He socialized frequently with Charles Boyer and the recent Parisian transplant Preston Sturges and went to Longchamps racetrack with John Huston and Huston's friend the former jockey Billy Pierson. Huston, who didn't find Hawks to be his kind of boon companion but didn't mind his company, observed that Hawks seemed to place only moderate bets. When Billy Wilder came to town and joined Hawks for drinks at Hawks's hotel, Hawks boasted to Wilder about how he had just made $2 million on a lucky oil investment. Wilder knew from experience to take this with a grain of salt, and when Hawks excused himself, a member of the hotel staff approached Wilder and asked if he knew his companion very well. Wilder said he did, whereupon the hotel man explained that he was concerned only because Hawks had been at the hotel for more than a month now and had not paid for anything. Beneath his casual countenance, however, Hawks was highly agitated about his lack of a new project and insisted upon seeing Feldman every day and called him up to ten times a day. Feldman complained in a wire home, "I have been besieged daily by Hawks to extent I am going nuts!"

When it became evident that nothing was going to break soon, Hawks and his family again returned to the South of France for the summer, splitting their time between the exclusive Hotel de Paris in Monte Carlo and the Villa Loi et Moi in tony Saint-Jean-Cap-Ferrat. It was the usual round of golf for Hawks, Dee tanning by the pool or at the beach, cocktails and long dinners with whoever happened to be around, plus a rather loud little boy approaching his second birthday. One visitor reported frequently "hearing words" between the husband and wife, while another said it was clear that "Dee wanted more excitement" than she was getting sitting around the glamorous but languid pleasure capitals of Europe with a child in tow.

During one of Dee's trips to Los Angeles, Hawks met a woman who would remain in his life until he died. Hawks was at the Longchamps racetrack with a small group when one of his party, the actress-model Lise Boudin, saw a friend and asked her to join them. She was Chance de Widstedt, generally known just as Chance, a twenty-year-old Chanel model. Tall, slim, and with a natural look rather like Bacall's, Chance made an immediate impression on Hawks, and the feeling was mutual. Chance had never heard of Howard Hawks and had no idea who he was but found him "tall, handsome, very elegant, très chic, athletic, attentive." The fact that he was older was even a plus, "because I was attracted to a father figure. I'd had no father."

Quite taken with this stylish young beauty, Hawks took her out to dinner, always in the company of other people, two or three times in Paris. Although her limited English and his nonexistent French made communication difficult, Hawks found out that she was born in Clichy, just outside Paris, was raised by her maternal grandmother, had begun her working life at sixteen as a figure skater with the Bouglione Circus, and was rebaptized Chance by Ted Lapidus of Dior in the back of a taxi as they sped through the Place de la Concorde. At the time Hawks met her, Chance was on the verge of quitting modeling and launching a career as a photojournalist.

During the time they knew each other in Paris, Hawks did not come on to his elegant new friend. "He was too scrupulous for that. Hawks," Chance said, "was not the type of man to have affairs. Dee, from what I heard, did have affairs, but not Howard." Chance felt Hawks was too much of a gentleman to provoke something tacky. "He liked women, lots of them, but one after the other, not all at the same time. At least that's what I believe."

By the fall of 1956, Hawks was living at the Hotel Prince de Galles on Avenue Georges V, but with nothing clicking into place with projects in Europe, he began to feel it was time to return home. When he returned to California at year's end, Hawks had been away for just short of four years, during which time he had made one film, sired a son, entered the seventh decade of his life, had a good deal of fun, spent quite a bit of money, become acquainted with some of the French critics who would further promote his reputation over the next few years, and, toward the end, reassessed the kinds of movies he had been making recently and what he wanted to be doing.

34

Bravo

The home front looked markedly different when Howard Hawks returned to Los Angeles after nearly four years in Europe. Hog Canyon was no longer his, and he took up residence for a short time in an apartment hotel, the tastefully understated but far from luxurious Westwood Manor on Wilshire Boulevard, just a few blocks east of Westwood Village. The previous summer, his daughter Barbara, now twenty, had married Donald McCampbell, a gregarious, athletic man three years her senior. Barbara was a theater arts major at UCLA before she went to work for the writers Bill Orr, Jack Warner's son-in-law, and Hugh Benson at Warner Bros., while Don studied music before trying his hand at different fields. Hawks hadn't bothered to return for the wedding, but Barbara said, "Slim was wonderful to Don and me when we got married. She and Leland and Kitty were at my wedding, they invited us for dinner a lot, and they visited us at our apartment in Westwood when Carrie was born." Carrie Dane McCampbell, Hawks's first blood grandchild, was born on May 30, 1957, her grandfather's sixty-first birthday.

Kitty, now eleven, had spent much of the last few years in California but had entirely missed seeing her father because of his stay in Europe. Peter Hawks, who was working as a district manager for TWA at the San Francisco Airport and hadn't seen his adoptive father in years, already had three daughters, Jamin, Kate, and Celia. David, now twenty-seven, had been working as an engineer at Douglas Aircraft in Santa Monica since graduating from Princeton in 1952.

Professionally, Hawks was raring to go. His four-year layoff, he said, "sort of gave me a fresh attitude," and he was sure that the frustration built up over his several unrealized projects would be broken by his return. No sooner did he arrive than Feldman presented him with a tantalizing "adulterous comedy" that struck a particularly responsive chord in Hawks. The agent-producer had bought a play in Europe about a handsome rogue

547

whose ability to juggle a wife and mistress becomes more difficult when he meets a beautiful young woman. Feldman hired I. A. L. Diamond, who had just begun his collaboration with Billy Wilder on *Love in the Afternoon*, to write the script. Hawks liked it very much and had Diamond rewrite the lead for Feldman's client and their mutual friend, William Holden. Capucine, Feldman's new twenty-three-year-old French amour, would play the wife, Brigitte Bardot was proposed as the mistress, while it could be left to Hawks to make a new discovery for the girlfriend. The project, however, stalled while Holden, on location in Ceylon for *The Bridge on the River Kwai*, delayed making any future commitments, and Hawks's attention soon turned elsewhere.

One thing that surprised and impressed Hawks upon his return to the States was television. When he had left at the beginning of 1953, TV was mostly variety, comedy, and game shows supplemented by a measure of serious live drama. Now, prime time was dominated by filmed series, and it can't have escaped Hawks's attention that fully a third of them were Westerns, including the number-one show, *Gunsmoke*, starring his embarrassed "Thing," James Arness. Lots of good actors, both veterans and young, good-looking kids, were now appearing on television, and Hawks watched a lot of it to bring himself up-to-date. In fact, Westerns seemed so commonplace and unexceptional in 1958 that Jack Warner yawned when Hawks told him he wanted to do a Western for his return to the screen. The director told a journalist at the time, "I got bored and decided I might as well be doing what I know best." Although highly identified with the genre because of the success of *Red River* and his general demeanor, Hawks had only made two Westerns in his career to date; of the six films still ahead of him, however, half would be Westerns.

Famously, *Rio Bravo* was born out of Hawks's visceral abhorrence of Fred Zinnemann and Carl Foreman's highly acclaimed 1952 hit, *High Noon* (for which Hawks's friends Gary Cooper and Dimitri Tiomkin won Oscars), a simple tale of a middle-aged small-town sheriff who asks for help from the local citizenry when faced with the return of some revenge-minded criminals. The picture was also seen as a liberal political allegory for the McCarthy era (surprising, given the highly conservative Cooper's involvement), in which normal people are shown as being easily cowed and afraid to take action against intimidating tyrants. Hawks's objections were not aesthetic but deeply personal and, one could even say, ideological; the film ran counter to everything he believed in. As he put it, "I didn't think a good sheriff was going to go running around town like a chicken with his head off asking for help, and finally his Quaker wife had to save him." He decided to "do just the opposite, and take a real professional viewpoint: As Wayne says when he's offered help, 'If they're really good, I'll take them. If not, I'll just have to take care of them.' We did everything that way, the exact opposite of what annoyed me in *High Noon* and it worked, and people liked it."

Hawks was to have similar objections to another film, Delmer Daves's *3:10 to Yuma*, based on a story by Elmore Leonard, when it came out in August. In that one, as Hawks remembered it, "the sheriff caught a prisoner, and the prisoner taunted him and made him perspire and worry and everything by saying, 'Wait till my friends catch up with you.' And I said, 'That's a lot of nonsense, the sheriff would say, 'You better hope your friends *don't* catch up with you, 'cause you'll be the first man to die.'" Though Hawks's interpretation is off (the "sheriff" he spoke of was actually just an impoverished rancher, not a professional), *Rio Bravo* arose from Hawks's reaction *against* aspects of two popular Westerns of the period, which made it easy for him to create certain key scenes by just taking scenes he disliked and turning their attitudes upside down or inside out.

As it happened, John Wayne also hated *High Noon*, and the idea of working together again after more than a decade appealed enormously to both Hawks and the star; whatever animosity Wayne may have harbored over having had to sue Hawks to receive his full payment from their previous film had long since subsided. There was no actor in Hollywood busier or more popular than Wayne, but he had recently been in a bit of a slump; he hadn't appeared in a Western since Ford's *The Searchers* in 1956, and his four films in the interim had not measured up to the star's usual commercial standards. So perhaps a good Western was what both actor and director needed.

To write the script, Hawks turned to the two writers who, aside from Faulkner, he liked the best and trusted the most, Jules Furthman and Leigh Brackett, although he had worked with neither since *The Big Sleep* some twelve years before. Furthman, now seventy, had grown more cantankerous and disagreeable than ever and hadn't worked much since the early 1950s. For her part, Brackett had left Hollywood entirely, marrying the pioneer science-fiction writer Edmond Hamilton and moving to Kinsman, Ohio, where she turned out many sci-fi, fantasy, and mystery stories and novels, including the highly regarded *The Sword of Rhiannon* and *The Long Tomorrow*. When she returned in July 1957, taking an apartment above the beach at Ocean Avenue and Wilshire in Santa Monica, it was only because it was Hawks who asked. Even though they were credited together, along with Faulkner, on the script to *The Big Sleep*, Brackett had never met Furthman. Fortunately, she said, "We got on famously." The writing responsibilities were divided up, but not as they had been with Faulkner on *The Big Sleep*. On what was initially entitled *El Paso Red* and then briefly called *Bull by the Tail*, the two writers would huddle with Hawks for hours as the director offered up his ideas. As Brackett explained the process, "I was used to writing by myself, alone with my typewriter in a little room. Jules Furthman, on the other hand, just hated to put anything down on paper. So, in story conferences with Howard Hawks, Jules did most of the ball-carrying. He and Mr. Hawks would talk the scenes out, and I'd contribute as much as I could. . . . Basically, though, I would put down on paper the scenes that Mr. Hawks and Furthman had talked out, shape them, reshape them if necessary, and put them together, adding a few things of my own in the process." The two writers' pay scales were outrageously disproportionate: Furthman received $2,500 a week, while Brackett, who did the lion's share of the actual writing, got only $600 weekly.

The first written document pertaining to the film, dated August 3, 1957, a thirteen-page incomplete treatment, has virtually nothing to do with *Rio Bravo* as it ultimately emerged but bears every resemblance to a Western remake of *To Have and Have Not*. From this short sketch began the real work. Clicking now, Hawks, Brackett, and Furthman came up with a new story line in August and finished a preliminary draft before the end of September. They then went through it again, fleshing out characters, adding and strengthening scenes, and sharpening dialogue, until a 123-page first draft, signed by Brackett alone, was completed on November 13. In terms of the basic dramatic situation, centering on the efforts of a sheriff and his motley crew to hold a man prisoner in their small jail while under siege by an outlaw gang, the script was quite well along at this stage. The relationship of Sheriff John T. Chance, named after the beautiful French model Hawks had on his mind, and a gambler woman called Feathers, the name of the female lead in Sternberg's *Underworld*, was all there. But the central male relationship was very different from what finally ended up on-screen. The second lead here was a man named Jim Ryan, a hired gun whom the sheriff, initially wary, finally takes on. Ryan resembled a combination of the eventual Dude and Colorado characters; at the same time, in the way he makes those around him uncertain of his sympathies because of his tendency to go where the money is, Ryan recalls Bogart's Harry Morgan and prefigures John Wayne's Cole Thornton in *El Dorado*. As Hawks explained, "When we came to a certain place in *Rio Bravo*, we had our choice between going in this direction and going in that direction. But we made notes to remember, because we said, 'This is so good we can use it sometime.' We ended up with enough good notes to make another movie, so we made another movie." The final shootout, including the throwing of dynamite into the barn where Burdette's men are hiding, exists in this early version, although there is no exchange of prisoners by the two sides beforehand.

The dynamite lobbing was a bit of business that appeared in *Gunga Din*, so it is possible that Hawks, perhaps unconsciously, was stealing from himself. Officially, however, the idea came from Hawks's daughter Barbara, accounting for the on-screen story credit to B. H. McCampbell. As Barbara put it, her father "came back from Europe with a basic idea for a Western, but he didn't know how to resolve the story, to get them all out of jail." Barbara said she and Don worked out a long story with numerous situations for the characters to confront, but the Warner Bros. legal department never saw the "original McCampbell material," and the credit was based on an "unpublished story" without documentation.

The screenplay's last major transformation took place in December and January. In a script dated January 28, 1958, the Jim Ryan character has been jettisoned and replaced by Chance's broken-down former deputy Dude and Wheeler's hired hand, a young fast gun named Colorado who, in his mercenary ways, recalls John Ireland's Cherry Valance in *Red River*. Dude is described as "a small man, almost frail-looking," and was derived, as Feathers was, from Hawks's and Furthman's recollections of *Underworld*, in which the leading character helps to reform his drunken best friend. The opening scene is very different, with Dude, already a deputy, warning cattleman Wheeler about the danger represented by Burdette. The celebrated initial scene of a man in the saloon throwing a silver dollar into a spittoon to humiliate Dude, spurring Chance's defense of his pathetic friend, was written only at the moment of shooting in June (and was also lifted from *Underworld*). What's more, the famous low-angle shot of Chance looking down at a groveling Dude, plus the camera tilt that underlines the connection between the men, were indicated in the script, although it is impossible to know who was behind this rare insertion of camera instructions in a Hawks screenplay. A final draft was worked on through February to modify and refine certain elements, but Hawks was so pleased with the January version that he submitted it to the MPAA, which objected to the "excessive number of specified individualized killings" and the clear indication of "a sex affair" between Chance and Feathers. In response, Hawks promised to downplay the killings by cutting away and not dwelling on them and proposed ending the most direct romantic scene "on a comic note" rather than with an implication that sex was to follow.

The MPAA also objected to the following ending, in which Dude and Stumpy walk down the street at night while Chance and Feathers are upstairs in her hotel room:

STUMPY

Looks like our sheriff just switched from one trouble to another.

DUDE

He's good at trouble.

Hawks shot this finale, but the censors still didn't like it, so he substituted his alternate in the release version of the picture.

Up to and during the shoot, Hawks continued to make small changes, but they mainly consisted of tinkering, almost always for the better. The dialogue in the finished film is uniformly smarter, more assured, and insolent than that in the final screenplay, attesting to Hawks's continual vigilance in these matters, as well as his constant openness to others' ideas at all times.

Hawks's major contribution in the late phase of writing was devising the opening sequence to eliminate dialogue. The four-minute interlude establishes all the important plot dynamics: the pathetic Dude will do anything for a drink, Chance is still inclined to help his old friend, Joe Burdette kills an unarmed man, and the men are willing to stand alone against the Burdette gang to see justice served. It all seems simple, but that is its beauty; it is a reduction to the essence of filmmaking, to the basic tools and lessons of the silent cinema, a demonstration of total mastery so subtle and confident that the casual observer doesn't even notice it. It is the kind of artistry that would disappear from the Hollywood cinema over the next two decades as the directors with origins in the silent days faded out, and its elemental strength would never be recaptured. Hawks acknowledged that he deliberately withheld dialogue from the picture until it became absolutely necessary, as a way of "getting back" to the fundamentals from which he may have strayed. At the same time, he admitted that he was inspired to create this prologue by the way television shows hooked the viewer and established a basic dramatic situation through the use of opening teasers.

In trying to regain "a little of the spirit with which we used to make pictures," Hawks focused on a few principles. Since *The Big Sleep*, he had shown increasing disdain for the primacy of a linear, logical plot. He remained committed to the overarching importance of telling a story, but he had now come to prefer almost covertly telling a story through the desires and motivations of his characters. Hawks had been leaning in this direction for more than a decade—particularly in *Red River*, and *The Big Sky*—but now the arrival of television was pushing him further away from wanting to rely upon plot. Because of television, he reasoned, audiences were becoming tired of plots, making them feel that they've seen it all before. "But if you can keep them from knowing what the plot is you have a chance of holding their interest." This approach made the writing process more difficult, but also more challenging. It is from this perspective, then, that the remainder of Hawks's films should be viewed, to judge how well he accomplished this tricky task he set for himself; there is, after all, a fine line between the rigor of concealing a story within characterization and the laziness of not sufficiently developing a story line, and disagreement over which side of the line his late films fall on has persisted ever since they were made.

Hawks determined to inject comedy into his work when at all possible, something he felt was a hallmark of the movies' early days more than recently, when, as he said, "I think we got too serious about it." While in one sense Hawks was becoming more conservative by retreating to the traditional values of the silent cinema, finding solutions in his past work and comfort in established genres, in another he was becoming more daring in his narrative methods. When it worked perfectly, as in *Rio Bravo*, the result could easily and justifiably be called "classical." Subsequently, in *Hatari!*, he went so far in working without a net that it often looked radically modern, while when the elements didn't gel, as in *Man's Favorite Sport?* and *Red Line 7000*, his style simply looked stiff and archaic. In any case, it becomes clear that, in the final decade of Hawks's career, his greatest fun came from the challenge of devising fresh and inventive narrative strategies, the antidote to the conventional view that he was tiredly rehashing the same old stories.

Perhaps surprisingly, given the acrimonious dispute between Hawks and Jack Warner that provoked the director's lawsuit, there was never a question of this new project being made anywhere but at Warner Bros.; in fact, the film served as a way of settling the suit. Warner was not overly excited by the idea of Hawks doing a Western, but with John Wayne in the package he couldn't go too far wrong, and the prospect of Hawks shooting much of the picture on the soundstages in Burbank seemed like protection against the director's going too much over budget or schedule. Hawks set up a new company, Armada Productions, and the deal with Warner Bros.

stipulated for the dismissal of Hawks's breach of contract and fraud suit, the cancellation of the second picture under the old Continental Company deal with Warners, a budget for *Rio Bravo* of $1.95 million, and $100,000 up front to Hawks, with Warners and Armada splitting the profits fifty-fifty after distribution, production, and advertising costs. To settle the nagging matter of the money Hawks had invested in the *Africa* script, $50,000 of the *Rio Bravo* budget was slipped to Hawks in the guise of Continental.

The fact that the sheriff's character in the initial treatment was actually called John Wayne left no doubt as to who would play the role. Nonetheless, before Wayne signed, a list of eleven actors was prepared in case of unforeseen circumstances, including Gregory Peck, Kirk Douglas, Burt Lancaster, and Sterling Hayden, but it is impossible to imagine any of them playing Chance with anything approaching Wayne's authority.

The other parts were wide open, and the many possible alternate castings of Dude, Feathers, Colorado, and Stumpy provide fodder for endless speculation as to what *Rio Bravo* would have been like had other actors played the roles. Would there have been a painful, Brechtian second level of meaning to Dude's alcoholic torture if Hawks's first choice, Montgomery Clift, had played him? Possibly Clift recognized the character's trials as too close to home, or maybe he just didn't want to mix it up with Wayne and Hawks and the rest of the macho bunch again, but he turned it down. Ironically, he had just acted with Dean Martin in *The Young Lions*, and one can only wonder if a hit on the order of *Rio Bravo* would have helped turn his career and life around in any way.

In all events, Hawks then made a list of nineteen potential actors for Dude, and Martin was not among them. Heading the list, in fact, was Frank Sinatra; others included James Cagney, John Cassavetes, Richard Widmark, Edmund O'Brien, Rod Steiger, and, surprisingly, John Ireland; a subsequent list also included Robert Mitchum, Spencer Tracy, Tony Curtis, Lancaster, Douglas, Glenn Ford, William Holden, Henry Fonda, Van Johnson, Ray Milland, and, most intriguingly, Cary Grant. Jack Warner was all in favor of Cagney, but Hawks, despite his great regard for his long-ago leading man, remained undecided. When Dean Martin's agent urged Hawks to meet his client, Hawks agreed, provided Martin would meet him in his office early the next morning. Martin turned up looking bedraggled; he apologized, explaining that he was working in Las Vegas and had had to get up early, charter a plane, and fly down for the meeting. This effort made a big impression on Hawks, who hired him on the spot. "I *knew* that if he'd do all that, he'd work hard and I knew that if he'd work hard we'd have no trouble because he's such a personality." Hawks sent the actor down to wardrobe, which outfitted him like "a musical comedy cowboy," whereupon Hawks instructed him to go back and get something that made him look like a real drunk. He did, finding the outfit he wore in the film.

For the hired gun Colorado, originally envisioned as an older man, Hawks first considered twenty-one possibilities, including Mitchum, James Garner, Jack Lemmon, Tony Curtis, Lee Marvin, Lloyd Bridges, Chuck Connors, and Jack Palance. By March, having reconceived the role as much younger, he was looking into such pretty-boy candidates as Michael Landon, Rod Taylor, and Stuart Whitman, and the football player Frank Gifford. But then Hawks had a brainstorm. He had known the former bandleader Ozzie Nelson for some time, and at that moment, *The Adventures of Ozzie and Harriet*, the family show starring the Nelson parents and their two sons, was at the peak of its popularity. Over the previous year, the younger son, seventeen-year-old Ricky, had also become a rock 'n' roll singing sensation; after the box-office muscle Elvis Presley had recently demonstrated, it seemed logical that Nelson might have similar pull. Hawks asked Ozzie to send over the most recent episodes, liked what he saw, and signed the boy up, even though Ozzie was demanding $150,000, an astronomical fee for a virtual screen newcomer.

Although, like Chance, the role of ornery old Stumpy seemed conceived for one actor and one actor alone, there were many initial candidates for it, including Arthur Hunnicutt, Gabby Hayes, Burl Ives, William Demarest, Lee Marvin, Buddy Ebsen, and Lee J. Cobb. But it was no surprise when the part went to Walter Brennan, who, like Ricky Nelson, was now a big TV star because of the downhome program *The Real McCoys*, which was just finishing its first season.

Feathers, of course, was the plum, a perfect role for Hawks to fill with a terrific new actress. All the same, Hawks had been away for four years, had no American actresses under contract, and didn't have enough time to look around and then tutor a complete novice. Therefore, his list of contenders was dotted with actresses who had been around for a while, in addition to the up-and-comers: Rhonda Fleming, Jane Greer, Martha Hyer, Mari Blanchard, Diane Brewster, Beverly Garland, Carolyn Jones, Piper Laurie, Julie London, Sheree North, Janis Paige, and TV star Donna Reed were initially considered.

Then someone new was brought to Hawks's attention. For months, Chris Nyby kept telling Hawks about a great-looking young actress he had twice directed on television. Finally, Hawks watched Angie Dickinson in a

Nyby *Perry Mason* episode and immediately had her come see him. He may also have been spurred on by John Wayne, who had recently made a cameo appearance in the innocuous comedy *I Married a Woman*, with Dickinson as his wife. She had also costarred opposite James Arness in the minor 1956 Western, *Gun the Man Down*, produced by Wayne's company, Batjac. The twenty-six-year-old beauty from North Dakota, who had appeared unremarkably in a handful of films since breaking in in 1954, came in for several meetings with Hawks before shooting a test in which Frank Gifford played John Chance. The test went well, but Dickinson never believed she had a chance against Capucine, Charles Feldman's protégée and girlfriend. But Capucine's French accent was too heavy, so Hawks gave Dickinson the good news. Dee told her husband that she was surprised at his choice, and he said, "Good. I'm glad you're surprised." According to Dickinson, "He wanted something different."

Enthusing to Hawks about having gotten the part, Dickinson confided to him, "I'd always been told, if I could do a picture with George Cukor or Howard Hawks, I'd be in clover." Hawks said, "Do you know why that is? It's because we do all your thinking for you." The lean, leggy actress recalled, "Hawks said, 'You've got a pretty good figure, but it could be better.' So I got into pretty good shape for the movie. But that was an order." Hawks and Dickinson also discussed changing her name. Challenged by Hawks to come up with something, Dickinson agonized over it for some time. "I came up with one name," she said. "I wrote it down, I couldn't speak it to him. So I gave him a slip of paper with the name on it: Anna Rome. Howard said, 'I like your own name better.'" To get the part, Dickinson had to sign a personal contract with Armada, which Hawks then split with Warner Bros.; it also gave John Wayne the right to borrow her for one picture and specified Bill Hawks and Chris Nyby as "preferred borrowers." So while it can't truly be said that Howard Hawks discovered Angie Dickinson, he certainly gave her her big chance.

Although it is easy to overlook in retrospect, the cast of *Rio Bravo* was filled out with television performers to a remarkable degree; given the box-office calculation involved in the casting of Ricky Nelson, this can only have been deliberate on Hawks's part. Ward Bond, who played the cattleman Wheeler, had to squeeze his work in between episodes of *Wagon Train*, then one of the most popular shows on TV. John Russell, the veteran character actor who portrayed Nathan Burdette, had just completed the pilot to the eventual successful series *Lawman* when he reported to Hawks. Pedro Gonzalez-Gonzalez, who appeared as the Mexican hotel proprietor, had become famous a couple of years before on Groucho Marx's *You Bet Your Life*, and Estelita Rodriguez, who played his wife, was a Cuban-born night-club singer.

Hawks called on numerous familiar faces to fill out the crew: the increasingly invaluable Paul Helmick came on as assistant director, Russell Harlan would man the camera (both for exteriors and interiors this time), and Meta Carpenter Rebner, now one of the leading and most senior women in her field, was back as script supervisor after not having worked for Hawks in well over a decade. As usual, Hawks decided to shoot the exteriors first and in March went with John Wayne to Arizona to check out the facilities in Old Tucson, a replica of the original walled city of Tucson built in 1940 by Columbia for the film *Arizona*. Uninterested in scenic splendors for a story essentially confined to a single street, Hawks found everything he needed here but didn't want the setting to resemble what had by then appeared in numerous other films, so he had the art director, Leo K. (Kay) Kuter, spend five weeks and $100,000 building a new main street about four blocks long. Ultimately, Hawks found Old Tucson so congenial that he returned for *El Dorado* and *Rio Lobo*.

A longtime mystery for Western buffs has centered on the whereabouts of Harry Carey Jr. in *Rio Bravo*, billed eleventh as a man named Harold, but no one has ever been able to spot him in the picture. Carey explained, "I really messed myself up with him. I was a full-fledged drinker when they called me over to do *Rio Bravo*. It would have been a ten-week job for me." Cast as one of the local citizens whose help Wayne's sheriff refuses in fighting off Burdette's men, Carey arrived in Tucson for the beginning of shooting and met with Hawks and Wayne to do a costume check and rehearse his first scene. "I was in a cowboy outfit, and Hawks said, 'I don't think I want Doby in a cowboy outfit. I want him as a townsperson in a top hat.' I left for a while and went back to the hotel and had three or four shots of vodka. I was feeling good, and I went back to rehearse the scene with Wayne. I had on a purple-colored cowboy hat, and Duke said, 'Where'd you get that hat? It's a good thing we're just rehearsing.' Hawks said, 'Okay, you get a new hat and we'll shoot that tomorrow,' and I said, 'Okay, Howard,' and I went off. And as I was getting in the car, I heard Duke say, in a very pronounced way, 'Well, Mr. Hawks . . . ,' and I felt awful. It was the only time I called him Howard and it screwed me up with him."

Carey's character was pared down to two shooting days, with Wayne's dialogue rewritten to say, "We can handle it. Besides, you have a wife and kids." The scene, along with Carey's role, was later dropped from the pic-

ture, although the actor's billing was retained. Harold is never referred to
by name, but Chance does glancingly refer to local men with "wife and
kids" who would be of no use to him in the stand-off. As Carey pointed out,
the *Rio Bravo* cast was full of big drinkers, led by Wayne, Dean Martin,
and Ward Bond, which Hawks didn't mind as long as it didn't affect their
work. Carey's familiarity with Hawks probably would have been excused, had
it not demonstrated that his drinking could adversely affect his judgment.

Carey quit drinking in 1963 and had his last contact with Hawks in
1976, when Hawks lent Carey a print of *Red River* for a show for schools
about Wayne and John Ford. "He was a strange man, but he treated me
like a million bucks," Carey said, despite the Tucson rupture.

The cast and crew of ninety-one people headed for Arizona in late
April, with most staying at the Santa Rita Hotel in Tucson, and filming began
on the planned fifty-five-day shoot on May 1 with scenes of Wheeler and
the rest of his men, including Colorado, arriving in town. The only actor
who needed any special preparation for his role was Ricky Nelson. Hawks
assigned his daughter Barbara, an expert horsewoman, the job of teaching
the teenage idol how to look good in the saddle, even though the riding he
had to do in the film was very rudimentary. Realizing that Nelson had no
special skills as an actor, Hawks decided to give him something to do with
his hands, notably rubbing the side of his nose with his index finger to show
he was thinking, as Clift had done in *Red River*. The director also forced
him to roll and smoke cigarettes, which Nelson hated. Ironically, Hawks
himself was off cigarettes at the time, in his umpteenth attempt to give them
up, and he told Angie Dickinson, "Everybody hates me because I'm so
impossible when I'm trying to quit." Hawks was skating on thin ice handing such a prominent role to someone so inexperienced, and he just got by
thanks to the terse dialogue and his own skill at directing young performers
(usually women) to project an insolence more left unspoken than said. Also,
the film was so strongly carried by the four other leads that it didn't particularly need support from Nelson the way *Red River* relied upon Clift or even
the way *El Dorado* derived comic mileage from the relative newcomer James
Caan. On May 8, Nelson's eighteenth birthday, Wayne and Martin gave
him a gift of a three-hundred-pound bag of steer manure, then, as a rite of
passage, tossed him into it.

Nelson's awkwardness is evident in the stiff, posed way he stands and
his not knowing what to do with his hands, but Hawks felt Nelson did well
enough in the picture and was convinced that his presence added enormously to its box-office draw. They did have a major disagreement, how-

ever, over what songs Nelson would perform on-screen. Disliking Dimitri Tiomkin and Paul Francis Webster's tune "My Rifle, My Pony, and Me," Nelson wanted to use a number Johnny Cash had written for him, "Restless Kid." Nelson recorded the Cash number as well as another song, "Cindy," at Capitol Records, but only the latter made it into the film, as Hawks, Tiomkin, and even Ozzie Nelson joined forces and prevailed upon the kid to see things their way. Dean Martin ended up singing "My Rifle" with a little harmonizing from Nelson. Hawks's decision to have Nelson and Martin sing in the film has often been ridiculed, but Hawks tossed off the objections simply by saying that the crooning "entertained me." Hawks also had a song in mind for Feathers, a tune called "The Bull by the Tail" (one of the film's earlier titles). But when he played it for Angie Dickinson, "I had the balls to tell him I didn't like it," she recalled. "He said, 'Everybody "yesses" me all the time,' and I think he was impressed that I told him what I thought."

With the script long since in very fine shape and the majority of the cast and crew utterly in its element, the production proceeded in a very relaxed, smooth manner. From the beginning, Hawks needed very few takes to get what he wanted, often just one. Unlike on *Land of the Pharaohs*, he knew just how all these characters should talk, but he obliged Wayne, Brennan, and the others when they wanted to alter their dialogue a bit to make themselves more comfortable. He let scenes run to indulge his whims and tastes, such as showing Wayne make a long approach toward Ward Bond just because he liked the star's inimitable "big cat" walk. Hawks needed to give Wayne only the minimum indication of how he wanted a scene to be played, and the actor always came on time, prepared and able to memorize new dialogue within minutes. Even more than he had twelve years earlier, Hawks loved working with Wayne. "He never squawks about anything," the director said. In the role of John T. Chance, Wayne wore his customary neckerchief and the Red River D belt buckle Hawks had made for him. Through most of the story, he also carried with him, almost as if it was part of his anatomy, the unique pump-action rifle he had first used in *Hondo*.

Hawks was pleased when Dean Martin justified his faith in him. As he later did with Robert Mitchum, Hawks saw through the actor's nonchalance and could tell that he really was taking his work seriously. Martin privately was advised by his *Young Lions* costar Marlon Brando on how to get to the bottom of his character, and Hawks gave the actor some critical direction that set him unerringly on track: initially afraid that Martin was going to do a sort of "nightclub drunk," Hawks told him he "knew a guy with a hangover who'd pound his leg trying to hurt himself to try and get some feeling in it." Martin said he knew exactly what Hawks was talking about and did it right the next time out, without even rehearsing. Making things considerably easier was Wayne, who, as usual, was generous with his costar. The two men warmed to each other at once, played chess together constantly between scenes, and remained lifelong friends. Hawks was impressed with how hard Martin worked and ended up considering him "a damn good actor, but he also is a fellow who floats through life. . . . He has to get some kind of a hint, . . . otherwise, hell, he won't even rehearse."

Surprisingly, the only actor Hawks had any trouble with at all was Walter Brennan, whose work for him had always been pure gold. On the first day, Hawks found the character actor, who was now sixty-three, merely recycling his hokey folksiness from *The Real McCoys*. The director rode him mercilessly until he finally left the set with John Wayne. When they returned, Brennan was so riled that he easily delivered the "crabby, evil, nasty old man" Hawks was looking for, albeit with an irrepressible vein of eccentric humor.

But Hawks needed to engage in very little of this sort of scene-making. As John Russell observed, "Hawks's game-playing was mostly with management, not on the set. He loved getting management steamed." As always, studio brass were not welcome on the set, and Hawks ran a disciplined but relaxed set that allowed for plenty of extracurricular activities. One weekend, Hawks, Wayne, and the entire inner circle drove across the border to Nogales to watch their director friend Budd Boetticher film a bullfight for a documentary. The director hoped to get shots of Wayne with the great matador Carlos Arruza in the ring for a nice publicity angle, but when Duke went out and doffed his hat to the crowd, he was, as Boetticher put it, "as bald as Eisenhower"; Wayne had spent the entire weekend so plastered that he'd forgotten to put on his hairpiece. No one else minded, however, as people seemed only to care about seeing Ricky Nelson, who drove the crowd into a frenzy. John Ford, fresh from finishing *The Last Hurrah*, dropped by the location on May 19 to see how the Duke was faring with Hawks this time out. Unbeknownst to Warner Bros., Ricky Nelson took part in a Tucson Speedway stock-car race the following week, and Hawks even allowed Sheb Wooley, of "Purple People Eater" fame, to play a bit in the opening scene. Dean Martin took off for New York one weekend to participate in his second annual telethon for the City of Hope. Dee and Gregg were around a good deal, and Hawks found time to help his son with some midget-car races. Visiting journalists, of whom there were quite a few, noted that *Rio Bravo* was a real "Big Guy" film: Wayne and John Russell were six foot four, Hawks and Ward Bond were six three, Ricky Nelson was six one, and Dean Martin was six feet.

The only consistent complaint made about *Rio Bravo* is that it dawdles in its storytelling, that it lacks the economy and snap of Hawks's best earlier films. But while this was to become a legitimate problem in some of his later films, with *Rio Bravo* the lingering over scenes stemmed directly from Hawks's desire to elaborate his characters and their relationships as fully as he could. Any rewriting Hawks did on the set was to deepen the sense of group interaction, to give further layers to their exchanges; to most people's minds, the resulting richness far outweighs the picture's casual tempo. For example, Hawks often used the exchange of inanimate objects, notably cigarettes, to communicate feelings between his characters. John Chance's continual rolling of cigarettes for Dude silently conveyed his willingness to keep helping his friend. At the same time, it is Chance's need for a light that prompts Colorado to go into the hotel, thus leaving the sheriff alone and vulnerable to the three gunmen who stick him up. After losing track of it in recent years, Hawks rediscovered his "three-cushioned dialogue" that stated important matters in indirect ways, especially in the relationship between Chance and Feathers.

Indeed, Hawks hadn't attempted one of his patented sultry girls-with-a-past roles in well over a decade, and he clearly was stimulated by doing so again. Unlike numerous other films, there could be no pretense here of trying to integrate the female character into the men's central activity, that of guarding the jail. John Chance literally has to commute between the jail, at one end of the street, and the hotel, at the other, to see Feathers. Once again, the woman is a vague combination of showgirl, gambler, and quasi-outlaw-prostitute, someone who has clearly been around but simultaneously can fall wholeheartedly and uncynically for the hero.

In Angie Dickinson, Hawks found one of the sexiest actresses who ever starred in one of his films, and he made sure to show her off to tantalizing advantage. Hawks personally supervised every detail of Dickinson's wardrobe, as, the actress said, "he wanted the clothes to be not the typical stiff things women from that time usually wore. He wanted soft, flowing, feminine clothes." The trick was to be able to play up Dickinson's allure while still pairing her convincingly with Wayne, who almost always seemed a bit awkward, even comical, in romantic scenes. Hawks pulled this off by teasing Wayne through the Feathers character, making knowing fun of the actor's discomfort by building it into the character. This proved so effective here that Hawks carried it to an even greater extreme in *Hatari!* As he had in *Red River*, Hawks again served up a watered-down variation on Bacall's immortal "It's even better when you help" line when Feathers, upon finally kissing Chance, says, "I'm glad we tried it a second time. It's better when two people do it." But her comic exasperation works beautifully, compared, for instance, to Joanne Dru's protestations in *Red River*, and she is given one key scene—throwing a flowerpot through the window when an unarmed Chance is threatened by three badmen, saving the sheriff's neck.

By the time Dickinson reported for her first day of work on May 19, temperatures coincidentally started to rise on location, hitting well over one hundred degrees on most days from that point on. Dickinson was only in Tucson for nine working days, as virtually all of her scenes were interiors; in the finished film, her only exterior is at the end of the flowerpot scene. Her first night there, she was given a rite of passage by the men. "They had me join them for dinner," she recounted, "and they cast me as the victim by trying me out on mountain oysters, and I loved them. So I passed." As a fabulously sexy woman on location with a virtually all-male cast and crew, Dickinson was obviously highly conspicuous. But it didn't bother Dickinson because the situation was essentially the norm in those days. "All films were like that, you rarely had many women around. Wardrobe and hair people were the only women. But it didn't ever bother me. I was just so thrilled to be a part of it." Dickinson spent most of her time on the set with Ricky Nelson, just sort of wandering around the desert location. As far as her feelings for Hawks were concerned, she said, "I felt intimidated and comfortable at the same time. Intimidated, but only properly so, respectfully. After all, he's the big boss. I wasn't afraid."

Still, Dickinson wasn't pleased with her first day of work, on an introductory scene of her character getting off the stage, which didn't make it into the film. "I hated my costume and I was intimidated in the acting because I felt I didn't look good. It was a very tough first day, with five or six takes of every shot. I just thought the laugh Howard wanted me to do was out of character. I have such a hearty laugh." She gradually learned that Hawks wasn't about to act things out for her. "He didn't want to show me how to do it. If he showed me what he wanted, it wouldn't be my own original approach. He was looking for me to be original. It made it tough because you didn't know what he wanted. . . . When he liked something, the most he would do was smile and nod his head. It was difficult and frustrating, but a thrill." Dickinson added, "I think he liked me, but I don't think he had a thing for me. I was so hung up on the fella I was with that I wouldn't have noticed." In general, Dickinson described Hawks personally as "pleasant and polite, but not overly friendly" with her. But as a director, she felt he was "subtle and classy."

For the climactic scene of Burdette's men being blown out of the barn with dynamite, the art director, Kay Kuter, put lots of colored paper inside to intensify the look of the explosion, but when the place blew on the first try, all the flying colors made it look, in Hawks's words, "like a big Chinese firecracker. We all started to laugh." Kuter had to rebuild the entire structure for a retake, which went according to plan.

On May 28, the company finished work in Tucson after twenty-four days—on schedule, something unheard of for Hawks. Shooting resumed in the jail set on Warner Bros. stage four in Burbank on June 2. For the next seven and a half weeks, filming proceeded in quiet, surefooted, good-natured fashion, which vastly enhanced the profoundly lovable nature of the picture; faced with the evidence on the screen, it is inconceivable that a film such as Rio Bravo could have resulted from an unhappy, stressful, strife-ridden shoot.

Now that they were back in the studio, concentrating on the more intimate scenes between handfuls of people, Hawks encouraged the actors more than ever to contribute, asking what they thought their characters would do in given situations. Brennan was the most adept at this, while Wayne was best when his lines were set and he could place the full force of his personality behind them. Hawks continued to rewrite and rearrange dialogue, often with the help of the ever-present Furthman, but not in significant ways, and he only rarely made more than two or three takes of any given shot, so assured were he, his actors, and his crew. A couple of exceptions were two key scenes with Wayne and Dickinson. Hawks found the scene in which Chance tells Feathers she has to leave town particularly difficult to stage, and Wayne had a lot of trouble with it as well; Hawks actually favors Dickinson considerably in the cutting, covering up Wayne's rare uncertain work in the scene. The final scene, in which Feathers interprets Chance's threat to arrest her as his way of saying he loves her, was also a big problem, and Hawks had the actors try it four or five different ways. Dickinson recalled, "Finally, Howard said, 'This time, half-way through, why don't you start crying?' So, with no preparation, we did it that way and that was the one we used." When filming was completed on July 23 in sixty-one days, Hawks was, amazingly, only six days over schedule.

Not holding his participation in *High Noon* against him, Hawks brought Dimitri Tiomkin in to write the score, which included the song for Ricky Nelson as well as one Dean Martin sings in jail. Most memorable, however, was "De Guello," the haunting theme for trumpet that was supposedly played by General Santa Ana's men at the Alamo and that Joe Burdette uses to spook Chance and his crew. The profoundly beautiful refrain is heard softly in the background at night and certainly sounds as though it could be authentic. Surprisingly, Tiomkin made it up when Hawks decided that the actual song was terribly banal. John Wayne liked it so much that he appropriated it for *The Alamo.*

Folmar Blangsted, the editor, got a rough cut assembled in less than three weeks, and the first screening in August convinced everyone at Warner Bros. that they had a big hit on their hands. Although the film was ready for release by late 1958, the studio decided to hold it back until March 18 of the following year, when it opened at the Roxy in New York City. Two days later, it took the country by storm, snaring the number-one spot nationally in its first week of release with giant numbers almost everywhere. It then lodged at number two for two weeks, behind *Some Like It Hot,* and enjoyed a sustained life through the spring. By the time it was done, *Rio Bravo* amassed rentals of $5.2 million, making it the tenth biggest box-office film of 1959 and the second highest earner of Hawks's career, after *Sergeant York.* It also did enormous business overseas, where Ricky Nelson was extraordinarily popular.

It almost goes without saying that *Rio Bravo* was not perceived as a serious piece of work at the time of its release. Even when they were directed by John Ford, John Wayne Westerns were only grudgingly praised by the critics of the time, for whom lofty intentions and aspirations counted for much more than storytelling talent and mise-en-scène. If a filmmaker then threw the likes of Dean Martin and Ricky Nelson into the mix, there was simply no hope that the film would be taken as anything other than an efficient popular entertainment. Besides, when was the last time Hawks had tackled material that was challenging or reputable? Since World War II, he had seen fit to do a mystery, a couple of Westerns and comedies, a musical and a quasimusical, a science-fiction cheapie, and a lousy epic. In the literary-oriented critics' minds, the last time Hawks had tackled truly ambitious subject matter was *Sergeant York* and, perhaps, *Air Force.* Moreover, Hawks's interests seemed to have gotten more generic and trivial since the war, while Oscar favorites such as George Stevens and William Wyler had become more brooding and deliberate.

All of this may help explain why Hawks, by the mid-1950s, had been relegated to the second tier of Hollywood filmmakers by much of the establishment, and why his reputation was in need of resuscitation by critics and buffs in the 1960s. Despite his track record and the absolute control he exercised over his projects, Hawks was viewed as being closer to the level of Michael Curtiz or William Wellman, fine directors who nonetheless worked mostly on assignment, than to the most respected figures of the moment, such supposedly finicky and meticulous filmmakers as Wyler, Zinnemann, Stevens, or Kazan. *Rio Bravo*, for instance, was not nominated for a single Academy Award, but the following year, even Wayne's rambling, verbose, undeniably deeply felt *The Alamo* was nominated for seven. *The Alamo* got attention partly because of Wayne's personal popularity but more because it was a grand, self-important picture that was "about" something bigger than just another Western standoff.

It is safe to say that very few people in the United States in 1959 looked at *Rio Bravo* within the context of Howard Hawks's entire career. Not long after, however, Peter Bogdanovich had the insight to observe that John Wayne's character in the picture was an extension of the roles played by Cary Grant in *Only Angels Have Wings* and Humphrey Bogart in *To Have and Have Not*, which suggested that there lurked within Hawks's work some consistencies, themes, motifs, and preoccupations that had previously gone undetected. It was a number of years, though, until the image of *Rio Bravo* was transformed from "one of the better class oaters of the year," as *Variety* called it at the time, into a film about which Robin Wood could say, "If I were asked to choose a film that would justify the existence of Hollywood, I think it would be *Rio Bravo*." Even for those unwilling to go that far, the film fully justifies serious appreciation of Hawks, since it represents the most detailed and elegant expression of his typical concerns—self-respect, self-control, the interdependence of select chosen friends, being good at what you do, the blossoming of sexual-romantic attraction—as demonstrated by characters utterly removed from the norms of routine existence. The Hemingway imperative of grace under pressure could not be rendered more perfectly, and the stoicism is shot through with fun, a full statement of a philosophy of life by a man whose instinctive but deeply thoughtful artistry lay in his seasoned ability to use a highly collaborative shooting process to his own ends.

Rio Bravo is also, of course, Hawks's consummate "boy's fantasy," fitting snugly with Hollywood mythmaking and escapism, which is what has helped make the film so enduringly appealing, especially to young men.

And while many films that one loves as a teenager reveal their shallowness later on, *Rio Bravo* ultimately shows itself to be an exceedingly mature film within the trappings of an adolescent adventure; *Rio Bravo* is Hawks's most resolved film in the sense that it is a thorough expression of the man, without any tension whatever among its narrative, genre, personal, and commercial ambitions. As Jean-Luc Godard put it, *Rio Bravo* "is a work of extraordinary psychological insight and aesthetic perception, but Hawks has made his film so that the insight can pass unnoticed. . . . Hawks is the greater because he has succeeded in fitting all that he holds most dear into a well-worn subject."

Robin Wood's analysis of Hawks's masterpiece still stands as a model of film criticism and exhibits as deep an understanding of, and appreciation for, what Hawks was all about as has ever been written. Not surprisingly, the film's richness has drawn out the best in numerous critics and scholars. While noting the exclusion of women from the atmosphere she found "clubby and reassuring in the male enclosure," Molly Haskell described it as "a movie one loves and returns to as to an old friend." Jean-Pierre Coursodon, in his book *American Directors*, found it "an all but perfect movie." Describing it as "rigorously abstract," Greg Ford confirmed the film's position as "the consummate working epitome of Hawks's most talked-about overview-blueprint for movies." Among the current generation of working filmmakers, *Rio Bravo* stands among the greatest of all movies: John Carpenter essentially remade it as *Assault on Precinct 13*, and Martin Scorsese excerpted it in his first film.

Ironically, while making so mellow and confident a film, both Wayne and Hawks were losing a grip on their marriages. Dependent on prescription drugs and alcohol, Wayne's wife, Pilar, sank into a deep depression with which Wayne was completely unprepared to deal. In September 1958, the couple separated, and soon thereafter, while Wayne was making *The Horse Soldiers*, Pilar attempted suicide. They eventually patched things up and remained married another fifteen years, but the period during *Rio Bravo* represented a low point in their relationship.

As for Hawks, his keen interest in Gregg was unlike anything he had shown in any of his previous children. Despite his age, Hawks displayed an enthusiasm for and an engagement in his young son that far surpassed the energy he was devoting to Dee. Various friends, notably Chris Nyby, suggested that Hawks's libido, low to begin with, all but vanished after Gregg's birth. Dee, barely thirty, certainly didn't feel like spending the next twenty years watching her husband slip into dotage. By 1958, it was clear that the marriage was beginning to gasp. Although Dee and Gregg temporarily continued to live with Hawks at the house at 914 North Roxbury Drive in Beverly Hills, they officially separated on September 15 of the following year, and Dee filed for divorce two weeks later, citing unspecified mental and physical cruelty. In her complaint, Dee listed among their holdings 13,924 shares of Lafitte, property at 930 Stradella Avenue in Los Angeles, as well as the house and a vacant lot in Palm Springs, several stories and screenplays, a Rolls-Royce, a Ford station wagon, a Thunderbird, a deposit on a Porsche, and interests in Hawks's various film companies. As of June 1959, she stated that they had $49,817.74 in the bank, whereas by August all of their accounts showed deficits because during the summer Hawks spent $74,000, including $20,000 on a racehorse. Dee also contended that in 1956 Hawks hid $85,000 "some place in Europe" and mentioned other expenses that were never accounted for.

While the divorce and disposition of their community property was being adjudicated, Hawks was ordered to pay Dee $3,450 per month. Dee and Gregg temporarily moved to New York City in April 1960, and when a settlement was finally reached in 1963, Dee got custody of Gregg, 37.5 percent of Armada Productions (that is, of Hawks's share of the *Rio Bravo* profits), the property on Stradella and the lot in Palm Springs, some furniture, and the Thunderbird. Hawks was also obliged to pay $500 a month in child support. After all of this, Hawks and Dee remained on good terms. Barbara said, "They became much better friends after they split up," and Hawks even gave Dee a small part in *Red Line 7000*.

Even before *Rio Bravo* wrapped, the word was around town that Hawks was back in a big way. In July 1958, he turned down an urgent request from Universal to quickly take on a Western called *Viva Gringo*, in which Kirk Douglas and Rock Hudson had agreed to star, and was also paged by Burt Lancaster and his partner Harold Hecht to direct a version of A. B. Guthrie's Pulitzer Prize–winning follow-up to *The Big Sky*, *The Way West*, which Hecht had to wait eight years to get made. Despite his stated objections to the wide-screen format, Hawks initiated plans to next team up with John Wayne on a big production in Cinemiracle, a new three-camera process akin to Cinerama that was first used on the semidocumentary adventure film *Windjammer*. At first they considered doing a Western, and subsequently discussed *Africa* for the format. When Cinemiracle didn't catch on, Hawks and Cinerama executives began months of talks; Hawks eventually passed because the heavy equipment wasn't portable enough for the mobile, spontaneous shooting needed for the animal-chasing scenes.

For some time, especially after the disappointment on *Africa*, Hawks had been feeling that Feldman wasn't doing a whole lot for him. Feldman himself was spending the majority of his time on his own pictures, and Hawks began to notice that the vast majority of projects his friend offered him were those he personally owned. Hawks, with some justification, felt that Famous Artists hadn't done much for him lately, that he wasn't being offered the best material, and that the deals he made, he basically made himself. But it wasn't Feldman's fault that *Land of the Pharaohs* flopped or that Hawks turned down *The Bridge on the River Kwai*. Pointing out to his longtime client that he had "the best deal in the business," Feldman nonetheless tried to placate Hawks by helping him with his continuing financial and tax problems by setting up a Swiss corporation in which he could stash some of his money.

Hawks and Feldman continued to socialize constantly. They spent New Year's 1958–59 and much of the winter in Palm Springs, where the season's crowd included William Holden, Sam Goldwyn, Buddy Adler, Sam Briskin, and Mervyn LeRoy, and their wives. Feldman also had some private tête-à-têtes with Dee, no doubt partly about the Hawkses' failing marriage. Hawks had bought land on Stevens Road in Palm Springs years before and had actually started construction on his own home there before leaving for Europe. Now he pushed ahead to complete the job, giving him a place in the desert he so loved.

In the wake of *Rio Bravo*, Warners gave Hawks the green light on a second Western. Hawks found a novel by Steve Franzee, *Desert Guns*, that he thought could be combined with elements of two of the writer's other stories, "Singing Sands" and "The Devil's Grubstake," to strong effect into one film. The director once again brought Leigh Brackett out from Ohio, and Feldman negotiated a new two-picture deal at Warner Bros., under which Hawks would receive $150,000 for the new screenplay, $250,000 as producer-director of each film, and 10 percent of the net profits—a deal, in other words, that gave him considerably more up-front cash but a significantly reduced percentage.

Brackett turned out a good script, peppered with lively dialogue, but Hawks dragged his feet in getting it moving; his real interest remained his great African adventure. In a meeting at the end of September 1959, Hawks and Feldman frankly told Jack Warner that they wanted to abandon *Gold of the Seven Saints*, as they were calling the Western, and proceed with something else, preferably *Africa*. Warner repeated his overwhelming lack of enthusiasm for that project and countered with a couple of properties the studio already owned, William Inge's hit play *The Dark at the Top of the Stairs* and something called *The Saga of Pappy Gunn*.

Thereafter came several weeks of secret skirmishing, mutual suspicion, and growing bad blood, culminating in a blowup that severed Hawks's forty-year relationship with Warner once and for all. Given Warner's lack of interest in *Africa*, Famous Artists started shopping it around town, with Paramount and Fox the first to bite. In early November, Warner got wind of this and fired off an angry letter to Feldman: "You are up to your old tricks again! Instead of working on the story both you and Howard promised would arrive here on October 30 you are selling Hawks to other studios. . . . [This] is uncalled for, unwarranted, unnecessary and unbusinesslike, and also unethical."

With Feldman out of town, one of his agents, Jack Gordean, responded, stating that Famous Artists had done nothing out of line, that Hawks's deal with Warners was nonexclusive, and that it was perfectly normal to take *Africa* elsewhere after Warner turned it down. He continued, "I am sure you know that Howard has been in great demand and that we have had many, many propositions offered to us for him. He is certainly one of the most sought-after directors in the business."

Unlike Hawks, Warner was still enthusiastic about *Gold of the Seven Saints* so, after more unpleasant exchanges and recriminations, Warner settled with Hawks by agreeing to let him keep the eighty thousand dollars the studio had already paid him to prepare the *Saints* screenplay. Warner quickly put the film into production, directed by Gordon Douglas; it is a film of no reputation, not even available on videotape. Initially, Warner had intended for Hawks's fee to be applied to another film, but a few days later, fed up with what he viewed as Hawks's and Feldman's game-playing, he simply canceled the contract altogether. After having watched Hawks walk out on him several times before, he no longer needed the aggravation.

Hawks always did what he wanted to do; loyalty, a mutually beneficial friendship, and professional understanding counted for nothing. He was bent on making the African film and would go where he could get the best deal he could. But within six weeks in October and November 1959, his third wife left him and he willingly concluded his relationship with the studio where he had entered the sound era, directed ten pictures, fought many battles that he usually won, and consistently got his pick of material and been allowed to shape and cast it his way. In short, Warner Bros., Hal Wallis notwithstanding, had been the studio most agreeable to letting Hawks be Hawks, and the result was much of his most successful work, both artistically and commercially. Now he closed the door on it, and there would be no going back.

35

Fun in the Bush: *Hatari!*

At Christmas 1959, Hawks wrote Chance de Widstedt a letter. For more than a year he had been thinking about her, he'd written and talked to her occasionally—and how many women had ever had a John Wayne character named after them? Since Hawks had last seen her in Paris, Chance had quit modeling to become a reportorial photographer, initially free-lance for the *Herald Tribune* and then, principally, for the photodominated magazine *Jours de France*. In his letter, Hawks informed her that he was now divorced from Dee and proposed to Chance that she come to Los Angeles and marry him. Although quite surprised, since she and Hawks didn't know each other that well and had never slept together, Chance did feel that there was something special between them. "I decided to go and have a look," she said, telling Hawks that she would like to come stay with him for a while.

When she arrived, early in 1960, she moved right into Hawks's house but stayed in a separate bedroom, as his wives always had. "This shocked me," she confessed, "because I thought it was more important to be tender. After all, *la nuit n'est pas seulement pour dormir.* But he had trouble sleeping sometimes because he had so much in his head. For his creativity he wanted to be alone, to read, to make notes, to dream, to wake up and write things down. He didn't need daily tenderness and affection. He liked to be solitary." Chance implied that they did become physically intimate during this period, but ambiguously explained that their relationship was one of "*sensualité, pas sexualité.* I admired him. I had no father. I was his friend, and he was my father and friend. And I wasn't with him because he was Howard Hawks."

Already busy working on his African project, Hawks would get up early every morning and go to work, while Chance would stay around the house, sometimes with six-year-old Gregg. "I'd have a dip in the pool, then go and get my hair done so that I would look impeccable when Howard came home from the studio," Chance said. "I was living in luxury, after coming from a two-bedroom apartment that I shared with my grandmother." All the same, Chance had tasted the good life in Paris, so she wasn't particularly overwhelmed by her newly adopted lifestyle. Hawks gave her a white Chevrolet Impala convertible to use around town, and when he came home from work, usually late, they would go out to dinner, most often at Dino's Place, Dean Martin's popular restaurant and club on the Sunset Strip, where Martin often performed casual impromptu sets. They also went to dinner with celebrities—once at Alfred Hitchcock's home and another time with Marilyn Monroe and John Wayne at the Beverly Hills Hotel. "But these things only happened maybe once every week," complained Chance. "In L.A. then there was not much I could do. I supposed it will have changed by now. But back then it was deadly. You couldn't even go have a coffee. You have no idea. I was used to Paris, where it was a wonderful time."

Finally, the boredom of so many hours alone and the aridity of life in Los Angeles became too much to bear. After three months, she told Hawks she'd had enough and was going back to Paris. "If Hawks had lived in Paris, then I suppose we would have married. . . . Maybe if I'd had some friends to pass the time of day, then I might have stayed. Maybe it was a stupid mistake not to have married him, but *c'est la vie*." Hawks was initially furious at her rejection, but he quickly came to understand the reasons for her discontent and her desire to pursue a career of her own. He also realized that they might be able to spend a good deal of time together very soon.

His bargaining power at its peak in the wake of *Rio Bravo* and with Warner Bros. definitively out of the picture, Hawks began setting up his African adventure in earnest. Jack Gordean, the Famous Artists agent handling most of Hawks's business now that Feldman was busy with so many producing projects, was in advanced discussions with Paramount about the project in early December 1959, when both Fox and Columbia stepped up with virtually identical offers. Paramount did finally land the production, with Hawks receiving $150,000 for the story, $150,000 for directing, and 50 percent of the profits after breakeven. At the same time, Feldman's client John Wayne agreed to star for $750,000 and 10 percent of the gross after the picture had pulled in $7.5 million.

Although it was not widely known at the time, Charles Feldman's life was in considerable danger during this entire period. In the fall of 1959, Feldman was diagnosed with an enlarged prostate. On April 26, Dr. Edward C. Parkhurst performed a suprapubic prostatectomy on him in Boston, and after two weeks in the hospital, Feldman departed with Capucine to convalesce in the South of France. The majority of Hawks's business, therefore, was handled with only the most cursory of attention from his agent.

Paramount announced *Hatari!* at the end of March, with shooting slated to begin within six months. Hawks had no more idea at this point what his story was going to be than he had more than four years before when Harry Kurnitz was trying to patch something together in Paris. (An advance from Paramount enabled Hawks to finally pay Kurnitz $29,750 for his earlier work.) In fact, he wasn't particularly interested in a story at all. "That was the year that Howard was not buying any story," moaned Leigh Brackett. "He didn't want plot, he just wanted scenes." All Hawks knew was that he wanted to make a picture about people who catch animals in Africa for zoos. It was a subject that had all the requisites: a dangerous profession, a colorful milieu, a group undertaking controlled by a boss to be played by a big star, and plenty of opportunity for exciting scenes, the likes of which had never been seen on-screen before. With its mix of people and animals against grand landscapes, it would even have the feel of a Western, albeit a modern and quite exotic one. Defending its decidedly loose-knit construction, Hawks said that "the form of the picture is a hunting season, from beginning to end. It's what happens when a bunch of fellows get together to hunt." He also rationalized that "you can't sit in an office and write what a rhino is going to do."

In fact, within a five-month period, the dramatic incidents and even the characters of *Hatari!* changed innumerable times. Based on various outlines and character notes, the tone of the piece was originally fairly dark and melodramatic, quite reminiscent of *Only Angels Have Wings* both in setting and attitude. As it evolved over the months, Hawks and his writers helped themselves to motifs from many of Hawks's other previous successes. Initially, Wayne and Clark Gable were meant to costar as two veteran hunters who, à la *A Girl in Every Port*, still competed for the same women. An overlay from *Rio Bravo* was added to this in that one of the men, an alcoholic, would have to be looked after by the other. Others may come and go but, as Leigh Brackett put it in one of her jottings, "Clint and Robbie are constants. There is a grim joke between them, a sardonic rivalry—which of them will last the longest. There is a special bottle of brandy on the top shelf, waiting to be drunk by the survivor. Though they quarrel over methods, they love each other." From *The Dawn Patrol* and *The Road to Glory* were drawn the ideas that casualties along the way would simply be replaced by others and that the man who used to receive the orders to place himself in harm's way would one day become the man who had to order others to do the same. From *Red River* came a marksmanship duel to prove which young man was better, from *Ceiling Zero* the character of an invalid who used to be a great hunter but is now, due to an accident, reduced to menial chores around the camp. From many films, notably *Only Angels Have Wings* and *To Have and Have Not*, was derived the stray beautiful woman who arrives, penniless, and is instantly resented by the tough hero, who has been burned by a woman before and has to be convinced to let her stay. In one draft, less than three months before photography began, there was a central *Moby Dick* theme of a wild rogue elephant, "old one-tusk," who kills a man in the opening sequence and must be hunted down by Clint by the close.

In mid-June, Hawks brought Leigh Brackett out to begin work, at $750 a week, but also hired the brothers Waldman, for a flat $35,000, to work separately from her, much as Brackett had worked apart from Faulkner on *The Big Sleep*. The sons of a Wall Street banker, Frank and Tom Waldman had been writing separately for television during the 1950s until teaming up to work for Blake Edwards on the *Peter Gunn* series and their first feature, the lightweight Bing Crosby comedy *High Time*. Aside from advising them about key incidents and ideas they might take from his previous pictures, Hawks gave them little guidance, and they hammered away in many directions that had no bearing on the finished film.

For the woman who shows up at the camp unannounced, Brackett came up with "a sexy cherub" named Scarlett who was invited there by the man killed in the opening scene and now finds herself at sea, and Hawks initially thought of including a blond seductress, inspired by Jean Harlow in *Red Dust*, who might be played by Stella Stevens and would throw all the men off balance. But he reconsidered, deciding that he didn't want anything to interfere with the basic focus of the material, and finally suggested a character based on the famous Ylla, a beautiful German considered the top animal photographer in the world, who was killed when she fell off a truck in South Africa.

For the other female role, Brackett invented a woman named Sandy, a "superbly able" deaf-mute who works, drinks, and sleeps with Clint but doesn't want him, or any man, to tie her down. Again, Hawks shied away from something so unusual and, again, found inspiration in real life, a girl with a well-known father who had been killed by a rhino but whose African farm she then continued to lease to other hunters. Brackett's draft also included a cocky Frenchman, "a tough kid with a chip on his shoulder and a rifle in his hand," as well as the death of Robbie, which occasions the drinking of the bottle of brandy and its replacement by a fresh bottle, "symbolizing that the game begins again."

Rightly judging that *Hatari!* was going to turn into a very expensive production and setting a provisional budget of $4,275,000, Paramount executives insisted that one enormous star salary was enough and that they weren't going to match Wayne's fee with an equal one for Clark Gable. (Gable was just coming off an arduous shoot on *The Misfits* opposite Marilyn Monroe for John Huston; he died on November 16, twelve days before *Hatari!* started filming.) To play the Frenchman, Hawks was leaning toward Yves Montand, having seen one reel of the unfinished *Let's Make Love.* Montand was interested, but, insecure about performing in English, he insisted upon seeing a script, which didn't exist, so he moved on. These casting problems created further delays in writing *Hatari!* and even in deciding what the characters would be. The Robbie role was diminished somewhat and reconceived for Peter Ustinov, just then at the apex of his popularity. Burly, British, and a droll scene-stealer, he would have been a curious foil indeed for John Wayne. But when he proved unavailable, the part was dropped altogether, although the need for some sort of equivalent comic relief was recognized. To this end, the quickly ascendant Peter Sellers was sought, followed by the Australian-British character actor Leo McKern, who retained vivid memories of his one meeting with Hawks: "I have never met anyone who spoke or moved slower; a broad gesture with an arm took so long that it became an effort not to take the eyes from his face and follow its movement like a stoat-thralled rabbit; and yet the word it accompanied . . . 'e-v-e-r-y-w-h-e-r-e . . .' lasted as long as the gesture. Not that there was any sense of weakness conveyed; on the contrary. I believe that it was simply that he had long ago decided that if anyone was going to come down with an ulcer, it was not H. H." While a previous commitment prevented Sellers from taking the role, McKern declined it for the simple reason that he could not fathom working with John Wayne, whose politics he abhorred.

Hawks, of course, was the producer of *Hatari!*, but with so much undecided in the writing and casting areas, more responsibility than ever would fall on the shoulders of Paul Helmick, who was put in charge of organizing the staggering logistics in Africa. Helmick and Paramount's production manager Don Robb had gone to Nairobi in January, but they soon wired Hawks that "new restrictions prevent photographing animal catching sequences in Kenya. . . . Tanganyika appears more suitable for our purposes." Moving on to Dar Es Salaam, the men secured full cooperation from Sir Ernest Vasey, acting minister of natural resources in Tanganyika, which was in its final year of British colonial rule. They also met sixty-five-year-old Willy de Beer, the only licensed game catcher in the country, who became the production's indispensable technical adviser. In all, Helmick and Robb's advance work was invaluable in terms of securing cooperation and choosing good locations where game could be found. Helmick shot lots of 16mm film for Hawks's perusal, and in preparation for the animal catching sequences, Hawks also looked at several documentaries on the subject, especially one called *Operation Rhino*, which he watched repeatedly.

Base camp was set up near Arusha, a colonial center sixty miles southwest of Mount Kilimanjaro and about eighty miles east of the enormous Ngorongoro Crater and the eastern edge of the wildlife-abundant Serengeti Plain. At Helmick's suggestion, a compound was built twenty-one miles from town to serve both as a ranch for the production's domesticated animals and as the fictional home base for the film's characters. Of course, all necessary equipment and amenities would have to be brought in, with the additional caveat that most of the shooting would be done from vehicles moving in unpredictable directions across very rough ground. Every make of all-terrain vehicle was tested, and forty were eventually ordered from Willys Motors in Toledo and then shipped from Brooklyn to Mombasa; alert to the new possibilities for product placement and promotional tie-ins in pictures, Hawks suggested lots of publicity ideas for Willys, just as he did for Nikon, which agreed to supply all the camera equipment seen in the film. A unique camera mount was designed to facilitate the smoothest possible action filming in the days before the Steadicam, and this would be placed on a special aluminum, automatic-transmission camera vehicle, which, like the beat-up-looking catcher's truck, was outfitted with the most powerful possible engine to enable it to zoom across the landscape at eighty miles per hour. Beyond that, there were dozens of animals to be gathered, kept, and, in some cases, trained. Animals arrived on trains prominently marked by the word *Hatari!*, or "Danger!" in Swahili.

Hawks was originally supposed to leave for Africa on August 29, but the casting remained entirely up in the air. He screened many new European films looking for attractive new faces. Among the pictures he saw was one of the key films of the French New Wave, Claude Chabrol's *Les Cousins*, which starred the darkly intense, compact Gerard Blain, who was being touted as "a French James Dean." Hawks didn't even watch the whole film, turning it off and immediately requesting a voice test by the actor in English. Blain's English was just passable, but Hawks had him brought to Hollywood and to his home in Palm Springs. Blain was stunned because "Hawks did everything. He cooked, he cleaned up, he brought all the drinks." There was a young woman hanging around whom Blain scarcely met and whose identity was a mystery to him. "She just sat in a rocking chair by the pool and did nothing," he recalled. For the other principal male role, Hawks looked at footage of the young British actor Patrick McGoohan but selected instead the blond German actor Hardy Kruger, who, unlike Blain, spoke excellent English.

Having decided to use an Italian leading lady, Hawks seriously considered Claudia Cardinale, a voluptuous, dark-haired knockout who was just beginning to emerge, but her English wasn't good enough. When Hawks had all but settled upon one of the most stunning actresses in Italian films, Antonella Lualdi, Paramount gave him an advance look at one of their upcoming releases, Roger Vadim's *Blood and Roses*, and he recalled that he had met one of its stars, Elsa Martinelli, who just happened to be a Feldman client, in Rome. A vivacious beauty whose career had actually begun in Hollywood five years before, courtesy of Kirk Douglas, Martinelli had natural, unaffected looks and a slim figure that were very much in the Hawksian mold. Hawks phoned her to check her English, had her make a test, and, when she agreed to play the role of the visiting photographer who becomes involved with John Wayne's group leader, won a five-hundred-dollar bet with Feldman, who had predicted she wouldn't take the part. In mid-September, Hawks met her in New York and took her directly to Brooks Brothers for the all-important wardrobe hunt. "He knew perfectly what he wanted for me," Martinelli explained, "but spent hours thinking over what type of ensemble a photographer would wear in the heart of Africa. He went with the saleswoman to choose the clothes I was to wear, then, when I came out of the dressing room, he sat there checking everything. . . . Only towards evening did Hawks make up his mind." They left the store having bought ten pairs of very simple safari clothes.

"We ate together, talking about everything except the movies," Martinelli continued. "He asked me questions about many things and was very witty, but in an obvious, almost childlike way, in contrast to his personality, his intelligence, his elegance. Leaving for California he said to me: 'I'm going to invent your role. Now that I've met you, you'll come out much nicer than I planned.'"

For the role of the girl raised in Africa who is both a sister and a wished-for lover to the young men, Hawks had tested, incredibly, Ingrid Thulin, a highly serious stage and screen actress from Sweden whose cool beauty had already graced several Ingmar Bergman films. Three French unknowns were also tried, and Hawks's choice, Michele Girardon, was brought to Los Angeles in mid-September. Attractive, open-looking, and a bit gawky, the twenty-five-year-old Girardon, who had appeared in a handful of films, including Louis Malle's *The Lovers*, struck Hawks's fancy at once, which got her the part but led to problems later on.

For the role that would provide the comic relief, Hawks still didn't know what he was going to do. He met with Art Carney and was considering Theodore Bikel when the agent Marty Baum heard about the part and promoted his client Red Buttons for it. A popular nightclub and television comedian who had won an Oscar for his serious performance in *Sayonara* in 1957, Buttons didn't know Hawks but had recently worked for his brother Bill, the producer of *Imitation General*. Buttons balked at going to Africa on a film without a script, but Baum insisted that with Hawks and Wayne, Buttons couldn't go far wrong. Also along for the ride was Wayne crony Bruce Cabot, whose injury in the opening scene sets the stage for the Frenchman's entrance. Hawks wanted a Latino for the final American animal catcher and, after noticing him in a small part in *The Magnificent Seven*, paged Valentin de Vargas, who had been so memorably menacing as the young hoodlum in Orson Welles's *Touch of Evil* a couple of years before. "During our two-hour interview," de Vargas recalled, "Hawks kept pointing out how dangerous it was going to be. He had me look at a documentary about how they caught animals and I was a little concerned, but then Paul Helmick said, 'You can be assured that you won't have to do any of that.'" Alone among the actors, de Vargas went to Africa with the advance crew weeks ahead of the start date in order to learn whatever he could. "As soon as I got over there, they told me they didn't have anybody to double me." De Vargas, like the rest of the cast, played the animal-catching sequences himself.

With no script in hand on what he knew would be a $6 million picture, Hawks left Los Angeles and stopped briefly in New York before flying to Paris on September 25. He was joined by his son David, who had thoughts of working in some capacity on *Hatari!* But these ideas were put aside when he met a young American woman named Judith Webb. Very soon they decided to marry, and as newlyweds they spent a month driving around Europe. When they embarked upon real life in Los Angeles, David found that Douglas Aircraft did not want him back because he had been gone too long. So he applied for membership in the Directors Guild of America, and during the nine-month wait for an assistant's job he was allowed to be an observer and unofficial trainee on various television shows.

From Paris, Hawks proceeded to Rome, where he remained longer than expected to work out final casting wrinkles. He had been preceded to

Arusha by the entire crew, but now the Fearless Leader, as Paul Helmick called him, would be arriving to crack the whip in his own quiet but firm way. Helmick and the cinematographer, Russ Harlan, had already been there a month, planning locations and working out how to cover different scenes. As a kind gesture to an old friend, Hawks had originally told Arthur Rosson, his trusty associate director from *Red River*, that he could supervise the second unit on the picture. This can only be seen as an exceedingly charitable gesture to a man on his last legs, as Rosson, now seventy-three, could never have handled such a rigorous job. As it happened, Rosson died on June 17, 1960, so Hawks told Russ Harlan that he could perform as an additional second-unit director along with Helmick before principal photography began, whereupon Harlan would join Hawks on the first unit and Joseph Brun would work with Helmick. Helmick and Harlan repeatedly tried to film one of the sequences Hawks most wanted for the picture; as Don Robb explained, the elephants "came right up to the tent line, wheeled and turned back. Mr. Hawks feels that the scene can be done in reduced scale with the five small elephants that we have. By split screen to double the numbers, and numerous cuts, he feels we can make it appear to be thirty to fifty elephants." They never succeeded.

Forty-one crew members in total were flown over from the United States to work on *Hatari!*, which became the final title. Hawks preferred *Tanganyika*, but this had been used by Universal in 1954. Some thirty other titles, including *Bring 'Em Back Alive*, *Africa Roars*, and *Untamed*, were proposed, but Paramount distribution executives felt that *Hatari!* had a ring to it and would catch on with kids.

Hawks landed in Nairobi at 2 A.M. on October 17 and was met by Don Robb, who accompanied him to Arusha. For the next several weeks, one and sometimes two units went out every day; Helmick was in charge of covering the small-game catches, while Harlan mainly concentrated on landscapes, general wildlife, and shots of vehicle caravans. As it would be throughout production, the film was sent to Technicolor in London for processing and then rushed back to Arusha so Hawks and his team could see what they were getting. Three local garages were busy day and night for ten days, adapting all the vehicles for motion picture use, outfitting them with radios, extra shock absorbers, and other special features. The animals that had been assembled were quickly growing tame; these included several rhinos, three lions, two leopards, and one hippo, one lynx, and one hyena. Although it had already issued its filming permit, the government continually pressed for a copy of the screenplay but received nothing but excuses; as Red Buttons said, "There was never a script, only pages." Hawks scouted final locations from a small plane, while much of his private time was spent plotting out who should be in the hunting sequences and what the characters' basic attitudes and behavior should be. Watching the film closely, it is easy to see that virtually all the dialogue covered on location was strictly functional and not tied to specific, unalterable dramatic developments, leaving Hawks maximum leeway to play with his plot, such as it was, when interiors were filmed in Hollywood later on.

Although it was not directly related to making of the picture, tragedy struck on November 1. A Nairobi-based British animal trainer not in Paramount's employ, Diana Hartley, had arrived at the de Beer compound with two cheetahs. When she learned that a lion she had known before, purchased for use in the film, was now at the compound, she approached it. Her friends heard her speak to the lion, then scream for help. When Hartley's body was pulled away, it became clear that the lion had bitten her on the neck, killing her. It later turned out that Hartley had mentioned to one of the other women at the compound that she was having her period; she was told in no uncertain terms not to go near the lion, but she ignored the advice.

It was kept quiet, but Valentin de Vargas said that during the shooting "there was a mishap every week." Three native Africans were accidentally killed during production, and while, miraculously, none of the actors or American crew members were ever seriously hurt, Willy de Beer was badly mauled when a baby leopard got loose and jumped on him from a tree. "He came back with his arm covered in bandages and throat completely wrapped, but he just shrugged it off," de Vargas recounted.

After de Vargas, Elsa Martinelli was the next cast member to turn up, at the beginning of November, arriving with her photographer boyfriend Willy Rizzo, who had the enviable double assignment of covering the shoot for *Paris Match* and working as the official Paramount stills man. A few days later, Hawks came down with a serious virus that landed him in the hospital for a week. While there, he heard from Feldman, who was in discussions with Spyros Skouras in London about a long-term deal for Hawks at 20th Century–Fox, for six to eight pictures at $150,000 apiece, $75,000 in annual expenses, and 50 percent of the profits, with Paris as Hawks's probable base of operations. Paramount would probably match this deal, Feldman said, while Columbia might be willing to go as high as $200,000 per picture.

By the third week of November, the principal cast members began filtering in. Some of the best homes in the area were vacated in order to accommodate the stars in luxury; Gerard Blain, along with much of the crew, stayed at the New Arusha Hotel. Hawks showed footage of some of the good catches to the enthusiastic actors, and then gave them a pregame pep talk, telling them that they were privileged to be going on perhaps the most expensive safari in the world, costing millions. "He told us he expected strong nerves and a lion's energy," Martinelli recalled. "He was witty and very calm, and for half an hour before shooting started, he told the actors all the good and bad things they'd have to face." When Hawks left the room, all the other actors ran over to John Wayne to ask if he had a copy of the script. "He paused a moment, as though posing for a fashion plate by Avedon," said Martinelli, "then he said, 'Listen, kids. I've shot a hundred movies. Well, the greatest directors, including Hawks, never handed me a script. I'm an actor, and when they call me for a film I know they need me, that's all. . . . You just have to trust them. If you're good, they'll show you to your best advantage day by day.'"

Privately, Hawks told his leading lady, "This is a film I wanted to make for years and I wanted to make it like it was a vacation." It became clear to Martinelli that the conditions under which they would be making the picture precisely paralleled those depicted in the story, with Hawks as the boss figure and the uncertainty prompted by the lack of a script directly analogous to the unpredictability of the animal hunts. It was a thought picked up on by François Truffaut when he saw *Hatari!*, which he always considered to be Hawks's disguised account of the process of filmmaking. In any case, for Hawks it was a realization of his lifelong urge to merge his fictional ideals with his real life, a boy's fantasy being played out every day. Even though the dreamer was now sixty-four years old, he couldn't have been happier.

Like the actors, Paramount simply had to trust Howard Hawks. With Jacob M. Karp having taken charge of production only in 1959, there was no veteran big boss like Jack Warner or Darryl Zanuck who had a clue how to control Hawks. All the studio could do was to pay the bills and hope for the best. There was no fixed budget per se and no absolute shooting schedule—what would it have been based on with no script?—although everyone, including Hawks, intended to finish in Africa by mid-February, before the rainy season arrived.

For the first part of principal photography, the company moved seventy-five miles west of Arusha to the shores of Lake Manyara, set in the middle of plains that teemed with all manner of game. While Hawks, the cast, and some top first-unit crew members stayed at the Lake Manyara Lodge, a sort of British colonial outpost, the general company, much as on

Red River, was put up in large canvas tents, in an area that was floodlit by portable generators all night to discourage animals from coming in. Principal photography started on November 28 with scenes involving Wayne, Martinelli, and Buttons at Ngasumet Wells, in the middle of the arid Masai Steppe. Martinelli recalled that on that first morning, "Hawks was there waiting for us, shaved and dressed as though for a garden party." She said that even after the longest of days, Hawks never tired. "He was the only one capable, after a day of wild adventure, of returning to camp with his shoes shined." He was a tough boss on his crew. He went through at least three first assistant directors on the picture, pushing the first one, Danny McCauley, to the breaking point and giving a hard time to the next, Bud Brill. "He was very hard on the people he worked with," Brill testified. "He wanted his own people, and the studio wouldn't let him."

Not only had Red Buttons not tested for the role, but he had never even met Hawks before he showed up to work. "Luckily for me, he dug me immediately. He found me amusing, and he and I paired off, he became my gin partner. He was the Gary Cooper of directors. He was a 'Yup,' 'Nope' guy. He was like a ventriloquist, he barely opened his mouth. I never heard him laugh, but I saw him smile a lot." Professionally, Buttons said, "He gave me a sense of freedom. From the first day he let me make up my own dialogue and we started to build from there. . . . There was something to be picked up from him that you don't get from many other people. Even though he was taciturn, he had a special quality about him. . . . He was different, somehow or other. He was like a counter-puncher, he'd see the openings and fill them in with his own cement. He had a great instinctive sense. . . . It would be a very tall order to second-guess him or argue with him." Unlike many people, Buttons called him Howard from the outset, and there was never a problem.

Work soon began on the action that made everyone the most nervous—the catching of rhinos. Although stunt doubles, notably Hawks's old friend Cary Lofton, were on hand, all the actors, at their director's encouragement, intended not to use them, particularly Wayne. Veteran hunter Willy de Beer's truck was rigged so that the animal catcher did his work from inside the cab, but that wasn't very photogenic, in Hawks's opinion, so a seat was affixed to the left front fender. This made the actors as visible as a large hood ornament but also very vulnerable. As soon as Wayne arrived, he grandly announced, "That de Vargas isn't going to ride in the bucket seat anymore. *I'm* going to ride in it!," and with very little practice, he proceeded to show everyone how it should be done. Buttons was cast in the role of a former New York taxi driver now at the wheel of the catcher's truck. "I'm the worst driver in the world, which is ironic, but they taught me," Buttons confessed. "They doubled me only for the long shots of really tough driving."

John Wayne always said, "The most fun I ever had on any picture was on *Hatari!*" But Hawks later revealed that Wayne, who admitted to being scared during much of the hunting action, "had the feeling with every swerve that the car was going to overturn as he hung on for dear life, out in the open with only a seat belt for support, motor roaring, body jarring every-which-way, animals kicking dirt and rocks and the thunder of hundreds of hooves increasing the din in his ears.

"Adding to the catcher's problems—and 'excitement,' as Duke preferred to call it—was the game's total unpredictability. They would, on a whim, suddenly switch from smooth plain to long grass, the whole territory being full of hidden holes or obstacles which could spell disaster in a second. Duke remarked that the zebras were the smartest at eluding the car as they headed for the rocky edges of the forest as though completely aware that no speeding vehicle could move through the boulders."

Throughout December, depending upon the animals, they shot sequences with rhinos, buffalos, giraffes, hartebeests and wildebeests, elephants, and zebras. "We were always on the alert, like a military alert," Red Buttons said, "for when the spotters would spot some animals, and then we'd all have to move out on the double." Enthusiasm ran strong, even though the drivers were getting lost all the time and it seemed to take forever to get the animals to do what was needed. As far as the performances were concerned, Hawks said very little to anybody. "At first, I thought, 'I am an *actor*,' you know, and I wanted to know what I should be doing," de Vargas recalled. "But we learned a lot just from being around the men who did this, and eventually I saw that Hawks had us mesmerized, because we actually became part of it. We *were* animal catchers."

Gregg arrived to spend Christmas with his father and ended up staying much longer than planned. Shortly after the first of the year, Hawks and the editor, Stuart Gilmore, put together some cut footage to send back to Hollywood to placate Paramount executives. Once they were caught, quite a few animals were shipped to Los Angeles, both for future use in the picture and for distribution, by agreement, to various zoos; Hawks was particularly concerned, probably as much for publicity reasons as emotional ones, that they be well cared for.

The last week of January, Hawks's unit returned to the Arusha base, where all the scenes set around the fictional compound were filmed. The baby elephants really did seem to come to think of Elsa Martinelli as their mother, as it appears in the film, and the sequence in which Red Buttons captures hundreds of monkeys by sending up a rocket to drop a giant net over a large tree was a particular nail-biter. The technique had been developed in England in the 1950s, but the special-effects man in charge was terribly nervous about proceeding with the scene. "He postponed it five days because he could feel a whisper of wind," Hawks recalled. "He didn't want any wind. We had to move people back a quarter of a mile behind barricades because we didn't know where the rocket was going to go. None of us thought it was going to work, really. But it worked beautifully the very first time."

That was the work side of things. Just as in the film, however, there were deep personal tensions working beneath the surface of what appeared to be a highly engaged, sympathetic group of people. Any film shoot creates a world of its own for the weeks or months it lasts, a feeling accentuated on a distant location that, in this case, was virtually out of touch with the rest of civilization. Red Buttons testified, "I found out for the first time that there was a world where nobody heard of Frank Sinatra." Buttons also explained that after hours, "It was not one big group. Duke and Howard, they'd have their little drink together. Some of us lived in private houses with lots of servants. There wasn't much social life except for those that lived in the hotel in Arusha, and they'd drink at the bar." Buttons did not know Wayne and didn't agree with him politically, but he was happy to find that Wayne seemed to be very fair. "We all got to Africa right after JFK was elected. John Wayne said, 'I didn't vote for him, but he's my president and I hope he does a good job." For Wayne, who was initially accompanied on location by his wife, Pilar, and his young daughter, this was a vacation, a relief after the rigors of producing, directing, financing, and acting in his $12 million personal project, *The Alamo,* which had opened in October. Elsa Martinelli was initially apprehensive that Wayne would take his cue from the story and make life difficult for her until she proved herself, but she found him a true gentleman; she became his chess partner throughout the shoot and often cooked pasta for him and Hawks at her house. According to Martinelli, later, after his wife left, Wayne started an affair with a blond woman who lived in Arusha, but he was so discreet that no one ever found out who it was.

At one point, there was a startling showdown between Wayne and Hawks. Assistant director Bud Brill said, "Duke Wayne got mad when Gregg Hawks slapped his lovely little girl or did something physical like that, and he said, 'If you do that one more time, I'll break your goddamned neck.' Then he looked up and saw Howard there with a big grin on his face."

The filming was a great adventure for everyone, but for a few it was a moving, life-altering experience. Hardy Kruger, accompanied by his wife, was so deeply affected by Africa that he arranged to purchase a portion of the compound after the shoot and has spent a good deal of his life there since. Although he didn't take a home, Red Buttons, also there with his wife, reacted the same way. "Of any of my locations, this one had the most profound effect on me. I never thought it would happen, but a tranquility came over me, gradually, and it really stayed with me. The reason it was so meaningful to me was that I was from cement, from the Lower East Side. . . . Looking at Mount Kilimanjaro, . . . on clear days, which they mostly were, . . . you'd see the snowcaps, and you could almost believe what the natives believed, that God resided up there. . . . Part of it has been in my soul ever since." Even Bud Brill, who was given such a hard time by Hawks, said, "I ended up falling in love with the country."

Most of the difficulties centered on the French contingent. Early on, Hawks confided to Martinelli that he was having trouble figuring out how to use Gerard Blain, for the simple reason that he looked so short next to all the other actors, especially Wayne. Just as he had dressed the slight Monty Clift in black to allow him to cut a stronger profile, Hawks realized he would have to do the same with Blain. "Unless I dress him up," he confessed, "nobody will believe he's a big game hunter in the heart of Africa capable of stealing his best buddy's girlfriend." His short stature also caused the director "to set him off from the others" visually and dramatically. "That's how Hawks worked," observed Martinelli. Red Buttons elaborated on Hawks's technique by saying, "It was improvisational, but then again it wasn't, because Howard had this all mapped out in his head. He played his people, he saw what they were and what they could do, who he could pair up, who he couldn't." It was Bud Brill's impression that with the possible exceptions of Wayne, Buttons, and Martinelli, "The actors were all scared to death of him, but he had a great knack of developing things as they went along." When Blain turned up all in black for his first scene—"he looked like he stepped out of a Fritz Lang movie," said Martinelli—Wayne could barely contain himself. That evening, she noted that he told Hawks, "'Dear Howard, only I know how much it took for you to make Montgomery Clift believable in *Red River.* . . . I hope you have the same success with this little French actor.' They knew each other so well nothing could escape them. Hawks simply answered: 'A great deal of Montgomery Clift's success belongs to you, so I hope you'll help me teach Blain at least two things, to fistfight and to hold a gun.'"

Blain recalled that, since Hawks had invited all the actors to feel free to contribute ideas for scenes, he suggested a way to climax the sharpshooting scene between him and Hardy Kruger, whose character had previously decked Blain with a punch. "I proposed to Howard Hawks, . . . what do you think if I give my rifle to Wayne and, in the same movement, turn around and hit Kruger, knock him down, then help him up and shake hands? This was my contribution, and Hawks used it." According to Martinelli, however, there was an unpleasant stinger to it. After the first run-through, Wayne supposedly told the Frenchman that the only way for a shorter man to knock down a taller rival was with an uppercut. After the scene was over, Blain pointedly told Wayne not to offer any more advice. The whole set froze, but Wayne just shrugged him off.

But things deteriorated between the two, mainly due to politics and Blain's undiplomatic decision to speak his mind to the right-wing star about capital punishment, the Bay of Pigs, and so on. Wayne, who didn't mind a legitimate argument, just got fed up. Blain should have known who would win this war, but he persisted, the result being that his part was diminished. The way Blain saw it, "At the beginning, my role was very important, more like Montgomery Clift in *Red River.* Little by little, it got changed. Unfortunately for me, he changed it during the shooting. He improvised a lot and, because Hardy Kruger knew English a lot better, I was at a great disadvantage."

But considerably more annoying to Hawks was Michele Girardon. The director had taken a great personal interest in her from the beginning, bringing her to Hollywood before the shoot and advising the inexperienced actress in his usual Pygmalionesque way. But there was much more to it than that. "Howard Hawks *loved* Michele Girardon," said Gerard Blain, "but she refused all his advances." This incensed Hawks, and he punished her as well by slicing her part to the minimum, although Blain felt that he "kept cutting and changing her role because he realized she wasn't much good. He really wasn't much of an actor's director. But if Michele had accepted the advances of Howard Hawks, it would have been a much different film." Hawks's frustration generated considerable tension on the set, which only increased when certain insiders realized that Girardon was carrying on the most furtive of affairs with Russell Harlan. No one knows if Hawks ever found out about that.

Instead, Hawks decided to forgive Chance for walking out on him in California and invited her to stay with him in Arusha. Chance arranged to cover the shoot for *Jours de France,* but this put her in direct conflict with Willy Rizzo, the representative of arch-competitor *Paris Match.* Chance and Rizzo hated each other on sight. "Since Rizzo was the lover of Elsa Martinelli, the lead, and I was the mistress of the director-producer, there was a rivalry," she said, and the Italian team won. "Martinelli would turn away from my camera whenever I tried to take her, and Rizzo was always running me down," Chance complained, and there wasn't much Hawks could do about it. Chance and Paul Helmick, who was sharing Hawks's house, didn't hit it off either, and then Chance and Red Buttons's wife were involved in a Jeep accident. It was all just too much for everybody, and Chance finally left to go on a real safari, returning periodically to pay brief visits to Hawks on location. According to Martinelli, Hawks also developed a serious interest in a beautiful woman who owned a ranch near Arusha.

Other visitors to the location included William Holden, who was co-owner of the Mount Kenya Safari Club to the north and spent much of the rest of his life in Africa; Rosalind Russell and Frederick Brisson; Ed Lasker; and the Italian writer and filmmaker Pier Paolo Pasolini, who surprised his friend Martinelli one night while on his way through Africa with Alberto Moravia. The company was advised, for diplomatic reasons, to give a luncheon for Julius Nyerere, the nationalist leader who would take control of Tanganyika when the British departed in December 1961; joined with the island of Zanzibar, the country would be renamed Tanzania. A fabulous spread of food was prepared at the compound, everyone was on his best behavior, and Nyerere even professed a familiarity with Hawks's work. Hawks was solicitous and friendly in return, but the decorous occasion suddenly turned acutely embarrassing when Hawks, who was seated at the table between Nyerere and his son Gregg, heard his son blurt out, "Dad, we never eat with black people at home. Why are we doing it now?" Hawks was at a total loss to recover from that one. After Nyerere left, Wayne privately disparaged him and everything he stood for, feeling that what Africa needed was a strong dose of capitalistic enterprise, not socialism and nationalization. He even said, "I really think that if conditions had remained more to the white establishment that I would have gone back there and started a company, a safari deal, in which the men could rope the animals and tag them instead of killing them." Blain recalled hearing Wayne say nasty things about the local blacks, but he felt that Hawks, whom he realized was an archconservative, "was neither one way nor the other" about them.

Hawks often got up very early in the mornings for brief hunting expeditions, although he never got the leopard he wanted to bag. For publicity reasons, it was felt that great white hunter John Wayne could not leave Africa without shooting an elephant, so it was arranged. As Red Buttons remembered it, it was a disgusting affair. "There was a lot of silent controversy about that. . . . They really let him take a pot shot. There was a queasy feeling about it." A still photograph shows the rifle-toting star standing uncomfortably in front of the slain beast, with Hawks looking on impassively. While he later admitted that "there's no particular thrill in killing an animal," Wayne added, "When you get over there and you wake up in the morning and you hear the savage sounds of these animals and everything, your hair curls and you grab that gun and you take a different attitude than you did when you were at home saying, 'Well, I'd never shoot a little deer.'" Wayne occasionally had to exercise his macho in other ways. One night, he decided to challenge Willy Rizzo, who was not much taller than Gerard Blain, to a cognac drinking match. After Rizzo matched him through twelve glasses of the stuff, Wayne finally said, "You're okay, a real man."

The rainy season arrived a month early in 1961, making it virtually impossible to shoot anything but the monkey-tree rocket launch during the first ten days of February. With mostly some chase scenes involving the baby elephants in downtown Arusha left to film, Hawks, Wayne, Martinelli, and Buttons all became ill for a few days, delaying completion of first-unit work until March 5. When the second unit wrapped things up the following day, the exodus out of Africa and back to Hollywood was on. By then, Red Buttons said, "We were ready to go home."

After a couple of weeks' layoff for travel and recuperation, production started up again on the soundstages of the Paramount lot in Hollywood. Ironically, it was the only major studio in town where Hawks had never made at least one film before, and he hadn't been employed there since working for Jesse Lasky nearly forty years earlier. Many of the animals that had been brought over were temporarily housed on the stages at Paramount. "They were in cages," Bud Brill remembered, "and they were so dejected." After the adventure of Africa, coming back to finish the picture on the faux-lodge sets was quite an anticlimax, even if working in Hollywood represented something of a dream come true for all the foreigners. Martinelli was flattered when John Wayne complimented her by inviting her and her four-year-old daughter to stay at his home for the duration of the shoot. "I realized that his way of showing his esteem for me was to insert me in his private sphere," she said. For moral support and a degree of protection from Hawks, Michele Girardon brought her mother over to stay with her.

Once the company was back home, the main challenge fell to Leigh Brackett: laying out all the action scenes and looking for ways to connect them. Brackett and Hawks approached it like a puzzle, and for Brackett, the chief satisfaction came from "doing a good job of putting all the pieces together, taking the disparate parts and making it look as though it grew that way." During the subsequent shooting, she acknowledged, "I was on the set every day, working till ten o'clock at night writing the scene they were going to shoot at nine o'clock the next morning." Although Bogart remained her favorite, Brackett was impressed with Wayne's professionalism: "I remember his working with the baby elephant in the scene at the end of *Hatari*, when the critter gets on the bed and it crashes down. They tried about eighteen takes, and he said, 'He's doing it right. I'm not.' The elephant had his cues down perfectly, but it was Duke who was blowing it. He's a much more complex person than people give him credit for being." Wayne was also personally ill at ease, at fifty-three, about playing the romantic scenes with twenty-eight-year-old Martinelli. Hawks took advantage of this by poking fun at his discomfort in the hilarious scene in which Martinelli's Dallas, forced to be forward if she wants anything to happen with Wayne's Sean Mercer, corners him and asks, "How do you like to kiss?" He's so adolescent about it that she's driven to inquire whether he's ever been kissed, whereupon he blusters, "Of course I've been kissed!"

Red Buttons was impressed with the atypical way Hawks handled the man-woman relationships. "He was completely unsentimental," he felt. "The word *nostalgia* is not in his vocabulary. You'd call him cool, especially the way he treated romance. It was the battle of the sexes, unvarnished." Gerard Blain found this approach downright weird; he is one of the few people who knew Hawks and worked with him (as opposed to film theorists and critics) who dared to say, "I detected a submerged homosexual in Howard Hawks."

Hawks stole from himself in sending Blain and Kruger off to Paris à la *A Girl in Every Port*, having Kruger say, "It turns out we both know a girl there." He lifted the ending from *The Front Page* when he had Wayne call the airport after Martinelli has left to tell authorities not to let her on a plane because "she stole something." Some of the work was good, some less so, the atmosphere was relaxed, businesslike, and less intense than in Tanganyika. As filming was winding down, word came on May 13 of the death of Gary Cooper, for whom *Hatari!* had originally been intended. After

Bogart, who had died in 1957, and Gable, here was another Hollywood giant gone.

Production finally came to a close on May 24. Including the break for travel, *Hatari!* was before the cameras for six months and cost $6,546,000 to make, an unusually high sum for the time, more than the contemporaneous *West Side Story*. Before the actors departed, Hawks thanked them and talked about doing a follow-up in India called *Bengal Tiger* with mostly the same cast. As assistant director Bud Brill remembered it, Hawks told a couple of Paramount executives that he had a great idea for a film that he'd like to sell to them. "So he started telling them the story of *Hatari!* and finally they said, 'But that's the story of the film you're making.' He said, 'No, not at all. That's the film we were *supposed* to make.'"

Dimitri Tiomkin had scored most of Hawks's films since *Red River* and assumed that he would be doing so on *Hatari!* Hawks, however, did not want a traditional, bombastic, swellingly exciting soundtrack for this picture, and he instructed the composer to use native instruments when possible and to absolutely avoid strings or woodwinds. Hawks recalled, "He said, 'That's a great idea, boss.' Then he called me the next day and said, 'You were fooling, weren't you?' And I said, "You're fired, Dimi.'" After a wrong turn with another composer, Hawks called the hottest up-and-coming music man in Hollywood. Henry Mancini had already written a few film scores, but he had recently stirred up excitement with his theme for Blake Edwards' television series *Peter Gunn* and was a particular pet at Paramount for his recently completed score for *Breakfast at Tiffany's*, due for release in the fall. Excited to work on such a big picture, Mancini was even more impressed when, at their first meeting, Hawks opened up a big box containing all sorts of exotic musical instruments he had brought back from Africa—thumb piano, shell gourds, and two-foot pea pods with seeds inside. "I was entranced and immediately decided to use them in the score," said Mancini, to whom Hawks also gave tapes of Masai chants.

Working more closely with Mancini than he normally did with a composer and making a point of sitting in on the recording sessions, Hawks came to him with the specific problem of what to do with a little vignette Stuart Gilmore had cut together of the three baby elephants following after Elsa Martinelli and splashing around in a muddy pond. He shot the unplanned sequence only because the elephants were so crazy about Martinelli, but he was leaning towards cutting it out unless Mancini had any bright ideas. The movements of the elephants put Mancini in mind of boogie-woogie, so he wrote the eight-to-the-bar "Baby Elephant Walk" and thereby created one of the most fondly remembered interludes in the picture.

For *Hatari!*, Mancini composed one of the genuinely great film soundtracks, full of lyricism, unusual rhythms, unfamiliar instrumentations, hints of jazz, and African motifs, music that quickened the pulse during the animal chases, deepened the mood created by the setting, accompanied the action perfectly, and also stood on its own. As Red Buttons put it, "The score *is* Africa. If you've been there, you know." The album was a best-seller, and Mancini remained a lifelong friend and fan of his director. "Howard was a great gentleman, and he never raised his voice," Mancini enthused.

Within three weeks of the wrap, Stuart Gilmore had the film in sufficiently presentable form for Hawks to host a private screening at Paramount. At dinner beforehand and over drinks afterward, Charles Feldman, who had recovered well from his prostate operation, predicted that *Hatari!* would be a smash, a cinch to gross $20 million or more, a sentiment echoed by Paramount executives, who boldly foresaw it becoming their second biggest hit of all time, behind only *The Ten Commandments*.

Feldman also apprised Hawks of the progress on negotiations on the Columbia contract. Columbia was still very interested in the deal, but Hawks was beginning to make impossible demands, such as final say in the event of any dispute with the studio over casting and cutting, from which Feldman had to dissuade him. Hawks told his friend that, for personal and financial reasons, he was leaning toward making his upcoming pictures in Europe. They also discussed John Wayne. Members of the inner circle knew there were concerns about his health, but more pressing was Wayne's insistence upon being paid tens of thousands of dollars for six weeks of overages on *Hatari!* It was a situation painfully reminiscent of what had happened on *Red River*, where the star felt he was getting shortchanged by his friend and boss. Hawks told Feldman he could take care of things man-to-man with Duke and get him to compromise, but Wayne wanted every penny owed him and had to threaten another lawsuit to get it.

In late June, after completing *Hatari!* to his satisfaction, Hawks decamped for Palm Springs to bake in the heat and unwind after the unceasing yearlong effort of making such an ambitious film. He was reasonably pleased, he said, that "the picture turned out to be pretty good, but I think we *could* have had a *hell* of a picture. You have to put Wayne with somebody who's good. Every time I put him with somebody who's good I end up with a good picture." For him, Gerard Blain and Hardy Kruger, while perfectly decent actors, simply didn't combine to equal one Montgomery Clift, Dean Martin, or, specifically, Clark Gable in screen weight or star power.

In late July, Hawks received a surprising offer. Darryl Zanuck was just then preparing his most ambitious personal project, an adaptation of Cornelius Ryan's best-selling book about the D-day invasion, *The Longest Day*. Part of the producer's plan to maintain absolute control over every aspect of the massive production was to hire three different directors, one to handle the French aspect of the story, another for the German angle, and a third for the Allied side. The last would be the most important, and Zanuck provisionally offered the job to Hawks, but when Hawks's agent Jack Gordean informed Zanuck that his client would require "a lot of money" and would need to see a script before discussing it, it was enough of a red flag for Zanuck. Another submission Hawks received during this time was *The Rounders*, a Max Evans novel about two contemporary cowpokes that Burt Kennedy brought to the screen in 1965. Hawks felt the material was initially very funny but ultimately a one-joke affair.

The first sneak preview of *Hatari!*, at the United Artists Theater in Long Beach on August 3, was a great success, as was a subsequent one at Stamford Theater in Connecticut. But Paramount, whose other year-end releases were scheduled to be *Breakfast at Tiffany's*, *Blue Hawaii* with Elvis Presley, and *The Errand Boy* with Jerry Lewis, decided that it wouldn't be able to book *Hatari!* into enough top theaters in December to maximize its potential, so the distributor put off its opening until the following summer. This was a disappointment to Hawks and, for this reason, the picture Wayne made at Paramount subsequent to *Hatari!*, John Ford's *The Man Who Shot Liberty Valance*, was released first. Wayne's next film, *Circus World*, was postponed, and Paramount and Hawks discussed a possible quick project with the actor. Jack Gordean then told Paramount executives that, "Howard has always liked *The Maltese Falcon*, and he feels he can make this a very exciting film with Wayne doing the Bogart role."

When the issue of script credit on *Hatari!* came up, Hawks strongly felt that credit should read, "Screenplay by Leigh Brackett, original story by Harry Kurnitz." Given that what Frank and Tom Waldman wrote bore only occasional resemblance to the finished film and that Brackett had been on the set to write virtually all the dialogue, Hawks said, "I do not think that the contribution the Waldman brothers made to the script warrants giving them credit on the screen." The brothers filed a protest with the Writers Guild but did not prevail.

Despite all the extra time Paramount had to generate publicity and its boast that it would back *Hatari!* with "the biggest all-media showmanship campaign in history," Hawks began to feel that the studio was blowing it and went to New York "to raise hell," as Paul Helmick put it, with marketing executives. There was another side to the publicity, however, that pleased Hawks enormously. Beginning on May 21, 1962, the highbrow Museum of Modern Art in New York launched a three-month retrospective of Hawks's career, the first of its kind in the United States. Today, such an event would seem richly deserved and nothing out of the ordinary. But just then the passion for, and achievement of, European art cinema was at its zenith, with gods such as Bergman, Antonioni, Fellini, Godard, Truffaut, Resnais, and Buñuel at the peak of their powers and reputation. In this climate, an extended tribute to a Hollywood entertainer whose last four films had been a comedy about a youth potion, a gaudy musical, a lackluster Egyptian epic, and a Western featuring John Wayne and a couple of pop singers, and whose new picture was being promoted with coloring books and baby-elephant music, was greeted at best with some skepticism, at worst with outright derision.

The series was the brainchild of Peter Bogdanovich, then an intense twenty-two-year-old film buff, occasional theater director, and aspiring critic, Hollywood chronicler, and film director. A couple of years earlier, his critic friends Andrew Sarris and Eugene Archer had been raving about Howard Hawks, and Bogdanovich had admitted that he hadn't seen much by him. "*Bringing Up Baby* hadn't been seen in New York in years," Bogdanovich recalled, "and Gene, Andy, and I made a list of all the Howard Hawks films we wanted to see." The young men then persuaded the New Yorker Theater's Dan Talbot to stage a two-week series called "The Forgotten Film" in January 1961. Of the twenty-eight films on the program, eleven were by Hawks. "I saw all the Hawks films and was blown away," Bogdanovich said. "On one Saturday we showed *The Big Sleep* and *To Have and Have Not*, and we had lines around the block. This was our first hint that this whole Bogart thing was happening. At *Bringing Up Baby*, people were screaming with laughter. I had to see it three times."

This, then, was the beginning of the Howard Hawks cult in America. When the *Hatari!* release date was firmed up, Richard Griffith, the curator of film at the Museum of Modern Art, agreed to stage the series if Bogdanovich could convince Paramount to pay for it. This done, Bogdanovich and his wife, Polly Platt, traveled to Hollywood to meet the great man and interview him in his Paramount office. "He was very cool, very straight," Bogdanovich remembered. "He sat there smoking Kents. He didn't laugh much, but when Polly made a mistake with the tape recorder and taped over a half hour, it didn't faze him at all; he said we could just do it again." The couple spent two or three days talking to Hawks.

When he was in New York for the *Hatari!* opening, Hawks appeared at the museum, where Bogdanovich saw him again briefly. The series "was very successful, very popular," Bogdanovich said. "It was unusual for its time. People were just getting hip to the idea that Howard Hawks was good." Bogdanovich's pioneering monograph, *The Cinema of Howard Hawks*, emphasized the irony of Hawks's relative neglect in his native land, given that "he is probably the most typical American director of all," and stressed the fact that domestic recognition was coming only in the wake of his discovery by the French. Also published in the wake of the series was Andrew Sarris's penetrating two-part article in *Films and Filming*, "The World of Howard Hawks," the first in-depth auteurist consideration of Hawks's career written in English. In December 1962, the young cutting-edge British critics added their voices in support of Hawks, as the bold *Movie* magazine put *Hatari!* on its cover and devoted most of the issue to the director, with articles by V. F. Perkins, Robin Woods, and Mark Shivas, among others.

Hatari! had its world premiere on June 19, 1962, at the Egyptian Theater in Hollywood as a black-tie benefit for Hollywood Friends of Africa. The next morning, Hawks flew to New York, where a marquee several stories tall on the De Mille Theater advertised "Howard Hawks' *Hatari!*" and the East Coast premiere took place that night. The reviews were decidedly mixed, with everyone agreeing on the merits of the animal footage but most critics deriding the egregious 159-minute running time and pointing out the lack of dramatic urgency in the story. Business started out strongly, the film bringing in just slightly less than Hitchcock's Paramount smash *Psycho* had at the same theater, but didn't hold at that high level. The film was very popular with kids that summer but was basically perceived as a pleasant and exotic diversion though not essential viewing for adults. A fine performer in the Midwest and Southwest, it did less well in bigger, more sophisticated markets. Hawks continued to feel that Paramount didn't make the most out of it and, after all the work and high hopes, was a bit disappointed with the commercial results.

By the time *Hatari!* was completely played out and removed from release at the end of 1964, Paramount had collected $4,755,913 in domestic film rentals on a box-office gross of $10,015,179. Overseas, it did well, particularly in Japan, where it had a huge opening at the Hibiya Theater in Tokyo and went on to earn more than $1 million. Still, as Paramount sank nearly $10 million into production, prints, advertising, and marketing, the film remained officially in the red until the 1970s, when television sales started generating residuals.

Even though Hawks had virtually unlimited control and power in the making of *Hatari!*, his particular way—both loose and strong—of creating films, the specific mix of personalities involved, and his willingness, even eagerness, to discover his film in the process of making it, meant that it turned out quite differently than the motion picture he'd had in his mind at the outset. Today, making a film in this manner at a Hollywood studio would be impossible, intolerable. And yet, despite the strain and discord among the troops, *Hatari!* is the most genial film in the world. As the critic Joseph McBride and other devoted fans of the picture have noted, there are few, if any, films that offer such enjoyable company, where one would like to just step into the screen and join in the action. If you don't like the film, it is legitimately open to criticism as being too long, juvenile, silly, undramatic, and inconsequential. If you do like it, none of this matters, and the more than two-and-a-half hours spent with the characters may not be nearly long enough.

Among the numerous individuals who "discovered" Hawks at the Museum of Modern Art during the summer of 1962 was the future film critic Stuart Byron. Years later, when he was asked to contribute to an anthology about favorite movies of all time, Byron chose to write about *Hatari!* Although he rivaled Jacques Rivette in critical extremism when he presumed that "even John Simon, forced to see *Hatari!* ten times, would understand its greatness," Byron astutely positioned Hawks at the center of the whole auteurist critical debate of the period, pointing out that "it is through Hawks that most people 'come to' auteurism," or "see the light." He then described *Hatari!* as the most perfect expression of everything Hawks believed in and represented; Hawks was, the critic maintained, "a Darwinian without regrets," a proponent of "a kind of atheistic humanism" who posited the value of personality and human beings against the "spiritual void" depicted in all of his films. Byron argued, "Inasmuch as he has no nostalgia for religion, Hawks is more starkly modern than Bergman (or for that matter, Wallace Stevens)—and . . . he can only be compared thematically, among the major modern figures, with Samuel Beckett."

Thus were drawn the battle lines—and such they were—in the dramatic debate over whether or not Howard Hawks was an "artist." As Hawks made his final films over the next few years, the argument would heat up to feverish, sometimes insanely passionate levels.

36

A Fishy Story:

Man's Favorite Sport?

By February 1962, Charles Feldman and Jack Gordean had already spent sixteen months trying to hammer out Hawks's rich deal with Columbia. In the usual Hollywood manner, it kept getting stalled and delayed, and after making his agents worry when he kept adding provisions that no studio would ever grant, Hawks decided he didn't want to go through with the deal after all. The reason he gave involved changes in the tax law that looked to pass shortly in Congress, laws that would put a financial damper on his plans to base his activities in Europe. After talking it over on the phone, Hawks and Columbia chairman Leo Jaffe mutually decided to call the whole thing off, but it was still embarrassing to Feldman, who had just produced *Walk on the Wild Side* for the studio and was also preparing Ian Fleming's *Casino Royale*, the one James Bond novel not owned by Hawks's old friend Cubby Broccoli and Harry Saltzman. Feldman and Hawks brought Leigh Brackett out to Los Angeles to discuss an approach to the script, and Hawks fancied the idea of Cary Grant in the role of the dapper 007. Later in the year, Feldman and Hawks got an advance print of *Dr. No* from England and thus were among the first Americans to see the initial Sean Connery Bond film. Hawks promptly lost interest in pursuing *Casino Royale*, but Feldman persisted.

For his part, Hawks quickly entered into a deal to stay at Paramount that was virtually identical to the one he had nearly consummated with Columbia: three pictures to be made by his Laurel Productions over five years, with Hawks receiving $200,000 a picture and 50 percent of the profits. There was briefly talk of the director reuniting with John Wayne and Dean Martin on a CinemaScope epic, tentatively entitled "The Yukon Trial," about a cattle drive to Alaska during the Gold Rush days. But Hawks, who had not made anything fully in the romantic-comedy vein in more than a decade, was more interested in a story by Pat Frank that had recently appeared in *Cosmopolitan* magazine, "The Girl Who Almost Got Away."

The modest tale centered on Roger Willoughby, a light-tackle specialist who, as the most successful salesman of the year, receives a bonus and a trip to the famous Wakapoochee Bass Tournament. This is a considerable challenge since, despite his profession, he has never fished in his life.

Still anticipating huge grosses from *Hatari!*, Paramount immediately approved the story, a $3.5 million budget, and the idea that Cary Grant, just then enjoying a late-career peak in popularity, would star as the befuddled would-be fisherman. Setting the production up was easy; almost nothing, after that, would go as Hawks planned. So pleased with her work and company on his last two pictures, he called Leigh Brackett to write the script for him, but she was headlong into a new novel and didn't care to put it aside for several months. Instead, he decided to try two relatively untested writers, John Fenton Murray and Steve McNeil; the former was for years Red Skelton's head writer on radio and TV and had just written *It's Only Money* for Jerry Lewis, while the latter was a busy television writer with ninety-seven *Saturday Evening Post* stories to his credit.

As he had done so many times before, Hawks held long meetings with his scribes, going over ideas for scenes and characterization, then sent them off on their own to work separately and deliver pages which would go straight into Hawks's bulging briefcase. Neither writer was entirely happy with this arrangement, and Murray, who never really hit it off with the director, quickly came to actively resent it. Paul Helmick dropped by Paramount a few times over the next couple of weeks and, in a note to Brackett, said, "You'd laugh if you could see how the two writers corner me to find out about Hawks, how he works, what he likes, how one knows if he likes something, etc. At first, they were quite relaxed and patient, but now, they're nervous wrecks."

Throughout June, Hawks was tied up with *Hatari!* openings and related events, and late in the month he traveled back to Paris, "looking for new talent," as Helmick said. While there, he received word of William Faulkner's death in Mississippi on July 6. Shortly after Hawks returned to California in July, Cary Grant took him to lunch to make a proposal: If Hawks would direct "The Great Sebastian," a project Grant wanted to do with the producer Saul Schwartz at Columbia, he, Grant, would definitely commit to star in Hawks's fish story. The actor should have known by now that Hawks would not take on a job for hire; in the event, the director did not like the "Sebastian" project, a sentiment that must have cooled Grant's interest in it. Grant, despite wanting to work with Hawks again, remained less than fully enthusiastic about his friend's new story, refusing to be pinned down, until he finally decided that he preferred a witty and romantic suspense script by Peter Stone called *Charade,* in which the director Stanley Donen wanted him to star opposite Audrey Hepburn.

Hawks was stuck, and Paramount was not pleased. Although the director felt that the Murray-Fenton screenplay needed some more work, he was still basically happy with the story and wanted to go ahead with the film, with Rock Hudson replacing Cary Grant. Having recently proven his mettle in such romantic-comedy hits as *Pillow Talk* and *Lover Come Back,* Hudson was then one of the biggest box-office draws in Hollywood, and Paramount agreed to arrange to borrow him from Universal. But in October, Hawks and the studio came to an impasse on the director's choice of a female lead. Although he was initially interested in a young actress named Joanna Moore, as soon as Hawks saw footage on Paula Prentiss, an attractive, twenty-three-year-old MGM contract player from Texas who had recently married the up-and-coming actor Richard Benjamin, he felt she was the perfect choice for the pretty, domineering woman who eggs on the flustered man. So strongly did he believe in her potential that he changed studios over her; when Paramount insisted on a bigger name to play opposite Hudson, "Howard went across the street for a meeting, came back, and said, 'We're going to be moving over to Universal right after lunch,'" as Paul Helmick remembered it. "It all happened within one hour. When we got to Universal our names were already painted on our parking places."

With shooting due to start in mid-November, Hawks quickly moved to fill the other parts. Very keen on Ursula Andress, even more so after *Dr. No,* Hawks tried to sign her for a long-term deal, beginning with the fishing film. But rightly suspecting that she would be hot once *Dr. No* was released, Andress and her husband John Derek decided to decline Hawks's offer. For the secondary woman's role of the daughter of the fishing-resort owner, he then considered using a Hungarian beauty he had found but settled on another discovery, the Austrian blonde Maria Perschy. As Hudson's fiancée, he cast Charlene Holt, a fun, spirited, twenty-three-year-old New York model who had already done tiny parts in *If a Man Answers* and *Days of Wine and Roses.* But Hawks spotted her in the course of one day in both a Revlon TV commercial and an ad in *Life* magazine. For her first interview with Hawks in November, the Texas native showed up straight from horseback riding, wearing tight Levi's, her hair in disarray. Nothing could have excited Hawks more, and he was quite pleased with her subsequent screen test. "I asked how much experienced she had," the director recalled. "She said this is the first time I've had more than two consecutive lines. Every time we worked she got better." Hawks liked Holt's laugh, and her charming manner and open, wholesome-looking face reminded him of Norma Shearer. Not only that, but she was unattached and quite amenable to going out with Hawks; for the next couple of years, she was his most frequent female companion.

Deciding to shoot virtually the entire picture on the Universal back lot, Hawks postponed the start week by week, until rolling cameras on December 11, 1962. He surrounded himself with familiar faces: Russell Harlan was back as the cinematographer, Stuart Gilmore as the editor, Paul Helmick as the associate producer, and Henry Mancini would compose the score. In the interim since *Hatari!*, David Hawks had become a working member of the Directors Guild of America, and he joined the crew as the official second assistant director. But most important, by delaying production, Hawks was able to have Leigh Brackett, now done with her novel, on-board, at one thousand dollars a week, to rewrite the script as he went. Determined to shoot in sequence, an increasing rarity in Hollywood, in order to enhance the spontaneity and allow for changes in the story, Hawks once again had Brackett by his side throughout the filming, writing and rewriting scenes again and again just before he staged them. When it made it into the press that old silent-film director Howard Hawks was making a picture with no script, Hawks came to his own defense by saying that predatory television producers always hungry for comedy gags and situations made it necessary for feature filmmakers to hide their ideas, lest they turn up on the tube before the films hit theaters.

The story was simple enough: Roger Willoughby is forced to endure endless frustrations and humiliations, both professional and personal, at the hands of a brash woman, Abigail Page, the head of public relations for the fishing lodge staging the competition, whose crazy idea it was in the first place for him to be entered. The whole idea turns upon Willoughby, the author of the highly regarded fishing manual *Fishing Made Simple,* being a fraud, a so-called expert who is the furthest thing from it. It gets so bad between the two of them that Willoughby keeps threatening to kill Abigail for getting him into all this, and the entire story is easily read as an allegory about sex, experience versus inexperience, and expertise versus ineptitude.

Hawks sent Helmick and Harlan to San Francisco to shoot the opening scene, in which the antagonism between the two leads is established during some driving up and down the hilly streets. "He didn't know what the hell he wanted," Helmick said, "except that he wanted them to dislike each other. The only thing he did was to pick the cars." The actors did not go on location, their close-ups in this sequence being inserted later with process shots. In the extended follow-up parking-lot scene, filmed on the studio back lot, of Willoughby diving headfirst through the sunroof in Abigail's car and flailing away upside down inside of it, it instantly becomes clear that the role was designed for Cary Grant. Rock Hudson doesn't exactly do a Grant impersonation, but in certain scenes the patterning is exceedingly pronounced. The effect is not displeasing, and even proves amiable, but it unavoidably points to the absence of the genuine article. As was his habit, before each scene Hawks would talk it over with his leading actors, asking them what they would do in the given situation, how they would react, what they would say. More than usual, he would demand a lot of takes in an attempt to get what he wanted from Hudson as well as Prentiss, thereby making them both more insecure than they were in the first place. Hudson gave it the college try throughout, even if it can't have been pleasant to know that he was second choice to Grant and was being encouraged to act like him. Prentiss, despite the fact that Hawks enormously liked her work, was unnerved by Hawks's approach, feeling that he was trying to overly channel her performance to resemble the great comediennes he had worked with in the past. On any number of occasions Hawks drove her to break down in tears; another time Norman Alden, who played the "Indian" John Screaming Eagle, did the honors when he attempted to comfort her about a bad review she had received that day in *Variety*. She started crying at the mere mention of it, "and she had a big scene to do that day, sort of a romantic scene with Rock," recalled Alden.

For his part, Alden was also a bit thrown off at first, resenting the fact that Hawks was constantly taking Hudson and Prentiss aside to talk to them about their performances but never said a word to him about his own work. Finally, he went to his director to say that he hoped he was doing his job well enough, to which Hawks replied, "Well, if they could act, I wouldn't have to do things like that." Alden found Hawks an amazing character, unlike anyone else he had encountered in Hollywood. "I adored him. He'd change clothes during the day and he'd come out and be very elegant. If he wanted a chair for me he'd call for 'Mr. Alden's chair.' He had all that old-time stuff that used to go on in pictures."

One day when Hawks, Hudson, Prentiss, and Norman Alden were having lunch on the lot, they were startled when a voice from behind them abruptly asked, "Do you mind if I join you?" It was Cary Grant, and the group spent a perfectly delightful noon hour with the man who was supposed to have starred in the picture. A less happy encounter came when

Angie Dickinson dropped by the set. Having been put under personal contract by Hawks only to find herself sold off to Warner Bros., Dickinson had always hoped, even expected, to work with the director again, but he had now made two films since *Rio Bravo* without ever contacting her. The actress had recently dyed her hair blond, and she recalled saying, "'Hi, Howard. Gosh, I'd love to make another picture with you,' and all he said was, 'I liked you better brunette.' It was a real put-down. I got the brush. You couldn't push him."

The executives at Universal found they couldn't push the old pro either. One morning when it was fast approaching ten o'clock and the company couldn't get the indoor lake set ready for a rehearsal, Hawks announced that he would leave and go home if he couldn't have a rehearsal by ten. Quickly, everyone was assembled and the actors were put in the water, whereupon Hawks turned to his young script supervisor, Bruce Kessler, and said, "'That's the silliest thing I've ever seen. Come on.' And he turns and starts walking out of the stage. I'm right on his tail. Everyone's grabbing at me and asking what's going on, but we went off and just rode around for a couple of hours. He went to a Buick agency, but he made sure that I could not get to a phone. I could not get out of his sight. Then he took me to lunch. He didn't eat lunch. Very rarely would he eat lunch. And I couldn't go to the bathroom. He sat there and never talked about what was in the scene, or what was wrong with the scene. . . . Finally, at two o'clock, we go back in. Our production manager is standing there, and he drove right by the man. Didn't even blink. He went back to work, having decided what he wanted to do, and we did it. But whatever his thought process was, what was going through his head, I'll never know. He wouldn't discuss the scene at all."

Hawks had the costume designer, Edith Head, create some custom-crafted scuba suits for Paula Prentiss and Maria Perschy. Molds were made of each actress's body, after which liquid rubber was sprayed over the molds to create the most form-fitting outfit possible. Costing ten thousand dollars apiece, the black suits were worth every penny, as they were astonishingly sexy, impossible to imagine getting in and out of. With women very much on his mind, Hawks also commissioned the photographer Don Ornitz to create an elaborate title sequence for which he shot six thousand Playboyesque color photos of thirty-three unknown models in various athletic pursuits.

Working at a deliberate but not painfully slow pace over three and a half months, Hawks wrapped the picture in the final week of March, and the editor, Stuart Gilmore, had it ready for its first sneak preview on May 31. At this point it ran 145 minutes, unimaginably long for a light romantic comedy, but Hawks claimed that it played tremendously well in this version, that Universal had never gotten such positive cards from a preview audience. Then executives decided that footage had to come out, and the next sneak, on June 7, was rather less successful than the first. At this, the suits began panicking and, rather than restoring material, deduced that more needed to be removed. The result was an even poorer third preview; inexplicably, this is the version that Universal decided to release.

Hawks always claimed, inaccurately, that forty minutes were cut—it was actually twenty-five—and insisted that the film was sabotaged in the process. "A comedy can really be ruined by being shortened," he told Peter Bogdanovich. "If you take out the scene which is planted to make the following scene funny, then the following scene is not funny. It suddenly becomes slow. And every 'plant' we had in *Man's Favorite Sport?* was taken out." But there are things that just don't add up in Hawks's account of what happened. Paul Helmick, the associate producer, doesn't remember the reactions to the various cuts having been appreciably different, and there was a full half year between the time of the final sneak preview and the film's release, time enough for Hawks to fight for a version he liked. At the time of the second preview, Hawks was "very high on his picture," according to Charles Feldman's secretary, Grace Dobish, and the director was very pleased with the attention and promotion Universal was lavishing on it. Even in retrospect, while admitting the film's failure, Hawks refused to blame its shortcomings on Rock Hudson. "Rock tried hard . . . but Rock is not a comedian," he told Joseph McBride. "And when you have visualized one person in it, and you're trying to get that, it's an awful tough job to do it because you just don't come out right. And even then we ended up with a pretty good picture."

Since his death from AIDS, much has been made of Hudson's private lifestyle and the veiled homosexual content of some of his films; critics might even point to the opening scene, in which he accidentally produces a driver's license that identifies him as Abigail, as one example of it. Paul Helmick swears that neither he nor Hawks "had any idea" that Hudson was gay, assuming, along with the public, that he was a he-man just as his image suggested.

One frustration for Hawks, Leigh Brackett, and everyone else was that Brackett was denied screen credit by the Writers Guild of America, despite the fact that Hawks pushed for it; even the initial writers, Murray and

McNeil, felt she deserved it. Brackett noted on her personal copy of the script, "I worked on this final version for four months, writing ahead of the cameras during the shooting but got no credit. The Guild said it was a polish rather than an original contribution." An outraged Paul Helmick wrote to her, "When I think of all the time you trudged from the office to the stage in the wind and the cold with five different versions of the same scene, it makes me wild to think that such an injustice could happen."

Even though numerous Hawks pictures—*The Air Circus, Scarface, Come and Get It, Red River*—were tampered with after they left the director's hands, *The Big Sky* and *Man's Favorite Sport?* are the only ones he felt were seriously compromised by studio cutting. The recent reappearance of the full, original *The Big Sky* proved that there was little qualitative difference between the two versions after all, and there is reason to suspect that Hawks exaggerated the damage done to *Man's Favorite Sport?* as well, as a way of rationalizing its relative commercial failure. In fact, the picture performed quite acceptably in its initial engagements, beginning February 5, 1964, and ranked sixth, ninth, and eighth at the box office for three weeks from late February through early March, a time when the top hits in the country were the more sophisticated and astringent comedies *Tom Jones* and *Dr. Strangelove,* and the broad, all-star slapstick farce *It's a Mad, Mad, Mad, Mad World. Man's Favorite Sport?* ended up with thoroughly average domestic rentals of $2,325,000, twenty-eighth on the charts for the year.

Mainstream critics, who had begun hearing the isolated proclamations of Hawks's genius, were not impressed, finding the film slow, old-fashioned, and not up to the level of the director's revered earlier comedies. It certainly looked bad, as Russell Harlan bathed the studio sets with what appeared to be floodlights, which only emphasized their artificiality, and the lakeside and forest "locations" fairly screamed "back lot." In addition, some of the early scenes, notably a visit to a touristy music gallery, where Hudson starts up all the machines so that he won't be overheard when he tells Prentiss and Pershy his deep secret, and a hokey interlude in a revolving hotel bar, where Hudson has to walk to keep up with the seated women, are as creatively impoverished as anything in Hawks, unimaginable in his work during his prime. Yet another reprise of the famous *Bringing Up Baby* gag, with Hudson walking in step close behind Pershy after she rips her dress, further suggested that Hawks had reached the point of merely recycling old ideas. This put more pressure on the cultists to defend their hero, and no doubt the brightest reading of *Man's Favorite Sport?* came from Molly Haskell, who, in a reappraisal seven years later, found herself "moved by the reverberations of a whole substratum of meaning, of sexual antagonism, desire, and despair." She saw Hudson and Prentiss as Adam and Eve figures in a Garden of Eden, where "Hudson is a virgin, who has written a 'How to' book on sex while harboring a deep, fastidious horror of it. His masculinity is a lie." Prentiss, therefore, "must take the initiative in Hudson's sexual initiation, for which the fishing exploit is metaphor. Fish are phallic symbols, of course, and there is even a scene in which a loose fish thrashes around inside Hudson's pants, causing him to jump and jerk uncontrollably." Haskell less convincingly argued that Hawks was not "an unconscious artist," positing that he was "far more deliberate and articulate in his vision of the American male than, say, John Cassavetes."

Of course, this is just the sort of analysis that Hawks would have gaped at in disbelief, but one could actually go further, to suggest that the film was a send-up, if not a devastating critique, of the entire, vaunted Hawksian ethos of professionalism. The film hinges on the fraudulence of the "expert," upon there being much less to the great professional than his reputation suggests. To Hudson, Prentiss says, "Of course you're a phony!" or something close to it, on several occasions. By the time Hudson's fiancée, played by Charlene Holt, turns up, he's got a reputation as a ladies' man, although nothing could be further from the truth. Finally, after winning the tournament, Hudson, in a very uncharacteristic scene for Hawks, confesses his unworthiness to his boss and the other contestants. For those who would make a case against Hawks, they have all the ammunition they need right here, a private confession from the director himself that he isn't all he's cracked up to be; it recalls Slim's indelible private put-down of him: "a great pillar of nothing."

But veiled, encoded, symbolic messages were not Hawks's way. For him, *Man's Favorite Sport?* was a decent comedy that was not quite as good as it might have been. In the context of his career, it marked another stage in the lessening of his artistic grip, of his absolute power to make a film come out the way he envisioned it. It was just a hint of how far off the track he would go next time out.

37

Fast Cars and Young Women

"Howard liked young people," the actor Robert Donner said. "And he had young people around him. I mean, for him it was fast cars and young women or fast women and whatever." As Howard Hawks got older, the circle he drew around him grew younger and younger; and it wasn't simply that he was turning into a dirty old man. "He loved the ladies," said Paramount producer A. C. Lyles, who recalled that for a while in the mid-1960s, there was a constant parade of young lovelies streaming through the Paramount gate to meet with the eminent producer-director. "You could always tell when someone was going to see Howard on the lot because it was always a willowy blonde with a husky voice." More than any other active director, the grey fox had the reputation of a starmaker, and while some budding starlets found him alternately intimidating, uncommunicative, and behind the times, others were struck by his extreme cordiality, youthful attitude, and great storytelling abilities.

But young actresses weren't the only people who attracted his interest. New actors, writers, assistants, and friends also entered his life. As Gregg entered his teens and found like-minded buddies interested in go-cart and dirt-bike racing, Hawks hung out a great deal with them, giving advice and continuing to ride motorcycles and drive a souped-up car himself. He continued to prefer men and women of action, who liked sports and the outdoors and whom he at least imagined shared his purposeful, uncomplaining, straight-ahead view of life. Hawks had few true close friends as it was; John Wayne he would sometimes see socially, while others, like Cary Grant, he would speak with occasionally over the phone. But his life in Palm Springs was not at all like that of the vast numbers of other desert dwellers in their seventies; due to his son, he was mostly around teenagers and, often, young women.

One woman who was as close to him as anyone was Cissy Wellman. Born in 1943, she was the fifth child of film director William Wellman and the former Dorothy Coonan, but she did not get along well with her father. "We were too much alike. We had friction and, you know, personality conflict. Dad loved me, but he said, 'I love you in my own way. I'm just a cantankerous son of a bitch.' And I loved my dad more than anything." Hawks was Cissy's surrogate father. "We understood each other so well that, you know, he was the dad that I always wanted." Her own father, she recalled, was actually jealous of her relationship with Hawks, with whom he had always maintained a friendly professional rivalry. "He used to say, 'How come you're always going out to Palm Springs . . . with Howard?' I said, 'Because we get along.' Simple. But he would be strange about it."

Living mostly in the desert, she felt, cut Hawks off a bit from what was happening in Hollywood, and he rarely attended new movies, preferring to watch television or look at magazines to spot models. Wellman reflected on how even as he entered old age, "Howard had a little-boy way about him. When he laughed, when he would get something, he would get this little-boy, cat-that-swallowed-the-canary grin and he would just . . . I loved the way he was and his . . . I miss *him*. The human, the man that was. . . . We were friends, we would get into fights, we would just talk and laugh. Go play golf, go fishing. Books he loved. He loved to cook, he taught me about baked potatoes and sour cream and caviar and artichokes. I'd do the artichokes, that would be our dinner. He loved my husband [Robert Donner] and used him in films and they became best friends. It was just wonderful to have that kind of relationship. I loved Howard. I miss him a lot."

Donner was impressed by Hawks's stamina both at work and at play. On the set, he recalled, "He very seldom sat down. Always remember he'd be standing alongside the camera and I was just amazed at his endurance." When he wasn't shooting, if he was in Los Angeles Hawks would get into his custom-engineered Corvette "and he used to pride himself on the fact that late at night he could make it from here to Palm Springs in about an hour and a half," a trip that normally takes two hours. "I mean he just screamed down there. Another thing I remember about him was that his idea of a dry martini was half vermouth and half gin. . . . And when we would go out to dinner, Howard would have a couple of martinis before dinner, and it amazed me at his age that he could put away a couple of those martinis. And then drive home."

Considerable speculation centered upon whether or not Hawks continued to enjoy a sex life in the 1960s and 1970s. Chris Nyby swore that Hawks was basically impotent from the late 1950s on. Robert Donner wasn't sure, but said that it was his gut feeling that Hawks "was active right up till the day he died." Pierre Rissient, a French publicist and friend who introduced him to many actresses and shot screen tests for Hawks in Europe, said, "It was very important for him to have the company of women, and there was the sexual impulse behind much of his casting, but he rarely took advantage of his position to do it. He was always trying to impress, but not to seduce. . . ." On one of Hawks's European trips, Rissient accompanied him to a festival in Gotenberg, Sweden, "where there were lots of sexy girls. Hawks was stimulated but didn't take advantage of the situation. But he was interested in the sport of it."

Hawks's good friend Bruce Kessler, a former race-car driver in his twenties who was the script supervisor on *Man's Favorite Sport?* and the second-unit director on *Red Line 7000,* insisted that Hawks did take advantage. "He was very active for a man his age, very interested in women. Not like a dirty old man, but interested. He admired women, and if I was sitting here talking to an attractive girl and Howard walked in, he would say, 'Well, let's screen-test her.' I'd say, 'Howard, she's a waitress here, she doesn't want to be an actress.' He'd say, 'Oh, that's okay, we'll screen test her anyway.'"

Hawks maintained an older man–younger man sexual camaraderie with Kessler. "Quite often after a picture was over, not before, he'd invite an actress with a bit part that he'd gotten friendly with to come down to his house in Palm Springs. Then he would call me and say, 'This girl's bringing a girlfriend. Would you please come down here?' . . . And Howard was sexually active. I mean he was a man who was seventy who was still sexually active. He also gave me some very sage advice. He once said to me, 'I've been married three times, Bruce. And I want to tell you something. Every one of my wives, they loved boating and fishing and playing golf and all these things, and hated Hollywood parties and going to premieres until the day they got married, and from that point on that's all they wanted to do. And they wouldn't care about doing the other things.'" Other visitors to Hawks's Palm Springs house remembered regularly seeing one or more young beauties lying around his pool topless or completely nude, although they never saw Hawks being physical with any of them.

Yet one more perspective came from George Kirgo, the young writer Hawks hired for *Red Line 7000.* One morning Kirgo arrived at the studio and was told that Hawks urgently wanted to see him. "I went into his office and he told me to close the door and come sit next to him. I drew up close to him and asked him what it was, and he had the most pleased look on his face and then, in a hushed, very confidential tone, he said in that drawling way of his, 'George, I got laid last night.' I didn't know what to say . . . and then he went on to explain that he was alone at home in Beverly Hills and he saw someone moving outside his window. He went to look and, of course, it was a beautiful woman who said she was lost or couldn't find an address or something. So he invited her in and talked to her and gave her a drink, and one thing led to another and so on. It was all just too fantastic, so I didn't know whether to believe it or not. . . . Howard did have a very active fantasy life."

What is certain is that Hawks needed to have beautiful young women, preferably with a good sense of humor, around him as "ornaments," as Chance put it, and that they did stimulate him and make him feel younger. Privately, some of his friends maintained that Hawks, in his old age, could become sexually excited given the right incitement, and one recalled overhearing two of the actresses in *Red Line 7000* comparing notes on their expertise at getting Hawks aroused. Chance, who saw him whenever he visited Paris, was sure that she was the last important woman in his life, but that doesn't account for Charlene Holt, who was regularly Hawks's date in Los Angeles during the mid-1960s and appeared in three of his films during that time. Hawks liked her enormously, and several of Hawks's friends swear that they were physically intimate; at the same time, no one would exactly describe her as his "girlfriend," and by 1966 she had married the multimillionaire Los Angeles real estate and construction executive William Alan Tishman. "She was a marvelous, impudent woman," Kirgo said of her. "No one could one-up Charlene."

Much further from his daily thoughts was his first wife, Athole, now sixty-two, who had been living quietly in West Los Angeles for years, seeing few people and basically holding her own. In late summer 1963, she had another relapse and was taken to Edgemont Hospital. Following doctors' advice, proceedings were initiated to have Athole declared legally incompetent, with her daughter Barbara declared official guardian. Thereafter, Athole was cared for in a series of nursing homes.

Before *Man's Favorite Sport?* came out, Hawks figured he might be staying at Universal and told top production executive Eddie Muhl that he was interested in doing a low-budget car-racing movie as his next production. When the studio manhandled his comedy after the sneak previews, however, he became disgusted with Universal and returned to Paramount, which gladly took him back. At that moment, his agents at Famous Artists tried to push Hawks into an intriguing new project, *The Americanization of Emily,* but as usual, Hawks preferred pursuing his own ideas.

Two ventures took precedence. Dating back to the silent days and his fascination with Marshall Neilan's multipart *Bits of Life,* Hawks had been intrigued with the possibility of telling multiple stories in one overall narrative. Finally, he saw his chance to try it. "I had three good stories about the racetrack, but none of them would make a picture, so I thought maybe I can put them together." Paul Helmick felt that Hawks embarked on this ensemble piece, his only film to deal with the 1960s generation, because he "wanted to show that he could make a film without paying John Wayne a million dollars. 'There are plenty of young people out there who can do it, and I don't have to pay.' He was trying to prove something." But Cissy Wellman, who was in the picture, said, "*Red Line* he only did because of his son. Gregg was ten and was into cars, and that's the only reason he did it."

The foreword to the screenplay, unsigned but betraying evidence of having been written by Hawks, begins as follows: "*Red Line 7000* is the story of three men and the women who love them. The three stories have little or no connection except that the men are race drivers. They are those prima donnas who handle incredibly fast combustions of steel and other metals and do it as a virtuoso plays a violin. Racing is the epitome of the dangerous professions, and while in some ways the men are similar in their abilities as men they are vastly different."

As he had on his last several pictures, Hawks wanted to put two writers on it simultaneously, but not in collaboration. Steve McNeil would be one, while the other would be a television drama writer from New York with no previous film experience, George Kirgo. "He picked me because he had seen a TV show I wrote, *Arrest and Trial,* in which Diane McBain told her hit-man boyfriend Richard Conte, 'I have bad luck with men.' Howard liked that and hired me on the basis of that one line."

Kirgo said Hawks "didn't have much story," just a few character ideas, such as the driver with only one hand, based on a well-known real driver named Allan Heath, and a woman who was considered "damaged goods." During the first week of May 1964, the writers, at $750 a week apiece, started work, listening to Hawks describe racetrack incidents and scenes from some of his old pictures. The director also prepared a story chart with a different color for each character. "He wanted to put in a character named Galveston," Kirgo remembered. "So I said, 'Why don't you just call her Fort Worth?' and that shut him up. But in honor of Howard, in *Don't Make Waves* I named a character Malibu, who was Sharon Tate."

With the script barely under way, Hawks began making plans to film some actual races that summer, and he saw in his new buddy Bruce Kessler, a former member of the world championship Ferrari team but not a stock-car driver, the ideal man for the job. Hawks had called the young man in the first place because of a short film Kessler was making about racing called *The Sound of Speed.* Hawks came to watch some of the shooting and later invited Kessler to the Palm Springs house, where they had rambling talk about nothing in particular. "But the feeling he expressed to me was that I understood life and death." Kessler intuited that Hawks felt "'We knew.' All of that was in his pictures, all of those guys not afraid of death. I wasn't that way at all, but he saw me in that light, and I listened to him, he said he'd like to have me work for him, and I said, 'Doing what?' and he was very oblique about that. You were with him or against him. That was how Howard kind of saw things. If you were one of his, he figured you could operate the camera, fly an airplane, do anything that was necessary to do on the picture."

Intent upon proving that he could make a commercial film quickly and cheaply, Hawks agreed to a $1.35 million budget, including 26 percent overhead. Of that, Hawks took $200,000, plus another $20,000 for the story. Quickly, he lined up cooperation from NASCAR to film at the organization's races and, over the next half year, Kessler shot several actual races: the Firecracker 400 at Daytona Beach, Florida, on July 4, 1964; the Southern 500 at Darlington, South Carolina, on September 7; the National 400 at Charlotte, North Carolina, on October 18, and the Motor Trend 500 at Riverside International Raceway near Los Angeles on January 17, 1965. Through most of this, there was no script, at least none that Hawks would show Kessler. "I didn't know what to shoot," the second-unit director confessed. "Howard told me, 'Use your own judgment.' So I just figured out how to stage, how to shoot everything." Except for the few dialogue scenes set at the tracks, Kessler shot all the location material in the picture, as well as the background plates used for the process photography.

Back at the studio, Hawks divided his time among the script, the casting, and promotional tie-ins. After decades of keeping brand names out of movies, Hollywood was just waking up to the financial potential of product placement in pictures, and Hawks and Jerry Lewis, also at Paramount at the time, led the way. With the help of an old carny character named Jack Meurice, Hawks lined up tie-ins with at least a dozen companies, which, for a certain consideration, would have their products prominently displayed on-screen; among them were Ford, Puroil, Pepsi-Cola, Honda, Rolex, Revell Toys, National Car Rental, and Holiday Inn. Some of the plugs were so blatant as to be embarrassing; after seeing the picture, Pepsi registered a complaint over the way the drink was featured, undoubtedly in reference to the phallic implications of the Pepsi bottles in the romantic scene between Marianna Hill and James Caan. *Newsweek*, in its reviews of the picture, sarcastically observed, "*Red Line 7000* is the first melodrama ever made in which the hero is plainly identified by a 'Pure' sign on his coveralls." Robert Donner half-joked, "Every shot in that movie is panning over to a Pepsi-Cola or Holiday Inn sign, and everybody's wearing logos. That picture didn't need to make a dime for Howard to make money. Anything it made was pure gravy because they had subsidized it so much with corporate entities."

In one respect, the casting process was a field day for Hawks, in that the large number of roles designed for young unknowns gave him the excuse to see an endless procession of sexy models and aspiring starlets. On the other hand, distressingly few of the aspirants had any talent to speak of, and Hawks was under pressure to cast the picture relatively quickly. Some roles would go to people he already knew: Charlene Holt, Norman Alden, Cissy Wellman, Robert Donner, and even Hawks's ex-wife Dee Hartford.

James Caan, a twenty-five-year-old actor from New York, was seen that summer in his first feature-film role, in Paramount's *Lady in a Cage*, and Hawks felt his brooding intensity would work for the nominal lead of the driver with a purity hang-up when it came to girls. For the two other main drivers, he wasn't so fortunate, choosing John Robert Crawford and James (Skip) Ward, both of whom were blond, bland, and nearly interchangeable.

For the women, Hawks went the route he'd been traversing ever since Bacall: he scoured TV shows, commercials, and magazines, looking for faces that caught his fancy. Bruce Kessler recalled, "We're driving down the street one day and he [sees] this girl on a billboard, and he says, 'Find out who that girl is. See if she wants a screen test. I think she's the type of girl I'm looking for to play this kind of part.'" It turned out that Kessler had known her when she was very young, before she went to New York and became a successful model, which is how Gail Hire, a dusky brunette, came to play the "bad luck" lead in the film. Laura Devon, a blonde who had made an impression on television's *The Richard Boone Show*, was cast as the more innocent tomboy, Julie, whom George Kirgo named after his own daughter.

Perhaps still inspired by Chance, Hawks decided that the third important female part would be a French girl, and he was determined to have one of the hottest young French actresses of the moment, Françoise Dorléac, play her. It's easy to understand why he wanted her, since no one ever fit the ideal of the Hawksian woman more than this willowy twenty-two-year-old beauty, whom many people felt was even more stunning than her younger sister, Catherine Deneuve. Hawks tried for weeks to pin her down through agents, raising his offer to $3,500 a week, far more than anyone else in the cast was getting—James Caan, for instance, earned $500 a week. But her European agent was hesitant, Dorléac herself proved elusive, and she ended up making her English-language debut in a terrible epic, *Genghis Khan.*

Instead, Hawks found one of the sexiest actresses he ever used in a film, Marianna Hill, to play the French girl whose "secondhand" status so bothers James Caan's tormented driver. Hill, who had done a bit of TV work, proved to be by far the most lively performer in *Red Line 7000*, and it would have seemed that she, of all of Hawks's discoveries of the 1960s, had what it took to become an effective screen personality; in the event, however, she popped up in films only sporadically over the years, notably in *Medium Cool* and *The Godfather, Part II.*

As the summer and fall wore on, George Kirgo assumed the dominant role in writing the picture since Steve McNeil was becoming unhappy and depressed; he spent an increasing amount of time in his cups at nearby Olblath's, until Hawks abruptly fired him in December. When the Writers Guild later assigned Kirgo sole screenplay credit, McNeil initially objected, but realized, he said, "The changes since I went off the picture have been so extensive that I see little point in protesting." When he came in from Palm Springs, Hawks would lunch with Kirgo at the studio's executive dining room. Hawks would tell stories—about Faulkner, Egypt, the old moguls—much more than he would discuss story with Kirgo, who came to love his boss but nonetheless found him "the most self-involved, self-obsessed man I've ever met," a considerable statement in Hollywood. "He was such a poseur. I remember he always laughed when someone would send him a copy of *Cahiers du Cinéma.* 'I just aim the camera at the actors,' he liked to say, 'and they make up all these things about me.'"

Another who found Hawks "very inside himself" was Howard W. Koch, a former director and producer who was appointed head of production for Paramount in the summer of 1964. "Paramount was a leaderless company when Howard Hawks was here," Koch explained. "Everything was all set up before I got here, the deals had been made, so there was nothing for me to do. The company was very rich at that time, partly because they sold their old titles to Universal for $50 million—it would be $1 billion today." This state of affairs suited Hawks just fine, since it guaranteed no executive interference, although Koch was a close friend of Jack Warner's, and the latter was not shy about confiding to Koch about some of Hawks's more devious methods.

While Kirgo was trying to give shape to Hawks's vaguely expressed ideas for the racing picture, Leigh Brackett was busy preparing a different script for the director. Even if Hawks was anxious to prove he could make a hit without John Wayne, he was also keen to work with him again. In March 1964, with Bill Hawks handling the deal, Paramount bought Harry Brown's Western *The Stars in Their Courses* for $35,000. Published in 1960 by Alfred A. Knopf, the epic novel, set in the late 1870s, was consciously crafted to be a Western *Iliad*. The story had three strong leading roles, considerable violence, and more than enough drama for a film. Hawks put Leigh Brackett to work in May, but after spending a couple of days with her to go over story points, he more or less left her alone while he concentrated on pulling *Red Line 7000* together.

Postponed from its original December 1 start date, principal photography on *Red Line 7000* got under way on January 19, 1965, two days after Kessler shot the final race in Riverside. Hawks hired Milton Krasner, his cinematographer on *The Ransom of Red Chief* and *Monkey Business*, to man the camera, and the director began putting his young cast through their paces on sets that looked even phonier than the ones on *Man's Favorite Sport?* Kirgo hadn't completed the script in any final sense, and in usual Hawks fashion, he stayed on through much of the shooting to make adjustments. Some problems arose after a draft was submitted to the Motion Picture Association of America for code approval. At a time when the decades-old censorship standards were on the verge of crumbling completely, the MPAA was still objecting to words like "bastard," the description "nice breasts," and the implication that two characters were having sex. In particular, the MPAA took offense at a bed scene (Hawks's first) between the tomboy, Julie, and her new, and possibly first, lover, Ned Arp, criticizing "pages of the dialogue which refer to the boy's past sex experiences and Julie's attitude that she desires to be the best sex companion possible. We do not wish to imply here that the problem is one of treatment. In our opinion, the fact that there is a sex relationship between the two could not be approved." Paramount and the MPAA went back and forth on this scene several times, the eventual compromise being a totally watered-down interlude that features no discussion of Ned's past experiences or of sexual performance; instead, Julie monotonously asks time and again what makes a woman sexy, to which the dim Ned has no reply. The MPAA also insisted that Julie's brother be given a scene in which he explicitly condemns Ned for his behavior with her.

Hawks labored to make the story and the actors come alive. Because of his cast members' limited experience, Hawks got much less creative input from them than he normally liked, and he had to deal with burgeoning egos. Caan, who called Hawks "Coach," was professional, although Norman Alden knew that "Jimmy always hated doing that picture"; in later years, Alden said, "he'd never want to hear about that." Cissy Wellman, who choreographed the musical number in the bar and appeared as a waitress, said that as much as she loved her surrogate father, she was very disappointed when she worked with him on the film. "He picked people who couldn't act," she said, "and some people needed direction. I think we all wanted it very much." She realized that her father, who was exactly Hawks's age but stopped making films in 1958, had gone through the same thing. "It's a question of age, of timing. It's called 'adapting.' . . . When he was directing, he would try to do Lauren Bacall all the time with every actress he had." James Caan felt the same way, allowing, "Hawks was a big believer in me. Unfortunately, I got Hawks when he was . . . well, not a little beyond his years . . . but a little behind the times, let's say." Intimidated by Hawks anyway, these young performers would tense up even more when they felt they were being molded to fit a preexisting image that the director had in mind, and it just didn't work. Hawks took to standing by and not saying anything at all. The reason there is an uncustomary amount of standard over-the-shoulder coverage in the picture is that instead of guiding and correcting his actors, Hawks would just cut when he didn't like the lines or the delivery and decide he would use a reaction shot and lay different dialogue over later on. He didn't know how to get what he wanted from his cast, and he may have realized that there was nothing there to get anyway.

Hawks felt that the production "started off half-cocked" because he didn't have the time to find a full cast of good actors, and things just got worse from there. Gail Hire did an excellent test, but once she had the part she changed from something of a headstrong rebel, which the director liked, to a star in her own mind. Laura Devon didn't pan out either, and the same went for John Robert Crawford and James Ward. Hawks liked the work of

Caan and Hill—"those two people could act and the others couldn't," he said flatly. There were many times Hawks's patience reached its limit, and Kirgo often saw him become red with anger, but Hawks still never blew his top. Because of the limitations of most of the actors, Hawks was also unable to steer his drama in a more comic direction, which had long been his natural instinct. Nor did he feel comfortable with the music, which consisted of corny "rock" versions of standards like "Bill Bailey, Won't You Please Come Home?" along with a silly Carol Connors—Buzz Cason number, "Wildcat Jones," "talked" by Gail Hire, and other odds and ends contributed by Nelson Riddle, whom Hawks probably engaged because of his celebrated theme for the *Route 66* TV show.

Hawks did have one bit of fun with an unexpected cameo performer. Jerry Lewis was the big man on the Paramount lot at the time, and one day, as Paul Helmick remembered, "Howard said, 'Wouldn't it be fun if we had Jerry Lewis driving one of the cars?' So I went to Jerry Lewis . . . and he said, 'I'll do it under one condition, that Hawks will pay me scale for one day's work.' So Howard did it, signed the check himself, and Jerry said, 'I'll never cash this.' So we put him in a black-and-white stock car, hunched over the wheel wearing a helmet. He mugged, of course, and it was kind of a mutual admiration society between him and Howard." Helmick maintained that Lewis is visible in one insert shot of a driver, but it is impossible to recognize him. Also in briefly are Terry (later Teri) Garr as a dancer and future Russ Meyer starlet Edy Williams.

Hawks prolonged the agony of the shoot, going about a month over schedule—he wrapped production on April 16—and in the process nearly doubled the budget, which soared to $2,425,176, effectively negating the reason he made the film in the first place. With Paramount hoping to release the picture as its Thanksgiving attraction, Hawks pushed through postproduction and went, with some of his colleagues, to its first sneak preview, at the Alex Theater in Glendale on Friday, August 20.

It may have been the worst night of Hawks's professional life. The showing was a nightmare, more catastrophic than anyone could have imagined. George Kirgo, who had left the picture in March and was seeing it for the first time, said, "Beginning with Gail Hire's soliloquy, the audience just started cracking up, laughing uncontrollably." Robert Donner remembered, "There was this roped-off section for us all to be in and you just got lower and lower in your seat." Norman Alden, who accompanied the director, recalled, "I didn't really know what to say. I felt embarrassed. No one was ever going to doubt him to say anything, and it wasn't my place . . . it wasn't anybody's place, I guess." George Kirgo, so mortified by the reaction that he said, "I lost most of my hair that night," left with the film's young star and said, "James Caan was suicidal." Paramount executives were so horrified that the studio discontinued all bidding by theaters for the picture. Hawks was able to take it more in stride than a younger person might have done, but he did react at once, instantly cutting fifteen of the film's 127 minutes and, on August 24, temporarily pulling Leigh Brackett off her Western script to prepare new dialogue for *Red Line 7000* which was dubbed in to try to improve things a bit. Kirgo was subsequently called back in to revise a few pages of Brackett's material.

But Hawks knew that no matter what he did, *Red Line 7000* was essentially unsalvageable. His basic reaction to this fiasco was to plunge immediately and deeply into the Western *El Dorado*. Due to John Wayne's busy schedule, filming would have to start on October 11, making this the fastest turnaround between pictures for Hawks in some twenty-five years. Therefore, Hawks was well and otherwise occupied when *Red Line 7000* had its world premiere at the Plaza Theater in Charlotte on November 9, 1965. Marianna Hill, Norman Alden, Gail Hire, and James Ward flew in for the occasion, and the picture actually did reasonably good business on the expected circuits in the South.

It was a different story when the picture hit major urban markets. Noting that it opened in New York City on a double bill with *Beach Ball*, starring Edd Byrnes, the Supremes, and the Righteous Brothers, the *New York Times*'s critic Bosley Crowther struck a common chord when he lamented, "It is dumbfounding that a filmmaker as distinguished as he could make a film as vulgar, witless and outrageously ponderous as this." Most aislesitters agreed wholeheartedly with Crowther, as did Hawks and his inner circle. Paul Helmick bluntly said, "It's a lousy picture." Cissy Wellman admitted, "Jimmy Caan, all of us would like to burn it." Aside from the obvious casting problems, Hawks blamed the failure on his jumping from one story to another, since "just as soon as you got interested in two people, you left them and got involved with someone else, and you couldn't get the momentum back again." To his credit, he assumed full responsibility for the debacle: "I just messed it up. It's as simple as that."

Not quite everyone agreed. Over the years, some devoted Hawksians have done contortions trying to assert that the film is great simply because the film's situations and motifs were so quintessentially Hawksian. In a long exegesis, Robin Wood went so far as to claim that *Red Line 7000* was possibly "the most underestimated film of the sixties"; the way he continually refers to the film's "intensity" and modernity and ignores the poor acting and artificial look, makes one wonder if he saw the same film as everyone else. Rather more convincing was the critic Richard Thompson, who, writing in the highbrow journal *December*, dealt with Hawks's own disillusionment with the film and paralleled the inexpertness of the cast with the immaturity and unprofessionalism of most of the characters. Thompson's persistent enthusiasm and decision to teach the film to students in Melbourne after moving there from the United States accounts for the rabid *Red Line 7000* cult that exists to this day in Australia.

Still, Peter Bogdanovich is closest to the mark in saying that "theoretically it's a good movie," as those who defend it are forced to ignore too many glaring shortcomings, even beyond the acting: the technical quality is pathetically poor, with a truly unpalatable mix of raw documentary footage, awful process work, and phony "exteriors" shot in the studio, most notably the announcer's tower and the spectators in the stands; the characters are largely uninteresting and shallow; and the movie is ostensibly more rooted in the real world than most Hawks films, and yet weirdly detached from it. To paraphrase Jacques Rivette: You only have to watch *Red Line 7000* to know that it is not a good film.

For *El Dorado*, the title Hawks gave to the adaptation of *The Stars in Their Courses*, Leigh Brackett felt she had outdone herself. "I wrote the best script I have ever written," she proudly said, "and Howard liked it, the studio liked it, Wayne liked it, and I was delighted." The story told of a Duke, "a meticulously dressed Englishman" (and *not* the John Wayne character) who is helped out of a jam by "rugged" Arch Eastmere, "one of the most dangerous hired guns on the range," when he is attacked in a bordertown cantina by the gunslinger Nelse McLeod and his gang. To return the favor, the Duke accompanies Arch to the town of Eldorado, where the powerful rancher Mark Lacy has hired Nelse McLeod to grab, by force, water rights controlled by the rancher Randal, whose son Hallock is the local sheriff.

Arch owes Hallock a favor. Acting as Hallock's deputies, Arch and the Duke help fight off McLeod's men and prevent them from blowing up a cliff on the riverbank. After becoming partially paralyzed from an old bullet wound, Arch "sacrifices his life to see that justice is done. Arch doesn't want to live the rest of his life as a helpless, paralyzed man. With Duke's help, he attacks and kills McLeod before he is cut down by hired guns himself. Duke turns Lacy over to the sheriff and the townspeople learn of his guilt for the first time. In death, Arch turns out to be the hero of Eldorado after all."

What specifically motivated Hawks to reject Brackett's initial script and force her into what she derisively called *The Son of Rio Bravo Rides*

Again is not entirely clear, but it was probably a combination of reasons. For starters, when he read Brackett's script, Hawks was struck by how tragic it was. "I read it and said, 'Hey, this is going to be one of the worst pictures I've ever made. I'm no good at this downbeat stuff,'" he told his writer. It is easy, and perhaps accurate, to speculate that Hawks, whose position as a reliable box-office director was beginning to be questioned in Hollywood, was simply anxious to retreat to the safe ground of *Rio Bravo*, to fall back on what he knew would work. But Hawks may also have rejected Brackett's script because after the 1930s, he had generally avoided killing off his leading characters once he'd developed interest and sympathy in them. Or he may have realized that his tendency to make his material more comic when working with Wayne would run counter to the contours of the grim, deterministic novel.

Hawks was far from shy about recycling discarded ideas from *Rio Bravo*. Put on the defensive about stealing from himself, as he phrased it, Hawks noted that Hemingway did it all the time (certainly not as blatantly as Hawks did) and argued that "if a director has a story that he likes and he tells it, very often he looks at the picture and says, 'I could do that better if I did it again,' so I'd do it again. . . . I'm not a damn bit interested in whether somebody thinks this is a copy of it, because the copy made more money than the original, and I was very pleased with it."

The first person he met resistance from was Brackett. "I have been at swords' points with him many a time because I don't like doing a thing over again, and he does. I remember one day he and John Wayne and I were sitting in the office, and he said we'll do such and such a thing. I said, 'But Howard, you did it in *Rio Bravo*. You don't want to do this over again.' He said, 'Why not?' And John Wayne, all six feet four of him, looked down and said, 'If it was good once it'll be just as good again.' I know when I'm outgunned, so I did it." Brackett wasn't happy about it and did her best to apply little zigzags to Hawks's blueprint. "Amazingly enough," Brackett noted, "very few people, except film buffs, caught the resemblance."

Hawks's way of bending the material to his own ends is visible in the first few minutes of the film. Instead of beginning with a violent attack in a cantina, the picture gets under way by firmly establishing what is by far the most important element in the story to the director: the friendship between the gunslinger (Wayne's Cole Thornton, formerly Arch Eastmere) and the sheriff (Robert Mitchum's J. P. Harrah, formerly Hallock). Their initial conversation is held while Harrah aims his rifle squarely at Thornton until he convinces his old friend not to go to work for the expansionist-minded rancher (Ed Asner's Bart Jason, formerly Mark Lacy). Within moments, the script has drawn upon several previous Hawks films: the pre–Civil War back story and postwar Texas setting call to mind *Red River,* Harrah's discovery that Thornton knew his girl Maudie (Charlene Holt) before he did is taken straight from *A Girl in Every Port,* and Maudie's recapitulation of her past (she was a penniless gambler's widow before Thornton took her under his wing) could pass for a biography of Feathers and John T. Chance in *Rio Bravo.*

The one significant scene retained from the novel and initial screen-play was Thornton's shooting of the rancher's son, whom he took to be fir-ing at him, and the wounded boy's ensuing suicide. Thornton's subsequent action of taking the boy's body back to his father's ranch and telling the man what happened is one of the most powerful expressions of a stoic's handling of death in all of Hawks, and as Robin Wood observed, its spare, beauti-fully articulated gravity makes one long to see the completely serious film Hawks chose not to make.

From there on, the narrative and character lines can be drawn directly back to *Rio Bravo,* with the situations or attributes generally reversed. This time the sheriff is the drunk who needs to be looked after by the gunslinger; the young newcomer on the scene (the novel's Duke character transformed into James Caan's Mississippi) can't shoot a lick, although he does throw a mean knife; the mercenary outlaw Nelse McLeod is a nonpareil professional whose men are dunces rather than the usual tough customers, and the ending once again involves an exchange of prisoners (Brackett refused to write this unless Hawks promised not to use dynamite again). Hawks also prominently lifted from *The Big Sleep* the scene in which Thornton forces a man out a door, only to have the man shot by his own men expecting someone else.

Through it all, the focus is on pain, disability, aging, and the fear of losing one's powers and abilities. Even though Hawks had dealt since his very first film, *The Road to Glory,* with characters' infirmities, injuries, and fears of not living up to what they once were, the explicit way he confronts issues related to human frailty and deterioration—from the vantage point of nearly seventy years—is what gives *El Dorado* its special poignance and highly personal feeling. Even if it may not be as accomplished as *Rio Bravo* or several of Hawks's earlier films, it still comes within shooting distance of what critics, and auteurists in particular, warmly regard as an old-age mas-terpiece, a summing-up film that shows that a great director always retains the potential to express himself eloquently. Hawks even threw the highbrows a bone this time in the form of the Edgar Allan Poe poem "Eldorado," from which the film draws its title; part of it, as spoken by James Caan in the picture, reads:

> *"Over the Mountains*
> *Of the Moon,*
> *Down the Valley of the Shadow,*
> *Ride, boldly ride,"*
> *The shade replied —*
> *"If you seek for Eldorado."*

The verse has always been interpreted as Hawks's most concise statement that since there is no El Dorado, with a pot of gold at the end of the rainbow, the key to human endeavor lies not in the goal but in the search itself. Typically, the director discouraged even this modestly intellectual analysis, maintaining that he included the poem, which he knew thanks to a Mexican jockey who used to recite it, only because he and Brackett liked it.

With a few days off to labor on *Red Line 7000* rewrites, Brackett worked right through the late summer and fall of 1965 on *El Dorado*, trying to give her boss what he wanted. As opposed to how it had been on his last three pictures, the casting fell into place perfectly. Due to receive a flat $750,000 with an additional participation that would bring his haul to at least $1 million, Wayne was looking forward to working with his old friend again. All the same, the star had undergone the biggest crisis of his life since their adventure in Africa, surviving a battle with cancer and the removal of half of his left lung in September 1964; rebounding with vigor, he then made *The Sons of Katier Elder* and *Cast a Giant Shadow* before reporting to Hawks.

To play the sheriff, Thornton's best friend, Hawks could use only someone capable of holding his own with Wayne, a man with something resembling the same physical and charismatic stature. Robert Mitchum is an actor Hawks should have worked with years before, so perfectly does his combination of authority and nonchalance fit into the director's world. Their paths had crossed, technically, more than twenty years earlier, when the young Mitchum played a bit in the Hawks-produced *Corvette K-225*, and Hawks had wanted him for *The Big Sky*, only to be double-crossed by Howard Hughes. It is also easy to imagine the actor taking on Matthew Garth in *Red River*, Dude in *Rio Bravo*, or the second lead in *Hatari!* that Hawks had to split in two. Mitchum said that Hawks simply called to ask him to be in the picture. When Mitchum asked what the story was, "He said, 'There is no story, just you and Duke.' I said, 'That's fine with me. Just tell me when to be there.'" Mitchum signed on for $300,000.

Carrying over from *Red Line 7000*, Hawks knew he wanted to use James Caan as the slightly off-center knife tosser who throws in with Thornton and Harrah, and he intended to give Charlene Holt, after two warm-ups, her big chance on this picture as the woman fancied by both men. Disappointingly, Walter Brennan was unavailable to reprise his patented old-coot part, so Hawks paged Arthur Hunnicutt, so good in *The Big Sky*, to fill in. Once again drawing from television, he got Johnny Crawford, who had a following from *The Rifleman*, to appear as the young man who kills himself after having been shot by Thornton. Edward Asner, then just starting his Hollywood career, was cast as the evil rancher Bart Jason, the Western stalwart Paul Fix was the doctor, and a few regulars, such as Robert Donner, John Gabriel, Diane Strom, and Anthony Rogers, also turned up. Hawks put Olaf Wieghorst, whose Western paintings are featured under the opening credits, before the cameras as the Swedish gunsmith who supplies Mississippi's shotgun.

For the second female part, of the impetuous MacDonald daughter who puts the bullet in Thornton's back, Hawks picked a fabulously sexy girl he had originally tested for *Red Line 7000*, only to decide that she wasn't yet ready to act a part. However, Hawks signed Michele Carey and started grooming her, so that by the time her next chance came around she could handle it. A child piano prodigy who began modeling in Denver and had done *The Man From U.N.C.L.E.* and a couple of other television roles before auditioning for Hawks, Carey may have looked and sounded very contemporary, but her impetuous attitude and bareback riding in skintight pants definitely added some spice to the picture. As Hawks enthused, "She's earthy, and girls like that who can act are hard to find these days."

As filming drew near, Paramount approved a budget increase to $3.85 million, but production head Howard W. Koch was worried. Knowing Hawks's reputation for slowness, Koch wrote to the company president, George Weltner, in New York, cautioning that they should by no means count on the picture being ready for release the following summer. After the director's substantial overages on his two previous projects for the studio, Koch had imposed a provision giving Paramount the right to take over the picture if Hawks exceeded the budget by 10 percent. Obviously, he admitted, such a move would involve "practical difficulties," adding that "business judgment would have to be carefully considered if we decide to take over because of the involvement of Wayne and Mitchum and the unavailability of substitute directors to complete a picture of this stature." Koch concluded that he believed in the film, but that Paramount even imagined that Hawks could be pushed off a film at this stage of his career, or that his stars would abide such a move, is incredible.

Russell Harlan was busy on the protracted shoot of *Hawaii*, so to photograph *El Dorado*, Hawks reached way back into his past, and no one was more surprised than Hal Rosson himself that Hawks wanted him for the job. The lone surviving Rosson brother, he was a year older than Hawks, and had retired in 1958. Many of his contemporaries were still working on top productions, but Rosson, who went all the way back with Hawks to *Quicksands* in 1923 and had also shot *Trent's Last Case*, really believed he had put away his light meter for good before Hawks convinced him to return. Rosson recalled that Hawks said, "'Oh come on, come back,' and I said, 'You don't want me,' and he said, 'Yes I do.' So I went back, and I was out of my mind I ever quit." As he acknowledged, "I would do anything for Howard Hawks, and I enjoyed doing it. It was fun."

With Old Tucson redressed once again so it wouldn't too closely resemble its appearance in *Rio Bravo* or any other picture, Hawks led the company to Arizona and starting filming on October 11, 1965. Oblivious to the fact that Paramount was watching him closely, he took his own sweet time as usual, and Leigh Brackett was on hand a good deal of the time to supply revisions; as Robert Donner put it, "the script was written in sand." Johnny Crawford, accustomed to the eye-on-the-clock rigors of television shoots, was astonished at Hawks's casual approach. "The atmosphere on this set was totally relaxed and ponderous, and I thought, 'Oh, yeah, this is the way I thought it would be.' I had read stories about powerful filmmakers who were like that. . . . What a luxury. Also what a cost. But I really enjoyed it." One day, according to Crawford, when the company was set to shoot his death scene at a ranch south of Tucson, some clouds moved in about noon. "Hawks looked up at the clouds and said, 'It looks like the sun's going to be behind the clouds for quite awhile,' so he and John Wayne jumped in their car and drove off for Nogales. We spent the rest of the day on location and they never came back."

To Crawford, Hawks "didn't seem like a man who was under any great amount of pressure. He seemed to be a very relaxed, confident, down-to-earth kind of a gentleman. A real gentleman. My first day on the set, Howard Hawks introduced me to Wayne and they invited me to sit with them at lunch. I was just thrilled. They were very interested in me and made me feel very special, asking me questions about *The Rifleman* and Chuck Connors just like anybody else. There were no airs about them."

As the majority of the story's action was to be played out at night, Hawks instructed Harold Rosson to study the nocturnal paintings of Frederic Remington, of which the director had several in his collection. In particular, Hawks wanted to catch the slashes of light that the painter often featured pouring out of doors and windows onto the street, and Rosson used yellow light to accomplish this, making sure to wash the actors with white light to avoid a jaundiced look. Encouraged by his boss's slow pace, Rosson took ever longer to set his lights, until it finally became too much, even for Hawks. "Trouble was," he said, "people started talking about an Academy Award, and he got slower and slower and slower and slower until it drove me crazy." All the same, Hawks defended Hally, as he called him, against the others' griping. "He'd say, 'Hally, you're doing just fine,'" Robert Donner recalled. "And Howard let it be known that if anybody had any problem, he was the guy to talk to. He was a stand-up guy and if you were his guy, that was it." After *El Dorado*, Rosson retired for good.

With Stuart Gilmore also tied up on *Hawaii*, Hawks took his recommendation of an editor, John Woodcock, who began cutting the picture together on location in Tucson. Woodcock said, "Hawks shot in conventional fashion, but when I tried to draw him into a discussion about the editing he gave me the brush-off, indicating that the editorial problems were all mine and to leave him out of it." Woodcock was also surprised, he said, that while most of the cast and crew chowed down every night on steak, ribs, chicken, and other meaty fare, "all that I ever saw Howard Hawks eat at any meal was a plate of assorted fresh fruit."

The camaraderie on the set was mostly casual and friendly, and Hawks and Wayne were buoyed when John Ford, frail and mostly confined to a wheelchair, came to the location for a visit. But relations between Wayne and newcomers could always be cause for concern. The way James Caan put it, "I was this little punk working with Wayne and Mitchum . . . Wayne? He'd push you. He was like a twelve-year-old kid. He took a liking to me but I lost it one day and almost took a whack at him. Mitchum broke it up, and from that day on it was fine." The young actor shortly became Duke's chess partner during the long waits while Rosson set up and Hawks retreated to his trailer to tinker with the dialogue. Caan, who had been so displeased about *Red Line 7000*, acted headstrong even with Hawks at times but was basically made to feel that this was a great opportunity for him and he shouldn't cross the line, so, as he did with Wayne, he advisedly backed off. According to Hawks, Caan never realized his role was supposed to be funny until he saw the finished film, and when the actor asked him why he hadn't told him, Hawks supposedly said, "You'd have spoiled it. You'd have tried to be funny." The way Caan remembered it, during the first week of shooting "I was playing all this for real and all of a sudden I realized that Jeeze, I'd better start smiling because some of this shit I've gotta say is pretty fucking ridiculous. So I started smiling. Everytime John Wayne would talk, I'd be standing alongside smiling."

For Caan, his personal relationship with Hawks was ultimately more important than his professional one. "I had a great time with him, I loved him," the actor reflected. "I don't remember him so much as a great director, but I do remember him as a great man. I don't remember him ever giving me direction as far as the way I should or shouldn't be feeling, but his writing was so pertinent that you had to be pretty much of a moron not to understand where you're supposed to be. I never felt Hawks put great importance on any film. It was like, 'We're doing a film, for Chrissakes. If they don't like it, give them their nickel back.' It wasn't all that important, we weren't curing cancer, like a lot of young people think they're doing today. You never heard Hawks say, 'We're losing the light,' or 'Oh, my God, I'm five days over schedule.' Who cares? It was nothing; it wasn't the end of the world. What we heard was, 'I'm hungry. Let's wrap it for the day. We'll pick it up tomorrow.'

"He was a guy who just deserved, and got, a lot of respect from everybody," Caan observed. "At the end of his career, he did what he liked, he did what would make it enjoyable for him, and for everybody around, pretty much. He had people around him, not necessarily because they were the best, but because they were decent and fun, people that he liked. There was nobody I ever remember that I disliked when I was around Howard. The guy earned the right to do things that he liked and be around people he liked and I find absolutely no fault with that whatsoever.

"For me," Caan concluded, "he became more of a father figure than a director. He taught me the meaning of life: 'She's good looking, she's not; that's a good steak, and that's not; and this is fun, and that's not.' So that's who Howard was to me." Caan, who had an infant daughter but whose marriage was going south at the time, started a romance during the shoot with his costar Michele Carey, who was divorced with a four-year-old son. The couple announced their engagement in June 1966, but they never married.

Robert Donner remembered, "I got engaged on *El Dorado* and Hawks and Duke Wayne and Bob Mitchum were having a little tequila one night. I was playing one of the heavies and they just thought it'd be hilarious if I had to get married looking as I looked. I mean, my hair was down to my shoulders, and I had a full beard, and the three of them were friends of Bill

Wellman, who would be my father-in-law. So they figured out a way to switch the schedule around so I was still on the picture when I got married, and I had to get married in my full beard and long hair. They thought that was very funny."

Donner also recalled the regular poker games in Ed Asner's Ramada Inn motel room, which was right next to Hawks's. One night the game got pretty loud. "Ed's saying, 'Keep it down, Jesus. You know, Hawks is next door.' And, well, we weren't keeping it down, I guess, because all of a sudden, there's this beating on the wall. We quieted down a little bit more, the game goes on, it gets a little louder . . . all of a sudden we hear, 'BAM! BAM! BAM!' Three shots. We go running outside, and there stands Hawks in his boots and a nightshirt, and he's got this .44 in his hand. And he says, 'Anybody I see in one minute is going home.' And you never saw people split faster in your life."

Ed Asner was one man John Wayne didn't take to, referring to him derisively as "that New York actor." Nobody, least of all Asner, could understand what provoked this, since nothing ever passed between them, although in later years, when Asner became an outspoken liberal, people joked that Wayne had been prematurely sensitive to Asner's political leanings.

As for Mitchum, Hawks hadn't been wrong in thinking that he'd be a perfect foil for Wayne. Given the actor's reputation for boozing and laziness, the director was pleasantly surprised by his work habits, even if Mitchum didn't mix with the rest of the company all that much, preferring to retreat to his trailer when not involved in a scene. Hawks said, "When the picture was half over I said, 'You know, you're the biggest fraud I've ever met in all my life.' He grinned and said, 'Why?' I said, 'You pretend you don't care a damn thing about a scene, and you're the hardest-working so-and-so I've ever known.' He said, 'Don't tell anybody.'"

Completing the Tucson part of the shoot after thirty-six working days, the 156-person company flew back to Los Angeles on November 22, the very week *Red Line 7000* was opening in Los Angeles. Six more weeks of production were scheduled at the studio, but Hawks, with Rosson's help, took nine, finally wrapping on January 28, 1966, three and a half months after he started. The $4,535,322 final price tag had certainly exceeded the intended budget by more than 10 percent, but Paramount, of course, hadn't said a word; by fall, the current regime would be out in the wake of Gulf + Western's takeover of the company, with Robert Evans installed as head of production.

There were no disputes about the writing credit this time, but Hawks got into extended disagreements about the title—he wanted *El Dorado* written as two words, Paramount wanted one—and the reference to Harry Brown's novel. The director now insisted that his film was based not on *The Stars in Their Courses* but on *Rio Bravo*. However, since Paramount had already paid a tidy sum for the rights to Brown's book—which Hawks was now saying, with a straight face, that he might want to make into a film one day—and was not inclined to pay an additional stipend to Warner Bros., this line of reasoning was soon dropped.

As the editor, John Woodcock put the picture together virtually alone, and he was astonished when, upon informing the director that the rough cut was ready for his appraisal, Hawks proceeded to invite about thirty people to see his new film at the studio theater without ever having seen it himself. Hawks gave Woodcock a few instructions during the projection, added a few more comments after the well-received screening, then took off into the night.

The initial public preview took place on April 22 at the Plaza Theater in Palm Springs, not far from Hawks's house on Stevens Road. The reaction was a world apart from that to Hawks's last film, producing relief all around. However, Hawks and Woodcock tinkered a bit more, eliminating a musical number reminiscent of *Rio Bravo* when Gregg Hawks told his father that "a sheriff shouldn't sing" and, in order to get the all-clear from the Catholic Legion of Decency, cutting the scene in which a topless Marina Ghane (who was spending a lot of time at Hawks's place in Palm Springs these days) tells James Caan which way the bad guys have gone. Paramount had long since given up the idea of putting the picture out that summer and, with the new regime in by fall, ended up holding back its domestic release for a year and a half from the time it finished shooting.

The world-premiere engagements actually began on December 17, 1966, in Tokyo and Osaka, where the film did outstanding business. By the time it opened in the United States, in June 1967, it was going head-to-head with another John Wayne Western, *The War Wagon*, produced subsequently by the Duke's own company, Batjac. This may have been unfortunate, but it probably didn't have much effect on business, which was strong for both pictures. Within a year, *El Dorado* had generated rentals of $6 million on box-office receipts of $12 million making it the twelfth biggest picture of 1967. Hawks had proved that, at least when working on familiar territory with big stars, he could still deliver the goods.

38

The Last Roundup

With the release of *El Dorado*, Howard Hawks was irrevocably thrust into the arena of the film buffs. The film's commercial success and reception by mainstream reviewers as a return to form after an eight-year lull (most critics truly did not note the close resemblance to *Rio Bravo*) gave it sufficient stature to be argued about, and *El Dorado* soon became one of the flashpoints in the raging battle between the auteurists and their enemies, of which there were at least three stripes. For the pro-Hawksians, who had been forced increasingly into a corner by his recent missteps, *El Dorado* provided proof once again that Hawks was one of the immortals who still walked among us. For Andrew Sarris, the guru of stateside auteurism, it was a masterpiece, the best American film of the year, "a poetic fantasy . . . tinged with melancholy." For his archrival, Pauline Kael, who had liked Hawks films in the past only to turn against him when she saw the cult building up around him, the picture looked like a TV movie. Inaccurately stating that it was entirely shot in the studio, "except for a few opening shots," she accused Hawks, as well as Wayne and Mitchum, of being too old and rich to care anymore. To Sarris, by contrast, Wayne's "oldness has become spiritually resurgent. His infirmities ennoble rather than enfeeble him, and every wrinkle on his skin has come to terms with his endless quest."

How could such opposing views ever be reconciled? In fact, they could not, which goes a long way toward explaining why Hawks, not to mention Wayne, remained caught in the cross fire of opposing critical factions for so long. To one side Hawks represented Hollywood classicism, tradition at its purest. To others, he was old-fashioned, conservative, worn out, someone not to be taken seriously or even valued anymore. Others resisting the acclamation of Hawks were modernist critics, literary-oriented and mostly Eastern intellectuals with a built-in bias against genres in general and Westerns in particular, and liberals and leftists for whom anything with John Wayne's name on it was automatically discredited.

But perhaps the most blistering evaluation of *El Dorado* came from Harry Brown, the author of *The Stars in Their Courses*. In a letter to Hawks, Brown claimed that the finished film bore no relation to his novel, and demanded that the attribution be removed from the picture's credits, adding, "Someday directors, Great [sic] or not, are going to stick to set-ups and camera-angles and let *writers* handle the scripts. I'd hate to be hanging until that day came, though."

Hawks brushed Brown's objections aside, and the credit stuck. The director didn't take the highfalutin claims made for his work by some of his ardent admirers very seriously either, but he was certainly grateful for their support and did nothing to discourage it. In an apparent first film festival appearance for a Hawks work, *El Dorado* was selected as the official United States entry in the San Sebastian Film Festival in June, and on the 23rd of that month Hawks flew to Paris to promote the picture. He spent a good deal of time with Chance, who took some particularly striking photographs of him in front of the film's giant poster on the Champs-Elysées that show him looking anything but tired and over-the-hill.

He also became fast friends with the picture's specially engaged publicist, Pierre Rissient, a great and gregarious film buff who sat in on and translated during his myriad interviews and dinners over the course of several days. Some of these interviews, notably the one conducted by Jean-Louis Comolli, Jean Narbon, and Bertrand Tavernier for the recently politicized *Cahiers du Cinéma*, became difficult when they touched on the subject of Hawks's intended next project, a drama about the Vietnam War.

Hawks said he intended to make "a film that is true, realistic." Like *Red Line 7000*, it would consist of "three stories blended into a single one. It's based on a true incident. It's the story of something concrete that the army wants to accomplish, and that they do accomplish in the course of the film." Asked his point of view about the war, Hawks said, "You know, it's a whole new sort of war, it doesn't resemble anything we've ever seen before. The Americans are fighting against very short men, who are right at home in their land. A tiny little bag is enough to carry all the equipment that a Vietcong needs to defend himself. . . . The Vietcong move around more easily. The people I've talked to say that it's the American soldiers who come from farms, from the country, who adapt the best. They're supposed to be awful good."

In his thinking about the project, Hawks was greatly inspired by a film to which Rissient took him, *The Anderson Platoon*, an hourlong French documentary shot the previous year about a black lieutenant who painstakingly leads his platoon on a mission to take a hill north of Saigon while under heavy attack. The men were shown to possess strong camaraderie and mutual feeling across racial lines, and while exposing the harshness of the war, the film ennobled the human effort expended in fighting it and was not overtly ideological. In other words, it was right up Hawks's alley. After dining with its director, Pierre Schoendorffer, himself a veteran of Dien Bien Phu who would, twenty-five years later, make an epic dramatic feature about that fateful battle, Hawks began openly stating that he was going to use Schoendorffer to shoot combat sequences in Vietnam, while he, Hawks, would film everything else in the States. As it happened, he discussed this arrangement only in the most general terms with Schoendorffer himself. Schoendorffer said, "Hawks asked me a lot of questions, he listened a lot. We had 'human' discussions, about the experiences of men that I had known. Politics was not my preoccupation, and it wasn't his either. I was full of admiration for Howard Hawks, and would have been interested to see the way it would have turned out."

During his interview, Hawks did manage to discomfort the otherwise worshipful *Cahiers* crowd by refusing to be goaded into a critique of American society and the Vietnam war. There is no evidence that Hawks or anyone else ever put pen to paper on the Vietnam project; Schoendorffer never heard from Hawks again after their handful of sessions in Paris. Hawks claimed to have abandoned the idea altogether when a little research showed that official army assistance would not be forthcoming without script approval, and Hawks would never have accepted such a condition. He also insisted that the film would not have made a statement about the war: "I *never* made a statement. Our job is to make entertainment. I don't give a God damn about taking sides." Bertrand Tavernier revealed that when he pressed Hawks further about it, the director said "he wanted to take some of the scenes deleted from *Sergeant York* and put them into his Vietnam film. That was frightening." One can only agree with Tavernier's conclusion that, given Hawks's naive refusal to engage the inevitable political implications of such a project and his lack of firsthand knowledge about the war, "It's good for him that he never made that film."

Not surprisingly, the project Hawks pursued much more seriously during this period was something completely unrealistic, a throwback to his silent days. In 1965, Hawks optioned the rights to his 1928 success *A Girl in Every Port*, and to Lewis Milestone's 1927 *Two Arabian Knights*, which concerned two devil-may-care adventurers who escape from a World War I German prison camp disguised as Arabs and make off to the United

States with a beautiful Arab girl. *Mr. Gus*, or *Now, Mr. Gus*, as Hawks variously called the project, went through a succession of story incarnations, winding up, a decade later, as a script that represented a virtual remake of *A Girl in Every Port*, about two men who circle the globe fighting oil-rig fires in the manner of the celebrated Red Adair. Whatever the premise, "the big erector project," as Hawks liked to call it, would be a buddy-buddy comedy on a very large scale.

Hawks originally considered John Wayne for one of the two leads, despite his advancing years and paunch, and it can hardly have been a complete coincidence that Wayne played a Red Adair figure named Chance Buckman in Andrew V. McLaglen's 1968 firefighting adventure, *Hellfighters*. This didn't deter Hawks, who frequently told George Kirgo he might hire him to write the script, received input from Peter Bogdanovich, and talked about it with any number of other creative friends. But it would be a few years before he had anything substantial on paper for his project.

Nor was it entirely coincidental that one of the men he spent the most time with from the mid-1960s onward was a Texas oilman named Ted Wiener. A millionaire many times over, Wiener had a home in Palm Springs and quickly became enthralled by Hawks's tales of Hollywood, the stars, and his own great accomplishments. The two played golf together regularly, and, in due time, Hawks persuaded his friend that putting money behind a slate of films that he would direct and produce would be just about the best thing he could possibly do with it. Hawks and Wiener spent a great deal of time cooking up schemes by which they could beat Hollywood at its own game, arrangements by which Hawks could make his choice of pictures and both men could rake in a small fortune.

That the old days were quickly coming to a close was signaled by any number of events. In 1967, Jack Warner, one of Hawks's oldest associates in Hollywood, sold controlling interest in Warner Bros. to Seven Arts. In May 1968, Hawks was devastated by the death of Charles Feldman, at sixty-three. Except for Victor Fleming, Hawks had probably been closer to Feldman than to anyone else at the peak of their friendship, and much of what Hawks had accomplished in his career could not have happened without him. Despite warnings at the time of his operation for prostate cancer, Feldman had, if anything, accelerated his career in its wake, producing a string of films through the 1960s that included *The Group*, the smash hit comedy *What's New, Pussycat?* and the extravaganza *Casino Royale*. Feldman had also brought Woody Allen into motion pictures with the latter two films and was preparing to produce Allen's directorial debut, *Take the Money and Run,* before his death. The month before he died, Feldman married a French socialite, Clotilde Barot, a move controversial among his friends since it entitled her to at least 50 percent of his vast estate. Hawks and Feldman's lives had not been as intimately entwined in recent years as they had been before, but his friend's death clearly marked the end of something for the director, and coincidentally gave him something less of a foothold in Hollywood. Eight months later, on January 10, 1969, Hawks's brother William died after enduring a three-month respiratory illness.

By now, Hawks was spending more time in Palm Springs and less in Los Angeles. In late 1967, he gave up his rented house at 502 North Hillcrest Drive in Beverly Hills, but he was charged by the owner for damage to the premises in a suit that was settled out of court. Hawks then moved to a penthouse apartment at the fabled Sunset Towers, a bit past its heyday but still a classy address, with its share of models and young actresses, whom Hawks liked to invite to his balcony to have a drink and watch the sunset. One of the resident girls he struck up a close friendship with was Sondra Currie, a petite redhead barely out of her teens who took to Hawks in a big way. "He was a gas," she enthused. "A tremendous sense of humor, a real old-fashioned man's man. I really didn't know that he was as important as he was. My mother did—she used to say, 'Sandy, don't you realize who he is?'

"We really hit it off. . . . I think I was more of a mild amusement to him, but we did have a close friendship for quite awhile." Currie often accompanied Hawks and Gregg on off-road racing trips to Baja California and had quasiromantic feelings about the old man. "I used to get very angry at him that there was such a big age difference," she admitted. "I felt very deprived, because we really, genuinely had such a good time together."

As Gregg entered his teens, Hawks spent an increasing amount of time with him, spoiling him with an array of dirt and racing bikes and riding with him and his friends in the desert around Palm Springs. If Hawks ever doted on anyone and loved someone completely, it was Gregg, who was far from the easiest kid to be around much of the time. But he became an excellent rider; he began entering races as soon as he could, winning quite a few of them.

In 1969, in the wake of the success of *Bonnie and Clyde,* Hawks briefly flirted with a story about the Kate (Ma) Barker–Alvin Karpis gang, which was written by William Faulkner's young brother, Murry Faulkner. Though the project was dropped, Murry Faulkner wrote to Hawks, saying that the director was "one of the two men in Hollywood of whom I heard my brother speak in frank and voluntary admiration."

Later that year, Hawks received overtures from a new company in town, Cinema Center Films, which had a distribution agreement with another start-up firm, National General Pictures. Developing a slate of pictures under the auspices of the company chief, Gordon Stulberg, and a young executive named Jere Henshaw, Cinema Center was anxious to sign some big names in order to establish instant credibility. Along with William Wyler, Hawks was one of the last of the great generation of directors who started in the silent era and could still, with the right project, deliver big stars and big grosses. As far as the company was concerned, Hawks's name meant money in the bank as long as he stuck to Westerns, so they offered him a choice.

First was *Monte Walsh,* an adaptation of a Western novel by Jack Schaefer about aging, obsolete cowboys that might conceivably have served as a vehicle for Wayne and another actor suitable to Hawks, such as Mitchum or Holden. But Lee Marvin was set to star, and the actor instantly dashed his hopes of working with Hawks by turning up for his meeting with the director roaring drunk. Jack Palance ended up costarring with Marvin under first-time director William Fraker, with dull results.

Hawks was always ready to work with Wayne if he could find a good story, an increasingly difficult proposition given the great star's age, girth, and health; in his one outstanding film after *El Dorado, True Grit,* Wayne virtually parodied his usual persona. Hawks found some potential in a story by Burton Wohl, who had written a handful of films through the 1960s, involving a series of train robberies of Union gold shipments by the Confederates and the efforts of a U.S. captain to track down the informers on his own side. Although at sixty-three now rather old to be playing the vengeful officer, Wayne would still be accepted in such a part, and Hawks was hopeful of getting Mitchum to play opposite him again as his Rebel counterpart who, after the war, teams up with him to find the culprits.

To write the script, Hawks tried straightaway to hire Leigh Brackett, but she was just about to leave on a trip around the world and could not accept. Instead, he went with Wohl, who, like numerous other writers who had never worked with Hawks, was unnerved by his lack of clear instructions and his long absences. As Brackett put it, "Howard drives writers right up the wall. He will throw you a whole bunch of stuff and say: 'This is what I want.' And then he goes away and you don't see him again for weeks. . . . He doesn't go into all the ramifications of motivation—that's what he's paying you for."

Motivation and background were particularly lacking in *Rio Lobo:* after two hours of the finished film, one knows absolutely nothing about John

Wayne's character except that he was in the army; he exists as a completely abstract creation, a functional figure only. It was Hawks's desire to bend the story as much as possible back toward *Rio Bravo* and *El Dorado*, which is what the second half of the tale became in reworked form. When Brackett returned from her travels at the beginning of December 1969, Hawks got rid of Wohl and brought her onboard, where she remained for nearly four months, working against her better instincts for avoiding repetition by providing just that, a reconfiguration of her, and her boss's, previous hits. "Most of what I did on *Rio Lobo* was to try and patch over the holes. . . . I was unhappy that he went back to the same old ending of the trade, because it was done beautifully in *Rio Bravo* and done over again in *El Dorado*."

In the form the script finally took, Wayne's Cord McNally, for strictly private reasons, becomes involved in yet another battle over land rights, trying to help the little guy fight off yet another big bully with a raft of gunslingers in his employ. This time, the ragtag group consists of his former Confederate foe, now his friend, the dashing New Orleans-born Lieutenant Pierre Cordona; a crazy old coot, Phillips, whose land is threatened; Phillips's son, Tuscarora, who lands in jail; and a beautiful young woman, Shasta, who has reasons of her own for fighting the bad men who have taken over the town. Working his variations, Hawks had his writers make the sheriff one of the villains so that Wayne and his cohorts had to break *into* the jail in order to hold out there until the federal marshal arrives, and he played with the exchange-of-hostages climax so as to have the outlaws attempt to throw the dynamite, with less successful results than in *Rio Bravo*.

Aside from Wayne and Jack Elam, whose walleyed looniness made him an excellent successor to Brennan, the casting was Hawks's biggest hobgoblin on the new picture. Like Paramount, Cinema Center was not disposed to paying another star salary in addition to Wayne's, and Mitchum's price had gone up since *El Dorado*. As he had done on *Hatari!*, Hawks split the intended second lead into two parts for younger men. For the southern lieutenant, Hawks made the unlikely choice of Jorge Rivero, the handsome young star of some two dozen Mexican movies who was being promoted for a Hollywood career after his first American picture, *Soldier Blue*; the director decided to go ahead with him after a screen test with Wayne. For Tuscarora, Hawks was determined to hire Chris Mitchum, Robert's second son. Jere Henshaw was just as adamantly against him, and the stand-off was resolved only when Hawks fulfilled his threat to shut down production in Mexico, which he did for two days, until Mitchum arrived. "I just asked if they wanted to go on their record or mine," Hawks said. "Chris was on the next plane."

For the female lead of Shasta, Hawks had no front-running candidates but was determined to follow his habit of finding a newcomer rather than casting an up-and-coming actress who might have demonstrated some acting talent. Pierre Rissient made tests of a dozen young European prospects for Hawks; one, a beautiful German named Katrine Schaake, interested Hawks greatly. She had played a bit in *What's New, Pussycat?* and, according to Rissient, Charles Feldman had been willing to give her a leading role if she would sleep with him, but she refused. Hawks was ready to cast Schaake as Shasta, but at a crucial moment, much as had happened with Françoise Dorléac on *Red Line 7000*, she couldn't be found; then, with the start date looming, immigration would not issue her a work permit.

With this, Hawks was forced into a hasty decision. Cinema Center had tested a beautiful twenty-three-year-old model named Jennifer O'Neill, who had already been under contract to Joseph E. Levine and Paramount but had acted in just one film, *Glass Houses*, directed by Alexander Singer, the director, coincidentally, of the Burton Wohl–written *A Cold Wind in August*. Hawks liked what he saw and hurriedly signed her. Married and the mother of a three-year-old daughter, the dark-haired, highly photogenic O'Neill was from a wealthy family; since she was seventeen, she'd been earning $100,000 a year as a model. But she had undergone little acting training, and Hawks had no time to groom her in his preferred fashion.

On a preproduction trip to Mexico City, Hawks found a local actress, Susana Dosamantes, who had been in a number of films, to play Maria. For the other Mexican woman, Amelita, he tested a model and actress who had appeared in Irvin Kershner's new film *Loving*, Sherry Lansing. "He had a very fixed image of what a woman should be," Lansing observed. "Tall, long hair, long legs, big eyes—a very specific type. Basically, she had to be Lauren Bacall, and I just fit right into the image.

"He made me go through the exercises. You'd strain your voice so you'd get a husky thing on your vocal cords, and there was a way to push it down to lower it," Lansing said. Once he cast an actress, "He attempted to control every aspect of your life, how you dressed, what you did in your spare time. The attitude was, 'If you do this movie, you are required to come to dinner, to be available.' In his world, you were required to be the image, not the person. It was all illusion."

Unlike many of Hawks's other would-be discoveries, Lansing was not easy to mold. College-educated and with a teaching degree, she was not certain she wanted to act at all and was in therapy at the time to try to resolve her dilemma. Her inclination to introspection and analysis made her a particularly bad match with Hawks, and she was frustrated that "talk with him never went beneath the surface. There was a lack of self-examination. It sounds cool when you read it, but it's terrible in real life." Allowing that she was "very conflicted and confused" through the entire experience, Lansing still confessed, "I liked him. I liked him a lot," adding, "we never had a *personal* relationship. He never did anything improper."

Along with script and casting difficulties, there were other annoyances. To save approximately $1 million in production costs, Hawks and Cinema Center agreed to base the production in Durango, Mexico. However, when the English director Michael Winner, who was preparing a Western called *Lawman* with Burt Lancaster, got wind of this, he immediately flew to Durango to nail down a lease on the standing movie set there, preempting Hawks by a matter of hours. The title was another problem. The story's original name was *San Timoteo*, which everyone knew needed to be changed. Sherry Lansing said, "I remember being in a liquor store with Hawks and he was looking at bottles to try to find a title for the film." Finally, in the hopes of reminding the public of past glories, *Rio Lobo* was settled upon.

Paul Helmick, who had now been with Hawks for more than twenty years, was back again as associate producer, and John Woodcock was paged for another stint as film editor. To shoot the film, Hawks picked William Clothier, who was nearly as old as Hawks, had shot a dozen of Wayne's pictures, and was known almost exclusively for his fine work on Westerns.

The film's most spectacular sequence would be the opening-reel train robbery and getaway, and shooting it required that the company work in Mexico, after all. A usable vintage train and sufficient track were found at Cuernavaca, not far south of Mexico City. A start date of March 16, 1970, was set; after two weeks, the company would move to the familiar standby, Old Tucson, for twenty-five days, followed by a week in Nogales. Twenty-two days back at the Cinema Center Studios in the San Fernando Valley would round out the sixty-five-day schedule on the $5 million production.

Although there were no dramatic parallels, the idea of a runaway train actually dated back to a sequence Hawks never got to shoot for his very first film, *The Road to Glory*, forty-five years before. For this elaborate episode, which involved the holdup, the placement of a sack of hornets inside a car, a skirmish between troops, Wayne's horseback pursuit of the detached cars down an incline, and the train's precarious stoppage by a series of ropes strung around trees, Hawks engaged the legendary stuntman and second-unit director Yakima Canutt. Though Hawks habitually delegated second-unit work, he was present and involved through the entire shooting of this critical scene. Since the only usable track was the heavily traveled line between Mexico City and Cuernavaca, at times regularly scheduled trains were held on sidings for hours so Hawks could get his shots, resulting in angry words and objects being thrown at the crew.

One day, an accident was averted when an engineer managed to jump on a rolling train that had lost its brakes and stop it fifty yards from a flatcar on which Hawks and Jorge Rivero were working. The very next day, however, they were back on the flatcar when a car appeared on the tracks, forcing the engineer to jam on the brakes. Hawks was thrown into the camera platform, his left leg cut to the bone, landing him in the Cuernavaca hospital. The seventy-three-year-old director shrugged off the incident, saying, "I get thrown off my motorcycle about once every three weeks when I go riding cross-country in the Palm Springs desert." In fact, his leg would be much more seriously injured shortly thereafter when, during a long delay in staging the train sequence, he disappeared for some dirt-bike racing and took a bad spill, shutting production down for nearly a week.

The high altitude at Cuernavaca was not friendly to Wayne, who huffed and puffed and was more reliant than ever upon his longtime double Chuck Roberson to handle the physical scenes; Roberson had exactly the same physique, had long since mastered the star's walk and movements and was still able to approximate the familiar old Wayne moves. "Hawks and Wayne were really kind of on their last legs at that point," John Woodcock observed. Hawks himself was a bit taken aback by how much the Duke had changed since they last worked together more than four years before: "Wayne had a hard time getting on and off his horse; he can't move like a big cat the way he used to. He has to hold his belly in; he's a different kind of person."

But no matter how old Wayne and Hawks were getting, they both still possessed plenty of authority, and Hawks handled himself the same way he always had. Peter Jason, a young actor cast in the secondary role of Lieutenant Forsythe, maintained that Hawks "was one of the clearest directors I've ever worked for, even though I never saw a script—he'd just tell you what to say. . . . So . . . you knew exactly what to do. But he left it open for you to do it any way you wanted. But there was no question in your mind what you were supposed to do."

Jason was also thoroughly impressed by Wayne, especially in the light of his jingoistic, even racist reputation in some circles. "My first day on the set, when John Wayne arrived, was the most amazing thing I've ever seen. Forty people lined up, forty Mexicans, and he walked up to every one of them, shook their hands, and knew their names—'Hi, Raoul'—knew their families, knew everything about all of them. So they'd all obviously worked on many movies together. It was very impressive to watch the real guys do it. As opposed to today, when nobody even knows who the hell's on the set. It was a great adventure."

Relieved to get the heavy action and Mexico behind them, the company flew by chartered jet to Tucson at the end of the month. The Academy Awards ceremony took place on April 7, and when John Wayne, a heavy sentimental favorite for his rambunctious performance as the one-eyed Rooster Cogburn in *True Grit*, was leaving for Los Angeles, Hawks told him, "Don't come back without it." He returned, victorious, to find the entire cast and crew of *Rio Lobo* waiting with their backs to him. When they turned around, Wayne was greeted by the sight of everyone, including his horse, wearing an eye patch.

Hawks rewrote as much as, and very likely more than, usual on location, forcing the actors to memorize several pages of dialogue on the spur of the moment just before the cameras rolled. Wayne was long since used to it, but some of the newcomers to the Hawks method had problems, particularly Jorge Rivero, who "had to translate everything from English to Spanish and back again," according to the director. But Peter Jason remembered that no matter how many times Hawks instructed Rivero to put some urgency behind his dialogue, "He did it exactly the same every time." Hawks quickly realized that Rivero "was really too slow, and he didn't have any authority at all."

As for his inclination to tinker with his script right up to the moment it was shot, Hawks explained it to a visitor on the set with great precision: "I don't change dialogue, I 'word' it how I feel it should be read. It's an instinct, I suppose, but it's how you tell a story. . . . To me, the difference between a good director and a bad director is how they tell a story. . . . My method is to—once I'm into a story—reword it." Overhearing this, John Wayne said, "You sure as hell get carried away," and added that as relaxed as a Hawks shoot seemed, "When the grey fox turns his steely blues on you, you get to work. No messing around."

Hawks's way of working and rewording dialogue was illustrated for the public and posterity in a film called *Plimpton! Shoot-out at Rio Lobo*, a promotional documentary that was shown on ABC-TV to coincide with the feature's release. It was arranged for George Plimpton, the well-known New York writer, editor, and professional dilettante, to play one of four gang members who come into a bar and threaten the sheriff, John Wayne, and Jennifer O'Neill at gunpoint, only to get mowed down. Plimpton would

44. Howard and Slim at home at the Hog Canyon Ranch, early 1940s.

45. and 46. Admiring Gary Cooper's marksmanship on *Sergeant York* (above), and giving him some fighting tips on *Ball of Fire* (right).

47. Slim and Howard with two of their hounds on the Goldwyn lot.

48. Howard with one of his racehorses.

49. Hawks casts a wary eye at Sam Goldwyn, with Barbara Stanwyck on the set of *Ball of Fire*.

50. Ella Raines happily examines her contract with her new bosses Charles Boyer and Hawks.

51. Who will blink first? Fearsome adversaries Hal Wallis and Hawks at Warner Bros., early 1940s.

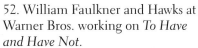

52. William Faulkner and Hawks at Warner Bros. working on *To Have and Have Not*.

53. Hawks has the attention of Dolores Moran and Lauren Bacall, but Humphrey Bogart has other things on his mind on *To Have and Have Not*.

54. Bogie and Bacall.

55. Hawks has John Ireland and Montgomery Clift compare their guns in *Red River*.

56. Assistant director William McGarry, David Hawks, and the director scout *Red River* locations in Arizona with the help of walkie-talkies.

57. Danny Kaye looks like the odd man out when Cary Grant visits the set of *A Song Is Born*.

58. Ann Sheridan and Hawks between set-ups in Germany on *I Was a Male War Bride*.

59. "If she'd only done *Red River*, she'd have been a big star," said Hawks of his discovery Margaret Sheridan, seen here opposite Kenneth Tobey in *The Thing*.

60. Hawks giving Kirk Douglas some pointed direction on *The Big Sky*.

61. Playing croquet in Palm Springs.

62. Helen Hawks congratulates her son William on his third marriage, to former Boston socialite Frances Koshland Judge, in Los Angeles, October 3, 1951.

63. Marilyn Monroe waiting for Hawks and Jane Russell to make a decision on *Gentlemen Prefer Blondes*.

64. and 65. Hawks's wedding to Dee Hartford at Hog Canyon, February 20, 1953. The groom was fifty-six, the bride twenty-four. They left for Europe the next morning. With Barbara and David, below.

66. In deep discussion about pharaohs with Faulkner and Harry Kurnitz,
Suvretta House, St. Moritz, Christmas, 1953.

67. The former mechanical engineering major demonstrates how to seal a pyramid.

68. Seven-month-old Gregg and Dee in Cannes, May 1955.

69. Hawks nursing his broken leg at Klosters, winter 1956.

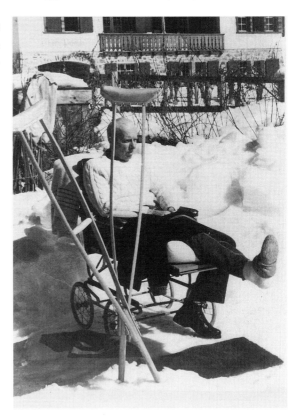

70. Back in action: the defining moment of *Rio Bravo*.

71. and 72. Dee, Gregg, and a friend visit the Tucson location of *Rio Bravo*. Below, John Wayne, John Russell, Walter Brennan, Angie Dickinson, and Dean Martin await the next move.

73. Chance de Widstedt and Howard.

74. and 75. Father and sons: with Gregg at the track, and with David in Beverly Hills, both 1960.

76. "There was a queasy feeling about it," said Red Buttons of the arrangements made for John Wayne to shoot an elephant during *Hatari!*

77. With Paula Prentiss on *Man's Favorite Sport?*

78. John Ford meets Michele Carey on the Tucson location of *El Dorado*, autumn 1965.

79. Hawks on the Champs–Elysées at the time of the Paris opening of *El Dorado*, June 1967.

80. Jean–Luc Godard's *hommage* in *Contempt (Le Mépris)*, 1964.

81. Publicist Pierre Rissient and Cinématheque Française head Henri Langlois with Hawks in Paris, June 1967.

83. In Ensenada for the Baja 500, June 9, 1971. From left to right: Peter Hawks's daughters Jamin and Kate; friend Doc Bertrand; Sondra Currie; Hawks; Norma Baldwin and her husband–to–be, Peter Hawks.

82. Dad with Gregg and the first of many race cars.

84. Backstage with John Wayne and Hawks's honorary Oscar, April 8, 1975.

85. With Raven, December 1977, about two weeks before his death.

have one line: pointing his rifle, he was to say, "This here's your warrant, mister." The documentary shows Plimpton arriving on the set, watching some tests, and, upon doing a few readings for the benefit of Hawks and Wayne, being advised by Hawks to get rid of his Harvard accent if he wanted to keep the line. The easterner is amusingly seen practicing his walk, mounting a horse, riding, and shooting a gun, up to the filming of his big scene. At the last second, Hawks tells Plimpton that after days of practicing his line as written, Plimpton is to point the gun and say, "I got a warrant right here, Sheriff." After the general hilarity dies down, Plimpton manages to get out the new line and is then yanked backward by a wire when his character is shot by Jorge Rivero.

For a while, Hawks seemed to get along well with Jennifer O'Neill, as they were seen walking around the set arm in arm and Hawks seemed to relish telling his stories to her. At a certain point in Tucson, however, Hawks saw the familiar pattern repeating itself, of an inexperienced actress suddenly deciding that she could behave like a star. Furthermore, as he watched dailies, he realized that on-screen she was "dull" and was bringing nothing to the picture. They had a major falling out, and afterward he wouldn't even speak her name, always calling her things like "a damn fool" and "stupid dame" in interviews.

Hawks responded to O'Neill's behavior as he had before, by cutting her part down. All through the story, O'Neill's character acquits herself outstandingly when things are on the line, managing to shoot the gang leader, Whitey, played by Robert Donner, in the bar, and gutsily driving a wagon onto the compound of Jack Elam's crazy man and figuratively disarming him. By any normal Hawksian standard, she had proved herself good enough to accompany the men on their big third-act mission. But because Hawks was fed up with his actress, he rewrote the script to give some key climactic action to Sherry Lansing.

"Jennifer O'Neill was supposed to kill the bad guy, but Howard got mad at her so he had me do it," Sherry Lansing acknowledged. For this reason, Lansing got to share, with John Wayne, the final scene, and the final shot, of Howard Hawks's long screen career. "Howard was yelling at me to try to get me to cry for the last scene," she said. "Duke went up to him later and said, 'Howard, you should lay off, she's pretty good. You should take it easy on her.' Howard said, 'Don't be ridiculous, she can take it.'" The climactic scene has Lansing securing revenge by gunning down the evil sheriff who has scarred her face, then hobbling off with Wayne, who has been shot in the thigh. "Mr. McNally, you . . . you make a person feel awful . . . ," she begins, whereupon Wayne replies, "Please don't say comfortable."

Lansing chomped at the bit of Hawks's often stern attitude with her. "I was standing around chatting with one of the grips and he told me, 'I can't talk to you too long or I'll be fired.' I think there was an unwritten code that you didn't fool with Howard's women.'" She was also put off by the way Hawks "talked glibly about his relationship with Kitty. He was very proud of her and he talked about her all the time, as if they were close," which couldn't have been further from the truth.

Despite all this, Lansing valued her experience on the picture, which was her last as well, because of the glimpse it gave her as to how filmmaking used to be. "It was much more fun," she insisted. "It wasn't life and death. He had a bigger-than-life attitude toward movies and life in general. It wasn't a 'serious' business the way it is today." After the shoot was over, Lansing admitted to herself that she hated acting and quit. "Howard started writing something else he wanted me to do," she said. "I didn't want to do it, and he started to get fed up with me. He thought I was being silly. He could be very abrupt." Lansing subsequently went on to become the first woman to run a motion picture studio, and she was saddened by her last encounter with Hawks: "When I got my first executive job at MGM, I called him up to tell him where I was, and all he said was, 'You could have been a great actress' and hung up."

It was clear to his collaborators that Hawks realized that the film wasn't working out the way he had hoped. "He knew it wasn't too good," the editor, John Woodcock, admitted. "He'd come out of dailies and say, 'That's a terrible scene, cut as much of it out as you can.'" Pierre Rissient came from Paris to spend several days on the Tucson location and reported, "You could feel that Hawks was letting the thing go. There was no intimacy or complicity between him and anyone on *Rio Lobo*. . . . I'd say he had already given up." After speaking with the veteran cinematographer at length, Rissient was sure that William Clothier was ready and willing to put considerably more effort and artistry into his work, "but he was made aloof by Hawks's attitude."

Rissient noted that John Wayne "was his own master" on the set, and Peter Bogdanovich, when he visited, was surprised by Hawks's extremely casual attitude. "Duke would actually direct the other actors some of the time," Bogdanovich observed. "And he would say, 'Isn't that right, Mr. Hawks?' And Hawks would say, 'Sure, Duke.'" Hawks told Bogdanovich of a chilling moment when John Ford, who had directed his last film in 1965, came to visit the set in Mexico. Bogdanovich recalled Hawks saying, "'Jack came down and we all had lunch. Everybody left and we were alone, and he just looked at me and said, "You S.O.B." I said, "What, Jack?" And that's all he said.' I think it had to do with the fact that there was Hawks, still directing Wayne, whom Ford had been so associated with, and Ford couldn't work anymore."

Hawks's lack of evident care shows in the finished film, which has all the visual élan of a TV movie of the time and isn't even distinctly recognizable stylistically as the work of Hawks. Many shots are lazily and clumsily reframed via zooms, and the camera often seems to readjust in an almost surprised way to the action and characters as they move. The lighting is not flattering to anyone, and one early-morning campsite scene, with the characters waking up, looks as though it was shot at high noon.

The company finished in Tucson and moved to the Studio Center in the San Fernando Valley. The facility had originally been Republic Studios, where John Wayne had made dozens of B Westerns in the 1930s and 1940s, and when someone asked Duke where his old dressing room was, he replied, "Dressing room? I didn't have a dressing room. I had a hook." Hawks worked out of a makeshift office in a trailer, a far cry from his resplendent bungalow in the old days of Warner Bros. and his spacious quarters, complete with a shower, at Paramount. Hawks gave his young actress friend Sondra Currie a small role as a hooker in the saloon, but she was all but cut out, visible only fleetingly. With the old censorship codes having broken down since he had last made a film, Hawks staged a repeat of the scene he was forced to cut from *El Dorado*, with Jorge Rivero barging in on a shirtless Sherry Lansing. Again, it was coyly staged, with Lansing strategically wrapping her arms around her breasts throughout the episode, during which she attempts to induce Rivero, a total stranger, to stay with her.

Hawks completed his final motion picture the second week of June, and "the minute he finished he headed for Palm Springs," John Woodcock recalled. "He gave me carte blanche in the cutting," trusting his editor to do his best and eliminate anything embarrassing. Hawks liked a few scenes, particularly the train robbery and its aftermath, but he felt that "with the main girl such a dud, scene after scene just backfired. . . . If you got *passable* scenes, you were awfully glad." On another occasion, he expressed his opinion of *Rio Lobo* more succinctly: "I didn't think it was any good."

When it was released at the very end of 1970, the film was generally recognized as a flat, below-par effort by both Hawks and Wayne. Given the built-in audience for virtually any John Wayne picture, it did reasonable business, but less than Cinema Center had hoped for and less than any of the three previous collaborations between the director and star. *Rio Lobo* generated $4.25 million in rentals, which earned it twentieth place among pictures for the year. By way of comparison, Wayne's next vehicle, a thoroughly average Western called *Big Jake,* earned rentals of $7.5 million, while the hip revisionist Western *Little Big Man,* released at exactly the same time as *Rio Lobo,* pulled in $15 million.

A few hardy souls spoke out for Hawks's last film. Most prominent among them was Roger Greenspun, the second-string critic for the *New York Times* and an arch-auteurist, who wrote that *Rio Lobo* was "close enough to greatness to stand above everything else so far in the current season." The review raised eyebrows in many quarters and provoked angry letters to the paper; in retrospect, with Hawks's critical reputation scarcely riding on the verdict, it is easy to see why. While not oblivious to the film's shortcomings, Greg Ford, in a scholarly *Film Heritage* essay, plausibly argued that if such artists as Matisse, Faulkner, and Wallace Stevens could be allowed many recapitulations of the same subjects, why not Hawks?

Still, however charitable one might care to be, the evidence of decline is too obvious to ignore. The film's lack of creative spark, of inspiration, of energy, of any driving force is palpable in every scene save for the train prologue. As shoddy as the visuals is the blandly utilitarian dialogue, much of which sounds dubbed in. If one were to compare the talk here with that in virtually any picture Hawks made before the 1950s, the staggering difference, in both words and pacing, would be instantly apparent. In fact, the dialogue is so functional, and the dramatic developments so basic, that one is put in mind of a silent film, albeit with little of the visual or storytelling economy. Wayne's preference for relaxation over action shows in his exceedingly "comfortable" performance, which may possess the authority but has little of the toughness of his work in *Rio Bravo.* Some detractors have gone so far as to call *Rio Lobo* a Hawksian self-parody, but it's not quite sharp enough for that. The film truly does feel tired and unengaged, with the repetition of previous situations and conceits this time played out to diminishing returns. Few great directors ever went out with a bang; like most of them, Hawks, at the estimable age of seventy-four, sort of faded away.

39

From Sand to Dust

The transformation of Howard Hawks from working director into living legend had its seeds planted in France in the 1950s, began taking noticeable shape in the 1960s, and assumed a life of its own in the 1970s. The first full-length critical study, *Howard Hawks* by Jean-Claude Missiaen, appeared in 1966, and the following year, for a BBC-TV series called *The Movies*, Peter Bogdanovich and Nicholas Garnham made a pioneering, hourlong documentary, *Howard Hawks: The Great Professional*, in which Hawks tells a number of his most familiar stories. While shooting the interview in Palm Springs, Bogdanovich had what was, for him, the harrowing experience of riding in a dune buggy with twelve-year-old Gregg at the wheel and getting stuck in the desert on a blistering day. "I started walking back for help," Bogdanovich recalled, "and I realized I didn't know where I was. Eventually I'm not feeling very well. There's a tiny bush. I'm going to get sunstroke, and I'm trying to figure out how to put my head under this bush. Then I hear a motorcycle and up rides Howard. When I got within hailing distance, I could see he looked terribly worried. Howard was riding through the sand and he looked very grim, like a man who knew tragedy. It was the most serious moment I ever saw him in."

In 1968, Robin Wood, the author of a previous volume on Hitchcock and one of the few brilliant critics ever to devote his career to film analysis, published a book on Hawks's films that still stands as the best critical investigation of the director's work and one of the most persuasive studies of any filmmaker. Succinct but fully argued, passionate but steeled by a rigorous critical method, Wood's intellectual, highly influential book did more to legitimatize high regard for Hawks than anything other than Andrew Sarris's installation of Hawks in the pantheon of great Hollywood directors in his landmark book *The American Cinema* that same year. Even then, Sarris felt compelled to point out that "Howard Hawks was until recently the least known and least appreciated Hollywood director of any stature," citing

Hawks's conspicuous neglect in the standard film histories published up to that time. Perceptively noting that "Hawks has lived a tightrope existence, keeping his footing in a treacherous industry for more than forty years without surrendering his personal identity," Sarris remarked on Hawks's concern for professionalism, his functional, eye-level visual style, and his ability to stamp "his distinctively bitter view of life on adventure, gangster and private-eye melodramas, Westerns, musicals, and screwball comedies, the kind of thing Americans do best and appreciate least." His conclusion: "That one can discern the same directorial signature over a wide variety of genres is proof of artistry." From a critical point of view, Wood and Sarris decisively confirmed Hawks's new standing, not just as an accomplished popular entertainer but as an American artist of the first rank. Hawks remained a major focal point of critical debate in Peter Wollen's enormously influential 1969 volume, *Signs and Meaning in the Cinema,* and 1971 saw the publication of another full-length study, by Jean Gili.

If Hawks ever read much of this adulatory analysis is unclear, but he willingly fostered the worship of critics by sitting for countless interviews about his career. His number was listed in the phone book, and he would tell anyone who called just to come on over. On the subject of himself, Hawks was inexhaustible, recounting the same colorful stories as if for the first time and outlasting interlocutors perhaps a third his own age; Joseph McBride remembered, "When I left Hawks's home after one of our visits, which seldom lasted less than five hours, I always felt exhausted, and *he* always looked great."

Hawks also played host to young directors who idolized him, unhesitatingly dispensing opinions and advice. The first of these was Bogdanovich, whose fealty to the master was such that he included excerpts from Hawks films in his first two features — *The Criminal Code* in *Targets, Red River* in *The Last Picture Show* — and blatantly, but unofficially, used a Hawks classic, *Bringing Up Baby,* as the basis for his third, and most successful, film, *What's Up, Doc?*

Bogdanovich remembered screening *Targets* for two director friends, Jean Renoir and Hawks, and felt that their reactions "shows the difference between the two men. . . . Renoir said, 'It is as good as the best Hitchcock,' and that's all. I showed the picture to Howard one night, just to him. He sat there. I sat there. Finally, he said, 'Well, the acting's not too good.' 'I know. Some of it.' 'Some of those scenes go on a little too long.' 'Maybe.' 'But the action's good, and that stuff's hard to do.' I lived on that for years. When we show the clip from *The Criminal Code,* there's a line, 'Howard Hawks directed that,' and he snorted when that came on. He liked and appreciated the *Red River* clip in *The Last Picture Show*. When I sent him the *What's Up, Doc?* script, I didn't hear from him for a couple of weeks. I was in the first day of rehearsal and the a.d. came up and said, 'It's Howard Hawks.' I got on the phone and he said, 'I read your script. You didn't steal the leopard, and you didn't steal the dinosaur. But it's pretty good. Who's in it?' I said, 'Barbra Streisand and Ryan O'Neal. I know they're not Hepburn and Grant. . . .' He said, 'That's for sure. But don't let 'em be cute, and you'll be fine.' That was it. He got a kick out of it's having been stolen from *Bringing Up Baby*. Then he went down to South America and came back and said, 'I've got some pictures for you,' and he'd taken pictures of the theater marquees where *What's Up, Doc?* was playing. He loved that it was a hit."

When the up-and-coming director William Friedkin was living with Kitty Hawks in New York for a couple of years in the early 1970s, the three spent some time together, which represented the possible beginnings of a rapprochement between a father and daughter who had scarcely ever seen each other. Friedkin naturally asked the old man what he thought of his films. Bluntly, Hawks said that he thought both *The Night They Raided Minsky's* and *The Boys in the Band* were "lousy" and warned Friedkin that he'd better make something entertaining if he wanted to keep getting work. Hawks said that he recommended that Friedkin "make a good chase. Make one better than anyone's done," and Friedkin confirmed that this piece of advice led directly to his decision to make *The French Connection*, for which he won an Oscar.

On a more personal and distressing level, when Kitty Hawks and Friedkin were in Los Angeles one February, Hawks invited them to dinner for her birthday. Friedkin recounted, "We met him at one of his favorite restaurants, Chianti, on Melrose. Kitty gave him a big hug and we noticed that he had a brown paper bag with him, like a grocery bag. We sat down and he said, 'Kitty, I've got something for you,' and she got very excited, not imagining what it could be. And he gave her the bag and she reached in and pulled out two men's shirts, and she just burst into tears." Kitty's lingering resentment of her absent father flooded to the surface once again, and while they saw each other sporadically, especially once Kitty moved to Los Angeles and became an agent, the two never reached any kind of accord.

One rather less illustrious filmmaker with whom Hawks became involved was Max Baer Jr. Best known for having played Jethro on *The Beverly Hillbillies* and as the son of the heavyweight boxer whom Hawks had briefly directed before being replaced on *The Prizefighter and the Lady* in 1932,

Baer sought and received Hawks's help in writing, producing and even editing his first production, *Macon County Line*, a cheap period melodrama. Hawks didn't think much of it but was genuinely impressed by how much money it made.

Hawks admitted that he didn't see much he liked. He hated Sam Peckinpah's *The Wild Bunch*, dismissing it with the often-quoted line, "I can kill four men, take 'em to the morgue, and bury 'em before he gets one down to the ground in slow motion." Nor was he thrilled with *The God-father*, suggesting that he had long since done it all, and better, in *Scarface*. *Easy Rider* he found interesting because "it was kind of a new style and it was well done." At the same time, he rightly predicted, "I don't think the picture is going to live as an outstanding picture." Pierre Rissient took him to see Abraham Polonsky's *Tell Them Willie Boy Is Here*, which he liked, as he did *Butch Cassidy and the Sundance Kid*. By inference, one can con-clude that Hawks was both a Robert Redford and a George Roy Hill fan, since the picture during this period that he seemed to like most was Hill's *The Sting*. It is easy to see why, since it recapitulated the best of Old Holly-wood and represented the sorts of things Hawks himself did well: it was centered on a strong buddy-buddy relationship, traded heavily upon star personalities, injected considerable humor into a dramatic story, and didn't pretend to be anything more than it was.

Hawks considered some of his early film festival visits to be promo-tional stops, since he very much considered himself an active filmmaker who intended to make more pictures. In November 1970, a month before *Rio Lobo* was released, he participated in a tribute at the Chicago Film Festival. He also made time to visit the Hawks-fanatical Doc Films group at the University of Chicago, which possessed one of the few prints of *Scarface* then available in the country and published the magazine *Focus*, which ran the legendary cover article "Who the Hell Is Howard Hawks?" Charles Flynn, who picked Hawks up at the airport on behalf of the group, recalled that the director asked to be taken directly downtown to Abercrombie & Fitch, where he spent a long time inspecting the store's stock of guns.

In July 1972, Hawks did what nearly every major director of his gen-eration did when they were perceived as being put out to pasture: he served as the president of a film festival jury. Hawks did the honors at the San Sebastian Film Festival, where he was forced to sit through quite a few European art films of the type he generally abhorred and avoided. But in the company of a few admirers, he made a pilgrimage to Pamplona for the running of the bulls, something he had considered filming twenty years before for his unrealized adaptation of *The Sun Also Rises*. While in Spain, he was approached by the Russian delegation about directing what would have been the first U.S.–Soviet co-production, a dubious distinction that was subsequently claimed by George Cukor's *The Bluebird*. Hawks had been responsible for giving the Russian entry at San Sebastian a special prize and, apparently in return, he was told that he could have carte blanche to make whatever he wanted. Provocatively, he proposed "a story that you might call pretty political," but one that might also be called a direct steal from *Some Like It Hot*, about a pair of Americans who "are trying to get away from the Russian police, and they go in the back door of the Ballets Russes. And when the cops come in, they're dancing in the chorus." Discussions never went very far, but Hawks's idea was no doubt not quite what the authorities had in mind from the director of *Red River* and *Rio Bravo*.

During this period, the project Hawks spoke about more seriously was one based on the World War II friendship of Ernest Hemingway and the photographer Robert Capa. Aside from *Sergeant York*, Hawks had always steered clear of biographical stories, but he thought that putting the two colorful personalities together in a film could be effective; "the story of one man gets kind of boring, but the story of a friendship is something that lets you make better scenes," Hawks argued. He never developed a screenplay for it, but he seemed intent upon focusing on numerous seriocomic incidents in the two men's relationship that he had either witnessed or heard about firsthand; Hemingway he considered fascinating on any number of levels, while Capa was "crazy as a bedbug." To play Hemingway, Hawks had in mind George C. Scott, who in 1977 so effectively played the Hemingway figure in *Islands in the Stream*.

In October 1972, Hawks received a special tribute at the San Francisco Film Festival, where the other special guests that year were his old Warner Bros. colleague Raoul Walsh and his *Only Angels Have Wings* discovery, Rita Hayworth. Hawks and Walsh, who had never been close friends, were cordial and sociable with each other, but Hayworth, whom Hawks had not seen in many years, was in particularly bad shape at the time, embarrassing herself, and turning off Hawks, by becoming falling-down drunk at both the opening-night party and a VIP dinner at Étoile. The Sunday tribute to Hawks lasted practically all day long. Hawks attended a San Francisco 49ers football game while the packed house of mostly young buffs at the Palace of Fine Arts feasted on hours of clips from his films. When he finally appeared, to a standing ovation, he dazzled everyone with his deep tan, aviator glasses, snug suit, imperious air, and repertoire of fabulous sto-

ries. He conveyed the impression of a proud military commander who had
never lost a battle, a winner, a man apart.

While Hawks seemed quite formidable, intimidating and austere to
visitors, even if he was, as always, utterly approachable, Walsh was considerably warmer and more affable. Both Pierre Rissient and his sometime
publicity partner in Paris during the 1960s, Bertrand Tavernier, spent a good
deal of time with both men. Tavernier placed the comparison on the intellectual and artistic plane: "I can say Walsh is a *wider* director; his interests
were wide, but he . . . was never able to do anything as controlled as *To
Have and Have Not* and some of Hawks's comedies. Hawks is a great director, but narrow; he always did the same three or four films. There are people
who have a narrow vision of the world, and Hawks is one. You don't *feel* the
world as you do in a Walsh film. . . . From [Hawks's] range he made mas-
terpieces. Sometimes he was a genius."

In 1973, both Hawks and Walsh were moved significantly further into
mainstream recognition by Richard Schickel's widely seen documentary
series, *The Men Who Made the Movies*, which featured an installment on
each of them as well as on Capra, Hitchcock, Wellman, King Vidor, George
Cukor, and Vincente Minnelli. As he had done with Bogdanovich, Hawks
took Schickel out to the desert for his interview, and a good deal of footage
shows Hawks surrounded by off-road motorcyclists, including Gregg, during and after a cross-country race. Schickel guessed that "Howard sees these
little adventures as tests for would-be interrogators, a way of determining
that your intellectual understanding of his work is matched by a willingness to put theory into practice."

Schickel also surmised that after having abandoned Los Angeles for
good, Hawks led "a rather isolated life," one that revolved mostly around
Gregg for its social side. This was largely true. Hawks's routine in Palm
Springs consisted of twenty laps in the pool upon rising at seven, breakfast,
sketching out architectural or design plans and then going into town for a
haircut and a chat with his barber, who was one of his few close friends, or
just taking a walk before lunch. In the afternoons, he worked on one of his
stories or scripts, attended to some business, tinkered with motorcycles, or
did some wood or metal work. Some days he would get in a round of golf.
Almost every weekend was devoted to Gregg's teenage-level racing career,
starting with quarter midget racing and moving up to motorcycling, in which
he'd started winning races when he was fourteen. Among the most frequent
visitors to the house were two hulking young auto mechanics named Bunny
and Winkie, who helped work on all the Hawks vehicles. A good cook—

Hoagy Carmichael always remembered his outstanding lamb stew—Hawks ate healthy, "clean" food and often planned and prepared an entire weekend's menu in advance.

During the summer of 1973, when it was clear that John Ford was dying, Hawks went over to see his neighbor several times a week. Hawks said that his one acknowledged superior in the business of directing movies spent most of his time in bed watching old Westerns on television and that the two of them would have a drink and joke about who had stolen what from whom and how they approached things differently, with Hawks ribbing Ford about being so corny and Ford sniping right back about how sarcastic Hawks was. When Hawks visited Ford on August 30, he could tell the end was near. He called John Wayne, who chartered a helicopter to see the great man one last time. Ford died the next night in his sleep.

Among Hawks's few remaining old friends in the desert were Hoagy Carmichael and Frank Capra, although he saw neither of them often. Between Hawks and Capra there was always a lingering competitiveness and, on Capra's part, a bit of a condescending attitude that often came out in put-downs of varying tartness. One night Cissy Wellman prepared a dinner party for the two venerable directors, each of whom said, "I can't stay late," when he arrived. Naturally, they both stayed until three in the morning. George Kirgo, Ted Wiener, and their wives were among the other guests, and Kirgo swore that he never laughed harder than that night, when the two old men kept topping each other with increasingly far-fetched stories and outright lies. Kirgo recalled how they started getting their stories mixed up, with Capra saying, "Howard, that didn't happen to you, it happened to *me!*" and Hawks just sallying forth as if no one had noticed. Later in the evening, however, Capra turned, and, Kirgo recalled, "Capra was never so mean as he was that night. Capra kept putting Howard down, and Howard wouldn't defend himself. He just laughed. Finally I sensed that Howard felt out of his depth intellectually."

One reason Hawks felt more comfortable with young people than with old contemporaries is that they wouldn't challenge or doubt him and would accept whatever he said at his word. Certainly, he found willing acolytes whenever he ventured out. Between April and July 1974, Tom Luddy at the Pacific Film Archive in Berkeley ran the most complete Hawks retrospective ever organized to date, in that it included the silent films until then thought to be lost: *Paid to Love*, *The Cradle Snatchers*, and *Trent's Last Case*. Attending the long-delayed American premiere of *Trent* on the afternoon of April 24, Hawks was so appalled by it that he demanded that the print be thrown out immediately afterward. However, he recovered sufficiently to appear that evening for *His Girl Friday* and *To Have and Have Not*, which received the usual rapturous receptions.

At a small discussion with some students and locals, Hawks was challenged by some feminists as to why, *Gentlemen Prefer Blondes* aside, he had never made a female equivalent of his films about male friendship. Hawks replied straightforwardly that in all his life he had never witnessed the same kind of bonding relationship between women, but he good-naturedly challenged anyone in the group to come up with a good story on such a theme. One of the group, a young actress and writer named Robin Mencken, followed up and spent a couple of days with him. "Howard's initial problem," she explained, "was that he could never think of a compelling story that would lead two women to bond with a code of ethics." But together they fleshed out an idea about two women who become united when one of them has to go to jail and leaves her child with her best friend. Mencken found Hawks incredibly sharp, open, and generous with his time and ideas. Just then, Mencken was up for the leading female part opposite Warren Beatty and Jack Nicholson in *The Fortune*, a role that eventually went to Stockard Channing, and Hawks helped her enormously in preparing for her screen test, coaching her on movement, keeping her momentum going, and her best angles. Because she was in Hawks's hotel room for so many hours, everyone else suspected something else was going on, but Mencken said that there was never a hint of a sexual undercurrent between them.

While in Berkeley, Hawks agreed to speak with three representatives of a radical leftist film journal called *Jump Cut*. The interviewers' agenda was to try to pinpoint Hawks's politics, to steer him away from his usual anecdotes and get him to express his personal philosophy and outlook on relevant issues. From the outset, they knew what they were dealing with, since before the recording session even started, Hawks told them, "If I want to have fun at a party, I'll tell the Duke, 'See that guy over there?' He's a Red.'" But they wrote that they were prepared to suspend their "aversion to his reactionary romanticism and hail him as a closet subversive, a repressed populist, perhaps even a right-wing anarchist."

The result was undoubtedly the oddest, most rambling, but in some ways most personal interview with Hawks ever published. In it he railed, as much of his generation did, against the "biased" media that "has turned people against Nixon," against newfangled school textbooks, against messages—political and otherwise—in motion pictures, and against "sick" pictures, which he defined as "pictures of psychopaths, pictures of strange people, pictures that are nauseating, people that you don't like to look at or follow—those are sick pictures." He expressed a revulsion at politics in general and at the "gradual erosion" of ideals he attributed to political life. On the subject of Vietnam, he said, "America lost all over the world by fighting there." He agreed that it was never a winnable war, saying, "I think that whoever started it in the first place was wrongly advised. They should have said, 'Go over there and drop a couple of big bombs, and if you don't feel like doing that, stay out of it.'"

The interviewers actually tried to argue Hawks into supporting the actions of the Symbianese Liberation Army, which had recently kidnapped Patty Hearst, insisting that the radicals were independent, strong-minded individuals with an "adventurous spirit," just like Hawksian characters. Saying "I think you're nuts," Hawks called the SLA members "nitwits" and stated, "I have absolutely no respect for kidnappers or anybody else who tries to get something that way, 'cause I don't think they've got a chance in the world of getting it. I've yet to see that these protesters who come into a place and tie themselves up are gaining anything by doing it."

This, however, led Hawks into a rare discussion of rearing children and a telling illustration of his relationship with Gregg: "I have a youngster eighteen years old. I asked him to trim his hair. He says, 'I don't want to.' I said, 'O.K., fine.' I took his car and his motorcycle away from him. He said, 'Why'd you do that?' I said, 'I wanted to; I don't want you to have 'em.' I said, 'I have a perfect right to think just as you do. You can do what you want to, but I don't have to go along with it.'"

Asked what Gregg was withholding from him by not cutting his hair, Hawks said, "Any desire to do anything I asked him to do. I didn't like the way he looked. I just said, 'You don't want to do it, that's quite all right, I don't want to help you. You sail along.' Didn't take him very long before he said, 'I'd rather cut my hair and have some of the things that I get from you.' I said, 'Good. I think you're smart. If you know the way to get 'em, I think you're doing the right thing.'" Hawks added, "We get along a hell of a lot better now than we did before."

As his partisans often pointed out, Howard Hawks had never won an Oscar and was nominated only once, but in late 1974, efforts were put in motion to change that situation. Without Hawks's knowledge, George Kirgo spearheaded a movement to get the board of governors to present Hawks with a special Academy Award. Not only did the members of the board agree, but they also decided to give an honorary Oscar to Jean Renoir. The latter's health did not permit him to attend, but Hawks was pleased and excited by the long overdue recognition. He was sitting in the orchestra section of the Dorothy Chandler Pavilion during the rehearsal the day before when he was tapped on the shoulder. It was Lauren Bacall, there to present the costume design Oscar, to whom he had not spoken in nearly thirty years. Bacall was afraid that he might be gruff with her, but to her surprise he was warm and expressive, delighted to see her. He even invited her out to the desert for a couple of days after the awards, suggesting that it would be nice to catch up and talk about the old days. Unfortunately, Bacall's schedule ruled the idea out, and she regretted ever after not having had the opportunity to truly make peace with the man who changed her life.

On April 8, 1975, *The Godfather, Part II* walked off with six Oscars, all but shutting down its main competition, *Chinatown*. One of Hawks's most faithful champions, François Truffaut, was present at the ceremony, having been nominated for directing and writing *Day for Night*. Who else could have presented Hawks's honorary award but John Wayne, who ambled out, and claimed that he and Hawks had made four, not five, pictures together, omitting *Rio Lobo* from the list, and read off some of the more eminent titles in the Hawks filmography. "Now, he's made a lot of actors jump," Wayne declared, "so it's time we made him do the same. Tonight he's not the director, I am. Hawks, we're ready to roll! Get your skinny whatchamacallit out here!"

Hawks was greeted with a standing ovation to receive the award that was being presented to "a master American filmmaker whose creative efforts hold a distinguished place in world cinema." George Kirgo had written what he felt was a strong speech for Hawks to deliver, but the director decided he wanted to prepare his own. At first, he considered something "a little sarcastic," to wit: "People usually come up here and thank everybody connected with their film, all the people they worked with, but I could stand up here all night, so I'll just thank a few little people—like Darryl Zanuck, Jack Warner, Harry Cohn, Ernest Hemingway, and Bill Faulkner." Instead, he decided to recount a story about visiting John Ford out in the desert shortly before the latter's death. "We got to telling each other things that we'd stolen from each other. . . . One day he was laughing and he said, 'There's something I took from you that beats the whole thing. . . . I made a picture that wasn't so good and you made *Sergeant York*,' he said, 'I got the award.' And he stopped in the middle of laughing . . . and he said, 'Well, you're going to get an award,' and I said, 'I don't think so.' He said, 'Goddamn it, you're going to get an award.' So I would like to thank the Academy for making that prediction of his come true. Thanks very much." When he finished, Hawks and Wayne engaged in a little Alphonse-and-Gaston routine of trying to lead the other offstage in opposite directions, then retreated to the pressroom, where Wayne was instantly accused by some journalist of being a racist. The star merely said, "You're mistaken," and Hawks backed the Duke up. When the belligerent reporter persisted in his tirade, he was escorted out of the building by security guards.

In Hawks's mind, even then, little more than a year short of eighty, he was still going to make another film. He had a couple of fresh projects in mind, but still foremost in his plans was his globe-trotting oil-rigging yarn. He had always imagined that this was the project that Ted Wiener would back, although his financial involvement with his rich golf buddy had proved less than rewarding thus far, since the one scheme of Wiener's that Hawks had actually sunk money into resulted in Hawks losing a lot of money. (By contrast, Peter Bogdanovich, who got to know the Texan through Hawks, made some big profits on his investments with Wiener.)

Having received help from several writer friends at points along the way, Hawks finally sat down and, in July 1976, finished a full first-draft screenplay for the picture by himself. Called "When It's Hot Play It Cool," it now focused on two international oilmen roaming the globe for untapped deposits, an incredibly blatant metaphor for their simultaneous sexual exploration. Hawks considered Clint Eastwood and Steve McQueen for the leads but complained that both were too humorless for his type of film, that they wanted too much money, and that McQueen had gotten too fat. He once half joked that he would prefer Paul Michael Glaser and David Soul of *Starsky and Hutch*, and he more seriously proposed that he was considering Alan Alda, an actor whose comedic gifts he much enjoyed on *M*A*S*H*, and perhaps Al Pacino. He also had no idea who to get for the Bacall-inspired female lead, a character he named Rabbit "because she runs around a lot."

Having been shown studio facilities near Madrid at the time of his visit to San Sebastian, Hawks had the notion of basing the production in Spain, doing the interiors there, then nding Pierre Schoendorffer around the world to film the extensive locations. Reasonably enough considering the subject, he wanted scenes shot in Indonesia, Saudi Arabia, and Turkey, but he cited red tape and very real political inhospitability in these and other oil countries as reasons for the film's delay. As it happened, though, Hawks never spoke, even in a preliminary way, with Schoendorffer about any of this, suggesting that he had never pursued the production realities with professional seriousness.

But just as Bertrand Tavernier felt it was a good thing that Hawks never made his Vietnam War film, the same suspicion holds for "When It's Hot Play It Cool." In Hawks's own draft, not only are many of the characters and conventions archaic and tired but the attitudes expressed are by turns infantile, racist, politically naive, and embarrassingly out of touch. It was one thing to have two Yanks hightailing it through the Middle East in the 1920s, but to portray Arab sheiks in the 1970s as evil, lecherous buffoons with nothing but white slavery and throat-slitting on their minds—and to have the American ride roughshod over them to boot—would have been utterly unpalatable to contemporary audiences.

The two leads, called Bill and Spike, just as they are in *A Girl in Every Port*, first meet in Malaysia, where they are representing competing American oil companies. They fight immediately, but "at the bottom these two are the same man; tough, resourceful, cheerfully ruthless but always within limits, deeply loyal to a friend but never sentimental, equally needing women, adventure, and a spice of danger to make life worth living." The gag from the original film, in which Bill pulls Spike's dislocated finger, remains intact, and Hawks even inserted an in-joke about John Wayne: when Bill claims that the other man doesn't look like he should be named Spike, Spike replies, "If you were a red-blooded American boy with a name like Marion, what would you do?"

After adventures and misadventures in Kuwait, Beirut, Jakarta, and Central America, Spike and Bill are saved from a firing squad by a local strongman who has come under the influence of an all-American conwoman named Flo, Spike's ex-wife and Bill's current lover.

Soused beyond belief, the two Yanks end up in a small cottage somewhere in the wilderness, and the film's final sequence deserves to be recounted in full, not only because it would, if filmed, have been the final scene in the entire Hawksian oeuvre but because it undoubtedly represents the most outrageous and explicit manifestation of the naive, instinctive homoerotic undercurrent running through a good deal of the director's entire career.

> *They start for bed; unwittingly, both head for the same one and get into it on opposite sides.* BILL *and* SPIKE. *In the same bed. For a moment there are contented grunting as they settle themselves for sleep. Then we see their faces as each one becomes aware of something wrong; they're back to back.*

SPIKE (in a stage whisper)
Bill . . . there's somebody in my bed.

BILL
There's somebody in mine, too. What will we do?

SPIKE
You throw yours out, and I'll throw mine.

BILL
Right.

SPIKE
I'll count to five. One . . . 2 . . . 3 . . . 4 . . . 5.

Bill and Spike grapple with each other. They tumble out of bed. They fight and Bill ends up in a corner on the floor.

SPIKE
How did you do with yours, Bill?

BILL
Mine threw me out.

SPIKE
That's too bad. Never mind, you can sleep with me.

They go peacefully to sleep as we FADE OUT.

With his advancing years, Hawks was pried open emotionally, if ever so slightly, by his daughter Barbara, who knew that "Dad wasn't the type of man with whom you could sit around for hours talking about intimate details of things." However, her husband Don McCampbell, came from a very close-knit Nebraska family that hugged and kissed a lot, and he had never met anyone as uncommunicative and emotionally closed off as his father-in-law. In these later years, Barbara and Don came to Palm Springs from Los Angeles to visit at least once a month. "I told Don, 'He's never told me he loves me, and he doesn't hug me,'" Barbara recounted. "Don got him to try it, and the first time I tried it, I felt his whole body tense up. But I didn't let go, and after a month, it was amazing, he loosened up. But my mother said he was always that way."

In the mid-1970s, Hawks began slowing down just a bit, and friends noticed certain telltale signs of aging. His hands shook somewhat, which doctors later confirmed was a sign of the early stages of Parkinson's disease, and this, combined with an injury to his right thumb, made him shun typing and writing in favor of dictating into a tape recorder. In addition, his injury on the flatcar during *Rio Lobo* had never healed properly. When the ankle of the same leg was ripped up when he hit a cactus bush with his off-road motorcycle in late fall of 1975 (when Hawks was seventy-nine, no less), he contracted blood poisoning, and the leg was never the same again. Gregg continued to mostly live with his father, although he stayed in Los Angeles after Peter Bogdanovich hired him as an assistant on *At Long Last Love*, a film Hawks tried to talk his young friend out of, although he visited the set a few times. In the wake of this film and his subsequent flop, *Nickelodeon*, Bogdanovich and Hawks had something of a falling out. After about a year, Hawks gave Richard Schickel a message to pass along to Bogdanovich: "Tell him to come out for some more lessons." Hawks continued work on "When It's Hot Play It Cool," asking Paul Helmick to figure out a budget. In Helmick's opinion, "he wanted to make films, he really did," although it was obvious it wasn't going to happen.

Hawks kept reading popular fiction, mostly pulp detective stories and Western novels by Louis L'Amour, and in early 1977 had one more idea for a film. It was the story of three men diving for gold buried in a sunken Nazi submarine. He insisted that the men should all hate one another, although that stuck him with a question he couldn't answer: Why, if the three couldn't stand each other, were they together on the same mission? Just as he had turned to his daughter and her husband to find the dynamite ending of *Rio Bravo*, so now did he ask them to solve his dilemma on the new idea. This time, however, no one had any brainstorms.

That July, two film magazines on different sides of the Atlantic published significant, and significantly opposing, issues pertaining to Hawks. *Positif,* long the competitor of *Cahiers du Cinéma* in France, came out with a special Hawks number with an interview and new critical commentaries. By contrast, *Film Comment* in New York carried a long piece by the veteran critic Raymond Durgnat called "Hawks Isn't Good Enough," which was the first major negative assessment of the director's career to appear since Hawks had essentially been installed in the pantheon some ten years before. Durgnat complained about many things: Hawks was partial to "skimming over pain"; he compared unfavorably to such other directors as Wyler, Huston, Milestone, and even Wellman and Hathaway on similar subjects; he kept "so great a distance from the nitty-gritty of the lives that he describes . . . that he's condemned to be an entertainer." The writer proclaimed, "As an entertainer Hawks is a real artist; but as an artist he's a very minor master." Durgnat scored a number of points in shotgun fashion, but his argument was so discursive, filled with factual errors, and simply wrongheaded at times that it finally proved unpersuasive. In a way, the piece's title was the most lastingly memorable thing about it, and this wasn't even the author's but rather the invention of the magazine's editors. The article did, however, provoke what *Film Comment* called the Great Hawks Debate, between Durgnat and Hawks champion William Paul, which lasted beyond Hawks's own death.

In 1977, Hawks led one more documentary filmmaker into the desert. This time it was a German, the former critic Hans C. Blumenberg, who interviewed Hawks for what became a very good documentary on the director's career, *Ein Verdammt Gutes Leben* (*A Hell of a Good Life*). Unavoidably, Hawks told many of his most familiar stories, but he told them well and by no means looked like a man about to depart this world.

Howard Hawks's last major public appearance was a memorable one for everyone present. On October 21–23, 1977, the Directors Guild of America's Special Projects division, under the guidance of David Shepard, and a small organization called the Los Angeles Cinémathèque cohosted a Weekend with Howard Hawks. About fifty DGA members and film buffs spent the weekend at the oceanfront Surf and Sand Hotel in Laguna Beach. Hawks drove in alone from the desert in his Volkswagen Scirocco, and the entire weekend, from Friday evening through Sunday afternoon, consisted of a total immersion in Hawks, the man and his films. Fourteen of his films were shown, and Joseph McBride, who by now had interviewed Hawks numerous times, knowledgeably hosted Hawks's public appearances, at which visitors asked the master dozens of questions. Hawks seemed to positively beam, reveling in the limelight, outlasting many of the guests at night and beating them to breakfast in the mornings. As his daughter Barbara told McBride, "The timing was perfect. And of all the things like that he'd done, I think that was the one he appreciated the most." The event also provided an opportunity for his son Gregg, Barbara, and Barbara's daughter Carrie to see a number of Hawks's films for the first time. For a man with a reputation for coldness, it was a remarkably warm and intimate occasion. To one observing him for the first time, Hawks came across as very happy and vigorous, and it was inspiring to sense that here was a rare resolved man who had, indeed, lived a hell of a good life. The man and his films, it seemed, were one.

Hawks cut such a trim, vigorous figure at the Laguna Beach weekend that no one could possibly have imagined that he would be dead within two months. As Barbara later said, "We thought he would live forever—it was as if he had beaten the system." Hawks was looking forward to a holiday season with Chance de Widstedt, who was flying in from Paris on December 4 and was due to stay with him at the house through the month. The night before, Saturday, December 3, Hawks had dinner alone at home. Shortly thereafter, he tripped over his one-hundred-pound black Belgian shepherd, Raven, and hit his head on the stone floor. According to what Hawks later told a reporter from the *Desert Sun*, the local Palm Springs newspaper, Raven "came over to me and whined a little bit. I patted her and told her it was okay. She tried to get me up."

Hawks, who was dazed with a head gash and had broken a bone in his back, struggled to lift himself up or pull himself along the floor so he could get to a phone, but he couldn't do it. He knew that no one would be coming by or checking in on him until at least the next day. All the while, Raven kept nudging her master. As it got later, Hawks became "cold and tired." He recounted, "I finally went to sleep, and the dog had her leg around my neck and curled up on my chest."

The next morning, two friends from town passed by and, alerted by Raven's barking, came in and found Hawks on the floor. He was immediately taken to nearby Desert Hospital, where he was treated for his head and back wounds and a serious concussion. Chance arrived in Los Angeles that afternoon and, informed by Gregg, who had been away motorcycling, as to what had happened, proceeded immediately to the hospital. According to what Hawks told Chance, his fall may have been abetted by other factors. "Hawks had taken a whiskey or two earlier in the evening, then forgot about them and took some medicine," she said, adding that doctors suspected he may have suffered a slight stroke or heart seizure either before or after he fell. Hawks credited his dog with saving his life by staying next to him for hours and sharing her body warmth through the long night.

Hawks's children visited him in the hospital, where he remained for two weeks. Had he been taken in and treated immediately, he would no doubt have been fine, as the injuries he had sustained were not themselves very serious. But he had suffered considerable dehydration that had affected his entire system, and he had other ailments that had not been detected before, the most important of which was arteriosclerosis. With Hawks confined to his bed and a wheelchair, Chance came by everyday to see him, give him a massage, and talk. She was there when Hawks had a farewell telephone conversation with John Wayne, who himself would die of cancer within less than two years. Photographs taken at the hospital reveal Hawks, for the first time, looking like a genuinely old man, something like the elderly William Randolph Hearst with his jowels and long robe. All the same, he flirted shamelessly with the nurses, obtaining their phone numbers for future reference, and Chance was impressed that he "kept his extraordinary look" ("*son regard extraordinaire*") until the end. "He didn't know that he was going," she insisted. "Which of us ever does? We always hold out hope till the very end. It was sad that such a man was departing. He was so passionate about life." Barbara remarked, "He kept his spirits and his sense of humor right to the end, but he just hated being hospitalized and hated being treated like an elderly gentleman the way the nurses treated him. He kept saying, 'What a horrible place this is—what am I doing here?'"

On December 17, after thirteen days, Hawks demanded to be taken home. That, however, was the end of his time with Chance, who said she was viewed with suspicion by some members of the family as a possible inheritance seeker, in the vein of Charles Feldman's last-minute French wife, and was declared persona non grata in the household. Hawks did indeed invite one of the nurses over for a "date"; after arriving home, having a martini, and watching a football game on TV, Hawks warned his daughter, "By the way, there may be a girl coming over for a swim."

Over the course of his last ten days, Hawks was lucid most of the time, a bit confused at others. He joked about the circumstances of his accident, and he finally told Barbara that he loved her. "It was the first time I can ever remember him saying it," she confessed. The last thing he said to her was, "Hi, Squirt," using his pet nickname for her, before he fell into unconsciousness on Christmas Day. With Barbara and Gregg at his side, he slipped away at 6:50 P.M. the following evening.

Officially, his death was attributed directly to "arteriosclerotic vascular disease with stroke," a consequence of arteriosclerotic heart disease and acute heart fibrillation. According to his wishes, Hawks's remains were taken to Desert Lawn Memorial Park in Calimesa and cremated, the ashes then scattered over the desert from the air. Obituaries and write-ups of his life and career were appreciative of his contributions, much more so than they probably would have been a decade earlier, but Hawks's death was still vastly overshadowed by that of Charles Chaplin, who had passed away the day before and who naturally dominated news coverage for some time thereafter.

A memorial service for Howard Hawks was held on December 29 at All Saints' Episcopal Church in Beverly Hills. John Wayne, who read a brief elegy, was by far the biggest name in attendance, and he repeated the lines he had read over the dead in *Red River:* "We brought nothing into this world, and it's certain we can take nothing out." No one else, not even any churchman, spoke, nor was there any music or ritual. Frank Capra, James Stewart, Angie Dickinson, and Sherry Lansing were among the two hundred or so people on hand, but several friends and devoted crew members noted with dismay how many people who owed their careers to Hawks were not present, a result, no doubt, of the emotional distance Hawks maintained between himself and many of those in his orbit and of how little he remained in touch even with people who had been very important to him at various times in his life. "It was kind of sad," one of his confidants said, "after everything he had done for so many people and for the industry, how little he seemed to be appreciated."

In his will, Hawks divided up his holdings among all his children but Kitty, whom he excluded on the basis that "her mother is well able to make such provision." Royalties rolled in on many of Hawks's films, and do so to this day, which David, Barbara, and Gregg continue to collect. Gregg inherited the Palm Springs house and was the beneficiary of a considerable trust set up by Hawks and Dee upon their divorce.

In the months after Hawks died, Cary Grant would periodically telephone Peter Bogdanovich, a brilliant vocal mimic, and say, "Peter, do Howard for me." Bogdanovich said, "The last times I saw both Cary Grant and John Wayne, they both talked about Howard, about missing him." Hawks was gone, but there was no forgetting him.

40

Posterity

All of Howard Hawks's wives outlived him. Athole spent the remainder of her years in a country club–like nursing home in the San Fernando Valley. Though she lived the quietest of lives and could not have been further from the limelight, she still managed to stir up some unwanted controversy before she died when a tabloid journalist visiting the home under false pretenses managed to get her to say some scurrilous things about her famous sister Norma's deteriorated condition toward the end. Athole passed away, at eighty-four, on March 17, 1985.

Slim, after her generally exciting and socially illustrious marriage to Leland Hayward came to an end in 1959, wed an even wealthier man, the British banker Kenneth Keith, in 1962; when he was knighted, she became Lady Nancy Keith. However, this marriage was virtually stillborn from the outset, and it ended in 1972. Slim spent the remainder of her years as a doyenne of New York society, with a circle that included Babe Paley, Lauren Bacall, Irene Selznick, Jerome Robbins, Mike Nichols, and, most famously, Truman Capote; she was one of Capote's closest confidants until she broke with him forever over what she saw as his betrayal of her in his catty story "La Côte Basque." She died on April 6, 1990, and her entertaining autobiography, *Slim: Memories of a Rich and Imperfect Life,* was published posthumously later that year.

Married to the fabulously wealthy, CIA-connected businessman Stuart W. Cramer III, who was formerly wed to Jean Peters and Terry Moore, Dee was a fixture on the Bel-Air–Beverly Hills social circuit until she and her husband moved to Palm Springs several years ago. Dee says she intends to write a book about both Hawks and Groucho Marx, claiming, "No one understands them the way I do. I know things nobody else knows."

Peter John Ward Hawks, Athole's son by John Ward adopted by Howard Hawks, worked in aviation in the San Francisco area all his life. His first wife, Shirley Godfrey, died in 1973, and he subsequently married

659

and was divorced from Norma Baldwin, who piloted her own private chartered plane. Peter and Shirley had three daughters. The eldest, Jamin, is
an attorney, while Kate, who has a son, and Celia, who has two sons, work
in aviation as did their father, who died on July 22, 1989, at his home in
Woodside, south of San Francisco.

David Hawks, married in 1975 to the film costumer Virginia (Ginger) Hadfield after his divorce from Judy Webb, had a long career as an
assistant director, working for many years on the *M*A*S*H* TV series before retiring in the early 1990s. He has two daughters by his first marriage,
Darren and Jessica. In the early 1990s, producer-director Irwin Winkler
asked David to appear as his father in *Guilty by Suspicion*, a film about the
Hollywood blacklist that included a scene of Darryl Zanuck watching dailies from *Gentlemen Prefer Blondes*. When David turned the offer down,
Winkler decided not to actually show "Hawks" on-screen in the picture.

Barbara Hawks McCampbell and her husband, Don, moved from the
western San Fernando Valley near Los Angeles to Palm Springs in the early
1990s, as Barbara always wanted to do. She works in real estate in the area
and rides her horse regularly. Both of their daughters, Carrie and Tracey,
are married, and Carrie has a daughter and a son.

Kitty Hawks worked for a number of years as a Hollywood agent with
ICM. From 1976 to 1983 she was married to Ned Tanen, a high-powered
executive and producer who, at the time of their marriage, was in charge of
production at Universal Pictures. After their divorce, Kitty returned to New
York City, where she works in interior decoration.

Gregg Hawks sold his father's Palm Springs house, has continued
racing motorcycles, and for some years now has run a motorcycle repair
and customizing business called Sport Engineering in Van Nuys, California. He and his wife, Penny, live in Santa Monica.

With several of Hawks's films more or less officially installed as classics by the time he died, his work enjoyed renewed life on the revival, retrospective, university, and museum circuits in the years that followed. Five
years after his death, three major books on his work were published: Joseph
McBride's career interview, *Hawks on Hawks*, assembled from the many
discussions the author had with the director over the years; academic Leland
A. Poague's learned critical study *Howard Hawks*; and the late Gerald Mast's
Howard Hawks, Storyteller. Dauntingly detailed, impressively erudite, and
exhausting at times in its thorough reading of the films, Mast's work stands,
after Robin Wood's book, as the most convincing and strongly argued full-
length case on behalf of Hawks's status as a major artist. Then, in 1987, came

the exceedingly bizarre labor of love, Clark Branson's *Howard Hawks; A Jungian Study.*

Any number of other spirited celebrations of Hawks's achievements appeared over the years. Molly Haskell's essay in Richard Roud's *Cinema: A Critical Dictionary* is particularly outstanding, and in a 1993 selection of the thirty best American movies ever made, the *L.A. Weekly,* a very film-wise alternative newspaper, ranked *Rio Bravo* third and *His Girl Friday* fifth; Chaplin and Welles were the only other directors to also claim two titles on the list.

In this light, it is surprising that James Bernardoni would assert, in his stimulating 1991 book *The New Hollywood,* that there was a "lack of solid, definitive criticism in support of Hawks's growing reputation" within the literature on film. In evaluating the work of significant directors since the late 1960s, the late Bernardoni persuasively writes that Hawks and Hitchcock have yielded by far the greatest influence on younger filmmakers, but that this influence has not been very much to the good, for complex reasons that he carefully elucidates. Bernardoni felt that it was the lack of strong criticism that "resulted in a rather misleading interpretation of his achievements gaining currency in the New Hollywood, an interpretation that seemed to hold that the lesson to be learned from Hawks was that the most blatantly escapist entertainments would be transformed by the same mysterious alchemy at work in Hawks's films into works of genuine art. The result was that a number of New Hollywood directors who apparently admired what Hawks had achieved . . . set out to work within the same genres without fully understanding how Hawks had managed to transcend their inherent limitations." Bernardoni pointed out *Jaws* as an example of "another indicator of the aesthetic decline that has befallen the American cinema during the New Hollywood era."

Bernardoni concluded that the legacies of both Hawks and Hitchcock were ill-served by their imitators. "The Hawksian tradition in film comedy has been all but ignored; the Hawksian adventure melodrama has been distorted into films that . . . [lack] Hawks's subtle (and audience-involving) renderings of action as the expression of morality."

The work of Howard Hawks has been called to mind by a great many films by young directors since the 1960s. These homages run from brief tips of the hat, such as Jean-Luc Godard's prominent placement of *Hatari!* posters in the background of shots in *Contempt,* to "stealing," such as Peter Bogdanovich's lift of *Bringing Up Baby* for *What's Up, Doc?* and John Carpenter's appropriation of the basic setup of *Rio Bravo* for *Assault on*

Precinct 13, to Carpenter's outright remake of *The Thing* and Brian De Palma's contemporary version of *Scarface*, written by Oliver Stone.

But the range of filmmakers who have felt moved to acknowledge Hawks's influence is exceptionally wide; the one consistent element is that most of them are, or have been at certain periods of their careers, very good directors. Other than the oblique, nonverbal one in *Contempt*, possibly the first explicit, self-conscious reference to a Hawks film in the work of another director came in Bernardo Bertolucci's second picture, *Before the Revolution*, in 1964. In it, the leading character spends a good little while trying to convince his friend to join the Communist Party, then bids him good-bye and heads off into a house. As the friend departs, the hero comes back out and shouts to him, "Agostino, go and see *Red River*. Don't miss it."

Four years later, Martin Scorsese, in his first feature, the low-budget *Who's That Knocking at My Door?*, devoted the first encounter between the central character, played by Harvey Keitel, and an attractive young woman, portrayed by Zina Bethune, to a protracted discussion of John Wayne and *The Searchers*. Later in the picture, Keitel and Bethune are seen emerging from a revival-house showing of *Rio Bravo*, discussing Angie Dickinson's performance. Keitel says, "Well, let me tell ya something. That girl in that picture was a broad." "What do you mean, a broad?" "A broad! You know, there are girls, and then there are broads. A broad isn't exactly a virgin."

Elsewhere, Scorsese has evinced a special enthusiasm for the "guilty pleasure" of *Land of the Pharaohs*, and the critic David Ehrenstein, the author of a book on Scorsese, has argued that Sharon Stone's character in *Casino*, aside from being based on an actual person, is drawn heavily from Joan Collins's Princess Nellifer. Scorsese has also said that *Scarface* was a particularly important influence on him; speaking of *Scarface* and *Bonnie and Clyde*, he remarked, with interesting application to his own career, "It's strange that we don't normally like people who are killing other people, but the way they're presented in these films is extremely glamorous."

Among other members of the late 1960s film school generation, Walter Hill, at his best, resembles Hawks in his proclivity for terse dialogue, lack of psychological orientation, taste for tough male characters, occasional bent for comedy, and definition of character through action. Although primarily a Fordian, John Milius also displays an affinity for Hawks, as does Michael Mann. Robert Zemeckis is an enormous fan of *Rio Bravo*, and when he was a critic, Paul Schrader wrote knowledgeably about Hawks's achievements.

John Carpenter, who was a student at the University of Southern California when Hawks spoke there, has said, simply, "I consider Howard

Hawks to be the greatest American director. He's the only director I know to have made a great movie in every genre. Critics mention the one-take, moving camera style of Ophüls and Welles but somehow never get around to the amazing one-take opening shot of the original *Scarface,* made in 1932. Hawks's sense of comic timing is unsurpassed. Just take a look at *His Girl Friday* if you're not convinced. In my opinion, the man literally invented American cinema. He showed us ourselves, the way we are, the way we should be." After his early success with *Halloween,* Carpenter announced that his dream was to do a remake of *Only Angels Have Wings.* Fortunately, he and everyone else who has considered this idea has dropped it, except for Jean-Jacques Annuad, whose medium-length IMAX 3-D venture, *Wings of Courage,* about real-life fliers in the Andes in the 1930s, draws heavily, and clumsily, upon Hawks's aviation classic. Equally unfortunate was a remake of *The Front Page* in 1988 called *Switching Channels,* which updated the story into the modern television age and reused Hawks's innovation of turning Hildy Johnson into a woman. Even the special-effects extravaganza *Twister* lifted its basic romantic triangle directly from *His Girl Friday,* with the central characters, who are obviously meant for each other, poised for a divorce, and Jami Gertz in the Ralph Bellamy part of the new fiancée who doesn't fit into the professional group.

In ways that didn't necessarily result in on-screen homages, some older directors had a keen appreciation of Hawks's talents. Some years ago there was a revealing exchange between the late, great English director Michael Powell and a good friend, the old-time Hollywood press agent Max Bercutt, also now gone:

BERCUTT

Hawks was a sour man, sour about himself and sour about other people.

POWELL

I think he had a very deep understanding of people, what was inside people.

BERCUTT

He was a mean man, he didn't like his wives and they didn't like him. He had some personality problem, which I think, frankly, concerned his libido. He couldn't hold his wives. He didn't have a coterie around him, he didn't have very close male friends.

Powell
POWELL
I think you have to dislike people in order to direct great comedy.

Not surprisingly, Clint Eastwood has named as his top three influences Ford, Hawks, and Anthony Mann, and two of his six favorite films of all time are by Hawks: *Red River* and *The Big Sky*. More surprisingly, Robert Benton, the cowriter of *Bonnie and Clyde* and the director of several films, including *Kramer vs. Kramer*, has also named Hawks as one of his decisive influences, noting, "I love Hawks. I don't pretend he's a greater director than Ford is, but I love who I love."

The most famous of the latest generation of Hollywood directors feels the same way about Hawks. Quentin Tarantino has expressed his love for Hawks in numerous ways. When asked to name his favorite director, the answer is always Hawks; identifying his favorite film, he has said that if he had one film with which to spend his last fifteen minutes on earth, it would be *Rio Bravo*, and he has insisted, "When I'm getting serious about a girl, I show her *Rio Bravo*, and she better fucking like it." When he was in Amsterdam writing *Pulp Fiction*, he spent many of his evenings attending a Hawks retrospective running at a local theater; he based the look of the giant restaurant-nightclub in his film partly on *Red Line 7000*, and he was inspired in writing his dialogue by *His Girl Friday*. Ultimately, he believes that "Howard Hawks is the supreme storyteller and entertainer. He's just too damn enjoyable."

One must not judge the master by the work of his pupils. By and large, however, Hawks has attracted a high caliber of students, and it is difficult to agree with Bernardoni that Hawks's lessons have been misunderstood, even if the salutes and imitations rarely measure up to the originals; after all, how could they? What Hawks achieved in the 1930s and 1940s, when the studio system was at full throttle and movie stars were designed to inhabit a glamorous and rarified world of the imagination, is no longer terribly feasible or even applicable. More important, the way Hawks asserted his personality, his view of the world, and his fantasies was complex and unique; there is no victory to be gained in trying to reproduce it.

As for Hawks's own thoughts of preserving his legacy, of ensuring that his accomplishments would live on, his vast, proud ego would certainly relish the appreciation of his work that has continued unabated since his death. As for the rest, as highly as he thought of himself, he never considered writing an autobiography; the thought of immaculately preserving the record of his life and career, as Capra, Cukor, and many others did, couldn't have been further from his mind. Years after water and mud destroyed many of his papers, scripts, and photographs in the barn at Hog Canyon, Hawks stashed the fraction that remained in his garage in Palm Springs, along with the cars, motorcycles, and tools. When James D'Arc, an enthusiastic young archivist from Brigham Young University, rang the great director's doorbell in the mid-1970s and asked if he had any papers he would consider donating to a permanent collection, Hawks said, "Sure. Whatever I've got is just sitting in the garage gathering dust. Take whatever you want." For Hawks, a man who lived completely in the present and, in his work, excelled at expressing the living moment between characters and actors, the moments those papers represented were already past. He had already lived them, and posterity was welcome to them.

Filmography

Films are listed in order of theatrical release, although some were shot in a different order.

Silent Period

Hawks directed a few scenes of *The Little Princess* (Artcraft Picture Corp. for Famous Players–Lasky, 1917) during the absence of director Marshall Neilan. He also had a hand in directing, probably uncredited, between three and five one-reel comedies starring Monty Banks. The first in the series was *His Night Out* (CBC Distributing Company, 1919), but documentation of titles and accurate credits is scant.

In 1919, Hawks became involved on the financial end of a company called Associated Producers with producer-directors Marshall Neilan, Allan Dwan, and Allen Holubar. Hawks was not a producer per se and exercised no control over the content or artistic aspects of the pictures, but he was involved on the production side and was present during some of the filming. Again, credits are imprecise at best, but Hawks had a hand in the following productions:

1920: *Go and Get It* (Neilan), *Dinty* (Neilan), *The Forbidden Thing* (Dwan)
1921: *A Perfect Crime* (Dwan), *Man-Woman-Marriage* (Holubar), *Bob Hampton of Placer* (Neilan), *A Broken Doll* (Dwan), *Bits of Life* (Neilan), *The Lotus Eater* (Neilan)
1922: *Penrod* (Neilan), *Fools First* (Neilan), *Hurricane's Gal* (Holubar)
1923: *Minnie* (Neilan), *Slander the Woman* (Holubar)

1923

Quicksands (Agfar Corp. for American Releasing Corp.)
Producer: Howard Hawks. Director: Jack Conway. Story and screenplay: Hawks. Cinematographers: Harold Rosson, Glen MacWilliams. Length: 6–7 reels. Filmed in Texas, late 1922. Released February 28, 1923. Subsequently acquired by Paramount Famous Lasky Corp., cut to 4,593 feet, rereleased May 21, 1927.

Cast: Helene Chadwick (girl), Richard Dix (1st lieutenant), Alan Hale (Ferrago), Noah Beery ("Silent" Krupz), J. Farrell MacDonald (Col. Patterson), George Cooper

(Matt Patterson), Tom Wilson (Sgt. Johnson), Dick Sutherland (Cupid), Hardee Kirkland (Farrell), Louis King (barfly), Jean Hersholt, Walter Long, Jack Curtis, William Dyer, Frank Campeau, Edwin Stevens, James Marcus, Lionel Belmore (members of dope ring).

1924

Tiger Love (Famous Players–Lasky/Paramount)

Producers: Adolph Zukor, Jesse L. Lasky. Director: George Melford. Screenplay: Howard Hawks, adapted by Julie Herne, from the opera *El Gato Montes* by Manuel Penella. Cinematographer: Charles G. Clarke. Length: 6 reels. Released June 30, 1924.

Cast: Antonio Moreno (The Wildcat), Estelle Taylor (Marcheta), G. Raymond Nye (El Pezuno), Manuel Camero (Don Ramon), Edgar Norton (Don Victoriano Fuentes), David Torrence (Don Miguel Castelar), Snitz Edwards (The Hunchback), Monte Collins (Father Zaspard).

1925

The Dressmaker from Paris (Famous Players–Lasky/Paramount)

Producers: Adolph Zukor, Jesse L. Lasky. Director: Paul Bern. Screenplay: Adelaide Heilbron, from an original story by Heilbron and Howard Hawks. Length: 8 reels. Released March 30, 1925.

Cast: Leatrice Joy (Fifi), Ernest Torrence (Angus McGregor), Allan Forrest (Billy Brent), Mildred Harris (Joan McGregor), Lawrence Gray (Allan Stone), Charles Crockett (mayor), Rosemary Cooper (mayor's daughter), Spec O'Donnell (Jim).

1926

The Road to Glory (Fox)

Executive producer: William Fox. Director: Howard Hawks. Screenplay: L. G. Rigby, from an original story by Hawks. Cinematographer (tinted prints): Joseph August. Length: 6 reels (5,600 feet), approximately 60 minutes. Filmed in Hollywood, December 1925–January 1926. Released February 7, 1926. (No prints known to exist.)

Cast: May McAvoy (Judith Allen), Rockliffe Fellowes (Del Cole), Leslie Fenton (David Hale), Ford Sterling (James Allen), Milla Davenport (Aunt Selma), John MacSweeney (butler), Hank (dog).

Honesty—the Best Policy (Fox)

Producer: William Fox. Director: Chester Bennett, with additional sequences directed by Albert Ray. Screenplay: L. G. Rigby, from an original story by Howard Hawks. Cinematographer: Ernest G. Palmer. Length: 5 reels. Filmed in Hollywood, spring 1926, additional sequences in July. Released August 8, 1926.

Cast: Rockliffe Fellowes (Nick Randall), Pauline Starke (Mary Kay), Johnnie Walker (Robert Dare and author), Grace Darmond (Lily), Mickey Bennett (freckled boy), Mack Swain (Bendy Joe), Albert Gran (publisher), Dot Farley (author's wife), Heinie Conklin (piano player).

Fig Leaves (Fox)

Producer: William Fox. Director: Howard Hawks. Screenplay: Hope Loring, Louis D. Lighton, from an original story by Hawks. Cinematographer (with two fashion sequences in Technicolor): Joseph August. Editor: Rose Smith. Art directors: William S. Darling, William Cameron Menzies. Costumes: Adrian. Titles: Malcolm Stuart Boylan. Length: 7 reels (6,498 feet), approximately 68 minutes. Filmed in Hollywood, March 1926. Released August 22, 1926.

Cast: George O'Brien (Adam Smith), Olive Borden (Eve Smith), Phyllis Haver (Alice Atkins), André de Beranger (Josef André), William Austin (André's assistant), Heinie Conklin (Eddie McSwiggen), Eulalie Jensen (Madame Griswald).

1927

The Cradle Snatchers (Fox)

Producer: William Fox. Director: Howard Hawks. Screenplay: Sarah Y. Mason, from the play by Russell Medcraft and Norma Mitchell. Cinematographer: L. William O'Connell. Editor: Ralph Dixon. Art director: William S. Darling. Assistant director: James Tinling. Titles: Malcolm Stuart Boylan. Length: 7 reels (6,282 feet), approximately 59 minutes. Filmed in Hollywood, January–February 1927. Released May 28, 1927.

Cast: Louise Fazenda (Susan Martin), Ethel Wales (Ethel Drake), Dorothy Phillips (Kitty Ladd), J. Farrell MacDonald (George Martin), Franklin Pangborn (Howard Drake), William Davidson (Roy Ladd), Joseph Striker (Joe Valley), Nick Stuart (Henry Winton), Arthur Lake (Oscar), Dione Ellis (Ann Hall), Sammy Cohen (Ike Ginsberg), Tyler Brook (osteopath), Sally Eilers, Arthur Walis.

Paid to Love (Fox)

Producer: William Fox. Director: Howard Hawks. Screenplay: William M. Conselman, Seton I. Miller; adaptation by Benjamin Glazer, from an original story by Harry Carr. Cinematographer (tinted prints): L. William O'Connell. Editor: Ralph Dixon. Art director: William S. Darling. Assistant director: James Tinling. Titles: Malcolm Stuart Boylan. Length: 7 reels (6,888 feet), approximately 80 minutes. Filmed in Hollywood, August–September 1926. Released July 23, 1927.

Cast: George O'Brien (Crown Prince Michael), Virginia Valli (Gaby), J. Farrell MacDonald (Peter Roberts), Thomas Jefferson (King), William Powell (Prince Eric), Marta Sterling (maid), Hank Mann (servant).

1928

A Girl in Every Port (Fox)

Producer: William Fox. Director: Howard Hawks. Screenplay: Seton I. Miller (and Reginald Morris, Marion Orth, Philip Klein, uncredited); adaptation by James Kevin McGuinness, from an original story by Hawks. Cinematographers (tinted prints): L. William O'Connell, Rudolph Berquist. Editor: Ralph Dixon. Art director: William S. Darling. Costumes: Kathleen Dax. Assistant director: Sidney Lanfield. Titles: Malcolm Stuart Boylan. Length: 6 reels (5,500 feet), approximately 64 minutes. Filmed in Hollywood, October–December 1927. Released February 26, 1928.

Cast: Victor McLaglen (Spike Madden), Robert Armstrong (Bill [Salami]), Louise Brooks (Marie [Mlle. Godiva]), Myrna Loy (Jetta), Maria Casajuana (Chiquita), Gladys Brockwell (Madame Flore), Sally Rand (girl in Bombay), William Demarest (man in Bombay), Natalie Joyce, Dorothy Mathews, Elena Jurado (girls in Panama), Francis McDonald (gang leader), Phalba Morgan (Lena, girl in Holland), Felix Valle (Lena's husband), Greta Yoltz (other girl in Holland), Leila Hyams (sailor's wife), Natalie Kingston (girl on South Seas island), Caryl Lincoln (girl from Liverpool), Michael Visaroff.

(Remade by British Lion and director Herbert Wilcox in Britain in 1952.)

Fazil (Fox)

Producer: William Fox. Director: Howard Hawks. Screenplay: Seton I. Miller, adaptation by Philip Klein, from the play *L'Insoumise*, by Pierre Frondaie. Cinematographer: L. William O'Connell. Editor: Ralph Dixon. Assistant director: James Tinling. Length: 8 reels (7,217 feet), approximately 75 minutes. With musical score and synchronized sound effects. Filmed in Hollywood, June–August 1927. Released June 4, 1928.

Cast: Charles Farrell (Prince Fazil), Greta Nissen (Fabienne), John Boles (John Clavering), Mae Busch (Helen Debreuze), Vadim Uraneff (Ahmed), Tyler Brooks (Jacques Debreuze), Eddie Sturgis (Rice), Josephine Borio (Aicha), John T. Murray (gondolier), Erville Alderson (Imam Idris), Dale Fuller (Zouroya), Hank Mann (Ali).

The Air Circus (Fox)

Producer: William Fox. Director: Howard Hawks; added dialogue sequences directed by Lewis Seiler. Screenplay: Seton I. Miller, Norman Z. McLeod, from an original story by Graham Baker and Andrew Bennison (and Hawks, uncredited). Dialogue: Hugh Herbert. Cinematographer: Dan Clark. Editor: Ralph Dixon. Dialogue director: Charles Judels. Assistant director: William Tummel. Titles: William Kernell. Running time: 88 minutes (8 reels, 7,702 feet). With musical score, synchronized sound effects, and 15 minutes of dialogue sequences. Filmed in Hollywood and Santa Monica, April–June 1928. Released September 30, 1928. (No prints known to exist.)

Cast: Arthur Lake (Speed Doolittle), David Rollins (Buddy Blake), Sue Carol (Sue Manning), Louise Dresser (Mrs. Blake), Charles Delaney (Charles Manning), Heinie Conklin (Jerry McSwiggen), Earl Robinson (Lt. Blake).

1929

Trent's Last Case (Fox)

Producer: William Fox. Production supervisor: Bertram Millhauser. Director: Howard Hawks. Screenplay: Scott Darling, adaptation by Beulah Marie Dix, from the novel by E. C. Bentley. Cinematographer: Harold Rosson. Assistant director: E. D. Leshin. Titles: Malcolm Stuart Boylan. Running time: 66 minutes (6 reels, 5,834 feet, with musical score and synchronized sound effects). Filmed in Hollywood, January–February 1929. Released in Great Britain September 23, 1929, never released in the United States.

Cast: Donald Crisp (Sigsbee Manderson), Raymond Griffith (Philip Trent), Raymond Hatton (Joshua Cupples), Marceline Day (Evelyn Manderson), Lawrence Gray (Jack Marlowe), Nicholas Soussanin (Martin), Anita Garvin (Ottilie Dunois), Edgar Kennedy (Inspector Murch).

Sound Period

1930

The Dawn Patrol (First National Pictures for Warner Bros.)

Producer: Robert North. Director: Howard Hawks. Screenplay: Hawks, Dan Totheroh, Seton I. Miller, from the story "The Flight Commander," by John Monk Saunders. Cinematographer: Ernest Haller. Editor: Ray Curtiss. Music: Leo F. Forbstein. Art Director: Jack Okey. Assistant director: Frank Shaw. Aerial adviser: Leo Nomis. Running time: 95 minutes. Filmed in Hollywood, Newhall, Triumfo, February–May 1930. Released July 10, 1930.

Cast: Richard Barthelmess (Dick Courtney), Douglas Fairbanks Jr. (Douglas Scott), Neil Hamilton (Major Brand), William Janney (Gordon Scott), James Finlayson (field sergeant), Clyde Cook (Bott), Gardner James (Ralph Hollister), Edmund Breon (Lt. Bathurst), Frank McHugh (Flaherty), Jack Ackroyd, Harry Allen (mechanics).

(Remade by Warner Bros. and director Edmund Goulding in 1938, incorporating aerial footage from Hawks's version, which was retitled *Flight Commander* for later television release.)

1931

The Criminal Code (Columbia)

Producer: Harry Cohn. Director: Howard Hawks. Screenplay: Seton I. Miller, Fred Niblo Jr., from the play by Martin Flavin. Cinematographers: James Wong Howe, Ted Tetzlaff. Editor: Edward Curtiss. Art director: Edward Jewell. Sound: Glen Rominger. Assistant director: David Selman. Running time: 97 minutes. Filmed in Hollywood, September–November 1930. Released January 3, 1931.

Cast: Walter Huston (Warden Brady), Phillips Holmes (Robert Graham), Constance Cummings (Mary Brady), Mary Doran (Gertrude Williams), DeWitt Jennings (Gleason), John Sheehan (McManus), Boris Karloff (Galloway), Otto Hoffman (Fales), Clark Marshall (Runch), Arthur Hoyt (Nettleford), Ethel Wales (Katie), John St. Polis (Dr. Rinewulf), Paul Porcasi (Spelvin), Hugh Walker (Lew), Jack Vance (reporter), James Guilfoyle (Detective Doran), Lee Phelps (Detective Doherty), Nicholas Soussanin.

(Filmed simultaneously in a French-language version, *Criminel*, directed by Jack Forrester and starring Harry Bauer and Jean Servais, using montage and action sequences from Hawks's version. Also filmed simultaneously in a Spanish-language version.)

1932

Scarface (Caddo Company–Atlantic Pictures for United Artists)

Producer: Howard Hughes. Director: Howard Hawks. Codirector: Richard Rosson. Screen story: Ben Hecht. Continuity and dialogue: Seton I. Miller, John Lee Mahin, W. R. Burnett (and Fred Pasley, uncredited), from the novel by Armitage Trail. Cinematographers: Lee Garmes, L. W. O'Connell. Editor: Edward Curtiss. Editorial advisor: Douglas Biggs. Music: Adolph Tandler, Gus Arnheim. Art director: Harry Oliver. Sound: William Snyder. Production manager: Charles Stallings. Running time: 90 minutes. Filmed in Hollywood, June–August 1931. Released March 31, 1932 in New Orleans; May 19 in New York in cut version. Reissued in 1947 by Astor Films and in 1979 by Universal.

Cast: Paul Muni (Tony "Scarface" Camonte), Ann Dvorak (Cesca), Karen Morley (Poppy), Osgood Perkins (Johnny Lovo), C. Henry Gordon (Ben Guarino), George Raft (Gino Rinaldi), Vince Barnett (Angelo), Boris Karloff (Gaffney), Purnell Pratt (publisher), Tully Marshall (managing editor), Edwin Maxwell (detective chief), Inez Palange (Mrs. Camonte), Harry J. Vejar (Louie Costillo), Henry Armetta (Pietro), Maurice Black (hood), Bert Starkey (Epstein), Paul Fix (Gaffney hood), Hank Mann (worker), Charles Sullivan, Harry Tenbrook (bootleggers), John Lee Mahin (MacArthur of the *Tribune*), Howard Hawks (man in hospital bed).

(Remade by Universal and director Brian De Palma in 1983.)

The Crowd Roars (First National–Vitaphone for Warner Bros.)

Producer: Bryan Foy. Director: Howard Hawks. Screenplay: Kubec Glasmon, John Bright, Seton I. Miller, Niven Busch, from a story by Hawks (and, from *The Barker: A Play of Carnival Life*, by Kenyon Nicholson, uncredited). Cinematographer: Sid Hickox. Cameraman for background racing footage: Hans F. Koenekamp. Editors: John Stumar, Thomas Pratt. Music: Leo F. Forbstein. Art director: Jack Okey. Automotive advisor: Fred Jackman. Running time: 85 minutes. Filmed in Hollywood, Ventura, December 1931–February 1932. Released April 16, 1932.

Cast: James Cagney (Joe Greer), Joan Blondell (Anne), Eric Linden (Eddie Greer), Ann Dvorak (Lee Merrick), Guy Kibbee (Dad Greer), Frank McHugh (Spud Connors),

William Arnold (Bill), Leo Nomis (Jim), Charlotte Merriam (Mrs. Connors), Harry Hartz, Ralph Hepburn, Fred Guisso, Phil Pardee, Spider Matlock, Jack Brisko, Fred Frame, Leo Norris, Dick Jones, Louis Meyer, Mel Kenaly (race drivers).

(Filmed simultaneously in a French-language version, *Le Foule Hurle*, directed by Jean Daumery and starring Jean Gabin. Remade by Warner Bros. and director Lloyd Bacon in 1939 as *Indianpolis Speedway*, incorporating racing footage from Hawks's version.)

Tiger Shark (First National–Vitaphone for Warner Bros.)

Producer: Bryan Foy. Director: Howard Hawks. Associate director: Richard Rosson. Screenplay: Wells Root (and John Lee Mahin, uncredited), from the story "Tuna," by Houston Branch. Cinematographer: Tony Gaudio. Cameraman for background fishing footage: Byron Haskin. Editor: Thomas Pratt. Music: Leo F. Forbstein. Art director: Jack Okey. Costumes: Orry-Kelly. Fishing consultant: Capt. Guy Silva. Running time: 80 minutes. Filmed in Hollywood, San Diego, Catalina Island, April–June 1932, with background fishing footage filmed along the Mexican coast. Released September 22, 1932.

Cast: Edward G. Robinson (Capt. Miguel "Mike" Mascarenas), Richard Arlen (Pipes Boley), Zita Johann (Quita Silva), Leila Bennett (Muggsy), Vince Barnett (Fishbone), J. Carroll Naish (Tony), William Ricciardi (Manuel Silva).

1933

The Prizefighter and the Lady (MGM)

Producer: W. S. Van Dyke. Directors: Van Dyke (and Howard Hawks, uncredited). Screenplay: John Lee Mahin, John Meehan, Frances Marion, from a story by Marion. Cinematographer: Lester White. Editor: Robert J. Kern. Running time: 102 minutes. Filmed in Hollywood, fall 1932. Released May 1933.

Cast: Myrna Loy (Belle), Max Baer (Steve), Primo Carnera (Carnera), Jack Dempsey (promoter), Walter Huston (professor), Otto Kruger (Willie Ryan), Vince Barnett (Bugsie), Robert McWade (adopted son), Muriel Evans (Linda), Jean Howard (cabaret girl).

(Hawks was the original director but was replaced by Van Dyke after a few days' filming.)

Today We Live (MGM)

Producer and director: Howard Hawks. Codirector: Richard Rosson. Story and dialogue: William Faulkner. Screenplay: Edith Fitzgerald, Dwight Taylor, from Faulkner's story "Turn About." Cinematographer: Oliver T. Marsh. Editor: Edward Curtiss. Art director: Cedric Gibbons. Gowns: Adrian. Sound: Douglas Shearer. Running time: 110 minutes. Filmed in Hollywood, December 1932–February 1933. Released March 3, 1933.

Cast: Joan Crawford (Diana), Gary Cooper (Richard Bogard), Robert Young (Claude), Franchot Tone (Ronnie), Roscoe Karns (McGinnis), Louise Closser Hale (Applegate), Rollo Lloyd (Major), Hilda Vaughn (Eleanor).

1934

Viva Villa! (MGM)

Producer: David O. Selznick. Directors: Jack Conway (and Howard Hawks, uncredited). Screenplay: Ben Hecht, from the book *Viva Villa: A Recovery of the Real Pancho Villa—Peon . . . Bandit . . . Soldier . . . Patriot*, by Edgcumb Pinchon and O. B. Stade. Cinematographers: James Wong Howe (in Mexico), Charles G. Clarke (in Hollywood). Editor: Robert Kern. Music: Herbert Stothart. Musical consultant: Juan Aguilar. Art director: Harry Oliver. Interior decoration: Edwin B. Willis. Costumes: Dolly Tree. Technical advisor: Carlos Novarro (Samaniegos). Technical associate: Matias Santoyo. Running time: 115 minutes. Filmed in Mexico (by Hawks), October–November 1933, in Hollywood (by Conway) December 1933–January 1934. Released April 27, 1934.

Cast: Wallace Beery (Pancho Villa), Leo Carrillo (Sierra), Fay Wray (Teresa), Donald Cook (Don Felipe), Stuart Erwin (Johnny), Henry B. Walthall (Madero), Joseph Schildkraut (General Pascal), Katherine De Mille (Rosita), George E. Stone (Chavito), Philip Cooper (Villa, as boy), David Durant (bugle boy), Frank Puglia (Villa's father), Francis X. Bushman Jr. (Calloway), Adrian Rosley, Henry Armetta (Mendoza brothers), Pedro Regas (staff), George Regas (aide), John Merkel (Pascal's aide), Mischa Auer (military attaché), Arthur Treacher (English reporter), William Van Brincken (German reporter), André Cheron (French reporter), Michael Visaroff (Russian reporter), Charles Stevens, Steve Clemento, Carlos De Valdez (old men), Harry Cording (majordomo), Sam Godfrey (prosecuting attorney), Nigel De Brulier (political judge), Charles Requa, Tom Ricketts (grandees), Clarence Hummel Wilson (jail official), James Martin (Mexican officer), Anita Gordiana (dancer), Francis McDonald (Villa's man), Harry Semels (soldier), Julian Rivero (telegraph operator), Bob McKenzie (bartender), Dan Dix (drunkard), Paul Stanton (newspaperman), Belle Mitchell (Spanish wife), John Davidson, Brandon Hurst, Leonard Moody (statesmen), Herbert Prior, Emile Chautard (generals), Shirley Chambers (wrong girl), Arthur Thalasso (butcher), Chris-Pin Martin, Nick De Ruiz (peons).

Twentieth Century (Columbia)

Producer and director: Howard Hawks. Screenplay: Ben Hecht, Charles MacArthur, from their play, adapted from the play *The Napoleon of Broadway*, by Charles Bruce Milholland. Cinematographer: Joseph August. Editor: Gene Havlick. Sound: Edward Bernds. Assistant director: Charles C. (Buddy) Coleman. Running time: 91 minutes. Filmed in Hollywood, February–March 1934. Released May 3, 1934.

Cast: John Barrymore (Oscar Jaffe), Carole Lombard (Mildred Plotka/Lily Garland), Walter Connolly (Oliver Webb), Roscoe Karns (Owen O'Malley), Ralph Forbes (George Smith), Charles Levison (Max Jacobs), Etienne Girardot (Matthew J. Clark), Dale Fuller (Sadie), Edgar Kennedy (McGonigle), Billie Seward (Anita), Clifford Thompson (Lockwood), James P. Burtis (conductor), Gigi Parrish (Schultz), Edward Gargan (sheriff), Snowflake (porter), Herman Bing (first beard), Lee Kohlmar (second beard), Pat Flaherty (Flannigan), Mary Jo Matthews (Emmy Lou), Fred Kelsey (detective on train), Ky Robinson (detective), Nick Copeland (treasurer), Howard Hickman (Dr. Johnson), Arnold Gray (stage actor), James Burke (Chicago detective), George Reed (Uncle Remus), Anita Brown (stage show girl), Irene Thompson (stage actress), Buddy Williams (stage actor), Clarence Geldert (Southern colonel), Lillian West (charwoman), Gaylord "Steve" Pendleton (brother in play), George Offerman Jr. (page boy), Frank Marlowe (stage carpenter), Lynton Brent (train secretary), Harry Semels (artist), King Mojave (McGonigle's assistant).

1935

Barbary Coast (Samuel Goldwyn Productions for United Artists)
    Producer: Samuel Goldwyn. Director: Howard Hawks. Screenplay: Ben Hecht, Charles MacArthur. Cinematographer: Ray June. Editor: Edward Curtiss. Music: Alfred Newman. Art director: Richard Day. Costumes: Omar Kiam. Sound: Frank Maher. Assistant director: Walter Mayo. Running time: 91 minutes. Filmed in Hollywood, June— August 1935. Released September 27, 1935.
    Cast: Miriam Hopkins (Mary Rutledge), Edward G. Robinson (Louis Chamalis), Joel McCrea (James Carmichael), Walter Brennan (Old Atrocity), Frank Craven (Col. Marcus Aurelius Cobb), Brian Donlevy (Knuckles), Harry Carey (Slocum), Matt McHugh (Bronco), Clyde Cook (Oakie), Donald Meek (McTavish), Rollo Lloyd (Wigham), J. M. Kerrigan (Judge Harper), Roger Gray (Sandy), Otto Hoffman (Peebes), Fred Vogeding (captain), Cyril Thornton (steward), Dave Wengren (quartermaster), Anders von Haden (McCreaty), Jules Cowles (pilot), David Niven (Cockney sailor).

1936

Ceiling Zero (Cosmopolitan Productions and First National for Warner Bros.)
    Producer: Harry Joe Brown. Director: Howard Hawks. Screenplay: Frank Wead (and Morrie Ryskind, uncredited), from his play. Cinematographer: Arthur Edeson. Editor: William Holmes. Music: Leo F. Forbstein. Art director: John Hughes. Wardrobe: B. W. King, Mary Dearry. Sound: Oliver Garretson. Asssistant director: Lee Selander. Technical advisor: Paul Mantz. Running time: 95 minutes. Filmed in Hollywood, October–November 1935. Released January 16, 1936.
    Cast: James Cagney (Dizzy Davis), Pat O'Brien (Jake Lee), June Travis (Tommy Thomas), Stuart Erwin (Texas Clark), Barton MacLane (Al Stone), Henry Wadsworth (Tay Lawson), Martha Tibbetts (Mary Lee), Isabel Jewell (Lou Clark), Craig Reynolds (Joe Allen), Richard Purcell (Smiley Johnson), Carlyle Moore Jr. (Eddie Payson), Addison Richards (Fred Adams), Garry Owen (Mike Owens), Edward Gargan (Doc Wilson), Robert Light (Les Bogan), James H. Bush (Buzz Gordon), Pat West (Baldy Wright), Gordon "Bill" Elliott (transportation agent), Mathilde Comont (Mama Gini), Carol Hughes (Birdie), Frank Tomick, Paul Mantz (stunt fliers).

The Road to Glory (20th Century–Fox)

Producer: Darryl F. Zanuck. Associate Producer: Nunnally Johnson. Director: Howard Hawks. Screenplay: Joel Sayre, William Faulkner (and Johnson, uncredited), from the film *Les Croix de Bois* (Pathé-Nathan, 1932), directed by Raymond Bernard, adapted from the novel by Roland Dorgelès. Cinematographer: Gregg Toland. Editor: Edward Curtiss. Music: Louis Silvers. Art director: Hans Peters. Set decorator: Thomas Little. Costumes: Gwen Wakeling. Sound: George Leverett, Roger Heman. Assistant director: Edward O'Fearna. Running time: 95 minutes. Filmed in Hollywood, January—March 1936. Released June 2, 1936.

Cast: Fredric March (Lt. Michel Denet), Warner Baxter (Capt. Paul Larouche), Lionel Barrymore (Papa Larouche), June Lang (Monique), Gregory Ratoff (Bouffiou), Victor Kilian (Régnier), Paul Stanton (relief captain), John Qualen (Duflous), Julius Tannen (Lt. Tannen), Theodore von Eltz (major), Paul Fix (Rigaud), Leonid Kinsky (Ledoux), Jacques Lory (courier), Jacques Vernaire (doctor), Edythe Taynore (nurse), George Warrington (old soldier).

(Incorporates considerable battle footage from *Les Croix de Bois*.)

Come and Get It (Samuel Goldwyn Productions, and Howard Productions, for United Artists)

Producer: Samuel Goldwyn. Associate producer: Merritt Hulburd. Directors: Howard Hawks, William Wyler. Director for logging sequences: Richard Rosson. Screenplay: Jane Murfin, Jules Furthman, from the novel by Edna Ferber. Cinematographers: Gregg Toland, Rudolph Maté (logging sequences). Additional second-unit photography: Chet Lyons. Editor: Edward Curtiss. Music: Alfred Newman. Art director: Richard Day. Costumes: Omar Kiam. Sound: Frank Maher. Special-effects photography: Ray Binger. Running time: 105 minutes. Filmed in Hollywood, June–September 1936, with logging footage filmed in Idaho, Wisconsin, Canada. Released October 29, 1936.

Cast: Edward Arnold (Barney Glasgow), Joel McCrea (Richard Glasgow), Frances Farmer (Lotta Morgan/Lotta Bostrom), Walter Brennan (Swan Bostrom), Andrea Leeds (Evvie Glasgow), Frank Shields (Tony Schwerke), Mady Christians (Karie), Mary Nash (Emma Louise Glasgow), Clem Bevans (Gunnar Gallagher), Edwin Maxwell (Sid Le Maire), Cecil Cunningham (Josie), Harry Bradley (Gubbins), Rollo Lloyd (Steward), Charles Halton (Hewitt), Phillip Cooper (chore boy), Al K. Hall (Goodnow), Robert Lowery (young man), Leoncie Rouy-Dementis part he played is missing.

(Reissued as *Roaring Timber*.)

1938

Bringing Up Baby (RKO)

Producer and director: Howard Hawks. Associate producer: Cliff Reid. Screenplay: Dudley Nichols, Hagar Wilde, from a story by Wilde. Cinematographer: Russell Metty. Editor: George Hively. Music: Roy Webb. Art director: Van Nest Polglase. Associate art director: Perry Ferguson. Set decorator: Darrell Silvera. Costumes: Howard Greer. Sound: John L. Cass. Special effects: Vernon L. Walker. Assistant director: Edward Donahue. Running time: 102 minutes. Filmed in Hollywood, September 1937–January 1938. Released February 18, 1938.

Cast: Cary Grant (David Huxley), Katharine Hepburn (Susan), Charles Ruggles (Maj. Horace Applegate), Walter Catlett (Constable Slocum), Barry Fitzgerald (Gogarty), May Robson (Aunt Elizabeth), Fritz Feld (Dr. Lehmann), Leona Roberts (Mrs. Hannah Gogarty), George Irving (Peabody), Tala Birrell (Mrs. Lehmann), Virginia Walker (Alice Swallow), John Kelly (Elmer), Jack Carson (roustabout), Richard Lane (circus manager), Ward Bond (motorcycle cop), George Humbert (Louis, the headwaiter), Ernest Cossart (Joe, the bartender), Stan Blystone (porter), Asta (George, the dog), Nissa (Baby, the leopard).

1939

Only Angels Have Wings (Columbia)
Producer and director: Howard Hawks. (Additional scenes directed by Charles Vidor, Norman Deming, uncredited). Screenplay: Jules Furthman (and Eleanore Griffin, William Rankin, Anne Wigton, John Trainor Foote, uncredited, based on the uncredited stories "Plane Number Four," by Wigton and "Plane Four from Baranca," by Hawks). Cinematographer: Joseph Walker. Aerial cameraman: Elmer Dyer. Second-unit director: Richard Rosson. Second-unit cameraman: Russell Metty. Editor: Viola Lawrence. Music: Dimitri Tiomkin. Musical director: M. W. Stoloff. Art director: Lionel Banks. Gowns: Robert M. Kalloch. Sound: Lodge Cunningham. Special effects: Roy Davidson (miniatures), Edwin C. Hahn. Technical advisor and chief pilot: Paul Mantz. Assistant director: Arthur S. Black. Running time: 121 minutes. Filmed in Hollywood, December 1938–March 1939, with flying footage filmed in California, Nevada, Utah. Released May 11, 1939.

Cast: Cary Grant (Jeff Carter), Jean Arthur (Bonnie Lee), Richard Barthelmess (Bat McPherson), Rita Hayworth (Judy), Thomas Mitchell (Kid Dabb), Allyn Joslyn (Les Peters), Sig Ruman (The Dutchman), Victor Kilian (Sparks), John Carroll (Gent Shelton), Donald Barry (Tex Gordon), Noah Beery Jr. (Joe Souther), Maciste (singer), Melissa Sierra (Lily), Lucio Villegas (Dr. Lagorio), Pat Flaherty (Mike), Pedro Regas (Pancho), Pat West (Baldy), Candy Candide (musician), Charles Moore (servant), Inez Palange (Lily's aunt), Rafael Corio (purser).

1940

His Girl Friday (Columbia)
Producer and director: Howard Hawks. Screenplay: Charles Lederer (and Ben Hecht, Morrie Ryskind, uncredited), from the play *The Front Page*, by Hecht and Charles MacArthur. Cinematographer: Joseph Walker. Editor: Gene Havlick. Musical director: M. W. Stoloff. Art director: Lionel Banks. Gowns: Robert M. Kalloch. Second-unit

director: Arthur Rosson. Assistant director: Cliff Broughton. Running time: 92 minutes. Filmed in Hollywood, September–November 1939. Released January 11, 1940.

Cast: Cary Grant (Walter Burns), Rosalind Russell (Hildy Johnson), Ralph Bellamy (Bruce Baldwin), Gene Lockhart (Sheriff Hartwell), Helen Mack (Mollie Malloy), Porter Hall (Murphy), Ernest Truex (Bensinger), Cliff Edwards (Endicott), Clarence Kolb (mayor), Roscoe Karns (McCue), Frank Jenks (Wilson), Regis Toomey (Sanders), Abner Biberman (Diamond Louie), Frank Orth (Duffy), John Qualen (Earl Williams), Alma Kruger (Mrs. Baldwin), Billy Gilbert (Joe Pettibone), Pat West (Warden Cooley), Edwin Maxwell (Dr. Egelhoffer).

(*The Front Page* was previously filmed in 1931, produced by Howard Hughes for United Artists and directed by Lewis Milestone, and was remade in 1974 by Universal, directed by Billy Wilder. *Switching Channels*, a sex-change version à la *His Girl Friday* set at a television news station, was made in 1988 by Tri-Star Pictures, directed by Ted Kotcheff.)

1941

Sergeant York (Warner Bros.)

Producers: Jesse L. Lasky, Hal B. Wallis. Director: Howard Hawks. (Additional scenes directed by Vincent Sherman, uncredited.) Screenplay: Abem Finkel, Harry Chandlee, Howard Koch, John Huston, from *Sergeant York: His Own Life Story and War Diary*, edited by Tom Skeyhill (and *War Diary of Sergeant York*, edited by Sam K. Cowan, *Sergeant York and His People*, by Cowan, and *Sergeant York: Last of the Long Hunters*, by Skeyhill, uncredited). Cinematographer: Sol Polito. Cinematographer for battle sequences: Arthur Edeson. Editor: William Holmes. Music: Max Steiner. Musical director: Leo F. Forbstein. Art director: John Hughes. Set decorator: Fred MacLean. Sound: Oliver S. Garretson. Second-unit director: B. Reeves Eason. Technical advisers: Donoho Hall, Paul Walters, Capt. F. A. R. William Yetter. Assistant director: Jack Sullivan. Unit manager: Eric Stacey. Running time: 134 minutes. Filmed in Hollywood, San Fernando Valley, Santa Susanna Mountains, February–May 1941. Released July 1, 1941.

Cast: Gary Cooper (Sgt. Alvin C. York), Walter Brennan (Pastor Rosier Pile), Joan Leslie (Gracie Williams), George Tobias (Michael T. "Pusher" Ross), Stanley Ridges (Maj. Buxton), Margaret Wycherly (Mother York), Ward Bond (Ike Botkin), Noah Beery Jr. (Buck Lipscomb), June Lockhart (Rosie York), Dickie Moore (George York), Clem Bevans (Zeke), Howard da Silva (Lem), Charles Trowbridge (Cordell Hull), Harvey Stephens (Capt. Danforth), David Bruce (Bert Thomas), Charles Esmond (German major), Joseph Sawyer (Sgt. Early), Pat Flaherty (Sgt. Harry Parsons), Robert Porterfield (Zeb Andrews), Erville Alderson (Nate Tompkins), Frank Wilcox (sergeant), Donald Douglas (Capt. Tillman), Lane Chandler (Cpl. Savage), Frank Marlowe (Beardsley), Jack Pennick (Cpl. Cutting), James Anderson (Eb), Guy Wilderson (Tom), Tully Marshall (Uncle Lige), Lee "Lasses" White (Luke, the target keeper), Charles Middleton (mountaineer), Victor Kilian (Andrews), Theodore von Bitz (prison camp commander), Jane Isbell (Gracie's sister), Frank Orth (drummer), Arthur Aylesworth (Martar, the bartender), Elisha

Cook Jr. (piano player), William Haade (card player), Joseph Girard (Gen. John Pershing), Jean Del Val (Marshal Foch), Douglas Wood (Mayor Hylan), Ed Keane (Oscar of the Waldorf), Ray Teal (soldier), Si Jenks, Herbert Heywood, Eddy Waller, Henry Hall (mountaineers), Pat West (sergeant).

1942

Ball of Fire (Samuel Goldwyn Productions for United Artists)

Producer: Samuel Goldwyn. Director: Howard Hawks. Screenplay: Charles Brackett, Billy Wilder, from the story "From A to Z," by Wilder and Thomas Monroe. Cinematographer: Gregg Toland. Editor: Daniel Mandell. Music: Alfred Newman. Art director: Perry Ferguson. Associate art director: McClure Capps. Set decorator: Howard Bristol. Miss Stanwyck's costumes: Edith Head. Sound: Frank Maher. Second-unit director: Arthur Rosson. Assistant director: William Tummel. Running time: 111 minutes. Filmed in Hollywood, August–October 1941. Released January 15, 1942.

Cast: Gary Cooper (Prof. Bertram Potts), Barbara Stanwyck (Sugarpuss O'Shea), Oscar Homolka (Prof. Gurkakoff), Dana Andrews (Joe Lilac), Dan Duryea (Duke Pastrami), Henry Travers (Prof. Jerome), S. Z. Sakall (Prof. Magenbruch), Tully Marshall (Prof. Robinson), Leonid Kinsky (Prof. Quintana), Richard Haydn (Prof. Oddly), Aubrey Mather (Prof. Peagram), Allen Jenkins (garbageman), Ralph Peters (Asthma Anderson), Kathleen Howard (Miss Bragg), Mary Field (Miss Totten), Charles Lane (Larsen), Charles Arnt (McNeary), Elisha Cook Jr. (waiter), Alan Rhein (Horseface), Eddie Foster (Pinstripe), Aldrich Bowker (justice of the peace), Addison Richards (district attorney), Pat West (bum), Kenneth Howell (college boy), Tommy Ryan (newsboy), Tim Ryan (motorcycle cop), Will Lee (Benny the Creep), Otto Hoffmann (stage doorman), Pat Flaherty, George Sherwood (deputies), Geraldine Fissette (hula dancer), Gene Krupa and His Orchestra.

(Remade as *A Song Is Born* by Goldwyn and Hawks in 1948.)

1943

The Outlaw (Howard Hughes Productions for United Artists)

Producer: Howard Hughes. Director: Howard Hughes (and Howard Hawks, uncredited). Screenplay: Jules Furthman (from an uncredited story treatment by Ben Hecht and Hawks). Cinematographer: Gregg Toland. Editor: Wallace Grissell. Music: Victor Young. Special effects: Roy Davidson. Assistant director: Sam Nelson. Running time: 121 minutes, later cut to 103 minutes. Filmed in Arizona (by Hawks), November–December 1940, in Hollywood (by Hughes), December 1940–spring 1941. Released February 5, 1943, San Francisco; withdrawn, rereleased in 1946; rereleased again (by RKO) in 1950.

Cast: Jack Buetel (Billy the Kid), Jane Russell (Rio), Thomas Mitchell (Pat Garrett), Walter Huston (Doc Holliday), Mimi Aguglia (Guadalupe), Joe Sawyer (Charley), Gene Rizzi (stranger).

Air Force (Warner Bros.)

Producer: Hal B. Wallis. Director: Howard Hawks. (Additional scenes directed by Vincent Sherman, uncredited.) Screenplay: Dudley Nichols (and William Faulkner, uncredited). Cinematographer: James Wong Howe. Aerial cameramen: Elmer Dyer, Charles Marshall. Editor: George Amy. Music: Franz Waxman. Art director: John Hughes. Set decorator: Walter F. Tilford. Costumes: Milo Anderson. Sound: Oliver S. Garretson. Second-unit director: B. Reeves Eason. Assistant director: Jack Sullivan. Unit production manager: Chuck Hansen. Special effects: Roy Davidson (director, miniatures), Rex Wimpy, and Hans F. Koenekamp (background photography). Chief pilot: Paul Mantz. Running time: 124 minutes. Filmed in Hollywood, Tampa, June–October 1942. Released February 3, 1943.

Cast: John Ridgely (Capt. Michael A. Quincannon), Gig Young (Lt. Xavier W. Williams), Arthur Kennedy (Lt. Tom McMartin), Charles Drake (Lt. M. W. Hauser), Harry Carey (Sgt. Skip White), George Tobias (Cpl. B. B. Weinberg), Ward Wood (Cpl. Gus Peterson), Ray Montgomery (Pvt. Henry Chester), John Garfield (Sgt. John B. Winocki), James Brown (Lt. Tex Rader), Stanley Ridges (Mallory), Willard Robertson (colonel), Moroni Olsen (commanding officer), Edward S. Brophy (Callahan), Richard Lane (Maj. Roberts), Bill Crago (Lt. Moran), Faye Emerson (Susan McMartin), Addison Richards (Maj. Daniels), James Flavin (Maj. Bagley), Ann Doran (Mary Quincannon), Dorothy Peterson (Mrs. Chester).

Corvette K-225 (Universal)

Producer: Howard Hawks. Director: Richard Rosson (and Hawks, uncredited). Screenplay: Lt. John Rhodes Sturdy, R.C.N.V.R. (and, uncredited, Edward Chodorov). Cinematographers: Tony Gaudio (studio), Harry F. Perry, and Bert A. Eason (location). Editor: Edward Curtiss. Art director: Robert Boyle. Special effects: John Fulton. Assistant director: William Tummel. Unit production manager: Vernon Keays. Running time: 99 minutes. Filmed in Hollywood, February–May 1943, Nova Scotia, Montreal, and Atlantic Ocean, May–July 1943. Released September 29, 1943.

Cast: Randolph Scott (Lt. Com. MacClain), James Brown (Paul Cartwright), Ella Raines (Joyce Cartwright), Barry Fitzgerald (Stooky O'Meara), Andy Devine (Walsh), Fuzzy Knight (Cricket), Noah Beery Jr. (Stone), Richard Lane (Admiral), Thomas Gomez (Smithy), David Bruce (Rawlins), Murray Alper (Jones), James Flavin (Gardner), Walter Sande (Evans).

1944

To Have and Have Not (Warner Bros.)

Producer and director: Howard Hawks. Screenplay: Jules Furthman, William Faulkner, from the novel by Ernest Hemingway. Cinematographer: Sid Hickox. Editor: Christian Nyby. Music: Max Steiner. Song ("How Little We Know"): music, Hoagy Carmichael; lyrics, Johnny Mercer. Art director: Charles Novi. Set decorator: Casey Roberts. Gowns: Milo Anderson. Sound: Oliver S. Garretson. Technical advisor: Louis

Comien. Special effects: Roy Davidson (director), Rex Wimpy (cameraman). Assistant director: Jack Sullivan. Running time: 100 minutes. Filmed in Hollywood, February–May 1944. Released October 11, 1944, in New York, January 1945 in the rest of the United States.

Cast: Humphrey Bogart (Harry "Steve" Morgan), Walter Brennan (Eddie), Lauren Bacall (Marie "Slim" Browning), Dolores Moran (Hélène de Bursac), Hoagy Carmichael (Cricket), Sheldon Leonard (Lt. Coyo), Walter Molnar (Paul de Bursac), Marcel Dalio (Gérard, or "Frenchy"), Walter Sande (Johnson), Dan Seymour (Capt. Renard), Aldo Nadi (bodyguard), Paul Marion (Beauclerc), Patricia Shay (Mrs. Beauclerc), Pat West (bartender), Emmett Smith (bartender), Janette Grae (Rosalie), Sir Lancelot (Horatio), Eugene Borden (quartermaster), Elzie Emanuel, Harold Garrison (children), Pedro Regas (civilian), Major Fred Farrell (headwaiter), Adrienne d'Ambricourt (cashier), Hal Kelly (detective), Ron Randell (ensign), Audrey Armstrong (dancer), Marguerita Sylva (cashier), Chef Joseph Milani (chef), Maurice Marsac, Fred Dosch, George Suzanne, Louis Mercier, Crane Whitley (de Gaullists).

(Remade as *The Breaking Point* by Warner Bros. and director Michael Curtiz in 1950 and as *The Gun Runners* by Seven Arts/United Artists and director Don Siegel in 1958).

1946

The Big Sleep (Warner Bros.)

Producer and director: Howard Hawks. Screenplay: William Faulkner, Leigh Brackett, Jules Furthman (and, Philip Epstein, uncredited), from the novel by Raymond Chandler. Cinematographer: Sid Hickox. Editor: Christian Nyby. Music: Max Steiner. Art director: Carl Jules Weyl. Set decorator: Fred M. MacLean. Wardrobe: Leah Rhodes. Special effects: E. Roy Davidson (director), Warren E. Lynch. Assistant director: Robert Vreland. Unit production manager: Chuck Hansen. Running time: 116 minutes (first version), 114 minutes (release version). Filmed in Hollywood, October 1944–January 1945; additional scenes filmed January 21–28, 1946. First version shown to U.S. troops overseas beginning August 1945. Final version released August 23, 1946.

Cast: Humphrey Bogart (Philip Marlowe), Lauren Bacall (Vivian Sternwood Rutledge), John Ridgely (Eddie Mars), Martha Vickers (Carmen Sternwood), Dorothy Malone (bookshop girl), Peggy Knudsen (Mona Mars; Pat Clark played Mona Mars in first version), Regis Toomey (Bernie Ohls), Charles Waldron (Gen. Sternwood), Charles D. Brown (Norris, the butler), Bob Steele (Canino), Elisha Cook Jr. (Harry Jones), Louis Jean Heydt (Joe Brody), Sonia Darrin (Agnes Lowzier), Theodore von Eltz (Arthur Gwynne Geiger), Tom Rafferty (Carol Lundgren), James Flavin (Capt. Cronjager), Joseph Crehan (medical examiner), Joy Barlowe (taxi driver), Tom Fadden (Sidney), Ben Welden (Pete), Trevor Bardette (Art Huck), Emmet Vogan (Ed, the deputy), Forbes Murray (furtive man), Pete Kooy (motorcycle cop), Carole Douglas (librarian), Jack Chefe (croupier), Paul Weber, Jack Perry, Wally Walker (Mars's thugs), Lorraine Miller (hatcheck girl), Shelby Payne (cigarette girl), Janis Chandler, Deannie Bert (waitresses), Marc Lawrence.

(Remade by United Artists and director Michael Winner in Britain in 1978.)

1948

Red River (Monterey Productions for United Artists)

Producer and director: Howard Hawks. Codirector: Arthur Rosson. Screenplay: Borden Chase, Charles Schnee, from Chase's novel *The Chisholm Trail*, serialized in the *Saturday Evening Post*. Cinematographer: Russell Harlan. Editor: Christian Nyby. Music: Dimitri Tiomkin. Song ("Settle Down"): Tiomkin. Art director: John Datu Arensma. Sound: Richard DeWeese. Special effects: Donald Steward. Special photographic effects: Allan Thompson. Assistant director: William McGarry. Production manager: Norman Cook. Running time: 133 minutes (subsequent voice-over version cut to 125 minutes). Filmed in Arizona, Hollywood, September–December 1946. Released September 1, 1948.

Cast: John Wayne (Tom Dunson), Montgomery Clift (Matthew Garth), Joanne Dru (Tess Millay), Walter Brennan (Groot Nadine), Coleen Gray (Fen), Harry Carey Sr. (Melville), John Ireland (Cherry Valance), Noah Beery Jr. (Buster McGee), Harry Carey Jr. (Dan Latimer), Chief Yowlachie (Quo), Paul Fix (Teeler Yacey), Hank Worden (Simms), Mickey Kuhn (Matthew, as a boy), Ray Hyke (Walt Jergens), Hal Talliaferro (Old Leather), Ivan Parry (Bunk Kenneally), Paul Fiero (Fernandez), William Self (wounded wrangler), Dan White (Laredo), Tom Tyler (quitter), Lane Chandler (colonel), Glenn Strange (Naylor), Shelley Winters (dance-hall girl).

(Remade for television in 1988.)

A Song Is Born (Samuel Goldwyn Productions for RKO)

Producer: Samuel Goldwyn. Director: Howard Hawks. Screenplay: No screen credit given (Harry Tugend, Phil Rapp, Daniel Fuchs, Melville Shavelson, Robert Pirosh, Ken Englund, Everett Freeman, Roland Kibbee, uncredited); from the screenplay *Ball of Fire* by Charles Brackett and Billy Wilder (uncredited), based on the story "From A to Z," by Wilder and Thomas Monroe. Cinematographer (Technicolor): Gregg Toland. Editor: Daniel Mandell. Musical directors: Emil Newman, Hugo Friedhofer. Songs ("A Song Is Born" and "Daddy-O"): words and music by Don Raye and Gene De Paul, orchestrations by Sonny Burke. Art directors: George Jenkins, Perry Ferguson. Set decorator: Julia Heron. Costume designer: Irene Sharaff. Sound: Fred Lau. Special photographic effects: John Fulton. Running time: 112 minutes. Filmed in Hollywood, June–September 1947. Released October 19, 1948.

Cast: Danny Kaye (Robert Frisbee), Virginia Mayo (Honey Swanson), Benny Goodman (Prof. Magenbruch), Tommy Dorsey, Louis Armstrong, Lionel Hampton, Charlie Barnet, Mel Powell, Buck and Bubbles, The Page Cavanaugh Trio, The Golden Gate Quartet, Russo and the Samba Kings (as themselves), Hugh Herbert (Prof. Twingle), Steve Cochran (Tony Crow), J. Edward Bromberg (Dr. Elfini), Felix Bressart (Prof. Gerkikoff), Ludwig Stossel (Prof. Traumer), O. Z. Whitehead (Prof. Oddly), Esther Dale (Miss Bragg), Mary Field (Miss Totten), Howard Chamberlain (Setter), Paul Langton (Joe), Sidney Blackmer (Adams), Ben Welden (Monte), Ben Chasen (Ben), Peter Virgo (Louis), Harry Balaban (bass), Louis Bellson (drums), Alton Hendrickson (guitar).

1949

I Was a Male War Bride (20th Century–Fox)

Producer: Sol C. Siegel. Director: Howard Hawks. Screenplay: Charles Lederer, Leonard Spigelgass, Hagar Wilde, from the autobiographical story by Henri Rochard (Dr. Roger H. Charlier). Cinematographers: Norbert Brodine, O. H. Borradaile (and Russell Harlan uncredited). Editor: James B. Clark. Music: Cyril Mockridge. Art directors: Lyle Wheeler, Albert Hogsett. Set decorators: Thomas Little, Walter M. Scott. Sound: George Leverett, Roger Heman. Special photographic effects: Fred Sersen. Assistant director: Arthur Jacobson. Running time: 105 minutes. Filmed in and around Heidelberg, Zuzenhausen, and Bremerhaven, West Germany, and at Shepperton Studios, England, September 1948–January 1949, also in Hollywood and San Pedro, May 1949. Released August 19, 1949.

Cast: Cary Grant (Capt. Henri Rochard), Ann Sheridan (Lt. Catherine Gates), Marion Marshall (Kitty), Randy Stuart (Mae), William Neff (Capt. Jack Rumsey), Eugene Gericke (Tony Jowitt), Ruben Wendorf (innkeeper's assistant), Lester Sharpe (waiter), Ken Tobey (seaman), Robert Stevenson (lieutenant), Alfred Linder (bartender), David McMahon (chaplain), Joe Haworth (shore patrol), John Whitney (Trumble), William Pullen, William Self (sergeants), Otto Reichow, William Yetter (German policemen), André Charlot (French minister), Alex Gerry (waiter), Russ Conway (Commander Willis), Harry Lauter (lieutenant), Kay Young (Maj. Prendergast), Lillie Kenn (innkeeper's wife), Carl Jaffe (jail officer), Martin Miller (Schindler), Paul Hardmuth (burgermeister), John Serrett (French notary), Bill Murphy (sergeant), Patricia Curts (girl in door).

1951

The Thing from Another World (Winchester Productions for RKO)

Producer: Howard Hawks. Director: Christian Nyby (and Hawks, uncredited). Screenplay: Charles Lederer (and Ben Hecht, uncredited), based on the short story "Who Goes There?" by John W. Campbell Jr. Cinematographer: Russell Harlan. Editor: Roland Cross. Music: Dimitri Tiomkin. Art directors: Albert S. D'Agostino, John J. Hughes. Set decorators: Darrell Silvera, William Stevens. Ladies' wardrobe: Michael Woulfe. Sound: Phil Brigandi, Clem Portman. Makeup supervisor: Lee Greenway. Special effects: Donald Stewart. Special photographic effects: Linwood Dunn. Associate producer: Edward Lasker. Running time: 87 minutes. Filmed in Montana, San Fernando Valley, Hollywood, October 1950–March 1951. Released April 6, 1951.

Cast: Margaret Sheridan (Nikki), Kenneth Tobey (Capt. Patrick Hendry), Robert Cornthwaite (Prof. Carrington), Douglas Spencer (Skeely), James Young (Lt. Eddie Dykes), Dewey Martin (Crew Chief), Robert Nichols (Lt. Ken Erickson), William Self (Cpl. Barnes), Eduard Franz (Dr. Stern), Sally Creighton (Mrs. Chapman), James Arness (The Thing).

(Remade as *The Thing* by Universal and director John Carpenter in 1982.)

1952

The Big Sky (Winchester Productions for RKO)

Producer and director: Howard Hawks. Screenplay: Dudley Nichols, from the novel by A. B. Guthrie Jr. Cinematographer: Russell Harlan. Editor: Christian Nyby. Music: Dimitri Tiomkin. French Lyrics: Gordon Clark. Art directors: Albert S. D'Agostino, Perry Ferguson. Set decorators: Darrell Silvera, William Stevens. Costume designer: Dorothy Jeakins. Sound: Phil Brigandi, Clem Portman. Special effects: Donald Steward. Second-unit director: Arthur Rosson. Associate producer: Edward Lasker. Assistant director: William McGarry. Unit manager: Arthur Siteman. Running time: 138 minutes (later cut to 122 minutes). Filmed in Wyoming, Hollywood, August–November 1951. Released August 6, 1952.

Cast: Kirk Douglas (Jim Deakins), Dewey Martin (Boone Caudill), Elizabeth Threatt (Teal Eye), Arthur Hunnicutt (Zeb Calloway), Buddy Baer (Romaine), Steven Geray (Jourdonnais), Henri Letondal (Labadie), Hank Worden (Poordevil), Jim Davis (Streak), Robert Hunter (Chouquette), Booth Colman (Pascal), Paul Frees (McMasters), Frank de Cova (Moleface), Guy Wilkerson (Longface), Don Beddoe (townsman), Barbara Hawks (Indian).

Monkey Business (20th Century–Fox)

Producer: Sol C. Siegel. Director: Howard Hawks. Screenplay: Ben Hecht, I. A. L. Diamond, Charles Lederer, from a story by Harry Segall. Cinematographer: Milton Krasner. Editor: William B. Murphy. Music: Leigh Harline. Musical director: Lionel Newman. Art directors: Lyle Wheeler, George Patrick. Set decorators: Thomas Little, Walter M. Scott. Wardrobe director: Charles LeMaire, Costume designer: Travilla. Sound: W. D. Flick, Roger Heman. Special photographic effects: Ray Kellogg. Running time: 97 minutes. Filmed in Hollywood, March–April 1952. Released September 5, 1952.

Cast: Cary Grant (Prof. Barnaby Fulton), Ginger Rogers (Edwina Fulton), Charles Coburn (Oliver Oxly), Marilyn Monroe (Lois Laurel), Hugh Marlowe (Harvey Entwhistle), Henri Letondal (Dr. Siegfried Kitzel), Robert Cornthwaite (Dr. Zoldeck), Larry Keating (Mr. Culverly), Douglas Spencer (Dr. Brunner), Esther Dale (Mrs. Rhinelander), George Winslow (Little Indian), Emmett Lynn (Jimmy), Jerry Sheldon (guard), Kathleen Freeman (nurse), Mary Field (clerk) Harry Carey Jr. (reporter), Joseph Mell (barber), George Eldredge (auto salesman), Heine Conklin (painter), Olan Soule (hotel clerk), Gil Stratton Jr. (Yale man), Ruth Warren, Isabel Withers, Olive Carey (laundresses), John McKee (photographer), Faire Binney (dowager), Billy McLean (bellboy), Paul Maxey, Mack Williams (dignitaries), Marjorie Holliday (receptionist), Harry Carter, Harry Bartell, Jerry Paris (scientists), Harry Seymour (clothing store salesman), Dabbs Greer (cab driver), Russ Clark, Ray Montgomery (cops), Robert Nichols (garageman), Forbes Murray, Roger Moore, Melinda Plowman, Terry Goodman, Ronnie Clark, Rudy Lee, Mickey Little, Brad Mora, Jimmy Roebuck, Louis Lettieri.

The Ransom of Red Chief (The fourth episode in O. *Henry's Full House*) (20th Century–Fox)

Producer: André Hakim. Director: Howard Hawks. Screenplay: Nunnally Johnson (and, Ben Hecht and Charles Lederer, uncredited), based on the short story by O. Henry. Cinematographer: Milton Krasner. Editor: William B. Murphy. Music: Alfred Newman. Art director: Chester Gore. Running time: 27 minutes (entire film: 117 minutes). Filmed in Hollywood, May 1952. Released September 19, 1952.

Cast: Fred Allen (Sam), Oscar Levant (Bill), Lee Aaker (J. B. Dorset), Kathleen Freeman (Mrs. Dorset), Irving Bacon (Mr. Dorset), Alfred Mizner (storekeeper), Gloria Gordon (Ellie Mae), Robert Easton, Robert Cherry, Norman Leavitt (yokels).

(Other episodes were directed by Henry Koster, Henry Hathaway, Jean Negulesco, Henry King. Hawks's episode was cut from the film after its initial engagement.)

1953

Gentlemen Prefer Blondes (20th Century–Fox)

Producer: Sol C. Siegel. Director: Howard Hawks. Screenplay: Charles Lederer, from the musical comedy by Joseph Fields and Anita Loos, based on the novel by Loos. Cinematographer (Technicolor): Harry J. Wild. Editor: Hugh S. Fowler. Music and lyrics: Jules Styne, Leo Robin. Songs ("When Love Goes Wrong" and "Ain't There Anyone Here for Love?"): music and lyrics by Hoagy Carmichael, Harold Adamson. Musical director: Lionel Newman. Choreographer and director of musical numbers: Jack Cole. Art directors: Lyle Wheeler, Joseph C. Wright. Set decorator: Claude Carpenter. Wardrobe director: Charles LeMaire. Costumes: Travilla. Sound: E. Clayton Ward, Roger Heman. Special photographic effects: Ray Kellog. Assistant director: Paul Helmick. Running time: 91 minutes. Filmed in Hollywood, November 1952–January 1953. Released July 15, 1953.

Cast: Jane Russell (Dorothy Shaw), Marilyn Monroe (Lorelei Lee), Charles Coburn (Sir Francis Beekman), Elliott Reid (Monroe), Tommy Noonan (Gus Esmond), George Winslow (Henry Spofford III), Marcel Dalio (magistrate), Taylor Holmes (Gus Esmond Sr.), Norma Varden (Lady Beekman), Howard Wendell (Watson), Steven Geray (hotel manager), Peter Camlin (gendarme), Henri Letondal (Grotier), Leo Mostovoy (Philippe), Alex Frazer (Pritchard), George Davis (taxi driver), Alphonse Martell (headwaiter), George Dee, Jimmy Saung, George Charkiris (dancers), Jimmy Moultrie, Freddie Moultrie (boy dancers), Harry Carey Jr. (Winslow), Jean Del Val (ship's captain), Ray Montgomery (Peters), Alvy Moore (Anderson), Robert Nichols (Evans), Charles Tannen (Ed), Jimmy Young (Stevens), Charles De Ravenne (purser), John Close (coach), William Cabanne (Sims), Philip Sylvestre (steward), Jack Chefe (proprietor), John Hedloe (athlete), Alfred Paix (porter), Max Willenz (court clerk), Rolfe Sedan (waiter), Robert Foulk, Ralph Peters (passport officials), Harry Seymour (captain of waiters), Donald Moray (airport porter), Deena Dikkers (hotel clerk), Fred Stevens (stagehand), Jean De Briac, Harris Brown, A. Cameron Grant, Richard La Marr, Robert Fuller.

1955

Land of the Pharaohs (Continental Company Ltd. for Warner Bros.)

Producer and director: Howard Hawks. Screenplay: William Faulkner, Harry Kurnitz, Harold Jack Bloom. Cinematographers (Warnercolor, CinemaScope): Lee Garmes, Russell Harlan. Supervising editor: Rudi Fehr. Editor: Vladimir Sagovsky. Music: Dimitri Tiomkin. Art director: Alexandre Trauner. Costumes: Mayo. Sound: Oliver S. Garretson. Special effects: Don Steward. Second-unit director: Noël Howard. Associate producer: Arthur Siteman. Assistant director: Paul Helmick. Unit manager: Chuck Hansen. Running time: 106 minutes. Filmed in Egypt, April–May 1954, Rome, June–August 1954. Released June 24, 1955.

Cast: Jack Hawkins (Pharaoh Cheops), Joan Collins (Princess Nellifer), Dewey Martin (Senta), Alexis Minotis (Hamar), James Robertson Justice (Vashtar), Luisa Boni (Kyra), Sydney Chaplin (Treneh), James Hayter (Mikka, Vashtar's servant), Kerima (Queen Nailla), Piero Giagnoni (Prince Zanin), Carlo d'Angelo (overseer).

1959

Rio Bravo (Armada Productions for Warner Bros.)

Producer and director: Howard Hawks. Screenplay: Jules Furthman, Leigh Brackett, from a short story by B. H. McCampbell. Cinematographer (Technicolor): Russell Harlan. Editor: Folmar Blangsted. Music: Dimitri Tiomkin. Original songs: music, Tiomkin; lyrics, Paul Francis Webster. Art director: Leo K. Kuter. Set decorator: Ralph S. Hurst. Costume designer: Marjorie Best. Sound: Robert B. Lee. Assistant director: Paul Helmick. Running time: 141 minutes. Filmed in Old Tucson, Hollywood, May–July 1958. Released March 18, 1959.

Cast: John Wayne (Sheriff John T. Chance), Dean Martin (Dude), Ricky Nelson (Colorado Ryan), Angie Dickinson (Feathers), Walter Brennan (Stumpy), Ward Bond (Pat Wheeler), John Russell (Nathan Burdette), Pedro Gonzalez-Gonzalez (Carlos Remonte), Estelita Rodriguez (Consuelo), Claude Akins (Joe Burdette), Malcolm Atterbury (Jake), Harry Carey Jr. (Harold; part cut from film), Bob Steele (Matt Harris), Myron Healey (barfly), Fred Graham (gunman), Riley Hill (messenger), Tom Monroe (henchman), Bob Terhune (Charlie, the bartender), Ted White (Bart), Nesdon Booth (Clark), George Bruggeman (Clem), Jose Cuchillo (Pedro), Eugene Iglesias (bystander), Joseph Shimada (Burt, the funeral director).

1962

Hatari! (Malabar Productions for Paramount)

Producer and director: Howard Hawks. Screenplay: Leigh Brackett, from a story by Harry Kurnitz. Cinematographer (Technicolor): Russell Harlan. Associate photographer: Joseph Brun. Editor: Stuart Gilmore. Music: Henry Mancini. Song ("Just for Tonight"): lyrics, Johnny Mercer; music, Hoagy Carmichael. Art directors: Hal Pereira, Carl

Anderson. Set decorators: Sam Comer, Claude E. Carpenter. Costumes: Edith Head. Men's wardrobe: Frank Beetson Jr. Sound: John Carter, Charles Grenzbach. Special photographic effects: John F. Fulton. Special mechanical effects: Richard Parker. Associate producer and second-unit director: Paul Helmick. Assistant directors: Tom Connors, Russ Saunders, Bud Brill. Unit manager: Jim Henderling. Production manager: Don Robb. Technical adviser: Willy de Beer. Running time: 159 minutes. Filmed in Tanganyika, East Africa, November 1960–March 1961, Hollywood, March–May 1961. Released June 19, 1962.

Cast: John Wayne (Sean Mercer), Hardy Kruger (Kurt Mueller), Elsa Martinelli (Anna-Maria "Dallas" D'Alessandro), Red Buttons (Pockets), Gerard Blain (Charles "Chips" Maurey), Bruce Cabot (Indian), Michele Girardon (Brandy Delacourt), Valentin de Vargas (Luis Francisco Garcia Lopez), Eduard Franz (Dr. Sanderson), Queenie Leonard (nurse), Jon Chevron (Joseph), Emmett E. Smith (bartender), Henry Scott (Sikh clerk), Jack Williams (native), Eric Rungren (Stan), Umbopa M'Beti (Arga), Koume Samburu (Saidi).

1964

Man's Favorite Sport? (Gibraltar-Laurel Productions for Universal)

Producer and director: Howard Hawks. Screenplay: John Fenton Murray, Steven McNeil (and, Leigh Brackett, uncredited), from the story "The Girl Who Almost Got Away," by Pat Frank. Cinematographer (Technicolor): Russell Harlan. Editor: Stuart Gilmore. Music: Henry Mancini. Song ("Man's Favorite Sport"): lyrics, Johnny Mercer, music: Mancini. Art directors: Alexander Golitzen, Tambi Larsen. Set decorator: Robert Priestley. Costumes: Edith Head. Men's wardrobe: Pete Saldutti. Sound: Waldon O. Watson, Joe Lapis. Special mechanical effects: Ben MacMahon. Special title photography: Don Ornitz. Associate producer: Paul Helmick. Assistant director: Tom Connors Jr. Unit production manager: Terence Nelson. Running time: 120 minutes. Filmed in Hollywood, December 1962–March 1963. Released February 5, 1964.

Cast: Rock Hudson (Roger Willoughby), Paula Prentiss (Abigail Page), Maria Perschy (Isolda "Easy" Mueller), John McGiver (William Cadwalader), Charlene Holt (Tex Connors), Roscoe Karns (Maj. Phipps), James Westerfield (policeman), Norman Alden (John Screaming Eagle), Forrest Lewis (Skaggs), Regis Toomey (Bagley), Tyler McVey (Bush), Kathie Brown (Marcia), Molly Bee (singer), Paul Bryar (bartender), Bill Cassady (escort), Edy Williams (second girl), Ed Stoddard, Joan Tewksbury, Betty Hanna (people in elevator), Dianne Simpson (elevator operator), Holger Bendixen (fisherman), Joan Boston (Joan).

1965

Red Line 7000 (Laurel Productions for Paramount)

Producer and director: Howard Hawks. Screenplay: George Kirgo (and Steve McNeil, Leigh Brackett, uncredited), from a story by Hawks. Cinematographer (Technicolor): Milton Krasner. Editors: Stuart Gilmore, Bill Brame. Music: Nelson Riddle. Songs:

"Wildcat Jones" by Carol Connors and Buzz Cason, "Let Me Find Someone New" by Connors and Riddle. Art directors: Hal Pereira, Arthur Lonergan. Set decorators: Sam Comer, Claude E. Carpenter. Costumes: Edith Head. Sound: John Carter, John Wilkinson. Special photographic effects: Paul K. Lerpae. Process photography: Farciot Edouart. Second-unit director: Bruce Kessler. Assistant director: Dick Moder. Unit production manager: Andrew J. Durkus. Running time: 110 minutes. Filmed in Hollywood, January–April 1965; second unit races filmed in Florida, South Carolina, North Carolina, California, July 1964–January 1965. Released November 9, 1965.

Cast: James Caan (Mike Marsh), Laura Devon (Julie Kazarian), Gail Hire (Holly MacGregor), Charlene Holt (Lindy Bonaparte), John Robert Crawford (Ned Arp), Marianna Hill (Gabrielle "Gaby" Queneau), James Ward (Dan McCall), Norman Alden (Pat Kazarian), George Takei (Kato), Diane Strom (receptionist), Anthony Rogers (Jim Loomis), Carol Connors, Cissy Wellman, Beryl Hammond, Leslie Sommers (waitresses), Forrest Lewis (Jenkins), Dee Hartford (Dinah), Anne Morell (girl in café), John Gabriel (Jake), Robert Donner (Leroy), Thomas A. Stears, Craig Chudy (drivers), Joel Allen (rector), Jerry Lewis (driver).

1967

El Dorado (Laurel Productions for Paramount)

Producer and director: Howard Hawks. Screenplay: Leigh Brackett, from the novel *The Stars in Their Courses* by Harry Brown. Cinematographer (Technicolor): Harold Rosson. Editor: John Woodcock. Music: Nelson Riddle. Song ("El Dorado"): lyrics, John Gabriel, music, Riddle, sung by George Alexander, accompanied by the Mellomen. Art directors: Hal Pereira, Carl Anderson. Set decorators: Robert Benton, Ray Moyer. Costumes: Edith Head. Sound: John Carter, Charles Grenzbach. Original paintings: Olaf Wieghorst. Special photographic effects: Paul K. Lerpae. Process photography: Farciot Edouart. Associate producer: Paul Helmick. Assistant director: Andrew J. Durkus. Unit production manager: John Coonan. Running time: 126 minutes. Filmed in Old Tucson, Hollywood, October 1965–January 1966. Released in Japan December 17, 1966; in the United States June 9, 1967.

Cast: John Wayne (Cole Thornton), Robert Mitchem (J. P. Harrah), James Caan (Alan Bourdillon "Mississippi" Traherne), Charlene Holt (Maudie), Paul Fix (Doc Miller), Arthur Hunnicutt (Bill Harris), Michele Carey (Joey MacDonald), R. G. Armstrong (Kevin MacDonald), Edward Asner (Bart Jason), Christopher George (Nelse McLeod), Marina Ghane (Maria), John Gabriel (Pedro), Robert Rothwell (Saul MacDonald), Robert Donner (Milt), Anthony Rogers (Dr. Donovan), Victoria George (Jared's wife), Jim Davis (Jason's foreman), Anne Newman (Saul's wife), Diane Strom (Matt's wife), Johnny Crawford (Luke MacDonald), Adam Roarke (Matt MacDonald), Charles Courtney (Jared MacDonald), Olaf Wieghorst (Swedish gunsmith).

1970

Rio Lobo (Malabar Productions and Cinema Center Films for National General)

Producer and director: Howard Hawks. Screenplay: Burton Wohl, Leigh Brackett, from a story by Wohl. Cinematographer (Technicolor): William Clothier. Editor: John Woodcock. Music: Jerry Goldsmith. Production designer: Robert Smith. Set decorator: William Kiernan. Costume designer: Leah Rhodes. Men's costumer: Ted Parvin. Women's Costumer: Patricia Norris. Sound: John Carter. Special effects: A. D. Flowers, Clifford P. Wenger. Technical adviser (train sequence): William Byrne. Title designer and director: Don Record. Associate producer: Paul Helmick. Second-unit director: Yakima Canutt. Assistant director: Mike Moder. Unit production manager: Robert M. Beche. Running time: 114 minutes. Filmed in Cuernavaca, Mexico; Old Tucson; Nogales; Hollywood, March–June 1970. Released December 18, 1970.

Cast: John Wayne (Capt. Cord McNally), Jorge Rivero (Lt. Pierre Cordona), Jennifer O'Neill (Shasta), Jack Elam (Phillips), Chris Mitchum (Tuscarora), Victor French (Ketcham), Susana Dosamantes (Maria Carmen), Sherry Lansing (Amelita), David Huddleston (Dr. Jones), Mike Henry (Sheriff Hendricks), Bill Williams (Sheriff Cronin), Jim Davis (Riley), Dean Smith (Bitey), Robert Donner (Whitey), George Plimpton, Robert Rothwell, Chuck Courtney (Whitey's henchmen), Edward Faulkner (Lt. Harris), Peter Jason (Lt. Forsythe).

Hawks appeared in the following documentary films devoted to his work:

1967

Howard Hawks: The Great Professional (BBC-TV)

Producer: Barrie Gavin. Director, writer, and narrator: Nicholas Garnham. Director (of Hawks interview) and interviewer: Peter Bogdanovich. Editor: Howard Billingham. Running time: 60 minutes. First broadcast: July 10. Segment of the BBC-TV series *The Movies.*

1970

Plimpton! Shoot-out at Rio Lobo (David L. Wolper Productions for ABC-TV)

Producer and director: William Kronick. Executive producer: David L. Wolper. Writers: George Plimpton, Kronick. Cinematographers: Michael Margulies, Jules Brenner. Editor: Robert K. Lambert. Music: Walter Scharf. Running time: 52 minutes. First broadcast: December 9.

1973

The Men Who Made the Movies: Howard Hawks (WNET/13, New York, for the Public Broadcasting Service)

Producer, director, writer, and interviewer: Richard Schickel. Cinematographers: John A. Morrill, Erik Daarstad. Editor: Geof Bartz. Narrator: Cliff Robertson. Running time: 58 minutes. First broadcast: November 18.

1978

Ein Verdammt Gutes Leben (*A Hell of a Good Life*) (Sunset Mark Productions, Munich, in association with Bayerischer Rudfunk, Munich)

Director, writer, and interviewer: Hans C. Blumenberg. Cinematographer: Bodo Kessler. Editor: Inge Gielow. TV Editor: Silvia Koller. Sound: Pat Shea. Production coordinator: Juergen Hellwig. Running time: 58 minutes. First shown: March 2, Berlin Film Festival.

1997

Howard Hawks, American Artist (British Film Institute)

Producer: Paula Jalfond. Director, writer, and interviewer: Kevin Macdonald. Running time: 58 minutes. First shown: January 27, National Film Theatre, London.

Acknowledgments

Even though it only began to take shape years later, this book was truly born at the Directors Guild of America's Weekend with Howard Hawks in Laguna Beach, California in October 1977. This outstandingly in-depth tribute was organized by David Shepard, then head of special projects for the guild, and moderated by Joseph McBride. It was the intensity of seeing so many Hawks films in the presence of their maker, and then having the opportunity to talk to him immediately and at length, that ignited my excitement for the man and his work that endured throughout the long period of research and writing. Joe McBride, who had edited *Focus on Howard Hawks* and would eventually edit his numerous interviews with the director into *Hawks on Hawks*, put the challenge to me to write a biography, and I thank him for all his insight, enthusiasm, and assistance.

Hawks on Hawks and Peter Bogdanovich's unpublished full-length career interview with the director, now published in condensed form in *Who The Devil Made It*, were the sources for the majority of Hawks quotes used in the text, and I thank Joe and Peter, who generously provided me with original, unedited copies of their manuscripts.

At the same time, many other Hawks interviews, most of which are listed in the bibliography, have been consulted. Among these, the most useful were the text stemming from the Directors Guild of America's weekend with Hawks; Kevin Brownlow's unpublished investigation into Hawks's silent movie career, and John Kobal's Q & A in his anthology of show-business interviews, *People Will Talk*.

The one centralized collection of Hawks-related material is the "stuff" Hawks himself gave to the Archives and Manuscripts Division of the Harold B. Lee Library at Brigham Young University in Provo, Utah. Hawks maintained his personal papers in haphazard fashion, and only a fraction of what he once possessed was still in his garage when he donated his holdings to BYU shortly before his death. But archivist James V. D'Arc did an immaculate inventory job, and his register of the collection, "The Papers of Howard W. Hawks," itemizes every piece available for study, from a list of Hawks family doctors in the mid-1940s to William Faulkner's personal script copy of *Dreadful Hollow*.

Almost equally valuable is the Charles K. Feldman Collection at the Louis B. Mayer Library at the American Film Institute in Los Angeles. Inventoried and maintained by Alan Braun, the collection represents a treasure trove of inside Hollywood history in general and of Feldman and Hawks's activities in particular. The papers provide ample evidence that one of the great unwritten Hollywood biographies is that of Feldman.

The Hollywood motion picture studios have proved highly variable in their accessibility and their cooperation with scholarly inquiry into Hawks's filming activities. Full information on the director's abundant work at Warner Bros. is available at the Doheny Library at the University of Southern California in Los Angeles. Leith Adams, who admirably oversaw the collection for years, is now at Warners, and the material is presently under the knowledgeable purview of Ned Comstock, as is some archival material from the old Fox Film Corporation and 20th Century–Fox, as well as Universal. The late Peter Knecht generously permitted further access to corporate and legal files at Warner Bros.

The late John Hall opened wide the RKO Pictures files before they were deposited with Special Collections at the University of California, Los Angeles. At UCLA, Brigitte Kueppers meticulously oversees the holdings donated by Fox, which were vital in connection with Hawks's silent career. Samuel Goldwyn Jr. was exceedingly generous in arranging special access to his father's massive collection, which provided a full account of Hawks's work for Goldwyn.

Gaining access to Columbia Pictures files, now that the company is owned by Sony, is not a simple matter for scholars, but Su Lesser and longtime archivist Dennis Wilson proved extraordinarily helpful in permitting a look at the invaluable records pertaining to Hawks's significant work at Columbia. Sherry Lansing, Howard W. Koch, and A. C. Lyles similarly were of great assistance in securing information regarding Hawks's work at Paramount Pictures, but even they could not turn up records from the studio's early years, which have apparently been destroyed.

With the exception of the limited amount of material on file at USC, Universal remains as impenetrable to the film scholar as the image of its famous Black Tower would suggest, and the records of MGM are now, for all intents and purposes, off-limits by policy of the owner of its library, Ted Turner.

The archives of United Artists, especially helpful in regard to *Red River*, are maintained at the Wisconsin State Historical Society in Madison. The Howard Hughes Collection at the Texas State Archives in Austin provided unexpected insight into the long relationship between Hughes and Hawks, although the production, story, and legal files of Hughes's motion picture operation, the Caddo Company, remain buried somewhere within the inaccessible Hughes empire. The reporting of *Variety* over the decades provides an unmatched source of information on the ebb and flow of the film business, as well as of increasingly precise information on the commercial fortunes of individual pictures. Wherever possible, however, budget and box-office figures have been drawn from internal studio records. Many other trade journals, especially more obscure ones from the industry's early days, have been consulted as well, notably *Motion Picture News*, *Kinematograph Weekly*, and *Bioscope*.

Also important was the Archives Department of Los Angeles District Court, where microfilm copies can be found of all the many lawsuits in which Hawks played a part.

Censorship-related correspondence from the Motion Picture Association of America is on file at the Margaret Herrick Library of the Academy of Motion Picture Arts and Sciences in Beverly Hills.

I would like to greatly thank Hawks's two eldest children, David Hawks and Barbara Hawks McCampell, who, with their respective spouses Ginger and Donald, opened their homes to me on numerous occasions and generously answered any and all questions I posed to them. Gregg Hawks and his wife, Penny, also had me to their home and guided me through several fascinating scrapbooks of old clippings and personal and professional photographs.

Many dozens of individuals who knew Hawks and/or worked with him were interviewed for this book. I conducted most of them myself, but several additional interviews were done by Ari Bass, Jonathan Benair, Joan Cohen, Philip Kemp, Kevin Macdonald, and Stephen O'Shea, and I thank them very much for their outstanding help.

By the late 1990s, those with firsthand knowledge of Hollywood's silent era and the golden age of filmmaking are members of an increasingly rare breed. The same project begun today would be impossible to duplicate in its present form simply because so many of the participants have passed away. Among those no longer with us who were particularly helpful were Meta Carpenter Wilde, Hawks's on-and-off secretary and scriptgirl and the epitome of Southern hospitality and graciousness, and Allan Dwan, whose early friendship and collaboration with Hawks provided unique insights into both Howard and Kenneth Hawks. Others now departed who gave interviews or were helpful in other ways were Max Bercutt, Pandro S. Berman, Rafe Blasi, Niven Busch, Stuart Byron, Frank Capra, Hoagy Carmichael, William Clothier, J. J. Cohen, Marcel Dalio, Carl Foreman, John Houseman, Noël Howard, John Huston, Don Hutter, Alfred S. Keller, John Kobal, Hans Koenekamp, Sheldon Leonard, May McAvoy, John Lee Mahin, Sam Marx, Gerald Mast, Earl Miller, Christian Nyby, L. W. O'Connell, Michael Powell, George Raft, Ella Raines, Wells Root, John Russell, Dan Seymour, Alexandre Trauner, Francois Truffaut, King Vidor, and Joseph Walker.

I also want to thank the following people for their important contributions to my work: Mark Adams of the British Film Institute, Norman Alden, Georg Alexander, Army Archerd, Lauren Bacall, Mary Lea Bandy at the Museum of Modern Art, Jeanine Basinger, Hercules Belville, Edward L. Bernds, Barbara Bione, Gerard Blain, Harold Jack Bloom, Peter Bogdanovich, Budd Boetticher, Ken Bowser, Bud Brill, Meredith Brody, Pat H. Broeske, Josh Bryant, Red Buttons, Paul Byrnes, Harry Carey Jr., Al Clark, Robert Cornthwaite, Johnny Crawford, Constance Cummings, Sondra Currie, Jon Davison, Edouard L. Desrochers at Phillips Exeter Academy, Bill Dewhurst, Angie Dickinson, Robert Donner, Clint Eastwood, David Ehrenstein, Bernard Eisenschitz, Ken Eisner, Derek Elley, Patricia Evans, Douglas Fairbanks Jr., Rudi Fehr, Michael Fisher, Sally Fleming, Charles Flynn, William Friedkin, Sam and Christa Fuller, Jack Friend, Michael Friend at the Academy of Motion Picture Arts and Sciences, Doug Galloway, Sam Gill at the Academy of Motion Picture Arts and Sciences, Bob Gitt, Arnold Glassman, Celise Goldman at the Directors Guild of America, Gary Graver, Jane Greer, Lawrence Grobel, Curtis Harrington, Virginia Hawks, Paul Helmick, Mark Horowitz, Jean Howard, Keline Howard, Joe Hyams, Sam Jaffe, Paula Jalfond, Peter Jason, Martin Jurow, Greg Kachel, Richard Keinen, Bruce Kessler, Leonid Kinsky, George Kirgo, Leonard Klady, Erle Krasna, Bill Krohn, Miles Krueger, Edward Lasker, Larry Lasker, Emanuel Levy, Lorraine LoBianco, Serge Losique, Glenn Lovell, Tom Luddy, Don McGlynn, Leonard Maltin, Pat Marlowe, Andy Marx, Arthur Marx, Dick May, Virginia Mayo, Myron Meisel, Robin Mencken, Clive Miller, Robert Mitchum, Dick Moore, D'Arcy O'Brien, Jeannie Olander, Pierre Rissient, Jonathan Rosenbaum, Jane Russell, Gary Salt, Andrew Sarris, Velvet Sheckler, Pierre Schoendorffer, Ben Schwartz, David Schwartz of the Museum of the Moving Image, William Self, David Shepard, Eric Sherman, Vincent Sherman, Lorrie Sherwood, George Sidney, Tony Slide, Dennis Sullivan, Jeffrey Sweet, Bertrand Tavernier, Elaine Thielstrom, David Thompson, Ken Tobey, Andre de Toth, Leonardo Garcia Tsao, Valentin de Vargas, Gwen Verdon, Catherine Verret, Juanita Walker, Cissy Wellman, Chance de Widstedt, Arthur Wilde, Billy Wilder, John Woodcock, Adrian Wootten of the British Film Institute, Fay Wray, Deborah Young, and the staff of the Polytechnic School in Pasadena.

Several people have provided a combination of long-term support and prodding, and I especially thank Florence Dauman, Charles Higham, David Thomson, Patrick McGilligan, and Luc Nemeth on this score. Michael Hamilberg was an early believer and was of great assistance in the early stages of the project.

Sustained encouragement and confidence also came from my parents, Daniel and Barbara McCarthy. My sister Kerry McCarthy Stilwell and her husband Richard Stilwell provided me with a place to work in their home in Virginia during a crucial period, and my wife's parents, Burton and Barbara Alpert, generously made available their home in Santa Fe for a long period of sustained writing.

My editor at *Variety*, Peter Bart, was incredibly understanding, as perhaps only another author can be, of the demands of writing a book, and I thank him for giving me such tremendous latitude at the paper during my stretches of intensive work.

My agent Harvey Klinger applied the cattle prod with an acute sense of timing; Bonnie Thompson was an exacting and exemplary copy editor; and Grove Press's Amy Hundley attended to countless details, large and small, with unfailing scrupulousness. I am deeply indebted to my editor, James Moser. How Jim forged his unique combination of patience, tact, enthusiasm, intelligence, and good humor I may never know, but they were all essential in seeing me through the job to completion.

I will never be able to properly thank my wife, Sasha Alpert, for being so exceedingly tolerant of the demanding rival for my attention that this book has represented, and I hope that our daughter, Madeleine, will excuse her father's bringing up another baby during the first two years of her life.

Notes

Introduction: The Engineer as Poet

Robert Capa's view of Hawks's mythomania was related by Noël Howard.

Hawks's unusual ability to manipulate the big studio bosses was especially stressed to the author by the former Famous Artists agent Martin Jurow.

Truffaut made his remark about Hawks's intelligence and intellectual qualities in numerous interviews, as well as repeatedly in conversation with the author.

Molly Haskell's quote comes from her entry on Hawks in *Cinema: A Critical Dictionary*, volume 1, edited by Richard Roud.

Paul Helmick's remark was made in conversation with the author.

1 Origins

Much background information on the Hawks family and local Indiana history comes from the following sources: Virginia Hawks, the widow of John Hawks, the only surviving member of the Hawks family in Goshen; "History of Waterford," by Harriet Yoder, English Department, Goshen College, January 1934; Elkhart County, Indiana, Index of Names of Persons and of Firms, compiled by the Works Progress Administration of Indiana, Work Project No. 6-20205, volume 1, sponsored by the Indiana State Library, Indianapolis, 1939; *Pioneer History of Elkhart County, Indiana, with Sketches and Stories*, by Henry S. K. Bartholomew, President, Elkhart County Historical Society, Goshen Printery, 1930. *A Twentieth Century History and Biographical Record of Elkhart County, Indiana*, edited by Anthony Deahl, Chicago and New York, Lewis Publishing Co., 1905; *A Standard History of Elkhart County Indiana*, under the editorial supervision of Abraham E. Weaver, 2 vols., Chicago and New York, American Historical Society, 1916; Violett Cemetery, Waterford, Indiana; *Index to Marriage Records Elkhart County, Indiana 1850–1920 Inclusive*, vol. 2, Letters F–K, compiled by Indiana Public Works Administration, 1940; Archives of the *News-Times*, Goshen; *News-Times Goshen City Directory*, 1912; *Goshen City Directory*, 1885–86; *Moore's Standard Directory of Goshen*,

Indiana, 1908–09; Manual of Goshen, Butler & Knox, 1889; *Goshen Sesquicentennial Edition, 1831–1981,* Goshen, News Printing Co.; *History of Neenah,* by G. A. Cunningham, Gazette Printing Establishment, 1878, reprinted by Neenah Historical Society, 1948; *Factories in the Valley—Neenah-Menasha, 1870–1915,* by Charles N. Glaab and Lawrence H. Larsen, State Historical Society of Wisconsin, 1969; *A History of Neenah,* compiled by S. F. Shattuck, in collaboration with the Neenah Historical Society, Neenah, Wisconsin, published privately, 1958; *History of the Fox River Valley, Lake Winnebago and the Green Bay Region,* vols. 1–3, edited by Hon. William A. Titus, Chicago, S. J. Clarke Publishing Co., 1930; *Family Letters: A Personal Selection from Theda Clark's Life,* edited by Suzanne Hart O'Regan, Neenah, Wisconsin, Palmer Publications, 1983; *Ghosts in Sunlight: A Remembrance of Things Past,* by Suzanne Hart O'Regan, Neenah, Wisconsin, Neenah Historical Society, 1985; *Bunn's Winnebago County Directory,* John V. Bunn, publisher, Oshkosh, Globe Printing Co., September 1, 1900; *Bunn's Directory of Winnebago County,* John V. Bunn, publisher, Oshkosh, Globe Printing Co., June 15, 1905; *Dictionary of Wisconsin Biography,* Madison, State Historical Society of Wisconsin, 1960; Hall of Records, Oshkosh, Winnebago County, Wisconsin; Edward Sherry Papers, State Historical Society, Madison, Wisconsin; Neenah Historical Society.

The account of the Howard-Hawks wedding is drawn from the *Neenah Daily Times,* June 6, 1895, p. 1. The account of Howard Hawks's birth is from the *Neenah Daily Times,* June 1, 1896. The account of C. W. Howard's death and funeral comes from the *Neenah Daily Times,* January 6 and 7, 1916, and the *Daily Northwestern,* Oshkosh, January 6, 1916.

2   Boy of Privilege

Information on Pasadena, the Hawks family's life there, and Howard Hawks's education comes from: Barbara Hawks McCampbell; *Pasadena Community Book,* 1951 edition; *Auld Lang Syne,* vols. 43–44, Pasadena Historical Society; Polytechnic Elementary School Announcement, 1912–1913; Pasadena directory, 1909; Private institutional records of the Polytechnic Elementary School (Pasadena), Pasadena High School/Pasadena City College, Citrus Union High School/Citrus College (Glendora), Phillips Exeter Academy (Exeter, New Hampshire), Cornell University (Ithaca), and the University Club (New York City); "Life at Phillips Exeter," bulletin of the Phillips Exeter Academy, vol. 9, no. 3, October 1913; *The 1914 Edition of the Pean,* published by the Senior Class of the Phillips Exeter Academy.

Sources on Victor Fleming include Sam Marx, Allan Dwan, Pat Marlowe, John Lee Mahin, Barbara Hawks McCampbell, and Sally Fleming; a 1928 Paramount biography; a purported "autobiography," *Action Is the Word,* published by MGM in 1939; Norma Shearer's unpublished autobiography; an interview in the *Los Angeles Daily News*, by Virginia Wright, February 2, 1948; obituaries and follow-up stories in the *Los Angeles Times*, *Los Angeles Examiner*, *Hollywood Citizen-News*, *Variety*, the *Hollywood Reporter*, and *Motion Picture Herald*; "Fleming: The Apprentice Years," by John Howard Reid, in *Films & Filming*, January 1968; *The Making of* The Wizard of Oz, by Aljean Harmetz, New York, Alfred A. Knopf, 1977, and the Eddie Sutherland interview, February 1959, conducted by the Popular Arts Project, Columbia University.

Information on Hawks's entry into the film industry and his early work comes from the author's interviews with Allan Dwan; *Allan Dwan*, by Peter Bogdanovich; the Cecil B. DeMille collection at Brigham Young University, and several interviews with Hawks, notably the London session with Kevin Brownlow.

3   Rich Boy in Hollywood

Sources on Hawks's early Hollywood years include the author's interviews with Allan Dwan; Norma Shearer's unpublished autobiography; *Motion Picture News*, published weekly in New York, 1913–1930; *The American Film Institute Catalogue, 1921–1930*; "Famous Players-Lasky Corporation Studio Directory, August 1924"; the Cecil B. DeMille collection at BYU; *Variety*; *Allan Dwan*, by Peter Bogdanovich; the Eddie Sutherland interview for the Popular Arts Project, Columbia University; Victor Fleming's 1928 Paramount biography and 1939 MGM "autobiography," *Action Is the Word*; and the following lawsuits filed in District Court, Los Angeles: J. D. Bach vs. Howard W. Hawks and Kenneth Hawks, January 13, 1921; H. W. Hawks vs. Marshall Neilan, June 9, 1923; Collection Service Corp. vs. H. W. Hawks, January 26, 1923; and William Shea vs. H. W. Hawks and Walter Mitchell, a.k.a. Walter Morosco, December 1, 1923.

4   Showtime

Sources on Hawks's silent-era directing career include the author's interviews with Allan Dwan, May McAvoy, L. W. O'Connell, D'Arcy O'Brien, Barbara Hawks McCampbell, David Hawks; the Fox Film Corp. story, legal, and executive records at the University of California, Los Angeles, and the University of Southern California; the Hawks papers at BYU; *Variety*; *Motion Picture News*; *The American Film Institute Catalogue, 1921–1930*; *Hollywood Filmograph*, a weekly show-business trade paper published in Hollywood throughout the 1920s; *Lulu in Hollywood*, by Louise Brooks; *Louise Brooks*, by Barry Paris; the Louise Brooks interview in *People*

Will Talk, by John Kobal; the British trade papers the *Bioscope* and the *Kinematograph Weekly;* Norma Shearer's unpublished autobiography; *Norma Shearer: A Life,* by Gavin Lambert; *Norma: The Story of Norma Shearer,* by Laurence J. Quirk; *My Story,* by Mary Astor. Henri Langlois's comment is taken from his article "Hawks Homme Moderne," *Cahiers du Cinéma,* January 1963, translated by Russell Campbell and reprinted as "The Modernity of Howard Hawks" in *Focus on Howard Hawks,* edited by Joseph McBride.

5   The Sound Barrier

Sources for this chapter include documents in the Fox Film Corp.; story files at UCLA and USC; *Variety;* the *Bioscope;* the *Kinematograph Weekly;* Tom Luddy; and the following lawsuits filed in District Court, Los Angeles: First National Prods. Corp. vs. H. Hawks and The Caddo Company, March 6, 1931, and Fox Film Corp. vs. Howard and Athole Hawks, May 3, 1932.

6   A New Dawn

Sources for this chapter include Douglas Fairbanks Jr., Fay Wray Rothenberg, and David Hawks; *On the Other Hand: A Life Story,* by Fay Wray; the Warner Bros. legal, story, and production files at USC; the interview with Richard Barthelmess conducted by Arthur B. Friedman of UCLA in 1956, on deposit at the Popular Arts Project collection at Columbia University; *Inside Warner Bros. (1935–1951),* edited by Rudy Behlmer; *Variety; Starmaker: The Autobiography of Hal Wallis,* by Wallis and Charles Higham; documents in the Howard Hughes Collection at the Texas State Archives in Austin, notably a deposition of Hawks taken on September 28, 1977, in connection with the estate case of Howard Robard Hughes Jr. in Probate Court No. 2 of Harris County, Texas; the books on Howard Hughes by Charles Higham and by Peter Harry Brown and Pat H. Broeske. The picture of Kenneth Hawks's death is drawn from the author's interview with L. W. O'Connell; *My Story,* by Mary Astor, and several contemporary accounts, especially those in *Variety,* the *New York Times,* and the *Los Angeles Times.*

7   *The Criminal Code*

Sources for this chapter include the story, legal, and production files of Columbia Pictures at Sony Entertainment; *Variety;* and Philip Kemp's interview with Constance Cummings, conducted on behalf of the author in London.

8   Tough Guys: Hughes, Hecht, Hays and *Scarface*

Sources for this chapter include interviews by the author with George Raft, John Lee
Mahin, and L. W. O'Connell; the Howard Hughes Collection at the Texas State
Archives in Austin; the lawsuit of First National Prods. Corp. vs. H. Hawks and
The Caddo Company, filed in District Court, Los Angeles, March 6, 1931; the
script drafts in the Hawks Collection at BYU; Ben Hecht's papers at the Newberry
Library in Chicago; the biographies of Hughes by Higham, by Brown and Broseke,
and by Donald L. Bartlett and James B. Steele; *Crime Movies: From Griffith to the
Godfather and Beyond*, by Carlos Clarens; *Actor: The Life and Times of Paul Muni*,
by Jerome Lawrence; *George Raft*, by Lewis Yablonsky; *Variety*; *Bashful Billion-
aire*, by Albert B. Gerber, New York, Lyle Stuart, 1967; *United Artists: The Company Built by the Stars*, by Tino Balio, Madison, University of Wisconsin Press,
1976; the W. R. Burnett and John Lee Mahin interviews in *Backstory: Interviews
with Screenwriters of Hollywood's Golden Age*, edited by Pat McGilligan; *Writers
in Hollywood*, by Ian Hamilton; the Ben Hecht entry in *Talking Pictures*, by Richard Corliss; "*Scarface* Returns After 45 Years," by Todd McCarthy, *Daily Variety*,
October 12, 1979; the 1964 Ben Hecht interview in the Popular Arts Project,
Columbia University; *Ben Hecht: The Man Behind the Legend*, by William
MacAdams. The information on the long censorship battle, publicity campaign,
and eventual release of *Scarface* is largely drawn from the Lincoln Quarberg Collection at the Margaret Herrick Library of the Academy of Motion Pictures Arts
and Sciences in Beverly Hills.

9   Back to Warners: *The Crowd Roars*

Sources for this chapter include the author's interviews with Niven Busch, George Raft,
and David Hawks; *Actor: The Life and Times of Paul Muni*, by Jerome Lawrence;
George Raft, by Lewis Yablonsky; the Hawks deposition about his relationship with
Howard Hughes in the Hughes Collection in Austin; the Warner Bros. produc-
tion, story, and legal files at USC; *Cagney: The Actor as Auteur*, by Pat McGillian;
"Niven Busch: A Doer of Things," an interview by David Thomson in *Backstory:
Interviews with Screenwriters of Hollywood's Golden Age*, by Pat McGilligan.

10   *Tiger Shark*

Sources for this chapter include the author's interviews with David Hawks, Barbara Hawks
McCampbell, John Houseman, Wells Root, John Lee Mahin, and King Vidor;
the Warner Bros. production, story, and legal files at USC; *All My Yesterdays: An*

Autobiography, by Edward G. Robinson with Leonard Spigelgass; *Run-Through*, by John Houseman.

11   Sidetracked at MGM: Faulkner, Thalberg and *Today We Live*

Sources for this chapter include the author's interviews with Sam Marx, John Lee Mahin, Wells Root, and Meta Carpenter Wilde; papers in the Hawks Collection at BYU; the lawsuit of Fox Film Corp. vs. Howard and Athole Hawks filed in District Court, Los Angeles, May 3, 1932; the biographies of William Faulkner by Joseph Blotner and Stephen B. Oates; *Faulkner and Film*, by Bruce F. Kawin; *Faulkner's MGM Screenplays*, edited by Kawin; MGM files at Turner Entertainment; *Variety*.

12   *Viva Villa!*

Sources for this chapter include the author's interviews with John Lee Mahin and Sam Marx; papers in the Hawks collection at BYU; *Showman: The Life of David O. Selznick*, by David Thomson; the Ben Hecht papers at the Newberry Library in Chicago; *Ben Hecht: The Man Behind the Legend*, by William MacAdams; the MGM files at Turner Entertainment; *Merchant of Dreams: Louis B. Mayer, MGM and the Secret Hollywood*, by Charles Higham; U.S. Ambassador to Mexico Josephus Daniels's official report on the Lee Tracy incident on file at the National Archives, Washington, D.C.; accounts of the incident in *Daily Variety, Los Angeles Daily News, Los Angeles Evening News, Los Angeles Times, Los Angeles Herald, Los Angeles Post Record, Hollywood Citizen; Mexico Visto por el Cine Extranjero*, vol. 1, by Emilio Garcia Riera, Ediciones ERA, Universidad de Guadalajara, 1987; *El Universal*, Mexico City, November 20, 23, 24, 1933; *Excelsior*, Mexico City, November 22, 23, 1933.

13   Screwball: *Twentieth Century*

Sources for this chapter include the author's interview with Edward Bernds; the Columbia Pictures story, production, and legal files at Sony Entertainment; *The House of Barrymore*, by Margot Peters, New York, Alfred A. Knopf, 1990; *Variety*; the Ben Hecht papers at the Newberry Library; *Ben Hecht: The Man Behind the Legend*, by William MacAdams; the Ben Hecht interviews in the Popular Arts Project at Columbia University.

14   *Barbary Coast*

Sources for this chapter include the author's interview with Meta Carpenter Wilde; the production, story, and legal files of Samuel Goldwyn; the interview with Joel McCrea in *People Will Talk*, by John Kobal; *All My Yesterdays: An Autobiography*, by Edward G. Robinson with Leonard Spigelgass; the Hawks Collection at BYU; *Ben Hecht: The Man Behind the Legend*, by William MacAdams; the Ben Hecht and Walter Brennan interviews in the Popular Arts Project at Columbia University.

15   Flying High: *Ceiling Zero*

Sources for this chapter include the Warner Bros. production, story, and legal files at USC; *Cagney: The Actor as Auteur*, by Pat McGilligan; *I Shot an Elephant in My Pajamas: The Morrie Ryskind Story*, by Morrie Ryskind and John H. Roberts, Lafayette, Louisiana, 1993, 1994; *Variety*.

16   *The Road to Glory*

Sources for this chapter include the author's interviews with Meta Carpenter Wilde and Andre de Toth; the 20th Century–Fox files at UCLA; the Faulkner books by Blotner, Kawin, and Oates; *Variety*; *A Loving Gentleman*, by Meta Carpenter Wilde with Orin Borsten.

17   Include Me Out: *Come and Get It*

Sources for this chapter include the author's interviews with Meta Carpenter Wilde, David Hawks, Samuel Goldwyn Jr., and Sam Marx; the production, story, and legal files of Samuel Goldwyn; *William Wyler*, by Axel Madsen; *Goldwyn: A Biography*, by A. Scott Berg; *Will There Really Be a Morning?*, by Frances Farmer; *Frances Farmer: Shadowland*, by William Arnold; the Walter Brennan interview in the Popular Arts Project at Columbia University; the Joel McCrea interview in *People Will Talk* by John Kobal; *A Loving Gentleman*, by Meta Carpenter Wilde with Orin Borsten; *Variety*; the lawsuit of Howard Hawks vs. Universal Pictures Corporation filed in District Court, Los Angeles, June 16, 1936.

18   Big Spender: RKO, *Gunga Din,* and *Bringing Up Baby*

Sources for this chapter include the author's interviews with Meta Carpenter Wilde, Douglas Fairbanks Jr., Barbara Hawks McCampbell, John Lee Mahin, King Vidor, Frank Capra, Christian Nyby, Vernon Harbin, and Pandro S. Berman; the production, story, and legal files of RKO Pictures; the Faulkner books by Blotner, Kawin, and Oates; *Me,* by Katharine Hepburn; *Kate: The Life of Katharine Hepburn,* by Charles Higham; the Cary Grant books by Beverley Bara Buehrer, Warren G. Harris, Charles Higham and Roy Moseley, Nancy Nelson, Jerry Vermilye, and Geoffrey Wasnell; *Ben Hecht: The Man Behind the Legend,* by William MacAdams; *Norma Shearer: A Life,* by Gavin Lamberg; *Variety;* the records of the Directors Guild of America; *Frank Capra: The Catastrophe of Success,* by Joseph McBride; the Joel McCrea interview in *People Will Talk,* by John Kobal.

19   Only Angels

Sources for this chapter include the author's interviews with King Vidor, Frank Capra, David Hawks, Andre de Toth, Joseph Walker, Al Keller, and John Kobal; the Columbia Pictures production, story, and legal files at Sony Entertainment; the lawsuit of Ben Kaufman vs. Howard Hawks and Donald Miller filed in District Court, Los Angeles, April 6, 1938; the records of the Directors Guild of America; *Variety; Slim: Memories of a Rich and Imperfect Life,* by Slim Keith with Annette Tapert; the Hawks Collection at BYU; the Cary Grant books by Buehrer, Harris, Higham and Moseley, Nelson, Vermilye, and Wasnell; the Richard Barthelmess interview in the Popular Arts Project at Columbia University; the *Chicago Reader.*

20   *His Girl Friday*

Sources for this chapter include the author's interviews with David Hawks, Barbara Hawks McCampbell, Joseph Walker, and Al Keller; the Columbia Pictures production, story, and legal files at Sony Entertainment; the interview with Ben Hecht in the Popular Arts Project at Columbia University; *Ben Hecht: The Man Behind the Legend,* by William MacAdams; the Cary Grant books by Buehrer, Harris, Higham, and Moseley, Nelson, Vermilye, and Wasnell; *Life Is a Banquet,* by Rosalind Russell and Chris Chase, New York, Random House, 1977; *The Columbia Story,* by Clive Hirschhorn, New York, Crown, 1989; the entry on Charles Lederer in *Talking Pictures,* by Richard Corliss; *I Shot an Elephant in My Pajamas,* by Morrie Ryskind; *Variety; Slim: Memories of a Rich and Imperfect Life,* by Slim Keith with Annette Tapert.

21 Slim, Hemingway, and an Outlaw

Sources for this chapter include the author's interviews with Jane Russell, Meta Carpenter Wilde, David Hawks, and Barbara Hawks McCampbell; the Howard Hughes papers at Austin; the Hughes biographies by Donald L. Barlett and James B. Steele, Peter Harry Brown and Pat H. Broeske, and Charles Higham; the interview with Lucien Ballard in *Behind the Camera: The Cinematographer's Art*, by Leonard Maltin, New York, Signet, 1971; *Jane Russell: My Paths and Detours—An Autobiography*, by Jane Russell; *Slim: Memories of a Rich and Imperfect Life*, by Slim Keith with Annette Tapert; the books on Ernest Hemingway by Carlos Baker, Kenneth S. Lynn, Norberto Fuentes, Jeffrey Meyers, and Frank M. Laurence; *Variety*; the divorce papers filed for Athole Hawks by Norma Shearer in Los Angeles, July 24, 1940.

22 *Sergeant York*

Sources for this chapter include the author's interviews with John Huston, Dick Moore, and Vincent Sherman; the Warner Bros. production, story, and legal files at USC; the Hawks Collection at BYU; the Charles K. Feldman Collection at the American Film Institute in Los Angeles; *Variety*.

23 Catching Fire

Sources for this chapter include the author's interviews with Jean Howard, Sam Jaffe, Lauren Bacall, Samuel Goldwyn Jr., Leonid Kinsky, David Hawks, and Billy Wilder; the Charles K. Feldman Collection at the AFI; production, story, and legal files of Samuel Goldwyn; the Hemingway books by Baker, Lynn, Fuentes, Meyers, and Laurence; *Jean Howard's Hollywood: A Photo Memoir*, by Jean Howard; *Merchant of Dreams: Louis B. Mayer, MGM and the Secret Hollywood*, by Charles Higham; *Slim: Memories of a Rich and Imperfect Life*, by Slim Keith with Annette Tapert.

24 *Air Force*

Sources for this chapter include the author's interviews with Christian Nyby, Hans Koenekamp, and Vincent Sherman; the Warner Bros. production, story, and legal files at USC; the Charles K. Feldman Collection at the AFI; the Hemingway books by Baker, Lynn, Fuentes, Meyers, and Laurence; *Slim: Memories of a Rich and Imperfect Life*, by Slim Keith with Annette Tapert; *The World War II Combat Film: Anatomy of a Genre*, by Jeanine Basinger; *Variety*.

25   The Bel-Air Front

Sources for this chapter include the author's interviews with Ella Raines, David Hawks, Barbara Hawks McCampbell, Sally Fleming, Andre de Toth, and Jean Howard; the Warner Bros. production, story, and legal files at USC; the Charles K. Feldman Collection at the AFI; the Faulkner books by Blotner, Kawin, and Oates; *Slim: Memories of a Rich and Imperfect Life*, by Slim Keith with Annette Tapert; *Variety*.

26   Not in the Script:
To Have and Have Not and *The Big Sleep*

Sources for this chapter include the author's interviews with Lauren Bacall, Christian Nyby, Hoagy Carmichael, Meta Carpenter Wilde, Dan Seymour, Marcel Dalio, Sam Marx, Pat Marlowe, Jean Howard, Sheldon Leonard, Miles Krueger; the Warner Bros. production, story, and legal files at USC; the Charles K. Feldman Collection at the AFI; the Hemingway studies by Baker, Fuentes, Lynn, Meyers, and Laurence; the Faulkner books by Blotner, Kawin, and Oates; *Slim: Memories of a Rich and Imperfect Life*, by Slim Keith with Annette Tapert; *By Myself*, by Lauren Bacall; *To Have and Have Not*, screenplay by Jules Furthman and William Faulkner, edited by Bruce F. Kawin; *The Big Sleep*, screenplay by William Faulkner, Leigh Brackett, and Jules Furthman, edited by George P. Garrett, O. B. Hardison Jr., and Jane R. Gelfman; *A Loving Gentleman*, by Meta Carpenter Wilde with Orin Borsten; *Humphrey Bogart*, by Bernard Eisenschitz; *Bogie: The Biography of Humphrey Bogart* and *Bogart and Bacall*, by Joe Hyams; *The Life of Raymond Chandler*, by Frank MacShane; *Selected Letters of Raymond Chandler*, edited by MacShane; "To Have and Have Not Adapted a Novel," by William Rothman; "Who Cares Who Killed Owen Taylor?," by Roger Shatzkin; *Howard Hawks, Storyteller*, by Gerald Mast; James Agee's comment from his review of *To Have and Have Not* in the *Nation*, 159, November 4, 1944; *Sometimes I Wonder: The Story of Hoagy Carmichael*, by Hoagy Carmichael with Stephen Longstreet, New York, Farrar, Straus and Giroux, 1965; *Mes Années Folles*, by Marcel Dalio, Paris, Éditions J. C. Lattes, n.d.; *Variety*; Cecelia Ager's review of *The Big Sleep*, published in *PM* on September 1, 1946; the Motion Picture Association of America files at the Academy of Motion Picture Arts and Sciences.
Material pertaining to Leigh Brackett comes from the Leigh Brackett Collection at Eastern New Mexico University; *Speaking of Science Fiction*, by Paul Walker, Oradell, N.J., Lava, 1978; an interview with Leigh Brackett and Edmond Hamilton conducted by David Turesdale with Paul McGuire, in *Tangent*, Summer 1976; "Leigh B. Hamilton," an oral history by Juanita Roderick and Hugh G. Earnhart, Youngstown State University Oral History Program, October 7, 1975; "A Conversation with Leigh Brackett," an unpublished, undated interview with Steve Swires; "A

Comment on the Hawksian Woman," by Brackett, *Take One*, July-August 1971; "Working with Hawks" by Brackett, *Take One*, October 1972; "From *The Big Sleep* to *The Long Goodbye* and More or Less How We Got There," by Brackett, *Take One*, September-October 1972; Brackett entry in *Dictionary of Literary Biography*, vol. 25, American Screenwriters, Hale Research Company, 1984; "Hawks bad mig skriva manus pa *The Big Sleep*, profile in *Chaplin 154*, Stockholm, February 1978.

27   The Urge to Independence: *Red River*

Sources for this chapter include the author's interviews with Christian Nyby, Harry Carey Jr., William Self, Samuel Fuller, David Hawks, Douglas Fairbanks Jr., Curtis Harrington, Jean Howard; the papers in the Hawks Collection at BYU; the Charles K. Feldman Collection at the AFI; the United Artists Collection at the Wisconsin State Historical Society in Madison; the Motion Picture Association of America files at the Academy of Motion Picture Arts and Sciences; "The Rise and Fall of the American West," an interview with Borden Chase by Jim Kitses, *Film Comment*, Winter 1970–71; the Borden Chase entry in *Talking Pictures*, by Richard Corliss; the Walter Brennan interview in the Popular Arts Project at Columbia University; *John Wayne: American*, by Randy Roberts and James S. Olson; *Shooting Star: A Biography of John Wayne*, by Maurice Zolotow; *Monty: A Biography of Montgomery Clift*, by Robert LaGuardia; *Montgomery Clift: A Biography*, by Patricia Bosworth; *Things I Did and Things I Think I Did*, by Jean Negulesco; *Slim: Memories of a Rich and Imperfect Life*, by Slim Keith with Annette Tapert; *The Making of the Great Westerns*, by William R. Meyer; *The BFI Companion to the Western*, edited by Edward Buscombe; *United Artists: The Company Built by the Stars*, by Tino Balio, Madison: The University of Wisconsin Press, 1936; *Howard Hughes: The Secret Life*, by Charles Higham; *Long Live the King: A Biography of Clark Gable*, by Lyn Tornabene; *Ernest Hemingway: Selected Letters, 1917–1961*, edited by Carlos Baker. Articles about Margaret Sheridan appeared in the *Hollywood Citizen-News*, September 19, 1946; the *Los Angeles Daily News*, January 3, 1951, and May 2, 1951; the *New York Times*, April 1, 1951; and the *Los Angeles Times*, April 22, 1951.

28   Slim Walks, Money Talks

Sources for this chapter include the author's interviews with Christian Nyby, Samuel Goldwyn Jr., David Hawks, Barbara Hawks McCampbell, Samuel Fuller, Edward Lasker, Jane Greer, Virginia Mayo; the production, story, and legal files of Samuel Goldwyn; the Charles K. Feldman Collection at the AFI; *Goldwyn: A Biography*, by A. Scott Berg; *Slim: Memories of a Rich and Imperfect Life*, by Slim Keith with

Annette Tapert; *Life; Variety; Please Don't Hate Me,* by Dmitri Tiomkin and Prosper Buranelli; the Montgomery Clift biographies by LaGuardia and Bosworth; *United Artists: The Company Built by the Stars,* by Tino Balio; the Howard Hughes papers at Austin; the Howard Hughes biographies by Barlett and Steele, Brown and Broeske, and Higham; *Howard Hawks, Storyteller,* by Gerald Mast.

29   Skirting Trouble: *I Was a Male War Bride*

Sources for this chapter include the author's interviews with Ken Tobey, William Self, David Hawks, Barbara Hawks, Edward Lasker, Jane Greer, Christian Nyby, Hoagy Carmichael, Frank Capra, Andre de Toth, A. C. Lyles, Vincent Sherman, John Lee Mahin, Paul Helmick; the Charles K. Feldman Collection at the AFI; the Hawks Collection at BYU; the 20th Century–Fox story files at UCLA; the Motion Picture Association of America files at the Academy of Motion Picture Arts and Sciences; the property settlement agreement between Howard and Nancy Gross Hawks executed on December 31, 1947, the interlocutory judgment of divorce filed May 28, 1949, and the final judgment of divorce granted in Los Angeles Civil Court June 6, 1949; *Variety; Kinematograph Weekly,* December 23, 1948, and February 2 and 17, 1949; "American Directors in Britain," by Irving Silas in *Film and Theatre Today: The European Scene,* edited by Gavin Lambert and J. Clifford King, London, Saturn Press, 1949; the Ann Sheridan interview in *People Will Talk,* by John Kobal; the Cary Grant books by Buehrer, Harris, Higham and Moseley, Nelson, Vermilye, and Wasnell; obituaries of Victor Fleming and follow-up stories in the *Los Angeles Times, Los Angeles Examiner, Hollywood Citizen-News, Variety,* the *Hollywood Reporter, Motion Picture Herald,* January 7–11, 1949; complaints of Athole Dane Hawks vs. Howard Hawks filed in Los Angeles Civil Court, August 31, 1949, and February 10, 1955.

30   An Old Boss, a New Mate

Sources for this chapter include the author's interviews with Christian Nyby, Edward Lasker, Lorrie Sherwood, Jane Greer, Larry Lasker, Ken Tobey, William Self, Robert Cornthwaite, Richard Keinen, Paul Helmick, George Sidney, David Hawks, Barbara Hawks McCampbell, Meta Carpenter Wilde, Arthur Marx, Erle Krasna; the RKO production, story, and legal files; the Charles K. Feldman Collection at the AFI; the Hawks Collection at BYU; the Motion Picture Association of America files at the Academy of Motion Picture Arts and Sciences; *The RKO Story,* by Richard B. Jewell with Vernon Harbin, New York, Arlington House, 1982; *Ben Hecht: The Man Behind the Legend,* by William MacAdams; "Christian Nyby Interview," by Jim Davidson, *Filmfax,* August-September 1992; "There's No Thing like an Old Thing," by Ted Newsome, *Filmfax*, May-June 1989; "Ken Tobey Interview" by Ted Newsome, *Filmfax*, May-June 1989; interview with Hawks by Ezra Goodman, *Los Angeles Daily News*, November 13, 1950; *New York Times* item, November 12, 1950; "The Real *Thing*," by Glenn Lovell, *San Jose Mercury News*, June 27, 1982; unpublished Hawks interview by Glenn Lovell, December 6, 1975; the estimations of *The Thing* by Michael Crichton, Arthur C. Clarke, and John W. Campbell Jr. from *Focus on Science Fiction Film*, Englewood Cliffs, N.J., A Spectrum Book, Prentice-Hall, 1972; *Groucho*, by Hector Arce, New York, G. P. Putnam's Sons, 1979; *The Ragman's Son*, by Kirk Douglas; *Variety*; Hollis Alpert's review of *The Big Sky* in the *Saturday Review*, August 16, 1952.

31 The Fox at Fox: *Monkey Business and Gentlemen Prefer Blondes*

Sources for this chapter include the author's interviews with Jane Russell, Gwen Verdon, Paul Helmick, David Hawks, Barbara Hawks McCampbell, Robert Cornthwaite, Miles Kreuger; the lawsuit of Howard W. Hawks vs. E. Steinkamp Inc., E. J. Neville Co., Inc., Elwain Steinkamp, Donna Steinkamp, J. A. Thompson, doing business as J. A. Thompson & Son, Frank F. Montank, Neil F. Montank, Donald F. Buhler, D. D. Koonce, and Doe I to Doe 350, filed in Santa Monica Civil Court, May 14, 1952; the Hawks Collection at BYU; the Charles K. Feldman Collection at the AFI; the 20th Century–Fox story files at UCLA; the Motion Picture Association of America files at the Academy of Motion Picture Arts and Sciences; the Cary Grant books by Buehrer, Harris, Higham and Moseley, Nelson, Vermilye, and Wasnell; the Jack Cole interview in *People Will Talk*, by John Kobal; *Jane Russell: My Paths and Detours—An Autobiography*, by Jane Russell; the Marilyn Monroe books by Janice Anderson, Richard Buskin, Fred Laurence Guiles, Donald Spoto, and Maurice Zolotow; *Variety*. The article on the shooting of *Gentlemen Prefer Blondes* appeared in the *Los Angeles Daily News*, December 12, 1952.

32 In the Land of the Pharaohs

Sources for this chapter include the author's interviews with Noël Howard, Alexandre Trauner, Harold Jack Bloom, Rudi Fehr, Paul Helmick, Lorrie Sherwood, David Hawks, Barbara Hawks McCampbell, John Huston; the Warner Bros. production, story, and legal files at USC; correspondence between Jack Warner and Hawks from Peter Knecht at Warner Bros.; the Charles K. Feldman Collection at the AFI; the Hawks Collection at BYU; "Genie de Howard Hawks," by Jacques Rivette, *Cahiers du Cinéma*, May 1953; *Variety*; *Hollywood sur Nile*, by Noël Howard, translated by the author in unpublished form as "Pharaohs I Have Known"; *Anything for a Quiet Life,* by Jack Hawkins; *Past Imperfect,* by Joan Collins; *Inside Joan Collins,* by Jay David; the Faulkner books by Blotner, Kawin, and Oates; *Robert Capa,* by Richard Whelan; *Please Don't Hate Me,* by Dimitri Tiomkin and Prosper Buranelli; "Comment Peut-on Être Hitchcocko-Hawksien?" by André Bazin, *Cahiers du Cinéma,* February 1955.

33　Sojourn in Europe

Sources for this chapter include the author's interviews with Chance de Widstedt, Carl Foreman, François Truffaut, John Huston, Lorrie Sherwood, Christian Nyby, David Hawks; Billy Wilder; the Hawks Collection at BYU; the Charles K. Feldman Collection at the AFI; *Variety;* judgment in favor of the plaintiff, Athole Dane Hawks, against the defendant, Howard Hawks, in Los Angeles Civil Court, May 3, 1955; "Howard Hawks" (interview), by Jacques Becker, Jacques Rivette, and François Truffaut, *Cahiers du Cinéma,* February 1956, reprinted in English in *Interviews with Film Directors,* edited by Andrews Sarris; *Groucho,* by Hector Arce; lawsuit of Nancy Gross Hayward vs. Howard W. Hawks & Doe I–X, Roe Corp. I–X, filed in Superior Court, Los Angeles, December 30, 1955; *Dangerous Friends: At Large with Hemingway and Huston in the Fifties,* by Peter Viertel; lawsuit of Howard Hawks doing business as Continental Company, Ltd., a Ltd. Partnership, and Howard Hawks, plaintiff, vs. Warner Bros., filed in Superior Court, Los Angeles, May 18, 1956.

34　Bravo

Sources for this chapter include the author's interviews with Chance de Widstedt, Angie Dickinson, John Russell, Harry Carey Jr., Meta Carpenter Wilde, Budd Boetticher, Paul Helmick, Barbara Hawks McCampbell, David Hawks, Christian Nyby; the Warner Bros. production, story, and legal files at Warner Bros.; the Hawks Collection at BYU; the Charles K. Feldman Collection at the AFI; the Motion Picture Association of America files at the Academy of Motion Picture Arts and Sciences; *John Wayne: American,* by Randy Roberts and James S. Olson; *Dino: Living High in the Dirty Business of Dreams,* by Nick Tosches; *Teenage Idol, Travelin' Man: The Complete Biography of Rick Nelson,* by Philip Bashe; *The Making of the Great Westerns,* by William R. Meyer; *The BFI Companion to the Western,* edited by Edward Buscombe; the Leigh Brackett Collection at Eastern New Mexico University; *Please Don't Hate Me,* by Dimitri Tiomkin and Prosper Buranelli; *Variety;* "Howard Hawks" by Jean-Pierre Coursodon in *American Directors,* vol. 1, edited by Coursodon with Pierre Sauvage; "Howard Hawks" by Molly Haskell in *Cinema:*

A *Critical Dictionary*, vol. 1, edited by Richard Roud; *Howard Hawks*, by Robin Wood; divorce suit of Donna H. Hawks vs. Howard W. Hawks filed in Santa Monica District Court, October 1, 1959.

35 Fun in the Bush: *Hatari!*

Sources for this chapter include the author's interviews with Chance de Widstedt, Red Buttons, Gerard Blain, Valentin de Vargas, Bud Brill, Edward Lasker, Paul Helmick, Peter Bogdanovich, David Hawks; Paramount Pictures files; the Hawks Collection at BYU; the Charles K. Feldman Collection at the AFI; *John Wayne: American,* by Randy Roberts and James S. Olson; *Sono come Sono: Dalla Dolce Vita e Ritorno,* by Elsa Martinelli; "High Adventure on Location" by Howard Hawks, *Hollywood Reporter,* November 14, 1961; the Leigh Brackett Collection at Eastern New Mexico University; the unpublished interview with Leigh Brackett by Steve Swires; interview with Leigh Brackett in *Speaking of Science Fiction,* by Paul Walker, Oradell, N.J., Lava, 1978; *Did They Mention the Music?,* by Henry Mancini with Gene Lees; *Variety; Just Resting,* by Leo McKern, London, Methuen, 1983; interview with John Wayne by Charles Higham, Hollywood Film Industry Oral History Project, July 6, 1971, at Columbia University; *The Cinema of Howard Hawks,* by Peter Bogdanovich; *Movie,* no. 5, December 1962; "The World of Howard Hawks," by Andrew Sarris in *Films and Filming* 8, nos. 10 and 11, July and August 1962, adapted from a 1961 article in the *New York Film Bulletin; Auteurism,* Hawks, *Hatari!* and Me," by Stuart Byron in *Favorite Movies,* edited by Philip Nobile.

36 A Fishy Story: *Man's Favorite Sport?*

Sources for this chapter include the author's interviews with Paul Helmick, David Hawks, Angie Dickinson, Norman Alden, Bruce Kessler; Universal files at USC; the Charles K. Feldman Collection at the AFI; the Leigh Brackett Collection at Eastern New Mexico University; *Variety; Rock Hudson: A Bio-Bibliography,* by Brenda Scott Royce; "*Man's Favorite Sport?* (Revisited)" by Molly Haskell, *Village Voice,* January 21, 1971, reprinted in *Focus on Howard Hawks,* edited by Joseph McBride.

37 Fast Cars and Young Women

Sources for this chapter include the author's interviews with George Kirgo, Paul Helmick, Howard W. Koch, A. C. Lyles, Christian Nyby, Pierre Rissient, Chance de Widstedt, Robert Mitchum, John Woodcock, Bruce Kessler, Cissy Wellman, Norman Alden,

Robert Donner, Johnny Crawford; Kevin Macdonald's interview with James Caan; Paramount Pictures files; the Charles K. Feldman Collection at the AFI; the Motion Picture Association of America files at the Academy of Motion Pictures Arts and Sciences; the Leigh Brackett Collection at Eastern New Mexico University; the incompetency case of Athole Dane Hawks filed in Superior Court, Los Angeles, September 5, 1963; James Caan interviews in *Game*, April 1975, and with Times Newspapers Ltd., May 5, 1991; the Harold Rosson interview in *Behind the Camera: The Cinematographer's Art*, by Leonard Maltin, New York, Signet, 1971; *John Wayne: American*, by Randy Roberts and James S. Olson; *Variety*; "The Namedropper Drops Howard Hawks, John Wayne, Robert Mitchum and James Caan, *El Dorado*, Part II," by John M. Woodcock in *Cinemeditor*, July 24, 1995; "The Namedropper Drops Arthur Hunnicut, Ed Asner, Chris George, Robert Donner, R. G. Armstrong, *El Dorado*, Part III" by John M. Woodcock, unpublished.

38   The Last Roundup

Sources for this chapter include the author's interviews with George Kirgo, Sherry Lansing, Sondra Currie, John Woodcock, Pierre Schoendorffer, Chance de Widstedt, Paul Helmick, Pierre Rissient, Bertrand Tavernier, Peter Bogdanovich, William Clothier, Peter Jason, Robert Donner; Paramount Pictures files; "Entretien avec Howard Hawks," by Jean-Louis Comolli, Jean Narboni, and Bertrand Tavernier, *Cahiers du Cinéma*, July-August 1967; "Journey into Light" (interview with Bertrand Tavernier), by Patrick McGilligan, *Film Comment*, March-April 1992; the Leigh Brackett Collection at Eastern New Mexico University; *Variety*; "The Gray Fox Is Back at It," by Wayne Warga, *Los Angeles Times*, May 24, 1970; *Plimpton! Shoot-out at Rio Lobo*, ABC-TV special broadcast December 9, 1970.

39   From Sand to Dust

Sources for this chapter include the author's interviews with Peter Bogdanovich, Chance de Widstedt, William Friedkin, George Kirgo, Lauren Bacall, Clint Eastwood, Pierre Schoendorffer, Sondra Currie, Tom Luddy, Robin Mencken, Angie Dickinson, Paul Helmick, Charles Flynn, Jonathan Rosenbaum, Pierre Rissient, Bertrand Tavernier, Barbara Hawks McCampbell, Cissy Wellman. *The American Cinema: Directors and Directions, 1929–1968*, by Andrew Sarris; unpublished Hawks interview by Glenn Lovell, December 6, 1975; "Journey into Light" (interview with Bertrand Tavernier), by Patrick McGilligan, Film Comment; *The Men Who Made the Movies*, by Richard Schickel; "Hawks on Film, Politics, and Childrearing," interview with Hawks by Constance Penley, Saunie Salyer, and Michael Shedlin, *Jump Cut*, January-February 1975; "Hawks Isn't Good Enough," by Raymond

Durgnat, *Film Comment*, March-April 1978; "Hawks vs. Durgnat," by William Paul, *Film Comment*, January-February 1978; "Durgnat vs. Paul: Last Round in the Great Hawks Debate" by Durgnat, *Film Comment*, July-August 1978; "Hawks," by Joseph McBride, *Film Comment*, March-April 1978; "Director's Life Saved by His Dog," by Lynn Burns, *Desert Sun*, December 14, 1977; "Hollywood Doesn't Live Here Anymore," by Robert Parrish; obituaries in world newspapers, December 26 and 27.

40   Posterity

Sources for this chapter include the author's interviews with Barbara Hawks McCampbell, David Hawks, Michael Powell, Max Bercutt, Clint Eastwood, James D'Arc; *The New Hollywood: What the Movies Did with the New Freedoms of the Seventies*, by James Bernardoni; John Carpenter interview, *DGA Magazine*, July-August 1966; "'There's Something Deeply Moving About Ordinary Life,'" interview with Robert Benton by Christian Keathley, *Film Comment*, January–February 1995. Quentin Tarantino comments are from an interview by Lynn Hirschberg, *Vanity Fair*, July 1995, an interview in the *Village Voice* by Lisa Kennedy, October 25, 1994, and *Quentin Tarantino: The Cinema of Cool*, by Jeff Dawson, New York, Applause Books, 1995.

Bibliography

Adair, Gilbert. "Bringing Up Baby." *Flickers: An Illustrated Celebration of 100 Years of Cinema*. London: Faber & Faber, 1995.

Anderson, Janice. *Marilyn Monroe*. New York: Crescent Books, 1983.

Apra, Adriano, and Patrizia Pistagnesi, eds. *Il Cinema di Howard Hawks*. Venice: La Biennale di Venezia, 1981.

Arce, Hector. *Groucho*. New York: G. P. Putnam's Sons, 1974.

Arnold, William. *Frances Farmer: Shadowland*. New York: McGraw-Hill, 1978.

Astor, Mary. *My Story*. New York: Doubleday, 1959.

Bacall, Lauren. *By Myself*. New York: Knopf, 1979.

Baker, Carlos. *Ernest Hemingway: A Life Story*. New York: Charles Scribner's Sons, 1969.

——, ed. *Ernest Hemingway: Selected Letters, 1917–1961*. New York: Charles Scribner's Sons, 1981.

Barllett, Donald L., and James B. Steele. *Empire: The Life, Legend and Madness of Howard Hughes*. New York: W. W. Norton, 1979.

Bashe, Philip. *Teenage Idol, Travelin' Man: The Complete Biography of Rick Nelson*. New York: Hyperion, 1992.

Basinger, Jeanine. *The World War II Combat Film: Anatomy of a Genre*. New York: Columbia University Press, 1986.

Bazin, Andre. "Comment Peut-on Être Hitchcocko-Hawksien?" *Cahiers du Cinéma* February 1955.

Becker, Jacques, Jacques Rivette, and François Truffaut. "Howard Hawks." Interview. *Cahiers du Cinéma* February 1956. Rpt. in English trans. in *Interviews with Film Directors*. Ed. Andrew Sarris. New York: Avon Books, 1967.

Behlmer, Rudy, ed. *Inside Warner Bros. (1935–1951)*. New York: Viking, 1985.

Bellinger, Martial, ed. *Est Cine Club: Howard Hawks* Metz. 22 (Spring 1963).

Belton, John. "Hawks and Co." *Cinema* (U.K.) 9 (1971). Rpt. in *Focus on Howard Hawks*. Ed. Joseph McBride. Englewood Cliffs, N.J.: Prentice-Hall, 1972.

——. *The Hollywood Professionals*. Vol. 3 of *Howard Hawks, Frank Borzage, and Edgar G. Ulmer*. New York: A. S. Barnes, 1974.

Berg, A. Scott. *Goldwyn: A Biography*. New York: Knopf, 1989.

Bernardoni, James. *The New Hollywood: What the Movies Did with the New Freedoms of the Seventies*. Jefferson, N.C.; London: McFarland & Co., 1991.

713

Bernstein, Judith. "The Valley of the Shadow." *Focus!* 8 (1972).

Blotner, Joseph. *Faulkner: A Biography*. Vol. 1 and 2. New York, Random House, 1974. Revised, updated, and condensed one-volume edition, 1984.

———. ed. *Selected Letters of William Faulkner*. London: Scolar Press, 1977.

Blumenberg, Hans C. *Die Kamera in Augenhöhe: Begegnungen mit Howard Hawks*. Kohn: DuMont Buchverlag, 1979.

Bogdanovich, Peter. *Allan Dwan: The Last Pioneer*. New York: Praeger, 1971.

———. *The Cinema of Howard Hawks*. New York: Museum of Modern Art Film Library, 1962. Interview reprinted in *Movie* (December 1962) and in French translation in *Cahiers du Cinéma* (January 1963).

———. *"Hatari!" Film Culture* 25 (Summer 1962).

———. *Pieces of Time: Peter Bogdanovich on the Movies*. New York: Arbor House–Esquire, 1973.

———. *Who The Devil Made It*. New York: Alfred A. Knopf, 1997. Contains edited version of the author's career interview with Hawks.

Bosworth, Patricia. *Montgomery Clift: A Biography*. New York: Harcourt Brace Jovanovich, 1978.

Bourget, Jean-Loup. "Hawks et le Mythe de l'Ouest American." *Positif* 195–96 (July-August 1977).

Brackett, Leigh. "A Comment on the Hawksian Woman." *Take One* July-August 1971.

———. "From *The Big Sleep* to *The Long Goodbye* and More or Less How We Got There." *Take One* 4.1 (September-October 1972).

———. "Working with Hawks." *Take One* 3.6 (October 1972). Rpt. in *Women and the Cinema*. Ed. Karen Kay and Gerald Peary. New York: E. P. Dutton, 1977.

Branson, Clark. *Howard Hawks: A Jungian Study*. Santa Barbara: Garland-Clarke Editions, Capra Press, 1987.

Brantley, Robin. "What Makes a Star? Howard Hawks Knew Best of All." *The New York Times* January 22, 1978.

Brooks, Louise. *Lulu in Hollywood*. New York: Alfred A. Knopf, 1982.

Brown, Peter Harry, and Pat H. Broeske. *Howard Hughes: The Untold Story*. New York: Dutton, 1996.

Brownlow, Kevin. *Howard Hawks*. Unpublished interview covering his silent career, conducted in London, June 30, 1967.

———. *The Parade's Gone By . . .* New York: Alfred A. Knopf, 1968.

Buehrer, Beverley Bare. *Cary Grant: A Bio-Bibliography*. New York: Greenwood Press, 1990.

Buscombe, Edward, ed. *The BFI Companion to the Western*. New York: Atheneum, 1988.

Buskin, Richard. *The Films of Marilyn Monroe*. Lincolnwood, Ill.: Publications International, Ltd. 1992.

Byron, Stuart. "*Auteurism*, Hawks, *Hatari!*, and Me." In *Favorite Movies*. Ed. Philip Nobile. New York: Macmillan, 1973.

Carcassonne, Philippe. "Candide et l'Ombre de la Loi." *Cinematographe* March 1978.

Carey, Gary. *Doug and Mary: A Biography of Douglas Fairbanks and Mary Pickford.* New York: E. P. Dutton, 1977.

Cary Grant: In the Spotlight. New York: Galley Press, 1980.

Chase, Borden. "The Rise and Fall of the American West." Interview with Jim Kitses. *Film Comment* Winter 1970–71.

Ciment, Michel. "Entretien avec Howard Hawks." *Positif* 195–96 (July-August 1977).

———. "Hawks et l'Ecrit." *Positif* 195–96 (July-August 1977).

Clarens, Carlos. *Crime Movies: From Griffith to the Godfather and Beyond.* New York: W. W. Norton, 1980.

Clark, Al. *Raymond Chandler in Hollywood.* London, Proteus, 1982. Rpt. Beverly Hills: Silman-James Press, 1996.

Collins, Joan. *Past Imperfect.* New York: Simon and Schuster, 1978, 1984.

Comolli, Jean-Louis. "Howard Hawks Aujourd'hui." *Cahiers du Cinéma* 160 (November 1964).

Comolli, Jean-Louis, Narboni, Jean, and Tavernier, Bertrand. "Entretien avec Howard Hawks." *Cahiers du Cinéma* 192 (July-August 1967).

Corliss, Richard, ed. *The Hollywood Screenwriters.* New York: Avon Books, 1972.

———. *Talking Pictures.* Woodstock, New York: Overlook Press, 1974.

Cornell, Brian. *Knight Errant: A Biography of Douglas Fairbanks, Jr.* New York: Doubleday, 1955.

Coursodon, Jean-Pierre. "Howard Hawks." In *American Directors*, vol. I. Ed. Jean-Pierre Coursodon with Pierre Sauvage. New York: McGraw-Hill, 1983.

Dardis, Tom. *Some Time in the Sun.* New York: Charles Scribner's Sons, 1976.

David, Jay. *Inside Joan Collins.* New York: Carroll & Graf, 1988.

Davidson, Jim. "Christian Nyby Interview." *Filmfax* 34 (August-September 1992).

Decaux, Emmanuel. "Delicates Balances." *Cinématographe* March 1978.

Devillers, Michel. "Frontieres de l'Eldorado." *Cinématographe* March 1978.

Dirigido por . . . Howard Hawks 24 (June 1975). Special issue. Barcelona: Climent, Edmundo Orts.

Douglas, Kirk. *The Ragman's Son.* New York: Simon & Schuster, 1988.

Durgnat, Raymond. "Durgnat vs. Paul: Last Round in the Great Hawks Debate." *Film Comment* March-April 1978.

———. "Hawks Isn't Good Enough." *Film Comment* July-August 1977.

Eisenschitz, Bernard. *Humphrey Bogart.* Paris: Le Terrain Vague, 1967.

Eyquem, Olivier. "Howard Hawks, Ingenieur." *Positif* 195–96 (July-August 1977).

Farber, Manny. "Howard Hawks." *Artforum* April 1969. Rpt. in *Negative Space*. Manny Farber. New York: Praeger, 1971. Rpt. in *Focus on Howard Hawks*. Ed. Joseph McBride. Englewood Cliffs, N.J.: Prentice-Hall, 1972.

———. "Underground Films." *Commentary* November 1957. Rpt. in *Negative Space*, Manny Farber. New York: Praeger, 1971.

Farmer, Frances. *Will There Really Be a Morning?* New York: G. P. Putnam's Sons, 1972.

Faulkner, William, Leigh Brackett, and Jules Furthman. *The Big Sleep.* Screenplay, from the novel by Raymond Chandler. In *Film Scripts One*. Ed. George P. Garrett, O. B. Hardison Jr., and Jane R. Gelfman. New York: Appleton-Century-Crofts, 1971.

Fieschi, Jacques. "Négligé et Tweed Bourru." *Cinématographe* March 1978.

Film Dope 23 (September 1981).

French, T. L. [Krohn, Bill]. "*Land of the Pharaohs.*" *Modern Times* 4 (April 1990).

Fuentes, Norberto. *Hemingway in Cuba*. Secaucus, N.J.: Lyle Stuart, 1984.

Furthman, Jules, and William Faulkner. *To Have and Have Not*. Screenplay, from the novel by Ernest Hemingway. Ed. Bruce F. Kawin. Madison: University of Wisconsin Press, 1979.

Gallagher, John, and Sam Sarowitz. "Truffaut: The Man Who Loved Movies." *Grand Illusions* Winter 1977.

Gili, Jean A. *Howard Hawks*. *Cinema d'Aujourd'hui* (series). Paris: Editions Seghers, 1971.

Goodwin, Michael, and Naomi Wise. "An Interview with Howard Hawks." *Take One* 3.8 (November-December 1971; published March 1, 1973).

Guiles, Fred Laurence. *Legend: The Life and Death of Marilyn Monroe*. New York: Stein & Day, 1984.

Hamilton, Ian. *Writers in Hollywood, 1915–1951*. New York: Harper & Row, 1990.

Harris, Warren G. *Cary Grant: A Touch of Elegance*. New York: Doubleday, 1987.

Haskell, Molly. *From Reverence to Rape*. New York: Holt, Rinehart and Winston, 1973.

———. "Howard Hawks." In *Cinema: A Critical Dictionary*, vol. I. Ed. Richard Roud. London: Secker and Warburg, and New York: Viking Press, 1980.

———. "Howard Hawks: Masculine Feminine." *Film Comment* March-April 1974.

Hawkins, Jack. *Anything for a Quiet Life*. New York: Stein & Day, 1974.

Hecht, Ben, Seton I. Miller, John Lee Mahin, W. R. Burnett, and Fred Pasley. *Scarface*. Screenplay, in French translation, from the novel by Armitage Trail. In *L'Avant-scene du Cinema* 132 (1973).

Hemingway, Ernest. *To Have and Have Not*. New York: Scribner, 1937.

Hepburn, Katharine. *Me: Stories of My Life*. New York: Knopf, 1991.

Higham, Charles. *Howard Hughes: The Secret Life*. New York: G. P. Putnam's Sons, 1993.

———. *Kate: The Life of Katharine Hepburn*. New York: W. W. Norton, 1975.

———. *Merchant of Dreams: Louis B. Mayer, MGM and the Secret Hollywood*. New York: Donald I. Fine, 1994.

Higham, Charles, and Roy Moseley. *Cary Grant: The Lonely Heart*. New York: Harcourt Brace Jovanovich, 1989.

Hillier, Jim, ed. *Cahiers du Cinéma: the 1950s: Neo-realism, Hollywood, New Wave*. Cambridge, Mass.: Harvard University Press, 1985.

Hillier, Jim, and Peter Wollen. *Howard Hawks, American Artist*. London: British Film Institute, 1997.

Hotchner, A. E. *Papa Hemingway: A Personal Memoir*. New York: Random House, 1966.

Houseman, John. *Run-through*. New York: Simon and Schuster, 1972.

Howard Hawks: A Weekend with the Director and His Films. Los Angeles: Directors Guild of America, Educational and Benevolent Foundation, Special Projects, 1979.

Howard, Jean. *Jean Howard's Hollywood: A Photo Memoir*. New York: Harry N. Abrams, 1989.

Howard, Noël. *Hollywood sur Nile*. Paris: Librairie Artheme Fayard, 1978.

Hyams, Joe. *Bogart and Bacall*. New York: Warner Books, 1976.

———. *Bogie: The Biography of Humphrey Bogart*. New York: Signet, 1967.

Jameson, Richard T. "People Who Need People." *Movietone News* 40 (April 1975).

———. "Talking and Doing in *Rio Bravo*." *Velvet Light Trap* 12 (Spring 1974).

Kawin, Bruce F. *Faulkner and Film*. New York: Frederick Unger, 1977.

———, ed. *Faulkner's MGM Screenplays*. Knoxville: University of Tennessee Press, 1982.

Keith, Slim, with Annette Tapert. *Slim: Memories of a Rich and Imperfect Life*. New York: Simon and Schuster, 1990.

Kepley, Vance, Jr. "Spatial Articulations in the Classical Cinema: A Scene from *His Girl Friday*." *Wide Angle* 5.3 (1983).

Kidd, Charles. *Debrett Goes to Hollywood*. New York: St. Martin's Press, 1986.

Kobal, John. *People Will Talk*. New York: Knopf, 1985.

LaGuardia, Robert. *Monty: A Biograpyhy of Montgomery Clift*. New York: Arbor House, 1977.

Lambert, Gavin. *Norma Shearer: A Life*. New York: Alfred A. Knopf, 1990.

Laurence, Frank M. *Hemingway and the Movies*. New York: Da Capo Press, 1981.

Lawrence, Jerome. *Actor: The Life and Times of Paul Muni*. New York: G. P. Putnam's Sons, 1974.

Legrand, Gerard. "Petit Discours de la Méthode de H.H." *Positif* 195–96 (July-August 1977).

Lehman, Peter, et al. "Howard Hawks: A Private Interview." *Wide Angle* Summer 1976.

Lovell, Glenn. *Howard Hawks*. Unpublished interview, conducted in Palm Springs, December 6, 1975.

Luhr, William. "Howard Hawks: Hawksthief." *Wide Angle* 1.2 (Summer 1976).

Lynn, Kenneth S. *Hemingway*. New York: Simon & Schuster, 1987.

MacAdams, William. *Ben Hecht: The Man Behind the Legend*. New York: Charles Scribner's Sons, 1990.

MacShane, Frank. *The Life of Raymond Chandler*. New York: E. P. Dutton, 1976.

———, ed. *Selected Letters of Raymond Chandler*. New York: Columbia University Press, 1981.

Madsen, Axel. *William Wyler*. New York: Thomas Y. Crowell, 1973.

Majlos, Lester [James Stoller]. "Hawks at 70: 'Red Line 7000.'" In *Moviegoer* No. 3 (Summer 1966), p. 60.

Mancini, Henry, with Gene Lees. *Did They Mention the Music?* Chicago: Contemporary Books, 1989.

Martinelli, Elsa. *Sono come Sono: Dalla Dolce Vita e Ritorno*. Milan: Rusconi, 1995.

Masson, Alain. "Organiser le Sensible." *Positif* 195–96 (July-August 1977).

Mast, Gerald. *Howard Hawks, Storyteller*. New York: Oxford: Oxford University Press, 1982.

Mate, Ken, and Pat McGilligan. "W. R. Burnett: The Outsider." Interview. *Backstory:*

Interviews with Screenwriters of Hollywood's Golden Age. Berkeley: University of California Press, 1986.

McBride, Joseph, ed. *Focus on Howard Hawks.* Englewood Cliffs, N.J.: Prentice-Hall, 1972.

——. *Frank Capra: The Catastrophe of Success.* New York: Simon and Schuster, 1992.

——. "Hawks." *Film Comment* March-April 1978.

——. *Hawks on Hawks.* Berkeley: University of California Press, 1982.

McCarthy, Todd. "Phantom Hawks." *Film Comment* 18.5 (September-October 1982).

McCarthy, Todd, and Joseph McBride. "Bombshell Days in the Golden Age." Interview with John Lee Mahin. *Film Comment* March-April 1980. Rpt. in *Backstory: Interviews with Screenwriters of Hollywood's Golden Age.* Ed. Pat McGilligan. Berkeley: University of California Press, 1986.

McGilligan, Pat. *Backstory: Interviews with Screenwriters of Hollywood's Golden Age.* Berkeley: University of California Press, 1986.

——. *Cagney: The Actor as Auteur.* San Diego: A. S. Barnes, 1982.

Meyer, William R. *The Making of the Great Westerns.* New Rochelle: Arlington House, 1979.

Meyers, Jeffrey. *Hemingway: A Biography.* New York: Harper & Row, 1985.

Milner, Michael. *Hatari!* New York: Pocket Books, 1962.

Missaien, Jean-Claude. *Howard Hawks. Classiques du Cinéma* (series). Paris: Editions Universitaires, 1966.

Monaco, James. "Notes on *The Big Sleep* Thirty Years After." *Sight and Sound* 44.1 (Winter 1974-75).

Murphy, Kathleen. "Howard Hawks: An American Auteur in the Hemingway Tradition." Ph.D. diss. University of Washington, 1977.

——. "Of Babies, Bones and Butterflies." *Movietone News* 54 (June 1977).

Negulesco, Jean. *Things I Did and Things I Think I Did.* New York: Linden Press–Simon & Schuster, 1984.

Nelson, Nancy. *Evenings with Cary Grant: Recollections in His Own Words and by Those Who Knew Him Best.* New York: William Morrow, 1991.

Newsome, Ted. "Ken Tobey Interview." *Filmfax* 15 (May-June 1989).

——. "There's No Thing like an Old 'Thing.'" *Cinéfantastique* 13.2–3 (November-December 1982).

Nichols, Dudley. *Air Force.* Screenplay. Ed. Lawrence Howard Suid. Madison: University of Wisconsin Press, 1973.

Oates, Stephen B. *William Faulkner: The Man and the Artist.* New York: Harper & Row, 1987.

O'Regan, Suzanne Hart. *Family Letters: A Personal Selection from Theda Clark's Life.* Neenah, Wisc.: Palmer Publications, 1983.

——. *Ghosts in Sunlight: A Remembrance of Things Past.* Neenah, Wisc.: Neenah Historical Society, 1985.

Orr, Christopher. "Authorship in the Hawks/Wyler Film, *Come and Get It." Wide Angle* 6.1 (1984).

Paris, Barry. *Louise Brooks.* New York: Alfred A. Knopf, 1994.

Paul, William. "Hawks vs. Durgnat." *Film Comment* January-February 1978.

Peary, Gerald, and Stephen Groark. "Hawks at Warner Brothers: 1932." *Velvet Light Trap* 1 (June 1971).

Penley, Constance, Saunie Salyer, and Michael Shedlin. "Hawks on Film, Politics, and Childrearing." *Jump Cut* 5 (January-February, 1975).

Perkins, V. F. "Comedies." *Movie* 5 (December 1962). Rpt. as "Hawks' Comedies" in *The Movie Reader.* Ed. Ian Cameron. New York: Praeger, 1972.

———. *"Hatari!" Movie* 5 (December 1962). Rpt. in *The Movie Reader.* Ed. Ian Cameron. New York, Praeger, 1972.

Plimpton, George. "The Amateur Strikes Again." *TV Guide* December 5, 1970.

Poague, Leland A. *Howard Hawks.* Boston: Twayne Publishers, 1982.

Quirk, Laurence J. *Norma: The Story of Norma Shearer.* New York: St. Martin's Press, 1988.

Richards, Jeffrey. "The Silent Films of Howard Hawks." *Focus on Film* Summer-Autumn 1976.

Rivette, Jacques. "L'Essentiel." *Cahiers du Cinéma* 32 (February 1954).

———. "Genie de Howard Hawks." *Cahiers du Cinéma* 23 (May 1953). Rpt. in English translation as "The Genius of Howard Hawks" in *Focus on Howard Hawks.* Ed. Joseph Mcbride. Englewood Cliffs, N.J.: Prentice-Hall, 1972.

———. "Notes sur une Revolution." *Cahiers du Cinéma* 54 (Christmas 1955).

Roberts, Randy, and James S. Olson. *John Wayne: American.* New York: The Free Press, 1995.

Robinson, Edward G., with Leonard Spigelgass. *All My Yesterdays: An Autobiography.* New York: Hawthorne Books, 1973.

Rohmer, Eric. "Redecouvrir l'Amérique." *Cahiers du Cinéma* 54 (Christmas 1955).

Rothman, William. "To Have and Have Not Adapted a Novel." In *The Modern American Novel and the Movies.* Ed. Gerald Peary and Roger Shatzkin. New York: Frederick Ungar Publishing Co., 1978.

Royce, Brenda Scott. *Rock Hudson: A Bio-Bibliography.* Westport, Connecticut: Greenwood Press, 1995.

Ruddy, Jonah, and Jonathan Hill. *The Bogey Man: Portrait of a Legend.* London: Souvenir Press, 1965.

Russell, Jane. *Jane Russell: My Paths and Detours—An Autobiography.* New York: Franklin Watts, 1985.

Sarris, Andrew. *The American Cinema: Directors and Directions, 1929–1968.* New York: E. P. Dutton, 1968.

———. "Hawksian Comedy." In *Movie Comedy.* Ed. Stuart Byron and Elisabeth Weis. New York: Penguin Books, 1977.

——. "The World of Howard Hawks." *Films and Filming* 8.10 and 11 (July and August) 1962, adapted from a 1961 article by Sarris in *The New York Film Bulletin*. Rpt. in *Focus on Howard Hawks*. Ed. Joseph McBride. Englewood Cliffs, N.J.: Prentice-Hall, 1972.

Schickel, Richard. *His Picture in the Papers: A Speculation on Celebrity in America Based on the Life of Douglas Fairbanks Sr.* New York: Charterhouse, 1973.

——. *The Men Who Made the Movies*. New York: Atheneum, 1975.

——. *Schickel on Film*. New York: William Morrow, 1989.

Shatzkin, Roger. "Who Cares Who Killed Owen Taylor?" In *The Modern American Novel and the Movies*. Ed. Gerald Peary and Roger Shatzkin. New York: Frederick Ungar Publishing Co., 1978.

Shearer, Norma. "Autobiography." Unpublished, uncompleted memoir covering the author's life through the mid-1930s.

Shivas, Mark. "Blondes." *Movie* 5 (December 1962). Rpt. in *The Movie Reader*. Ed. Ian Cameron. New York: Praeger, 1972.

Silke, James R., Serge Daney, and Jean-Louis Noames. "Entretien avec Howard Hawks." *Cahiers du Cinéma* November 1965.

Sijan, Slobodan. "Un Image de *Rio Bravo*." *Positie* 400 (June 1994).

Simsolo, Noel. *Howard Hawks*. Paris: Edilig, 1984.

Spoto, Donald. *Marilyn Monroe: The Biography*. New York: HarperCollins, 1993.

Tavernier, Bertrand, and Jean-Pierre Coursodon. *50 Ans de Cinema Americain*. Paris: Nathan, 1991.

Thomson, David. *The Big Sleep*. London: British Film Institute, 1997.

——. *A Biographical Dictionary of Film*. New York: William Morrow, 1976. Rpt. 1981. 3rd ed. New York: Alfred A. Knopf, 1994.

——. *Showman: The Life of David O. Selznick*. New York: Alfred A. Knopf, 1992.

Tiomkin, Dimitri, and Prosper Buranelli. *Please Don't Hate Me*. Garden City, N.Y.: Doubleday, 1959.

Tornabene, Lyn. *Long Live the King: A Biography of Clark Gable*. New York: G. P. Putnam's Sons, 1976.

Tosches, Nick. *Dino: Living High in the Dirty Business of Dreams*. New York: Doubleday, 1992.

Truffaut, François. *Les Films de Ma Vie*. Paris: Flammarion, 1975. Trans. Leonard Mayhew. *The Films in My Life*. New York: Simon & Schuster, 1978.

Tusca, Jon. *Close Up: The Contract Director*. Metuchen, N.J.: The Scarecrow Press, 1978.

Vermilye, Jerry. *Cary Grant*. New York: Galahad Books, 1973.

Viertel, Peter. *Dangerous Friends: At Large with Hemingway and Huston in the Fifties*. New York: Nan A. Talese–Doubleday, 1992.

Walker, Joseph, and Juanita Walker. *The Light on Her Face*. Hollywood: The ASC Press, 1984.

Wallis, Hal, and Charles Higham. *Starmaker: The Autobiography of Hal Wallis*. New York: Macmillan, 1980.

Wasnell, Geoffrey. *Haunted Idol: The Story of the Real Cary Grant.* New York: William Morrow, 1984.

Whelan, Richard. *Robert Capa.* New York: Alfred A. Knopf, 1985.

Wilde, Meta Carpenter, with Orin Borsten. *A Loving Gentleman.* New York: Simon & Schuster, 1976.

Willis, Donald C. *The Films of Howard Hawks.* Metuchen, N.J.: The Scarecrow Press, 1975.

Wise, Naomi. "The Hawksian Woman." *Take One* 3.3 (April 1972).

Wollen, Peter. *Signs and Meaning in the Cinema.* London: Thames and Hudson; Bloomington: Indiana University Press, 1969.

Wood, Robin. "Acting Up." *Film Comment,* March-April 1976.

———. "Hawks De-Wollenized" and "Reflections on the Auteur Theory." In *Personal Views: Exploration in Film.* London: The Gordon Fraser Gallery, Ltd., 1976.

———. *Howard Hawks.* London: Secker and Warburg; Garden City, New York: Doubleday, 1968. Rpt. with a new afterward. London: BFI Publishing, 1981.

———. "Rio Bravo." *Movie* 5 (December 1962).

———. "To Have (Written) and Have Not (Directed): Reflections on Authorship." *Film Comment* May-June 1973.

———. "Who the Hell Is Howard Hawks?" *Focus!* 1 and 2 (February 1967 and March 1967).

Wray, Fay. *On the Other Hand: A Life Story.* New York: St. Martin's Press, 1989.

Yablonsky, Lewis. *George Raft.* New York: McGraw-Hill, 1974.

Yule, Andrew. *Picture Shows: The Life and Films of Peter Bogdanovich.* New York: Limelight Editions, 1992.

Zolotow, Maurice. *Marilyn Monroe.* New York: Harcourt, Brace & Co., 1960.

———. *Shooting Star: A Biography of John Wayne.* New York: Simon & Schuster, 1974.

Index

Photo Credits

1. Courtesy of David Hawks
2. Courtesy of David Hawks
3. Courtesy of David Hawks
4. Neenah Historical Society
5. *Goshen News-Times*
6. *Goshen News-Times*
7. *Goshen News-Times*
8. Neenah Historical Society
9. Todd McCarthy
10. Neenah Historical Society
11. Courtesy of David Hawks
12. Courtesy of Barbara Hawks McCampbell
13. Courtesy of David Hawks
14. 20th Century–Fox
15. 20th Century–Fox
16. 20th Century–Fox
17. From the author's collection
18. From the author's collection
19. From the author's collection
20. Warner Bros., courtesy of David Hawks
21. Courtesy of David Hawks
22. The Caddo Company, courtesy of David Hawks
23. Courtesy of David Hawks
24. Courtesy of David Hawks
25. Courtesy of Barbara Hawks McCampbell
26. Courtesy of David Hawks
27. The British Film Institute
28. MGM, courtesy of David Hawks
29. Columbia Pictures, courtesy of David Hawks
30. The Samuel Goldwyn Company
31. Courtesy of David Hawks
32. Warner Bros., courtesy of David Hawks
33. The Samuel Goldwyn Company
34. The Samuel Goldwyn Company
35. RKO Pictures, courtesy of David Hawks
36. Columbia Pictures, courtesy of David Hawks
37. Columbia Pictures, courtesy of David Hawks
38. Courtesy of David Hawks
39. Columbia Pictures, courtesy of David Hawks
40. John Engstead, courtesy of the Hawks collection at Brigham Young University
41. John Engstead, courtesy of the Hawks collection at Brigham Young University
42. From the author's collection
43. From the author's collection
44. Courtesy of the Hawks collection at Brigham Young University
45. Warner Bros., courtesy of the Hawks collection at Brigham Young University

46. The Samuel Goldwyn Company
47. The Samuel Goldwyn Company
48. From the author's collection
49. The Samuel Goldwyn Company
50. From the author's collection
51. Warner Bros.
52. Warner Bros., courtesy of the Hawks collection at Brigham Young University
53. Warner Bros., courtesy of David Hawks
54. Warner Bros., courtesy of David Hawks
55. United Artists
56. Courtesy of David Hawks
57. The Samuel Goldwyn Company
58. 20th Century–Fox, courtesy of the Hawks collection at Brigham Young University
59. RKO Pictures
60. RKO Pictures
61. Courtesy of the Hawks collection at Brigham Young University
62. Courtesy of David Hawks
63. 20th Century–Fox, courtesy of David Hawks
64. Courtesy of David Hawks
65. Courtesy of David Hawks
66. Courtesy of the Hawks collection at Brigham Young University
67. Courtesy of the Hawks collection at Brigham Young University
68. Courtesy of Gregg Hawks
69. Courtesy of David Hawks
70. Warner Bros.
71. Warner Bros., courtesy of the Hawks collection at Brigham Young University
72. Warner Bros.
73. Chance de Widstedt
74. Chance de Widstedt
75. Chance de Widstedt
76. Paramount Pictures, courtesy of the Hawks collection at Brigham Young University
77. Universal Pictures
78. Paramount Pictures
79. Chance de Widstedt
80. Embassy Pictures
81. Chance de Widstedt
82. Courtesy of Gregg Hawks
83. Courtesy of Sondra Currie
84. The Academy of Motion Picture Arts & Sciences
85. Chance de Widstedt